Stanley Gi

GREAT BR

Specialised Stamp Catalogue
Volume 1: Queen Victoria

Mulready envelope addressed to Mr W Gibbons, Chemist, Plymouth, the father of Edward Stanley Gibbons, who founded the publishers of this catalogue at the same premises in 1856.

Stanley Gibbons have been celebrating the 150th anniversary of that event in 2006.

Stanley Gibbons
GREAT BRITAIN
Specialised Stamp Catalogue
Volume 1: Queen Victoria

14th EDITION

Stanley Gibbons Ltd
London and Ringwood

By Appointment to Her Majesty The Queen
Stanley Gibbons Ltd., London
Philatelists

Published by **Stanley Gibbons Limited**
Editorial Sales Offices and Distribution Centre:
Parkside, Christchurch Road, Ringwood,
Hants BH24 3SH

1st edition—October 1963
Reprinted—October 1963, November 1963
2nd edition—May 1967
3rd edition—July 1970
Reprinted—September 1970
4th edition—November 1973
5th edition—October 1977
6th edition—December 1979
7th edition—September 1983
8th edition—November 1985
9th edition—January 1989
10th edition—June 1992
11th edition—June 1997
12th edition—February 2001
13th edition—January 2004
14th edition—December 2006

Item No. 0285 (06)

ISBN 13: 978–0–85259–628–9
ISBN 10: 0–85259–628–6

Typeset and Printed in Great Britain by
Piggott Black Bear Ltd., Cambridge

Contents

Preface .... *page* vii

Introductory Notes viii

Historical Introduction
The Early Posts 1
The Origins of the Adhesive Postage Stamps and Mulready Stationery ... 3

The Mulready Letter Sheets and Envelopes (Section AM)
General Notes 13
Priced List 16

The Line-Engraved Issues (Sections A to G)
Essays, Die Proofs, Plate Proofs, Colour Trials and Reprints of the Line-Engraved Stamps 19
General Notes 36
Cancellations found on the Line-Engraved Issues 54
Condition: Line-Engraved Issues 64
Section A: One Penny Black, Type A1, Imperforate 66
Section BA: One Penny Red, Type A1, Imperforate, Die I, Alphabet I (Plates 12 to 131) 97
Section BB: One Penny Red, Type A1, Imperforate, Die I, Alphabet II (Plates 132 to 177), Treasury Roulette 166
Section CA: One Penny Red, Type A1, Experimental forms of Separation 178
Section CB: One Penny Red, Type A1, Officially Perforated 180
Section D: Twopence Blue, Type D1 (No Lines), Imperforate 215
Section E: Twopence Blue, Type E1 (White Lines Added), Imperforate .. 220
Section F: Twopence Blue, Type El, Perforated 226
Section G: Line-Engraved Stamps with Letters in all Four Corners and with Plate Numbers incorporated in the Design 231

The Embossed Issues (Section H) 239

The Surface-Printed Issues (Sections J to KE)
Section J: 1855–83 Surface-Printed Issues 243
General Notes on 1880–1900 Surface-Printed Issues 298
Essays and Die Proofs of the 1880–1900 Surface-Printed Issues 303
Section KA: The "Provisional" Issue (1880–81) 310
Section KB: The First Unified Stamp 1d. Lilac (1881) 315
Section KC: The Unified Issue (1883–91) 320
Section KD: Before and After the 1884 Stamp Committee 337
Section KE: The "Jubilee" Issue (1887–1900) 349

Departmental Official Issues and Government Mail (Section LA)
General Notes 379
Inland Revenue 380
Government Parcels 383
Office of Works 386
Army 387
Board of Education 390

The Postal Fiscal Stamps (Section LB)
General Notes 391
Receipt and Draft Stamps (1853–57) 392
Surface-Printed Inland Revenue Stamps 395
Embossed Inland Revenue Stamps 406

The Post Office Telegraph Stamps (Section LC)
General Notes 410
Telegraph Stamps (1876–81) 417

Appendixes
Appendix 1: The Mulready Letter Sheets or Envelopes Printed with Advertisements, etc 431
Appendix 2: Protective Overprints or Underprints 455
Appendix 3: "Specimen" and "Cancelled" Overprints 472
Appendix 4: Postage Rates (1839–1900) 474
Appendix 5: Circular Delivery Companies 476
Appendix 6: College Stamps 485

Further Reading 493

Indexes and Checklists
Checklist of Essays, Die Proofs, etc. of the Line-Engraved Issues 19
Checklist of the Line-Engraved Issues 65
Index to Plate 1b of the 1d. Black 70
Index to Catalogued Varieties in Section A 95
Index to Catalogued Varieties in Section BA 162
Index to Catalogued Varieties in Section BB 176
Index to Catalogued Varieties in Section CB 213
Checklist of the 1855–83 Surface-Printed Issues 250
Checklist of the 1880–1900 Surface-Printed Issues 309

Preface

It is not quite three years since the publication of the 13th edition of this catalogue, a period in which we have seen a level of activity in the market for Queen Victoria Great Britain stamps that we have not experienced for a quarter of a century.

As this catalogue demonstrates, it is scarce to rare material that is currently driving the GB market, most notably proofs, essays and colour trials. Also performing strongly are the Mulready letter sheets and envelopes, the listing of which has been expanded to include examples with distinctive cancellations, bringing them into tune with the listings of the first line-engraved stamps.

Although the Mulreadys were widely ridiculed and lampooned, leading to their eventual withdrawal, one group of Victorian entrepreneurs welcomed them with enthusiasm, taking advantage of the new cheaper postage rates and the handy medium provided by the Post Office to disseminate a variety of commercial messages—creating, in effect, the world's first "junk mail". Unfortunately, just as today, the vast majority of this mail must have been consigned straight to the waste paper basket. These Mulready advertisements have been extensively studied over the years and a listing of them has been provided as an appendix to this catalogue, added to with each edition as new items are discovered. For the 14th edition, Tom Slemons has carried out a complete revision of the list, increasing the number of recorded advertisements by about 50 and simplifying the descriptions to facilitate correct identification.

Thanks to Ray Simpson and Peter Sargent there are several improvements to the notes on perforating and a number of double-perforated varieties are listed for the first time.

In the short time between this and the last edition there have been few discoveries in the fiscals, college stamps and underprints, but thanks to Dr. Conrad Graham there are three new watermark varieties in the telegraph stamps. Following the publication of Peter Langmead's book, these issues have staged a revival in popularity.

Research goes on and new discoveries are made, but the present editorial team owe it to our eminent predecessors to ensure that additions and amendments to this work of considerable scholarship which they created and maintained will also stand the test of time. We are aware of newly published information but have always required to see material ourselves before listing it and remain happy to meet with collectors and view items to this end.

The 'back of the book' has the interesting new listing of Mulready Advertisements mentioned above. Like the Victorian proofs, they are scarce to rare and are unpriced in this catalogue. Finally, John Holman, editor of the *British Philatelic Bulletin* has kindly given us the benefit of his experience, adding 18 new titles to the "Further Reading" bibliography.

Hugh Jefferies
Robert Oliver
Vince Cordell

Acknowledgements

We thank the many collectors, specialists and correspondents who have helped us since the publication of the 13th edition. Without this assistance and that from our London office this work would not have been possible. Among those that warrant special mention are Messrs. Ray Simpson and Peter Sargent, Peter Mollett, W. P. "Bill" Bird, Barry Fitzgerald, Andrew Lajer and Tom Slemons. Specialists in their field who have again advised us are Dr. J. A. Parrish, Scott Treacey, Mike Batty, Doug McGill, Tim Burgess and others. All are to be congratulated for their contributions to this Catalogue.

Members of the Great Britain Philatelic Society who have contacted us have again given their assistance with the text and illustrations. We also thank the members of staff at the British Postal Museum & Archive (formerly the NPM).

We acknowledge permission from the following to reproduce various illustrations. The Post Office for two illustrations on p.36 showing platemaking: British Postal Museum & Archive, London, for Figs. 4 and 11 in the Historical Introduction, the Mulready proof on p.13, Figs. 2,4,5,7,9 and 15 in the essays and die proofs of the 1880-1900 Surface-Printed issues and the Boucher essay for Telegraph stamps: Spink, for Fig.23 on p.12, and the three illustrations of mounted die proofs ex-De La Rue archives on p.245 and Fig.J22, a hand-painted De La Rue essay on p.303.

STANLEY GIBBONS PUBLICATIONS

Introductory Notes

The aim of this catalogue is to classify in specialised form the stamps of Great Britain, to give distinguishing numbers to them and to quote prices which are current with Stanley Gibbons Ltd. at the time of going to press and at which they will supply if in stock.

Catalogue Numbers

All *Specialised Catalogue* numbers include a prefix letter or letters; shades normally have a number in brackets and subsequent varieties have letter identifications.

Where specialisation has become intensive, as in the Line-Engraved, there is first a listing of the basic stamp, followed by separate listings of the plates of that stamp. For example, referring to Section BA in this volume, B1(1)d is a major re-entry in the commonest shade, without plate identification. From the list, BS6a is a re-entry, on stamp FA or stamp MJ, on the 1d. Plate 17, commonest shade. A more detailed identification is "BS6a (stamp FA)".

For each basic stamp a cross-reference is included to the S.G. catalogue number in the 2007 edition of the Gibbons *Commonwealth and Empire Stamps 1840–1952* Catalogue.

It has of course not always been possible nor even advisable to give specific catalogue numbers (e.g. for the varieties of the later Penny Red plates), as will be understood when the lists are studied. Nor are catalogue numbers given to Essays, Die Proofs, etc. (other than in the Line-Engraved issues), or to Plate Proofs, Colour Trials, Trial Cancellations, etc., which should therefore be described in full.

Prices

Prices quoted in this catalogue are the selling prices of Stanley Gibbons Ltd. at the time the book went to press. They are for stamps in fine condition; in issues where condition varies prices may be higher for the superb and lower for the average or sub-standard. In the case of unused stamps, the prices are for stamps lightly hinged. Prices for used stamps refer to postally used copies. All prices are subject to change without prior notice and no guarantee is given to supply all stamps priced, since it is not possible to keep every catalogued item in stock.

Prices for re-entries and varieties occurring in the margins of stamps are for single stamps unless otherwise stated. They may be increased or reduced according to how much of the re-entry or variety is shown, e.g. a badly centred stamp with the variety complete is worth more than an otherwise well-centred stamp which only shows part of the variety.

Prices quoted for stamps "on cover" are for a single example of the stamp concerned on cover. Covers bearing either multiples of the stamp or other values used in conjunction with it will generally command a higher price.

Guarantee

All stamps supplied by Stanley Gibbons Ltd. are guaranteed originals in the following terms:

If not as described, and returned by the purchaser, we undertake to refund the price paid to us in the original transaction. If any stamp is certified as genuine by the Expert Committee of the Royal Philatelic Society, London, or by B.P.A. Expertising Ltd., the purchaser shall not be entitled to make any claim against us for any error, omission or mistake in such certificate.

Consumers' statutory rights are not affected by the above guarantee.

Expertisation

We do not give opinions as to the genuineness of stamps. Expert Committees exist for this purpose and enquiry can be made of the Royal Philatelic Society, 41 Devonshire Place, London W1G 6JY, or B.P.A. Expertising Ltd., P.O. Box 137, Leatherhead, Surrey KT22 0RG. They do not undertake valuations under any circumstances and fees are payable for their services.

Correspondence

Letters should be addressed to the Catalogue Editor, Stanley Gibbons Publications, 7 Parkside, Christchurch Road, Ringwood, Hants BH24 3SH, and return postage is appreciated when a reply is sought.

New information and unlisted items for consideration are welcomed.

To order from this Catalogue

Always quote the *Specialised Catalogue* number, mentioning *Volume 1, 14th Edition,* and where necessary specify additionally the precise item wanted, this applying naturally where, for example, several check letter combinations are listed under one number.

Detailed Introductory Notes

Before using the catalogue it is important to study the "General Notes" as these explain the technical background of the issues in question. They are to be found at the beginning of the relevant sections.

Items Excluded

In dealing with varieties we record only those for which we can vouch, namely items we have seen and verified for ourselves.

Watermark Illustrations

The illustrations show watermarks as seen from the *front* of the stamp, except for those on page 412 which intentionally show the watermarks as seen from the *back* of the stamp in conjunction with the explanatory notes which accompany them.

Symbols and Abbreviations

†	(in price column)	does not exist
—	(in price column)	exists, but no market price is known (a blank conveys the same meaning)
*	(in price column)	an "Abnormal" (see the General Notes to Section J)
from	(preceding price column)	several items listed, such as a number of different letterings, for which only the commonest is priced
I.	(above price column)	control imperforate selvedge (partially perf. margins are regarded as imperf.)
P.	(above price column)	control selvedge perforated through
A/H	(die proofs)	After hardening
A/S	(die proofs)	After striking
B/H	(die proofs)	Before hardening
B/S	(die proofs)	Before striking
LC	(watermark)	Large Crown
(M/S)	(die proofs)	in manuscript
N.P.M.		The National Postal Museum, London (now the British Postal Museum & Archive)
Pl.		plate
R.		row (thus "R. 6/4" indicates the fourth stamp from the left in the sixth horizontal row from the top of a sheet of stamps)
SC	(watermark)	Small Crown
TRL	(line-engraved)	Transfer roller line

Stanley Gibbons Holdings Plc. Addresses

STANLEY GIBBONS LTD, STANLEY GIBBONS AUCTIONS
399 STRAND, LONDON, WC2R 0LX

Telephone 020 7836 8444, Fax 020 7836 7342, E-mail: enquiries@stanleygibbons.co.uk and Internet: www.stanleygibbons.com for all departments

Auction Room and Specialist Stamp Departments. Open Monday–Friday 9.30 a.m. to 5 p.m.

Shop. Open Monday–Friday 9 a.m. to 5.30 p.m. and Saturday 9.30 a.m. to 5.30 p.m.

STANLEY GIBBONS PUBLICATIONS
PARKSIDE, CHRISTCHURCH ROAD, RINGWOOD, HANTS BH24 3SH

Telephone 01425 472363 (24 hour answer phone service). Fax 01425 470247 and E-mail info@stanleygibbons.co.uk

Publications Mail Order. FREEPHONE 0800 611622. Monday–Friday 8.30 a.m. to 5 p.m.

Stanley Gibbons Publications has overseas licensees and distributors for Australia, Belgium, Canada, Denmark, Finland, France, Hong Kong, Israel, Italy, Japan, Luxembourg, Netherlands, New Zealand, Norway, Saudi Arabia, Singapore, Sweden, Switzerland and the United States.

Please contact the Ringwood address for details.

FRASER'S
(a division of Stanley Gibbons Ltd)
399 STRAND, LONDON WC2R 0LX

Autographs, photographs, letters and documents

Open Monday–Friday 9 a.m. to 5.30 p.m. and Saturday 10 a.m. to 4 p.m.

Telephone 020 7836 8444, Fax 020 7836 7342, E-mail: info@frasersautographs.co.uk and Internet: www.frasersautographs.com

---

Great Britain Philatelic Societies

Great Britain Philatelic Society. Hon. Membership Secretary: Peter Tanner, 'High Standings', 13 Huberts Close, Gerrards Cross, Bucks SL9 7EN.

The Modern British Philatelic Circle. Hon. Membership Secretary: A. J. Wilkins, 3 Buttermere Close, Brierley Hill, West Midlands DY5 3SD.

The Great Britain Collectors' Club. Secretary-Treasurer: Parker A. Bailey, 17 Greenwood Road, Merrimack, NH 03054, USA.

Historical Introduction

The Early Posts

The origins of the Royal Mail can be traced back to the medieval period when messengers from the, often peripatetic, Royal Court carried the sovereign's commands to his representatives throughout the realm. Such messengers provided no public service and other letters were carried by private couriers or merchants.

In 1635 King Charles I, casting about for sources of extra-parliamentary revenue, opened the Royal Post to the public. Charges were expensive, being calculated on the distance covered by each letter. Succeeding administrations continued to view the postal service primarily as a source of revenue and from 1653 to 1677 the right to run, and profit from, the post office was "farmed out" to various concessionaries. Henry Bishop, who ran the postal service during the early 1660s, is credited with the introduction of the first postmark to provide details of the date of posting.

As trade developed use of the postal service grew considerably and the increased revenue prompted the government to exercise direct control through the Treasury. There was considerable dissatisfaction, however, with the poor service provided by the Post Office in the capital with the result that the Royal monopoly was challenged in March 1680 by a post organised by William Dockwra which delivered letters within London for 1d. The courts supported the Post Office and Dockwra's service was closed down in November 1682 only to reopen as part of the government system the following month.

The Struggle for Postal Reform

The postal system developed in a haphazard fashion during much of the eighteenth century. Improvements in organisation and in communications, notably the introduction of the mail coach by John Palmer in the 1780s, did not lead to a better postal service and the system of postage rates became even more complex and expensive as the weekly contribution made by the postal revenues to the Exchequer increased. By the 1830s demands by the newly-enfranchised middle classes for administrative and philanthropic reforms were being directed at the postal service. A Commission of Inquiry into the Government Revenue published five Reports on the Post Office during 1829 and 1830. Although only relatively minor changes were subsequently made the Reports led to considerable agitation for postal reform, both in the House of Commons and amongst the mercantile classes.

The Parliamentary campaign was led by Robert Wallace, M.P. for Greenock, and resulted in a Commission of Inquiry into the management of the Post Office in 1835.

It was at this stage that Rowland Hill, a businessman not previously connected with postal affairs, published the first edition of his pamphlet "Post Office Reform" which advocated the introduction of lower postal charges which would be uniform within the inland system. In November 1837 a Parliamentary Select Committee was appointed to consider postal rate charges. By 1839 the campaign for postal reform was reaching its climax. Petitions from the public, encouraged by propaganda circulated by the influential Mercantile Committee, flooded into Parliament and the Liberal Government of Lord Melbourne, disregarding the misgiving of the Post Office officials, swung behind the popular demand. The Uniform Postage Act received the Royal Assent on 17 August 1839. The fight for cheap postage had been won.

The reforms had still to be implemented against the passive opposition of much of the Post Office hierarchy. The Chancellor of the Exchequer, Francis Baring, appointed Rowland Hill to a post at the Treasury to put his theories into practice. Over the next few years Hill and his assistant Henry Cole were to revolutionise the postal service and introduce a workable concept of prepayment using postal stationery and adhesive postage stamps.

Uniform Fourpenny Postage. Although it had been accepted that the uniform postal rate would be 1d. per half-ounce for any distance, Rowland Hill considered that such a drastic reduction in the rates would attract too much mail for the Post Office to be able to handle. The reduction was therefore made in two stages. On 5 December 1839 the rate in London was brought down from 2d. to 1d. per $\frac{1}{2}$ oz. if prepaid, but left at 2d. or 3d. if unpaid. Elsewhere the rate was fixed at 4d. per $\frac{1}{2}$d. oz. irrespective of distance within the British Isles. District offices were set up to deal with the additional mail.

The 4d. rate applied until 9 January 1840 and during this period nearly all letters had a manuscript "4" but some towns used a handstruck "4", generally only for a few days. Letters not prepaid had the "4" in black. Prepaid letters had it in red.

The experiment of charging more for unpaid letters in London caused a large increase in the volume of prepaid letters. This saved the postmen much time as they no longer had to wait to collect money, and perhaps give change; it also quickly led to the introduction of letter boxes to enable mail to be delivered when the addressee was away.

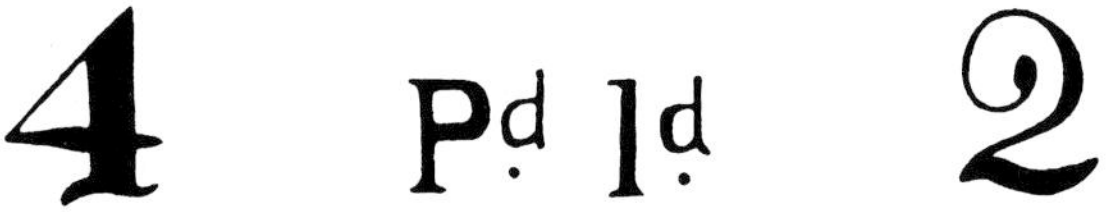

Fig. 1. Three examples of handstruck stamps from Nottingham. Left, Fourpenny Post; centre, Penny Post; right, Postage Due

Uniform Penny Postage. This was introduced on 10 January 1840 and represented Hill's major postal reform, the culmination of years of persuasion and preparation. The rate was 1d. per $\frac{1}{2}$ oz. anywhere in the British Isles if prepaid, or 2d. if unpaid. It was an immediate success, the number of letters carried in 1840 being more than double that of 1839 and by 1850 the number had increased more than fourfold.

Nearly every town used handstruck stamps in red on the mail in a wide variety of types, from a simple figure "1" ("2" or "4" for overweight letters) or incorporating "P", "Pd" or "Paid" and some times with the name of the town added. *See Fig. 1* Similarly figures were handstruck double the rate in black to denote postage due. Their use continued after the introduction of the Mulreadys and adhesive postage stamp until about 1853.

Prepaid Private Letter Sheets. With the introduction of Uniform Penny Postage some private individuals produced prepaid letter sheets. One type was sold by J. Baraclough, Bookseller, Nuneaton, of which only two examples are known. One is printed in brown in the R. M. Phillips collection and the other, in blue, is in private hands. *Price* £80000.

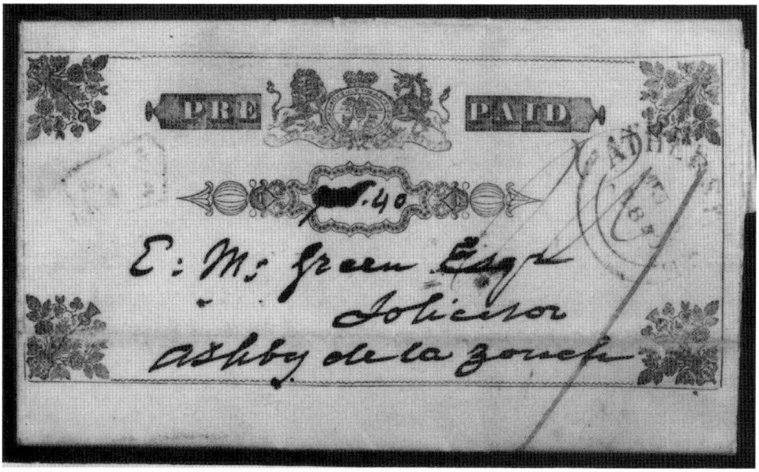

Fig. 2. The second type of the Buchanan letter sheet. The illustration is reduced in size

Four types were produced by J. W. Buchanan, also of Nuneaton. They are all printed in shades of blue. The first is a simple design showing a 30 mm scroll at top centre for the insertion of the date with "PRE" and "PAID" at either side as shown in *Fig. 2.* Several examples are known with dates ranging from 17 January 1840 to 5 May 1840. *Price* £14000.

The second type is known dated 7 June 1840. *Price* £17500.

The third type differs in that "PRE PAID" is omitted and the central scroll is repeated at foot and dated, the first scroll bearing the initials "JWB". A copy is in the R. M. Phillips Collection dated 19 July 1841 and the only other known copy in private hands is dated 10 July 1841. *Price* £60000.

The fourth type is as last but the "PRE" and "PAID" inscriptions are arranged at each side of the coat-of-arms as *Fig. 2.* The piece is a front only and is believed to be unique. It is undated but it is interesting to note that the addressee is the same as on the third type which is in the R. M. Phillips Collection.

Parliamentary Envelopes. When the Uniform Penny Postage was introduced on 10 January 1840 the free franking privileges of Members of Parliament were abolished. Rowland Hill arranged for the introduction of the following envelopes for the use of Members of Parliament so that they would not suffer inconvenience as a result of the cessation of free franking. They were the first postal stationery to prepay postage (*see Fig. 3*). Sold by Mr. Vardon, the librarian, the sale of these envelopes continued until May 1840 when the Penny Black labels and Mulready stationery were issued. The Parliamentary envelopes are priced in used condition only.

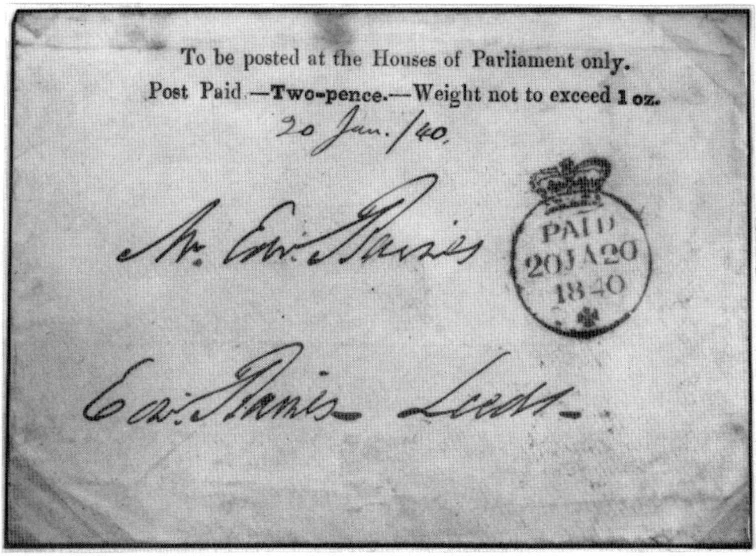

Fig. 3. Houses of Parliament 2d. envelope PE2

Inscribed "Houses of Parliament". Issued on 16 January 1840.

PE1	1d. envelope printed in black	*from*	£10000
PE2	2d. envelope printed in black	*from*	£30000

Inscribed "House of Lords". Issued in January 1840.

PE3	1d. envelope printed in vermilion	*from*	£22000
PE4	2d. envelope printed in vermilion		

Inscribed "House of Commons". Issued in January 1840.

PE5	1d. envelope printed in black	*from*	£2750

The Origins of the Adhesive Postage Stamps and the Mulready Stationery

The first suggestion concerning the use of franks to indicate the prepayment of postage appears to have come from Charles Whiting, a printer and inventor, who wrote to the Secretary of the Post Office in 1830 submitting a scheme for the use of "go free" franks similar in appearance to banknotes already being printed on machinery for which he held the patents (*see Fig. 4*). The idea was rejected due to a perceived possibility of fraud and because it was felt that the mail coaches would be unable to cope with the extra business which might result!

Hill's scheme was also, of course, based on prepayment and, although much of his effort was directed towards the Mulready postal stationery, his evidence to the Duncannon Committee on 13 February 1837 included the concept of the adhesive stamp "a bit of paper just large enough to bear the stamp, and covered at the back with a glutinous wash. . .".

Others were also thinking along similar lines and in December of the same year James Chalmers of Dundee suggested the use of "slips" or stamps to seal letter sheets (*see Fig. 5*).

Fig. 4 Charles Whiting's "Go Free" Frank, 1830

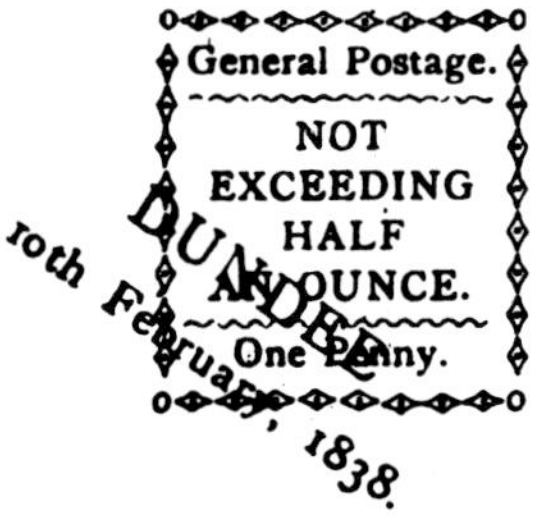

Fig. 5. Chalmers' 1d. essay of 1838

Meanwhile, John Dickinson, the papermaker, submitted proposals for prepaid letter sheets and produced the first essays for 1d. and 2d. letter sheets, together with 1d. envelopes. These showed silk threads running through the paper as a protection against forgery (*see Fig. 6*). They were inscribed "LONDON DISTRICT POST", the 1d. for up to 1 oz. (in yellow-buff) and the 2d. in another design for up to 2 oz. (in green). The adoption of this scheme was recommended by the Commissioners of Post Office Inquiry in July 1837.

In 1838 W. H. Ashurst published *Facts and Reasons in support of Rowland Hill's plan for a Universal Penny Postage* in which he illustrated two typographed designs for letter sheets by John W. Parker. One is illustrated in *Fig. 7* and the other reads "Cambridge Bible Warehouse" instead of "Publisher". Both were printed in yellow.

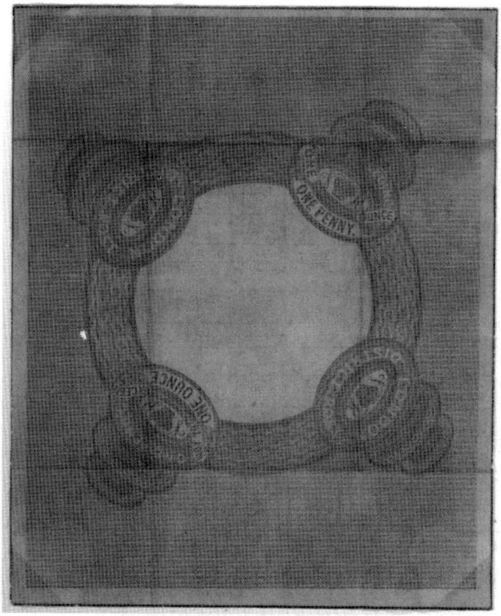

6. *Dickinson's 1d. letter sheet of 1837. The illustration is reduced in size*

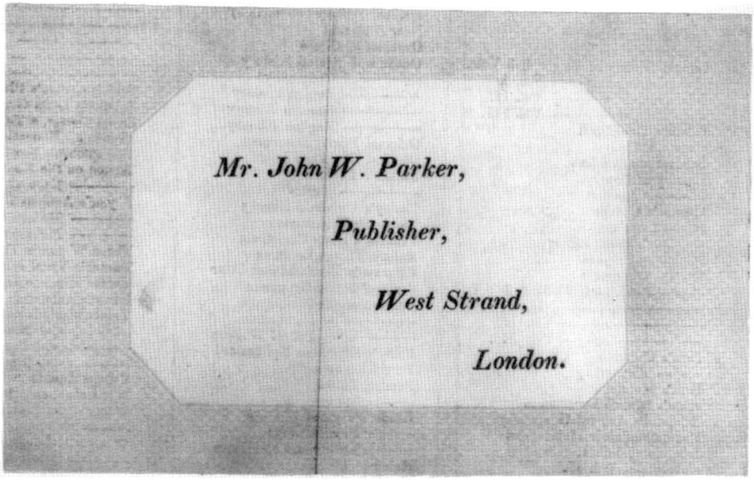

7. *J. W. Parker's letter sheet of 1838. The illustration is reduced in size*

In the following year *The Post Circular* printed a number of designs for letter sheets prepared by Charles Whiting. These were to be printed in various colours and inscribed "POST OFFICE PERMIT" (*see Fig. 8*).

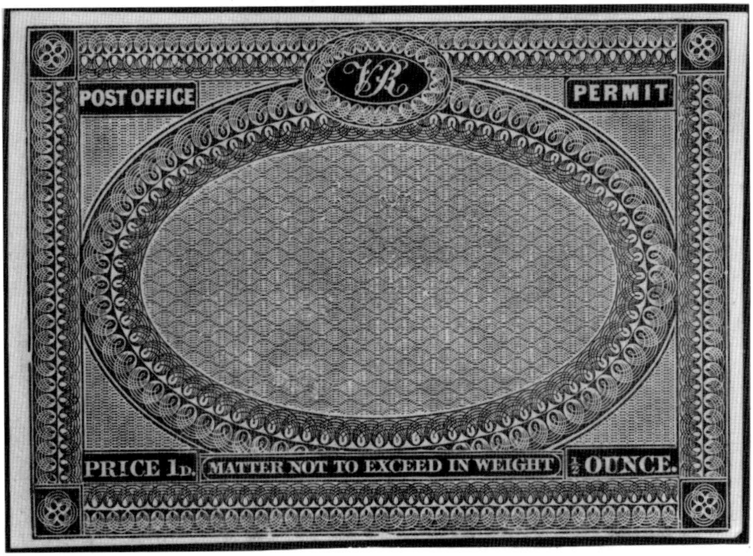

Fig. 8. "Post Office Permit Letter Sheet" by Charles Whiting, 1839

In May 1839 Rowland Hill published a pamphlet entitled *On the Collection of Postage by means of Stamps* which elaborated on his earlier proposals and in which he said: "I still looked upon stamped covers or envelopes as the means which the public would most commonly employ; still believing that the adhesive stamps would be reserved for exceptional cases".

The 1839 Treasury Competition. By a Treasury Minute of 23 August 1839, later published in *The Times* of 6 September, an invitation was issued to artists, scientists and the general public to submit ideas and designs for stamped covers, adhesive labels and for their security against forgery. *The Postal Reform and the Penny Black* by Douglas Muir contains the full list of competitors. Awards of £200 and £100 were offered for the two best proposals and the closing date was set for 15 October.

Over 2,600 suggestions were submitted, but only a small number related to adhesive postage stamps, and it fell to Rowland Hill to assess them and make his recommendations. The number of awards was increased, £100 each going to Benjamin Cheverton, Henry Cole and Charles Whiting and £50 each to James Bogardus and Francis Coffin for a joint entry.

No submission was ideal, however, although aspects from a number of them were subsequently incorporated by Hill into his own scheme.

Many of the entries have since been lost or destroyed, but it is believed that the following may have been connected with the competition:

Anonymous. These were found among Rowland Hill's papers and exist in black on coloured gummed paper, varying in size according to value. The denominations range from 1d. to 16d. in a circle and from 18d. to 2s. 8d. in a diamond. They were intended to be fixed so as to be destroyed on opening the letter. More recently they have been attributed to James Bogardus (*Fig. 9*).

Fig. 9 Anonymous essay, possibly by James Bogardus

Fig. 10. Essay by James Chalmers

James Chalmers. One of a number of essays submitted to the competition is shown in *Fig. 10*. Those shown in *Fig. 11* were reproduced in a circular entitled *A Comparative Statement of the Expense of Stamped Envelopes with Stamped Slips* on the back of which Chalmers wrote a letter to Rowland Hill dated 8 October 1839.

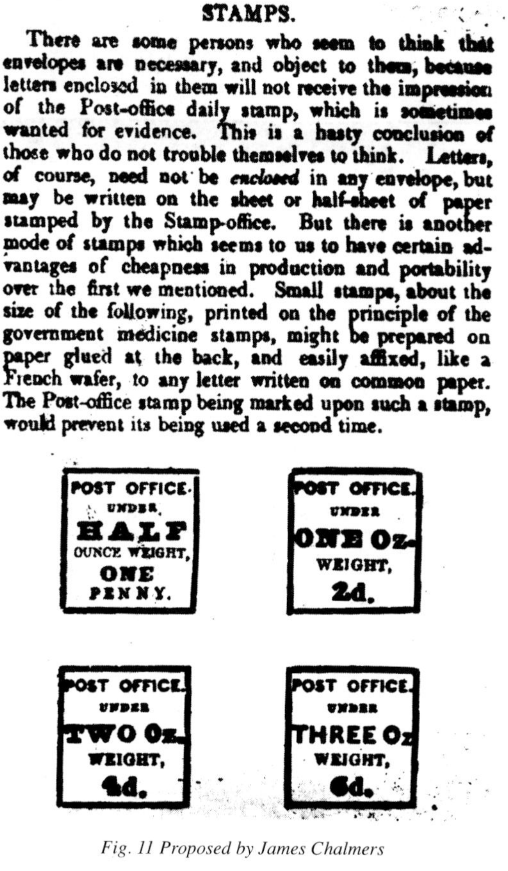

STAMPS.

There are some persons who seem to think that envelopes are necessary, and object to them, because letters enclosed in them will not receive the impression of the Post-office daily stamp, which is sometimes wanted for evidence. This is a hasty conclusion of those who do not trouble themselves to think. Letters, of course, need not be *enclosed* in any envelope, but may be written on the sheet or half-sheet of paper stamped by the Stamp-office. But there is another mode of stamps which seems to us to have certain advantages of cheapness in production and portability over the first we mentioned. Small stamps, about the size of the following, printed on the principle of the government medicine stamps, might be prepared on paper glued at the back, and easily affixed, like a French wafer, to any letter written on common paper. The Post-office stamp being marked upon such a stamp, would prevent its being used a second time.

Fig. 11 Proposed by James Chalmers

Benjamin Cheverton. Cheverton's award was for "consultation", which presumably refers to his very practical suggestions that stamps should be printed in rolls of 240 on security paper with a watermark. As a guard against forgery he advocated "the embossment of a female head of the greatest beauty to be executed by Mr. Wyon" on the grounds that any differences in the features of a well-known face resulting from forgery would be much more easily recognized than variations in a mechanical or ornamental device.

In 1910 (see *The London Philatelist* Nov. 1910) some of Cheverton's original correspondence came to light including this Treasury Competition Essay in which he mentions a specimen described as a strip with one head and spaces for a further eleven to give a shilling value.

The item shown in *Fig. 12* has been associated with Cheverton over the years but there is no evidence so far to connect it with him other than it was originally a strip of 6 "stamps". A strip of 4 is in the Royal Collection and two singles in private hands.

Fig. 12. VR Monogram associated with Benjamin Cheverton

Fig. 14. R. W. Sievier essay which incorporated embossing and engine-turning

John Dickinson Letter Sheets. The essays referred to previously were entered for the competition but were printed by Charles Whiting and may have been prepared by him. They were probably a joint entry.

Robert W. Sievier. This engraver, and later a noted sculptor, produced several essays. The one illustrated as *Fig. 14* has the central pattern embossed and it was proposed that the engine-turned surround be printed in two or three colours so each of his essays was produced in several combinations of two or more colours. It was stitched up in No. 65 of the *London and Westminster Review. Price for complete page from* £3000.

Another design has a scallop-edge instead of an outer frame and a third shows the Royal Arms in the centre. He also constructed a printing machine and estimated that he could produce one million impressions per day for as little as £6 5s. He concluded that stamps printed in such a complicated design in two processes and several colours would be extremely difficult to forge.

Charles Whiting. Whiting submitted about one hundred designs and proposals over a period of time, some embossed and others using the Congreve method of printing simultaneously in two colours by the use of interlocking plates which were separately inked. Three of these essays are shown in *Fig. 15*. The Congreve Machine had been used at Somerset House since 1821 to print some of the revenue stamps. The two essays shown in *Fig. 16*, also produced on this machine, introduced the idea of using corner check letters, with "A 3" at the top and Charles Whiting's initials at the bottom.

The essay by Whiting shown in *Fig. 17* was made in 1840 and printed by the Congreve principle on thin paper. It is known in black and red, deep blue and red and green and red. *Price from* £1800 *each.*

The essay for the Harwoods envelope (*Fig. 18*) was also produced by Whiting, some examples being known with the manuscript note "Submitted by Mr. C. Whiting".

In a Minute, drafted by Rowland Hill, dated 26 December 1839 the Lords of the Treasury directed the means for the prepayment of postage: first, stamped covers; second, stamped envelopes; third, adhesive stamps; and fourth, stamps to be impressed on paper of any description which the public may send to the Stamp Office. It brought the Treasury Competition to a close and gave official status to Rowland Hill's plans for prepayment and the work that had already been put in hand for the production of stationery and adhesive stamps.

William Wyon. Wyon was one of a distinguished family of engravers. His position at the time of the competition was Chief Engraver of Seals to the Queen and to the Royal Academy. The sketch shown in *Fig. 19* known as the Wyon essay (Royal Collection), was probably a first sketch. The essay is in Indian ink, mounted on card was later annotated by Pearson Hill, Rowland Hill's son "Original sketch for the Postage Stamp, by Wyon". Although little is known about this sketch, it was probably submitted to Rowland Hill in November or December 1839. The size of the sketch is 19 × 19.75 mm. which is almost that required for the labels, rather than for the postal stationery essays which were to follow in 1840.

The City Medal of 1837 (*Fig. 20*) shows the engraving of the Queen's head which was the model for the portrait employed on all Great Britain stamps of the reign. *Prices bronze from* £900, *silver from* £2500 *each.*

Embossed Essays for Stamping Paper. Between January and September 1840 William Wyon and Charles Whiting produced a number of embossed essays for the stamped paper. Whiting made essays of the uncrowned Queen's head (embossed head with ornamental surround) and Wyon used the crowned head for a series of embossed essays for which Whiting (through his engraver Alfred Deacon in some instances) made the engine-turned surrounds.

Whiting's embossed essay (*Fig. 21*) is generally in black and is known dated 22 February 1840. *Price* £1600.

Two embossed Wyon essays are shown in *Fig. 22*. The one on the left occurs in black, blue or green and is known dated 25 January 1840. The one on the right is known struck in deep blue on card.

Fig. 15. Three essays by Charles Whiting

Fig. 16. Two essays by Whiting, with check letters in the corners

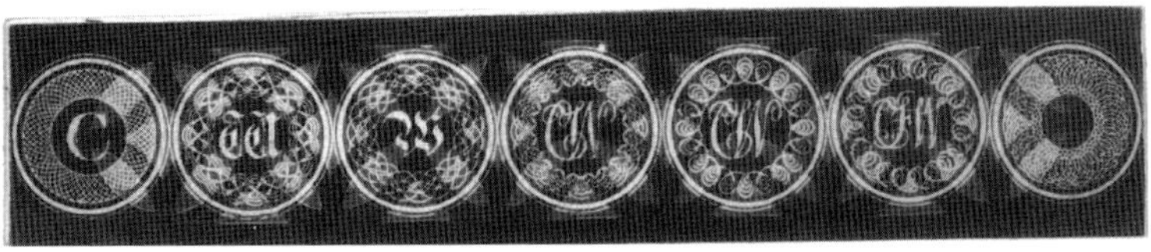

Fig. 17. Further essay by Whiting

Fig. 18. Essay for the Harwoods envelope, submitted by Charles Whiting. The illustration is reduced in size

Fig. 19. Wyon essay in India ink

Fig. 20. The Wyon City Medal of 1837

Fig. 21. Whiting's embossed essay

Fig. 22. Two embossed essays by William Wyon, the one on the right being used later for postal stationery

It appears that there were technical problems over adapting the essays for reproduction by machinery and then the Treasury officials became worried that they might be forged by electrotyping. On 13 October 1840 an entry in Rowland Hill's journal records that embossed receipt stamps which could be applied to any paper would be insecure against forgery. By then it was clear that the public disliked the Mulreadys but that the adhesive stamps were a success contrary to all predictions. Rowland Hill judged that there was no real public demand for the stamping of paper and so the project came to an end.

Wyon's work was not wasted, however, as when it became necessary to replace the Mulreadys, Rowland Hill adopted the second essay (*Fig. 22, right*) and used it on envelopes made from Dickinson paper. The earliest 1d. value known is dated 25 January 1841, and the 2d. envelope followed in April. The Wyon head was again used with his initials on the Queen's neck for the embossed postage stamps of 1847-54. The Treasury Lords agreed to paper being stamped to order in October 1855 when the Wyon design was at last used for its original purpose.

Combination Proof. Illustrated as *Fig. 23* is a proof of the Mulready design pulled from the original engraving on brass by John Thompson and completed on 1 April 1840. This formed the basic design for the letter sheets and envelopes, the additional matter being prepared separately and then proofed together.

On the left is the embossed essay of the Queen's head by Wyon with the engine-turned pattern in blue by Whiting, which was completed in January 1840. This essay, with the outer frame removed, was adopted for making the 1d. and 2d. embossed dies for stamping the Post Office envelopes of January and April 1841 respectively, which replaced the Mulready design. On the right is a complete die proof of the Penny Black completed by Charles and Frederick Heath in March 1840. The endorsement is believed to be in the writing of Rowland Hill.

Several examples are known of *Fig. 23* printed in blue, but without the manuscript endorsement.

Fig. 23. Combination proof showing, from left to right, the embossed head for envelopes, the Mulready design and the Penny Black. The illustration is reduced in size

SECTION AM

The Mulready Letter Sheets and Envelopes

General Notes

History. It was the Chancellor of the Exchequer, Francis Baring, who recommended William Mulready, R.A., to Rowland Hill with a view to designing the stationery. Henry Cole visited him first on 12 December 1839 and again three days later by which time Mulready had drawn the design which was adopted. It was a romantic conception of the world-wide benefits of cheap postage. Britannia, with shield depicting the Union Jack and with the British Lion at her feet, is shown presiding over the ocean and despatching a winged messenger to each of the four points of the compass. Below the messengers there are sailing ships on the left, and on the right a Laplander on a sleigh drawn by a reindeer. To the left were oriental groups: Chinese with pigtails, laden camels, elephants, someone writing a letter and a child apparently reading some bad news to a bedridden parent. To the right were a group probably representing William Penn negotiating with some Red Indians, women and children under a palm tree, a planter supervising the heading up of two casks and finally a mother reading a letter of good news to her children. Artistically, an excellent design, but hardly practicable for its purpose.

The design was approved on 4 January 1840 and John Thompson was commissioned to engrave it on brass. The engraving was not completed until 1 April, when the first proof was made.

Full-size layout essays are known printed in light blue or black on white, wove paper showing the layout of the side panels and experimental background with "POSTAGE" in the top panel. *Price* £7500, or light blue £12000. Other proofs of various stages are held by The Post Office Heritage Services. Die proofs of the design in black, usually on India paper, exist. *Price* £2500, or printed in blue. *Price* £12000.

On 18 March 1840 arrangements were made with William Clowes for printing the letter sheets and envelopes. On 10 April Rowland Hill went to the National Gallery with specimens of the letter sheets which were greatly approved by the Council of the Royal Academy. The letter sheets and envelopes were put on sale in London on 1 May and brought into use on 6 May. A few examples are known to have passed through the post prematurely.

The letter sheets have been variously described, in the past, as "covers" or "wrappers", but the term "letter sheet" is more accurate. This was their purpose, although by their nature they were capable

Proof for the Mulready One Penny Envelope

of accepting an enclosure. The term "cover" is more frequently used to describe an envelope, "entire", or "wrapper" bearing adhesive stamps or indication of cash payment for postage. The term "entire" usually refers to a letter written on plain paper, folded and sealed, with the front bearing the address and the indication of postage paid, either by cash or stamp. A "wrapper" is only the outer sheet of paper folded around a letter or enclosure, sealed, addressed, and with the indication of postage paid, either by cash or stamp. Prior to the changes in postage rates which began in December 1839, envelopes were simply an extra postage expense, so virtually never used in Great Britain. Folding plain paper to form an "entire" or "wrapper" was the norm. The Mulready envelopes were intended to change this, but their design, printing format and sales requirements, hindered their full acceptance. Initially, adhesive stamps were always referred to as "labels" and the term "stamp" was used to describe any impression struck to indicate prepayment of postage, including postage for the Mulreadys.

Description. The Mulready letter sheets and envelopes were printed in sheets of 12. The price of a full sheet was 15 pence, 12 pence for the postage and 3 pence for the paper. They were shipped to post offices and other vendors or users in this form with a discount for volume purchases. The large sheets of letter sheets could be cut into individual items and sold in that manner at a price of one and a quarter pence each. The large sheets of envelopes could not be cut and had to be sold in full sheets of 12 at 15 pence each. These pricing requirements applied to post offices and sub-offices, receivers, stamp distributors, and sub-distributors. Private firms such as stationers, printers, booksellers, and other private firms soon recognized a marketing opportunity and began the practice of printing advertisements on the letter sheets and envelopes, then selling these to the public at less than face value.

Each letter sheet has post office instructions and rates printed in four panels, two on each side of the design, or what is the "front" when folded for mailing. Below the design is a panel that encloses the word POSTAGE against an engine-turned background. Below this panel is a letter and a number. The envelopes were not printed with the post office instruction panels. They were printed with the POSTAGE panel and the letter and number. Each envelope, when cut from the sheet, is in a diamond shape with the "front" lying squarely between the points of the diamond. Once it was addressed and ready for mailing, all that needed to be done was to fold the four points of the diamond together and seal it.

Paper. The paper for the Mulreadys was produced by John Dickinson. It is commonly known as Dickinson "silk" thread paper. The threads were imbedded in the paper as a security measure to prevent postal fraud or forgery. Scientific examination of both a Mulready envelope and its successor, the 1841 embossed envelope, showed that the threads were an all-cotton folded yarn. The letter sheets have three pink threads crossing above the design and two blue threads crossing below the design. The envelopes have two pink and one blue thread crossing the flaps on the left and right sides of the design. There is no true watermark in the paper, but what appears to be a watermark occurred randomly in the manufacture of the paper and is sometimes seen. This has become known as a "stitch" watermark.

The Formes and the Stereos. A brass engraving was made from William Mulready's artwork. From the brass engraving individual casts were made and called Stereos. At Rowland Hill's suggestion, these were numbered for security purposes. From twelve Stereos, a Forme was made to print the large sheets. A range of Stereo numbers was allocated to prepare each Forme. Surviving full sheets, reconstructions, and "plating" have provided us with some of the Stereo layouts within the Formes. Some Stereos were moved from their original Forme or Forme allocation and incorporated into other Formes displacing, it is believed, worn or damaged Stereos. Some Stereos have remained unplaced in a Forme. One penny letter sheets and envelopes have the Stereo numbers preceded by a capital letter "A". Stereos on two penny letter sheets and envelopes are preceded by a lower case letter "a".

Advertisements. A large number of letter sheets and small number of envelopes were used for purposes other than purely correspondence. Various firms, organizations, government agencies, banks, merchants, stationers, printers, booksellers, and others used them to convey all sorts of messages. Although these messages are not advertisements in the strictest sense, they have become known under the all encompassing title of "Advertisements". They are of great historical interest and provide an amazing insight into the period of their brief life. All presently known examples are listed in Appendix I.

Public Ridicule, Caricatures, and Withdrawal. The Mulreadys were widely greeted by the public with ridicule, derision, and abuse. Their design was far too "radical" for their time. Rowland Hill recognized this within a week of their release and wrote "I fear we shall be obliged to substitute some other stamp for that designed by Mulready". At the same time they were being ridiculed verbally and in the press, numerous artists and printers created caricatures lampooning them in typical Victorian style. Amongst the many prepared, the better known are by John Leech, "Phiz", and William Spooner. Replacement one and two penny envelopes appeared in early 1841 and sold individually instead of in sheets of 12. Remaining stocks of Mulready envelopes were withheld from circulation. The letter sheets, although not popular, were more widely used and not replaced until 1844. By then the envelope was fully accepted and the use of letter sheets dwindled. Eventually all remaining stocks of envelopes and letter sheets of Mulready's design were recalled and destroyed.

The Known Arrangements and Details of the Formes.

One Penny Letter Sheets, First Series.

FORME 1

A15	A7	A8	A2
A9	A6	A14	A5
A4	A10	A1	A11

FORME 2

A25	A19	A30	A26
A16	A21	A24	A27
A23	A22	A18	A17

In Forme 1, A14 was later replaced by A71; A4 was replaced by A31; A11 was replaced by A47.

Mulready 1d. letter sheet

FORME 3

A57	A64	A63	A34
A50	A67	A65	A66
A54	A69	A68	A35

FORME 4

A51	A36	A40	A81
A78	A71	A70	A80
A37	A42	A44	A77

In Forme 3, A65 was later replaced by A231 and A68 by A229. A76 is known but it is not known which stereo it displaced. Formes 2 and 3 are known in complete sheets.

One Penny Letter Sheets Second Series.

FORME 5

A247	A241	A242	A240
A254	A243	A246	A244
A251	A249	A250	A255

FORME 6

A230	A232	A233	A226
A234	A223	A235	A236
A239	A224	A238	A237

Stereos A219, A220, A221 and A228 are known but have not yet been allocated to a forme.

One Penny Envelopes, First Series.

Forme 1				Forme 2			
A133	A134	A137	A141	A150	A156	A148	A149
A132	A135	A138	A142	A144	A146	A147	A145
A131	A136	A139	A140	A154	A153	A151	A143

In Forme, 1, A137 was later replaced by A173.

Forme 3				Forme 4			
A167	A165	A158	A170	A172	A175	A164	A174
A162	A160	A155	A159	A182	A181	A176	A177
A163	A157	A161	A166	A179	A178	A180	A189

Stereos known but not allocated are A183, A186, A187, A193, A194. Formes 3 and 4 are known in complete sheets.

One Penny Envelopes, Second Series.
These Stereos are all extremely rare. In many cases only one copy is recorded. Stereos A275 to A323 were allocated to Formes 5 and 6. No reconstruction of these Formes is possible. They may have been substituted Stereos in Formes 1 through 4, but there is no evidence to support that theory. Recorded examples:

A275—A proof on India paper in the Post Office Heritage Collection.

A276—One used.	A277	A278	A279
A280	A281—One used.	A282	A283
A284	A285	A286—One used.	A287
A288	A291	A293	A294
A295	A296	A297	A298
A299	A300	A302	A305
A310	A320	A321	A323

Two Pence Letter Sheets. Only one Forme was used.

a92	a90	a97	a104
a94	a103	a96	a105
a95	a98	a99	a91

Complete sheets are known unused.

Two Pence Envelopes. Only one Forme was used.

a196	a200	a199	a204
a203	a202	a201	a198
a210	a197	a209	a208

a211—Exists as either a displaced Stereo or a substituted Stereo. One example of a195 is known. The only surviving sheets and reconstructions give no clue, but being the highest Stereo number used, it was probably a substituted Stereo. Three examples are known, one used with a red Maltese cross, one used with a black Maltese cross and one used.

Priced List

1840 (6 May).

ME1		1d. letter sheet (printed in black)	£300	£400
		Used pair	†	£2500
		Used with 1840 1d. black adhesive	†	£8000
		Used with 1841 1d. red adhesive	†	£8000
		Used with 1840 2d. blue adhesive	†	£20000
		Used with 1841 2d. blue adhesive	†	£20000
		Used before 6 May 1840 *from*	†	£18000
		Used on 6 May 1840 *from*	†	£12000
		Used on 7–9 May 1840	†	£2000
		Used on Sunday 10 May 1840	†	£12000
	b.	Unused sheet of twelve (Forme 2 or Forme 3)	£5000	†
	c.	Original stereos from Forme 1, excluding A4, A11, A14 *each*	£300	£400
	d.	Displaced stereos from Forme 1 (A4, A11, A14) *each*	£325	£475
	e.	Substituted stereos A31 or A47 from Forme 1 *each*	£325	£475

	ea.	Substituted stereo A71 from Forme 1	£325	£400
	f.	Stereos from Forme 2 *each*	£300	£400
	g.	Original stereos from Forme 3, excluding (A65 and A68) *each*	£300	£400
	h.	Displaced stereos from Forme 3 (A65 and A68) *each*	£325	£500
	i.	Substituted stereos from Forme 3 (A229 and A231) *each*	£375	£550
	j.	Stereos from Forme 4 *each*	£425	£550
	k.	Stereos from Forme 5 *each*	£425	£600
	l.	Stereos from Forme 6 *each*	£450	£600
	m.	Unplaced stereos A76, A219, A220, A221, A228 *each*	£475	£600
	n.	With advertisement, etc. printed inside *from*	£650	£650
	o.	"Stitch watermark"	£550	£550
	s.	"Specimen", Type 2 (stereos A14, A65) *from*	£6000	

The 1d. letter sheet exists with 1d. and 2d. of 1840, making the 4d. rate. Other combinations are known, notably three 1d. and two 2d. of 1840 on a Mulready addressed to Boston, U.S.A.

ME2		1d. envelope (printed in black)	£325	£425
		Used with 1840 1d. black adhesive	†	£8000
		Used with 1841 1d. red adhesive	†	£8000
		Used with 1840 2d. blue adhesive	†	£20000
		Used with 1841 2d. blue adhesive	†	£20000
		Used before 6 May 1840 *from*	†	£18000
		Used on 6 May 1840	†	£12000
		Used on 7–9 May 1840	†	£2000
		Used on Sunday 10 May 1840	†	£12000
	a.	Unused sheet of twelve (Forme 3 or Forme 4)	£5500	†
	b.	Original stereos from Formes 1 to 4, excluding A137 *each*	£325	£425
	c.	Displaced stereo A137	£375	£500
	d.	Substituted stereo A173	£375	£500
	e.	Unplaced stereos A183, A186, A187, A193, A194 *each*	£400	£525
	f.	Stereos from Formes 5 and 6 *each from*	£500	£650
	g.	With advertisement, etc. printed inside *from*	£1800	£2500
	h.	"Stitch watermark"		
	i.	Printed double, one albino and inverted stereo A134	†	—
	s.	"Specimen", Type 2 (stereos A141, A158, A276, A288) *from*	£6000	
ME3		2d. letter sheet (printed in blue)	£375	£1500
		Used pair	†	£5500
		Used with 1840 1d. black adhesive	†	£30000
		Used with 1841 1d. red adhesive	†	£30000
		Used with 1840 2d. blue adhesive	†	£20000
		Used with 1841 2d. blue adhesive	†	£18000
		Used on 6 May 1840	†	£65000
		Used on 7–9 May 1840 *from*	†	£9000
	b.	Unused sheet of twelve	£5000	†
	c.	Any stereo *each*	£375	£1500
	d.	"Stitch watermark"	£450	£1600
	e.	With advertisement, etc. printed inside *from*		£2500
	s.	"Specimen", Type 2 (stereos a91, a96) *from*	£6500	
ME4		2d. envelope (printed in blue)	£400	£1500
		Used with 1840 1d. black adhesive	†	£30000
		Used with 1841 1d. red adhesive	†	£30000
		Used with 1840 2d. blue adhesive	†	£20000
		Used with 1841 2d. blue adhesive	†	£20000
		Used on 6 May 1840	†	
		Used on 7–9 May 1840 *from*	†	£9000
	a.	Unused sheet of twelve	£5250	†
	b.	Any stereo, except a211 *each*	£375	£1500
	c.	Unplaced stereo a211, a195	£550	£1800
	d.	"Stitch watermark"	£550	£1700
	s.	"Specimen", Type 2 (stereos a208, a209) *from*	£6750	

Mulready Lettersheets and Envelopes

Prices refer to the Cancellation on a Mulready lettersheet or envelope

Coloured Maltese Cross Cancellations

	1d. Mulready	*2d. Mulready*
Red Maltese Cross	£350	£2200
Black Maltese Cross	£300	£1800
Blue Maltese Cross	£15000	*
Violet Maltese Cross (Market Street/ Glasgow)	£40000	*
Magenta Maltese Cross (Shades)	£10000	*
Ruby Maltese Cross (Aberdeen)	£4000	*
Orange Maltese Cross (Liverpool)	£1500	*
Vermilion Maltese Cross (Bristol)	£2250	*
Yellow-bistre Maltese Cross (Ayton)	£25000	*
Brown Maltese Cross (Haddington)	£5000	*
Red and Blue Maltese Cross	£18000	*
1844 in Black	£700	£1900

Distinctive Maltese Crosses

	1d. Mulready	*2d. Mulready*
Coventry	£6000	*
Dublin in Red	£1250	£4000
Dublin in Black	£1250	£4000
Dursley	*	£25000
Greenock	£2750	*
Kelso	£12500	*
Leamington	£2800	*
Leeds	£4500	*
Limerick	£3000	*
London Type I	£650	*
London Type II	£800	*
Manchester	£6000	*
Mullingar	£25000	*
Norwich	£6000	£12000
Wotton-under-edge	£30000	*
York	£15000	*
Scottish Type I or II	£1000	*
Stonehaven red	£30000	*

"Numbers in Maltese Crosses" Cancellations

		1d. Mulready	*2d. Mulready*
Number 1 in Cross	*from*	£2000	£6000
Number 2 in Cross	*from*	£2000	*
Number 3 in Cross	*from*	£2000	*
Number 4 in Cross	*from*	£2000	£6000
Number 5 in Cross	*from*	£2000	*
Number 6 in Cross	*from*	£2000	£6000
Number 7 in Cross	*from*	£2000	£6000
Number 8 in Cross	*from*	£2000	£6000
Number 9 in Cross	*from*	£2000	£6000
Number 10 in Cross	*from*	£2750	£6000
Number 11 in Cross	*from*	£2750	£6000
Number 12 in Cross	*from*	£3000	£6000

Town and "Penny Post" Postmarks

	1d. Mulready	*2d. Mulready*
Penny Post as sole pmk	£5000	*
Town Datestamp as sole pmk	£5000	*

SECTIONS A–G

The Line-Engraved Issues

Essays, Die Proofs, Plate Proofs, Colour Trials and Reprints of the Line-Engraved Stamps

---

Introduction. Within the confines of a catalogue of this nature it is possible to include only a brief description of the material that exists in these categories. Some of the items mentioned are unique, since the only existing specimens are in the Royal Collection, The Post Office Heritage Services, the Victoria and Albert Museum, the British Library or similar permanent repositories. Such items are therefore not priced.

The material is classified in the order of sequence of the events leading to the production of the issued stamps, and each value is dealt with separately. The following checklist will aid location of the various sections:

Section	*Cat. Nos.*	*Description*
First Experiments for the Stamps	DP1–3	*page* 19
Gum and Paper Trials	DP3a	20
The First (Later Rejected) Die for the One Penny Stamp	DP4–9	20
The One Penny (Accepted Die I)	DP10–20G	21
"The One Penny Blue" (Plate 8)	DP21–25	24
The One Penny Dickinson Silk-thread Paper Trial	DP22	24
The One Penny Retouched Die (Die II)	DP26A–36	25
The One Penny "Plate Number" Issue	DP37–40	27
The Twopence Stamp of 1840	DP41–41A	27
The Twopence Stamp of 1841	DP42–44	28
Experiments for a new Blue Colour for the Twopence Stamp	DP45	29
The Twopence Die II (Retouched Die)	DP46–50	29
The Three-Halfpence Stamp	DP51–58	30
The Halfpenny Stamp	DP58A–69	31
Essays for a Farthing Stamp	DP70	33
The Prince Consort Essays	DP71	34
Dr. Perkins Paper Trials	DP72	34
Postal Notices	PN1–5	34

First Experiments for the Stamps

One of the main reasons in choosing the Queens' head for the stamps was that it was instantly recognised so that any attempt at imitation would be easily detected. The intricate engine-turned background was another deterrent against the forger.

On 2 December 1839 Henry Cole visited Perkins, Bacon and Petch to enquire about printing the adhesive stamps and on 13 December the firm agreed to prepare a die to be composed of "the best Engraving of Her Majesty's Portrait which we can get executed by the best Artist" and Rowland Hill ordered the die on 16 December, "the Queen's head to be drawn from the City Medal". This had been designed by William Wyon and struck to commemorate Queen Victoria's visit to the Guildhall on 9 November 1837. The printers were first asked to produce a sketch of the prepared stamp before engraving was started.

DP1–3. **December 1839.** Three essays in black exist on white paper of engine-turned backgrounds. On the first two, paper cut-outs of the Queen's head are pasted; on the third the "head" is a cleared space with "HALF OUNCE POST OFFICE ONE PENNY" in hand-printed lettering encircling it. These items are in the Victoria and Albert Museum.

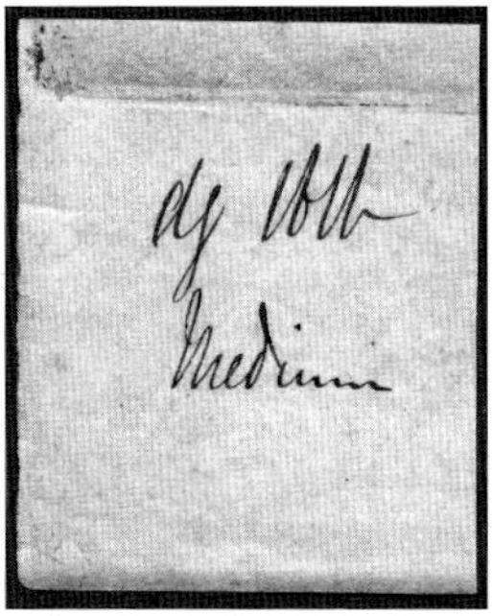

DP3a

DP3a. Paper and Gum trials. During this period, paper and gum trials were carried out by Perkins Bacon to establish the preferred combination for the stamps. These trials were endorsed in manuscript with the paper weight, 12, 16, 17 and 20 lbs, the type of gum, lg (light), og (ordinary) and dg (dark) together with any chemicals added. Ca (calcium), Po (potassium), Mag (magnesium). Also noted in manuscript are, Dickinson, fcap and medium. *Price for the single example shown* £3500.

The First (Later Rejected) Die for the One Penny Stamp

The printers commissioned Henry Carbould to draw the Queen's head and began experimenting with the engine-turned background. By January the die was ready for an engraving of the head. This was undertaken by Charles Heath, one-time partner of Perkins, who enlisted the engraving skill of his son Frederick, and the die was ready by the middle of January.

January 1840. Four black die proofs exist, showing different stages in development of the head on a light engine-turned background:

DP4. **First Stage.** With the head in an early stage with only part of the engraving completed (*illustrated*).

DP5. **Second Stage.** With the head completed but having uncleared spaces around. The only known proof of this has the spaces deepened by indian ink (Royal Collection).

DP6. **Third stage.** The spaces around the head having been engraved (*illustrated*).

DP7. **Fourth stage.** Completed and with the addition of the words "POSTAGE ONE PENNY" (*illustrated*). (*Prices from* £50000.)

DP8. **1840–1935. Reprints.** The die in its final form remained with Perkins, Bacon & Co. and reprints were made from time to time. These reprints have smudges below "ONE" and "NNY" which vary but are not always present. The reprints are:

(a) On white card in black. (*Prices from* £18000.)
(b) On cream wove paper in black, yellow-green, ultramarine, rose-carmine, orange-red. (*Prices from* £17000.)
(c) On paper watermarked Small Star in yellow-green, ultramarine, rose-carmine. (*Prices from* £15000.)
(d) On paper watermarked Large Broad Star in yellow-green. (*Prices from* £10000.)

DP4

DP6

DP7–8

DP9. **1849. Background Trials.** The above die was rejected and trials were made of a darker background.

Prints from the plate itself exist in black (on card) and in carmine, blue, green, purple and orange. (*Prices from* £3500.)

A proof exists in black of the central band of the plate, which was the background finally adopted (Royal Collection) and there is a proof of the central bank taken from the roller. (*Prices from* £10000.)

In the Royal Collection there is a unique die proof showing the Queen's head from the rejected die in conjunction with the darker background.

The One Penny (Accepted Die I)

Work started on the second die (the accepted Die I) in mid January and Charles Heath completed it on 23 January. On 30 January Rowland Hill gave instructions for the inscription to read simply "POSTAGE ONE PENNY", thus dispensing with the "HALF OZ" which had figured on the Wyon essays. On 20 February the die was returned to Perkins, Bacon and Petch. The Queen expressed high satisfaction with the proof on 2 March.

DP10. **January 1840.** Die proof on India paper of the darker background with space cleared for the head. In black (*illustrated*). (*Price* £75000).

DP10

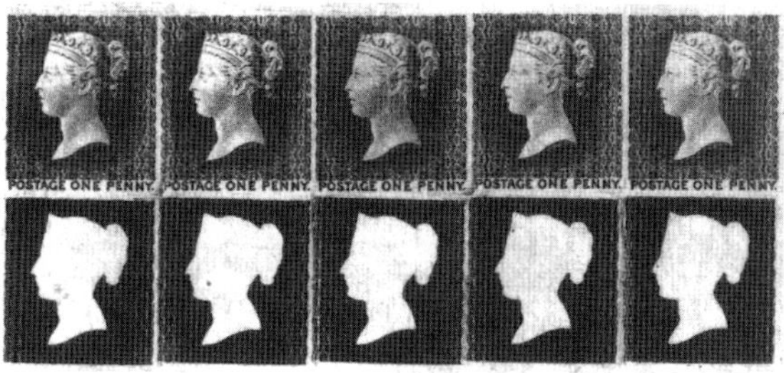

DP11 (illustration reduced in size)

DP13

DP15d

DP11. **January 1840.** Five impressions as DP7 above, together with five of DP10, all in blue. This proof is of an experimental plate made for comparison of the two backgrounds and as a trial in spacing (*illustrated*). (*Price the complete piece,* £125000.)

DP12. **February 1840.** The next step, that of engraving the head in the vacant space, was now taken. Die proofs in black exist of a first stage with head complete but showing white area behind the head. (*Price* £125000.)

DP13. A later die proof shows these to have been filled in and some fine lines added down the back of the neck (*illustrated*). (*Price* £125000).

DP14. **February 1840.** While the head was being engraved Perkins, Bacon & Petch made use of duplicate impressions in the form of DP7 above, for colour trials and other purposes. These trials are on thick, spongy white paper in purple-blue, deep blue, blue, light blue; dark brown, red-brown, umber-brown, light umber; brick-red, deep red, pale red. These colour trials are sometimes found cancelled with the Maltese Cross or a cancellation stamp of Charles F. Whiting which included the monogram "VR". (*Prices from* £12000.)

DP16

Black *Blue*

DP17a

DP17b

Essays for the Top and Bottom Labels

DP15. **February 1840.** Attention was now turned to essays for the top and bottom labels. For these, background proofs in the style of DP10 were used.

(a) Essays on white card with "POSTAGE ONE PENNY" in small black sans-serif capitals at the bottom.

(b) Essays on white card with "POSTAGE" at the top and "ONE PENNY" at the bottom in white sans-serif capitals and "AB", "VR" in the four corners in black capitals.

(c) Essays on white paper with lettering at top and bottom similar to, though smaller than, the eventually accepted form. The four corners were cut away and small squares of white paper were pasted in; these were given a hand-drawn thin frame line. "BR", "VR" were insicribed in the corners in pencil. Annotated "Approved R.H. 2.21.40" on reverse.

(d) As (c) but with the "BR", "VR" letters engraved in small Roman capitals in the centre of starlike ornaments (illustrated). (Price £175000.)

(a) and (b) are only known in the Victoria and Albert Museum. The whereabouts of (c) is unknown. Three specimens of (d) exist, one being in the Royal Collection, one in The Post Office Heritage Services and the other in private hands.

DP16. **February 1840** (*Illustrated*). Four rough water-colour sketches of the stamps, two each of the 1d. in black and the 2d. in blue, were made in February 1840. Originally on one white card with the lower two marked "1d." and "2d." in pencil on the heads, these were divided to make two pairs. The lower part is in the Royal Collection, the upper part is in The Post Office Heritage Services.

DP17. **March 1840.** The lettering of "POSTAGE" and "ONE PENNY" had now reached the form eventually approved for the issued stamps, as is shown in the die proofs of March 1840 on India paper on soft card.

(a) This die proof is in the form of the issued stamps save that the corners are blank (*illustrated*). Two of these proofs, differing very slightly through later work on one by the engraver, are in the Royal Collection. A further example is in The Post Office Heritage Services. It is believed that two exist in private hands, one of which was sold at auction in 1995. (*Price* £175000.)

(b) As (a) but with the "stars" in the upper corners (*Illustrated*). (*Price* £135000.)

(c) As (b) but reversed, on thin bluish wove paper. One example, underinked, is in the Royal Collection and one other is in private hands. The purpose of this proof is unknown. (*Priced from* £75000.)

The First Plate Proof

DP18. **1 April 1840.** A complete plate proof of 240 impressions, taken from Plate 1 on plain paper before either the letters had been inserted in the corners or the marginal inscriptions had been added. This plate proof, formerly in possession of Sir Rowland Hill and signed on the reverse, is now in The Post Office Heritage Services. No other similar proofs are known.

DP19, "Rainbow" colour trials, first trial plate of three

The "Rainbow" Colour Trials of 1840 (May 1840 unless stated)

These were produced to test various combinations of stamp and cancellation ink.

DP19. **First 1d. Trial Plate.** This was a small plate of three impressions without corner letters and with the top right corner of each impression void (*illustrated*). All three impressions show the "O" flaw, later seen on issued stamps from Plates 7, 8, 9 and 10. Proofs are known:

(a) On paper watermarked Small Crown in mauve-pink, lilac-brown, blue-black.
(b) On similar paper dipped in prussiate of potash in blue-black.
(c) On white wove paper in deep blue.
(d) On white wove paper dipped in prussiate of potash in deep blue.

The Small Crown watermark of proofs (a) and (b) above was not exactly similar to that used for the issued stamps. Trial proofs as above are known obliterated with "No. 712" in black and showing evidence of attempts made later to clean off the cancellation. (*Prices of all the above from* £120000.)

Second Trial Plate. This succeeded the small plate of three impressions. On this latter plate there were twelve impressions (none with "O" flaw). There are no corner letters.

Complete Sheet without Voided Corners. The only known complete sheets from this plate are in the Royal Collection and in The Post Office Heritage Services. This is probably the first proof taken. On the top right-hand stamp there is a thick ink line which is presumably an indication to the printer that this corner of each impression was to be void.

DP20. **Sheet with Voided Corners.** The voiding of the coners was effected by filling the grooves in the plate with wax.

State 1 (*illustrated*). Proof sheets (4 × 3) in this state are known in black, orange-red, reddish brown and deep blue. (*Prices: Singles from* £4500; *Sheets from* £65000.)

State 2. As State 1 but a tiny dash appears on the bottom line of the S.E. corner square of the second stamp of the third row. Proof sheets are known:

(a) On white wove paper dipped in prussiate of potash in lilac-pink, lilac-rose, dull rose-red, deep blue.
(b) On stout roughish white wove paper in black, rose-red, deep blue.
(c) On thin white wove paper in bright pink, lilac-rose, dull rose-red, deep rose-red, lilac-brown, deep red-brown, black, red, blue, deep dull blue, Prussian blue, dull lilac.
(d) On thick bluish laid paper (June 1840) in dull red, brownish rose-red, deep rose-red.
(e) A proof in black on paper stained with prussiate of potash, logwood and cochineal, giving a lilac-rose tinge to the paper (August 1840).

(*Prices: Singles from* £4000; *Sheets from* £50000.)

State 3 (*illustrated*). The voided corners are more uniform in shape compared with the ragged corners of States 1 and 2. Proof sheets are known:

(a) On white wove paper dipped in prussiate of potash in red, red-brown, rose-red, deep blue, black.

DP20, State 1

DP20, State 3

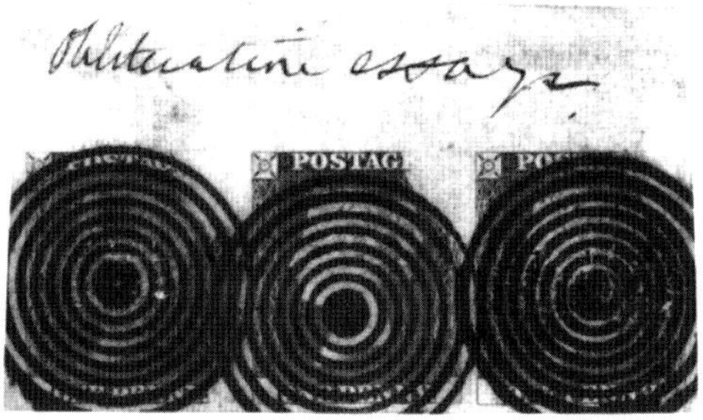

Typical cancellation experiments

(b) On white wove paper in red, pale red, red-brown, crimson-red, dull blue, deep blue, Prussian blue, yellow-green, deep green.

(c) On small Crown Wmk paper, usually sideways (September 1840), in red-brown, blue.

(d) On thick bluish laid paper (20 November 1840), in blue, dull blue, green, bluish green, dark olive-green, drab.

(e) On thick bluish laid paper dipped in prussiate of potash (November 1840), in dark olive-green. Sheets from this plate in all three states are known. (*Prices: Singles from* £4000; *Sheets from* £50000.)

Variations of the numerous shades are found resulting from the addition to the inks of prussiate of potash or oil. Varnish was applied to the face of some sheets and a few sheets were gummed.

DP20F. **Cancellation Experiments.** Experiments were made on these colour trial sheets using various different cancellers (including the Maltese Cross) and different black inks. A vermilion ink was used on some black prints. Attempts to clean off the obliterations were made with various agents. (*Single examples from* £12000.)

There are other rare documents bearing examples of the "Rainbow Trials", one of the most interesting being a document bearing 20 different in shades of red and red-brown. (*Price* £250000.)

DP20G. Experiments were made in June 1840 with different weights of paper and some sheets were printed from Plate 7. The paper used was of weights 24, 26 and 28 lb. (the normal weight being 30 lb. per ream). Interesting examples of these experiments are to be found in The Post Office Heritage Services. (*Prices from* £40000.)

"The One Penny Blue"

DP21. **15 December 1840. Trial use of the 1d. Plate 8.** Four entire sheets of 240 stamps were printed in each of three colours, red-brown, full deep blue and Prussian blue. These were printed for Rowland Hill as he wished to see the chosen colour of the 1d. in sheet form. Also he wished to make a decision on the shade of the 2d. He chose the "full deep blue". Some of these 1d. blue proofs reached the public and were used as stamps. What became of the bulk of the twelve sheets is not known. (*Price* £125000.)

One Penny (Plate 11) Trial on Dickinson Silk Thread Paper

DP22. **1 May 1841.** Following the trial printing of the 2d. value of March 1841 (see DP44), a trial was made in full deep red using the 240 unit Plate 11. The first and last vertical columns of the stamps had no silk threads. The ink used blued the paper deeply. Eight sheets were printed, six of these being gummed, two ungummed, but we have only seen examples without gum. This paper was not considered to be as safe as the watermarked paper. This trial, S.G. 16, was formerly listed as A1m in this catalogue. (*Price* £4500.)

Trials to Frustrate Copies Being Made by the Anastatic Process

DP23. **1852.** Alarm having been caused by persons called Glynn and Appel, professing to be able to produce imitations of the 1d. stamp by the anastatic process, experiments were made with new colours. For these trials (which resulted in no change in the inks in regular use) the small 1d. plate of 1840 with voided corners was used. Printings were (a) in dull greyish black on thick wove paper and (b) in dull pale purple on stout wove paper dipped in prussiate of potash.

Late Proofs from the One Penny Original Die

DP24. **January 1858.** A proof of the 1d. Original Die in rose-red on India paper on white card. Of the known examples of this proof one bears the manuscript initials "J.O.P." at top left and is also endorsed "Proof taken from the original Heaths Head taken 29 Jany 1858", the second in black is endorsed "Proofs from the original die taken 9 Feb 1858". Both these items are in The Post Office Heritage Services.

DP25 (*illustration reduced in size*)

DP29b (*illustration reduced in size*)

DP25. **1860–1871.** Between 1860 and 1871 the numeral "1" and the words "Old Original" were engraved on the die in two lines below the stamp. The words are in sans-serif capitals and are reversed on the prints.

Of this state of the die, proofs are known in black, pale blue, pale and deep orange-vermilion, sage-green, yellow and orange-yellow, purple and deep purple (*illustrated*). Specimens cut close to the design do not show the "1" or the "Old Original". (*Prices from* £12000 in black.)

DP26. **April 1890. "Guildhall Proof".** Proof impressions in black on thin yellowish white wove paper on soft white card. Printed in connection with the celebrations of the jubilee of uniform inland penny postage, 16 May 1890. The inscriptions and lower numerals are inked and the paper was deeply sunk and usually partly torn by the edges of the dies with considerable staining of the creases so formed. (*Price* £12000.)

For the 1d. Die II, 2d., $1\frac{1}{2}$d. and $\frac{1}{2}$d. of this series see DP31, DP48, DP58 and DP69.

The One Penny Retouched Die (Die II)

The new Die II was made from an impression of Heath's original Die I by retouching, after the Board of Inland Revenue had agreed to the request of Messrs. Perkins, Bacon that a new deeper-cut die be employed. William Humphrys carried out the re-engraving.

DP26A. **1854.** First state of die proof showing lines in the upper part of the downswept hair broken and the S.E.–N.W. diagonal lines on the neck are very short and do not touch the continuous ones of the other diagonal. (*Prices from* £45000.)

A die proof endorsed "2nd state" exists in the Royal Collection.

DP27. **September 1854.** A die proof exists which was rejected as it was considered to be too unlike the original. This proof is in The Post Office Heritage Services.

DP28. **November 1854.** Die proof impressions were taken from a second new die also prepared by Humphrys: (a) before hardening in black; (b) after hardening, showing cracks on the surface. The word "NEW" was engraved above the impression in positive, therefore appearing reversed on the print. This again was in black. (*Prices from* £25000.)

Late Impression from the One Penny Die II (Retouched Die)

February 1871. Ormond Hill Die Proofs. At this time Mr. Ormond Hill instructed the printers to prepare a series of proofs in various colours. Die proof with the "NEW" and the numeral "3" reversed above and below the impression respectively. Rust marks show below the letters "PENN" and fine horizontal lines show at the right and left of the centre of the impression.

DP29. Proofs with "NEW" and "3" uninked (a) on white thin paper on card in black, rose; (b) on thin hard yellowish white wove paper in black, Prussian blue, cobalt, orange-vermilion, pale carmine, sage-green, emerald-green, deep carmine, violet (*illustrated*). (*Prices from* £18000 in black.)

For the 2d., $1\frac{1}{2}$d. and $\frac{1}{2}$d. of this series see DP46, DP56 and DP64.

DP30. **October–November 1878. Die Proof Trials for Lighter and more Fugitive Colours.** Group 1 on yellowish white wove paper, watermarked Small Star, in dull ultramarine, rose-red, purple. (*Prices from* £20000).

All three are known overprinted "Specimen", Type 10 and the 1d. purple with "Specimen" written across it in black ink. Examples are found which show evidence of tests of the inks to see if they were fugitive. (*Prices from* £20000.)

For the 2d., $1\frac{1}{2}$d and $\frac{1}{2}$d. of this series see DP47, DP57 and DP67 and for Group 2 see DP39 and DP40.

DP31. **April 1890. "Guildhall Proof".** Die proof on thin yellowish white wove paper on soft white card, in black. (*Price* £12500.)

For fuller description see DP26 and for 2d., $1\frac{1}{2}$d. and $\frac{1}{2}$d. of this series, see DP48, DP58 and DP69.

DP32. **1911. Die Proofs:** (a) on soft yellowish white card, in black; (b) by surface-print on similar card in black, showing the black and white parts of the design reversed. (*Prices from* £12500.)

DP33. **Secondary Dies.** (a) On India paper, on white card with numerals reversed above the impressions. All in black: No. "2", No. "3", No. "4", No. "5", No. "6". (*Prices from* £16000.)

(b) 1890. On thin yellowish white paper, on soft white card, in black: No. "2". (*Price* £12500.)

An Official Imitation of the One Penny Stamp

DP34. **November 1856.** By order of the Board of Inland Revenue, Somerset House, an imitation of the One Penny stamp was made to ascertain whether a skilful engraver could exactly reproduce the design of the stamp. The imitation exists today only as a print in red of portions of each of a pair of "stamps", on proof paper mounted on card. Three examples are known, one in the Royal Collection, another in the R. M. Phillips Collection at The Post Office Heritage Services, and one in private hands.

The So-called "Royal" Reprints

DP35. **September 1865.** Plate proof impressions were taken from the 1d. Plate 66, Die II, after it had been withdrawn from use (*illustrated*). Prints were made on paper watermarked Large Crown, imperf:

(a) In black with watermark inverted. (*Price* £2000.)
(b) In carmine-rose. (*Price* £1600.)
(c) In carmine-rose overprinted "Specimen", Type 2. (*Price* £12000.)

The South Kensington Exhibition Proofs

DP36. **February 1872.** With official permission for the International Exhibition at South Kensington in 1872, Perkins, Bacon printed proofs on thick white card, imperforate from Die II, Plate 27 in black. The printers were allowed to retain this sheet. Upon the liquidation of this firm in 1935 the sheet was sold and broken up for sale, 1d. black, proof. (*Price* £800.)

At the same time proofs were also printed in the same manner from the current plates as follows: (a) $\frac{1}{2}$d. rose, Plate 3; (b) 1d. carmine-rose, Die II, Plate 126; (c) $1\frac{1}{2}$d. rose-red, Plate 3; (d) 2d. blue, Plate 14, but these items are only known in pairs overprinted "Specimen" in the Royal Collection.

At the Stamp Show 2000 an original press, once owned by Perkins Bacon & Petch, was used to print 1d. blacks minus corner letters. These were sold in presentation packs. The modern plate was created from an original die held by Post Office Heritage Sevices.

DP35
1d. Plate 66, Die II

DP37
Die I

The One Penny "Plate Number" Issue

DP37. **1858.** Essay was taken from 1d. Die I. A special transfer impression was taken up and the stars were removed from the top corners. An assumed plate number "123" was engraved in both the side panels. A plate impression was laid down and letters BA–AB were engraved in small sans-serif capitals. The essay was in red. (*Price* £18000.)

Late Proofs from the Penny "Plate Number" Issue

DP38. **April 1867. Paris Exhibition Proofs.** Proof sheets were taken from Plate 103 on soft white card and were imperforate. They were specially printed for this exhibition, where blocks of 20 cut from the sheets were shown. Proofs in black or rose. (*Price* £1600 *each.*)

For the 2d. and $1\frac{1}{2}$d. of this series see DP49 and DP54.

DP39. **1878–79. Plate Proof Trials for Lighter and more Fugitive Colours.** Group 2. The following trials are known, all from plates and on paper then in regular use. All were imperforate, trial cancellations were mentioned, some in manuscript: (a) mauve, Plate 191; (b) as (a) but with trial cancellation; (c) mauve-pink, Plate 212; (d) rose-red, Plate 146 with trial cancellation; (e) rose-red, Plate 191 with trial cancellation. (*Prices from* £10000 in rose-red.)

For the 2d. and $\frac{1}{2}$d of this series see DP50 and DP68. For the first group of similar trials see DP30.

DP40. **Plate Proof Impressions.** These are apparently of the same series as above. The 1d. Plate 214 is known printed in rose on thick, yellowish vertically laid card. (*Price* £12000.)

The Twopence Stamps of 1840

DP41. **April 1840.** The die for this stamp was taken from a modified roller relief of the One Penny die. Printed in black on India paper the lower corners are of course blank and "stars" appear in the upper corners. Six examples are known including one each in the Royal Collection and The Post Office Heritage Services (*illustrated.*) One cover exists with an example cancelled by a black Maltese Cross. (*Single examples from* £180000.)

DP41A. A similar die proof was struck about 1868 in black on white wove paper with a *se-tenant* impression to the left of the prepared background; the latter appears to be defaced or corroded.

DP41

DP42a

DP42b

The Twopence Stamp of 1841

It was decided to modify the design of the original 2d. to be issued at the same time as the change of colour of the 1d. stamp from black to red. Essays for this stamp were taken from two dies, both having two impressions (one above the other). They were taken from a roller relief of the original twopence die.

DP42. **23 October 1840. With value blocked out.**

(a) In black with white line below "POSTAGE" only.

(b) In black with a white line below "POSTAGE" and an additional line above the value tablet.

26 October 1840. With the value unaltered.

(c) In blue as (a); (d) in blue as (b). (*Prices from* £15000.)

DP43 (illustration reduced in size)

DP43. **15 January 1841. Small Trial Twopence Plate.** The small plate of 12 impressions was made because the first 2d. plate of the new type "with white lines" was not ready and specimens were required for distribution with the announcement of the forthcoming issue. There were no letters in the lower corners. Printings were in full deep blue.

(*Price per single* £1500.)

(*Price per single, watermark inverted* £3000.)

(*Price for complete sheet* £20000.)

Postally used examples are known. Price for 1844 type cancellation *from* £12000. Maltese Cross cancellation *from* £18000.

DP44

DP45

DP46

Trial Printings on "Dickinson" Paper

DP44. **9 March 1841.** It being desired to experiment with the "Dickinson" paper with "silk" threads embedded in it, the small plate of twelve 2d. stamps without letters in the corners (see under DP43 above) was utilized. The top right corner of each impression was voided in the same manner adopted with the small 1d. plate used for the "Rainbow" trials (*see illustration*). Only five pieces of paper were supplied by Dickinson & Co. and these were so small as to allow only two of the three rows on the plate to be printed. Three pieces were printed in red-brown from the top two rows and two pieces in blue from the lower two rows. All five pieces were blued by chemical action and all were gummed. One sheet in each colour is in the Royal Collection. (*Prices red-brown* £22000; *blue* £27000.)

For the 1d. red on Dickinson paper see DP22.

Experiments for a new Blue Colour for the Twopence Stamp

DP45. **April 1867.** A special single unit plate was made of the 1d. value, using the transfer roller of Plate 75, Die II. Before any prints were made the upper left corner of the design was erased (*see illustration*). Prints were made: (a) on thin hard yellowish white wove paper in bright blue, Prussian blue and rose-red; (b) on deep blue diagonally laid paper in red. Examples are found cancelled and showing evidence of tests to remove the cancellation. (*Prices from* £12500. *With trial cancellation* £9000.)

The Twopence Die II (Retouched Die)

This shows the "stars" in the upper corners and the words "NEW DIE" "1" and "34" reversed and uninked. It was completed on 8 April 1858, but no 1858 proof impressions are known. Later impressions are recorded:

DP46. **February 1871. Ormond Hill Die Proofs.** Die proofs (*illustrated*) (a) on thin white paper, on card in black, deep blue; (b) on thin hard yellowish white wove paper in black, ultramarine, chrome-yellow, pale sage-green, brownish orange, deep lilac-rose. (*Prices from* £18000 in black.)

For the 1d., 1½d. and ½d. of this series see DP29, DP56 and DP64.

DP47. **October–November 1878. Die Proof Trials for Lighter and more Fugitive Colours.** Group 1 on yellowish white wove paper on card, watermarked Small Star in mauve-pink, dull rose-pink and bright ultramarine. All three are known overprinted "Specimen", Type 10. (*Prices from* £15000 *in either state*).

For the 1d., 1½d. and ½d. of this series see DP30, DP57 and DP67 and for Group 2 see DP50.

DP48. **April 1890. "Guildhall Proof".** Die proof on thin yellowish white wove paper on soft white card, in black. (*Price* £10000.)

For a fuller description see DP26 and for the 1d. Die II, 1½d. and ½d. of this series see DP31, DP58 and DP69.

Late Proofs from the Twopence "Plate Number" Issue

DP49. **April 1867. Paris Exhibition Proofs.** Proof sheets were taken from the 2d. Plate 9 on soft white card imperforate. These were specially printed for the Paris Exhibition where blocks of 20 cut from the sheets were shown with the exception of the 2d. black. The sheets were printed in (a) black; (b) blue. (*Prices from* £2000 in black, £2500 in blue.)

For the 1d. and 1½d. of this series see DP38 and DP54.

DP50. **1878–79. Plate Proof Trials for Lighter and more Fugitive Colours.** Group 2. The following trials are known from plates and paper then in regular use. All were Plate 15, imperforate. Trial cancellations were mentioned: (a) pale ultramarine, (b) bright ultramarine, (c) lake-red, (d) purple. (*Prices from* £15000.)

For the 1d. and 1½d. of this series see DP39 and DP68. For the first group of similar trials see DP47.

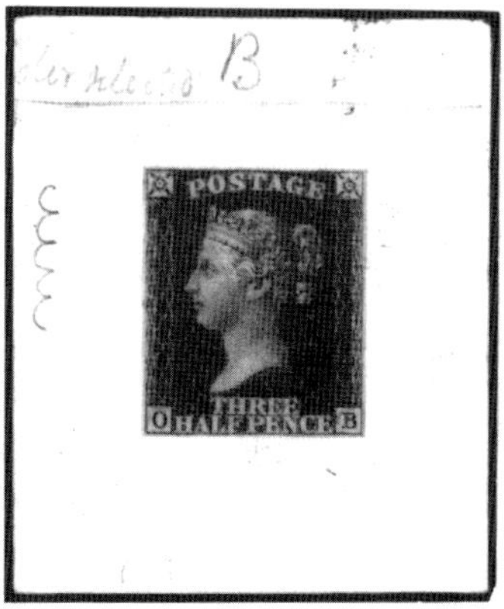

DP51c

DP52b

DP53b

DP56–57

The Three-Halfpence Stamp

DP51. **February 1860.** Three essays were prepared by altering specimens of the 1d. Die II rose-red stamp with crosses in the upper corners:

(a) With "POSTAGE—ONE PENNY" obliterated and the words "THREE"—"HALF"—"PENCE"—"POSTAGE" added in flake white at the four sides ("POSTAGE" being at the foot).

(b) With all four corners cleared and letters BA–AB inserted; "POSTAGE" is in a slightly curved form about the head and "THREE" "HALFPENCE" in two lines below the head.

(c) Similar in appearance to (b) but retains the stars in the upper corners. The top and bottom panels were painted out in red and labels were pasted over them giving a final effect as in (b). The lettering is in white on a pale rose ground. (*See illustration.*) Of these three essays (a) is in the Royal Collection, (b) was in the Berlin Postal Museum and (c) The Post Office Heritage Services.

DP52. **March 1860.** (a) An essay in form very similar to that approved, made by altering a 1d. stamp printed in mauve-pink. The heart-shaped band is painted around the head in flake white and the words "POSTAGE" "THREE" "HALFPENCE" painted on the band in mauve-pink; the stamp is on a card bearing writing and the initials "O.H." of Ormond Hill.

(b) The approved essay, similar to the above and in mauve-pink but with the wording higher up on the band and the neck shortened (*illustrated*). A specimen of this in the Royal Collection bears a note written by Ormond Hill below the essay, "Approved 12.3.60 O.H.". A similar essay is in The Post Office Heritage Services.

DP53. **March 1860.** (a) Die proof in mauve-pink on white card submitted to Ormond Hill. The spaces between the words on the white heart-shaped band are filled in with fine scroll ornamentation in pencil.

(b) Another specimen of the above with a pattern inserted in pencil between "THREE" and "HALFPENCE". This example bears the words at the foot "Proof from die recd. 17.3.60" and at the back of the card: "suggested a light engine turning or chain pattern between the words" (*illustrated*).

(c) Proof in black on white card of the die used for the stamps. An example of this is also known marked in pencil: "Proof from hardened die. 20.3.60". (*Price* £15000.)

DP54. **March 1860.** A supply of 10,000 sheets of the 1½d. value was printed in March and April 1860, from Plate 1 on Large Crown watermarked paper, perf. 14 in rosy mauve. The colour of the ink stained the paper a bluish tinge. The stamps were never issued for postal use and 8,962 sheets were destroyed in 1867. It is rare, and is listed as G5.

In March 1860 an experiment was made with some imperforate examples of the 1½d. mauve-pink to see whether the colour was fugitive. A card exists in The Post Office Heritage Services with four examples all overwritten "Specimen" in black, two having been exposed to sunlight for four days, the other two having been kept in the dark. The test resulted in a noticeable fading of the pink shade from the exposed stamps. A block of twenty of this 1½d. mauve-pink, perforated, was shown at the Paris Exhibition of 1867 together with proof blocks of the 1d. and 2d. stamps (see DP38 and DP49).

Late Proofs from the Three-Halfpenny Die

DP55. **1870.** These were colour trials for the halfpenny stamp of 1870.

(1) On soft yellowish white wove paper: (a) pale yellow-green, numbered in pencil "1"; (b) yellow-green, numbered in pencil "2"; (c) dark blue-green, numbered in pencil "3"; (d) deep green, numbered in pencil "1" and "3"; (e) pale rose-red, signed in ink, "J.O.P. 13.5.70"; (f) chrome-yellow, ditto; (g) orange-yellow, ditto: (h) orange-red, ditto. (*Prices from* £16000 *each*).

(2) On the blue wove paper: (a) pale yellow-green, numbered in pencil "1"; (b) yellow-green, numbered in pencil "2"; (c) dark blue-green, numbered in pencil "3"; (d) deep green, numbered in pencil "1" and "3". (*Prices from* £16000.)

DP56. **February 1871. Ormond Hill Die Proofs.** As last, with the number "35" reversed below the design (*illustrated*).

(a) On thin white paper on card in black, rose. (*Prices from* £15000.)

(b) On thin hard yellowish white wove paper in black, deep ultramarine, chrome-yellow, orange-yellow, pale sage-green, carmine-rose, deep lilac-rose, pale purple. (*Prices from* £14000 in black *each.*)

For the 1d., 2d. and ½d. of this series see DP29, DP46 and DP64.

DP57. **October–November 1878. Die Proof Trials for Lighter and more Fugitive Colours.** Group 1 on yellowish white wove paper, watermarked Small Star, in deep yellow-green, dull rose and deep mauve. All three are known overprinted "Specimen", Type 10. (*Prices from* £15000.)

Examples of the above trials are known overwritten "Specimen" in black ink and some show evidence of tests for fugitive inks. (*Prices from* £15000.)

For the 1d., 2d. and ½d. in this series see DP30, DP47 and DP67.

DP58. **April 1890. "Guildhall Proof".** Die proof on thin yellowish white wove paper on soft white card, in black. (*Price* £14000.)

For a fuller description see DP26 and for the 1d. Die II, 2d. and ½d. of this series see DP31, DP48 and DP69.

The Halfpenny Stamp

DP58A. **1865.** On 5 October 1865 Ormond Hill requested De La Rue to submit a design for a stamp of this value for the Postmaster-General; (a) In black on matt card (*Price* £10000); (b) in 1975 De La Rue placed on the market an essay in claret on card, which had been prepared in 1865. (*Price* £10000.)

DP58B. **April 1870.** De La Rue submitted a card containing eight hand-painted designs for complete stamps in red-brown and white together with four hand-painted designs for frame only in black and white, to be printed by surface-printing. This piece was put on the market by De La Rue in 1976 and is in The Post Office Heritage Services.

At the same time, the four frame designs (from a duplicate set) were offered for sale individually. (*Price* £6500 *each*).

DP59. **April–May 1870.** Nineteen essays for the new halfpenny stamp were submitted by Perkins, Bacon & Co. Of six that are in the Royal Collection three, marked A, B and C, show a large head against an engine-turned background with lettering at the sides. Another, marked "3", incorporates the Chalon Head as used for Grenada and other colonies. The last two show the later adopted form of a small head in a white circle; the last, initialled "W.H.S. 12.5.70" is nearest to the issued stamps.

DP60. **May 1870.** A proof specimen of the background adopted for the ½d. stamp. It is an exact reverse of that used for the other line-engraved stamps. In black on thin white card.

DP61. **May 1870.** A preliminary pencil drawing of the Queen's head believed to be by Frederick Heath who engraved the head on the ½d. die.

DP64, DP65, DP67

DP62. **May 1870.** (a) A ½d. proof in black on India paper, on white card, taken before the engraving of the head was strengthened. (b) Die proofs in black and in rose taken after the engraving of the head was strengthened and the die was hardened. (*Prices from* £15000.)

DP63. **December 1870. Reserve Die.** A reserve die was prepared and was engraved "No. 2" above the design. This die was held in case of loss or damage to the original. There are slight differences from the original in that the tip of the nose and lips of the Queen are only slightly shaded. A die proof in black on white wove paper is to be found in the British Museum. The actual die, which is now in The Post Office Heritage Services, was used in April 1967 when a further die proof was struck in black on thin white card which is also to be found in The Post Office Heritage Services.

DP64. **February 1871. Ormond Hill Die Proofs** (*illustrated*).

(a) Die proofs of the ½d. on thin white paper, on card in black, rose, emerald-green, brownish orange.

(b) Die proofs on thin hard yellowish white wove paper in dull lilac-rose, bright ultramarine, umber, brownish orange, orange-red, chrome-yellow, pale sage-green. (*Prices from* £15000.)

For the 1d., 2d. and 1½d. of this series see DP29, DP46 and DP56.

Colour Trials for the Halfpenny Stamp

DP65. **April–May 1870.** It was originally intended that the ½d. stamps should be green but technical difficulties caused a change to lake-rose. A number of trials of colours were made using the original flat die of the engine-turned background used for the stamp.

(1) On soft white wove paper: (a) green, marked in pencil "No. 1"; (b) yellow-green, marked in pencil "No. 2"; (c) dark blue-green, marked in pencil "No. 3"; (d) chrome-yellow; (e) orange-yellow; (f) orange-red.

(2) On blue wove paper: (a) dark-green, marked in pencil "No. 1"; (b) dark blue-green, marked in pencil "No. 3"; (c) dark blue-green, marked in pencil "1 and 3"; (d) yellow-green. (*Prices from* £12000.)

Some of the 1870 colour trials for the ½d. stamp were struck from the die of the 1½d. value. They will be found listed under DP55.

DP66. **April–May 1870.** Proof impressions were struck from a small plate of six incomplete impressions of the New South Wales 1d., 2d. and 3d. "Diadem" issue: (1) on white wove paper in yellow-green marked in pencil "2"; (2) on white, vertically laid paper in (a) blue-green, marked in pencil "1"; and (b) blue-green, marked in pencil "3". (*Prices from* £10000.)

Late Proofs from the Halfpenny Die

DP67. **October–November 1878. Die Proof Trials for Lighter and more Fugitive Colours.** Group 1 on yellowish white wove paper, watermarked Small Star in rose-lake and purple. Both are also known overprinted "Specimen", Type 10. (*Prices from* £10000.)

For the 1d., 2d. and 1½d. of this series see DP30, DP47 and DP57.

DP68. **1878–79. Plate Proof Trials for more Fugitive Colours.** Group 2. The following trials are known all from plates and on paper then in regular use. All were imperforate. Trial cancellations were mentioned: (a) lilac-rose, Plate 14; (b) as (a) but with trial cancellation; (c) pale lilac-rose, Plate 19; (d) blue-green, Plate 20. (*Prices from* £12500.)

For the 1d. and 2d. of this series see DP39 and DP50.

DP69. **April 1890. "Guildhall Proof".** Die proof on thin yellowish white wove paper on soft white card in black. (*Price* £14000.)

For a fuller description see DP26 and for the 1d. Die II, 2d. and 1½d. of this series see DP31, DP48 and DP58.

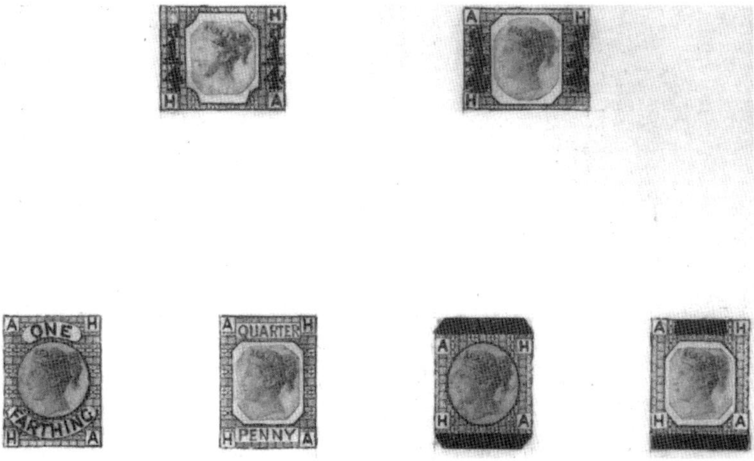

DP70

Essays for a Farthing Stamp

DP70. **November 1874.** Under the date 20 November 1874, the Engraving book of Perkins, Bacon & Co. contains an entry "Drawg. 6 postage stamps ¼d. for trial". A card bearing these six designs came to light in 1935 (*illustrated*) and with it another card bearing seven designs prepared by De La Rue & Co. Previous to this nothing was known of any suggestion that the Post Office might introduce a farthing value. These cards are believed to be unique (Heritage Services). The six drawings of the Perkins, Bacon essay have the head of the Queen cut out from actual specimens of the halfpenny stamp. The frames consist of engine-turned backgrounds printed in black and the value and corner letters were added by hand in black ink.

The Prince Consort Essays

Evidence given to the 1851 House of Commons Select Committee indicates that these essays were prepared for Henry Archer in connection with his offer to produce surface-printed postage stamps on more favourable terms than the existing contract with Perkins, Bacon. Their relationship, if any, with Archer's perforation experiments is unclear. The die was probably engraved by Samuel W. Reynolds, apparently acting on behalf of Robert E. Branston, but the check letters may refer to Ferdinand Joubert, although there is no evidence connecting him with these essays. The sheets were gummed before being printed. Edwin Hill, Supervisor in the Stamp Department of Somerset House cautioned Archer's engraver, Reynolds, against use of the Queen's head. Therefore Archer used the head of the Prince Consort. Although the essays were surface-printed they are included in this section for convenience as they are part of "Line-Engraved" history.

DP71a

DP71c

DP71. **1850.** Essay of Head of the Prince Consort, by Henry Archer. Surface-printed in sheets of 36 (3 horizontal rows of 12), in sheets of 240 and in sheets of 252 (21 panes of 12). The panes of 12 are plateable.

(a) Unfinished Imperforate in blue (*illustrated*). (*Price* £18000.)

(b) Finished Imperforate in brown, red-brown or black. (*Price from* £2000 *each.*)

(c) Finished Perforated 16 in brown, red-brown, red or black (*illustrated*), (*Price from* £9000.)

There are single finished perforated examples in blue in The Post Office Heritage Services, the Royal Collection and a third in private hands.

Dr. Perkins Paper Trials

DP72. **1870–71. Trials on Paper Chemically Treated by Dr. Perkins.** Dr. Perkins, a chemist of Brixton, informed the authorities that he knew of a process which would ensure against the stamps being tampered with. He was supplied with sheets of each kind of paper used for postage stamps and after he had treated them he returned them to the G.P.O. The sheets were then passed on to Perkins, Bacon & Co. and De La Rue & Co. for printing stamps but the sheets were so discoloured by a bluish hue that the experiment was not a success. The stamps printed by Perkins, Bacon & Co. were on Large Crown watermark paper. The following were printed, all in the current shades: 1d. Plate 121, imperf.; 1½d. Plate 1, imperf.; 2d. Plate 9, imperf, Plate 13, imperf. and perf. 14; 3d. Plate 5, imperf.; 4d. Plate 12, imperf.; 6d. Plate 9, imperf.; 1s. Plate 4 (Spray), imperf. In addition all these exist also perf. 14 and overprinted "Specimen" similar to Type 8 but measuring 21½ × 2½mm. All these are listed under their respective normal stamps.

Postal Notices

To instruct Post Office staff and to inform the general public it was usual to send a postal notice. Many have been issued since the conception of the Postal Service; most of them were without actual stamps or die proofs attached. Below are mentioned the more important ones.

1840 Postal Notices

PN1. A circular from the General Post Office, Edinburgh dated "April 1840" and sent by order of Sir Edward Lees, Secretary of the Post Office in Scotland, to the postmasters under his control, referring to the usage and cancellation of the 1d. and 2d. stamps. These notices are usually found with a pair of Penny Blacks attached. (*Price* £55000.)

Owing to delays in the delivery of paper and problems which had arisen over the gumming (which was done after printing), instructions were given to concentrate on the production of 1d. stamps. Printing of the 2d. did not commence until 1 May on ungummed paper. Eighteen sheets on imperfectly gummed paper were delivered by hand to Edwin Hill on 5 May for enclosing with Postal Notices of 7 May 1840.

PN2. The Postal Notice from W. L. Maberly from the General Letter Office dated 7 May 1840 reads in part: "I now enclose two Specimens of the Twopenny Adhesive Labels, which you will preserve with the Specimens already sent to you … I also enclose, for your information, two Specimens of the Label Stamp bearing the letters V. R. at the upper corners, which are to be applied to the correspondence of Public Departments …". This notice usually has no stamps attached but it is known with stamps, presumably applied by the receiving Postmaster, or later by a collector.

1841 Postal Notices

PN3. The original Postal Notice sent to all Postmasters, Sub-Postmasters, and Letter Receivers from the General Post Office in Edinburgh in 1841 refers to the issue of the new 1d. and 2d. stamps as well as the stamped Postal Stationery and is usually found with an example of the 1d. as issued as well as a proof copy of the 2d. with void corners, plus the two types of the 1d. postal stationery envelope, the latter being overprinted with large "SPECIMEN". It was stated that the 2d. envelope would be sent when ready. (*Price* £7000.)

PN4. A Postal Notice was sent by E. S. Lees from the General Postal Office, Edinburgh dated April 1841, enclosing two specimens of the 2d. envelope overprinted with large "SPECIMEN". (*Price* £2500.)

PN5. A similar notice issued in London from W. L. Maberly of the General Post Office, dated April 1841, reads in part: "I now enclose you Specimens of the New Two-penny Envelopes, which you will permit to pass at the rate of Postage marked upon them. The Sale of these, as well as the New Penny Envelopes, is for the present confined to the Limits of the London Two-penny Post." The notice was sent with two specimens of the 2d. envelope overprinted with large "SPECIMEN".

One example of this notice has been reported.

SECTIONS A–G

1840–1879 Line Engraved Issues

General Notes

Introduction. The early ½d., 1d., 1½d. and 2d. stamps were printed by Perkins, Bacon & Petch of 69 Fleet Street, E.C. (from 1852 Perkins, Bacon & Co.). That firm had in use a machine known as the "Rose" engine, originally invented by Mr. Perkins for making the complicated backgrounds of banknotes. Since the authorities were greatly concerned with the possibility of fraud against the Post Office the availability of this security device may well have been the deciding factor in gaining Perkins, Bacon & Petch the contract. They were destined to hold the contract for nearly forty years during which time the designs of the stamps were altered only in minor details.

Arrangement. By reason of their long term of currency and because of features of unique philatelic interest the Line-Engraved issues present an unequalled field for intensive study. No other large group of stamps has received more attention from specialists. The cataloguing of such a volume of information presents many problems if it is to be done in a manner comprehensible to all types of collectors from beginners to advanced specialists. The aim throughout this part of the catalogue is to combine maximum information with maximum clarity.

The basic principle followed is to present a general listing of each major issue (e.g. the 1d. black, 1d. red, 2d. blue) giving a full list of shades and of all varieties not restricted to one plate or one stamp. Where possible there follows a specialised listing of all states of each plate together with short explanatory notes on the history of that plate. This principle is followed through as far as Plate 45 of the 1d. red, beyond which so intensive a plate-by-plate treatment is not yet practicable, but more information is becoming available and it may be possible to provide more detailed lists in future editions.

The Line-Engraved issues offer unlimited opportunities for the collector who is prepared to give time and enthusiasm to their study. Not only is the study itself a fascinating one, it can also be profitable; the issues include almost countless rarities which are not recognized as such by any except the fully informed. Stamps worth considerable sums await discovery by the keen student. The price lists, particularly of the more obscure plates of the 1d. red, show rare stamps which can still be found as often as not unrecognized and purchased quite cheaply.

To become a specialist the collector needs first to have a sound understanding of the methods used in the laying down of the plates.

Invalidation. Line-engraved issues were declared invalid along with some early surface-printed stamps from 1 June 1901. Those Victorian issues not included were demonetised later on 1 July 1915, also included with the stamps were revenues and postal stationery not demonetised in June 1901.

The Printing Method. The basic principle of line-engraving or *intaglio* printing is that those details which will appear in colour on the stamps are recessed into the plate. The printer covers the whole surface of the plate with ink, works it into the recessed areas and then proceeds to wipe the surface clean. Ink remains in the recesses. In printing, dampened paper is placed on the wiped plate, a circular roller then forcing it under considerable pressure into the recessed areas, there to pick up the ink. On the finished stamps the ink tends to stand up from the surface of the paper. In this respect line-engraving differs from all other types of printing used for British stamps.

The Original Die (Die I). This die, the origin of all British line-engraved stamps except the ½d. for almost forty years, was not in fact the first to be made. An earlier die had been rejected as having too light a background. The accepted die was engraved by Charles and Frederick Heath who worked from a sketch made by Henry Corbould of the head on William Wyon's City Medal of 1837. This sketch is to be found along with others in the R. M. Phillips Collection in The Post Office Heritage Services. The fine interlacing lines of the background and the trellis-like side ornamentation were typical work of the Rose engine, mechanically transferred to the die by a roller. The head, the corners, corner stars, "POSTAGE" and the value tablet were all engraved by hand. The story behind the making of this die and its unsuccessful predecessor is dealt with in the section on essays, die proofs, etc.

When first completed the die was still in the original softened state necessary for the engraver. It was finally hardened and was then ready for the application of the transfer rollers.

The Transfer Rollers. These were circular steel cylinders, at this stage in a softened condition. Impressions were taken up on the curved face of the cylinders by rocking them back and forth over the die. Considerable pressure was mechanically applied to obtain a clean and firm impression on the roller.

Many roller impressions were taken from the die, most of these for the production of the printing plates but some for the preparation of dies for the twopence value. All variations of the design such as the cutting away of corner stars were effected by the excision of upstanding metal on a roller die; the original die was never altered.

In the case of the first twopence die a roller impression from the original die was altered by having the whole value tablet cut away; a new die was then made from the altered roller die, the value was then engraved, the block hardened and new roller impressions taken.

On any one roller a maximum number of seven impressions could be taken. It is thought that it was usual to use a different roller die for each plate, as indeed was later obligatory with the issues which incorporated the plate numbers in the designs. However, the presence of minor flaws throughout several plates, particularly in the early years, proves that one impression was often used on more than one plate. A good illustration of this is the presence of the "O" flaw on certain stamps of Plates 7 and 8 and on nearly all of Plates 9 and 10. This flaw and others which are found on early plates are most useful to specialists as their presence narrows the field and makes plating considerably easier. The flaws were mainly the result of the breaking off of a tiny ridge of metal on the roller impression. This resulted in an absence of a groove on the plate impressions from that particular roller die with the result that the flaws are usually white. Flaws in colour, though less commonly found, do exist; they are apparently the result of a small piece of foreign matter adhering to the face of the roller during the transferring operation. White flaws were often of a progressive nature, the defect on the roller gradually becoming more extensive with continued use. Such progressive deterioration as shown on the stamps is philatelically important in that it reveals the order of the laying down of the impressions on the plate.

The roller dies used for the plates for 1840 until the introduction of letters in all corners carried "stars" in the top corners but had the lower corners blank. For the issues with letters in all four corners the roller dies had all corners blank but as well as these there seem to have been some early roller dies with top corners blank. This is inferred from the appearance of some repaired impressions. (See "Later States of the Plates" following illustrations of "The Alphabets".)

Before use on the plates all transfer rollers were hardened.

The Printing Plates. The plates were of softened steel and the necessary size to take 240 impressions in twenty horizontal rows of twelve. To make each impression on the plate the roller die was rocked in contact with the plate and under great pressure. The order of laying down was not always the same but generally speaking was in vertical columns starting at the bottom of the right hand column. (This column, by natural reversal in printing, became the first left hand column of the sheet, that is, the vertical "A" column.) There were numerous exceptions to this rule, such as the early Plates 2, 7 and 8 which, as is shown by the presence of absence of certain roller die flaws, were laid down in horizontal rows. It has elsewhere been stated that the impressions on the transfer rollers were placed vertically on their periphery but in the case of the above-mentioned black plates it is possible that the roller impression was placed horizontally.

The philatelic importance of the roller dies will at this stage be more fully realized; any flaw or defect on a roller die was inevitably reproduced on every plate impression laid down by means of that die.

To aid in the correct placing of the impressions on the plates, fine guide lines were ruled on the early plates. These are further dealt with below.

Owing to the heavy pressure used in the laying down, small ridges of metal were raised around each impression. These, known as *burrs*, had to be burnished off carefully.

As laid down, the impressions carried no corner letters and the plates no marginal plate numbers or inscriptions. When these had been added the plate was ready for use. The first two 1d. plates and apparently a few others were put to press without prior hardening. The best-known example of this is Plate 1 which wore very rapidly and had to have every impression re-entered. The wearing had the effect of lessening the depth of the impression detail so that insufficient ink remained on the plate after wiping. The stamps showed weak greyish patches, in fact in some sheets printed from Plate 1 before it was withdrawn for repairing and hardening the stamps were in a pale grey shade around the head with the greatest wear below and to the right of the neck.

Even when the plate was hardened, as became the usual course, wear occurred after it had been used for a long time. For reasons not now known some plates wore much more rapidly than others. In particular, 1d. reds showing advanced plate wear are often seen though for the most part plates were withdrawn and destroyed before wear become too obvious. This was achieved by steam grinding the plate's surface so that it could be used again. This process was carried out in the presence of officers from the Inland Revenue and Chief Inspector's departments when batches of rejected plates were destroyed.

Burrs, corner letters, marginal markings and re-entering are all further dealt with below.

Although the above illustrations are modern, they show the basic principles as employed by Perkins, Bacon. Above, top, taking an impression from the original die. Above, transferring the impression onto the printing plate.

Sheet Layout. All 1d., 1½d. and 2d. plates were of 240 impressions in 20 horizontal rows of 12. The ½d. plates were of 480 impressions and are described in the notes on that value in Section G.

The Dies. The original die (Die I) was used to provide roller dies for the laying down of all the line-engraved stamps from 1840 to 1855. In that year a new master die was laid down (by means of a Die I roller die) and the impression was retouched by hand engraving. This retouched die, always known to philatelists as Die II, was from that time used in the preparation of all new roller dies.

A new series of 1d. Plate numbers was commenced for the new die but the old sequence was continued for the 2d. although from the commencement of the issue with letters in all four corners the 2d plates were laid down by means of roller dies taken (indirectly) from the 1d. Die II. It should be noted that all 2d. stamps with "stars" in the upper corners are from Die I.

In this catalogue, illustrations and description of points of difference between the two dies are based on those of A. B. Creeke Jnr. in *Adhesive Stamps of the British Isles* by Wright and Creeke. They were originally published in *The Stamp Collectors' Fortnightly* in 1897.

Some difficulty may be experienced by the collector who approaches the problem of the recognition of the 1d. dies relying solely on the detection of the differences given below the two illustrations. These differences are slight and they require a good magnifying glass to be seen. But even to the moderately experienced collector there is a very distinct difference in general appearance. Collectors will find it helpful to compare an undoubted Die I stamp (1d. black, 1d. red imperf. or any 2d. with "stars") with an equally certain Die II stamp (any line-engraved 1d. or 2d. with letters in all corners). Familiarity with these examples will soon promote an ability ro recognize the two dies at sight, without any need of close study. The Die II head has a coarser, fuller appearance than Die I.

The Corner Letters. The corner letters on early British stamps were intended as a precaution against forgery, each stamp on each plate having a different combination of letters from any other on the same plate. The theory was that a forger would make a plate of one stamp only or at least of very few different combinations, so that his letterings would be repetitive and thus detectable.

The plates of the 1d. black, 1d. red and 2d. blue with "stars" in the top corners all carried 240 impressions in twenty horizontal rows of twelve, thus:

Row 1: AA, AB, AC, etc. to AL.
Row 2: BA, BB, BC, etc. to BL, and so on to
Row 20: TA, TB, TC, etc. to TL.

Commencing with the 2d. in 1858, all the line-engraved stamps eventually appeared with letters in all four corners. This was intended as an added precaution against both forgery and the possibility of piecing together of unmarked portions of used stamps to form apparently unused wholes. The principle of the lettering was unchanged since the upper corners merely repeated the letters of the lower corners, though in reverse. Thus, for example, the first stamp in the second row of any plate, previously lettered BA in the lower corners, continued to be so lettered but was now also lettered AB in the upper corners.

Except in the case of the 1d. Die II Plates 50 and 51 (*q.v.*) on which the corner letters were hand-engraved, all plates had the letters inserted by hand-punch. Especially in the earlier plates, positioning was highly variable. In some cases a letter would be so misplaced as almost to touch the sides of its square; in others a letter would be struck twice or a wrong letter might be struck; the human element was of course the cause of such varieties.

Whether or not this rather elaborate security system was necessary, the incorporation of corner letters in the designs has had the happiest consequences for British philatelists. The study of the letters, their shape size and positioning was the first step towards the fascinating pastime (it might justifiably be called the science) of plating. Without the "Alphabets" it is certain that the task would never have been attempted.

"Plating" and the "Alphabets". *Plating* is the reconstruction, using single stamps or multiple pieces, of the whole sheet as it came originally from the plate, with every stamp in its correct position and every stamp assigned to its correct parent plate. The corner letters are of such importance because they immediately give the position on the plate so that the task is reduced, not perhaps to easy, but certainly to manageable proportions. When, as in the last types, plate numbers as well as letters formed part of the design it is a simple task to reconstruct sheets, a task calling for no particular skill, but with the earlier stamps, which have corner letters but no plate numbers, plating is a task calling for a high degree of application and intelligence. In this task, in addition to their function of indicating postion, the letters prove to be of the greatest assistance. It is found that letters of a certain identity of shape or size form groups. Even though on one plate letters may vary (for example the tall and the broad F's on 1d. Plate 29), in size there is a similarity. Collectors learn to recognize the peculiar characteristics of four "Alphabets": Alphabet I, small letters; Alphabet II, larger and heavier; Alphabet III, taller and generally thinner' Alphabet IV, mostly large hand-engraved letters.

Die I. May 1840.

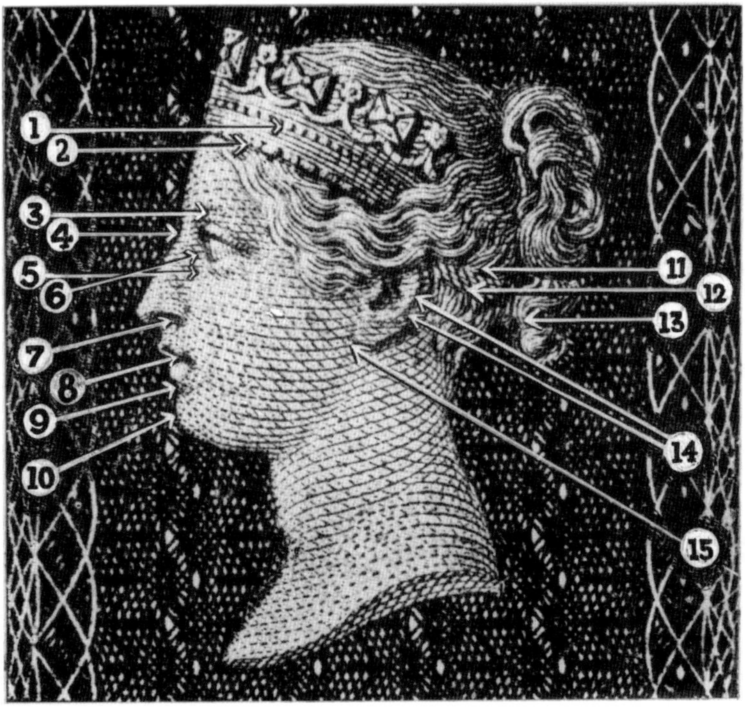

Die I of the 1d. The distinguishing features are:

1. The upper of the two rows of jewels, in the band of the diadem, appears to be of round stones

2. The shading below the band of the diadem is very light

3. The shading on the eyelids is faint, that of the lower lid being in the form of dots

4. The nose is practically straight

5. The cheek is delicately shaded

6. The eyeball is faintly shaded

7. The nostril is comparatively straight

8. The mouth has a slightly open appearance

9. The point of juncture of chin and lower lip is a gentle curve

10. The bottom of the chin is shaded with dots

11. The top of the band behind the ear is faint

12. The lower edge of the band is formed of two faint lines

13. The penultimate twist of curl goes almost straight down to the last twist

14. The shading of the external rim of the ear is comparatively heavy

15. The outline of the ear lobe curves upwards as it reaches the cheek

Die II. Introduced February 1855.

Die II of the 1d. The distinguishing features are:

1. The stones have a diamond-shaped appearance

2. The shading is very heavy

3. The shading of the eyelids is heavy, that of the lower lid being in the form of strong lines

4. The nose at the juncture with the forehead is concave, this giving the bridge a curved appearance

5. The shading of the cheek is heavier, giving the face a fuller, more mature appearance

6. The eyeball is heavily shaded

7. The nostril is larger and arched

8. The mouth appears to be closed and the upper lip is longer

9. There is a distinct indentation giving a fuller lower lip

10. A new line follows the curve of the chin up to the above-mentioned indentation

11. The top of the band is distinct

12. There is one thick line

13. The penultimate twist of curl curves round above the last twist

14. The shading of the external rim of the ear is lighter

15. The lobe outline ends without any upward curve

The Alphabets then, in the aid they give in plating, are of the first importance; almost as important are the various roller die flaws, the recut corners (1d. Plate 87 onwards) the recut frames (1d. Plate 76, 90) the Maltese Cross postmark as an indication of period and similar use of certain known peculiarities of shade. All these are clues which the plater uses to lead him to his objective, the identification of the plate of every stamp.

The work of the early pioneers was largely concentrated on the plating of the 1d. black and the relatively simple 2d. blues; these stamps have been fully understood and documented for many years. But the very large number of plates used for the 1d. red, "with stars", nearly 300 in all, has made the complete plating of that stamp a work beyond the capability of any single collector.

The Post Office collection of imprimatur sheets is housed at Heritage Services in Freeling House. The following is a list of publications concerning plating with reference to the imprimatur sheets and further details will be found in the Bibliography at the end of this volume: *The Plating of the Penny, 1840–1864, Die I, Plates 1 to 204, Reserve Plates 1 to 6,* edited by H. W. Fisher; *The Plating of Alphabet II, Plates 1 to 21,* by W. R. D. Wiggins; *The Plating of Alphabet III, Plates 22 to 68 & R17 together with Alphabet IV (Pl. 50 & 51) and Alphabet II (R15 & R16)* by Dr. W. R. D. Wiggins and G. C. Tonna.

Study of this catalogue will show the would-be plater the possibilities of the various groups. The collector with limited time may prefer to try his hand on a small group, possibly the 1d. reds with Maltese Cross cancellations, or the perforated 2d. blues. Perhaps the best group for the collector of limited means is the 1d. "rose-reds" of 1857 to 1864. The knowledgeable plater has the chance of picking up great rarities (e.g. any stamp from Plates 64 or 65), unrecognized and priced at a nominal rate.

It should not be supposed that plating is the only or most usual course open to collectors of the Line-Engraved stamps; their attraction lies in the infinite variety of ways in which they can be studied or, more simply, collected. Even the finding of one stamp from each plate of the One Penny, say from 1840 to 1857, would result in quite a large and valuable collection. The further refinement of seeking one stamp of identical lettering from each plate would transform a relatively simple task into one calling for considerable application and patience. Whatever the chosen line of approach, the Line-Engraved stamps can be relied upon to provide almost endless enjoyment and the thrill of the chase for the collector with any bent towards specialisation.

Imprimatur Sheets. By official regulations, whenever a plate was laid down, an impression on the same watermarked paper and in the selected colour to be used for the issued stamps was submitted to Somerset House for approval. This sheet, when approved and placed in the archives, was known as the imprimatur sheet. The collection of imprimatur sheets, in The Post Office Heritage Services, is incomplete, some sheets being missing. Some stamps (about 21 in all) have been removed at different times from the existing sheets and are in the Royal Collection and private collections. Imprimatur examples frequently show shades somewhat different from the issued stamps and very occasionally, due to unusual circumstances, they are in a different colour. Imprimatur stamps of the line-engraved issues are always ungummed. When they are corner examples with selvedge showing plate number they are considerably more valuable than examples without the plate number. Quotations for imprimatur examples appear in the price lists where they apply and are for marginal examples without plate numbers.

Orders for photographs of the imprimatur sheets should be sent to Heritage Royal Mail, Freeling House, Phoenix Place, London, WC1X 0DL.

The Alphabets

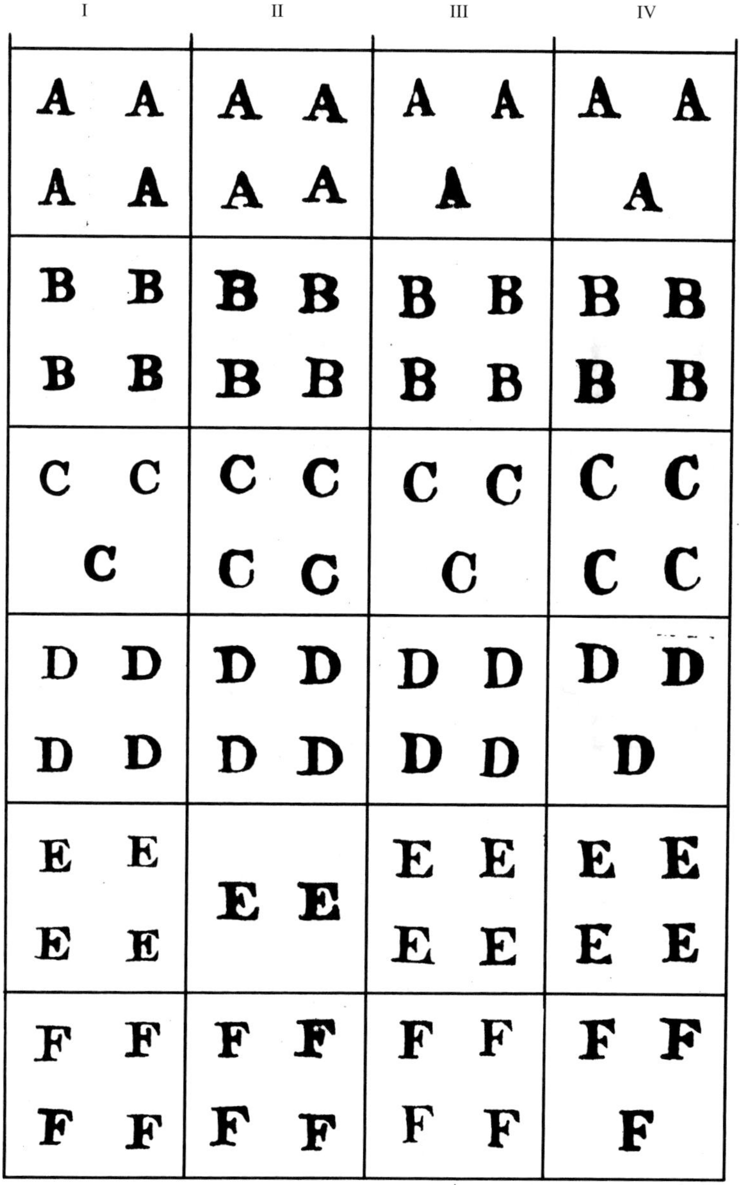

The chart above and those which follow on pages 44 and 45 are a guide to the general characteristics of the four Alphabets. Letters typical of certain plates or groups of plates are illustrated separately at the relevant points in the lists

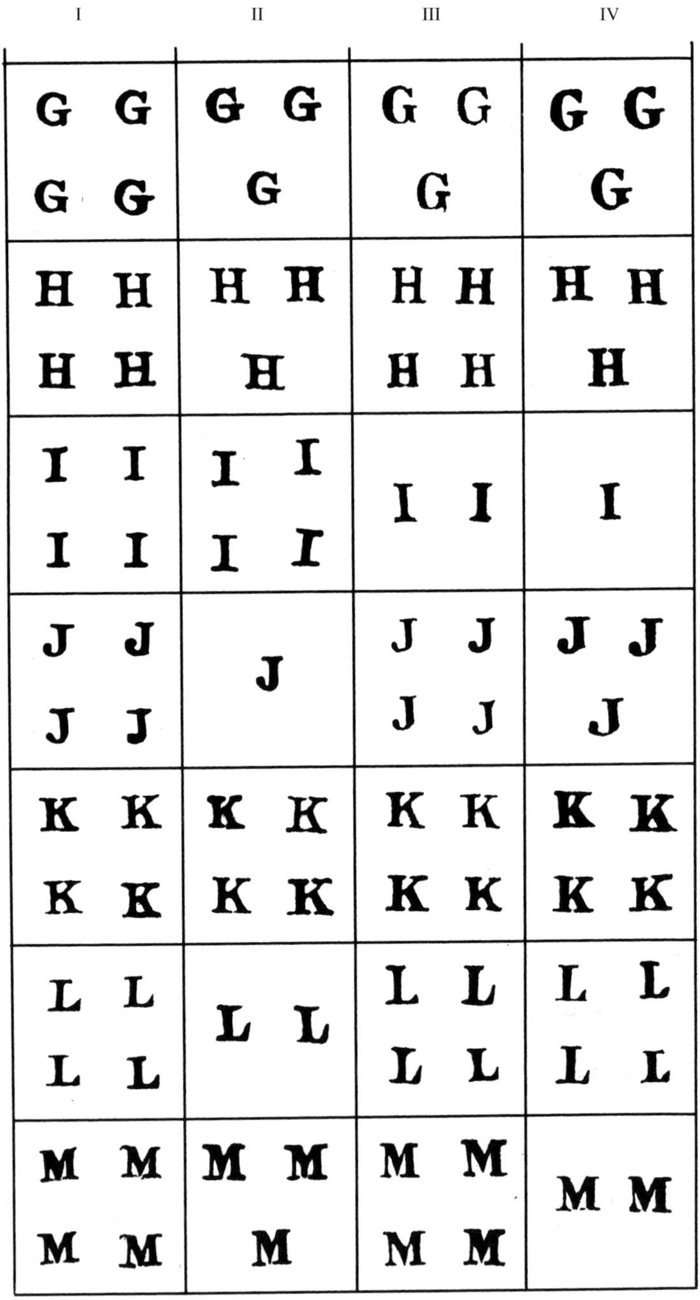
I
II
III
IV
G G G G G G G G
G G G G G
H H H H H H H H
H H H H H H H
I I I I I I
I I I I I
J J J J J J
J J J J J
K K K K K K K K
K K K K K K K K
L L L L L L L L
L L L L L L
M M M M M M M M
M M M M M

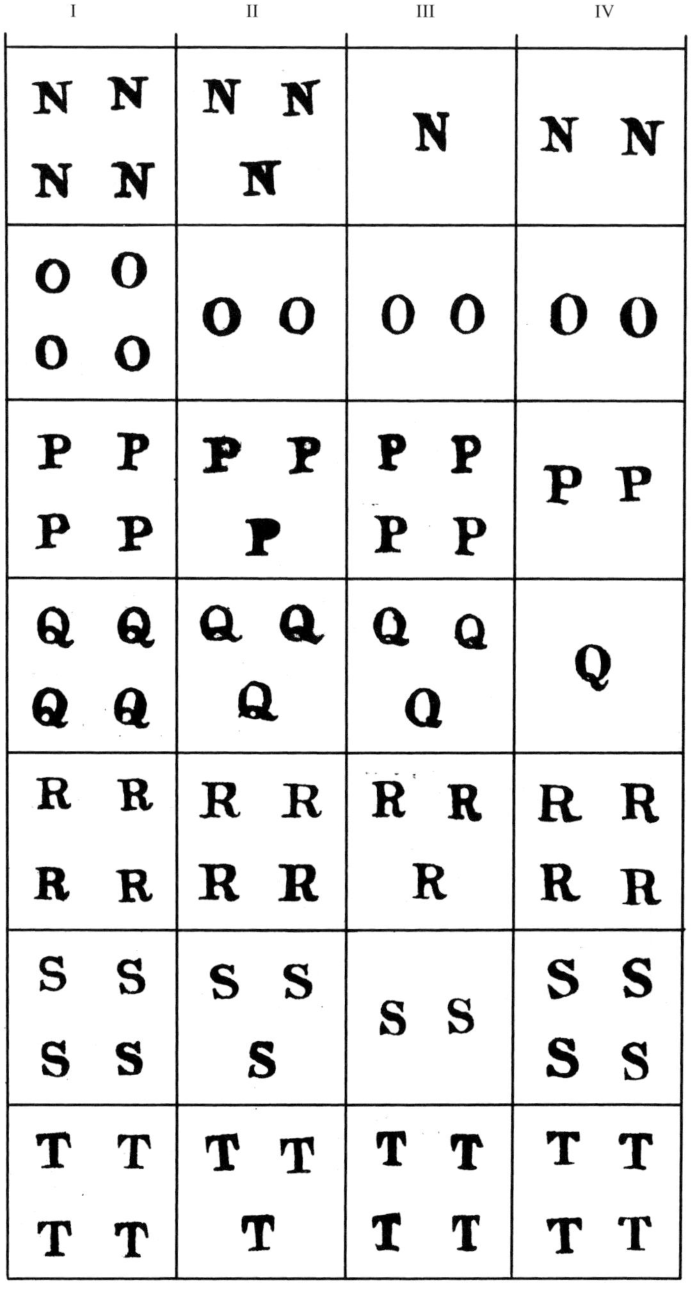
I
II
III
IV

Later States of the Plates. In numerous cases there is evidence of plates having been repaired after considerable use; in some cases a plate is found to have been repaired on more than one occasion. An extreme example is Plate 1 used first for the 1d. black printings, then for the 1d. red printings; of some impressions on this plate five different states exist. A very similar series of events occurred with Plate 5, likewise printed from in both black and red. These and other series can be traced in the lists which in the early plates are based on notes by Dr. H. Osborne.

Repairing, thereby creating a new state of that particular impression on the plate, was generally effected by use of a roller die. All roller dies lacked corner letters so that the effect of a new rolling-in (i.e. re-entry) was, by pressure, to weaken the corner letters of the old impression while deepening the lines of the main body of the design. It follows that except in cases where the re-entering of an impression was carelessly done so that doubling of the design can be seen, the best evidence of repairing is usually a weakness of the corner letters accompanied by better definition of the rest of the design. Sometimes the weakening of the corner letters would be so pronounced as to necessitate a recutting of those letters. For an example of letters weakened in the second state, see the illustrations of the 1d., EB, Plate 30. Such recutting is more likely to have been necessitated by a re-entering than by wearing or an original weakness in the letters. In some cases the classic features of a repaired impression, weak corner letters and strong main design, are accompanied by a weakness of the corner "stars". These indicate the use of a roller die with all corner squares blank.

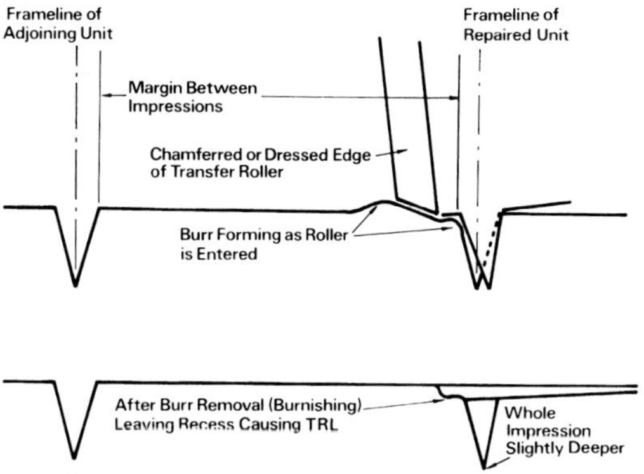

FIG. 1. UNEVENLY ROCKED &/OR MALALIGNED TRANSFER ROLLER

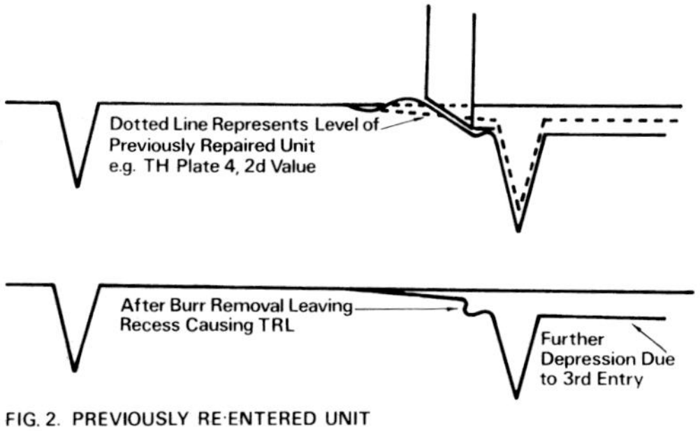

FIG. 2. PREVIOUSLY RE-ENTERED UNIT

Transfer Roller Lines (TRLs). Research on the 2d. blue, Plate 4 (see Figs. 1 and 2), has provided very substantial evidence that the repaired impressions on the early 1d. and 2d. values in many instances exhibited a well-defined mark on one or both sides of their margins which was more than just a random mark produced by local burr removal. This mark, or defined line, was shown to have similar characteristics on each impression repaired on a particular plate and led to the conclusion that it must have been produced by the edge of the transfer roller. Hence we refer to it as a transfer roller line or TRL in the text (see Fig. 3).

Three repaired impressions (LE, PB, QC) on the 2d. blue, Plate 3 were the subject of an article published in Gibbons *Stamp Monthly*, October 1991.

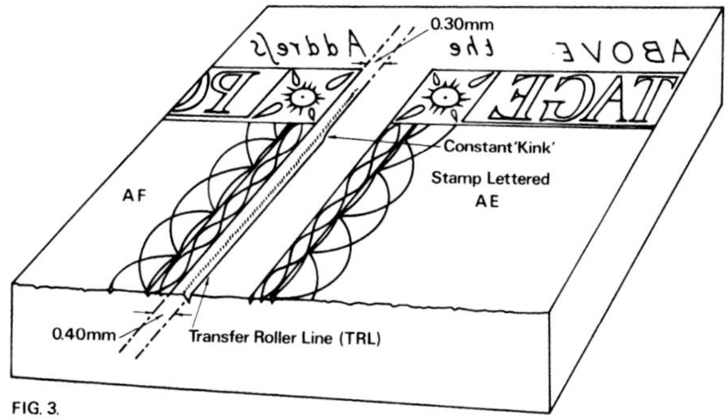

FIG. 3.
DIAGRAMATIC IMPRESSION OF TRL FORMED BETWEEN STAMPS AE & AF AFTER REPAIR TO AF, DIMENSIONALLY SIMILAR TRL OCCUR ON AE, AI, TF, TG & TH AFTER REPAIR (LEFT HAND SIDE OF STAMP)

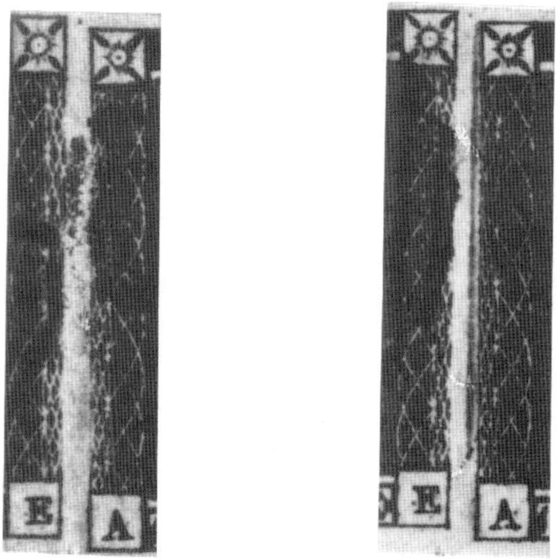

2d. imperforate, Plate 4, stamps AE and AF. Left, slight linear corrosion. Right, re-entered with TRL and stronger sideline

Typical re-entry

Transfer shift

Re-entry. This term is commonly, and sometimes incorrectly, used to describe any stamp which shows doubling of part of the design other than the corner letters. In fact such doubling can result from three different causes:

Fresh Entry. When an impression has been twice entered on a plate, before that plate has been put to press, the term *fresh entry* is correctly used. The second entering may have been accidental or deliberate; if it has failed exactly to coincide with the earlier impression some doubling of the design may be visible. If coincidence were exact no variety will be recognizable.

Re-entry. This term, precisely used, covers the re-entering of an impression after the plate has been at press. As with a fresh entry, if the new impression did not coincide exactly with the old, some doubling will be seen on the stamp. This is known as a *non-coincident re-entry*. When exact coincidence of impressions was achieved no doubling will be seen. This is known as a *coincident re-entry.* Unlike coincident fresh entries, coincident re-entries can sometimes be recognized by the comparison of late and early prints from the same impression; where the later print is clearer and stronger than the early print it is reasonable to assume that re-entering has taken place. In this connection readers are referred to the earlier notes on "Later States of the Plates".

Owing to the difficulty experienced in many cases of deciding whether a stamp showing some doubling is a fresh entry or a re-entry the latter term is generally used in this catalogue to cover both, except in cases where more precise information has to be conveyed.

Shifted Transfer. This term and the equivalent *basal shift* are used to cover stamps which show doubled or thickened top or bottom lines, not as a consequence of re-entering but as a result of a squeezing or roll-over of metal under the heavy pressure used in laying down the plate. It is probable that some stamps commonly accepted as re-entries are in fact shifted transfers. But the term re-entry cannot correctly be used to include shifted transfers as no re-entering has occurred.

Marginal Markings. All the plates of the line-engraved issues bore a plate number at each of the four corners. This appeared on the printed sheets and in some cases corner stamps are found with sufficient selvedge to show part or all of the plate number. Such pieces are of extreme rarity and are eagerly sought by specialists.

In the margins of all 1d. plates was the inscription "Price 1d. Per Label. 1/- Per Row of 12. £1 Per Sheet. Place the Labels ABOVE the Address and towards the RIGHT HAND SIDE of the Letter. In Wetting the Back be careful not to remove the Cement". On the 2d. (Plates 1 to 3, and 4 as originally issued) a similar inscription with values altered (2d., 2/-, £2) appeared. Stamps with attached selvedge showing part of the inscription are always popular and of enhanced value.

In the $\frac{1}{2}$d. stamp of 1870 the values in the inscription naturally differed from the 1d. and the second line read "Place the Labels Above and at the Right-hand Side of the Address".

While the 2d. Plate 4 was in use the inscription was changed to "£1 Per Sheet" from the earlier "£2 Per Sheet", as it was intended to divide the sheets of 240 into two panes, and the amended inscription was continued on later plates.

Beginning with the 1d. (Die II) Plate 98 and the 2d. Plate 12 the plate numbers were enclosed in a circle and a *current number* was engraved (except in the $\frac{1}{2}$d. value) above the first two stamps in the top row and below the last two stamps in the bottom row. This number indicated the printers' order of production and was applied in sequence to each plate made, irrespective of value or function. The $\frac{1}{2}$d. current numbers were above the seventh stamp in the top row and below the eighteenth in the bottom row.

Marks for pinning the sheets for the Archer perforation trials were introduced in 1849. The original pin marks took the form of a centrally placed small dot above the inscription opposite the gap between the sixth and seventh stamps. A vertical line was placed in a similar position on the bottom selvedge. These marks were applied to existing plates 89 to 92, and to all new plates from 93 onwards. Plate 4 of the 2d. was also amended. Revised marks were introduced in 1854. These took the form of a small cross placed above the original dot at the centre of the top margin with a similar cross to the left of the vertical line at the bottom (this appears to the right on the printed sheets). These crosses first appeared in this form on the 1d. Red plates registered on 13 February 1854 and on others registered up to 11 August 1854. (Die I Plates 178 to 193 and Reserve Plate 14). As the changes were coincidental with the introduction of officially perforated stamps it is probable that plates already at press (Plates 155, 157, 162 to 177) had these marks added so that they could be perforated on the new Napier machines. The marginal marks were further revised in September 1854 so that the printed sheets show a vertical line to the left of the central top cross. At the bottom of the sheet the original centrally-placed vertical line was converted to a cross with a simple vertical line replacing the cross added in February. Plates 194 to 204 and Die II Plates from 5 onwards were the first to show these alterations. The marking on Plate 4 of the 2d. Blue was altered likewise, so that both 1849 and September 1854 marks are found on this plate and possibly those of February 1854 also. The imprimatur of at least one plate (204) shows a hybrid of the September 1854 pin mark at the top and the February 1854 mark at the bottom. Plates 202 and 203, registered on the same date, and Plates 1 to 4 (Die II), registered 15 January 1855, may also be hybrids. Such markings were almost certainly amended before printing from these plates began.

Marginal markings for the $1\frac{1}{2}$d. were similar to the September 1854 type for the 1d.

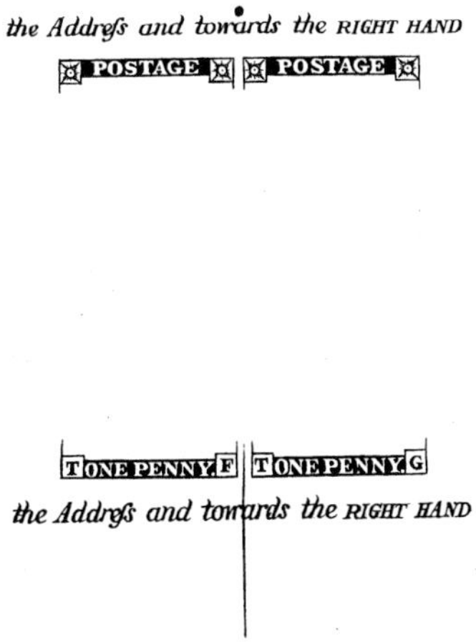

1849 Pin marks

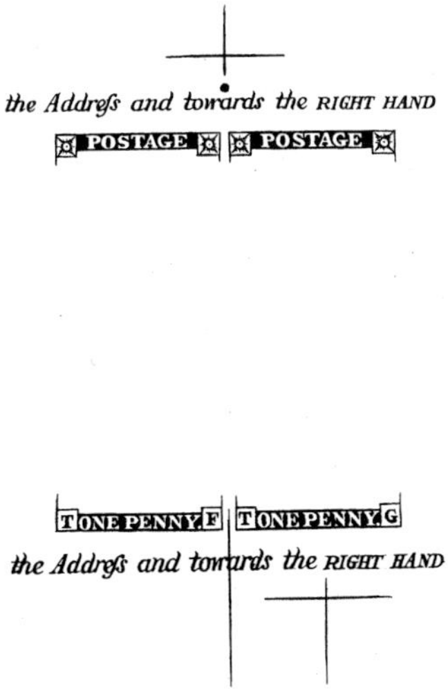

Feb 1854 Revised pin marks

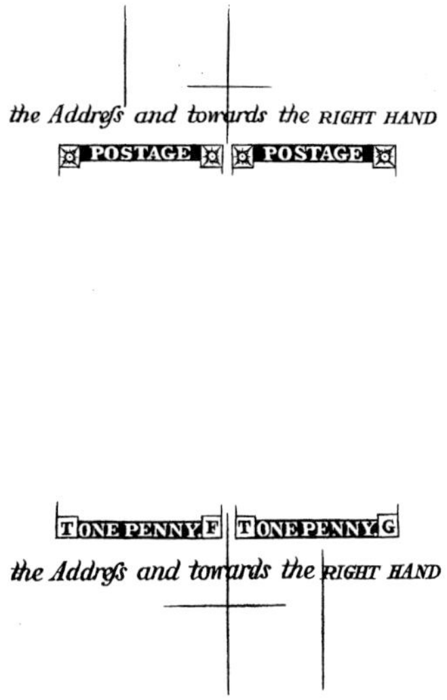

Sept 1854 Revised pin marks

In 1851, to facilitate horizontal division of sheets, an ornament was engraved on each side-margin between the J and K horizontal rows. The first type (Type A) was applied to the 1d. plates in current use at the time (December 1851) these being Plates 116, 118 to 131. This marking, which is restricted to these plates, is rare and seldom seen complete. All the mentioned plates may exist with, and without, the ornaments.

The ornaments without the circle as Types B, C and D were used on the following 1d. plates.

Type B	Type C	Type D
132–146	147	98
148 and 149	161	150–152
153–160	167–170	178
162–166	173	181 and 182
171 and 172	175–177	R4–R6
184–186	179 and 180	
190 and 191	183	
194–197	187 and 188	
199–203	192	
R1 and R3	198	
	204	
	R2	

In addition Type C was used on the later plates of the 1d. including the series with the plate number incorporated in the design of the stamp. The 1½d. Plate (1) had Type D and Plate 3 is found only with Type C.

A fan-shaped ornament, Type E, was added at the sides of the 2d. plates, Plate 4 being the first and therefore existing uniquely with and without the ornaments. At the same time the 2d. plates had the dot and line markings changed to a line and a cross on both upper and lower margins.

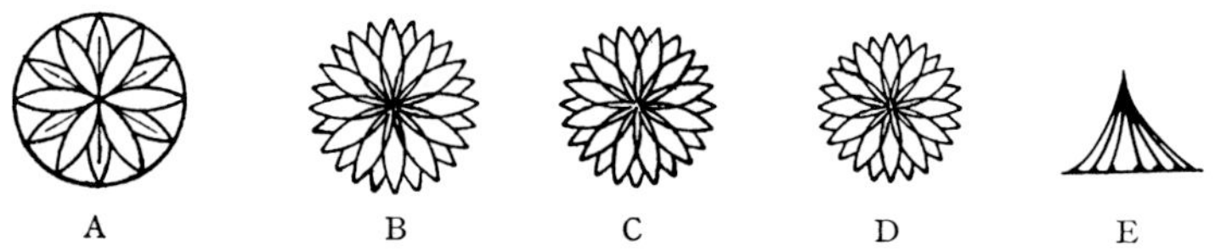

Marginal markings

The ½d. plates also had the fan-shaped ornaments, Type E, on the top and bottom margins between vertical rows L and M together with crosses and guide lines in the side margins.

Paper, Gum and Ink. The paper was made by Stacey Wise of Rush Mills, Hardingstone, near Northampton and, being handmade, varied a good deal in thickness. Supplies of the small crown watermarked paper produced under the initial contract were in triple sheets so that Perkins, Bacon & Co. had to guillotine them into stamp-size sheets of 10½ + 19¾ inches. From 28 August 1840 under the second contract with Mr. Wise, the paper supplied was in single sheets. These were ungummed with "deckled" edges. The width of the paper was increased by ½ inch in 1874 in preparation for the introduction of perforating machines with continuous feed mechanism..

The gum, applied by Perkins, Bacon & Petch, was made of potato starch, variable in colour, efficiency and taste. After 1855 some gelatine was added and in 1864 double-gumming was adopted. Gum was always applied after the sheets were printed, but before perforation.

The inks used for the 1d. and 2d. during the first year of issue were not fugitive and numerous cases of stamps being cleaned and re-used came to the notice of the Post Office. Accordingly in 1841 the 1d. colour was changed to red-brown (commonly called "red") and the ink was made fugitive by the addition of prussiate of potash. The 2d. was not changed in colour as a fugitive blue was available but white lines were added to the design of this value to allow identification of the stamps printed in the new ink.

The original paper was greyish white but as a result of chemical action between the paper and the fugitive inks introduced in 1841, a bluish discoloration was usual. In 1857 the blueing was eliminated, either by not using the prussiate of potash or by introducing a neutralizing agent. Double fugitive ink was first used on the 1d. Lilac of 1881.

Watermarks. The watermark "bits" were stitched to flat wire-mesh tray-like moulds. The Small Crown bits were hand-shaped of fine brass wire, consequently small differences of shape and size are encountered. The Large Crown (Type I) bits were stamped out of sheet brass and show no variation other than the "errors" illustrated. The "errors" resulted from the insertion on the wire-mesh tray of two new bits (presumably hand-made). They occupied positions which resulted in their appearing normally on stamps lettered MA and TA, but when the paper was reversed (during printing) they appeared on ML and TL. When the paper was inverted the stamps affected were HL and AL, and when inverted and reversed, HA and AA. The first listing is on No. C8d from Plate 42. The MA variety can be found on the 1857 rose-red stamps with letters in lower corners from Plates 42, 43, 47, 52, 55, 56, 57, 66, 67, R16 and R17 on normal paper and the reversed paper stamp lettered ML on Plates 57 and 60. These are also recorded on stamps from a large range of the 1864 plates with letters in all corners: MA variety Plates 72 to 74, 78 to 96; ML variety (MA reversed) Plates 76 and 84. The TA variety is recorded as existing on the 1857 rose-red with letters in lower corners from Plates 27, 34, 36, 38, 39, 42, 43, 46, 52, 55, 56, 58 to 62, 66, 68, R16 and R17 and the TL variety (TA reversed) on Plates 34, 39, 59, 67 and R15. Our information here is possibly incomplete. There is no record of these "error" watermarks on any 2d. stamps other than some from Plate 8 TA or TL (TA reversed), Plate 9 MA or ML (MA reversed) and TA or TL (TA reversed) of the 1858 issue.

The Large Crown watermark (Type I) was modified in about March 1861 by the deletion of the two small lines in the lower arches and the new type (Type II) is slightly larger. The One Penny stamps C10 and C12/13 exist with both types of the watermark and the plates recorded for each type are stated in footnotes in the text. The 2d. No. G2 from Plate 9 also exists in both types. All other issues exist only in one of the types and this is indicated in the headings.

The sheets used by Perkins, Bacon & Co. for the 1d., 1½d. and 2d. values carried the watermark "POSTAGE" once on both top and bottom selvedges in outlined Roman capitals, the words being a fraction more than 2½ inches long. The side selvedges carried the same watermark, twice to each side. The latter words were the same length but the letters were appreciably smaller than those of the top and bottom selvedges. There were of course 240 Small or Large Crowns to each sheet and the space occupied by these was enclosed in a frame of five straight parallel watermark lines. These are occasionally seen on marginal stamps.

Small Crown watermark

Large Crown watermark Type I

Large Crown watermark Type II

Large Crown TA error

Large Crown MA error

In November 1856 30 reams of the Large Crown paper were supplied from which all the marginal "POSTAGE" watermarks had been omitted. We have no knowledge of any pieces surviving to illustrate this incident. It should be noted that if examples lettered AE, AF, AG, AH, TE, TF, TG, TH show more than one of the horizontal parallel marginal watermark lines, or stamps EA, FA, GA, HA, MA, NA, OA, PA, EL, FL, GL, HL, ML, NL, OL and PL show more than one vertical parallel marginal line, then these could originate from such sheets.

The $\frac{1}{2}$d. value had its own peculiar watermark (**W3**), which extended to the width of three stamps (see G4). A selvedge watermark consisting of the words "Postage Stamps" in script characters appeared at each side of the sheet.

From early 1863 as a result of an official request the paper-makers introduced watermark "mould letters" in the upper and lower margins of the Large Crown sheets. The letters A to Z were used and from 1870 double letterings AA to ZZ. The $\frac{1}{2}$d. paper had watermark mould numbers, 1 to 8, instead of letters.

Perforations. An early trial roulette by Henry Archer is dealt with in Section CA, as are the gauge 16 trial perforations made on Archer's machine. Some uncertainty remains if the machine ever saw service after it was purchased, along with the patent, in June 1853. Available evidence suggests that, at best, it was used only very briefly.

Two new machines for postage stamps (and two for the large format revenue stamps – see L101 and L104) were subsequently ordered from David Napier & Son, York Rd. and Vine St., Lambeth. The postage stamp machines began work in January 1854 four months after the revenue machines. A third machine, primarily for the line engraved stamps, was acquired in 1858. The Napier machines were originally equipped with gauge 16 punch sets, but these proved to be too prone to damage and also weakened the paper excessively. During 1855 they were replaced with gauge 14 sets. The two gauges were used concurrently until the summer of 1855, after which peforation 14 became the standard. At least one gauge 16 punch set was held in reserve and this was utilized for a brief period in 1857. All the punch sets of both gauges were of the single comb type which perforates three sides of one row of stamps at each strike.

The Napier machines originally transported the sheets under the punches in a tympan/frisket assembly, which typically left the top margin unperforated. From 1875 tympans began to be superseded by continuous feed mechanisms which greatly increased productivity. Conversion of all three machines used for the line engraved stamps was not completed, however, until 1878. The continuous feed machines perforated the top margin. The standard batch size was originally 5 sheets and average daily production per machine was 3200 sheets at a rate of 600 sheets an hour. The batch size was later increased to a maximum of 7 sheets. With the new continuous feed mechanism the daily production rate increased to 5500 sheets per machine.

Short and Long Stamps. Stamps which are short by one or two rows of perforations are not listed although they may be of some interest. As already mentioned the imperforate sheet was fed into the perforator and the A row would be perforated on three sides. If the horizontal perforations touched the design the second row would be adjusted which made the top row in the sheet short. Inserting the imperforate sheet from the bottom would leave stamps in the T row short if an adjustment was made. Examples have been noted among all stamps perforated at Somerset House on this machine up to 1878 including perf. 14. Long stamps also result from an adjustment to the position of the sheet under the punches. Double perforations can also occur for the same reason and these are listed. See also the Surface-printed Section J.

Guide line in corner

Guide line through value

Varieties of the Line-Engraved Stamps. Varieties of a minor nature, other than shade or colour variaions, are listed below the main listing of the stamp concerned.

Guide Lines. These lines, traces of which are found only on the earlier stamps, were lightly drawn on the plates to assist in the alignment of the impressions during the rolling in. Traces are found mainly in the corner squares but occasionally through "POSTAGE" and the value. Guide dots and cuts, used to indicate the spacing of the guide lines, are found occasionally on stamps or in the margins.

Double Letters. Since the corner letters were punched on to the printing plate by a hand punch, the human element resulted in varieties occurring. In some cases a letter would be badly misplaced or perhaps impressed in the wrong corner square. Not all misplaced and otherwise defective letters were corrected, but where they were it is not uncommon to find traces of the original letter remaining. These are the varieties known as "double letters", though some may be merely the result of a slight movement of the punch in the workman's hand.

Constant Varieties. Although described as such a few of them are not to be found on the imprimatur sheets. These presumably occurred in the course of printing and may turn out to be second states. However, until evidence of first states is forthcoming they will continue to be described in this catalogue as constant varieties.

It has been suggested that the origin of some of the extra lines found in or near the letter squares of the 1d. red, printed from plate 82 onwards, was in the way that the letter punch was used. A slightly angled blow, when placing the letter in the square, would cause the punch holder to impinge on the plate, forming a superfluous line which in some instances (see plate 114 TF) would show a trace of a similar line at right angles. The letter most commonly affected was M and this was probably due to the short punch used. See also articles by Harold W. Fisher in the October 1979, January and May 1980 issues of *The GB Journal.*

"J" Flaws. The flaw on letter J illustrated occurs on the earlier plates with Alphabet I lettering with square-footed J and resembles a double letter but was caused by a blemish on the letter punch. It is known on the Penny Die I Plates 10, 12, 15, 18–24, 26–28, 32, 34–44, 46, 48–53, 57, 61, 63, 65–66, 72, 75 and on the Twopence Plate 3. They are listed in with the constant varieties except where they occur in conjunction with another more major variety on the same stamp in which case they are shown with that variety. The variety is stronger in some plates than others and may also vary in different positions on the same plate, depending upon the angle at which the punch was applied.

Double letter

Ivory head

"J" flaw

Retouches. Evidence of retouching is commonly found on Line-Engraved stamps. The term denotes a deepening or recutting of weak or absent detail, the instrument used being the graver or burin, a hand tool.

The need for retouching probably arose in most cases following a burnishing off of burrs or guide lines but the prevalence of recutting of corners, especially on the 1d. Die I from Plate 89 onwards, suggests that the fine corner lines were not transferring well, probably as a result of much use of the original die. The side frame lines also appear to have given a good deal of trouble and some retouching of one or both sides of the design is very commonly seen. The many "Extended Frame Lines" so useful for platers' identifications are the result of corner recutting. Recut corner letters, already discussed in the notes on "Later States of the Plates" above, are of course retouches.

Burr Removal and Corrosion Marks. Foggy patches of colour (usually found in the side margins) are caused by ink which is picked up from shallow recesses on the printing plate. These recesses are caused by over removal of burrs when the tool has cut into the plate or by corrosion of the printing surface. These should not be confused with Transfer Roller Lines mentioned above.

Ivory Heads. These quite striking varieties seen on the backs of stamps usually take the form of a white head on a deep blue ground and are the result of uneven blueing. As the prussiate of potash was in the ink it is not surprising to find the blueing deepest where the ink is thickest; the head area, being lightly printed, shows least blueing. In most cases because the paper was damp when used, diffusion of the blue occurred and no ivory head appeared. Other forms of ivory head appear in blue on a yellowish ground, probably due to secondary reaction in used stamps, and in blue on a paler blue ground. It is possible that these are from sheets dipped in prussiate of potash.

The "VR" One Penny Black. This stamp, of similar design to the normal except that it has the letters V R in the upper corner squares, was prepared for official use but not issued. It is listed at the end of Section A.

"Specimen" Stamps. Stamps overprinted "Specimen" were generally used for purposes of presentation to foreign Postal Departments or of circularising Postmasters concerning new issues. While not, correctly speaking, postage stamps they form an interesting sideline in much the same way as do imprimaturs and proofs.

"Specimens" are not numerous among the Line-Engraved issues. The overprints are illustrated in Appendix 3.

Cancellations

Maltese Cross Cancellations. These handstamps were officially issued for use with the first postage stamps and Mulready covers in May 1840. They were made individually and by hand so that no two are exactly alike. Great interest is taken in the more unusual forms that are found and we illustrate some of these. Some crosses can be found with what appear to be small numerals (1 or 11) and also circle, large and small dots. These latter are possibly due to the canceller being repaired by means of pins.

A red ink was first employed, but was superseded by black (after some earlier experiments) in February 1841. Maltese crosses in black and red on the same stamp exist on the 1d. black from Plates 1b, 2, 8, 9, 10 and 11. Several other colours were used in certain areas and these are listed separately but we do not distinguish between the various shades of red which include scarlet, carmine, red-brown and purple-brown.

It should be noted that the red Maltese Cross is less common than the black on Penny Blacks from Plates 8 and 9. It is scarce on Plate 10 and very rare on Plate 11. The black Cross is less common on Plates 1 to 7. The red Cross is of considerable rarity on the Penny Red stamps.

Normal

Number in Cross

From the middle of March 1843, until it was superseded in 1844, a series of crosses, numbered 1 to 12 in the centre, was in use at the London Head Office. The top of the obliterator was indicated by a small cross. No. 3 usually shows no cross as it was not repaired after the cross broke off soon after its introduction. These occur on the 1d. and 2d. of 1841 and are rare on the 1840 issues. They are also known on the Mulready envelopes and covers.

The Maltese Cross is a valuable plating aid for collectors of the Penny Red imperf. Its presence on a stamp is strong evidence that that stamp is from a plate put to press before 1845.

Belfast

Brighton

Channel Is.

Cork

Coventry

Dublin I

Dublin II

Dursley

Eyreçourt

Greenock

Hollymount

Kelso

Kilmarnock

Leamington

Leeds (special)

Limerick

London I

London II

Manchester

Montrose

Mullingar

Norwich and Plymouth

Perth

Settle

Scottish (small centre)

Scottish (large centre)

Stirling

Stonehaven

Welshpool

Whitehaven

Wotton-under-Edge

York

"Penny Post" Postmarks. These cancellations are of the straight line type and were applied at the Penny Post receiving offices, usually on the envelope, the stamp then being obliterated at the Head Office. Some of these were in use before 1840 but they are known on the Penny Black, the Penny Red imperf. and the Twopence Blue of 1840 and they come with or without the Maltese Cross.

Typical "Penny Post" Postmarks

Town Dated Postmarks. These were used in 1842 in several post offices in the South West of England in place of the Maltese Cross. The more common of these are Dorchester, Honiton, Lyme and Totnes but Amesbury, Bridport, Chard, Shaftesbury and Wincanton are scarce. They vary in size and are usually found at the back of the letter as they were not originally intended as obliterators. Owing to the size of the mark, single stamps usually only show a part of it. They are found on the Penny Red imperf. and on Plates 1, 2 and 3 of the Twopence Blue.

"Penny Post" (Handsworth)

Town Dated Postmark

1844-type Cancellations. The Maltese Cross cancellers did not prove satisfactory and following a suggestion put forward by Mr. Francis Abbott, a senior clerk in the Post Office, numbered cancellers were introduced. Those for England and Wales were issued in April 1844 while those for Scotland, Ireland, the London Chief Office (London City) and the London District Post appeared in May of the same year.

The cancellers differed in style, those of the London Chief Office having the number enclosed in a diamond within bars while those of the London District Post had a circle or oval in place of the diamond. Likewise the styles of the English, Scottish and Irish cancellers each followed a distinctive pattern. Our illustrations of these marks which follow are not intended to do other than indicate general types. For a detailed study readers are referred to *The Postmarks of Great Britain and Ireland, 1660–1940*, by R. C. Alcock and F. C. Holland (Alcock, Cheltenham, 1940).

The following illustrations show a wide range of 1844-type cancellations:

LONDON TYPES

Single

Double

Triple
London Chief Office (London City)

Double
London Chief Office

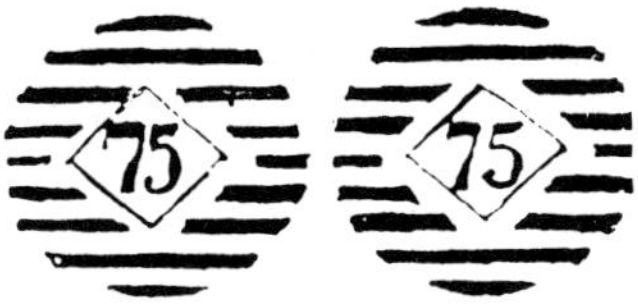

Double (also known triple)
Foreign Newspaper Office, 1860

LONDON DISTRICT OFFICES

Chief Offices, 1850

Numbered Districts, from 1857

PROVINCIAL TOWNS

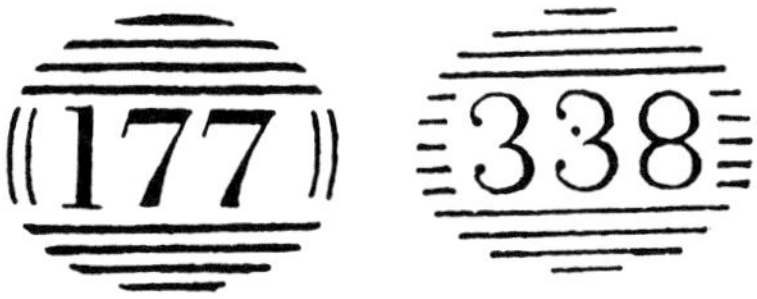

English Towns

Welsh Town (Cardiff)

Scottish Town

Stars at Sides (Edinburgh, 1850s)

Irish Town

Duplex Cancellations. The following are typical of the Duplex types introduced from the 1850s:

DUPLEX TYPES FOR LONDON

Used for "Too Late" mail, from 1853

Inland Section, from 1858

London Chief Office (London City)

Heavier Types (thicker bars)

London Chief Office (London City), about 1867

London District Office, from 1863

ROTARY OR ROLLER TYPE

Birmingham, 1850s

DUPLEX TYPES FOR ENGLAND

Early "Spoon", 1854

Modified "Spoon"

Rugby "Shoe", 1857

Sideways Duplex, 1857

Normal Duplex, from 1860

So-called "Creswell"

DUPLEX TYPES FOR WALES

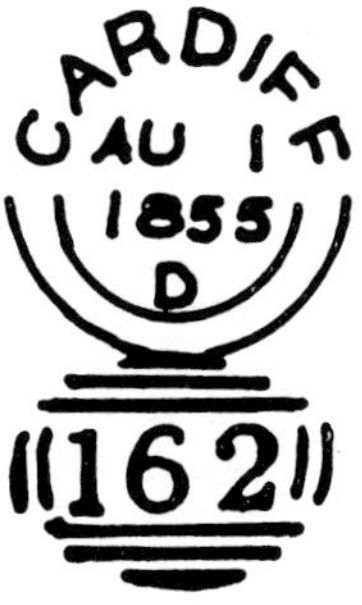

From 1854

From 1857

From 1858

DUPLEX TYPES FOR SCOTLAND

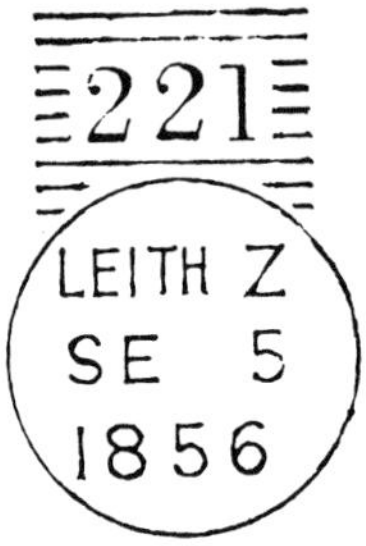

From 1856

Dotted Circle

Experimental Types

The normal Scottish type is like the Greenock example but with continuous circle

Edinburgh Brunswick Star Obliterators

Posted after Last Collection

St. Andrew's Cross
(The normal type is without white cross)

DUPLEX TYPES FOR IRELAND

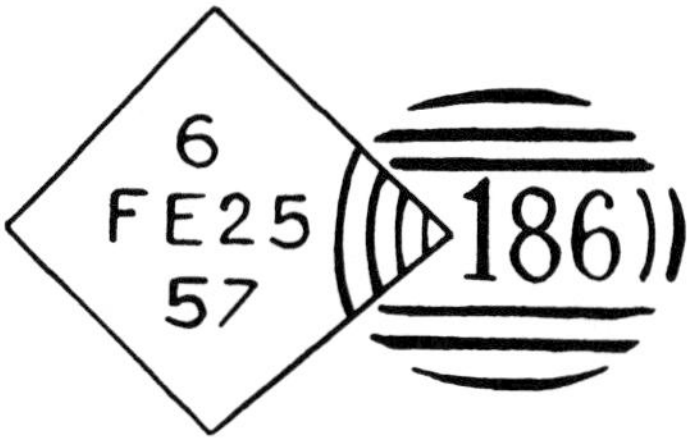

Dublin, from 1855

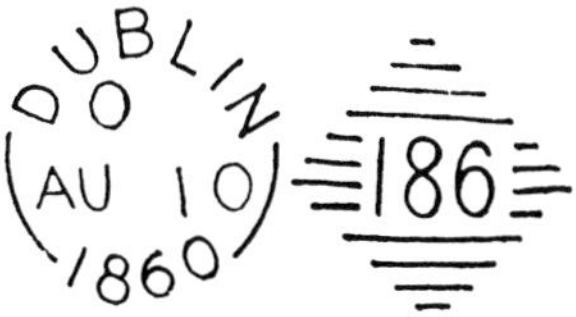

From 1859

Various Other Types. The following is a selection of the various other types of cancellations found on the Line-Engraved issues:

Travelling Post Office

N° 712

Experimental

Dotted Circle

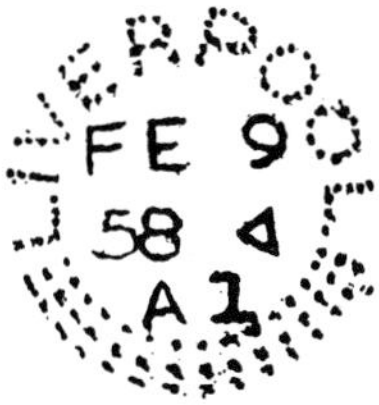

Liverpool dotted

Salisbury

Pearson Hill Early Machine Cancellations

Azemar (Machine)

Hoster (Machine)

"Squared" Circles

Newspaper Branch

Local Cancellations. These are cancellations, without date, applied at local or sub-offices.

For Scotland. From 1841 to 1845 name stamps in the following type were used at local offices and the mail was to be further cancelled in the normal way on reaching the Chief Post Office. However, correspondence for local delivery did not pass through the C.P.O.

From October 1854 to February 1860, when local cancellations were officially discontinued, local offices were permitted to use their name stamps to obliterate the stamps instead of applying them to the back of the correspondence. The C.P.O. cancellation was not normally employed in addition except where the local cancellation was wrongly impressed on the back. We illustrate the main types, but there are a number of sub-types.

SCOTTISH UNDATED NAME STAMPS

From 1841

From 1854
Serifed letters from 1855

From 1854
Italic letters from 1856

From 1854

From 1854

Double. From 1855

From 1856

Kirkwall. From 1858

For Ireland. These were used as in Scotland but less extensively.

From 1852

From 1859

For England, Ireland and Wales the use of undated name stamps as cancellers was never officially authorised as it was in Scotland.

For Wales. The circular type was also used at local offices in Wales.

For England. A wide range of types has been noted: straight line with upright or italic capitals, with or without serifs, usually unframed; straight line with capitals and lower case, upright or italic; unframed or framed circular with capitals, with or without serifs, sometimes with one or two arcs below; other miscellaneous types.

Condition—Imperforate Line-Engraved Issues

The prices quoted for the 1840 and 1841 imperforate Line-engraved issues are for "fine" examples. As condition is most important in assessing the value of a stamp, the following definitions will assist collectors in the evaluation of individual examples.

Four main factors are relevant when considering quality.

(a) Impression. This should be clean and the surface free of any rubbing or unnatural blurring which would detract from the appearance.

(b) Margins. This is perhaps the most difficult factor to evaluate. Stamps described as "fine", the standard adopted in this catalogue for pricing purposes, should have margins of the recognised width, defined as approximately one half of the distance between two adjoining unsevered stamps. Stamps described as "very fine" or "superb" should have margins which are proportionately larger than those of a "fine" stamp. Examples with close margins should not, generally, be classified as "fine".

(c) Cancellation. On a "fine" stamp this should be reasonably clear and not noticeably smudged. A stamp described as "superb" should have a neat cancellation, preferably centrally placed or to the right.

(d) Appearance. Stamps, at the prices quoted, should always be without any tears, creases, bends or thins and should not be toned on either the front or back. Stamps with such defects are worth only a proportion of the catalogue price.

Good

Fine

Very Fine

Superb

The above actual size illustrations of 1840 1d. blacks show the various grades of quality. When comparing these illustrations it should be assumed that they are all from the same plate and that they are free of any hidden defects.

Key to the Line-Engraved Issues. The table below is intended to give the user of this cataogue a condensed view of these issues, in relation to the different dies, plates and "Alphabets" and the watermarks and perforations. The page numbers in the extreme right-hand column and rapid location of the relevant part of the catalogue listing.

The Imperforate Issues

Spec. Cat. Nos.	*S.G. Nos.*	*Description*	*Date*	*Wmk*	*Perf*	*Die*	*Alphabet*	*Plates*	*Page*
A1	1–3	1d. black	6.5.40	SC	Imp.	I	I	1–11	66
D1	4–6	2d. no lines	6.5.40	SC	Imp.	I	I	1, 2	215
A2	7	1d. red-brown	10.2.41	SC	Imp.	I	I	1, 2, 5, 8–11 ("black" plates)	67
B1	8–12	1d. red-brown	Feb. 1841	SC	Imp.	I	I	12–131	97
B2	8–12	1d. red-brown	6.2.52	SC	Imp.	I	II	132–177	166
E1	13–15	2d. white lines	13.3.41	SC	Imp.	I	I	3, 4	220

The Perforated Issues

One Penny Value

Spec. Cat. Nos.	*S.G. Nos.*	*Description*	*Date*	*Wmk*	*Perf*	*Die*	*Alphabet*	*Plates*	*Page*
CE1	16a	1d. red-brown	1848	SC	Roul.	I	I	70, 71	178
CE2	16b	1d. red-brown	1850	SC	16	I	I	90–101	179
CE3	16c	1d. red-brown	1853	SC	16	I	II	Various	179
C1	17–18	1d. red-brown	Feb. 1854	SC	16	I	II	155, 157, 162–204, R1–R6	181
C2	22	1d. red-brown	Jan. 1855	SC	14	I	II	194–204, R1–R6	183
C3	24–25	1d. red-brown	27.2.55	SC	14	II	II	1–21	188
C4	21	1d. red-brown	22.2.55	SC	16	II	II	1–15	188
C5	26	1d. red-brown	15.5.55	LC	16	II	II	1–15	189
C6	—	1d. red-brown	June 1855	LC	14	II	II	1–21	189
C7	—	1d. red-brown	August 1855	SC	14	II	III	22–27	194
C8	29–33	1d. red-brown	10.1.56	LC	14	II	III	22–38, 40, 42–49	194
C8A	37	1d. red-brown	Nov. 1856	LC	14	II	III	Various from 23–45	200

Transitional Issues on Yellowish Paper

Spec. Cat. Nos.	*S.G. Nos.*	*Description*	*Date*	*Wmk*	*Perf*	*Die*	*Alphabet*	*Plates*	*Page*
C9	—	1d. orange-brn	1857	LC	14	II	III	Various from 27–55	200

Rose-red on White Paper

Spec. Cat. Nos.	*S.G. Nos.*	*Description*	*Date*	*Wmk*	*Perf*	*Die*	*Alphabet*	*Plates*	*Page*
C10	38–41	1d. rose-red	Mar. 1857	LC	14	II	III	Various from 23–58, R17	201
C11	36	1d. rose-red	26.12.57	LC	16	II	III	Various from 27–60	203
C12	42	1d. rose-red	1861	LC	14	II	IV	50, 51 engraved	209
C13	—	1d. rose-red	1862	LC	14	II	II	Reserve 15, 16	211

Two Pence Value

Spec. Cat. Nos.	*S.G. Nos.*	*Description*	*Date*	*Wmk*	*Perf*	*Die*	*Alphabet*	*Plates*	*Page*
F1	19, 20	2d. blue	1.3.54	SC	16	I	I	4	226
F2	23	2d. blue	22.2.55	SC	14	I	I	4	227
F3	23a	2d. blue	5.7.55	SC	14	I	II	5	228
F4	20a	2d. blue	18.8.55	SC	16	I	II	5	228
F5	27	2d. blue	20.7.55	LC	16	I	II	5	228
F6	34	2d. blue	20.7.55	LC	14	I	II	5	228
F7	35	2d. blue	2.7.57	LC	14	I	III	6	229
F8	36a	2d. blue	1.2.58	LC	16	I	III	6	229

Letters in All Four Corners

Spec. Cat. Nos.	*S.G. Nos.*	*Description*	*Date*	*Wmk*	*Perf*	*Die*	*Alphabet*	*Plates*	*Page*
G4	48, 49	$\frac{1}{2}$d rose-red	1.10.70	**W3**	14	—		1, 3–6, 8–15, 19, 20	237
G1	43, 44	1d. rose-red	1.4.64	LC	14	II		71–74, 76–125, 127, 129–225	233
G5	53a	$1\frac{1}{2}$d. rosy mauve	1860	LC	14	II		1	238
G6	51–53	$1\frac{1}{2}$d. rose-red	1.10.70	LC	14	II		1, 3	238
G2	45	2d. blue	July 1858	LC	14	II		7–9, 12	235
G3	46, 47	2d. thinner lines	7.7.69	LC	14	II		13–15	236

SECTION A

One Penny Black, Type A1, Imperforate

A1

1840 (6 May). Introduction of Postage Stamps. Die 1. Alphabet I. Wmk Small Crown. Imperf.

A1 (=S.G. 1/3)	(1)	1d. intense black	£8500	£375
	(2)	1d. black	£6500	£275
	(3)	1d. grey-black (worn plate)	£7500	£350
		Pair	£30000	£850
		Block of four	£80000	£15000
		Used on cover	†	£475
	d.	*Bleuté* paper (Plates 1–8)	—	£500
	e.	Watermark inverted	£18000	£1750
	f.	Re-entry	£7000	£325
	g.	Double letter in corner	£6750	£300
	h.	Guide line in corner	£6750	£300
	i.	Guide line through value	£6750	£325
	j.	Guide dots	£6500	£275
	k.	Extended frame line	£6500	£275

Imprimaturs (*from Plates* 1, 2, 3, 5 *and* 8): *from* £20000.

The prices above are for examples from the cheapest plate or plates. The rest of Section A contains separate lists for each plate, which include the varieties and the printings in red.

Early Usage: 1d. Black used on cover during May 1840

ta.	6 May	*from*	£90000
tb.	7 May	*from*	£12000
tc.	8 May	*from*	£6000
td.	9 May	*from*	£3500
te.	10 May (Sunday)		£40000
tf.	11 to 16 May		£2500
tg.	17 May (Sunday)		£12000
th.	18 to 23 May		£2000
ti.	24 May (Sunday)		£11000
tj.	25 to 30 May		£1500
tk.	31 May (Sunday)		£10000

The ld. stamps were put on sale at post offices on 1 May for use from 6 May and a few authentic covers bearing earlier dates than 6 May are known.

One Penny Printings in Red from "Black" plates

To prevent the cleaning and fraudulent re-use of black stamps the colour was changed to red-brown in 1841. The plates then available were used for printing the new colour so that it is possible to match black and red prints from the same plate with identical features: corner lettering, peculiarities, varieties, etc.

Plates lb, 2, 5, 8, 9, 10 and 11 which had been printed in black, were also printed in red and are thus listed under the ld. Black Plates. This course has been followed as being the most logical in view of the fact that printings in red were made from at least some of these "Black" plates *before* the final printings in black. This situation arose through a shortage of black stamps occurring after supplies of red stamps had been printed, but before the authorities were ready to issue them. Though always referred to as one of the "Black" plates, Plate 11 was in fact first printed from and registered in red. The black printings from this plate were of course issued before the reds and, with the other black stamps (from Plates 5, 8, 9 and 10) which were specially printed to relieve the shortage, are correctly considered to be a provisional issue.

Later One Penny Red stamps from plates never used for black printings are listed in Sections BA, BB, CA and CB.

1841 (10 February). Printed from "Black" plates in Red-brown shades on blued paper. Die I. Alphabet I. Wmk Small Crown. Imperf.

A2 (=S.G.7)		1d. red-brown (shades)	£1500	£100
		Pair (plate 9)	£6000	£325
		Block of four (plate 10)	£10000	
		Used on cover (plates 9, 11) . . . *from*	†	£200
	d.	Watermark inverted (plate lb, 8 and 10)	—	£1500

No. A2d is also recorded from plates 8 and 10 but the price quoted is for plate lb.

Distinctive Maltese Cross Cancellations

		No. A1 *off cover*	*No.* A1 *on cover*	*No.* A2 *off cover*	*No.* A2 *on cover*
ua.	Leeds Cross	£2000	£7000	£750	£2500
ub.	Manchester Cross	£1000	£2500	£750	£1800
uc.	Plymouth/Norwich Cross	£3000	£8500	£900	£3000
ud.	Wotton-under-Edge (red)	£4500	£14000	†	†
ue.	Wotton-under-Edge (black)	£4000	£12500	£5000	—
uf.	Stonehaven Cross	£2500	£12500	£3000	—
ug.	Mullingar Cross (red)	£6000	£20000	†	†
uh.	Kilmarnock Cross (red)	£5000	—	†	†
ui.	Dublin Cross	£2000	£6000	£300	£900
uj.	Greenock Cross	£2000	£6000	£500	£1000
uk.	Welshpool Cross	£4000	—	£950	—
ul.	Dursley Cross	—	£2800		
um.	Perth Cross	—	£5500		

Coloured Maltese Cross Cancellations

		No. A1 *off cover*	*No.* A1 *on cover*	*No.* A2 *off cover*	*No.* A2 *on cover*
va.	Red	£300	£475	£4500	£30000
vb.	Black	£275	£475	£100	£200
vc.	Blue	£6000	£20000	£1200	£4500
vd.	Magenta (shades), see below	£2000	£7000	†	†
ve.	Ruby (Aberdeen)	£800	£2800	†	†
vf.	Violet (Glasgow)	£6000	—	†	†
vg.	Orange (Liverpool)	—	£1800	†	†
vh.	Vermilion (Bristol)	—	£2000	†	†
vi.	Brown (Haddington)	£2500	£6000	†	†
vj.	Yellow (Newnham-on-Severn)	—	—	†	†
vk.	Red + black	£2000	£7000	£3000	—

The best examples of the Magenta Cross shades are those from Preston, Glasgow and Burton-on-Trent.

A 1840 1d. Black and 1d. Red-brown from Black Plates

"Numbers in Maltese Cross" Cancellations

	No. A1 *off cover*	*No.* A1 *on cover*	*No.* A2 *off cover*	*No.* A2 *on cover*
wa. No. 1 in Cross	£7000	—	£500	£1250
wb. No. 2 in Cross	£7000	—	£500	£1250
wc. No. 3 in Cross	£7000	—	£500	£1250
wd. No. 4 in Cross	£7000	—	£750	£2000
we. No. 5 in Cross	£7000	—	£500	£1250
wf. No. 6 in Cross	£7000	—	£500	£1250
wg. No. 7 in Cross	£7000	—	£500	£1250
wh. No. 8 in Cross	£7000	—	£500	£1250
wi. No. 9 in Cross	£7000	—	£500	£1250
wj. No. 10 in Cross	£7000	—	£600	£2000
wk. No. 11 in Cross	£7000	—	£750	£2000
wl. No. 12 in Cross	£7000	£20000	£750	£2000

Town Postmarks without Maltese Cross (cancelling the stamps)

	Large portion of p/m on the stamp	*Complete p/m on stamp and piece*	*Complete p/m on stamp and cover*
1d. Black. No. A1			
xa. Black	£5000	£7000	£15000
xb. Red	£5000	£7000	£20000
xc. Yellow (Horsham)	—	£22000	—

All known examples of No. A2*xc* are on piece or cover.

"Penny Post" Postmarks (cancelling the stamps) in Black, Blue, Green, Red

	Large portion of p/m on the stamp	*Complete p/m on stamp and piece*	*Complete p/m on stamp and cover*
1d. Black. No. A1			
ya. Comblined with Maltese Cross . *from*	£1500	£2000	£5000
yb. Without Maltese Cross .... *from*	£3000	£4500	£15000
yc. Framed type ("PyP No. 15", Handsworth)	£2000	£2500	£6500

1844-Type Cancellation

A1 *za.* Black	£1200	£1700	£5000
A2 *za.* Black	£500	£650	£2200

Plate Numbering. Plates numbered from 1 to 11 were used for printing the 1d. Black. A plate lettered A was used for printing the unissued "VR" Official stamp. Several of the plates underwent one or more attempts at repairing. The list below gives the dates of registration, first use and destruction of these plates:

Plate	*Registered*	*Earliest Known Postal Use*	*Destroyed*
1	15 and 27 April 1840	6 May 1840 ("Plate 1a"); 12 June 1840 ("Plate 1b")	11 December 1841
2	22 and 27 April 1840	2 May 1840	19 November 1841
3	9 May 1840	16 May 1840	October 1840
4	19 May 1840	23 May 1840	9 January 1841
5	1 and 11 June 1840	17 June 1840	November 1841
6	17 June 1840	29 June 1840	9 January 1841
7	8 July 1840	by 6 July 1840	9 January 1841
8	31 July 1840	5 September 1840	8 September 1841
9	9 November 1840	18 November 1840	7 October 1843
10	8 December 1840	2 January 1841	21 February 1843
11	27 January 1841 (in red)	4 February 1841 (in black)	15 January 1842
A	15 April 1840 and 9 May 1840	not issued	not known

Repaired Impressions—Prices for Original States

Although they are not separately listed, it must be understood that wherever impressions are repaired, creating second states, the prices for the letterings in original states may be higher than those for normal unrepaired letterings that exist in only one state. This applies throughout the Line-Engraved issues.

One Penny Black, Plate 1a

Plate 1 of the ld. Black was registered on 15 April 1840. As the plate had not been hardened it soon showed signs of wear. A second sheet is recorded as having been registered on 27 April 1840. The plate was later withdrawn and extensive repairs were undertaken. It is usual to refer to the plate in its original state as "Plate 1a" and to the repaired state as "Plate 1b".

AS1		1d. intense black (early impression)	£10000	£400
AS2		1d. grey-black (showing moderate plate wear)	£8500	£300
AS3		1d. grey-black (very worn)	£9500	£400
		Pair	£35000	£1400
		Block of four	£95000	£19000
		Used on cover	†	£550
	aa.	No ray flaw (intruding impression): CL	—	£325
	a.	No ray flaw: RL, SK, SL, TK, TL	—	£325
	b.	Re-entries: HB, HD, OA, PB	—	£425
	c.	Shifted transfer: PL, RL, SL, TL (basal shifts)	—	£325
	d.	Double letters: A*E*, C*D*, *F*A, F*I*, G*I*, *M*F, *Q*A, R*I*, *T*K	—	£300
	e.	Constant varieties: DG (smudge in D square), DA, EA, GA all smudge in A square). JA (the A is blind), MK (mark on left margin at top of M square) *from*	—	£325
	f.	Cancelled with black Maltese Cross	—	£850
	g.	Watermark inverted	—	£3000
	h.	*Bleuté* paper	—	£550

Imprimatur. First registration sheet (*before hardening*): £20000. Stamps removed from the imprimatur sheet are AL, SB to SL, TA to TL. *Imprimatur. Second registration sheet* (*after hardening?*) £20000. Stamps removed from the imprimatur sheet are AL, SC to SL, TA to TL.

Plate Characteristics, Plate la. Apart from the ten o'clock ray flaw, which appears on all stamps of the sheet with the exception of CL, RL, SK, SL, TK and TL, the *lower* segment of the left "star" presents identification characteristics of importance. It will be noted that the seven o'clock ray is generally exaggerated and the five o'clock ray is almost absent. This relation of the two rays is preserved throughout the whole plate. The one exception is the stamp CL, on which the rays five, seven and ten are normal; evidently CL is an intruding impression, due perhaps to the accidental turning of the transfer roller.

For distinguishing Plate 1a impressions from those of the second state (Plate 1b), the characteristic corner star of Plate la should be a sufficient guide in all cases except FG, FI and LG; but other features of the first state help to distinguish it from the repaired state, for instance: (1) the thicker baselines; (2) the thicker check letters; (3) the more pronounced guide-lines seen in the right upper corners of some letterings; (4) the woolly appearance of early impressions and the very worn appearance of the late impressions; (5) the "plate dot" (a marginal dot just outside the left side-line, opposite the Queen's mouth) is frequently seen on Plate 1a stamps, but is almost entirely absent from the second state (1b).

Plate 1a

Plate 1b

Characteristic corner stars

One Penny Black, Plate 1b

As the first Penny Black plate was put to press without previous hardening, it wore rapidly giving rise to the grey impressions so frequently seen in Plate la. Owing to extreme wear, the engraved lines of the Queen's head became very faint, and this necessitated the restoration of every one of the 240 units of the plate. This could only be satisfactorily carried out by re-entry, and it is believed that the transfer roller impression which had been used for laying down Plate 2 of this value was employed for the purpose of re-entering the worn Plate 1. This procedure had the effect of profoundly modifying the character of the left star, which in the great majority of the 240 plate impressions now resembled more that of the final stage of Plate 2. 23 May 1840 is the date on which it is thought that this first repair of Plate 1 was carried out. The earliest recorded use of Plate 1b for printing is 8 June 1840 and its earliest known date of postal use is 12 June 1840.

AS4	1d. intense black	£8500	£375
AS5	1d. black	£6500	£275
	Pair	£30000	£950
	Block of four	£80000	£16000
	Used on cover	†	£475
	a. The "original" Plate 1a re-entries: HB, HD, OA, PB	£8000	£400
	b. Non-coincident re-entries showing portions of the original impression: CL, GA, GC, GK, GL, HK, IB, ID, II, JI, JK, MH, MI, MK, NG, OI, QL	£6750	£300
	c. Non-coincident re-entries showing recut and enlarged letters: EJ, IL, JC, PA *from*	£6750	£425
	d. Twisted re-entry altering position of check letters EK and GK	£6750	£375
	e. Retouched check letters: *N*C to *N*J, O*I*, *P*J, *P*K, R*I*	£6750	£300
	f. Double letters: A*E*, *CD*, *F*A, *F*I, G*I*, *M*F, *Q*A, *T*K	£6750	£325
	g. Burr rubs (NE of ONE joined, or nearly so): CF, DF, FD, NA, OB, OD, OF, PD, QD, RE	£6750	£300
	h. Complete or partial recut side-lines, necessitated by burr rub following re-entering—left side: AJ, BJ, FH, GB, GF, HC, HL, IG, IH, IJ, JJ, JL, KD, KF, KG, KH, KL, LA, LB, LL, MC, ME, MG, OD, OF, PC, PD, PF, QG, RB, RD, RF; right side: KE, KL, LB, MD, TC	£6750	£300
	i. Recut corners: BH, BL, FH, GB, HL	£6750	£300
	j. Constant varieties: AL, IE, JB, PG, SI	£6750	£325
	k. Roller flaw in N.E. segment of left star: strong on DE, DG; faint on DB, DC, DD, DF, DH *from*	£6750	£275
	l. Watermark inverted	£10000	£1750
	m. Thin paper	—	£375
	n. *Bleuté* paper	—	£500

The thin paper variety may be from the balance of the experimental thin paper used with Plate 7.

Index to Plate 1b Varieties. As Plate 1b contains a large number of distinctive stamps this separate index is provided. It can be used both for the black printings (AS4/5) and for the red printings (AS6). It does not include the letterings of those repaired impressions which are found only printed in red.

Only the key letter to the variety is given; thus the entry "GF: *h*" is a reference to AS4/5*h* or to AS6*h*, depending on the colour of the stamp.

AE: *f*	DH: *k*	HC: *h*	JJ: *h*	MF: *f*	OB: *g*	QL *b*
AJ: *h*	EJ: *c*	HD: *a*	JK: *b*	MG: *h*	OD: *g,h*	RB: *h*
AL: *j*	EK: *d*	HK: *b*	JL: *h*	MH: *b*	OF: *g,h*	RD: *h*
BH: *i*	FA: *f*	HL: *h,i*	KD: *h*	MI: *b*	OI: *b,e*	RE: *g*
BJ: *h*	FD: *g*	IB: *b*	KE: *h*	MK: *b*	PA: *c*	RF: *h*
BL: *i*	FH: *h,i*	ID: *b*	KF: *h*	NA: *g*	PB: *a*	RI: *e*
CD: *f*	FI: *f*	IE: *j*	KG: *h*	NC: *e*	PC: *h*	SI: *j*
CF: *g*	GA: *b*	IG: *h*	KH: *h*	ND: *e*	PD: *g,h*	TC: *h*
CL: *b*	GB: *h,i*	IH: *h*	KL: *h*	NE: *e*	PF: *h*	TK: *f*
DB: *k*	GC: *b*	II: *b*	LA: *h*	NF: *e*	PG: *j*	
DC: *k*	GF: *h*	IJ: *h*	LB: *h*	NG: *b,e*	PJ: *e*	
DD: *k*	GI: *f*	IL: *c*	LL: *h*	NW *e*	PK: *e*	
DE: *k*	GK: *b,d*	JB: *j*	MC: *h*	NI: *e*	QA: *f*	
DF: *g,k*	GL: *b*	JC: *c*	MD: *h*	NJ: *e*	QD: *g*	
DG: *k*	HB: *a*	JI: *b*	ME: *h*	OA: *a*	QG: *h*	

CD FA FI MF QA TK

Double letters, Plates 1a and 1b

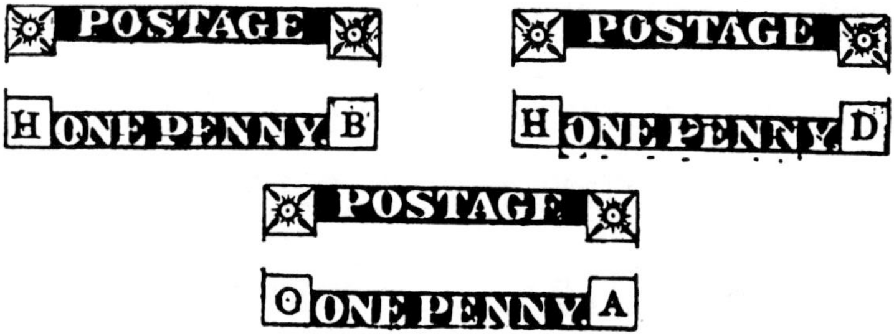

Re-entries, Plates 1a and 1b

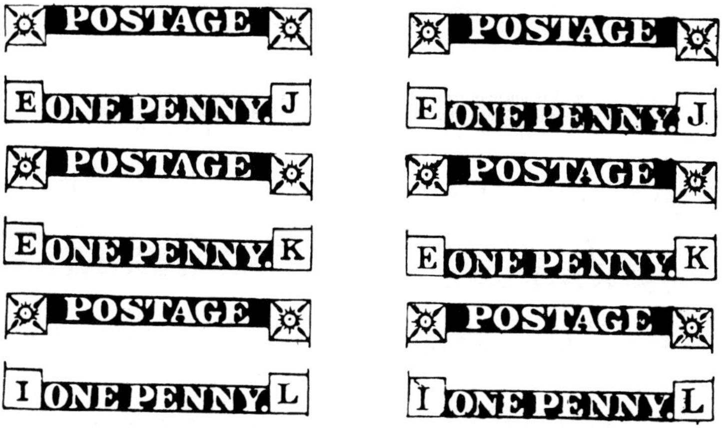

Recut letters EJ, EK, IL. Left, the early forms (Plate 1a). Right, the changed forms (Plate 1b).

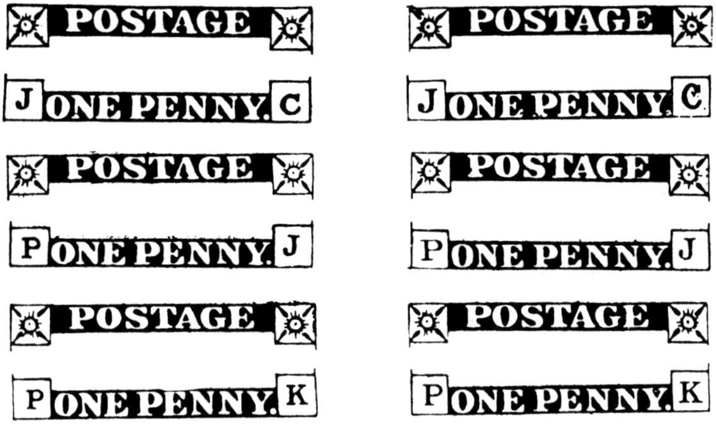

Recut letters JC, PJ, PK. Left, the early forms (Plate 1a). Right, the changed forms (Plate 1b)

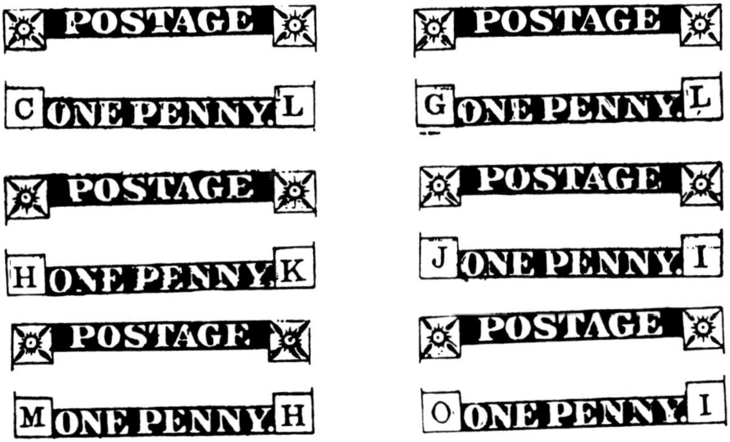

Re-entries, Plate 1b

AL IE JB PG SI

(Late printing) *Constant varieties, Plate 1b*

Plate 1b, Printing in Red

In August 1840 it was decided to change the colour of the ld. value to red but printing was delayed while extensive experiments were conducted to find a new type of black ink for obliterating the stamps in order to prevent the removal of postmarks and re-use of the stamps. This was achieved but as an additional precaution a new type of ink was developed for printing the stamps in red and the use of these inks was approved by a Treasury Minute dated 17 December 1840. Printing in red commenced on 30 December and the stamps came into use about 10 February 1841.

Not all of the 240 letterings exist in the second state in red, as after all printing in black had finished in 1840, but before the plate was used for any printing in red, it was decided to carry out a plate repair involving some 45 impressions: these State 3 impressions may only be found in the red printing: no later states than State 2 (Plate 1b) are known in the black printings. It is doubtful whether the plate was again hardened after repairs later than the first; hence the more rapid wear after the later repairs.

AS6	1d. red-brown	£8500	£275
	Pair	—	£750
	Block of four	—	—
	Used on cover	†	£475
	a. The "original" Plate 1a re-entries: HB, HD, OA, PB	—	£400
	b. Non-coincident re-entries showing portions of the original impression: GA, GC, GK, GL, HK, ID, II, JI, JK, MH, MI, MK, NG, OI	—	£350
	c. Non-coincident re-entries showing recut and enlarged letters: EJ, IL, JC *from*	—	£400
	d. Twisted re-entry altering position of check letters EK and GK	—	£375
	e. Retouched check letters: *N*C, *N*E to *N*J, O*I*, *P*J, *P*K, R*I*	—	£300
	f. Double letters: A*E*, *CD*, *F*A, *F*I, G*I*, *M*F, *Q*A	—	£325
	g. Burr rubs (NE of ONE joined, or nearly so): DF, FD, NA, OB, OD, OF, PD, QD, RE	—	£300
	h. Complete or partial recut side-lines, necessitated by burr rub following re-entering—left side: BJ, FH, GB, GF, HC, HL, IG, IH, IJ, JJ, JL, KD, KF, KG, KH, KL, LL, MC, ME, MG, OD, OF, PC, PD, PF, QG, RD, RF; right side: KE, KL	—	£300
	i. Recut corners: BH, FH, GB, HL	—	£300
	j. Constant varieties IE, PG, SI	—	£325
	k. Roller flaw in N.E. segment of left star: strong on DE, DG; faint on DB, DC, DD, DF, DH *from*	—	£300
	l. Watermark inverted	—	£1500

The above varieties that exist in black and in red-brown are indexed below the listing of AS4/5.

The Second Repair to Plate 1, Printings in Red

Plate 1c, State 3 Impressions following the Second Plate Repair. State 3 and later state impressions exist only in the red printings. The second repair gave rise to the following State 3 impressions, namely AA, AB, AD, AH, AI, AJ, AK, AL, BL, CF, CG, CL, IB, IC, JA, JB, LA, LB, LC, MD, ND, PA, PL, QL, RA, RB, RL, SA, SB, SC, SD, SE, SL, TA, TB, TC, TD, TE, TF, TG. TH, TI, TJ, TK, TL. Practically all these impressions show thinning of the upper corner stars as well as of the check letters, which points to a transfer roller impression with blank upper corners as well as blank lower corners having been used for this re-entering. In all but two instances the re-entering was coincident and without duplications: the two exceptions are TC and TL. In JA and LA, the check letters J and L are extremely faint.

AS7	1d. red-brown. JA and LA (faint first letters)	—	£450
AS8	1d. red-brown. TC and TL (non-coincident re-entries)	—	£500
AS9	1d. red-brown. Remaining letterings (see above)	—	£400

The Third Repair to Plate 1, Printings in Red

This, carried out fairly early in 1841, included some 21 stamps. In this number are included 14 stamps which had not been dealt with at the second repair, thus constituting an additional group of third states, and also seven stamps which, although included in the second repair, were again re-entered, so constituting fourth states.

Plate lc, State 3 Impressions following the Third Plate Repair. This group comprises the letterings: ID, JC, JD, JE, JF, JG, JI, KC, OA, QC, QD, RG, RK and SG. Many of the stamps of this group show "faint re-entry marks" in the upper star corners, the engravings of these corners not being further compressed, and the lower background restored, facts which point to a partial re-entering from below POSTAGE downwards, so excluding the upper parts of the impressions. Of this group RK (State 3) is a noncoincident re-entry, showing duplication and distortion on the left and QD (State 3) shows a strengthening of the bottom line.

AS 10	1d. red-brown. RK State 3 (non-coincident re-entry)	—	£700
AS10A	1d. red-brown, QD State 3 (strengthened bottom line)		
AS11	1d. red-brown. The remaining letterings as above (coinciding State 3 re-enterings)	—	£500

Re-entries, Plate 1c

Plate 1d, State 4 Impressions following the Third Plate Repair. The stamps operated on for the third time, so becoming fourth states, are: QL, RL, TB, TG, TH, TJ and TK. All in this group show faint re-entry marks in the star corners, also thinned check letters and restored lower background, pointing to a partial re-entering from below POSTAGE downwards.

AS12	1d. red-brown. The above State 4 letterings .... *each*	—	£550

The Fourth Repair to Plate 1, Printings in Red

Plate 1e, State 5 Impressions following the Fourth (last 1841) Repair. The stamps QL, RL and TK were again re-entered. This last repair, like the third, was evidently a partial re-entering from below POSTAGE downwards. Unlike the fourth state, these fifth state stamps have much more pronounced and extensive marks in the star corners in place of the "faint re-entry marks": there is further thinning of the check letters, and a restoration of worn background below.

AS13	1d. red-brown. QL, RL and TK State 5 .... *each*	—	£600

One Penny Black, Plate 2

Plate 2 was registered and put to press on 22 April 1840 and a second sheet was registered on 27 April. This was the only plate other than Plate 1a to provide stamps for the first day, 6 May 1840, and it is known used as early as 2 May. The plate was destroyed on 19 November 1841.

Examination of the left corner star is of great assistance in identifying stamps from this plate. The star in this left corner is normal in only 55 stamps out of the 240, lettered FF to JL. In the remaining 185 stamps on the sheet, the left star shows a complete absence of the left ray of the lower segment (the 7 o'clock ray): and of these all except 33 (lettered Cl to FE) show an additional flaw in the left segment, the upper (10 o'clock) ray being absent.

The three forms of the left corner star on Plate 2. Left, normal. Centre, 7 o'clock flaw. Right, 7 and 10 o'clock flaws

It is a noteworthy feature of ld. Plate 2 that where horizontal guidelines exist in stamps from the upper half of the sheet, they are always found at the base of the impressions, whereas in the lower half of the sheet they are always near the upper borders. This also applies to shifted transfers, which appear as duplications, coloured projections or thickenings; when these occur in the upper half of the sheet, they are always found at the base of the stamps, whereas on the stamps of the lower half of the sheet, they occur only at the upper borders, then giving rise to swollen coloured parts of the corner stars, doubled central dots and coloured projections. The check letter D is distinctive in the upper half of the sheet, where it is broader than usual, and leaning slightly to the left. Curiously this letter is normal in the lower half of the sheet. The check letter E resembles that of Plate 1 leaning to the left and its lower limb projecting slightly beyond the upper.

Normal *Broad* E

Distinctive letters, Plate 2

Plate 2 in Black, 1st State

AS14	1d. intense black	£9250	£375
AS15	1d. black	£6000	£275
AS16	1d. grey-black	£7500	£350
	Pair	£30000	£850
	Block of four	£80000	£15000
	Used on cover	†	£475
	a. Re-entries AD, HL, SA	£6500	£375
	b. Shifted transfers: basal shifts (GC, IL): upper shifts (e.g. “S” row)	£6250	£300
	c. Double letters: *D*G, *E*A, F*G*, K*E*, *M*E, *P*A, *T*L	£6250	£300
	d. Recut letter square: PB (both squares), PD, PG, PI, RF	£6250	£300
	e. Burr rubs, NE of ONE nearly joined: KJ, KK, NC; right margin: SK	£6250	£300
	f. Without ray flaws: FF to JL (JA and JF are listed under variety k	£6250	£300
	i. Showing horizontal guide-lines at top	£6250	£300
	j. Very worn plate	£7500	£350
	k. Constant varieties: B*D*, *H*A, *J*A, JF, LE, PL, QL	£6250	£300
	l. Watermark inverted	£18000	£1900
	m. Cancelled with black Maltese Cross	†	£550
	n. *Bleuté* paper	—	£550

Imprimatur. First registration sheet (*before hardening*): £20000. *Imprimatur. Second registration sheet* (*after hardening?*): £20000. Stamps removed from both imprimatur sheets AL, SC to SL, TA to TL.

Plate 2 in Black, 2nd State: First Repair (May or June 1840)

Stamps in black of the first repair are not easy to distinguish, but SD, TA, TB, TC, and TE to TH all show stronger engraved lines on the face. In addition, stamps TA, TB and TC show recut frame lines, particularly on the right side, together with signs of burr removal marks or TRLs

AS17	1d. black. SD, TA, TB, TC, TE, TF, TG, TH	£8000	£325

Plate 2, Printings in Red

AS18	1d. red-brown (shades)	£6000	£240
	Pair	—	£650
	Block of four	—	—
	Used on cover	†	£325
	a. Re-entries AD, HL, SA	—	£325
	b. Shifted transfers: basal shifts (GC, IL): upper shifts (e.g. “S” row)	—	£275
	c. Double letters: *D*G, *E*A, F*G*, K*E*, *M*E, *P*A, *T*L	—	£275
	d. Recut letter square: PB (both squares), PD, PG, PI, RF	—	£275
	e. Burr rubs, NE of ONE nearly joined; KJ, KK, NC; right margin: SK	—	£275
	f. Without ray flaws: FF to JL (JA and JF are listed under variety k)	—	£275
	i. Showing horizontal guide-lines at top	—	£275
	j. Very worn plate	—	£325
	k. Constant varieties: B*D*, *H*A, *J*A, JF, LE, PL, QL	—	£300

Plate 2 in Red, Second Repair

Sometime in 1841, after all printing from this plate in *black* had finished, there was a second plate repair; red stamps from this plate showing restored engraving, all without the 7 o'clock ray flaw and some of these also without the 10 o'clock ray flaw, have been found (TH to TL).

AS19	1d. red-brown. TG, State 3; TH, State 3; TI to TL, State 2	—	£600

PB PI

Recut corners, Plate 2

Re-entries, Plate 2

DG EA FG KE ME PA TL

Double letters, Plate 2

BD HA JA JF LE PL *and* QL

Constant varieties, Plate 2

One Penny Black, Plate 3

Plate 3 was registered on 9 May 1840 and put to press on 12 May. It is known used on 16 May 1840.

No distinctive roller flaws have been noted on this plate, but there are certain other features which help in identification, particularly the base-lines of the letter blocks, which are generally thinner than in any other Penny Black plate.

Greyish impressions resembling those of Plate 1a are common, but the thin base-lines and the normal left star make the distinction between the two plates easy. Several of the check letters of Plate 3 are distinctive, particularly the letter P, which has a very small loop. The letter M is smaller than normal, and the letter K is generally narrower. The E is more like the letter on Plates 1 and 2 than that on the subsequent plates, and the letter A is blind on one or two stamps. Guide-lines are few and faint in this plate. There is no evidence of plate repairs having been carried out; in fact the plate was destroyed in October 1840, and was not printed from in red.

AS19A	1d. intense black	£10000	£425
AS20	1d. black	£9250	£325
AS21	1d. grey-black (worn)	£9750	£375
	Pair	£35000	£1500
	Block of four	£85000	£18000
	Used on cover	†	£575
	a. Letter P with small loop: PA to PL	£9500	£375
	b. Double letters: *F*D, *H*A, *K*C	£9500	£375
	c. Constant varieties: KF, T*E*, *T*K	£9500	£375

d.	Watermark inverted	—	£2750
e.	*Bleuté* paper	—	£575
f.	Recut letter square: PD	£9500	£350

Imprimatur: £20000. Stamps removed from the imprimatur sheet are AL, SC to SL, and TA to TL.

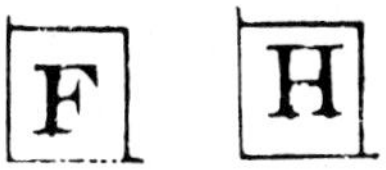

FD HA KC

Double Letters, Plate 3

KF TE TK

Constant Varieties, Plate 3

PD

Recut letter square, Plate 3

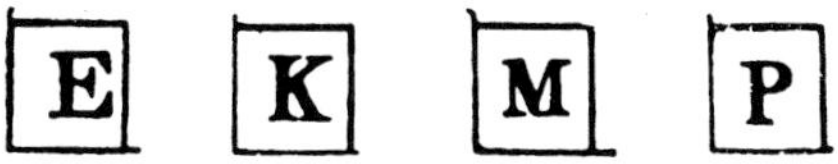

E K M P

Distinctive Letters, Plate 3

One Penny Black, Plate 4

Plate 4 was registered on 19 May 1840. It is known used on 23 May. It is known as a "spotted plate" because many of its stamps show spots. These minute black dots are to be seen scattered in the margins and in the clear parts of the stamps, such as the corner squares. The base-lines of the letter blocks are much thicker than those in Plate 3. The check letters "L" in the twelfth *horizontal* row of stamps are distinctive, as the foot slopes upwards, and the angle made with the upright is slightly acute. Curiously enough the letters "L" in the twelfth *vertical* row are quite different, and the angle formed by the foot and the upright is slightly obtuse. Greyish impressions indicating wear of the plate are sometimes found, but there is no evidence of repair to Plate 4. Some very fine examples of bleuté paper are to be found in this plate. The plate was not printed from in red, and it was destroyed on 9 January 1841.

AS22		1d. intense black	£9000	£375
AS23		1d. black	£6500	£300
		Pair	£30000	£950
		Block of four	£80000	£16000
		Used on cover	†	£500
	a.	Re-entries: SC, SD	£7000	£350
	b.	Double letters: *DA*, *DB*, *DD*, *DF*, *PA*, *QA*, *RG*	£6750	£325
	c.	Recut letter square: IE	£6750	£325
	d.	Defective H and dots at right of N.E. corner: AH	£6750	£325
	e.	Watermark inverted	—	£2750
	f.	*Bleuté* paper	—	£550

No imprimaturs of this plate have been reported.

L (horizontal row) *L (vertical row)*

Distinctive Letters, Plate 4

AH

Defective Letter, Plate 4

Re-entries, Plate 4

DA DB DD DF PA QA RG

Double Letters, Plate 4

THE PROVISIONAL BLACK PRINTING

The printing of stamps of the 1d. value in red had only been in progress for some three weeks of January 1841, when there came an order for a further supply of stamps in black, as it was proposed to carry on with black stamps until the supply of black obliterating ink for cancelling the red stamps had been received. This limited supply of further black stamps, known as the provisional black printing, is believed to have been obtained from five plates then at press, namely Nos. 5, 8, 9, 10 and 11. In the case of Plates 5, 8, 9 and 10 certain impressions on each plate were repaired just before any black prints were taken. This plate repair of January 1841 may be referred to as "the provisional issue repair"; it resulted in the appearance of certain black letterings in a later state than corresponding red letterings which had been produced in early January. Such red stamps, in an earlier state than the corresponding provisional black prints, may be referred to as pre-provisional red prints. Thus in the case of 1d. Plate 5 we have the well-known provisional issue black print PB State 3 following the provisional issue repair of January 1841, and the pre-provisional red print PB State 2 following a plate repair of 1840, the printing being made in early January and prior to the provisional issue repair. In the same way we have AC State 2, AK State 2, CC State 4, EA State 3, EB State 3, EC State 3, FB State 2, FC State 2, FD State 2, GA State 2, HA State 2, HB State 2, JB State 2, KA State 2, MA State 2, QA State 2, QB State 2, QC State 2, RA State 2, RC State 2, RD State 2, SA State 2, SB State 2, SC State 2, SD State 2, TA State 3, TB State 2, TD State 2 and TK State 2, all ld. blacks of the provisional printing and of the same order of rarity as PB State 3 black, along with ld. reds of prior states from the first pre-provisional printing, all with the same lettering as the above. These pre-provisional red prints prove that the blacks of the later states are from the provisional printing, and like the black provisionals, these red prints are very scarce.

One Penny Black, Plate 5

Plate 5 was put to press on 28 May 1840 and registered twice: on 1 and 11 June. Its earliest known date of use is 17 June.

A noteworthy plate feature is the bulging of the base-line under each side of the "O" in "ONE"; this occurs on a large number of stamps from Plate 5.

Another condition commonly found on this plate is a pronounced weakness of the side-lines (particularly at the left) and of the outer line in the right upper corner. It was probably because of these weaknesses, as well as the wear of the engraved lines of the Queen's head, that so many impressions on the right side of the plate (left side of the printed sheets) were repaired. In the repaired impressions these defects are no longer seen.

The check letters "E" on this and the two following plates (6 and 7) are much alike, but they are distinct from those of Plate 4 as they (Plate 5) are narrower, have a thicker upper limb, and the serifs are less pronounced. The check letter "J" on Plate 5 is characteristic, its vertical stroke sloping downwards and to the left.

Plate 5, unlike the other middle plates (4, 6 and 7), was used for printing red stamps, and the possession of red prints is helpful in differentiating some of the more difficult letterings. 1d. Plate 5 was one of the plates used for printing the 1d. black provisional issue of early 1841; the other four plates also used for this purpose being plates 8, 9, 10 and 11.

Plate 5 was a much-repaired plate, repairs being carried out on at least four separate occasions, namely twice in 1840, again in January 1841 (the provisional issue repair) and again later in 1841 after all printing in black had ceased and the plate was being used only for red printings. The plate was destroyed in November 1841.

Plate 5 in Black, 1st State

AS24	1d. intense black	£7500	£375
AS25	1d. black	£6500	£275
	Pair	£30000	£850
	Block of four	£80000	£15000
	Used on cover	†	£500
	a. Re-entries: LL and ND	£7000	£350
	b. Double letters: DB *E*B, *H*B, *H*E, *H*I, K*E*, P*H*, P*J*, T*H*	£6750	£325
	c. Retouched letter: *B*A, *N*A	£6750	£300
	d. Constant varieties: *B*G, QC, QF *from*	£6750	£325
	e. Watermark inverted	—	£2750
	f. *Bleuté* paper	—	£400

Imprimatur. First registration sheet (before hardening): £20000. Stamps removed from the imprimatur sheet are AL, SB, SD to SL, TA to TL. *Imprimatur. Second registration sheet (after hardening?)*: £20000. Stamps removed from the imprimatur sheet are AL, SC to SL, TA to TL.

NOTE. The units DB, EB and HB (double letter), BA and NA (retouched letter) and QC (constant variety) exist as later repaired states, in both black and red-brown. These varieties in their later states may attract a slight premium by virtue of their relative scarcity.

Plate 5 Later States in Black, 1840 Repairs

Two separate plate repairs were carried out in the year 1840, during which time only black stamps were being printed. The impressions selected for repair in 1840 came from the last five vertical rows of the plate (first five vertical rows of the printed sheet). The repairs were by re-entry, and a noteworthy effect was that not only were the check letters thinned, but also the engraving of the upper star corners likewise, the inference being that the roller used for re-entering this ld. black plate (as well as for later ld. black plates up to Plate 10) was one with blank upper corners instead of stars. Where the same impressions were re-entered twice, i.e. at each of the 1840 repairs, the second repair (giving rise to a third state) produced more thinning of check letters and upper stars than did the first re-entering. The amount of strengthening of the engraved lines of the head and of the engine-turned background was similar in each case. While a number of impressions were repaired twice in 1840, others were only repaired once—at the first or second operation.

First 1840 Repair

AS27	1d. black. State 2: AA, AB, BB, CA, CB, CC, CD, CE, DA, DB (double letter), DC, DD, DE, EA, EB (double letter), EC, ED, FA, JA, OA, OB, PA, TA	—	£425

Second 1840 Repair

AS28	1d. black. State 2: Repaired for first time at second 1840 operation BA (retouched letter), BC, NA (retouched letter), PB	—	£525
AS29	1d. black. State 3: BB, CB, CC, CD, CE, DA, DB (double letter), DC, DD, ED	—	£625

For the next printing in black, see Nos. AS30/31.

Plate 5 in Red, Earliest State

AS26	1d. red-brown (shades) *from*	£2250	£150
	Pair	—	£300
	Block of four	£15000	—
	Used on cover	†	£275
	a. Re-entries: LL and ND	—	£175
	b. Double letters: *H*E, *H*I, K*E*, P*H*, P*J*, T*H*	—	£175
	d. Constant varieties: *B*G, QF	—	£175

NOTE. Double letter unit HB and constant variety unit QC exist as the 1st state in red only in the scarce pre-provisional printing (see No. AS35) as they were repaired again in the Provisional Issue.

Double letter units DB and EB plus the retouched letter units BA and NA exist in red only in 2nd or later states (DB 3rd and 4th states only in red) as a result of one or both 1840 repairs.

Red Printings Repaired at One or Both 1840 Repairs

The following letterings printed in red were not subject to the later repairs and can therefore be matched with the letterings listed under Nos. AS27/29.

AS27A	1d. red-brown. State 2: units existing in red *only in 2nd State* from first 1840 repair, and remaining in State 2 throughout red printings: AA, CA, DE, FA, JA, OA, OB, PA	—	£175
AS28A	1d. red-brown. State 2: unit existing in red *only in 2nd State* from second 1840 repair, and remaining in State 2 throughout red paintings: NA (retouched letter)	—	£175
AS29A	1d. red-brown. State 3: units existing in red *only in 3rd State* from repairs at both 1840 operations and remaining in State 3 throughout red printings: CB, CE, DD	—	£175

Certain units repaired at either or both of the 1840 repairs commenced their life in red in a second or later state, but were subsequently repaired again at the fourth repair in late 1841. These units are listed as Nos. AS37 and AS38 in their 3rd or 4th States, but may have a certain scarcity value in their earlier state.

Pre-provisional Printing in Red

This printing was carried out on 30 December 1840 with the plate which included the repaired impressions listed under their latest states under Nos. AS27/29. This printing included some impressions which were repaired once again before the provisional black printing of 22 January and hence produced a very scarce issue with a life of only three weeks.

AS34	1d. red-brown. State 2: PB	—	£3500
AS35	1d. red-brown. State 1: AC, AK, FB, FC, FD, GA, HA, HB (double letter), JB, KA, MA, QA, QB, QC (constant variety), RA, RC, RD, SA, SB, SC, SD, TB, TD, TK; State 2: EA, EB, EC, TA; State 3: CC	£2500	£550

Provisional Printing 1841, in Black (Third Repair)

The provisional black printings were made during the period 22 January to 3 February 1841. In the case of Plates 5, 8, 9 and 10, these printings were preceded in each case by a plate repair (the provisional issue repair). In the case of Plate 5, some two dozen impressions were re-entered in this repair, one of the resulting repaired impressions being the well-known, non-coincident re-entry PB State 3: the remaining units are all concident re-entries, and though less conspicuous than PB State 3, are of the same order of rarity.

The effect of this repair was similar to the earlier 1840 repairs: where units had already been repaired at these earlier operations, they show increased thinning of the stars and check letters.

AS30	1d. black. Provisional printing. State 3: PB (non-coincident re-entry)	—	£6000
AS31	1d. black. Provisional printing (all coincident re-entries). State 2: AC, AK, FB, FC, FD, GA, HA, HB (double letter), JB, KA, MA, QA, QB, QC (constant variety), RA, RC, RD, SA, SB, SC, SD, TB, TD, TK; State 3: EA, EB (double letter), EC, TA; State 4: CC	—	£800

1841 Printings in Red from Provisional Repair

Printings in red-brown were resumed on 4 February 1841 with the plate in the same state as used for the black printings, Nos. AS30/31.

AS32	1d. red-brown. State 3: PB (non-concident re-entry)	—	£1750
AS33	1d. red-brown (all coincident re-entries of provisional issue repair)		
	State 2: AC, AK, FB, FC, FD, GA, HA, HB (double letter), JB, KA, MA, QA, QB, QC (constant variety), RA, RC, RD, SA, SB, SC, SD, TB, TD, TK	—	£250
	State 3: EA, EB (double letter), EC, TA	—	£300
	State 4: CC	—	£375

Printings in Red Only, Fourth Repair (late 1841)

This repair is characterised by a marked strengthening of the SE large ray of the NE star and of both stars where thinned through wear or earlier repair. Some weakening of check letters is apparent and many units show marginal burrs.

No. AS39 with same letterings in the earlier state in red-brown may also have a scarcity value according to the time between repairs and the number of examples now surviving.

AS39	State 2: AD, AH, BD, EE, FE, GB, GC, GE, GH, HC, IA, IB, IC, LA, LB, MB, NB, NC, OC, RB, RG, SH, TC, TE, TF, TG	—	£175
AS38	State 3: AB, AC, BA (retouched letter), BC, FA	—	£210
AS37	State 4: BB, CD, DA, DB (double letter), DC, EA, EB (double letter), ED	—	£210
AS36	State 4: EC	—	£325

Re-entry, Plate 5

Third State Re-entry, Plate 5

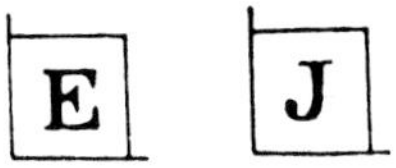

E J
Distinctive Letters, Plate 5

BA *Normal* *NA* *Normal*
Re-engraved *Re-engraved*
Recut Letters, Plate 5

EB HB HE KE PH PJ
Double Letters, Plate 5

BG QC QF
Constant Varieties, Plate 5

One Penny Black, Plate 6

This plate was put to press on 15 June 1840 and registered on 17 June; its active life was some six months, and defacement was carried out on 9 January 1841. It was therefore not used for any of the printings in red. A few stamps in Plate 6 are spotted as in Plate 4, though the dots are fewer and less pronounced. Generally the base-lines are thinner than those of Plate 4 but thicker than those of Plate 3. Impressions showing weak lateral borders are more frequent than in Plate 4 and they resemble Plate 5 in this respect. Probably for the same reason repairs were carried out on this plate, but many of the units so dealt with are in the D and E vertical rows of the lower part of the plate. As some units of Plate 6 are really difficult to distinguish from the corresponding units of Plate 5 (for example, the stamps lettered RD), *red* prints of Plate 5 are a useful guide.

Plate 6, State 1

AS40		1d. intense black	£9500	£375
AS41		1d. black	£7000	£275
		Pair	£30000	£1000
		Block of four	£80000	£16000
		Used on cover	†	£500
	a.	Re-entries: OB, QJ. QK, SA	£7500	£325
	b.	Double letters: *B*G, F*K*, *L*B, *M*K. *P*F	£7250	£300
	c.	Constant varieties: EK, MG, *T*B	£7250	£300
	d.	Watermark inverted	£18000	£2750
	e.	*Bleuté* paper	—	£525

No imprimaturs of this plate have ever been recorded.

The two repairs of Plate 6. It seems likely that the same relief which was used for the earlier repairs of Plate 5 was also used for the repairs of Plate 6. There is the same tendency to thinning and occasional faintness of one or both of the upper corner stars, more pronounced after the second repair and strongly suggestive of the employment of a re-entering relief having *blank* upper corners, such as appears to have been used in the second repair of Plate 1, as well as in the earlier repairs of Plates 8 and 9 and in the repair of Plate 10.

Plate 6, State 2

AS42		State 2: FF, FG, KD, KE, KF, KG, LD, LE, LG, MD, ME, MK, NA, NB, NC, ND, NE, NL, OC, OD, OE, OG, OK, OL, PD, PE, PF, PG, PH, PL, QC, QD, QL, RD, RE, SE, TA, TB, TC, TD, TE	£7500	£450
	a.	Original re-entry: OB	—	£500

Plate 6, State 3

AS43		State 3: MD, ND, PD, PE, PG, QE (State 3 only)	—	£500

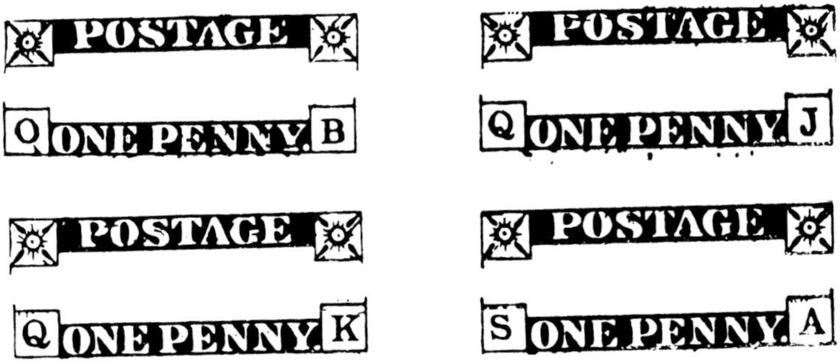

Re-entries, Plate 6

BG FK LB MK PF

Double Letters, Plate 6

EK MG QE State 3 only TB

Constant Varieties, Plate 6

THE WHITE FLAWS OF PLATES 7 TO 10

The "O" Flaw. The "O" flaw appears on most of the stamps of Plates 7, 8, 9 and 10. In its most complete form, as seen in the majority of impressions in the upper four rows of Plate 10, this flaw may be said to consist of three stages. The three components of the complete flaw, as described below and as illustrated in the accompanying illustrations, represent *successive stages* in its development.

Stage 1. A narrow white break in the base-line, passing downwards and to the left, from a point just to the right of centre of the base of "O" of "ONE".

This stage of the flaw occurs in a number of impressions of One Penny Plates 7 and 8. Thus in Plate 7 it is found in the majority of the stamps from GG to IL, and it may even be discerned in one or two of the first stamps of the "J" row. In Plate 8 it occurs more widely, and may be seen in nearly the whole of the impressions of the lower part of the sheet from OK to TL. This is a point of practical importance, since both black and red stamps from the lowest rows of Plate 8 can be "plated" from the presence of this little flaw alone. A further point of interest is the disappearance of the flaw after the repair of an impression.

Stage 1 *Stage 2* *Stage 3*

Stage 2. A white tail-like flaw, breaking the base-line, and generally separated on the left from Stage 1 by a narrow band of colour, whence it passes upwards and to the right towards the lower part of "N" of "ONE".

This is seen quite definitely in nearly all of the stamps lettered AA to GF of Plate 7, after which it vanishes, to reappear in a faint and indefinite form in a few stamps of the H horizontal row. In Plate 8, Stage 2 is well defined in nearly all of the impressions from AA to OJ, after which the tail-like portion disappears, leaving only the little gap of Stage 1 in the lower units of the sheet. Plate 9 shows the second stage of the flaw throughout, the only exceptions being the repaired impressions. Plate 10 shows Stage 2 in all of the stamps (except KB) of the lower four-fifths of the sheet, and also in the stamps DK and DL.

Stage 3. An extension of the base-line break of Stage 2, which passes beneath the left half of the foot of "N" of "ONE".

The final extension of the flaw is of diagnostic importance, as it only occurs in Plate 10, where its incidence is limited to the stamps of the four upper rows, AA to DJ excluding the flawless exceptions BE, BF, BH, BJ and BK and also AF in which the base-line under the flaw has been touched by hand, so obscuring the expansion.

The "Right Star" Flaw. Another characteristic flaw, which falls within the same category of white blemishes, is the weakness of the south-east large ray of the right star, so frequently seen in the stamps of Plates 8, 9 and 10. As in the case of the "O" flaw, its career ends with Plate 10, for it does not occur in Plate 11 or subsequent plates.

Early State *Late State*

This weakness, while often latent in the earlier printings, may be seen, even in the unrepaired states, as a small white streak within the large ray; it is more evident in the red printings than in the black

Between the earliest recognizable state and the most extreme state there is a gradual transition, the appearance and extent of the flaw being influenced by plate wear, and also through compression of the engraving by a re-entering operation. The flaw is most evident in those impressions which were repaired by re-entry in the year 1840, and at the beginning of 1841 (the provisional issue repair); in fact, in some of these repaired states, we find obliteration of the major part of the coloured "ray".

One Penny Black, Plate 7

Plate 7 was put to press on 26 June 1840. It was registered on 8 July, and the earliest date of use known, is 6 July 1840.

In Plate 7, nearly all the stamps from AA to GF show Stage 2 of the "O" flaw; as also, though faintly, do a few stamps of the H horizontal row. Most of the other stamps in the G and H horizontal rows show Stage 1 of the flaw; so do stamps of the I row and the first two stamps of the J row.

Some of the stamps from the lower part of the sheet are rather difficult to distinguish from those of the preceding plate, but generally in Plate 7 the sidelines are firmer and the baselines are thicker.

In most of the stamps of the twelfth horizontal row the letter L is distinctive, as its lower left serif is almost entirely absent. The E is narrower than in earlier plates. The double letters are rather poor examples and generally ill-defined.

An experimental printing, using this plate, was made in 1840 on lighter thinner paper. The remaining supply of this paper may have been used up on printings from Plates 1b, 8, 9 and 10. Examples from other plates may also be found on thin paper due to normal variations in paper thickness.

Greyish impressions from a worn state of the plate are often found, but there is no evidence on this plate of repairs, such as were carried out in Plates 5 and 6. This plate was not printed from in red, and was destroyed on 9 January 1841.

AS44	1d. black	£7250	£300
AS45	1d. greyish black	£7500	£375
	Pair	£35000	£1900
	Block of four	£85000	£18000
	Used on cover	†	£600
	a. Re-entries: KK, QI	£7500	£400
	b. Double letters: *C*A, *D*A, *F*A, *N*B, *N*F, P*E*	£7500	£350
	c. Experimental thin paper	£7750	£400
	d. Constant varieties: *B*A, C*F*, M*D*	£7250	£350
	e. Watermark inverted	—	£2750
	f. *Bleuté* paper	—	£500
	g. Guide line through value	£7250	£325

No imprimaturs of this plate have been recorded.

Re-entries, Plate 7

E LB

Distinctive Letters, Plate 7

BA CF MD

Constant Varieties, Plate 7

One Penny Black, Plate 8

Plate 8 was put to press on 3 July 1840 and registered on 31 July. Its earliest known use is 5 September.

The "O" flaw occurs on the great majority of impressions from Plate 8. Most of the stamps from AA to OJ show Stage 2 of the flaw and Stage 1 occurs in nearly the whole of the remaining stamps from OK to TL. As many units on the plate were subsequently repaired, certain of the later printed stamps appear in a second state not showing the flaw. Plate 8 was evidently one of the plates used for the provisional black printing carried out in the period 22 January to 3 February 1841. The proof of this rests on the finding of black prints showing repairs which were executed subsequently to the commencing of printing in red. There are certain letterings of which both black and red printings exist in the original and the repaired states, for example the ten letterings, DK, PG, RF, RG, SE to SG, TE, TG and TH. In all these instances the repair must have been executed after printings in red had commenced, and before the provisional printing in black took place, and therefore sometime during the first three weeks of January 1841. As in other Die I plates, repair was by re-entry. Incidentally, owing to the employment for this repair work of a roller lacking the "O" flaw, the flaw suffered obliteration in practically all repaired units. That this particular re-entering roller impression had blank upper corners, may be inferred from the tendency to compression of the engraving in the star corners, resulting in the extension and increased prominence of the white right star flaw.

The above "provisional issue repair" was the second such plate operation. An earlier plate repair of the units GE and HE was evidently carried out in 1840, during the period Plate 8 was being used for regular 1d. black printings and before it was used for printing in red, for red stamps of these two letterings showing the "O" flaw of State 1 have never been seen.

A third plate repair was evidently carried out later in 1841 after *all* printing in black had ceased, giving rise to a large number of Plate 8 letterings in red, in which no corresponding repaired states in black have been noted. This last re-entering operation had, as in the earlier repairs, the effect of obliterating the "O" flaw in almost every case, so pointing to the employment of a relief impression not having the flaw. On the other hand, there was no thinning of the engraving of the star corners on this occasion, but rather a definite strengthening, so that the little white right star flaw seen in the earliest states of the red prints was completely eliminated. It is to be inferred that this relief had normal upper corners while also lacking the "O" flaw. The faulty re-entries of the top row AE to AL resulted from this late repair, as no corresponding repaired states in black have been noted.

The thin paper variety may be from the balance of the experimental thin paper used with Plate 7.

This plate was destroyed on 8 September 1841.

Plate 8, 1st State, in Black

AS46	1d. black	£9000	£350
	Pair	£42000	£2100
	Block of four	—	£22000
	Used on cover	†	£675
	a. Re-entries: DL, RL, TA, TJ	£9250	£450
	b. Double letters: H*A*, *M*I	£9250	£425
	c. Constant varieties: BL, HL, TL *from*	£9250	£425
	d. Watermark inverted	£20000	£3000

	e. Thin paper	—	£500
	f. *Bleuté* paper	—	£600

Imprimatur: £22000. Stamps removed from the imprimatur sheet are AL, SB, SD to SL, TA to TL.

Plate 8, 1st State, in Red

AS47	1d. red-brown (shades)	£2250	£150
	Pair	—	£325
	Block of four		
	Used on cover	†	£225
	a. Re-entries: DL, RL, TA, TJ	—	£200
	b. Double letters: H*A*, *M*I	—	£175
	c. Constant varieties: BL, HL, TL	—	£175
	d. Watermark inverted		

Plate 8, 2nd State (1840 repair) in Black and in Red

AS48	1d. black: GE, HE (no "O" flaw)	—	£600
AS49	1d. red-brown: Ditto	—	£300

Plate 8, 1st State, Pre-provisional Printings in Red

AS52	1d. red-brown. State 1 of the same letterings as below (AS50)	—	£600

Plate 8, State 2 (Provisional Printing in Black and Post-provisional in Red)

These printings were made during the period 22 January to 3 Febuary 1841 and were preceded by a plate re-entering (provisional issue repair) on some of the impressions, namely DK, PG, RF, RG, SE, SF, SG, TE, TG, TH. These black prints are all in State 2, and are distinguished by having no "O" flaw, and by having an early state (State 1) in red.

AS50	1d. black, State 2, provisional black printings of the above letterings	—	£950
AS51	1d. red-brown, State 2, printings of the above letterings	—	£275

Plate 8, Late Repair of 1841, Printed in Red Only

AS53	1d. red-brown. Non-coincident re-entries AE to AL State 2	—	£225
AS54	1d. red-brown. Coincident re-entries State 2: AD, BH, BI, BJ, BK, BL, CJ, CK, CL, DI, DJ, EG, EH, EI, EJ, EK, EL, FG, FH, FI, FL, GL, HK, HL, II, IJ, IK, IL, NE, NF, NG, NH, NI, NJ, OD, OE, OF, OG, OH, OI, OL, PA, PD, PE, PF, PH, PI, PJ, PK, PL, QE, QF, QG, QH, QI, QJ, QK, QL, RD, RE, RH, RI, RJ, RK, SD, SH, SI, SJ, TB, TC, TD, TF, TI	—	£210
	a. Original re-entries: DL, RL, TJ	—	£250
AS55	1d. red-brown. Coincident re-entries State 3: DK, PG, RF, RG, SE, SF, SG, TE, TG, TH	—	£210

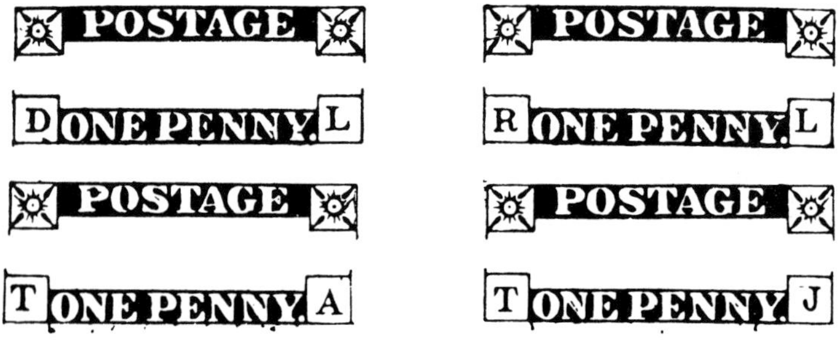

Re-entries, Plate 8

Distinctive Letter, Plate 8

HA

MI

Double Letters, Plate 8

BL

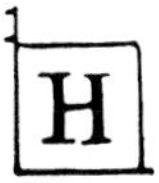

HL

TL

Constant Varieties, Plate 8

One Penny Black, Plate 9

Plate 9 was registered on 9 November 1840 and its earliest known use is 18 November.

In the original unrepaired state of the plate every stamp from Plate 9 showed Stage 2 of the "O" flaw.

An early repair to the four stamps AE, AG, AH and AI must have been made before the close of the year 1840 as no *red* printings of any of these letterings showing the flaw have ever been discovered. There was formerly in existence the upper half of a sheet of ld. Plate 9 printed in red, and in this half sheet, all of the impressions except six had the "O" flaw (Stage 2). These six exceptions bore evidence of having been re-entered. The curious point about the six is that only two, namely AD and AF have been found to exist in red with the "O" flaw. It is to be inferred, therefore, that the four stamps AE, AG, AH and AI were repaired before red printing began, and that AD and AF were re-entered just after the commencement of red printing, and just before the re-entering of the six remaining stamps of the "A" row, namely AA, AB, AC, AJ, AK and AL, all of which appear in the repaired state in the provisional black printing.

Plate 9 was in use long after the red printings from other black plates had finished. It is by no means unusual to find red stamps from this plate bearing the 1843 (number in cross) cancellation, and these stamps have the colour and appearance of printings from the plates of this period. That late plate repairs were carried out is proved by the existence of red printings in repaired states which are not known in black prints with corresponding letterings.

Vertical guidelines are to be found in the right upper corner of a large number of the stamps; also guide dots may be seen above the right upper corners on most of the A row stamps and inside the lower right corner on BL, IL, JL, KL, LL, TA and TE; and outside the lower right corner on SL and TC. Distinct horizontal guide-lines run through the value on all stamps of the 'K' horizontal row. The check letters are, on the whole, very similar in shape to those of the preceding plate: the letter J, however, is slightly square-footed, though decidedly less so than on the following two plates.

Plate 9 was destroyed on 7 October 1843.

Plate 9, in Black

AS56	1d. black	£9500	£420
	Pair	£42000	£2100
	Block of four		
	Used on cover	†	£800
	a. Re-entries: EH, NK	£10000	£475
	b. Basal shifts: FA to FG, FI, FL	£9750	£450
	c. Double letters: *B*E, *B*L, *C*K, *D*C, E*B*, *H*B, *JL*, L*B*, *LL*, *M*A, *O*A, O*B*, *T*B	£10000	£475
	d. Constant varieties: *E*A, JA	£10000	£475
	e. Watermark inverted	£20000	£3250
	f. Thin paper	—	£575

No imprimaturs of this plate have been recorded.

Plate 9, Printings in Black and Red

Plate 9, Printed in Red (1st repair)
Unrepaired stamps

AS57	1d. red-brown (shades)	£2250	£150
	Pair	—	£325
	Block of four	£12500	—
	Used on cover	†	£225
	a. Re-entries: EH, NK	—	£175
	b. Basal shifts: FA to FG, FI, FL	—	£160
	c. Double letters: *B*E, *B*L, *C*K, *D*C, E*B*, *H*B, J*L*, L*B*, *LL*, *M*A, *O*A, O*B*, *T*B	—	£170
	d. Constant varieties: *E*A, JA	—	£170

Stamps from the 1st repair (for printings in *black*, see No. AS58 overleaf)

AS59	1d. red-brown AE, AG, AH, AI State 2 (without "O" flaw)	—	£300

The first repair. As the four Plate 9 red stamps, AE, AG, AH and AI, have never been seen with the "O" flaw, these units must have been repaired before red printing started. But since second state black prints of the above do not appear to be appreciably more abundant than second state black prints of the remaining "A" row units, it might be inferred that this first plate repair was carried out towards or even after the cessation of the regular black printing in 1840.

Stamps subsequently repaired (see Nos. AS60/1, below)
State 1 (with "O" flaw (Stage 2))

AS62	1d. red-brown AA, AB, AC, AD, AF, AJ, AK, AL	—	£500
AS63	1d. red-brown BB, EC, ED, FC, FD, FE	—	£475

Plate 9, Printed in Black (1st and 2nd repairs)

AS58	1d. black AE, AG, AH, AI State 2 (without "O" flaw)	—	£850

The second or Provisional issue repair. The repair of January 1841 included the eight remaining units of the "A" row not previously repaired, namely AA, AB, AC, AD, AF, AJ, AK, and AL. Other units included were BB, EC, ED, FC, FD, and FE. The results of this repair closely resemble those of the earlier operation. Roller compression effects are seen in the right star and in the south-east coloured diagonal of the right star: the "O" flaw is obliterated.

AS60	1d. black. State 2 provisional black prints of the above letterings	—	£850

Plate 9, Printed in Red (2nd repair)

AS61	1d. red-brown. State 2 printings of the above letterings	—	£225

As in the case of other plates used for the provisional issue, *earlier* states in red of letterings repaired in January 1841 are scarce.

Subsequent Printings in Red

Late Repair of 1841, Printed in Red Only. The eight "A" row stamps, AC, AD, AE, AF, AG, AH, AI and AJ, and also EC must have been submitted to a further repair operation after *all* printings in black had finished, for in addition to restoration of Queen's head and background, this late operation had the effect of restoring to normal the right cross, in which faintness of the star and of the south-east diagonal had followed the first re-entering. In these third states, the above cross diagonal is actually stronger than in the original state: the "O" flaw remains obliterated.

Plate 9, Known in Red Only

AS64	1d. red-brown State 3 of AC to AJ and also EC	—	£250

Plate 9, Known in Red Only. There is a further group of Plate 9 red printings in which no corresponding black prints have been seen. These are all in State 2 and include the following letterings: BC, BD, FA, FB, FF, GA, GB, GC, GD, and GE: all are without the "O" flaw, and the first four are without the "right cross" flaw.

AS65	1d. red-brown State 2 of BC, BD, FA, FB, FF, GA to GE	—	£225

Re-entries, Plate 9

BL CK DC EB HB LB LL

Double Letters, Plate 9

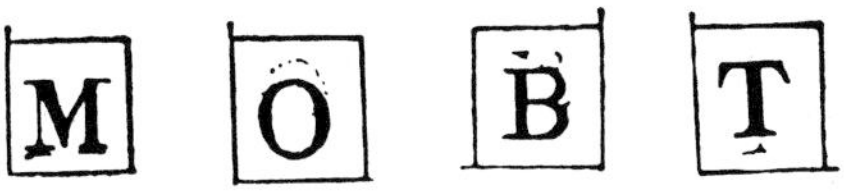

MA OA OB TB

Double Letters, Plate 9

EA JA

Constant Varieties, Plate 9

One Penny Black, Plate 10

Plate 10 was registered and put to press on 8 December 1840. Its earliest known date of use is 2 January 1841.

Stamps from Plate 10 are comparatively easy to identify, owing to the distinctive character of several check letters. The short stumpy H of Plate 10 is found on no other Penny Black plate; and the same may be said of the long-tailed R which occurs throughout the eighteenth horizontal row, and which is really a letter P with a hand-cut tail. Again the letter Q with its less curved tail is peculiar to this plate. Furthermore, there are a number of check letters of distinctive shape found only on Plates 10 and 11: the longer I, the square-footed J, the short-footed L, the short, broad M with distinct serifs, the tall, narrow N, the P with characteristic loop (cf. Plate 11), and the short stumpy T.

In its early state Plate 10 shows the "O" flaw on all stamps except BE, BF, BH, BJ, BK and KB. In the upper four rows of the sheet from AA to DJ, the flaw is in Stage 3; these stamps can at once be identified, as no other plate shows the "O" flaw in the third stage.

Probably owing to wear in its upper part, this plate had certain impressions in the B, C and D rows repaired later on: in these repaired impressions the flaw practically disappears.

Red printings of 22 impressions of this plate have been found to exist in two states, the original state with the "O" flaw, and the repaired state without the flaw. These are the stamps lettered BA to BD, BG, BI, BL, CA to CL, DH, DK and DL. As most of these letterings exist also in two states in black, it is evident that the repairs were carried out after printings in red had begun, and before the final (provisional) printings in black had been made.

It is known that the repairs were carried out in two stages as single examples of CB and CG exist with enough of the base of BB and BG above to show that in both cases the upper stamps are with the "O" flaw and are therefore still in State 1.

Plate 10 was withdrawn from use fairly early in 1841, probably owing to a complaint from Rowland Hill about " badly printed" stamps (worn plate?). It was destroyed on 21 February 1843.

Of the black printings Plate 10 is considered to be the most difficult to obtain in blocks.

Printings in Black

State 1

AS66	1d. black	£12500	£600
AS67	1d. grey-black	£13500	£625
	Pair	£45000	£2750
	Block of four		
	Used on cover	†	£1600
	a. Without "O" flaw (original state): BE, BF, BH, BJ, BK, KB	£13000	£625
	b. Re-entries: PG, PK, SI, TA	£13500	£650
	c. Check letter P converted into R by hand engraving: RA to RH and RJ	£13500	£650
	d. Basal shifts + long-tailed R: RK, RL	£13500	£675
	e. Re-entry + long-tailed R: R1	£13750	£700
	f. Double letters, G*J*, *H*A, K*L*, P*A* *from*	£13000	£625
	g. Constant varieties: JK, *M*A, *M*D and "J" flaw on E*J*, *J*F, N*J*, O*J*, P*J*, S*J*, T*J*	—	£650
	h. Cancelled with *red* Maltese Cross	†	£1000
	i. Thin paper	—	£750

No imprimaturs of this plate have ever been recorded.

State 2, Provisional Printing

AS68	1d. black: BA to BD, BG, BL, CA to CH, CK, DH, DK, DL	—	£950

Printings in Red

State 1

AS69	1d. red-brown (shades)	£1500	£150
	Pair	—	£300
	Block of four	£6000	—
	Used on cover	†	£225
	a. Without "O" flaw (original state): BE, BF, BH, BJ, BK, KB	—	£180
	b. Re-entries: PG, PK, SI, TA	—	£200
	c. Check letter P converted into R by hand engraving: RA to RH and RJ	—	£200
	d. Basal shifts + long-tailed R: RK, RL	—	£200
	e. Re-entry + long-tailed R: RI	—	£225
	f. Double letters: G*J*, *H*A, K*L*, P*A*	—	£180
	g. Constant varieties: JK, *M*A, *M*D and "J" flaw on E*J*, *J*F, N*J*, O*J*, P*J*, S*J*, T*J*	—	£180
	h. Watermark inverted		

The used example of No. A69*h* is ED.

State 1, Pre-provisional Red Prints

AS70	1d. red-brown: BA to BD, BG, BI, BL, CA to CL, DH, DK, DL	—	£325

State 2

AS71	1d. red-brown: BA to BD, BG, BI, BL, CA to CL, DH, DK, DL	—	£200

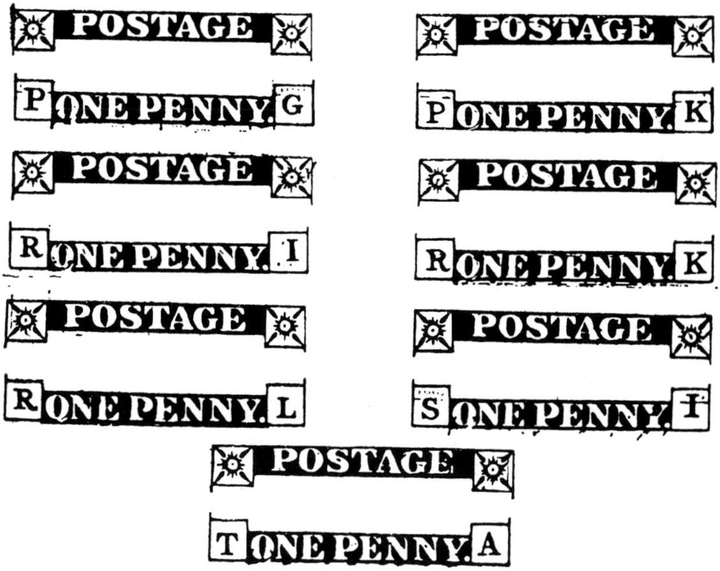

Re-entries and Basal Shifts, Plate 10. *Showing also Long-tailed Rs on* RI, RK, RL

Distinctive Letters, Plate 10

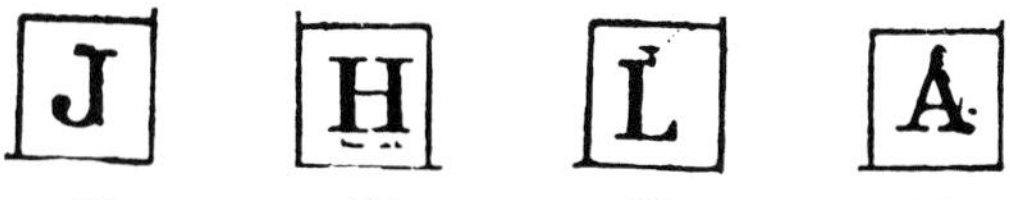

GJ HA KL PA

Double Letters, Plate 10

JK MA MD

Constant Varieties, Plate 10

The "J" flaw is illustrated and described under Varieties of the Line-Engraved Stamps in the Line-Engraved General Notes.

One Penny Black, Plate 11

The black printing usually displays a grey tone unlike examples from a worn plate, indeed black impressions are scarce. Another feature is that it is usual to find the Maltese Cross in black, the red cancellation is exceptional.

This plate, finished on 19 January 1841, was registered in *red* on the 27th of the same month. It was printed from in red on 29 and 30 January. On 1 and 2 February, 700 sheets were printed from it in *black*, and on 3 February and for some weeks on, it continued to be used for printing sheets of stamps in red. As the total black printing of 700 sheets was carried out in two consecutive days, there could hardly have been time for plate repairs during this period: thus repaired states of Plate 11 impressions have been found in the red printings only.

There is a roller flaw which occurs on practically the whole of the eight upper rows of Plate 11 (excepting GE and GF), and that is a small gap at the left end of the upper line of the right corner square. This same corner square shows a constant roller flaw in all stamps of the S row (SA to SL). Minor variations of assistance to platers: TA and TH, thick bottom lines; TC, marks (re-entry) in the NE square.

The broad check letter "E" of Plate 11 is unlike that of any other Penny Black plate, and of the remaining check letters "I", "J", "L", "M", "N", "P" and "T" are like those of Plate 10, but Plate 11 stamps do not have the "O" flaw which occurs on Plate 10.

A further peculiarity often seen on Plate 11 stamps is a weakness of the right side-line.

The first repair gave rise to second states of the red stamps AF, AG and AH, each of which is distinguished by the presence of "faint re-entry marks" in the north-east corner; apparently the re-entering was incomplete and did not include the upper star corners, the upper frame-line break flaw therefore not being affected by the operation. Another feature which distinguishes the first repair of these three letterings is the remarkable firmness of the right border of each stamp after repair.

The second repair of the stamps AF, AG and AH was accompanied by the disappearance of the "faint re-entry marks" from their north-east corners, as well as by a certain amount of thinning of the check letters "A". The third state of AH shows the presence of a very distinct linear burr in the left margin.

The remaining repaired units, which seem to have been re-entered but once, should perhaps be included under the heading of "late repair", as none shows the features which characterize the first repair. In all these repaired stamps, fresh burr marks appear in one or both margins, and in AE and FA, the re-entering has caused faintness of the second check letter.

Plate 11 was destroyed on 15 January 1842.

Printings in Black

AS72	1d. greyish black	£11500	£3800
AS73	1d. black	£14000	£4000
	Pair	£40000	£12000
	Block of four	£95000	—
	Used on cover	†	£8500
	a. Re-entries: BC, OA, TC, TD, TK	—	£4250
	b. Double letters: B*B*, *D*D, *J*E, K*A*, N*H*, *P*H, R*D*	—	£4000
	c. Roller flaw: north-east corner (SA to SL)	—	£4000
	d. Constant varieties: *A*H, HB, NA, NB, NH, OF, *R*L	£12000	£4000
	e. Cancelled with *red* Maltese Cross	†	£17500
	f. Watermark inverted	—	£15000
	h. Cancelled with *blue* Maltese Cross	†	£20000
	i. Cancelled with black and red Maltese Cross	†	£17500

No imprimaturs of this plate have ever been recorded

Printings in Red

AS74	1d. red-brown (shades)	£1500	£100
	Pair	—	£225
	Block of four		
	Used on cover	†	£225
	a. Re-entries: BC, OA, TC, TD, TK	—	£150
	b. Double letters: B*B*, *D*D, *J*E, K*A*, N*H*, *P*H, R*D*	—	£125
	c. Roller flaw northeast corner (SA to SL)	—	£125
	d. Constant varieties: *A*H, HB, NA, NB, NH, OF, *R*L	—	£125

AS75	1d. red-brown. Repaired impressions. State 2: AE, AF, AG, AH, AI, AJ, DC, EF, FA, FB, FF, GA, TA . . . . *from*	—	£225
	a. Original re-entry: TK	—	£275
	State 3: AF, AG, AH . . . . *from*	—	£225

For trial printing in red-brown on Dickinson "silk" thread paper see DP22 under Line-Engraved Essays, Proofs, etc.

7 O'clock Ray Flaw and top line break, Plate 11

Distinctive Letters, Plate 11

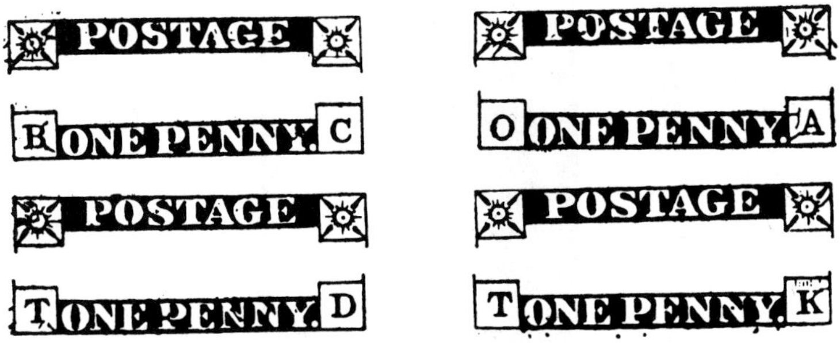

Re-entries, Plate 11

BB DD JE KA NH PH RD

Double Letters, Plate 11

AH HB, NA, NB, NH, OF RL

Constant Varieties, Plate 11

SECTION AV

The "VR" Official Stamp

This stamp, s.g. V1, was prepared for use in April 1840 but was not issued. The upper corners bore the letters V and R instead of "stars". The watermark was Small Crown and it was imperforate.

The plate bore the letter A in all four corners instead of the usual plate number. It was registered twice, on 15 April and 9 May 1840.

VR1

Imprimatur pair showing part of the margin inscription and the letter A

After 3,323 good sheets had been delivered, the idea of special stamps for government offices was abandoned and 3,302 sheets were destroyed on 25 January 1843.

Of the surviving 21 sheets, 13 were used for distribution with the Postmasters' Notice. A few specimens passed through the post. Rowland Hill used examples from a sheet sent to him in April 1840 for experiments with trial obliterators including the Maltese Cross and concentric circles cancellations, using various black inks, after which attempts were made to remove the cancellations by means of chemical agents.

VR1 (=S.G. V1)	1d. black	£18000	£25000
	Obliterated with trial concentric circles	†	£22000
	With trial Maltese Cross cancellation	†	£25000
	Pair	£50000	—
	Block of four	£125000	—
	Used on cover	†	—
	a. Re-entry: SH	£22000	
	b. Double letters: *F*A, *H*E; *PD* (both letters), *R*F ..... *from*	£22000	

Imprimatur: First registration sheet (*before hardening*): £24000. Stamps removed from the imprimatur sheet are AL to NL, OK, OL, PK, PL, QK, QL, RI to RL, SI to SL, TA, T1 to TL. *Second registration sheet* (*after hardening?*): £24000. Stamps removed from the imprimatur sheet are AL, QJ, QK, QL, RJ, RK, RL, SE to SL, TA, TI to TL.

Index to Catalogued Varieties in Section A

"Colourless" roller flaws such as the various Ray flaws and the "O" flaw are not included in this index. Similarly, as a general rule, characteristic letters such as the square Js of Plates 10 and 11 are not indexed but an exception has been made of the Rs of Plate 10 which are really Ps with added tails.

Printings in red from the black plates are included as well as repaired states, whether in black or in red. Although a separate index to Plate 1b appears after the listing of AS4/5, Plate lb varieties are included below also.

AA 1c, 5, 9
AB 1c, 5, 9
AC 5, 9
AD 1c, 2, 5, 8, 9
AE 1a, 1b, 8, 9, 11
AF 8, 9, 11
AG 8, 9, 11
AH 1c, 4, 5, 8, 9, 11
AI 1c, 8, 9, 11
AJ 1b, 1c, 8, 9, 11
AK 1c, 5, 8, 9
AL 1b, 1c, 8, 9

BA 5, 7, 10
BB 5, 9, 10, 11
BC 5, 9, 10, 11
BD 2, 5, 9, 10
BE 9
BG 5, 6, 10
BH 1b, 8
BI 8, 10
BJ 1b, 8
BK 8
BL 1b, 1c, 8, 10

CA 5, 7, 10
CB 5, 10
CC 5, 10
CD 1a, 1b, 5, 10
CE 5, 10
CF 1b, 1c, 7, 10
CG 1c, 10
CH 10
CI 10
CJ 8, 10
CK 8, 9, 10
CL 1a, 1b, 1c, 8, 10

DA 1a, 4, 5, 7
DB 1b, 4, 5
DC 1b, 5, 9, 11
DD 1b, 4, 5, 11
DE 1b, 5
DF 1b, 4
DG 1a, 1b, 2
DH 1b, 10
DI 8
DJ 8
DK 8,10
DL 8,10

EA 1a, 2, 5, 9
EB 5, 9
EC 5, 9
ED 5, 9
EE 5
EF 11
EG 8
EH 8, 9
EI 8
EJ 1b, 8, 10
EK 1b, 6, 8
EL 8

FA 1a, 1b, 5, 7, 9, 11
FB 5, 9, 11
FC 5, 9
FD 1b, 3, 5, 9
FE 5, 9
FF 6, 9, 11
FG 2, 6, 8, 9
FH 1b, 8
FI 1a, 1b, 8, 9
FK 6
FL 8, 9

GA 1a, 1b, 5, 9, 11
GB 1b, 5, 9
GC 1b, 2, 5, 9
GD 9
GE 5, 8, 9
GF 1b
GH 5
GI 1a, 1b
GJ 10
GK 1b
GL 1b, 8

HA 2, 3, 5, 8, 10
HB 1a, 1b, 5, 9, 11
HC 1b, 5
HD 1a, 1b
HE 5, 8
HI 5
HK 1b, 8
HL 1b, 2, 8

IA 5
IB 1b, 1c, 5
IC 1c, 5
ID 1b, 1c
IE 1b, 4
IG 1b
IH 1b
II 1b, 8
IJ 1b, 8
IK 8
IL 1b, 2, 8

JA 1a, 1c, 2, 5, 9
JB 1b, 1c, 5
JC 1b, 1c
JD 1c
JE 1c, 11
JF 1c, 2, 10
JG 1c
JI 1b, 1c
JJ 1b
JK 1b, 10
JL 1b, 9

KA 5, 11
KC 1c, 3
KD 1b, 6
KE 1b, 2, 5, 6
KF 1b, 3, 6
KG 1b, 6
KH 1b
KJ 2
KK 2, 7
KL 1b, 10

LA 1b, 1c, 5
LB 1b, 1c, 5, 6, 9
LC 1c
LD 6
LE 2, 6
LG 6
LL 1b, 5, 9

MA 5, 9, 10
MB 5
MC 1b
MD 1b, 1c, 6, 7, 10
ME 1b, 2, 6
MF 1a, 1b
MG 1b, 6
MH 1b
MI 1b, 8
MK 1a, 1b, 6

NA 1b, 5, 6, 11
NB 5, 6, 7, 11
NC 1b, 2, 5, 6
ND 1b, 1c, 5, 6

A 1840 1d. Black Variety Index

NE 1b, 6, 8
NF 1b, 7, 8
NG 1b, 8
NH 1b, 8, 11
NI 1b, 8
NJ 1b, 8, 10
NK 9
NL 6

OA 1a, 1b, 1c, 5, 9, 11
OB 1b, 5, 6, 9
OC 5, 6
OD 1b, 6, 8
OE 6, 8
OF 1b, 8, 11
OG 6, 8
OH 8
OI 1b, 8
OJ 10
OK 6
OL 6, 8

PA 1b, 1c, 2, 3, 4, 5, 8, 10
PB 1a, 1b, 2, 3, 5
PC 1b, 3
PD 1b, 2, 3, 6, 8
PE 3, 6, 7, 8
PF 1b, 3, 6, 8
PG 1b, 2, 3, 6, 8, 10
PH 3, 5, 6, 8, 11
PI 2, 3, 8
PJ 1b, 3, 5, 8, 10
PK 1b, 3, 8, 10
PL 1a, 1c, 2, 3, 6, 8

QA 1a, 1b, 4, 5
QB 5
QC 1c, 5, 6
QD 1b, 1c, 6
QE 6, 8
QF 5, 8
QG 1b, 8
QH 8
QI 7, 8
QJ 6, 8
QK 6, 8
QL 1b, 1c, 1d, 1e, 2, 6, 8

RA 1c, 5, 10
RB 1b, 1c, 5, 10
RC 5, 10
RD 1b, 5, 6, 8, 10, 11
RE 1b, 6, 8, 10
RF 1b, 2, 8, 10
RG 1c, 4, 5, 8, 10
RH 8, 10
RI 1a, 1b, 8, 10
RJ 8, 10
RK 1c, 8, 10
RL 1a, 1c, 1d, 1e, 8, 10, 11

SA 1c, 2, 5, 6, 11
SB 1c, 2, 5, 11
SC 1c, 2, 4, 5, 11
SD 1c, 2, 4, 5, 8, 11
SE 1c, 2, 6, 8, 11
SF 2, 8, 11
SG 1c, 2, 8, 11
SH 2, 5, 8, 11
SI 1b, 2, 8, 10, 11
SJ 2, 8, 10, 11
SK 2, 11
SL 1a, 1c, 2, 11

TA 1c, 2, 5, 6, 8, 10, 11
TB 1c, 1d, 2, 5, 6, 8, 9
TC 1b, 1c, 2, 5, 6, 8, 11
TD 1c, 5, 6, 8, 11
TE 1c, 2, 3, 5, 6, 8
TF 1c, 2, 5, 8
TG 1c, 1d, 2, 5, 8
TH 1c, 1d, 2, 5, 8
TI 1c, 2, 8
TJ 1c, 1d, 2, 8, 10
TK 1a, 1b, 1c, 1d, 1e, 2, 3, 5, 11
TL 1a, 1c, 2, 8

SECTION BA

One Penny Red, Type A1, Imperforate Die I, Alphabet I (Plates 12 to 131)

1841 (February). Original Issue in Red-brown shades on blued paper. Die I. Alphabet I. Wmk Small Crown. Imperf.

B1 (=S.G. 8/12)	(1)	1d. red-brown	£425	25·00
	(2)	1d. red-brown on very blue paper	£475	25·00
	(3)	1d. pale red-brown (worn plates)	£550	35·00
	(4)	1d. deep red-brown	£650	40·00
	(5)	1d. lake-red	£3800	£675
	(6)	1d. orange-brown	£1300	£175
		Block of four (with black Maltese Cross canc.)	£2200	£650
		Block of four (with 1844-type cancellation)	£2200	£250
		Used on cover (with 1844-type cancellation)	†	30·00
	c.	Watermark inverted	£2500	£300
	d.	Major re-entry	—	75·00
	e.	Minor re-entry	—	45·00
	ea.	Basal shift	—	20·00
	f.	Double corner letter	—	30·00
	g.	Guide line in corner	—	20·00
	h.	Guide line through value	—	25·00
	i.	Open top, upper right corner	—	20·00
	j.	Thick outer frame to stamp	—	25·00
	k.	Ivory head	£450	25·00
	l.	On thicker, lavender-tinted paper (Plates 118 to 131) *from*	£1000	£225
	s.	"Specimen", Type 1 (Plates 90 and 95)	£3000	

The prices listed above for varieties vary upwards according to the plate or the prominence of the variety.

Imprimaturs (*from Plates* 12–21, 24–77, 77b, 78–131): *from* £650.

Coloured Maltese Cross Cancellations

		Stamp off cover	*Stamp on cover*
sa.	Black	45·00	£140
sb.	Red	£3500	£20000
sc.	Blue	£500	£1200
sd.	Green	£5000	£15000
se.	Violet	£6000	£20000

Distinctive Maltese Cross Cancellations (in Black)

ta.	Belfast	£200	£500
tb.	Brighton	£300	£750
tc.	Channel Is.	£5000	£40000
td.	Cork	£300	£900
te.	Coventry	£500	£1600
tf.	Dublin I or II	£110	£250
tfa.	Dursley	£750	£2000
tg.	Eyrecourt	£750	£2000
th.	Greenock	£200	£400
tha.	Hollymount	£1500	£8000
ti.	Kelso	£400	£1500
tj.	Kilmarnock	£1200	£3500
tk.	Leamington	£200	£600
tl.	Leeds	£400	£1500
tm.	Limerick	£400	£1500
tn.	London I	60·00	£150

to.	London II	80·00	£200
tp.	Manchester	£250	£600
tq.	Montrose	£250	£900
tr.	Mullingar	£2500	£8500
ts.	Norwich	£250	£800
tt.	Perth	£180	£600
tta.	Settle	£1500	£8500
tu.	Stirling	£125	£450
tua.	Welshpool	£600	£3500
tv.	Whitehaven	£1200	£5000
tw.	Wotton-under-Edge	£3250	£8500
tx.	York	£400	£1600
ty.	Scottish I or II	90·00	£180
tz.	Stonehaven Cross	£2000	£7500

"Numbers in Maltese Cross" Cancellations

		Stamp off cover	*Stamp on cover*
ua.	No. 1 in Cross	£135	£400
ub.	No. 2 in Cross	£135	£400
uc.	No. 3 in Cross	£160	£425
ud.	No. 4 in Cross	£400	£1500
ue.	No. 5 in Cross	£135	£400
uf.	No. 6 in Cross	£110	£325
ug.	No. 7 in Cross	£110	£325
uh.	No. 8 in Cross	£110	£325
ui.	No. 9 in Cross	£135	£400
uj.	No. 10 in Cross	£225	£750
uk.	No. 11 in Cross	£225	£850
ul.	No. 12 in Cross	£225	£850

For illustrations of these cancellations see after Line-Engraved General Notes.

Town Cancellations (on Stamps)

		Large portion of p/m on stamp	*Complete p/m on stamp and piece*	*On stamp on cover*
va.	Black	£550	£800	£2200
vb.	Blue	£1300	£1800	£3500
vc.	Green	£2400	£3000	£7500
vd.	Red	£6500	£9000	—
ve.	Yellow	—	—	—

"Penny Post" Postmarks (on Stamps), in Black

wa.	Combined with Maltese Cross	£250	£450	£1300
wb.	Without Maltese Cross	£550	£1300	£4250
wc.	Framed type "PyP No. 15" (Handsworth), in black, blue, or green	£450	£600	£3000

1844-Type Cancellations (on Stamps)

		Large portion of p/m on stamp	*Complete p/m on stamp and piece*	*On stamp on cover*
xa.	Black	15·00	18·00	30·00
xb.	Blue	£175	£250	£500
xc.	Green	£1750	£3000	£5000
xd.	Red	£5000	£8000	£12000
xe.	Violet	£2500	£3500	£9000
xf.	Olive-yellow	£1800	—	£6500

Repaired Impressions—Prices for Original States

Although they are not separately listed, it must be understood that wherever impressions are repaired, creating second states, the prices for the letterings in original states may be higher than those for normal unrepaired letterings that exist in only one state. This applies throughout the Line-Engraved issues.

THE ONE PENNY RED EARLY PLATES

The ld. red plates from Plate 12 to Plate 36 are mostly not difficult to "plate" from single stamps for the following reasons: (1) used examples are generally cancelled with the Maltese Cross; (2) the shades of the printed stamps are largely distinctive; and (3) they mostly fall into separate groups by reason of frame-line flaws or ray flaws; for instance, in the Plates 12 to 16 group there is a single gap or break in the upper line of the north-east corner, and this gap is larger in each successive plate of the group. The stamps of the Plates 17 to 20 group do not show roller flaws (except for the complete N.E. break in the E horizontal row of Plate 20), but each plate has some distinctive character or characters; in Plate 17 early impressions often appear in a rich brown shade; in Plate 18, very many of the stamps show pronounced basal shifts; Plate 19 is characterized by numerous horizontal guidelines towards the base of the stamps. The group including Plates 21 to 27 shows the development of multiple north-east breaks eventually fusing in Plates 26 and 27 to form complete upper line gaps of the north-east corner. Commencing with Plate 26 and carrying on to Plate 36, ray flaws appear in each of the upper corners, the 10 o'clock ray being absent from the left star and the 1 o'clock ray being absent from the right star. (In Plate 26 the 10 o'clock ray flaw is absent from RG to TL.) These two ray flaws absent from Plates 37 to 44 reappear in Plate 45, but the Maltese Cross cancellation is not so commonly seen on used stamps from Plate 45, and in subsequent plates the 1844 cancellations take its place. From Plates 12 to 77 all Js are square-footed except on Plates 14, 16, 17, 29 to 31 and 33. From Plate 77 through to the end of the 1d. red "with stars" the Js are all rounded. The letters D and E are helpful: on Plates 12 and 15 are found the "Broad E and "Slim D; Plates 13, 14 and 16 to 33 have both these letters slim; Plates 34 to 44 show both these letters broad.

Square-footed J — *Round-footed* J — *Tall narrow* E *and* D — *Short broad* E *and* D

Squat S *(Plate 29)* — *Narrow* F — *Normal* F

Prices

Plated stamps are not priced unused; hence BS1–29 are priced in *used* condition only.

One Penny Die I, Plate 12

Plate 12 was registered on 25 February 1841 and destroyed 15 January 1842. It is the first of a series of five plates of the One Penny value, all of which show a roller flaw in the form of a gap in the upper line of the north-east corner. The flaw is entirely absent from the impressions first laid down, namely TL, TK, TJ, TI, TH, TG, TF, TE, TD, TC, TB, TA, SL, SK, SJ and SI, the flaw being invisible because latent; the deficiency in the corresponding relief line of the transfer roller was of insufficient depth to avoid the marking of a complete plate incision, that is, there remained enough metal in the relief line to mark the plate. As the transferring proceeded, the deficiency in the roller relief line increased in depth, and the first sign of the flaw is seen as a single minute break in the top line of the north-east corner of the stamp SH, and this is repeated on the five neighbouring stamps to the left. In SB, SA and the R row stamps, there are two such minute breaks. In the Q row, the two small breaks have become united by the disappearance of the intervening portion of colour line, thus forming a single break, which gradually increases in size in passing upwards to the top of the plate.

Minor varieties are found: AC, dot below SE corner; DF, mark below E of ONE; GJ, possible upward doubling of J; IH, vert. line left of H; LD, diagonal scratch below L square.

Plate 12 check letters: E is broad, H is short, I is tall, and J is square-footed.

This plate was repaired on at least two occasions, and a number of letterings existing in three states have been found.

The first repair. As in the case of the preceding One Penny Plate 11, the impressions included in the first repair operation of Plate 12 are characterized by the presence of "faint re-entry marks" in the right star. As in Plate 11, the frame-line gap of the north-east corner remains unaffected by the earlier re-entering; thus the presence of "faint re-entry marks" points to the exclusion of the top of the stamp from the re-entering. In these re-entered impressions of the first repair, the right border of the stamp exhibits increased firmness.

The later repair. Of the 35 letterings included under this heading, twelve are third states, since they exist in two previous states, the second of which shows the "faint re-entry marks". The twelve third state letterings are AD, AE, AF, AG, AH, AI, BC, BD, BF, BH, BI and BJ. These third states are distinguished by increased thinning or faintness of the check letters, or doubling of the base-line under one or both letter blocks, or by the presence of fresh burr in the margin. In addition to these third states, there are some 23 second states which are considered to be due to this late repair; in over half of these the frame-line flaw has disappeared in the re-entering, owing to the employment of a relief which differed from that originally used for laying down the plate, in not having the frame-line flaw. "Faint re-entry marks" are not seen in these later re-enterings.

BS1		1d. red-brown (shades) . . . . . *from*	75·00
		Pair	£175
		Block of four	£625
		Used on cover	£175
	c.	Basal shifts: AG, PI, QE, QF, QG, QH, QL, RL, TB, TG, TH, TK . . .	80·00
	d.	Double letters: C*H*, *D*D, G*J*, *K*F, *O*C	95·00
	e.	Constant varieties: DF, *L* D and "J" flaw on D*J*, E*J*, I*J*, *J*G, *J*I, L*J*, M*J*, N*J*, O*J*, T*J*	95·00
	f.	State 2, following early repair: AD, AE, AF, AG, AH, AI, AK, BA, BB, BC, BD, BF, BH, BI, BJ, BK, KI, QG	£200
	g.	State 2, following later repair: AA, AB, AC, AJ, BE, BG, BL, CD, CE, CF, CH, CJ, CK CL, KJ, OA, OE, PA, PH, SJ, SK, TH, TI	£200
	h.	State 3, following later repair: AD, AE, AF, AG, AH, AI, BC, BD, BF, BH, BI, BJ	£200

Imprimatur: £675. Stamps removed from the imprimatur sheet are AL, SB to SL, TA to TL.

The N.E. *Corner Break, Plate* 12

The Distinctive E *and* H, *Plate* 12

DD KF OC

Double Letters, Plate 12

DF LD

Constant Varieties, Plate 12

The "J" flaw is illustrated and described under Varieties of the Line-Engraved Stamps in the Line-Engraved general notes.

One Penny Die I, Plate 13

Registered 27 April 1841 and destroyed 15 July 1841. Stamps from this plate are the scarcest of those from Plates 12 to 16. In this and the following Plate 14, a large number of shifted transfers resulted from the transferring operation. The north-east break, which occurs throughout this plate, is somewhat wider than the corresponding break in the preceding Plate 12. Check letter T is squat, as in 1d., Plate 10.

BS2		1d. red-brown (shade) . . . . *from*	£140
		Pair	£350
		Block of four	£1000
		Used on cover	£280
	a.	Re-entry: IK, MH	£250
	b.	Double letters: B*I*, B*J*, *C*F, *D*B, F*D*, G*D*, O*G*, P*H*, Q*D*, R*E*, *T*D	£175
	c.	Basal shifts (well marked): AA, AC, AD, AG, AH, BA, BC, BD, BF, BI, BJ, CD, CE, CF, CG, CJ, CK, DA, DE, DG, DK, DL, HD, HE, HF, MB, ML, NB, NE, NG, PI, PJ, PL, QB, QK, RB, RC, RE, RH, RJ	£160
	d.	Recut S.E. square: R*F*, S*A*	£175

Imprimatur: £675. Stamps removed from the imprimatur sheet are AL, SC to SL, TA to TL.

Re-entries, Plate 13

BJ DB OG PH RE

Double Letters, Plate 13

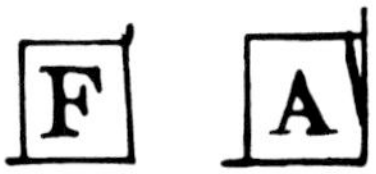

RF — *Recut Squares*; SA — *Constant Variety*

Plate 13

One Penny Die I, Plate 14

Registered 27 April 1841 and destroyed 8 September 1841. The north-east break is wider than in Plate 13, but not so wide as in Plate 15; this break is seen throughout the plate and is widest in the upper rows. The plate is remarkable for its numerous double check letters; the letter J is round-footed. Shifted transfers are numerous in the lower half of the plate, striking examples being OC, OH and OK. The plate did not undergo any repairs.

BS3		1d. red-brown (shades) . . . . *from*	90·00
		Pair	£200
		Block of four	£675
		Used on cover	£180
	a.	Re-entries: KF, SD (with D letter double)	£160
	b	Double letters: A*I*, *B*B, *B*F, *C*F, *C*G, *C*J, D*B*, D*D*, D*G*, D*H*, D*I*, D*J*, *E*E, E*I*, E*L*, F*C*, F*D*, H*B*, H*G*, I*B*, *I*E, *I*F, *I*K, *I*L, J*E*, *J*H, J*I*, *J*J, L*I*, N*C*, O*I*, *O*J, Q*I*, R*G*, S*I*, S*L*, T*H*, T*J*	£100
	c.	Basal shifts (clear double base): OC, OH, OK, PF	£110
	d.	Ditto (others): AA, AB, KD, KG, KH, KI, KK, KL, LJ, LK, LL, MA, MB, MD, MH, MI, MJ, MK, NK, NL, OA, OB, OD, OE, OG, OL, PI, QB, QH, QJ, RB, RC, RI, RJ, RL, SE, SG, SJ, TA, TD, TE, TG, TI, TK	95·00

Imprimatur: £675. Stamps removed from the imprimatur sheet are AL, SD to SL, TA to TL.

Re-entries, Plate 14

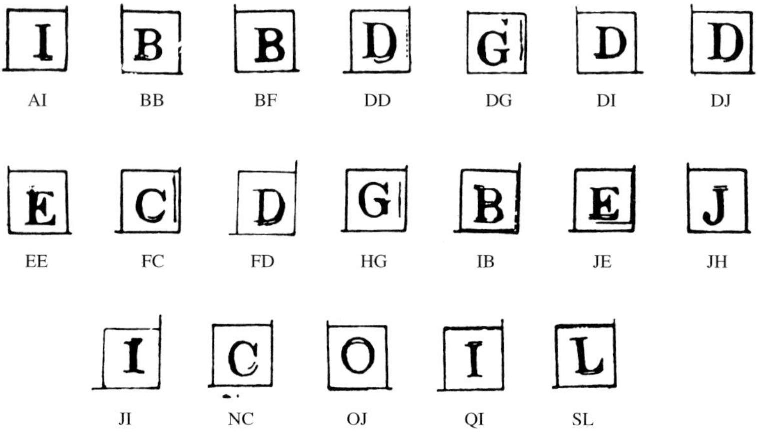

Double Letters, Plate 14

One Penny Die I, Plate 15

Registered 23 July 1841 and destroyed 21 February 1843. The north-east break in this plate is almost complete in the lower rows, and practically complete above. As in most of the plates of this group (12 to 16) basal shifted transfers are numerous, BH, TE and TJ being especially fine examples. In EL, PL and RF the upper line of the north-east corner is closed. Check letters—E is broad and J is square-footed; check letter A is closed above in CA, DA, EA (almost), FA, GA (almost), HA and IA.

BS4		1d. red-brown (shades) . . . . *from*	65·00
		Pair	£150
		Block of four	£500
		Used on cover	£120
	a.	Re-entries: PG, RE	£120
	b.	Double letters: *D*D, *H*H, *H*I, I*D*, O*H*, *S*C	90·00
	c.	Basal shifts: prominent examples BH, TE, TJ	90·00
	d.	Ditto (others): AB, AD, AG, AH, AI, AJ, BI, BK, BL, DE, FA, FB, FC, FD, FE, FF, FG, FH, FI, FK, GA, GB, GC, GD, GE, GF, GG, GH, GI, HC, HD, HE, HK, HL, IK, IL, LG, LK, LL, MC, ME, MH, MK, ND, NH, OC, OD, OE, OF, OI, PF, PH, PI, PJ, QE, QF, QG, QH, QI,RL, TA, TB, TC, TD, TF, TG, TH, TI, TK	85·00
	e.	Constant varieties: HF, *P*A, and "J" flaw on C*J*, E*J*, G*J*, H*J*, *J*B, *J*C, *J*D, *J*E, *J*F, *J*I, *J*J, *J*K, *J*L, L*J*, M*J*, N*J* plus minor basal shifts on B*J*, F*J*, I*J*, Q*J*, R*J*	90·00

Imprimatur: £675. Stamps removed from the imprimatur sheet are AL, SD to SL, TA to TL.

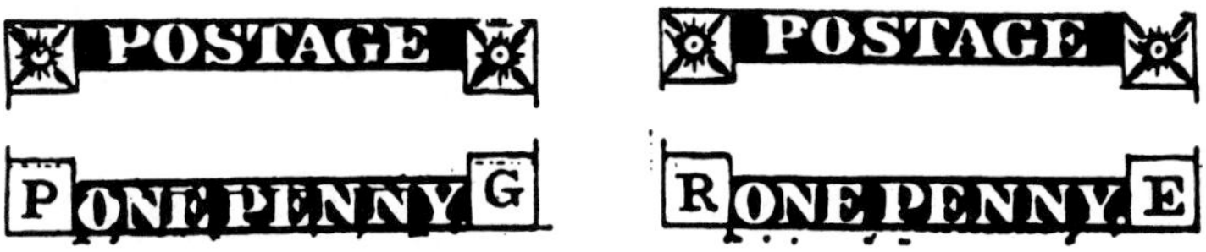

Re-entries, Plate 15

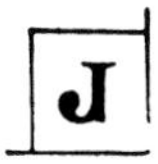

Square-footed J, *Plate* 15

DD HH HI ID OH SC

Double Letters, Plate 15

HF PA

Constant Varieties, Plate 15

One Penny Die I, Plate 16

Registered 23 July 1841 and destroyed 21 February 1843. The north-east break is practically complete throughout the plate in the original state, but in FF, HF and IH the top line of the north-east corner is unbroken. This plate was repaired after being in use for some time, and in some of the repaired impressions the upper north-east line has been restored. Check letters—in Plate 16 we note the return of the letter J to the round-footed variety, and the letter I is shorter than in the other plates of this group (12 to 16). Basal shifts occur in fair abundance, though not as numerous as in the preceding plate.

BS5		1d. red-brown (shades) . . . . *from*	60·00
		Pair	£150
		Block of four	£525
		Used on cover	£110
	a.	Re-entries: PC, RI, SI, SK	£110
	b.	Double letters: A*L*, G*C*, G*J*, *H*C, *H*G, *I*A, *J*C, *J*D, *O*D	85·00
	c.	Basal shifts: EL, FL, GA, GE, ID, IJ, IK, IL, ML, NA, OA, OE, OH, OK, PF, PH, PI, PJ, QA, QB, QG, RF, RG, SJ, SL, TB, TJ	80·00
	d.	No north-east break: FF, HF, IH	95·00
	e.	State 2 (repaired by re-entry): AC, AD, AE, AF, AG, AH, AI, BD, BE, RI, RJ, RK, SI, SJ, TC, TD, TE, TG, TH, TI, TJ, TK	£180

Imprimatur: £675. Stamps removed from the imprimatur sheet are AL, SD to SL, TA to TL.

The N.E. Corner Break, Plate 16

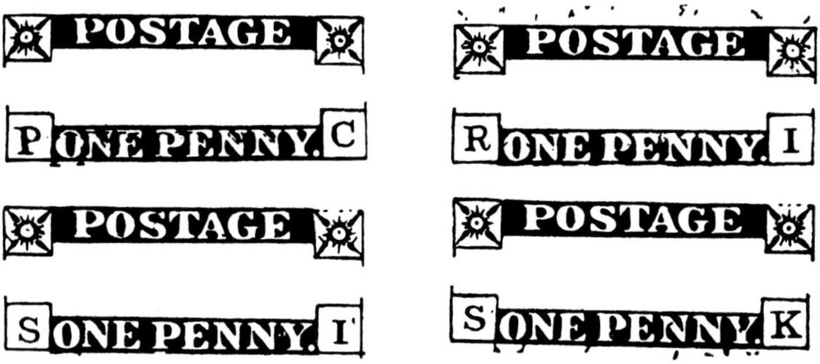

Re-entries, Plate 16

AL GC JC JD OD

Double Letters, Plate 16

One Penny Die I, Plate 17

Registered 10 September 1841 and destroyed 18 March 1842. The upper north-east corner frame-line is complete in this plate. The check letter J is round-footed throughout. Both upper and basal shifted transfers occur; the former may be found in the B, D, E., F, G and L horizontal rows; the latter in the H, I, P, Q, R, S and T horizontal rows. In the stamp NH the rays of the right star have been redrawn. In later printed sheets from the plate, a strong scratch line is seen passing from the right letter square of TK into the left letter square of TL. BL and EL show a spreading of' "GE", of "POSTAGE", BL being later repaired. GA and GB show some doubling at the top; QB and QC each show a thin line below the Q square. There may be a slight doubling of the P on PE.

After being in use for some time the plate showed signs of wear and repair by re-entry was carried out in the three upper rows of impressions; the margins of these repaired stamps show well-marked burr lines. In BB, BC and BL the first state shows a marked burr rub through the latter part of POSTAGE; in State 2 of these letterings the burr rub is absent.

BS6		1d. red-brown (shades) . . . . . *from*	65·00
		Pair	£175
		Block of four	£550
		Used on cover	£110
	a.	Re-entries: FA, MJ	£120
	b.	Double letters. *I*E, *J*D, M*B*, *O*B, *O*F, *O*G, *O*H, *O*J, *O*L, *P*E, T*D*, T*F* .	85·00
	c.	Upper border shifts: BA, BF, DK, DL, EA, EC, ED, FG, FL, GA. GB, GE, GG, GJ, LK	80·00
	d.	Basal shifts: HB, IA. PB, PC, PD, QA, QG, QI, RA, RE, RF, RI, RL, SA, SB , SE, SI, TH	80·00
	e.	TK or TL. Showing pronounced scratch mark in adjacent letter squares	95·00
	g.	Upper border shift plus burr rub: BB State 1, BC State 1, BL State 1 .	95·00
	h.	State 2 (repaired by re-entry): AB, AC, AD, AE, AF, AG, AH, AI, AJ, AK, AL, BA, BB, BC. BD, BE, BF, BG, BH, BI, BJ, BK, BL, CA, CB, CC, CD, CE, CF, CG, CH, Cl, CJ, CK, CL	£180
	i.	Constant varieties: *Q*B, *Q*C, *Q*D	85·00

Imprimatur: £675. Stamps removed from the imprimatur sheet are AA to AL, EK, EL, FF to FL, TL.

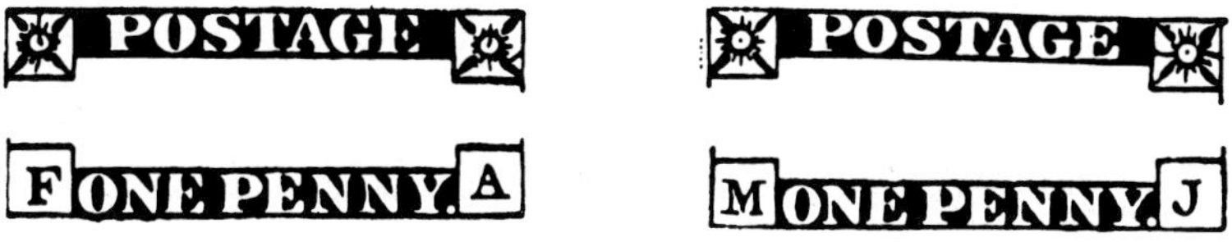

Re-entries, Plate 17

IE MB OB OL TD TF

Double Letters, Plate 17

TK–TL *Flaw, Plate* 17

QB QC QD

Constant Varieties, Plate 17

One Penny Die I, Plate 18

Registered 21 September 1841 and destroyed 5 March 1842. The plate shows no roller flaws, but the laying down of it gave rise to numerous shifted transfers, particularly in the lower half of the plate; A*D*, A*K*, *E*D, *N*A, T*E*, T*F* show weak or defective letters in the original state. The H of HB may be slightly double; "POSTAGE" is somewhat spread on NF and RL. Horizontal guide-lines are numerous and occur throughout the K horizontal row. The plate did not wear too well, and many of the impressions (54) had to be repaired by re-entering. The letter J is square-footed.

BS7		1d. red-brown (paper mostly well blued) . . . . *from*	£110
		Pair	£275
		Block of four	£925
		Used on cover	£200
	a.	Double check letters (minor): A*D*, *H*B	£120
	b.	Basal shifts: DC, EE, FE, FI, GD, GG, LB, LD, LF, LH, LI, LJ, LK, MB, MC, MD, ME, MF, NB, NC, ND, NE, OB, OC, OE, OG, OH, OI, PG, PI, PJ, QA, QB, QC, QD, QE, QF, QG, QH, QI, QK, QL, RA, RB, RC, RD, RE, RF, RH, RI, RK, SA, SB, SC, SD, SF, SG, SI, TB, TC, TD, TE, TF, TG, TH, TI, TK	£120
	c.	Burr rub POSTAGE: DL, FC	£130
	d.	"J" flaw: I*J*, M*J*, N*J*, S*J* plus basal shifts on O*J*, R*J*, T*J*	£130
	e.	State 2 (repaired by re-entry): AI, AJ, AK, AL, BG, BH, BI, BJ, BK, BL, CI, CJ, CK, CL, DI, DK, DL, EI, EJ, EK, EL, FI, FJ, FK, FL, GJ, GK, GL, QG, QK, RF, RG, RH, RI, RJ, RL, SD, SF, TB, TC, TD, TE, TF, TG, TH, TI	£180
	f.	State 2 (repaired by re-entry, non-coincident): QH, QI, QL, RE, RK, SE	£225
	g.	State 2 (repaired by re-entry) plus "J" flaw: D*J*, Q*J*	£250
	h.	Constant variety: T*F*	£130

Imprimatur: £675. Stamps removed from the imprimatur sheet are AA to AL, EK, EL, FG to FL, GL, TL.

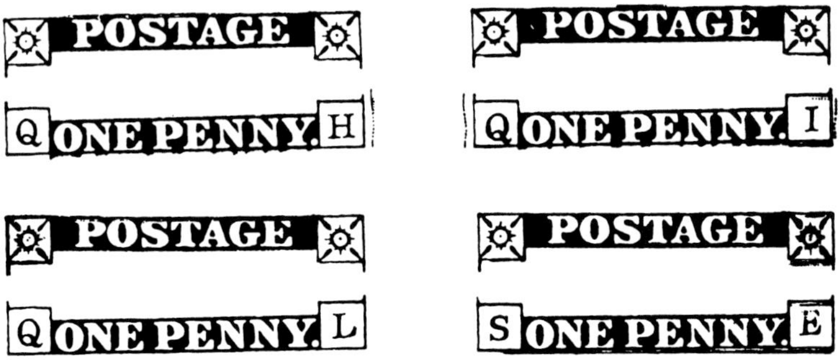

Non-coincident Second State Re-entries, Plate 18

AK ED TE

Defective Letters, Plate 18

TF

Constant Variety, Plate 18

One Penny Die I, Plate 19

Registered 3 November 1841 and destroyed 7 October 1843. Horizontal guide-lines, as BS8*g*, are very numerous on this plate; they are basal in position and are often found in pairs, one near the upper level and one near the lower level of the value. Shifted transfers are practically absent from the upper half of the sheet; in the lower half shifts may be found, basally situated, or at the upper border (reverse shifts), or at both upper and lower borders. F*K* and I*B* are notably defective letters. There is no evidence of plate repair. The letter J is square-footed.

BS8		1d. red-brown (shades) . . . . *from*	55·00
		Pair	£140
		Block of four	£450
		Used on cover	£110
	a.	Double check letters: *B*L, *D*B, *J*A, *J*B, *L*A, *L*B, *N*A, *Q*K, *SD* plus "J" flaw on *CJ*	65·00
	b.	Basal shifts: LE, NB, ND, NG, NH, OA, QI, SJ, TA, TB, TC, TD, TE, TF, TG, TH, TI, TK, TL	60·00
	c.	Upper (reverse) shifts: OE, PB, PI, PK, QA, QG, SB, SC	60·00
	d.	Double (basal and reverse) shifts: OD, OH, OI, OK, OL, PC, PL, QB, QC, QD, QJ, QL, SL	60·00
	e.	Constant varieties: A*L*, D*K*, F*K*, I*B*, K*L*, M*J*, N*I*, R*A*, plus "J" flaw on *JL* and "J" flaw only on A*J*, B*J*, D*J*, E*J*, G*J*, H*J*, I*J*, *J*J, K*J*, N*J*, P*J*, R*J* . . . . *from*	65·00
	f.	"J" flaw plus basal shift: T*J*; "J" flaw plus upper (reverse) shift: O*J* .	65·00
	g.	Horizontal guide line	65·00

Imprimatur: £675. Stamps removed from the imprimatur sheet are AA to AL, TA, TD to TL.

Example of horizontal guide line, Plate 19

Double Letters, Plate 19

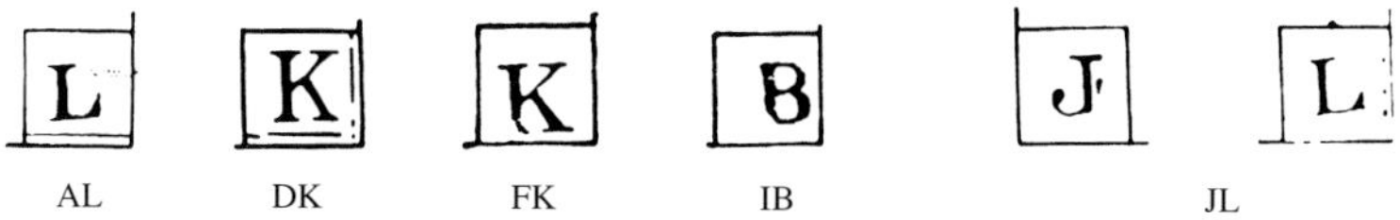

Double Letters, Plate 19

Constant Varieties, Plate 19

One Penny Die I, Plate 20

Registered 15 November 1841 and destroyed 7 October 1843. Many of the stamps (particularly in the upper rows) show scratches and smears in their margins. Shifted transfers are few and relatively poor; the best is the double shift (basal and upper) in N*L*. There are some striking double check letter varieties, notably *JB*, *O*K, *S*J. The plate is free from roller flaws, except in the E horizontal row, where in the north-east corner, the upper frame-line is missing throughout. These E row stamps also show the 10 o'clock ray flaw in the left star, but the 1 o'clock ray of the right star is normal (as in the lower row stamps RG to TL of Plate 26). This is important from the diagnostic point of view, because in E row stamps of other plates with complete north–east breaks (Plates 26 and 27) the 1 o'clock right ray flaw is present. Plate 25 E row stamps, like those of Plate 20, do not show the 1 o'clock right ray flaw. Careless corner recutting occurred on AD, AF, BK, HJ–HK, OH, SK. The right side line of the NE square is missing on KK; two scratches appear outside the A square on FA. The letter J is square-footed.

BS9		1d. red-brown (shades) . . . . *from*	55·00
		Pair	£140
		Block of four	£450
		Used on cover	£110
	a.	Re-entries (minor): NA, OI	65·00
	b.	Double and triple check letters (major): JB, *O*K, *S*J	65·00
	c.	Ditto (others): C*J*, G*I*, G*K*, KC, *L*A, *M*I, *M*L, PC, *P*L, *Q*D, Q*I*, S*D*, T*D*, T*F* plus "J" flaw on B*J*	60·00
	d.	Basal shifts: NC, ND, NH, NK, TK	60·00
	e.	Double (basal and reverse) shifts with double check letter L: N*L* .	70·00
	f.	Constant varieties: KK and "J" flaw on A*J*, I*J*, R*J*	65·00
	g.	South-east corner recut: A*D*, AF, BK, H*J*–*H*K, OH, SK	60·00
	h.	Open top north-east: stamps of the E horizontal row	60·00

Imprimatur: £675. Stamps removed from the imprimatur sheet are AA to AL, HJ to HL, IG to IL, TL.

ML OK PC PL SD SJ

Double Letters *Triple Letter, Plate* 20

AD HJ–HK KK

S.E. Corner Recut, Plate 20 *Constant Variety, Plate* 20

One Penny Die I, Plate 21

Registered 11 December 1841 and destroyed 21 February 1843. Stamps in the upper rows of this plate (AA to HE inclusive) show a minute break at the left end of the upper line of the north-east corner. Beyond this point to TL the little break is absent but the stamp HH shows a complete north-east gap like the E row stamps of Plate 20. The stamps of this plate are generally weak on the right side and particularly in the south-east corner. The plate is also remarkable for the large number of double check letters, some of which are very striking, particularly *LL*, *M*L, *R*L and *S*D. Apparently the letter K was erroneously punched in the left letter squares of all stamps of the last vertical row from LL to TL; in NL and QL the wrong letter K seems to have been completely burnished out, but in the seven other of these impressions some remains of the incompletely removed K can be seen, particularly in LL, ML and RL. AB and AC both show traces of extrinsic re-entries at top. The J of AJ is without top. The right side of the S.E. square is missing on GE, PD and PF. Owing to weakness, it was necessary to repair some of the plate impressions; see second states of OA, PA, QA, QB, RA, RB, SA, SB and TA. The letter J is square-footed.

Evidence has been produced showing that CB of plate 21 and BI of plate 22 exist in two states both appearing with and without hand retouches in the right margln. As suggested for plate 22, other letterings rnay exist.

BS10		1d. red-brown (shades) . . . . . *from*	55·00
		Pair	£140
		Block of four	£450
		Used on cover	£110
	a.	Extrinsic re-entries (above), AB, AC	65·00
	aa.	Double check letters: striking examples *R*L, *S*D, plus "J' flaw on F*J*	65·00
	b.	Ditto (others): *CC*, *D*E, E*D*, I*C*, I*D*, *J*C, K*A*, *K*B, *L*E, *M*A, M*C*, N*D*, O*J*, *O*L, P*I*, *P*L, *Q*C, S*E*, S*L*, *T*L, plus "J" flaw on E*J*, *J*B	60·00
	c.	Corrected check letters: *LL*, L over K; *M*L, M over K and basal shift	£100
	ca.	Defective check letter: A*J*	60·00
	d.	Basal shifts: OH, PG, TJ	60·00
	e.	Open top north-east, stronger right side + burr line: HH	75·00
	f.	"J" flaw: *J*L, L*J*, S*J*	65·00
	g.	State 2 (repaired by re-entry): OA, PA, QA, QB, RA, RB, SA, SB, TA	£180

Imprimatur: £675. Stamps removed from the imprimatur sheet are AA to AL, TA, TD to TL.

HH

Void Corner, Plate 21

AJ CC ED FJ IC JC JJ

KB LL MC ML OJ OL PL

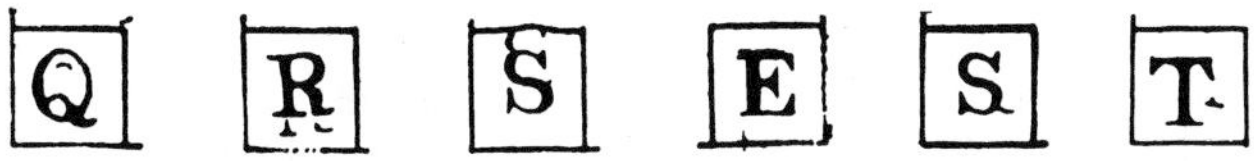

QC RL SD SE SL TL

Defective and Double Letters, Plate 21

One Penny Die I, Plate 22

Registered about 30 December 1841 and destroyed 21 February 1843. North-east breaks are as follows: (1) a single minute break at the left end of the upper line of the N.E. block in all impressions from JI to TL, and (2) a break, multiple in character, from AA to JH. Notable re-entries are QB and TA. Check letters: E is small, as also is M; L has a fairly long foot with a split serif at the end; T is squat with a thickened serif below. The letter J is square-footed and nearly all those on this plate show a defect possibly caused by foreign matter on the letter punch. There are no pronounced examples of shifted transfer on the plate. Almost all letterings show hand recutting of the letter squares, in some instances on all four sides.

BS11		1d. red-brown (shades) . . . . *from*	55·00
		Pair	£140
		Block of four	£450
		Used on cover	£110
	a.	Re–entries: QB, TA	£100
	b.	Double letters: A*F*, B*D*, L*I* plus "J" flaw on *IJ*, *JJ*, *KJ*, *LJ*, *OJ*	65·00
	c.	Constant varieties: *A*A, A*L*, EG, *F*F, F*I*, H*D*, *H*F, *I*A and "J" flaws on C*J*, D*J*, E*J*, H*J*, *J*A, *J*B, *J*C, *J*F, *J*I, *J*L, *L*C, M*J*, N*J*, P*J*, Q*J*, R*J*, S*J*, T*J*	60·00

No imprimaturs of this plate have ever been reported.

AA *to* JH JI *to* TL

N.E. Corner Breaks, Plate 22

Distinctive Letters, Plate 22

Re-entries, Plate 22

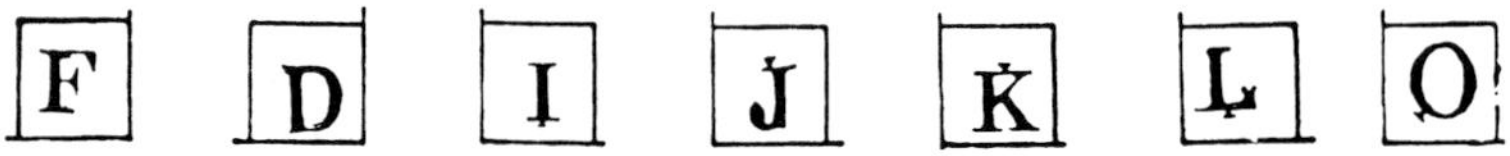

AF BD IJ JJ KJ LJ OJ

Double Letters, Plate 22

AA AL FF FI

HF IA LC

EG

Blob on neck

HD

Constant Varieties, Plate 22

One Penny Die I, Plate 23

Registered about 18 January 1842 and destroyed 21 February 1843. Triple north-east breaks appear throughout the plate. The only shifted transfers at all pronounced are the reversed (top border) shifts DL, EB and EG. In most cases the south-east frame-line is weak (as in Plate 21). Check letters: some of these are defective (e.g. the truncated P of PK), and many of the letter squares have smudge-like marks which, being superficial, tend to disappear with plate wear. The letter L in this plate is of the longer footed variety.

BS12		1d. red-brown (shades) . . . . . . *from*	55·00
		Pair	£140
		Block of four	£450
		Used on cover	£110
	a.	Reverse (top border) shifts: DL, EB, EG	60·00
	b.	Double letters: AC, F*F*, *G*A, N*I*, *S*H	60·00
	c.	Letter without foot: *P*K	£100
	d.	Smudges in letter squares: *A*E, D*F*. F*H*, *H*G, *H*I, *IB*, *IH*, IJ, *IL*, *J*G, *JH*, L*E*, L*F*, M*C*, *O*F, *PG*, PH, PI, *PJ*	60·00
	e.	Burr rub POSTAGE: HC	65·00
	f.	"J" flaw: *J*C, *J*D, R*J*	65·00

No imprimaturs of this plate have ever been reported.

N.E. *Breaks, Plate* 23

FF GA NI SH

Double Letters, Plate 23

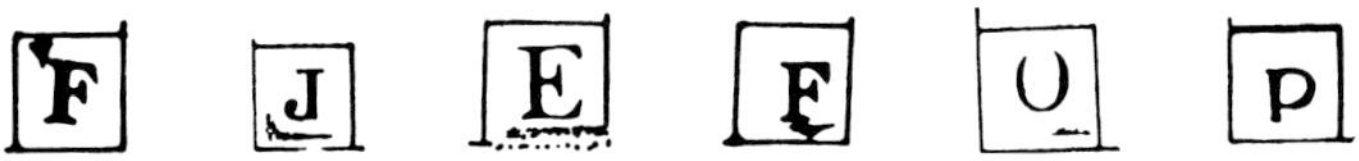

DF JG LE LF OF PK

Constant Varieties, Plate 23

One Penny Die I, Plate 24

Registered 4 March 1842 and withdrawn from press 18 August 1843. In this plate the upper four rows of impressions AA to DL all have closed tops in the north-east corner, with the exception of AF, CA, CB, CC and DH which have the triple north-east break. All the remaining impressions, from EA to TL, show the triple break in the north-east corner. There are no prominent shifted transfers to be noted. The stamp AA has the right side-line recut. The check letter L in this plate is of the short-footed variety. The letter J is square-footed and the T is stumpy as on Plate 22. Stamps HD and HE show smudge marks in the H square.

The right side of the N.E. square is missing on DI and EJ. The left serif of J on JA is missing and there is a short line to the top of M square on MJ.

BS13		1d. red-brown (shades) . . . . *from*	55·00
		Pair	£140
		Block of four	£450
		Used on cover	£110
	a.	Double check letters (not prominent): *C*F, *C*I, *H*J, *O*D	60·00
	b.	Recut right side–line: AA	65·00
	c.	Constant varieties: DI, EJ, *H*D, *H*E, *J*A plus "J" flaw on *MJ* and "J" flaw only on *CJ*, F*J*	60·00

Imprimatur: £675. Stamps removed from the imprimatur sheet are AA to AL, FK, FL, GG to GL, HL, TL.

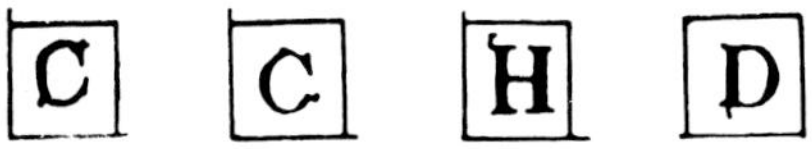

CF CI HJ OD

Double Letters, Plate 24

DI, EJ HD HE JA MJ

Constant Varieties, Plate 24

One Penny Die I, Plate 25

Registered 17 March 1842 and withdrawn from press 27 January 1843. The stamp AG is a fresh entry, showing a completely closed north-east top, and also duplication in the letters of POSTAGE. The stamps AH, AI and CB have unbroken tops in the north-east corner. The twelve stamps of the E horizontal row, like those of the E row of Plate 20, all have completely open tops north-east; they also show the 10 o'clock left ray flaw, but lack the one o'clock right ray flaw; a useful point of distinction from the E row stamps of ld. Plates 26 and 27. All the remaining impressions in the original state show the multiple north-east break, which, in most cases, is the triple break with the two right-hand gaps fused. The letter J is square-footed. Repaired impressions: AE, AF and AH have unbroken top north-east lines in State 2; other repaired impressions: second states of BA, CA, DA, RA, RB, RC, SA, SB, SC, TA, TB, TC and TD all show the multiple north-east break, and about half of them show "faint re-entry marks" in the north-east corner. This plate shows no prominent shifted transfers.

BS14		1d. red-brown (shades) . . . . . *from*	55·00
		Pair	£140
		Block of four	£450
		Used on cover	£110
	a.	Re-entry: AG	£100
	b.	Double letters: I*J*, I*K*, K*K*, *T*A	65·00
	c.	Blurrs in letter squares: F*F*, F*K*, *G*I, R*E*, R*L*	60·00
	d.	Open top north-east corner: stamps of the E horizontal row	60·00
	e.	State 2 (repaired by re-entry): AE, AF, AH, BA, CA, DA, RA, RB, RC, SA, SB, SC, TA, TB, TC, TD	£180
	f.	Recut frameline: DK	65·00

Imprimatur: £675. Stamps removed from the imprimatur sheet are AA to AL, FJ to FL, GG to GL, TA.

Re-entry, Plate 25

DK

Recut left frame, Plate 25

IJ IK

Double Letters, Plate 25

FK GL RL

Constant Varieties, Plate 25

One Penny Die I, Plate 26

Registered 22 June 1842 and withdrawn from press 27 January 1843. This is the first plate of a group (Plates 26 to 36) in which the stamps are characterized by a 10 o'clock ray flaw in the left star, and a short 1 o'clock ray flaw in the right, known as the 1842–3 ray flaws. In this Plate 26 the 10 o'clock left ray flaw is present throughout the plate, but the 1 o'clock right ray flaw is lacking in the stamps RG to TL; otherwise both ray flaws are present in all stamps of the plates of this group (26 to 36). This plate, as in the case of the following Plate 27, has the top of the north-east corner completely open. Check letter differences between the plates are as follows: in Plate 26 the letter L has a short foot; in Plate 27 the foot is longer. In Plate 26 the letter T is short and thick; in Plate 27 the T is more slender. The letter J is square-footed.

BS15		1d. red-brown (shades) . . . . *from*	55·00
		Pair	£140
		Block of four	£450
		Used on cover	£110
	a.	Re-entries: NC, RK	£100
	b.	Double letter: *G*L	60·00
	c.	Defective check letters: B*J*, E*E*, *E*K, *J*A, *T*E, *TL*	65·00
	d.	Inverted I and smudge in letter square: L*I*	65·00
	e.	Line through the top of F: RF	65·00
	f.	Badly recut south-east corner: IF	65·00
	g.	Constant variety: EA–FA (vertical pair)	£160
	h.	Constant varieties: C*A* and "J" flaw on D*J*, E*J*, F*J*, G*J*, K*J*, M*J*, O*J*, Q*J*	65·00
	i.	Defective south-east corner: IE	65·00

Imprimatur: £675. Stamps removed from the imprimatur sheet are AA to AL, KJ to KL, LG to LL, TL.

10 *O'clock Flaw* (N.W. *Square*)

1 *O'clock Flaw* (*and Open Top,* N.E. *Square*)

1842–43 *Ray Flaws*

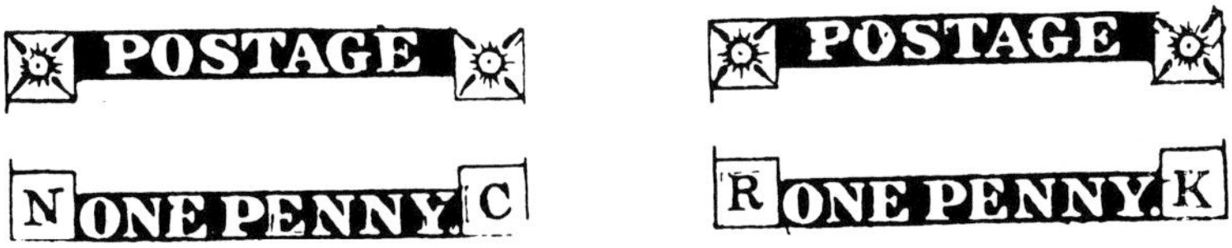

Re-entries, Plate 26

BJ CA EA-FA IE IF

LI TE TL

Constant Varieties, Plate 26

One Penny Die I, Plate 27

Registered 5 September 1842 and destroyed 7 October 1843. All stamps in the original state show the complete north-east break, and also the 1842–3 ray flaws. In this plate the check letters L and T differ from those of Plate 26 as indicated above. There are no prominent shifted transfers or double letters to be seen; the re-entries KK and MA are not very prominent. The frame-lines at the south-east corners of the stamps IF, KF and PB have been badly recut. The plate underwent repair by re-entry, a number of impressions in the F, G, H and I rows being operated on. These repaired stamps have the N.E. square complete and show the usual weakening of the corner letters. Guide lines, very prevalent in the original state of this plate, disappear from the repaired impressions. The letter J is square-footed.

BS16		1d. red-brown (shades) . . . . . *from*	55·00
		Pair	£140
		Block of four	£450
		Used on cover	£110
	a.	Re-entries: KK, MA	£100
	b.	Vertical row L squares showing guide dots	60·00
	c.	Badly recut south-east corner: HI, IF, KF, PB	60·00
	d.	Constant varieties: L*A*, T*K* and "J" flaws on B*J*, C*J*, D*J*, E*J*, I*J*, *J*C, *J*D *J*E, *J*F, *J*J, L*J*, M*J*, N*J*, O*J*, P*J*, Q*J*, R*J*	60·00
	e.	State 2 (repaired by re-entry): FC, FD, GB, GC, GD, GE, HB, HC, HD, HE, IC, ID, IE	£180

Imprimatur: £675. Stamps removed from the imprimatur sheet are AA to AL, RJ to RL, SG to SL, TL.

HI IF KF PB

Re-cut Corners, Plate 27

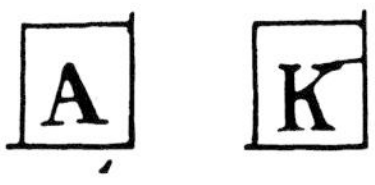

LA TK

Constant Varieties, Plate 27

One Penny Die I, Plate 28

Registered 14 September 1842, withdrawn from press 16 September and destroyed 7 October 1843. Stamps of this plate show the 1842–3 ray flaws. There is no north-east gap except on the three stamps QC, QD and QE and these have also the above ray flaws. Six consecutive stamps, OK, OL, PA, PB, PC and PD show a coloured roller flaw in the clear part of the N.W. corner star; this flaw is strongest in PD and weakest in OK, beyond which it disappears. The double check letters *F*A, *M*A and *O*F are not striking. Scratch lines through POSTAGE appear in the later printings of MD and QH. Some impressions of the lower part of the plate, namely TF to TL were repaired by re-entry resulting in thinning of the check letters by roller compression. The letter J is square-footed.

BS17		1d. red-brown (shades) . . . . . *from*	60·00
		Pair	£150
		Block of four	£500
		Used on cover	£120
	a.	Re-entries: HB, HC	£110
	b.	Double check letters: *F*A, *M*A, *O*F	70·00
	c.	Defective check letter: *Q*J	70·00
	d.	Coloured roller flaw: OK, OL, PA, PB, PC, PD	65·00
	e.	State 2 (repaired by re-entry): TF, TG, TH, TI, TJ, TK, TL	£190
	f.	Open top, north-east corner: QC, QD, QE	70·00
	g.	Constant varieties: *B*C, *I*B, K*E*, MD, PH–*P*I, QH and "J" flaw on E*J*, F*J*, *J*A, *J*L, M*J*	65·00

Imprimatur: £675. Stamps removed from the imprimatur sheet are AA to AL, GK, GL, HF to HL, TL.

Re-entries, Plate 28

FA MA OF

Double Letters, Plate 28

Roller Flaw,
PD, *Plate* 28

BC IB KE QC, QD, QE PH–PI

MD QH

Constant Varieties, Plate 28

One Penny Die I, Plate 29

Registered 14 November 1842, withdrawn from press 18 August and destroyed 7 October 1843. Stamps of this plate have the 1842–3 ray flaws. The north-east top frame-line is unbroken except in JK, KC and TC, which have the open top. Check letters: J is round-footed, and F in the vertical row is tall and narrow; R is normal: In this plate the squat letter S is distinctive and unlike the letter S in any other of these plates. Horizontal lines are seen in a number of the letter squares. The G letter square of GC and the C letter of IC show smears.

BS18		1d. red-brown (shades) . . . . . *from*	60·00
		Pair	£150
		Block of four	£500
		Used on cover	£120
	a.	Double letters: *B*C, *B*F, *C*A, *CJ*, D*H*, *D*J, *G*C, H*H*, *J*J, *J*L, L*B*, L*D*, *N*G, N*H*	70·00
	b.	Stamps from S row, showing squat letter S	£100
	c.	Open top north-east corner: JK, KC, TC	70·00
	d.	Constant varieties: AG, I*C*	70·00

Imprimatur: £675. Stamps removed from the imprimatur sheet are AL, GL, RK, RL, SG to SL, TA to TL.

1842–43 *Ray Flaw* *Normal* F *Tall Narrow* F *Squat* S *Wide* J

Distinctive Features of Plate 29

BF CA GC HH JL LB NG

Double Letters, Plate 29

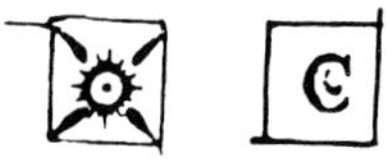

AG IC

Constant Varieties, Plate 29

One Penny Die I, Plate 30

Registered 6 December 1842, withdrawn from press 18 August and destroyed 7 October 1843. The check letters on this plate are irregular, often clumsy-looking and distorted, and frequently retouched. From the fifth horizontal row downwards the letters F are of the tall narrow type. The letter R of each stamp of the 18th horizontal row is really a punched-in P with hand-cut tail. The letter H generally shows heavy top serifs. The J is round-footed. The letters A of the vertical A row are practically all blind with the exception of DA in which the letter A is widely recut. Blurs occur in the letter squares of A*A*, *E*E, *EF*, S*E*, T*A*. The right frame is strengthened on JK, LG, MG. The K square of KD is recut and the L square of BL has a small extra fine. The 1842–3 ray flaws persist throughout the plate. This plate was repaired by re-entering 17 stamps of the B, C, D and E rows, namely BA to BD, CA to CD, DA to DE and EA to ED. The most prominent of these is the stamp EB State 2, which is a non-coincident re-entry with duplications in the star corners, and marked thinning of the check letters. The remaining (coincident) re-entries, 16 of them, show thinning of the check letters and restoration of the fine engraved lines is of the Queen's head and of the lateral borders (particularly the right).

BS19		1d. red-brown (shades) . . . . . . *from*	£110
		Pair	£250
		Block of four	£675
		Used on cover	£225
	a.	Double letters: A*D*, B*F*, C*F*, C*I*, *D*H, *E*E, F*L*, *P*F, *T*G	£130
	b.	Re-cut or retouched letters: A*C*, E*G*	£130
	c.	Defective letters: D*C*, E*C*, *G*E, *JJ*	£130
	d.	P converted to R (hand-cut tail) RA to RL	£150
	e.	Left side-line recut: AH	£130
	f.	Open top north-east corner: IJ, SE	£130
	g.	State 2, non-coincident re-entry: EB	£600
	h.	State 2, coincident re-entries: BA, BB, BC, BD, CA, CB, CC, CD, DA, DB, DC, DD, DE, EA, EC, ED	£225
	i.	Constant varieties: KH, SB	£130
	j.	Blur in letter square: *EF, TA*	£130

Imprimatur: £675. Stamps removed from the imprimatur sheet are AA to AL, GJ to GL, HG to HL, TL.

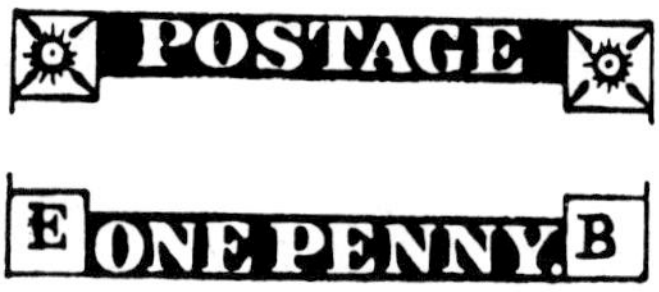

EB, *First State*

EB, *Second State* (*Re-entry*)

Re-entry, Plate 30

AD CF DH FL PF TG

Double Letters, Plate 30

AC EG GE JJ

Letter Variations, Plate 30

EF

Blurs in letter squares, Plate 30

KH SB TA

Constant Varieties Plate 30

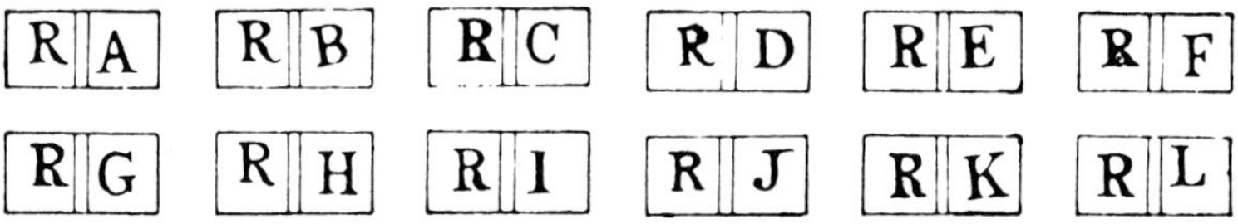

Hand recut tail to R: RA *to* RL, *Plate* 30

One Penny Die I, Plate 31

Registered 27 January 1843, withdrawn from press 16 September and destroyed 7 October 1843. The 1842–3 flaws persist throughout the plate. Check letters: the letter R in this plate is the long-tailed variety, which is really the letter P with a hand-cut tail; the letters F are nearly all of the arrow type (the letter F of FB is normal); the letter J is round-footed. Double check letters are fairly numerous, but not very prominent. Stamps with the check letters AF and KE have the open top at the north-east corner. The stamp BA shows a blur under the A. RK shows a partial break in the north-east corner.

BS20		1d. red-brown (shades) . . . *from*	55·00
		Pair	£140
		Block of four	£450
		Used on cover	£110
	a.	Double letters: A*D*, A*H*, B*F*, D*G*, F*A*, F*F*, I*F*, J*F*, O*H*, S*D*	65·00
	b.	P converted to R (hand-cut tail) RA to RL	85·00
	c.	Open top north-east corner: AF, KE	65·00
	d.	Smears in letter squares: B*A*, G*J*, *O*I, *P*K	65·00
	e.	Basal shifts: GL, JL	65·00

Imprimatur: £675. Stamps removed from the imprimatur sheet are AA to AL, GK, GL, HG to HL, IL, TA.

FA *Normal* F — FB *Wide* F — AH — BF — DG

Plate 31

FA — FF — IF — JF — OH — SD

Double Letters, Plate 31

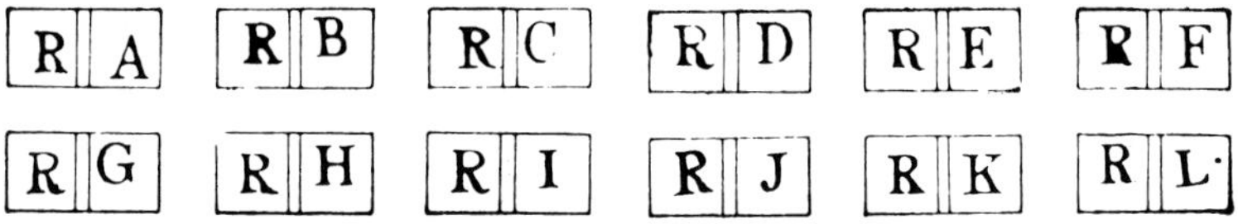

Hand recut tail to R: RA *to* RL, *Plate* 31

One Penny Die I, Plate 32

Registered 7 February 1843, withdrawn from press 16 September and destroyed 7 October 1843. The 1842–3 ray flaws persist throughout the plate. The stamps AL, LC and MC are fresh entries. The following stamps have open tops at the north-east corner: CH, KI, NK, OF, OJ. A considerable number of shifted transfers occur in this plate; these are mostly basal shifts but upper border shifts may be seen in the I and J horizontal rows. The letters B and BA and BL have been recut and are larger than normal; retouched letters occur in K*D*, *LD* and M*D*. The check letters R are mostly letters P with hand-recut tail, though these letters R differ from those long-tailed letters R of Plates 30, 31 and 33. The letter J is square-footed.

BS21		1d. red-brown (shades) . . . *from*	55·00
		Pair	£140
		Block of four	£450
		Used on cover	£110
	a.	Re-entries: AL, LC, MC	£100
	aa.	Re-entry and double letter: *O*E	£120
	b.	Double letters: *C*J, *G*H, *G*J	65·00
	ba.	Weak entry at top and double letter: *Q*K	£100
	c.	Letter B recut and enlarged: *B*A, *B*L	70·00
	d.	Retouched check letters: K*D*, *LD*, M*D*	65·00
	e.	Basal shifts: BJ, BK, GI, HD, HK, NE, NG, NH, NL, OH to OL, PG, SI	60·00
	f.	Upper border shifts: ID, IE, IF, IH, II, IJ, IK, JB, JC, JE	65·00
	h.	Blur in letter square: *HC*, *SD*	65·00
	i.	Mark in Y of PENNY: RF	65·00
	j.	Constant varieties: BB, E*F*, *E*G and "J" flaw on N*J*	65·00
	k.	Open top to north-east corner: CH	65·00
	l.	Hand recut tail to R: RB, RI	65·00

Imprimatur: £675. Stamps removed from the imprimatur sheet are AA to AL, BD to BL, TL.

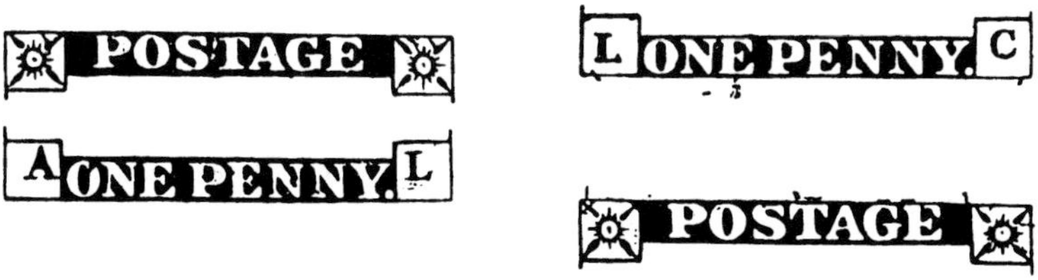

MC

Re-entries, Plate 32

Re-entry and Double "O", *Plate* 32

Weak entry and Double "Q", *Plate* 32

Basal Shift, Plate 32

Normal B BA BL

Recut Letters, Plate 32

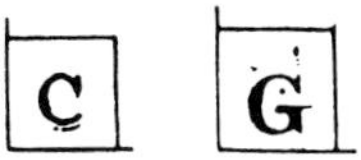

CJ GJ

Double Letters, Plate 32

BB EF EG

Constant Varieties, Plate 32

RB RI

Hand recut tail to R, *Plate* 32

One Penny Die I, Plate 33

Registered 20 February 1843 and destroyed 7 October 1843. The 1842–3 ray flaws persist throughout the plate. Three stamps have open tops at the north-east corner; these are FD, SF and SK. A considerable number of shifted transfers (mostly basal shifts) may be seen on this plate.

As in Plates 30 and 31 the stamps of the R row have the long-tailed check letter R, which is really letter P with a hand-cut tail; the check letters I are of the tall variety, and the J is round-footed. The letter P of PB has a very small (recut) loop, and the letter S of SE is distorted. Letters Q of QH and QL are defective. Practically all the letters C in this plate are much misplaced to the left in their letter squares. Minor marks or abnormalities of letters are seen on B*A*, B*B*, *I*H, K*I*, *N*B, P*I*.

Plate 33 has several of its impressions repaired by re-entering. PA State 2, a non-coincident re-entry, is the most prominent.

BS22		1d. red-brown (shades) . . . . . . *from*	55·00
		Pair	£140
		Block of four	£450
		Used on cover	£110
	a.	Double letters: A*I*, *D*A, D*G*, D*K*, *E*B, *E*F, E*K*, HG, K*K*, M*E*, P*D*, Q*E*, *T*B	75·00
	b.	Basal shifts: KE, KF, KJ, LF, LG, LJ, MH, MK, OC, OF, OG, OH, OI, OJ, OK, and TF to TL	65·00
	c.	P converted to R (hand-cut tail) RA to RL	£100
	d.	Abnormal letter P with small loop: PB	£100
	e.	Distorted check letter S: SE	75·00
	f.	Open top north-east corner: FD, SF, SK	75·00
	g.	State 2, non-coincident re-entry: PA	£700
	h.	State 2, coincident re-entries: QA, RA, TA	£180

Imprimatur: £675. Stamps removed from the imprimatur sheet are AA to AL, RG to RL, SJ to SL, TL.

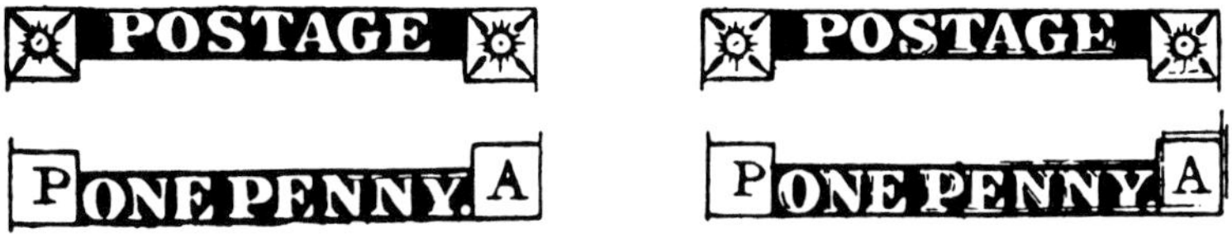

PA, *Plate* 33: *First and Second* (*Re-entered*) *States*

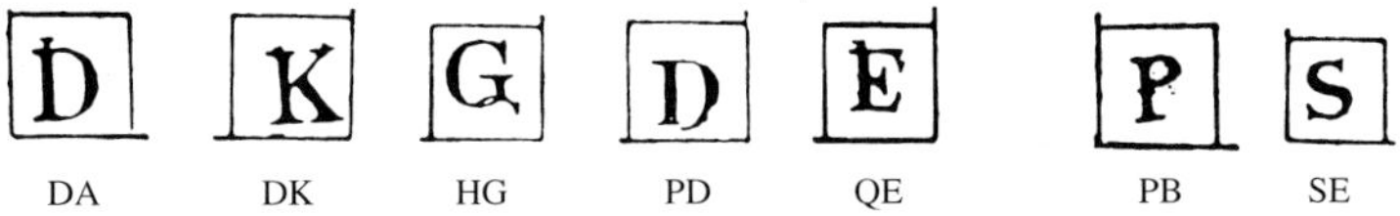

DA DK HG PD QE PB SE

Double Letters, Plate 33 *Abnormal Letters*

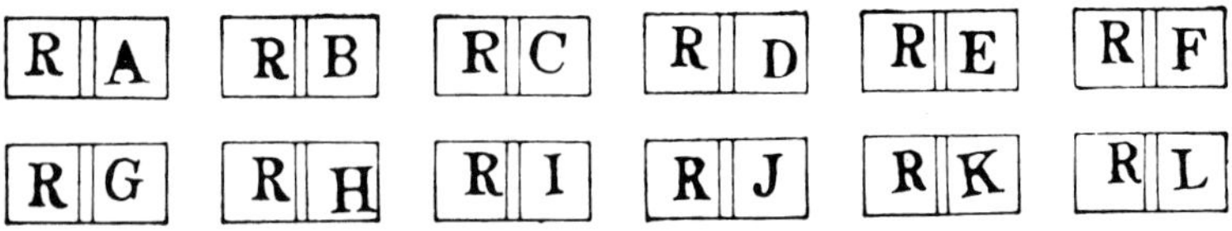

Long-tailed R: RA *to* RL, *Plate* 33

One Penny Die I, Plate 34

Registered 7 June 1843 and destroyed 25 June 1844. The 1842–3 ray flaws still persist throughout the plate. The stamp SI has the top of the north-east square open. Numerous horizontal guide-lines, passing through the letter squares and through the value near the upper level of the words ONE PENNY, occur in this plate. Check letters: in this and the following plates, the check letters E and D are broader than in the preceding plates; the letter J is square-footed, and many of the letters A are blind and placed high in the letter squares. Double letters are not generally pronounced. Repairs were carried out in the lower quarter of the plate. Letterings have been found in two states and at least one combination in three states; second states are known on: PA, PB, QA to QC, RA to RC, SA to SE, and TA to TH.

BS23 1d. red-brown (shades) . . . . *from* 60·00

Pair £150
Block of four £450
Used on cover £110
a. Basal shifts: KA, KB, LH, LL, MJ, NK, OF, OG, TF, TG . . . . 65·00
b. Double letters: *A*G, *D*A, *D*B, *D*D, *D*K, *D*L, *G*B, HG, *H*H, J*L*, N*H*, *O*K, *Q*C, *S*D, *SH* . . . . 70·00
c. Constant varieties: *I*C, *M*A, *P*J and "J" flaw on D*J*, F*J*, L*J* . . . . 70·00
d. Open top north-east corner: SI . . . . 80·00
e. State 2 (repaired by re-entry): PA, PB, QA to QC, RA to RC, SA to SE, and TA to TH £180
f. State 3 (repaired by re-entry): TC £200

Imprimatur: £675. Stamps removed from the imprimatur sheet are AA to AL, RL, SE to SL, TL.

AG DL JL QC IC MA PJ

Double Letters *Constant Varieties*

One Penny Die I, Plate 35

Registered 7 June 1843 and destroyed 27 February 1845. The 1842–3 ray flaws persist throughout the plate. Shifted transfers are not marked in this plate; FJ is one of the most prominent. SJ is a fresh entry. Frame-lines are recut on the right side of SH and SI. The stamp TI has the top of the north-east corner open. Check letters: D and E are of the broader type; J is square-footed. The letter D is retouched in OD; in PI the bottom serif of I is prolonged to the left.

BS24 1d. red-brown (shades) . . . . *from* 60·00

Pair £150
Block of four £450
Used on cover £110
a. Re-entry: SJ £110
b. Basal shift: FJ . . . . 65·00
c. Double letters: A*H*, *D*A, *H*J, I*K*, *J*K, *K*E, *K*I, L*A*, L*D*, *MF*, OE, PC, PE, *S*F plus "J" flaw on *KJ* . . . . 80·00
d. Open top north-east corner: TI . . . . 75·00
e. Recut letter D: OD . . . . 65·00
f. Right frame-lines recut: SH, SI; left frame-line recut: SC . . . . 65·00
g. Constant varieties: *J*K, KK, P*I*, TG and "J" flaw on M*J*, N*J*, P*J*, Q*J* . 80·00
h. Mark in G and "J" flaw: *GJ* . . . . 80·00

Imprimatur: £675. Stamps removed from the imprimatur sheet are AA to AL, SE to SL, TA, TL.

Re-entry, Plate 35

GJ KK PI TG

Constant Varieties, Plate 35

AH DA IK JK KE

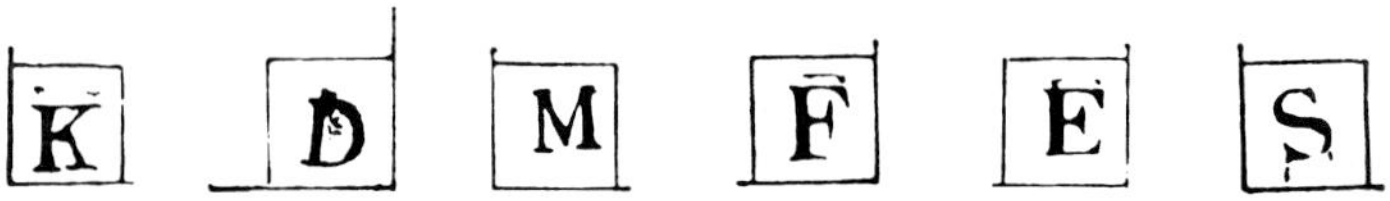

KI LD MF OE SF

Double Letters, Plate 35

One Penny Die I, Plate 36

Registered 7 June 1843 and destroyed 27 February 1845. The 1842–3 ray flaws persist throughout the plate. Basal shifts are fairly numerous; some have been mistaken for "re-entries" which are lacking, as are also fresh entries. Check letters D and E are of the broader type as in Plates 34 and 35. Double letters (doubling often slight) occur.

BS25		1d. red-brown (shades) . . . . . *from*	60·00
		Pair	£150
		Block of four	£450
		Used on cover	£110
	a.	Basal shifts: AF, AJ, CB, GE, GH, LJ, NF, OJ, QF, QQ QH, QI, RA, RJ, SH, SJ, SK, TB, TD, TF, TH	65·00
	b.	Double letters: A*D*, B*H*, B*K*, *D*D, D*K*, *E*H, *E*I, *J*H, K*H*, O*H*	75·00
	c.	Basal shift and double letter: P*E*, P*G*	80·00
	d.	Smears in letter squares: C*A*, E*B*, F*D*	65·00
	e.	Constant varieties: NL, *Q*C, T*J* and "J" flaw on C*J*, F*J*, G*J*, I*J*, *J*J, *J*K, *J*L, N*J*	70·00

Imprimatur: £675. Stamps removed from the imprimatur sheet are AA to AL, BA to BI, TA.

BH BK DK KH

Double Letters, Plate 36

NL QC TJ

Constant Varieties, Plate 36

ONE PENNY DIE I, PLATES 37 TO 45

This group of plates covers the transitional period of the change from the Maltese Cross to the 1844-type cancellations. The basic stamp of each plate is therefore priced for each type of cancellation, and it will be noted that the Maltese Cross becomes progressively scarcer with later registered plates. Listed varieties are priced with 1844-type cancellations.

It is impractical to price later uses of previous plates with 1844-type cancellations or to price stamps from later plates with Maltese Cross cancellations, but such items do exist.

Guide dots are found in or outside all TA to TL stamps in Plates 40 to 45, and also in or outside the L squares in every horizontal row. Throughout Plates 37 to 45 the D and E letters are both broad and the Js are all square-footed. Varieties such as vertical guide lines have not been listed separately as they vary in intensity and are fairly common, particularly in the north-east corner. They may therefore be confusing as a plating guide.

One Penny Die I, Plate 37

Registered 7 July 1843 and withdrawn from press 17 February 1844. This plate had a comparatively short life. Many stamps, particularly in the vertical K row, show spots and blemishes (see constant varieties) which may be confused with re-entry marks or double check letters. The "J" flaw occurs on a number of units.

BS26		1d. red-brown (shades)	
		with 1844-type cancellation . . . . . *from*	45·00
		with Maltese Cross cancellation . . . . . *from*	£100
		Pair	£100
		Block of four	£325
		Used on cover with 1844-type cancellation	65·00
	b.	Basal shifts: AF and TK with corrosion marks	60·00
	c.	Double letters: A*D*, *D*C, H*B*	70·00
	d.	Corrosion marks in value and letter squares: CK, DK, EK, MK, OK to SK	60·00
	e.	Constant varieties: E*J*, *L*F, MA, *M*E, NC, NK, O*H*, S*I*, T*D* and "J" flaws on *J*D, *J*I, *J*J, *J*K, *J*L, M*J*, P*J*, Q*J*, R*J*, S*J*	65·00

Imprimatur: £675. Stamps removed from the imprimatur sheet are AA to AL, BD to BL, TL.

LF

MA

NC, *Double dot*

Constant Varieties, Plate 37

One Penny Die I, Plate 38

Registered 26 July 1843 and destroyed 25 June 1844. This plate does not have any particular characteristics, though numerous stamps show a constant coloured blur in the N.W. star corner. Basal shifts are also numerous and the most well defined are listed. "J" flaws occur on many letterings. Horizontal guide lines through the value are also found and listed. The majority of impressions from the bottom row, the T row, were repaired by re-entry, due to weakness developing in the top and side margins. Those State 2 stamps known to exist are listed.

BS26A 1d. red-brown (shades)

with 1844-type cancellation . . . *from* 45·00
with Maltese Cross cancellation . . . *from* 90·00

Pair . . . £100
Block of four . . . £325
Used on cover with 1844-type cancellation . . . 65·00
b. Basal shifts: ED, OI, PI, PJ, PK, PL, RG, RH, RI, SA, SL, TA, TD, TJ plus "J" flaw on Q*J* . . . 60·00
c. Horizontal guide line through value: CB, CC, CD, FA, FB, FC, FD, FE, FF, FH, FI, FK, GE . . . 60·00
d. "J" flaw: I*J*, *J*E, *J*H, *J*I, *JJ*, K*J*, L*J*, M*J*, N*J*, O*J*, S*J* . . . 65·00
e. State 2 (repaired by re-entry): TB, TC, TE, TG, TI, TK, TL . . . £150

Imprimatur: £675. Stamps removed from the imprimatur sheet are AA to AL, BC, BE to BL, TL.

One Penny Die I, Plate 39

Registered 2 October 1843 and destroyed 25 June 1844. This plate shows no really marked identifying feature, though the N.E. corner star tends to have a short 11 o'clock ray on many stamps. As with Plate 38 the N.W. corner star has coloured blurs on several stamps. There are also prominent basal shifts. The plate was not very well laid out, causing some narrow and very wide spaces between the stamps. The well-defined re-entry marks on MA were most likely an attempt to realign this impression.

BS26B 1d. red-brown (shades)

with 1844-type cancellation . . . *from* 45·00
with Maltese Cross cancellation . . . *from* 90·00

Pair . . . £100
Block of four . . . £325
Used on cover with 1844-type cancellation . . . 65·00
b. Re-entry: MA . . . £120
c. Basal shifts: AF, BJ, FD, FE, GA, GB, GC, GF, QB, QD, QF, QG, QJ, QK, SC, TH, TI, TJ, TK, TL . . . 60·00
d. Recut top frame line: QA to QK (some combined with basal shifts as above) . . . 70·00
e. Horizontal guide line through value: AB, BL, PH . . . 70·00
f. "J" flaw: F*J*, M*J* . . . 70·00

Imprimatur: £675. Stamps removed from the imprimatur sheet are AA to AL, BD to BL, TL.

Re-entry, Plate 39

One Penny Die I, Plate 40

Registered 17 November 1843 and destroyed 25 June 1844. This plate was also badly set out with narrow to very wide spaces between some stamps. No special characteristics are present, though stamps lettered JG to JL and KA have a similar flaw to that on Plate 39 in the N.W corner star which must have been caused by foreign matter on the roller impression. There are numerous examples of recut frame lines both complete and local, often showing as extensions beyond the normal design. In fact there are so many minor varieties in the sheet that some units exhibit more than one. Second states exist on stamps lettered AF and AI which show well-defined transfer roller lines in the left margin with strengthening of the frame-lines. The plate had a short life and is best known for the various states of the KB re-entry.

The KB Re-entry

State 1a. As first issued this stamp shows a re-entry with duplication above and below; both check letters are misplaced to the right. The right side of the B square consists of two lines.

State 1b. After some sheets had been printed KB was apparently re-entered, its side frame lines being strengthened. The right side of the B square is now in triplicate and touching both loops of the B.

State 1c. The B square has received attention and the right side now consists of one thick line.

State 2. Finally, the original B has been erased and a new B struck in a central position. The square has been recut.

BS26C		1d. red-brown (shades)	
		with 1844-type cancellation . . . . *from*	60·00
		with Maltese Cross cancellation . . . . *from*	£125
		Pair	£130
		Block of four	£400
		Used on cover with 1844-type cancellation	£110
	b.	KB re-entry, State 1a	£475
	ba.	KB re-entry, State 1b	£1500
	bb.	KB re-entry, State 1c	£750
	bc.	KB re-entry, State 2	£1250
	c.	Second state with double top line: LB (occurred during repairs to KB)	£210
	d.	Double letters (slight): I*D*, K*A*, T*E*	70·00
	e.	Basal shifts. FG, IA, PA, PB, PC, PD, PE, PF, SA, TC, TE, TF, TH, TI, TK, TL	65·00
	f.	Recut left frame line: AE, BE, FH, IF, JI, MI, OK, PE, TB	65·00
	g.	Recut right frame line: AG, IE, JG, JH, KH, LG, MH, NJ	65·00
	h.	Roller flaw N.W. corner star: JG, *J*H, JI, JJ, JK, JL, KA (slight)	65·00
	i.	Constant varieties: A*C*, BB, B*H*, NL, *R*H and "J" flaw on I*J*, *J*B, *J*C, *J*D, *J*E, *J*F, *J*H, *J*I, *J*J, M*J*, N*J*	65·00
	j.	Additional State 2 (repaired by re-entry): AF, AI	£200

Imprimatur: £675. Stamps removed from the imprimatur sheet are AA to AL, GG to GL, HJ to HL, TL.

States 1a–1c

State 2

The KB re-entry, Plate 40

Roller Flaw AC BB BH NL RH

GE touches margin

Constant Varieties, Plate 40

One Penny Die I, Plate 41

Registered 6 November 1843 and destroyed 27 February 1845. This had a much longer life than Plate 40. The top line above the star squares and POSTAGE was generally weak and in some instances gives a broadening effect to the letters. A roller flaw developed when the lower rows were transferred and resulted in the top limb of the letter E of POSTAGE showing a coloured mark or blur. The right limb of the second N also shows a similar mark on several stamps. These may be found in various degrees on most units in rows Q, R, S and T.

BS26D		1d. red-brown (shades)	
		with 1844-type cancellation . . . . . . *from*	45·00
		with Maltese Cross cancellation . . . . . . *from*	£100
		Pair	£100
		Block of four	£325
		Used on cover with 1844-type cancellation	65·00
	b.	Major re-entries: IL, NA	£120
	c.	Double letters: *M*C, R*I*	65·00
	d.	Basal shifts (slight): TA to TL	60·00
	e.	Horizontal guide line through value: BC, DF, EB, ED to EI (others less pronounced exist)	60·00
	f.	Blur marks on E and N of PENNY: Q to T rows	60·00
	g.	Constant varieties: AL, F*D*, F*F*, *L*K, PL, T*A*, TL and "J" flaw on B*J*, C*J*, F*J*, H*J*, *J*B, *J*C, *J*D, *J*E, *J*F, *J*G, *J*H, *J*I, *J*J, *J*K, L*J*, P*J*	65·00

Imprimatur: £675. Stamps removed from the imprimatur sheet are AA to AL, GG to GL, HJ to HL, TL.

Typical blur mark on E *of* PENNY

Re-entries, Plate 41

MC RI AL FD FF PL TA

Double Letters *Constant Varieties*

Plate 41

One Penny Die I, Plate 42

Registered 23 January 1844 and destroyed 25 June 1844. This plate had a very short life. Many of the stamps show white highlights suggesting that the plate was lightly rolled-in and, with further compression during use, may have resulted in its early withdrawal on 25 June 1844. There are no other very pronounced plate characteristics, though the N.E. corner star shows a tendency to have a short 11 o'clock ray.

BS26E		1d. red-brown (shades)	
		with 1844-type cancellation . . . . . *from*	45·00
		with Maltese Cross cancellation . . . . . *from*	£125
		Pair	£100
		Block of four	£325
		Used on cover with 1844-type cancellation	65·00
	b.	Re-entry: QA	80·00
	c.	Double letters: K*F*, M*D*	65·00
	d.	Recut left frame line: AG	60·00
	e.	Recut N.E. square: IE	60·00
	f.	Horizontal guide line through value: EA to EG, KA, KD, KG, KH, PD, RK (others less pronounced exist)	60·00
	g.	Constant varieties: IH, P*I* and "J" flaws on C*J*, *J*A, *J*B, *J*C, *J*D, *J*F, *J*I, *JJ*, K*J*, L*J*	60·00

Imprimatur: £675. Stamps removed from the imprimatur sheet are AA to AL, GF to GL, HK, HL, TL.

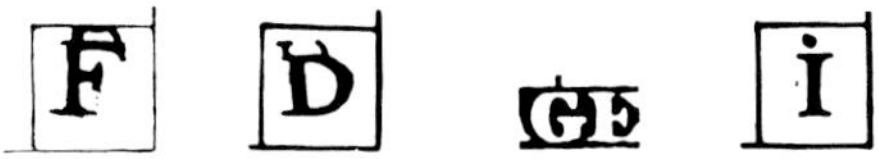

KF MD IH PI

Double Letters *Constant Varieties*

Plate 42

One Penny Die I, Plate 43

Registered 23 January 1844 and destroyed 27 February 1845. This plate was registered with Plate 42 and had a life of just over twelve months. No special characteristics are present, though the 11 o'clock short ray in the N.E. corner star which started on Plate 42 still persists.

BS26F		1d. red-brown (shades)	
		with 1844-type cancellation . . . . . *from*	45·00
		with Maltese Cross cancellation . . . . . *from*	£125
		Pair	£100
		Block of four	£325
		Used on cover with 1844-type cancellation	65·00
	b.	Recut left frame: DH	60·00
	c.	Horizontal guide line through value: LE, PA, QA, QH, QI (others less pronounced exist including some through letter squares)	60·00
	d.	Constant varieties: A*I*, EB, *P*D, *P*G, QF and "J" flaw on A*J* to D*J*, G*J*, H*J*, I*J*, *J*A, *J*B, *J*C, *J*D, *J*E, *J*F, *J*G, *J*H, *J*I, *JJ*, *J*K, *J*L, L*J* to O*J*, Q*J*, T*J*	65·00

Imprimatur: £675. Stamps removed from the imprimatur sheet are AA to AL, SF to SL, TA, TK, TL.

AI EB PD PG QF

Constant Varieties, Plate 43

One Penny Die I, Plate 44

Registered 29 February 1844 and destroyed 1 April 1846. These dates suggest a much longer printing life than most of the earlier plates in this group. A characteristic of the plate is a general weakness of the top of most units which was partially made good by local recuts on some letterings. It gives rise to the so-called "P" flaw which is chiefly found in the top rows and varies in occurrence and definition according to the amount of compression due to use and/or amount of inking (wiping).

BS26G		1d. red-brown (shades)	
		with 1844-type cancellation . . . . *from*	45·00
		with Maltese Cross cancellation . . . . *from*	£125
		Pair	£100
		Block of four	£325
		Used on cover with 1844-type cancellation	65·00
	b.	Re-entry: SI	£100
	c.	Double letter: G*E*	65·00
	d.	Horizontal guide line in right square: EL	60·00
	e.	"P" flaw (variable): BE, BF, BG, BI, DI to DL, HG, HH, ID	65·00
	f.	Constant varieties: *AF*, A*I*, D*L*, *H*D and "J" flaw on C*J*, E*J*, F*J*, I*J*, *J*C, *J*D, *J*F, *J*H, *J*I, *J*J, *J*K, *J*L, O*J*, P*J*, Q*J*	65·00

Imprimatur: £675. Stamps removed from the imprimatur sheet are AA to AL, BA to BF, CA to CC, TL.

"P" *Flaw*
(Semi-constant)

Re-entry, Plate 44

AF AI DL HD

Constant Varieties, Plate 44

One Penny Die I, Plate 45

Registered 29 February 1844 and destroyed 27 February, 1845. This plate has some definite characteristics in that the N.W. corner 10 o'clock ray flaw returns (as on Plates 26 to 36) and the N.E. corner shows generally shorter rays in the 9, 11 and 1 o'clock positions. As with Plate 44 there is a similar weakening to many units at the top margin and frame lines show some local hand-cutting. This weakness at the top leads to the appearance of the "E" flaw in POSTAGE which is illustrated under the next group of plates.

BS26H		1d. red-brown (shades)	
		with 1844-type cancellation . . . . *from*	45·00
		with Maltese Cross cancellation . . . . *from*	£125
		Pair	£100
		Block of four	£325
		Used on cover with 1844-type cancellation	65·00
	b.	Double letters (slight): *D*A, *D*H, K*L*	65·00
	c.	Horizontal guide line through value: GF, HE, through letter squares: D*I*, *MA*, M*C*	65·00
	d.	"E" flaw (variable): BC, BD, BF to BJ, BL, CJ, DD, DE, FC, FG, FJ, GF, GK, IA, IH, II, MA, NE, OC, TI	70·00
	e.	Constant varieties: DB, KD, *M*H, T*A*	65·00

Imprimatur: £675. Stamps removed from the imprimatur sheet are AA to AL, HG to HL, IJ to IL, TL.

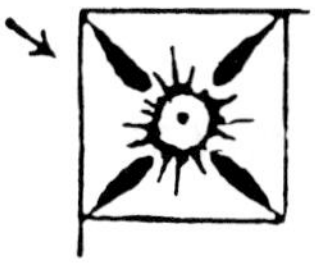

10 *o'clock Ray Flaw*

KL *Double Letter* MH TA *Constant Varieties*

Plate 45

One Penny Die I, Plates 46 to 58 (May 1844 to May 1845)

The "E" flaw, illustrated, is a helpful feature in this group. It is prominent in Plates 46, 47, 48, the upper half of 53 and on most stamps of Plates 54 to 56. It is not always well defined. A more minor flaw, the "T" flaw, illustrated, occurs plentifully on Plates 47 to 48 so that these two plates generally show both E and T flaws in POSTAGE.

All the plates of this group have the square J. On Plate 58 the I is short and the Rs have their tails hand-cut. Guide dots are found in or outside the S.E. squares of the last stamp in nearly all the horizontal rows and on all TA–TL stamps in this group up to Plate 56. Recut frame lines are numerous in addition to those mentioned under "Plating Aids", especially on Plates 52 to 56.

In this and subsequent groups only the more outstanding of the mentioned varieties are illustrated.

BS27		1d. red-brown (shades) . . . . *from*	25·00
	a.	"E" flaw	40·00
	b.	"T" flaw	40·00
	c.	"E" and "T" flaws together	55·00
	d.	P converted to R (hand-cut tail) (Plate 58)	60·00
	e.	Re-entry (Major, various)	60·00
	ea.	Second states: Plate 48, AD, AE, AF; Plate 49, TF . . . . *from*	£180
	f.	Double letter	30·00
	g.	Horizontal guide line	30·00
	h.	Basal shift . . . . *from*	30·00
	i.	Corner or part of side frame lines recut . . . . *from*	30·00
	j.	One or both side frame lines completely recut . . . . *from*	30·00
	k.	Constant varieties	40·00

Imprimatur: Plates 46 to 58, *each* £650. Stamps removed from the imprimatur sheets Plate 46: AA to AL, GJ to GL, HG to HL, TL; Plate 47: AA to AL, GF to GL, HK, HL, TL; Plate 48: AA to AL,

FG to FL, GJ to GL, TL; Plate 49: AA to AL, HK, HL, IF to IL, TL; Plate 50: AL, GL, RL, SE to SL, TA to TL; Plate 51: AA to AL, GG to GL, HJ to HL, TL; Plate 52: AA to AL, GG to GL, HJ to HL, TL; Plate 53: AA to AL, IG to IL, JJ to JL, TL; Plate 54: AL, RJ, SD to SL, TA to TL; Plate 55: AL, HL, RK, RL, SG to SL, TA to TL; Plate 56: AL, JG to JL, KJ to KL, TA to TL; Plate 57: AA to AL, HJ to HL, IG to IL, TL; Plate 58: AA to AL, GK to GL, HG to HL, IL, TL.

Plates registered: Plate 46, 4 May 1844; Plate 47, 24 May 1844; Plate 48, 19 June 1844; Plates 49, 50, 12 September 1844; Plate 51, 3 December 1844; Plate 52, 17 December 1844; Plate 53, 7 January 1845; Plate 54, 25 January 1845; Plate 55, 7 February 1845; Plate 56, 25 February 1845; Plates 57, 58, 9 May 1845.

Plated Used Examples

Plate 46	30·00	Plate 53	25·00
Plate 47	30·00	Plate 54	25·00
Plate 48	25·00	Plate 55	25·00
Plate 49	45·00	Plate 56	27·00
Plate 50	45·00	Plate 57	35·00
Plate 51	25·00	Plate 58	35·00
Plate 52	25·00		

Plating Aids

The abbreviations used in the list below and in similar lists throughout this section are as follows: ***R***, re-entry; ***D***, double letter; ***B***, basal shift; ***C***, corner or part of side frame lines recut; ***F***, one or both side frames completely recut; ***H***, horizontal guide line; ***CV***, constant variety; ***CVJ***, "J" flaw.

Plate 46: ***R***: LK; ***D***: B*D*; ***H***: EG, EK, HF, KG, LJ, MC, PI; ***CV***: LH, N*F*, *P*E, *R*B; ***CVJ***: I*J*, K*J*.

Plate 47: ***R***: SI; ***D***: L*D*; ***H***: NL; ***CV***: *AA* A*B*, A*C*, EG, E*H*, L*D*, QB.

Plate 48: ***R***: JE, TL; ***D***: *D*F; ***F***: CI, CJ, CK; ***H***: HD, HG, IB, IJ, JH, JJ, KA, NL, PL; ***B***: BJ, NI, NJ, OD, PG, PH, QH, and T row; ***CV***: *L*A; ***CVJ***: G*J*, O*J*. There is a mark on the left margin of the GI.

Plate 49: ***D***: *M*D; ***F***: BB, EI, MJ, MK, NH, TD, TE, TF (2nd state), TH, TI, TJ; ***H***: BJ, BK, CC, QI, SI, SK, TH; ***B***: OE, OF, OH, TF (1st state); ***CV***: D*J*, RH; ***CVJ***: G*J*, *J*C.

Plate 50: ***R***: CE, DE; ***F***: CL, DC, KA; ***C***: ED; ***H***: FA, OL. Double or defective letters S*D*, S*E*. Lines in S.W. squares, JK, PI; ***CV***: AC, A*L*, *N*A; ***CVJ***: K*J*.

Plate 51: ***D***: A*D*, MC, M*I*; ***F***: DE, FF, IE, TG; ***H***: EK; ***CV***: A*C*, I*F*, KB, LC, *L*G, QI, RI, SF; ***CVJ***: N*J*, R*J*, S*J*.

Plate 52: ***D***: SK; ***B***: NK; ***H***: DG, EL, IH, KG, OK; ***CV***: F*C*, *H*A, *Q*A, *Q*L; ***CVJ***: B*J*, *J*C, *J*E, *J*F, *J*J. The right side of the N.E. square is open on DB; several stamps have recut sides.

Plate 53: ***D***: *P*I, *T*D; ***B***: FL; ***CV***: A*B*, A*H*, A*I*, A*K*, CH, SD, *T*D, TE; ***CVJ***: G*J*, *J*D, *J*E, *J*F. On NA to NF the "E" flaw is "hooded"; on DI there is a large mark to the right of I; on EA "POST" is spread; many stamps have recut frames.

Plate 54: ***R***: DA, JL, TF, QD, SI; ***CV***: A*B*, A*D*, A*E*, A*I*, A*J*, F*I*, NJ, TG; ***B***: RD; SH, originally normal, was re-entered after the plate had been in use (State 2, re-entry). There is a large flaw on the crown on HK, DI, LE, NL have broken top to the N.E. square.

Plate 55: ***R***: KK, PL; ***D***: *M*K; ***B***: BG, DH; ***H***: *CL*, DG, DI, DJ, GH, HA, IH; ***CV***: B*D*, *SE*, *SH*.

Plate 56: ***R***: JG–KG; ***D***: *M*C; ***H***: IH, LF, LG, PB, PI, PK, QI; Recut right frame, LI; ***CV***: B*A*, *LE*, *M*H, *SF*, *SH*.

Plate 57: ***R***: IL, JF, JG (affects N.E. square and value), JH, JI, JJ, JK, NL, OL; ***B***: NA to NK, OA to OD, OH, OI, OK, PD, TE; ***H***: ED; ***CV***: BE, CE, G*D*; ***CVJ***: G*J*.

Plate 58: ***R***: FI, FJ; ***D***: A*B*, *D*H, RA, *S*B, *S*H; ***C***: DL, KD; ***H***: ED; ***CV***: *Q*B.

"E" AND "T' FLAWS

RE-ENTRIES, ETC.

Plate 47

Plate 48 (*Note also* T *and* E *Flaws*)

Plate 48

Plate 48, *Horizontal Guide line*

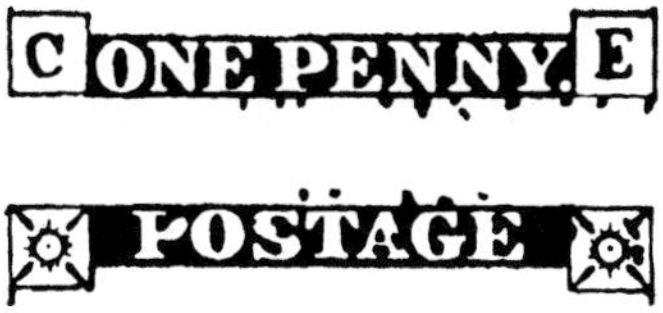

Plate 50

NA *to* NF *Plate* 53, *"Hooded* E" *Flaw*

HK *Plate* 54, *"Crown" Flaw*

Plate 54

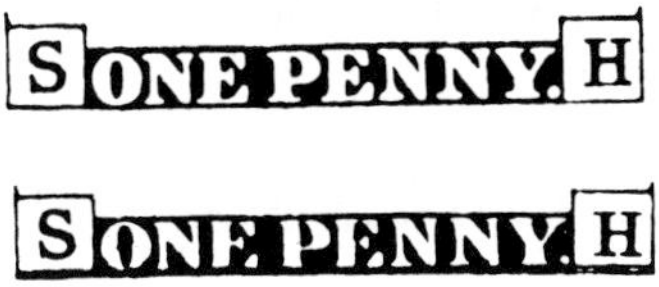

Plate 54 (1*st and* 2*nd States*)

Plate 54

Plate 54

Plate 55

Plate 56 (JG–KG)

Plate 57

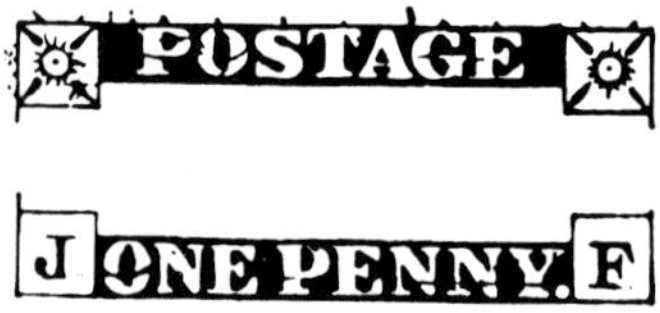

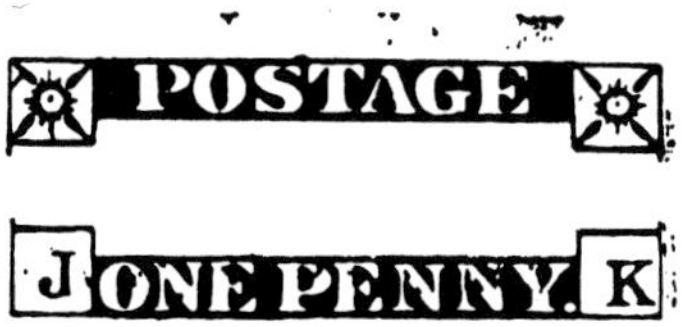

Second J *doubled by re-entry*

Plate 57

Plate 57, *Basal Shifts*

Plate 58, *Re-entries*

DOUBLE LETTERS

BD, Plate 46

DF, Plate 48

MC, Plate 56

AB

DH

RA

SB

SH

Plate 58

CONSTANT VARIETIES

LH

NF

PE

RB

Plate 46

AA

Plate 47

AB

AC

EG

EH

LD

QB

Plate 47

LA

Plate 48

DJ

RH

Plate 49

AC

AL

JK

NA

Plate 50

AC

IF

KB

LC

LG

QI

RI

SF

Plate 51

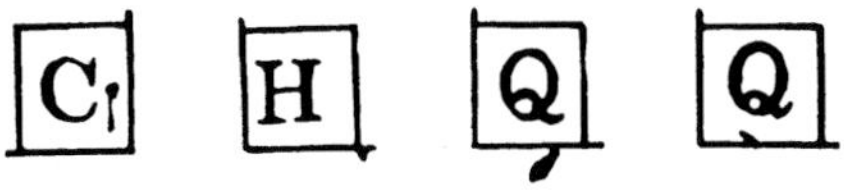

FC HA QA QL

Plate 52

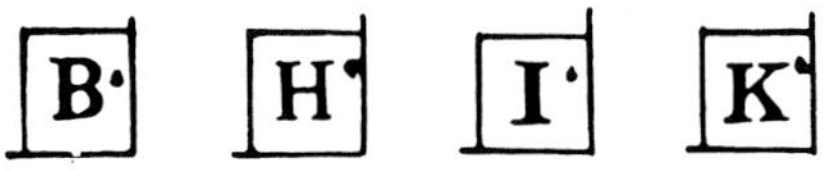

AB AH AI AK

Plate 53

CH SD TD TE

Plate 53

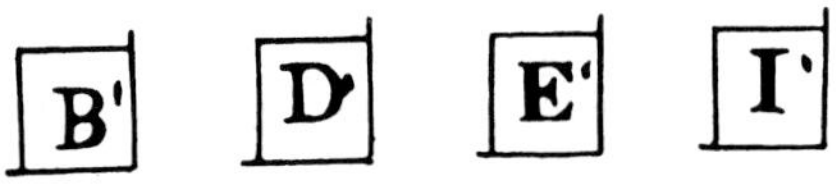

AB AD AE AI

AJ FI NJ TG

Plate 54

BD CL SE SH

Plate 55

BA LE MH SF SH

Plate 56

BE CE GI) QB, *Plate* 58

Plate 57

One Penny Die I, Plates 59 to 75 (June 1845 to April 1847)

This group is characterized by a distinctive oval "O" (the normal O of Alphabet I being round) and all the Js are square-footed. Plates 59 to 62 may be found in shades redder than usual and smudgy burrs are common, usually on the left. Some very fine re-entries occur, one being the notable "Union Jack" re-entry; see Plate 75 Plating Aids below. Sheets from Plates 70 and 71 were used by Henry Archer for experimental rouletting and are listed in Section CA.

BS28	1d. red-brown (shades)	*from*	—	25·00
	a. Oval "O"		—	28·00
	b. Re-entry (various major)	*from*	—	55·00
	c. Plate 75, LK, "Union Jack" re-entry		£15000	£2200
	d. Double letter (various)	*from*	—	28·00
	e. Basal shift	*from*	—	28·00
	f. One or both side frames completely recut	*from*	—	28·00
	g. Notable recutting of corners or part of side frames	*from*	—	28·00
	h. Constant varieties	*from*	—	32·00

Imprimaturs: Plates 59 *to* 75, *each* £450. Stamps removed from the imprimatur sheets are: Plate 59: AA to AL, HJ to HL, IG to IL, TL; Plate 60: AA to AL, GI, GK, GL, HG to HL, TL; Plate 61: AA to AL, BD to BL, TL; Plate 62: AA to AL, BC, BE to BL, TL; Plate 63: AA to AL, GJ to GL, HG to HL, TL; Plate 64: AA to AL, FL, GG to GL, HK, HL, TL; Plate 65: AA to AL, HJ to HL, IG to IL, TL; Plate 66: AA to AL, BD to BL, TL; Plate 67: AA to AL, GG to GL, HJ to HL, TL; Plate 68: AL, BL, SE to SL, TA to TL; Plate 69: AL, JL, RG, RH, SG to SL, TA to TL; Plate 70: AA to AL, HJ to HL, IG to IL, TA; Plate 71: AL, IF to IL, JJ, JK, TA to TL; Plate 72: AL, ID, to IL, TA to TL; Plate 73: AA to AL, JK, JL, KF to KL, TL; Plate 74: AA to AL, HF to HL, HL, IK to IL, TL; Plate 75: AA to AL, GK to GL HG to HL, TL.

Plates registered: Plates 59, 60, 25 June 1845; Plates 61, 62, 14 August 1845; Plate 63, 2 September 1845; Plate 64, 3 December 1845; Plates 65, 66, 2 February 1846; Plates 67, 68, 17 April 1846; Plate 69, 8 June 1846; Plate 70, 30 June or 30 July 1846; Plates 71, 72, 21 October 1846; Plates 73, 74, 14 January 1847; Plate 75, 19 April 1847.

Plated Used Examples

Plate 59	33·00
Plate 60	25·00
Plate 61	25·00
Plate 62	25·00
Plate 63	25·00
Plate 64	25·00
Plate 65	25·00
Plate 66	25·00
Plate 67	27·00
Plate 68	27·00
Plate 69	25·00
Plate 70	25·00
Plate 71	25·00
Plate 72	25·00
Plate 73	25·00
Plate 74	25·00
Plate 75	25·00

Plating Aids

The abbreviations used in the list below and in similar lists throughout this section are as follows: ***R***, re-entry; ***D***, double letter; ***B***, basal shift; ***C***, corner or part of side frame lines recut; ***F***, one or both side frames completely recut; ***H***, horizontal guide line; ***CV***, constant variety; ***CVJ***, "J" flaw.

Plate 59: ***R***: BK, BL, IH, JG, JH, JL, MC, RK; ***D***: AL; ***CV***: A*C*, *T*F.

Plate 60: ***B***: OK, RA, SL, TA, TB; ***D***: *K*A; ***F***: NG; ***CV***: *F*E, G*K*, *I*E, M*H*, *Q*B, *T*F.

Plate 61: ***R***: EJ, EK, FL, HK, IL, JL, MK–NK; ***B***: KB, KE, LE, LK; ***CV***: *D*G, FC, FJ, IG, KH, *M*J, N*B*, *P*B, *S*I; ***CVJ***: *J*B, *J*C, *J*D, *J*F, *J*G, *J*H.

Plate 62: ***R***: AD, AE, DL, EL, QF–RF, TJ, TK; ***B***: QG; ***D***: D*K*; ***CV***: B*E*, *C*L, I*C*, JK, *P*F, SG.

Plate 63: ***R***: CL, DK, LH, TA; ***D***: A*F*; ***F***: CG; ***CV***: A*H*, *C*E, DL, *F*H, IL, LB, *M*A; ***CVJ***: *J*E, *J*F, O*J*, P*J*; Q*J*.

Plate 64; ***R***: KK, KL, MC, MK, OJ; ***D***: *F*H; ***CV***: C*A*, DL, *L*C.

Plate 65: ***R***: IG (double top), IH; ***D***: C*D*; on BD the original state has the D sharp and clear, in the second state the lower loop of the D is faint; ***CV***: A*G*, KD, QC; ***CVJ***: H*J*.

Plate 66: ***R***: JI, QH–RH, QI–RI, RJ; ***D***: A*H*; ***CV***: A*D*, ID, ME, OF, QD, *R*E, S*J* (and "J" flaw); ***CVJ***: T*J*.

Plate 67: ***R***: MK; ***CV***: AI, *G*I, HE, HF, II, LG.
Plate 68: ***R***: HA; ***B***: ML, SB, SL; ***D***: GJ; ***CV***: B*G*, I*A*.
Plate 69: ***R***: SE; ***F***: AK; ***CV***: AL, *J*E, NF.
Plate 70: ***R***: HD, MJ; ***D***: *K*B; ***CV***: AA, *F*C, H*L*, *K*I, MF, *O*A.
Plate 71: ***R***: SG, TG; ***D***: M*D*, R*H*; ***CV***: *M*J, TD.
Plate 72: ***R***: HJ, LJ, PA; ***D***: GK; Recut letter, J*A*; ***CV***: *F*F, H*D*, KE, *Q*K, *T*C, *T*K; ***CVJ***: MJ to Q*J*.
Plate 73: ***R***: FJ, JC; ***D***: A*F*, *A*G, *R*B; ***CV***: *E*C, *J*E, *O*B.
Plate 74: ***R***: FD, GD, HJ, LG, LH, SG; ***CV***: *J*E, JK.
Plate 75: "Union Jack" re-entry, LK; ***R***: EA, EB, NF, RA; ***D***: *L*D, *R*E; ***F***: LE; ***C***: PC, QE, QG, QL, RL, TD; ***CV***: BC, BG, I*A*, *T*H; ***CVJ***: K*J*.

DOUBLE LETTER

CD — MD — RH — AF — AG — RE, *Plate* 75

Plate 65 — *Plate* 71 — *Plate* 73

RE-ENTRIES

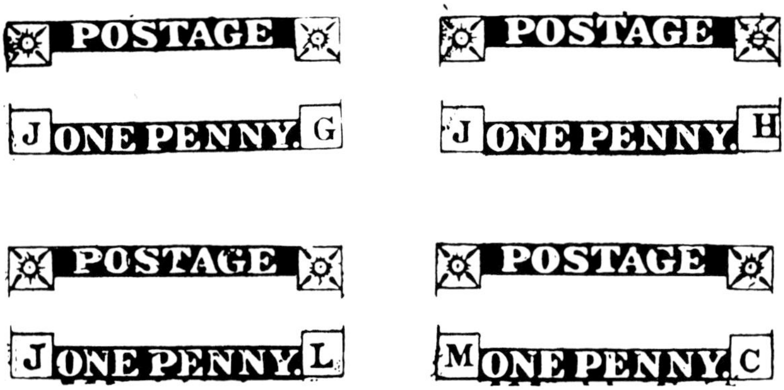

Plate 59

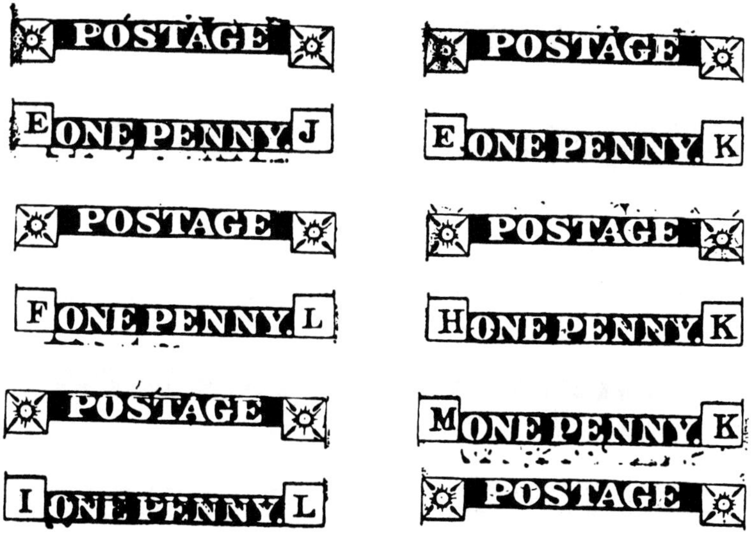

(MK–NK)

Plate 61

Plate 62

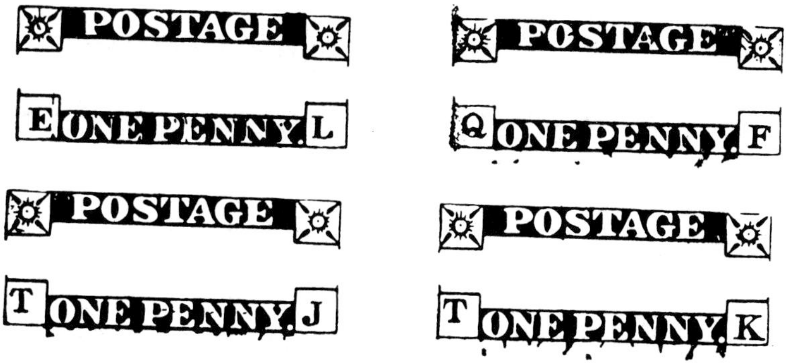

Plate 62

CL

DL

Plate 63

Plate 64

Plate 65 (*Re-entries*)

First State

Second State

Plate 65

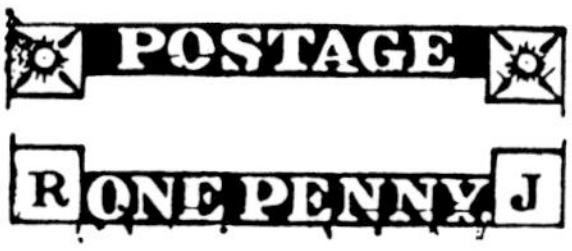

Plate 66

Plate 68

Plate 69

Plate 71

Plate 73

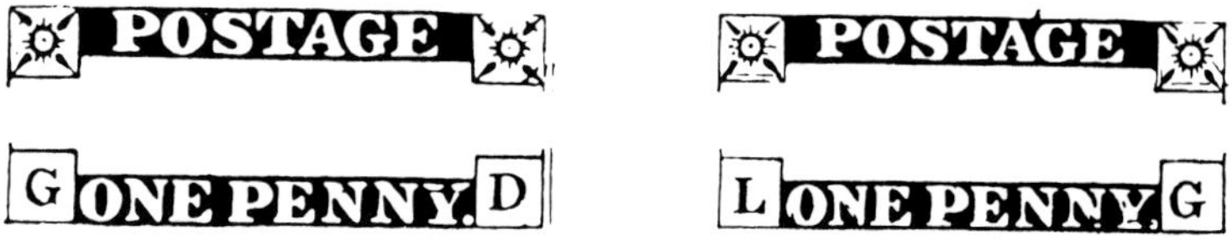

Plate 74

Plate 74

Plate 75

Plate 75, *"Union Jack" re-entry*

CONSTANT VARIETIES

AC TF

Plate 59

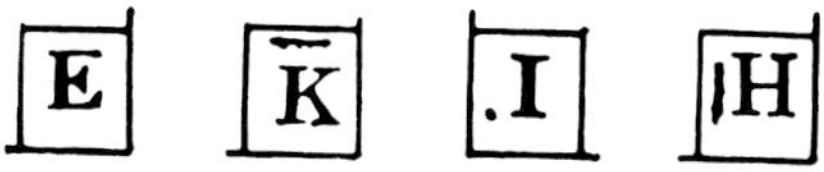

FE GK IE MH

Plate 60

QB TF

Plate 60

DG FC FJ IG

Plate 61

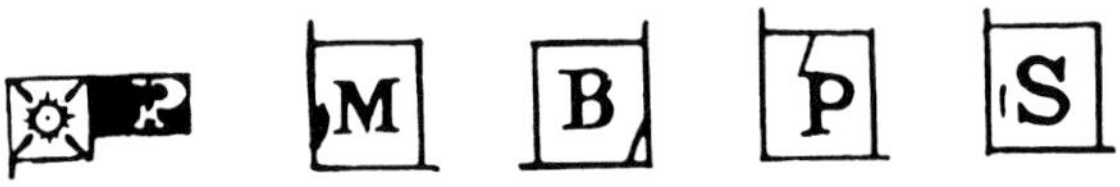

KH MJ NB PB SI

Plate 61

BE CL IC JK PF SG

Plate 62

AH CE FH IL LB MA

Plate 63

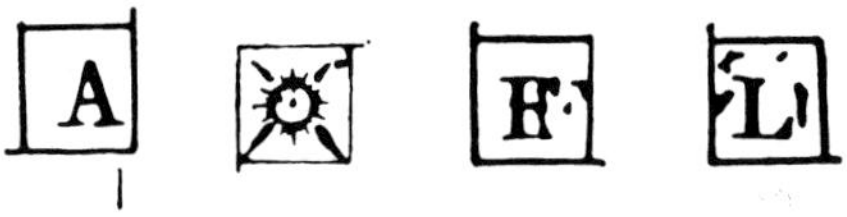

CA DL FH LC

Plate 64

AG KD QC AD ID (*flaw on neck*)

Plate 65 *Plate* 66

ME

OF (*triangular flaw below ear*)

QD (*flaw on check*)

RE

SJ

Plate 66

AI

GI

HE

HF

II

Plate 67

LG

Plate 67

BG

IA

Plate 68

AL

JE

NF

Plate 69

AA

FC

HL

KI

MF

OA

Plate 70

MJ

TD

Plate 71

FF

HD

KE

Plate 72

QK

TC

TK

Plate 67

EC

JE

OB

Plate 73

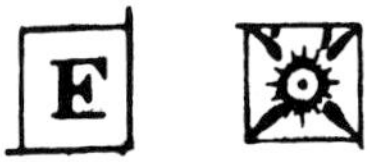

JE JK

Plate 74

BC BG IA TH

Plate 75

One Penny Die I, Plates 76 to 87 (April 1847 to October 1848)

Plate 76. In previous groups retouching of side lines, corners, etc., has been common; the present group includes a plate (Plate 76) where nearly every stamp has been provided with a thicker frame. This plate can be confused with Plate 90 of the next group but does have distinctive letters. In Plate 76 spreading of POSTAGE by burnishing is noticeable on BI, FH, FI, FL, GC, GD and similarly the E of PENNY is extended on KB, KC, LL, MD, ND, NE, PB, PE, EH to EL and some others show burrs. The letters A and E are broad and the J square-footed throughout Plate 76.

Malformed or Badly Misplaced Letters are prevalent throughout the group, Plates 79 and 80 being particularly notable for blind letters and other unsightly peculiarities. This has been ascribed to the plates having not been adequately softened so that the punches (of which a new set was used for Plate 79 onwards) were struck more heavily, causing slight depressions which trapped surplus ink. Every R on Plates 83, 86, 87 had the tail hand-cut. Recut frames are prevalent on Plate 77 as well as on Plate 76, already mentioned.

Missing Letter. A major error occurred on Plate 77. When it was laid down the stamp "BA" had the "A" omitted so that it is describable as "B blank". The "A" was added at a later date to make the stamp normal. It can be found in both states but the "B blank" state exists with only 26 examples known.

Inverted S. All the Ss on Plate 78 were inverted. Two later plates, 105 and 107, also have this peculiarity and readers are referred to the notes on them in their group, Plates 102 to 131.

BS29	1d. red-brown (shades)	*from*	25·00
	a. "B blank" (Plate 77)		£10000
	b. BA Plate 77b ("B blank", Plate 77, corrected)		£1500
	c. Re-entry (various major)	*from*	60·00
	d. Double letter (various)	*from*	30·00
	e. Blind or malformed letter		30·00
	f. P converted to R (hand-cut tail)		70·00
	g. Heavy outer frame (major retouching, Plate 76)		25·00
	h. Inverted "S", (Plate 78)		£120
	i. Basal shift	*from*	30·00
	j. One or both side frames completely recut	*from*	28·00
	k. Notable recutting of corners or part of side frames	*from*	28·00
	l. Constant varieties		35·00

Imprimaturs: Plates 76 *to* 87, *each* £650. Stamps removed from the imprimatur sheets are: Plate 76: AA to AL, BD to BL, TL; Plate 77: AA to AL, BE to BL, TK, TL (B blank still present); Plate 77b: AA to AL, RG to RL, SJ to SL, TL (BA present); Plate 78: AA to AL, BD to BL, TL; Plate 79: AA to AL, BE to BL, TK, TL; Plate 80: AA to AL, BD to BL, TL; Plate 81: AA to AL, BD to BL, TL: Plate 82: AA to AL, BD to BL, TL; Plate 83: AA to AL, BD to BL, TL; Plate 84: AA to AL, GK, GL, HF to HL, TL; Plate 85: AA to AL, FL, GG to GL, HK, HL, TL; Plate 86: AA to AL, II, IK, IL, JG to JL, TL; Plate 87: AA to AL, GJ to GL, HG to HL, TL.

Plates registered: Plates 76, 77, 19 April 1847; Plates 77b, 78 to 83, 12 January 1848; Plates 84 to 87, 11 October 1848.

Plated Used Examples

Plate 76	25·00	Plate 82	30·00
Plate 77	25·00	Plate 83	30·00
Plate 78	25·00	Plate 84	25·00
Plate 79	25·00	Plate 85	25·00
Plate 80	25·00	Plate 86	25·00
Plate 81	25·00	Plate 87	25·00

Plating Aids

For details of the abbreviations used see page 133.

Plate 76: ***R***: BD, CB, EH, EI, JK, MA, NE; ***D***: *AA*, *AB*, A*H*, A*J*, *B*B, H*D*, *J*B, K*D*, L*D*, *L*L, P*J*; ***CV***: BK, *C*I, *D*F, *G*A, GB, JE, OF, *P*B, QF. The recutting of side frames on Plate 76 was general so that it is necessary to mention only those stamps which are not wholly "framed". Three stamps show no signs of recutting: BL, EG, EL; stamps with only one side recut are EF, ML, PE, QA, QC; stamps with incomplete recutting but with both sides affected: OG, OK, OL.

Plate 77: ***R***: IK, LA; ***D***: *S*D; ***F***: (both sides recut), EC, ED, GD, TE, TL; ***C***: (mainly cases of one frame entirely recut): CB, CI, CJ, EE, EG, EH, FB, FC, GE, GK, HG, II, JI, JJ, KJ, LE, LI, LJ, MB, MD, OI, RB, RE, RJ, SC, SE, SF, SH, TC; NA (N recut very large); ***CV***: C*F*, F*G*, *Q*K.

Plate 78: ***D***: *E*J, *C*L, *F*C, H*E*; Letter Varieties: SA to SL (all Ss inverted); IB (B recut); ***C***: FF, OB, QC; ***CV***: A*B*, AL, *E*G, F*H*, L*C*, *L*D, *M*A, *R*I.

Plate 79: ***R***: SC; ***D***: B*G*, B*I*, *D*G, *D*L, H*G*, I*H*; ***CV***: *A*C, *C*A, *F*C, *I*A, I*H*, L*H*, *T*I.

Plate 80: ***R***: JK, KL; ***D***: B*B*, D*J*, *E*B, F*G*, G*H*, L*K*, M*H*, P*H*; ***CV***: *T*K. CJ has letter C recut and very large.

Plate 81: ***R***: EL, HC, HI; TI (second state) showing a weakness in the upper left corner, in the original state the corner fine is stronger; ***D***: C*D*, *G*J, KG, QG; ***C***: *K*A, ME; ***CV***: K*E*, *N*H, R*K*.

Plate 82: ***R***: IK, NK: ***D***: A*D*; ***C***: SH; ***CV***: O*C*, *T*F, T*J*.

Plate 83: ***R***: HK, IC, ID, IE, IF, IJ, IL, JB, KK, LK; ***C***: DI, LF; ***CV***: HI, OF; all Rs with hand-cut tails.

Plate 84: ***R***: EI, HJ, HK, IE, JJ, SH, SK, TA, TE, TH, TJ; ***D***: C*E*, C*F*, D*G*, I*C*, *O*C; ***B***: LJ, NH; NG (N recut very large); ***CV***: L*H*.

Plate 85: ***R***: AK–BK, CB, DA–EA, LK–MK, SF; ***D***: P*G*; C*F*, *L*E, T*A*, *T*D.

Plate 86: ***R***: EL; FB to FF and FH have "POSTAGE" affected by burr rub damage. All Rs with hand-cut tails; ***CV***: MG, *P*I.

Plate 87: ***R***: EI, GI, JJ, LK–MK; ***C***: BI, BJ; ***CV***: AH, CL, *N*G; all Rs with hand-cut tails.

ERROR

Letter A *omitted, stamp* B(A), *Plate* 77

Letter A *inserted, stamp* BA, *Plate* 77b

VARIETIES AND MALFORMED LETTERS

AA

AH

BB

HD

KD

LD

PJ

Double letters, Plate 76

SD, *double letter, Plate* 77

Inverted S, *stamps* SA *to* SL, *Plate* 78

EJ, *double letter, Plate* 78

IB, *recut* B, *Plate* 78

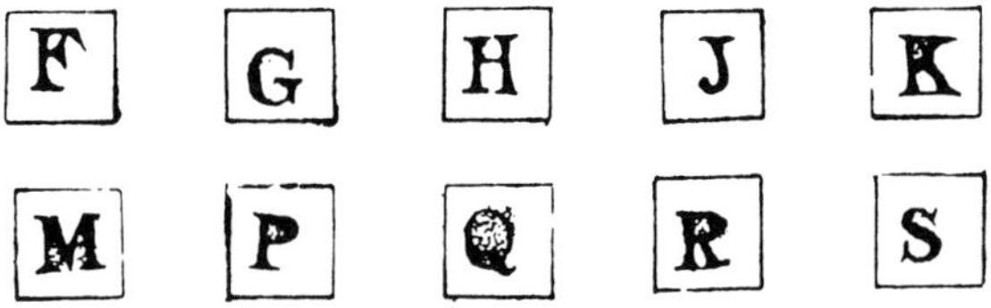

Characteristic malformed letters, Plate 79

Characteristic malformed letters, Plate 80

DJ EB FG GH LK MH PH

Double letters, Plate 80

RE-ENTRIES

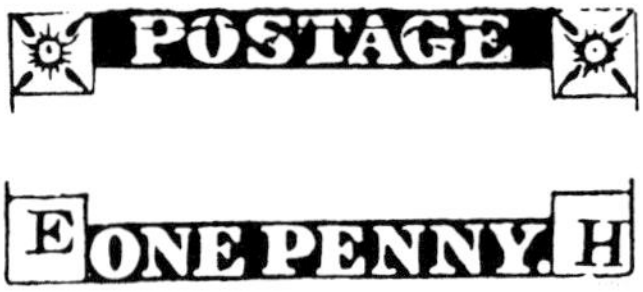

Re-entry; note also the enlarged (recut) M

Plate 76

Plate 76

Plate 77

Plate 79

Plate 80

Plate 80

Plate 81

Plate 81

Plate 82

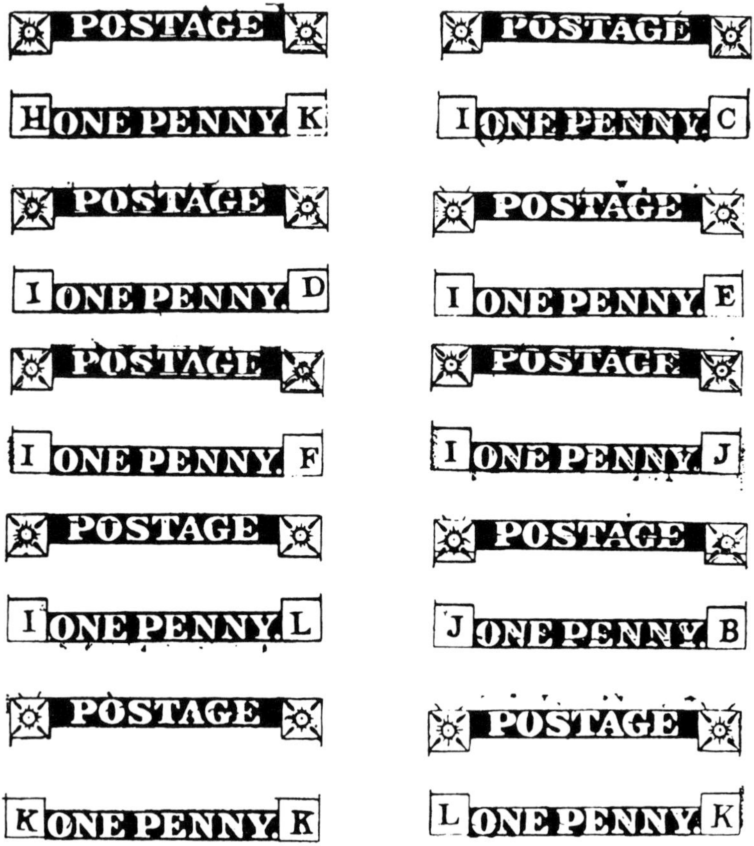

Plate 83

EI

Plate 84

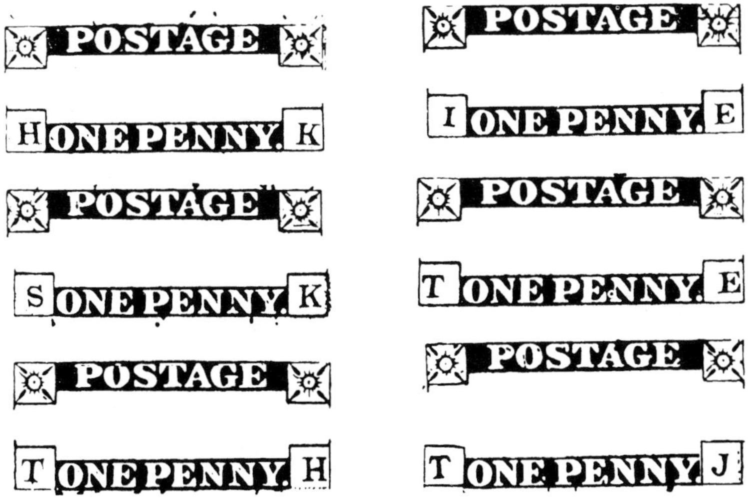

Plate 84

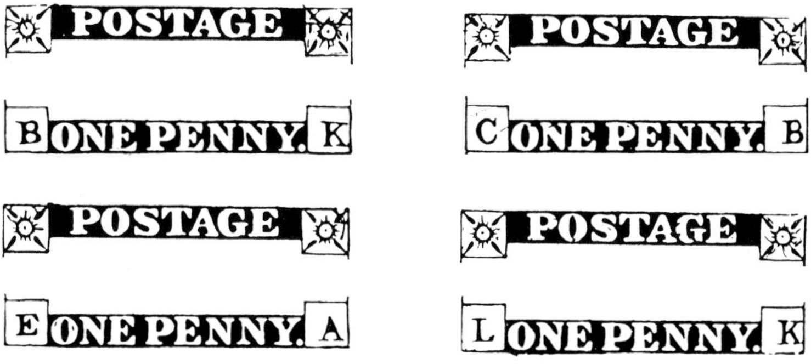

Plate 85

Plate 85

EI

Plate 87

Plate 87

CONSTANT VARIETIES

BK

CI

JE

GB

PB

DF

GA

OF

QF

Plate 76

CF, *long lower serif*

FG

QK

Plate 77

AB

AL

Plate 78

EG

FH

LC

LD, *long lower serif*

MA

RI

Plate 78

AC

CA

FC

IA

IH

LH

TI

Plate 79

CJ
Plate 80

TK

KA, *recut corner,*
Plate 81

KE

NH
Plate 81

RA

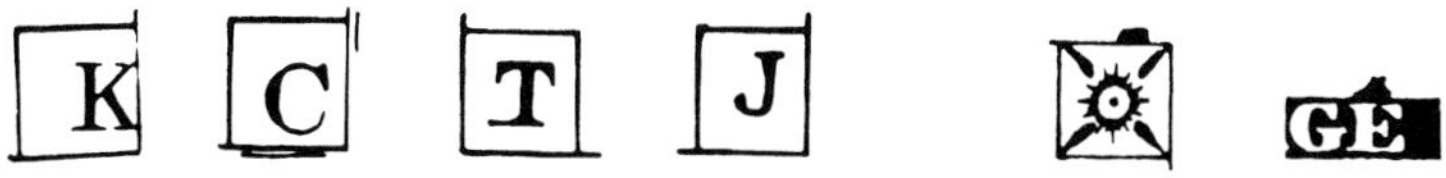

RK, *misplaced* K, OC — *Plate* 81; TF, TJ — *Plate* 83; HI, OF — *Plate* 83

LH, *Plate* 84; NG, N *recut*, *Plate* 84; CF, LE, TA, TD — *Plate* 85

MG, PI — *Plate* 86; AH, CL, NG — *Plate* 87

One Penny Die, I, Plates 88 to 91 (March to May 1849)

The Postage Stamps of Great Britain, Part I, gives numerous details whereby a number of the stamps of Plates 88 and 89 can be recognized. General distinctive features are not many but it can be said that the letters are neater and cleaner than in the previous group; though still often misplaced in their squares. There is a distinct tendency for the left letter to be to the left of its square. Plate 90 is the prominently "framed" plate mentioned above in connection with Plate 76. In Plate 90 every stamp has recut frame lines except BL, recut on left only. Stamps from this plate differ from those of Plate 76 in that the frames are thicker and the letters smaller. The J is rounded. Misplaced letters are again frequent.

BS30	1d. red-brown (shades)	*from*	—	28·00
	a. Re-entries, various	*from*	—	60·00
	b. Double letters	*from*		32·00
	c. Heavy outer frames (major retouching)		—	28·00
	d. One or both sides completely recut (Plate 88)	*from*	—	28·00
	e. Prominent recutting of corners or part of side frames (Plate 88)	*from*	—	28·00
	f. Constant varieties		—	35·00
	s. "Specimen", Type 1 (Plate 90)		£3000	

Plate 88 overprinted "Specimen" Type 1 has never been seen but there was a photograph of a complete sheet in the Berlin Postal Museum.

Imprimaturs: Plates 88 *to* 91, *each* £650. Stamps removed from the imprimatur sheets are: Plate 88: AA to AL, HJ to HL, IG to IL, TL; Plate 89: AA to AL, HL, IG to IL, JK, JL, TL; Plate 90: AA to AL, FL, GG to GL, HK, HL, TL; Plate 91; AA to AL, GK, GL, HF to HL, TL.

Plates registered: Plates 88, 89, 20 March 1849; Plates 90, 91, 24 May 1849.

Plated Used Examples

Plate 88	30·00	Plate 90	28·00
Plate 89	30·00	Plate 91	28·00

Plating Aids

For details of the abbreviations used see page 133.

Plate 88: ***R***: BL, LA, ***D***: *G*F, K*G*, Q*L*, ***CV***: B*J*, C*I*, *DK*, *KE*, *P*A, *PC*, *T*L; Both sides recut: LC, LD, ME, MG, OD, OG, OH; left side recut: KH, LE, LH, MF, MH, NH, OE, OF, OI, OJ, OK, OL; right side recut: DG, IG, LB, LG, MD, NG. Recutting of corner squares was widespread and prominent. The letters are usually well shaped but often struck at an angle and there is a tendency for the left letter to be at the left of its square. The J is rounded. All As are blind except HA, IA, KA. The spacing between G and H vertical rows was very contracted. Notably ill-placed letters appear on A*D*, *D*B, *E*F, *G*F, H*C*, *HJ*, J*C*, J*D*, J*K*, *K*I, M*D*, Q*J*, S*D*, *T*I.

Plate 89: ***R***: EG. Recutting was restricted to the corner squares which were all recut. The K is of slightly "Gothic" appearance, J rounded, E larger. ***CV***: *D*G, *F*C, G*K*, I*F*, I*K*, *OA*, *Q*K.

Plate 90: ***R***: ID, TB. Every stamp has recut frames except BL, recut on left only. Letters are usually clear and clean but often misplaced. Extreme examples are A*F*, A*H* (in both the foregoing cases A is blind), *D*C, E*B*, F*D*, H*D*, H*E*, *L*H, *M*H, N*F*, *N*I, P*J*; ***CV***: A*B*, *G*L, IG. The recut frame lines are thicker than on Plate 76 but some confusion may occur with fully recut stamps from Plate 88.

Plate 91: ***CV***: *B*L, E*F*, OB, TA, T*J*.

RE-ENTRIES

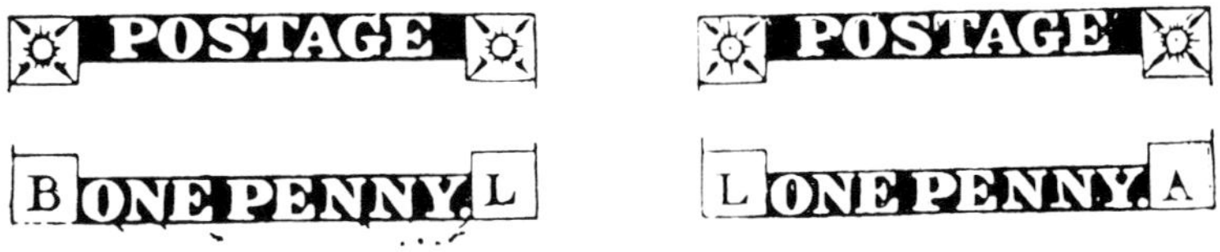

Plate 88

Plate 90

CONSTANT VARIETIES, ETC.

GF KG
Double letters, Plate 88

HJ TI
Misplaced letters, Plate 88

IG, *recut at right, Plate* 88

BJ

CI

DK

Plate 88

KE PA PC TL

Plate 88

DG FC GK IF IK

Plate 89

AB GL IG

Plate 90

BL EF OB TA TJ

Plate 91

One Penny Die I, Plates 92 to 101 (May 1849 to February 1850)

This group of plates is often loosely referred to as "Archers" because all were used by Henry Archer in his experimental perforating. See Section CA.

Characteristics common to the group as a whole are: shades generally in the pale red class, dark colours unusual; the check letters are small but much better cut than the previous group; with the exception of "O" and "Q" which are always upright, the placing of the letters was not usually straight; all corner squares were recut with consequent prevalence of extended frame lines; minor varieties such as marks, blurs and dots are common and are useful plating aids (there are not very many of these on Plates 95 and 96). Blocks are not uncommon except from Plate 99 which is scarce thus. Guide dots appear between AF and AG, FF and FG, OF and OG on Plates 92 to 98. They do not appear on Plates 99 to 101. These dots are at the top of the stamps in A and O rows and at the bottom in F row.

Readers are referred to Dr. Gardiner-Hill's *Archer Plates* for details of many minor varieties on Plates 92 to 101.

BS31	1d. red-brown (shades) . . . . . *from*	—	30·00
	a. Re-entry . . . . . *from*	—	65·00
	b. Double letter		32·00
	c. Notable recutting and/or extension of corner lines or partial recutting of side frame lines	—	35·00
	d. One or both sides completely recut		35·00
	e. Constant varieties . . . . . *from*	—	45·00
	s. "Specimen", Type 1 (Plate 95)	£3000	

Imprimaturs: Plates 92 *to* 101, *each* £700. Stamps removed from the imprimatur sheets are: Plate 92: AA to AL, HI, HK, HL, IG to IL, TL; Plate 93; AA to AL, GK, GL, HG to HL, IL, TL; Plate 94: AA to AL, GK, GL, HG to HL, IL, TL; Plate 95: AA to AL, FL, GG to GL, HK, HL, TL; Plate 96: AA to AL, FK, FL, GG to GL, HL, TL; Plate 97: AA to AL, HJ to HL, IG to IL, TL; Plate 98: AA to AL, GI, GK, GL, HG to HL, TL; Plate 99: AA to AL, HF to HL, IK, IL, TL; Plate 100: AA to AL, GI, GK, GL, HG to HL, TL; Plate 101: AA to AL, GJ to GL, HG to HL, TL.

Plates registered: Plate 92, 24 May 1849; Plates 93, 94, 96, 97, 98, 6 December 1849; Plates 95, 99, 7 January 1850; Plates 100, 101, 25 February 1850.

Plated Used Examples

Plate 92	35·00	Plate 97	30·00
Plate 93	30·00	Plate 98	30·00
Plate 94	30·00	Plate 99	40·00
Plate 95	30·00	Plate 100	33·00
Plate 96	30·00	Plate 101	30·00

Plating Aids

For details of the abbreviations used see page 133.

Plate 92: ***R***: AA, AG; ***D***: I*J*, L*I*; ***CV***: AC, B*F*, C*E*, C*J*, EJ, F*D*, I*D*, *P*A.

Plate 93: ***C***: AH, GB, IA, IB, NJ; ***F***: LA, MA, NA, OA, PA, QK, TA: ***D***: P*F*; ***CV***: B*E*, N*C*, TL.

Plate 94: ***C***: AA, AI, BD, BJ, DD, EB, ED, FC, HB, IA, IF, JD, LB, MF, ND, OD, OF, PJ, QC, QD, QL, RC, RD; ***F***: AK, IE, PL; ***CV***: AC, *B*C, DC, H*C*, *I*C, J*I*, K*E*, L*L*, *M*K, NF, O*E*, O*F*, *O*G, O*I*, *QC*.

Plate 95: ***R***: EJ; ***F***: TA; **C**: BD, BH, FJ, IB, IH, NA, ND, SK; ***CV***: B*F*, *D*B, *E*H, F*E*, *I*F, *JG*, K*E*, *NF*, *P*K, QA, T*D*–*T*E.

Plate 96: ***R***: TB; ***D***: *C*G, M*J*; ***C***: CB, JA, SI, TA; ***CV***: A*C*, AF, A*K*, *E*K, *K*B, MA, *P*I, Q*D*.

Plate 97: ***C***: LJ, RJ; ***CV***: *E*G, F*K*, *K*B, *L*D, M*A*, *N*A, N*B*, NJ, P*E*, R*A*, S*K*.

Plate 98: ***R***: AH, AL; ***D***: *G*L, L*G*; ***C***: BH, FA, GD, HD, JF, NH, OB, PH, SH, TG; ***F***: JH, TH; ***CV***: CA, *D*F, F*D*, GF, K*E*, *LK*, MI, *MK*, *O*F, OI, *P*A, *P*D, S*C*, S*D*.

Plate 99: ***R***: JD, SF; ***D***: CC; ***C***: AD, AJ, FJ; ***CV***: C*A*, *G*C, J*J*, L*I*, *L*J, *M*E, *M*G, *M*J, R*J*, SJ.

Plate 100: ***C***: AG, AK, DL, EK, GL, HL, LF; ***CV***: A*D*, B*D*, *D*J, *E*L, *F*I, GC, *H*E, H*I*, IC, K*K*, MD, *N*F, O*E*, *P*A, *PL*, RC, T*L*.

Plate 101: ***C***: BC, EB, IJ, JI; ***CV***: *A*J, *B*C, C*B*, *F*C, GC, IG, J*D*, K*E*, LE, MA, *N*A, OD, QD, SA, SE, TB.

RE-ENTRIES

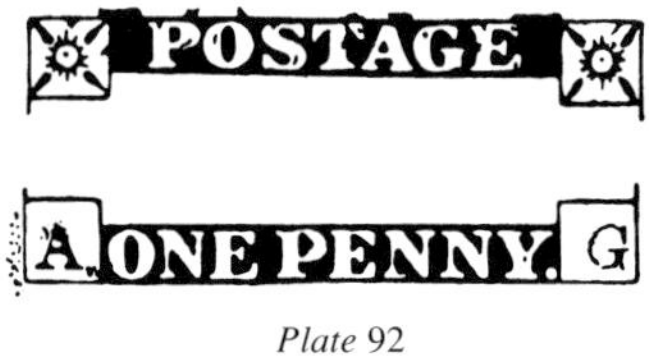

Plate 92

Plate 95

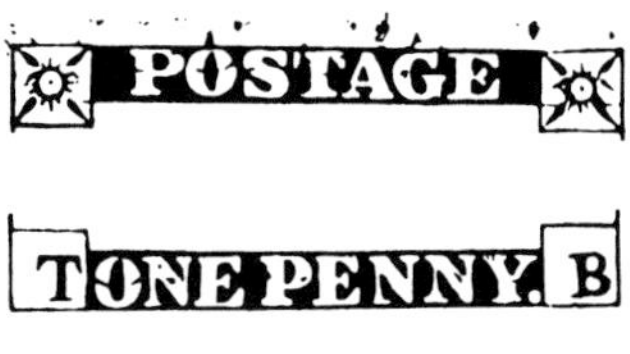

Plate 96

CONSTANT VARIETIES

AC BF CE CJ EJ FD

Plate 92

ID PA BE NC PF TL

Plate 92 *Plate* 93

AC BC DC HC IC

JI KE LL MK

Plate 94

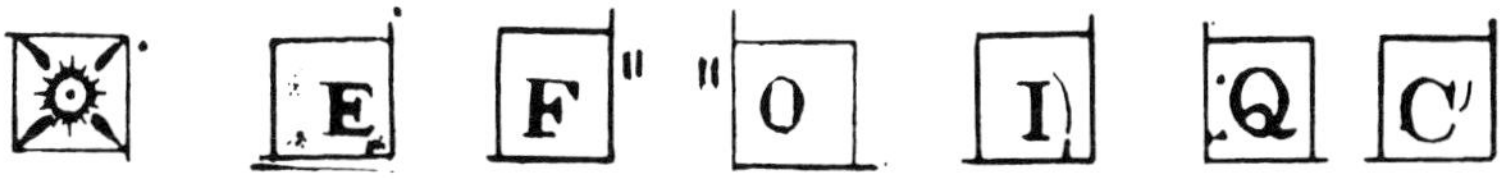

NF OE OF OG OI QC

Plate 94

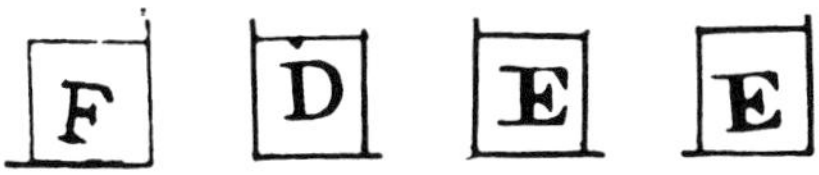

BF DB EH FE

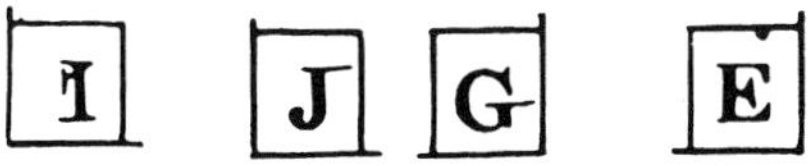

IF JG KE

Plate 95

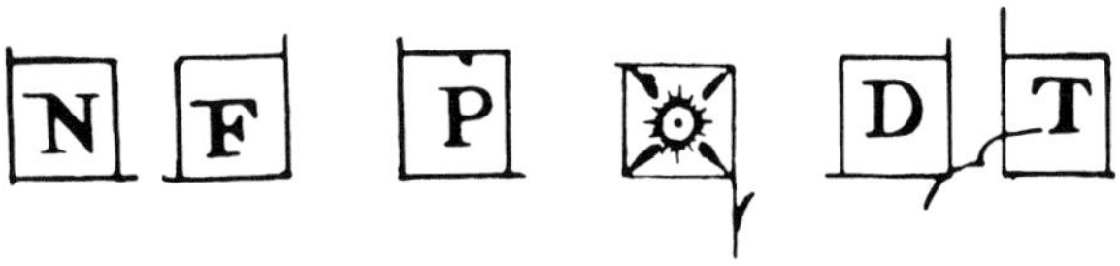

NF PK QA TD–TE

Plate 95

AC AF AK EK KB

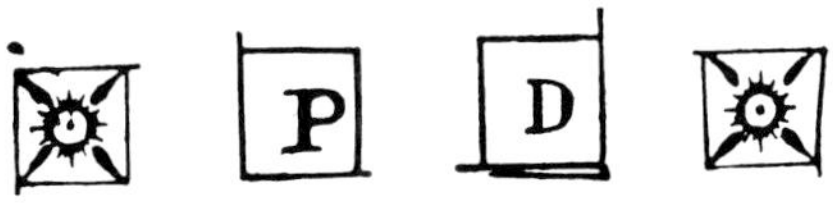

MA PI QD TA

Plate 96

EG FK KB LD MA

NA NB NJ PE RA SK

Plate 97

CA DF FD GF KE

LK MI MK OF

Plate 98

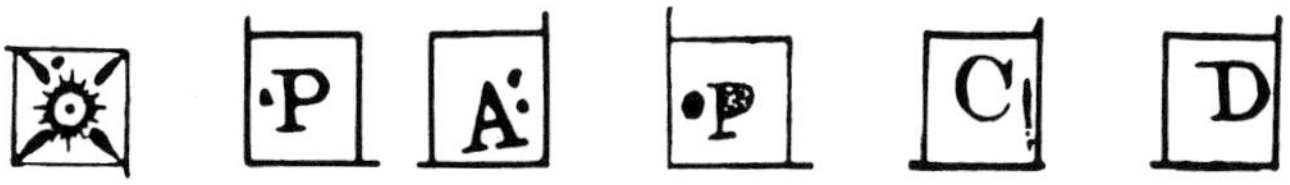

OI PA PD SC SD

Plate 98

CA GC JJ LI LJ

ME MG MJ RJ SJ

Plate 99

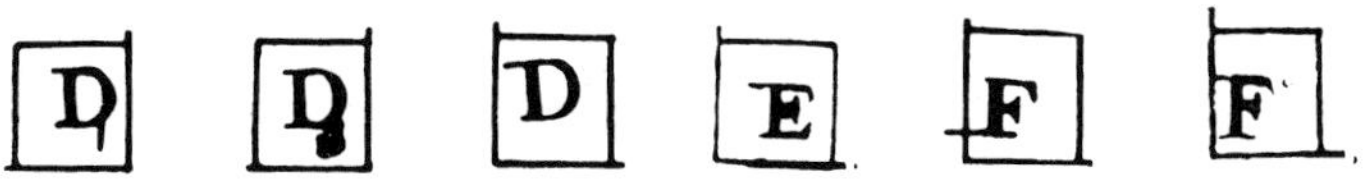

AD BD DJ EL FI FK

GC HE HI IC KK MD

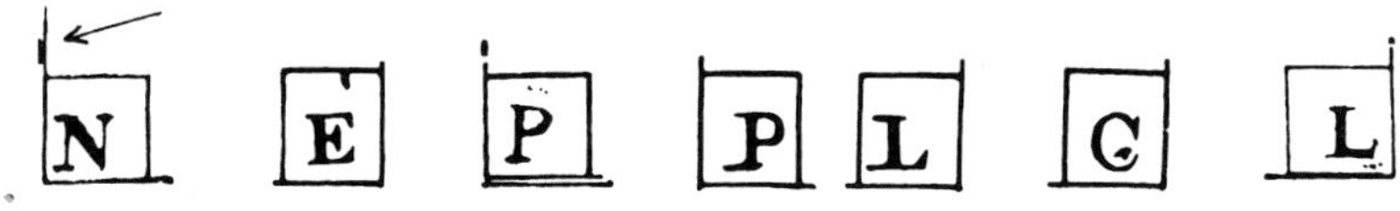

NF OE PA PL RC TL

Plate 100

AJ BC CB FC GC IG

Plate 101

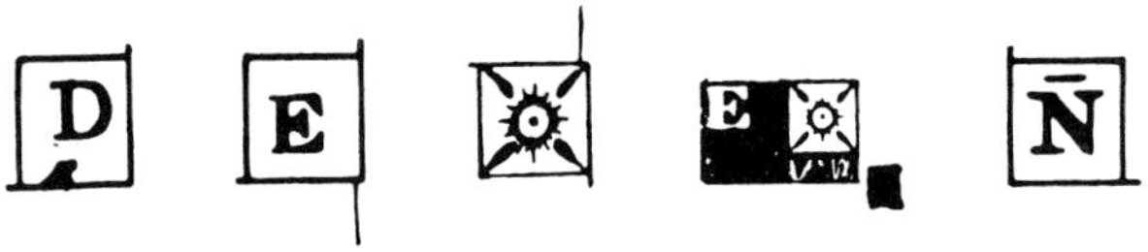

JD KE LE MB NA

Plate 101

OD QD SA SE TB

Plate 101

One Penny Die I, Plates 102 to 131 (July 1850 to October 1851)

This is not an easy group for the would-be plater. There are few group characteristics other than that all of the corner squares have been recut and the corner letters are uniformly small, well-cut and lightly outlined. There are hardly any double letters. From Plate 125 onwards the letters become slightly larger and more heavily cut and can be recognized at sight.

Shades are varied from pale red to deep red-brown. Plate 131 is frequently found in brick-red on very pale blue paper.

Lavender-Tinted Paper. Stamps used from about June 1851 can be found on a lavender-tinted paper of more than usual thickness. These are listed under No. B1*l*, Alphabet I and form an identifiable sub-issue for specialists. The same paper was used for printings of the 1d. Alphabet II (see No. B2*k*) and the 2d. Plate 4 (No. ES16). For further details see Section E, Plate 4.

All the Ss on Plates 105 and 107 are inverted. Compared with the corners of Plate 78, which also showed inverted Ss, the corners of Plates 105 and 107 are strong. In Chapter 15 of *The Postage Stamps of Great Britain, Part I,* there is a helpful list giving the positions of the corner letters on all S row stamps in Plates 78, 105 and 107.

In this group Plate 116 is the only plate showing a notable general feature throughout. A definite break is seen in the line of colour separating the letter P of POSTAGE from the upper margin. Though not always constant, this break is clear in the worn state of the plate.

On Plate 131 a notable coloured flaw, caused by a faulty roller die, showed on all stamps of the first vertical column from GA down to TA, in every stamp of the second column, AB down to TB, and also on AC, BC, and CC. The flaw takes the form of a gross enlargement of the 1 o'clock ray of the NE corner star.

Readers are referred to the late Dr. Gardiner-Hill's *Plates 102–131* for fuller information on the more minor varieties of this group.

BS32		1d. red-brown (shades)	*from*	30·00
	a.	Re-entry	*from*	75·00
	b.	"1 o'clock" roller die flaw (Plate 131)		45·00
	c.	Inverted "S" (Plate 105, 124)	*from*	£125
	ca.	Inverted "S" (Plate 107)		£300
	d.	"P" flaw (Plate 116)		45·00
	f.	Double letter	*from*	45·00
	g.	Partial recutting of side frame lines	*from*	40·00
	h.	One or both sides completely recut	*from*	40·00
	j.	Constant varieties	*from*	45·00

Imprimaturs: Plates 102 *to* 131, *each* £650. The Plate 129 imprimatur sheet has the watermark inverted. Stamps removed from the imprimatur sheets are: Plate 102: AA to AL, BD to BL, TL; Plate 103: AA to AL, BE to BL, TL; Plate 104: AA to AL, BE to BL, TL; Plate 105: AA to AL, BA to BH, TL; Plate 106: AA to AL, BE to BL, TL; Plate 107: AL, GK, GL, HG to HL, TA to TL; Plate 108:AL, HK, HL, IG to IL, TA to TL; Plate 109: AL, GK, GL, HG to HL, TA to TL; Plate 110: AL, GK, GL, HG to HL, TA to TL; Plate 111: AL, JK, JL, KG to KL, TA to TL; Plate 112: AL, IK, IL, JG to JL, TA to TL; Plate 113: AL, SE to SL, TA to TL; Plate 114: AA to AL, IK, IL, JG to JL, TL; Plate 115:

AA to AL, IK, IL, JG to JL, TL; Plate 116: AA to AL, HK, HL, IG to IL, TL; Plate 117: AA to AL, FL, GG to GL, HL, TL; Plate 118: AL, JK, JL, KG to KL, TA to TL; Plate 119: AA to AL, GK, GL, HG to HL, TL; Plate 120: AA to AL, SE to SL, TL; Plate 121: AA to AL, RK, RL, SG to SL, TL; Plate 122: AA to AL, JK, JL, KG to KL, TL; Plate 123: AA to AL, JK, JL, KG to KL, TL; Plate 124: AA to AL, JK, JL, KG to KL, TL; Plate 125: AA to AL, QK, QL, RG to RL, TL; Plate 126: AA to AL, GK, GL, HG to HL, TL; Plate 127: AL, RL, SF to SL, TA to TL; Plate 128: AA to AL, HK, HL, IG to IL, TL; Plate 129: AA to AL, GK, GL, HG to HL, TL; Plate 130: AA to AL, GK, GL, HG to HL, TL; Plate 131: AA to AL, HK, HL, IG to IL, TL.

Plates registered: Plates 102 to 106, June 1850; Plates 107 to 112, 1 January 1851; Plates 113 to 115, 26 February 1851; Plates 116 to 121, 20 May 1851; Plates 122 to 125, 25 July 1851; Plates 126 to 131, 23 September 1851.

Plated Used Examples

Plate 102	30·00
Plate 103	33·00
Plate 104	33·00
Plate 105	37·00
Plate 106	33·00
Plate 107	£250
Plate 108	37·00
Plate 109	50·00
Plate 110	50·00
Plate 111	37·00
Plate 112	30·00
Plate 113	33·00
Plate 114	45·00
Plate 115	40·00
Plate 116	30·00
Plate 117	45·00
Plate 118	30·00
Plate 119	30·00
Plate 120	37·00
Plate 121	30·00
Plate 122	30·00
Plate 123	33·00
Plate 124	30·00
Plate 125	30·00
Plate 126	30·00
Plate 127	30·00
Plate 128	30·00
Plate 129	37·00
Plate 130	33·00
Plate 131	33·00

Plating Aids

The abbreviations used in the list below and in similar lists throughout this section are as follows: ***R***, re-entry; ***D***, double letter; ***B***, basal shift; ***C***, corner or part of side frame lines recut; ***F***, one or both side frames completely recut; ***H***, horizontal guide line; ***CV***, constant variety; ***CVJ***. “J” flaw.

Plate 102: ***C***: BF, BH, *C*B, CC, GA, MA, MB, OB, OD, PB; ***F***: AF, AG; ***CV***: M*D*, PG.
Plate 103: ***C***: IL, MD; ***CV***: *A*A, O*C*.
Plate 104: ***C***: DJ, EA, PJ; ***CV***: A*E*, *A*F, FL, *G*A, G*B*, *SE*.
Plate 105: ***C***: AB, BD, CA, CB, DB, EA, EB; ***CV***: E*E*, *NH*, SI, All Ss inverted.
Plate 106: ***C***: CK, ***CV***: *A*D, *A*H, B*E*, *L*E, *O*C, *R*L, T*G*.
Plate 107: ***D***: F*I*; ***C***: AB, EB, HB; ***CV***: *L*D. All Ss inverted.
Plate 108: ***CV***: DE, *F*C, *I*C, *Q*G, *S*I.
Plate 109: ***CV***: *F*K, *L*A, *R*H, SD, *S*G, *S*K.
Plate 110: ***R***: TL; ***CV***: A*G*, *D*A, HG, *K*C.
Plate 111: ***C***: BK, CB, NB; ***F***: KK; ***CV***: D*E*, FC.
Plate 112: ***C***: JI, TJ; ***CV***: *A*L, N*I*, P*B*, Q*C*.
Plate 113: ***R***: TD, TE; ***CV***: CI, HG, *K*D, *L*C, O*K*, P*G*, R*E*, R*G*.
Plate 114: ***R***: RC; ***C***, RF; ***CV***: *C*H, *I*K, O*H*, T*F*.
Plate 115: ***CV***: G*E*, L*J*, M*C*.
Plate 116: ***CV***: C*D*, HL, *Q*D, *Q*E, R*F*, R*I*, RL.
Plate 117: ***C***: AF, AJ; ***CV***: ML, R*H*, TL
Plate 118: ***C***: 65 stamps; ***F***: IA, IB, IG, KH, KK, QA, QB, RA, RB; ***CV***: I*L*, T*G*.
Plate 119: ***C***: FG, ID, KD, MH, QD, QH, SD, SH, TC, TK; ***CV***: *D*A, HL, I*A*, IE, M*C*, O*B*.
Plate 120: ***C***: BB, BF, BI, BJ, BK, CB, EB, FB, *F*K, GB, HB, IB, JA, JB, KB, LB, MA, MB, MK, NB, NK, NL, OH, OJ, PA, PI, PJ, QJ, RL, SA, TA; ***F***: AF, AI, AJ, KA, OK, OL; ***CV***: *A*A, FJ, QF.
Plate 121: ***C***: CF, DD, EE, EF, FD, FF, HF, IJ, LB, LD, LE, LF, MD, MF, NF, PB, QA, QB, QD, QE, RB, RD, SB, SD, SF, TA, TB, TD, TE; ***CV***: PH, SK.
Plate 122: ***R***: ND; ***C***: AA, BA, CD, DA, DE, FB, GA, HA, HH, IA, KA, NA, OA, PA, QA, TC: ***CV***: CG, DG, *P*D, RB, *SC*

Plate 123: ***F***: GI, GJ; ***CV***: H*D*.
Plate 124: Inverted S, SB; ***R***: EI, FI, GI, HI, II, JI; ***C***: MA, MH; ***CV***: A*L*, SK, T*L*.
Plate 125: ***CV***: AL, *E*B, FB, ID, K*E*.
Plate 126: ***R***: CJ; ***C***: AD; ***CV***: AG, T*H*.
Plate 127: ***R***: TH, TL; ***C***: 53 stamps; ***F***: KF, LB; ***CV***: AH, E*C*, EJ, FC, H*G*, OD, RA.
Plate 128: ***F***: LB; ***CV***: *D*A, EJ, KL, *N*G, P*F*, S*L*.
Plate 129: ***R***: RL; ***CV***: FL, *G*G, ID, OL, P*B*.
Plate 131: ***C***: CF, DI; ***CV***: B*J*, C*J*, *K*C, LI, *LK*, *M*E, P*A*, P*J*.

RE-ENTRIES

TD

TE

Plate 113

Plate 114

ND, *Plate* 122

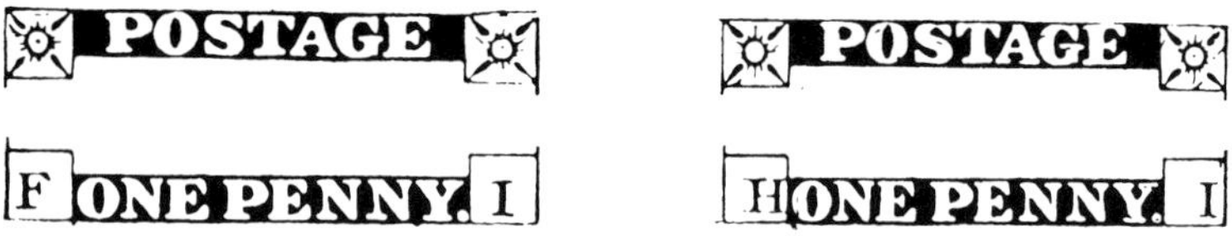

Plate 124

CJ
Plate 126

CONSTANT VARIETIES

CB

MD

PG

Plate 102

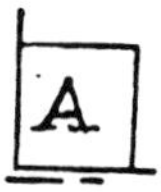

AA

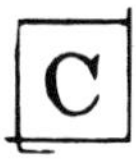

OC

Plate 103

AE AF FL GA GB SE

Plate 104

EE NH SI AD AH BE

Plate 105 *Plate* 106

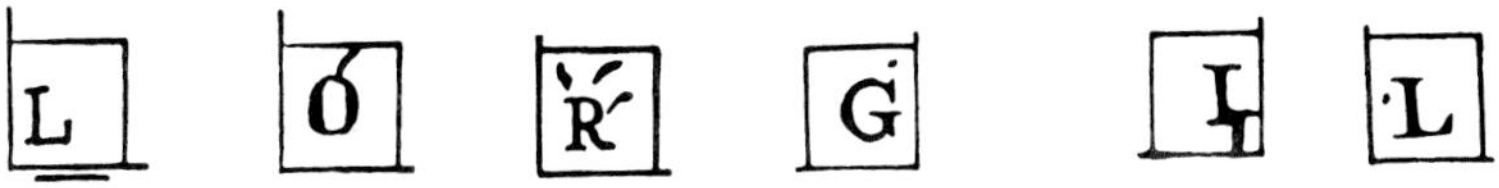

LE OC RL TG FI LD

Plate 106 *Plate* 107

DE FC IC QG SI

Plate 108

FK LA RH SD SG SK

Plate 109

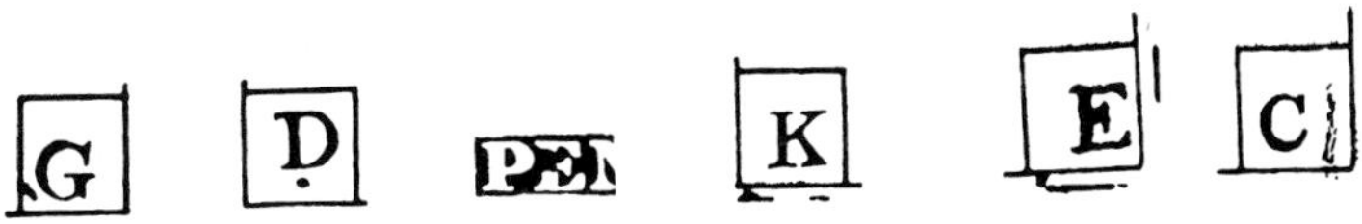

AG DA HG KC DE FC

Plate 110 *Plate* 111

AL NI PB QC CI HG

Plate 112 *Plate* 113

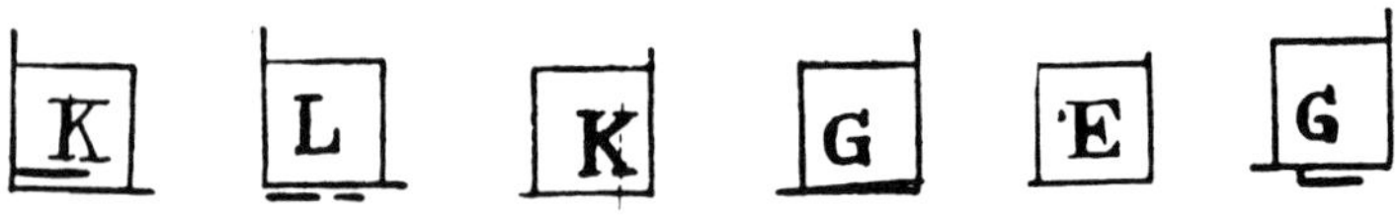

KD LC OK PG RE RG

Plate 113

CH IK OH TF

Plate 114

GF LJ MC

Plate 115

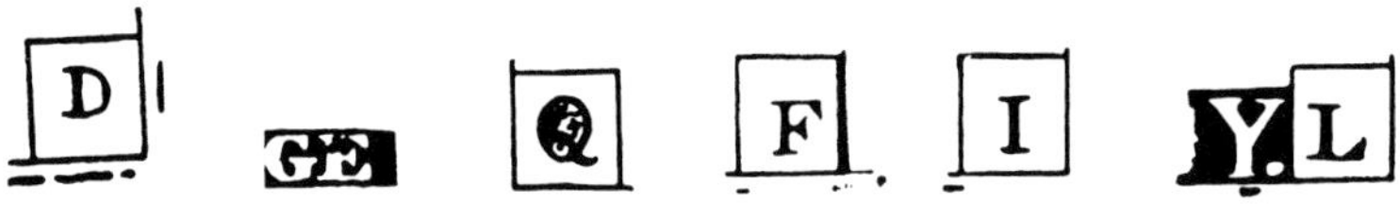

CD HL QD, QE RF RI RL

Plate 116

ML RH TL

Plate 117

IL TG

Plate 118

DA HL IA IE MC OB

Plate 119

AA FJ FK QF

Plate 120

PH SK

Plate 121

CG, DG

PD

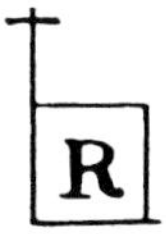

RB

SC

Plate 122

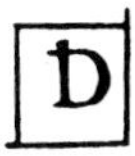

HD, *Plate* 123

AL

SK

TL

Plate 124

AL

EB

Plate 125

FB

ID

KE

Plate 125

AG

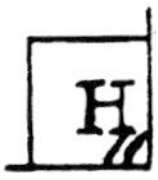

TH

Plate 126

AH

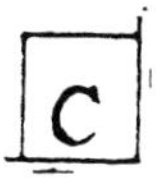

EC

EJ

FC

HG

OD

RA

Plate 127

DA

EJ

KL

PF

SL

Plate 128

FL

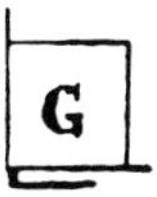

GG

ID

OL

PB

Plate 129

BJ

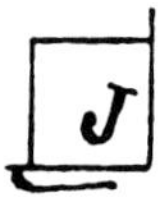
CJ

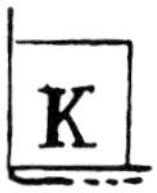
KC

LI

LK

ME
Plate 131

PA

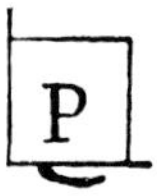
PJ

Index to Catalogued Varieties in Section BA

"Colourless" roller flaws such as the various Ray flaws and the "O" flaw are not included in this index. Similarly, characteristic letters such as the "square"' and "rounded" Js are not indexed. Plates 12 to 131 are included.

AA 12, 13, 14, 22, 24, 47, 70, 76, 88, 92, 94, 103, 120, 122
AB 12, 14, 15, 17, 21, 39, 46, 53, 54, 58, 76, 78, 88, 90, 105, 107, 131
AC 12, 13, 16, 17, 21, 23, 30, 40, 47, 50, 51, 59, 79, 88, 92, 94, 96, 131
AD 12, 13, 15, 16, 17, 18, 20, 30, 31, 36, 37, 48, 51, 54, 62, 66, 82, 88, 99, 100, 106, 126
AE 12, 16, 17, 23, 25, 40, 48, 54, 62, 88, 104
AF 12, 16, 17, 20, 22, 25, 31, 36, 37, 39, 40, 44, 48, 63, 73, 88, 90, 96, 102, 104, 117, 120
AG 12, 13, 15, 16, 17, 25, 28, 34, 40, 42, 65, 73, 88, 92, 100, 102, 110, 126
AH 12, 13, 15, 16, 17, 25, 30, 31, 35, 53, 63, 66, 76, 87, 88, 90, 93, 98, 106, 127
AI 12, 14, 15, 16, 17, 18, 33, 43, 44, 53, 54, 67, 88, 94, 120
AJ 12, 15, 17, 18, 19, 20, 21, 36, 40, 43, 54, 76, 88, 99, 101, 117, 120
AK 12, 17, 18, 53, 69, 85, 88, 89, 94, 96, 100
AL 16, 17, 18, 19, 22, 27, 32, 50, 59, 69, 78, 88, 98, 112, 124, 125

BA 12, 13, 17, 25, 30, 31, 32, 56, 77, 77b, 88, 122
BB 12, 14, 17, 30, 32, 40, 49, 76, 80, 120, 131
BC 12, 13, 17, 28, 29, 30, 41, 45, 75, 94, 101, 131
BD 12, 13, 16, 17, 22, 30, 45, 46, 55, 65, 76, 94, 95, 100, 105
BE 12, 16, 17, 40, 44, 57, 62, 93, 106
BF 12, 13, 14, 17, 29, 30, 31, 44, 45, 92, 95, 102, 120
BG 12, 17, 18, 44, 45, 55, 68, 75, 79
BH 12, 15, 17, 18, 36, 40, 45, 95, 98, 102
BI 12, 13, 15, 17, 18, 44, 45, 79, 87, 120
BJ 12, 13, 15, 17, 18, 19, 20, 26, 27, 32, 39, 41, 43, 45, 48, 49, 52, 87, 88, 94, 120, 131
BK 12, 15, 17, 18, 20, 32, 36, 49, 59, 76, 85, 89, 111, 120
BL 12, 15, 17, 18, 19, 27, 32, 39, 45, 59, 76, 88, 90, 91

CA 17, 25, 26, 29, 30, 36, 64, 79, 88, 98, 99, 105
CB 17, 30, 36, 38, 76, 77, 85, 96, 101, 102, 105, 111, 120, 131
CC 17, 21, 30, 38, 49, 99, 102, 131
CD 12, 13, 17, 30, 38, 65, 81, 116, 122
CE 12, 13, 17, 19, 50, 57, 63, 84, 92
CF 12, 13, 14, 17, 24, 30, 77, 84, 85, 121, 131
CG 13, 14, 17, 63, 96, 122
CH 12, 17, 53, 114
CI 17, 18, 24, 30, 48, 76, 77, 88, 113
CJ 12, 13, 14, 15, 17, 18, 19, 20, 22, 24, 27, 29, 32, 36, 41, 42, 43, 44, 45, 48, 77, 80, 92, 126, 131
CK 12, 13, 17, 18, 37, 48, 89, 103, 106
CL 12, 17, 18, 27, 50, 55, 62, 63, 78, 87

DA 13, 25, 30, 33, 34, 35, 45, 54, 85, 88, 110, 119, 122, 128
DB 13, 14, 19, 30, 34, 45, 52, 88, 95, 105, 131
DC 18, 30, 37, 50, 90, 94
DD 12, 14, 15, 30, 34, 45, 94, 121
DE 13, 15, 21, 30, 36, 45, 50, 51, 108, 111, 122
DF 12, 23, 41, 48, 76, 98
DG 13, 14, 31, 33, 52, 55, 61, 79, 84, 88, 89, 122
DH 14, 29, 30, 43, 44, 45, 55, 58
DI 14, 18, 24, 41, 45, 53, 54, 55, 83, 131
DJ 12, 14, 18, 19, 22, 26, 27, 29, 34, 43, 44, 49, 55, 80, 100, 104
DK 13, 17, 18, 19, 25, 33, 34, 36, 37, 44, 62, 63, 88, 89
DL 13, 17, 18, 23, 27, 34, 44, 58, 62, 63, 64, 79, 100

EA 17, 20, 25, 26, 30, 42, 53, 75, 85, 88, 104, 105
EB 20, 23, 25, 30, 33, 36, 41, 42, 43, 75, 80, 90, 94, 101, 105, 107, 120, 125, 131

EC 17, 20, 25, 30, 42, 45, 73, 77, 127
ED 17, 20, 21, 25, 30, 38, 41, 42, 50, 57, 58, 77, 94
EE 14, 18, 20, 25, 26, 30, 41, 42, 77, 105, 121
EF 20, 25, 30, 32, 33, 41, 42, 43, 76, 88, 91, 121
EG 20, 22, 23, 25, 30, 32, 41, 42, 46, 47, 76, 77, 78, 89, 97
EH 20, 25, 36, 41, 47, 76, 77, 95
EI 14, 18, 20, 25, 36, 41, 49, 76, 84, 87, 124
EJ 12, 15, 18, 19, 20, 21, 22, 24, 25, 26, 27, 28, 37, 44, 61, 78, 92, 95, 127, 128
EK 18, 20, 25, 26, 33, 37, 46, 51, 61, 89, 96, 100
EL 14, 16, 18, 20, 25, 27, 44, 52, 62, 76, 81, 86, 100

FA 15, 17, 26, 28, 31, 38, 50, 88, 98
FB 15, 38, 77, 120, 122, 125, 131
FC 14, 15, 18, 27, 38, 52, 61, 70, 77, 78, 79, 89, 94, 101, 108, 111, 127
FD 13, 14, 15, 27, 33, 36, 38, 39, 41, 74, 90, 92, 98, 121
FE 15, 18, 38, 39, 60, 95
FF 15, 16, 22, 23, 25, 31, 38, 41, 51, 72, 78, 121
FG 15, 17, 38, 40, 45, 77, 80, 119
FH 15, 23, 38, 40, 63, 64, 78
FI 15, 18, 22, 38, 54, 58, 100, 107, 124
FJ 15, 18, 21, 24, 26, 28, 34, 35, 36, 39, 41, 44, 45, 58, 61, 73, 95, 99, 120
FK 15, 18, 19, 25, 38, 89, 97, 100, 109, 120
FL 16, 17, 18, 27, 30, 53, 61, 104, 129

GA 15, 16, 17, 23, 39, 76, 88, 102, 104, 122, 131
GB 15, 17, 27, 34, 39, 76, 93, 104, 120, 131
GC 15, 16, 27, 29, 39, 99, 100, 101
GD 13, 15, 18, 27, 57, 74, 77, 98
GE 15, 16, 17, 27, 30, 36, 38, 44, 77, 115
GF 15, 39, 45, 88, 98
GG 15, 17, 18, 129
GH 15, 32, 36, 55, 80
GI 15, 20, 32, 48, 67, 87, 123, 124
GJ 12, 15, 16, 17, 18, 19, 26, 31, 32, 35, 36, 43, 48, 49, 53, 57, 68, 81, 123
GK 18, 20, 45, 60, 72, 77, 89
GL 18, 25, 26, 27, 31, 90, 98, 100

HA 52, 55, 68, 122, 131
HB 14, 17, 18, 27, 28, 37, 94, 107, 120, 131
HC 15, 16, 23, 27, 28, 32, 81, 88, 94
HD 13, 15, 22, 24, 27, 32, 44, 48, 70, 72, 76, 90, 98, 123
HE 13, 15, 24, 27, 45, 67, 78, 90, 100
HF 13, 15, 16, 22, 46, 67, 121
HG 14, 16, 23, 33, 34, 44, 48, 77, 79, 110, 113, 127
HH 15, 21, 29, 34, 44, 122
HI 15, 23, 27, 81, 83, 100, 124
HJ 15, 19, 20, 22, 24, 35, 41, 43, 65, 72, 74, 84, 88
HK 15, 20, 32, 54, 61, 83, 84, 89
HL 15, 27, 70, 100, 116, 119

IA 16, 17, 22, 40, 45, 68, 75, 79, 93, 94, 118, 119, 122, 131
IB 14, 19, 23, 28, 48, 78, 93, 95, 118, 120, 131
IC 21, 27, 28, 29, 34, 62, 83, 84, 88, 94, 100, 108
ID 15, 16, 21, 27, 32, 40, 44, 66, 83, 90, 92, 119, 125, 129
IE 14, 17, 26, 27, 32, 40, 42, 51, 60, 83, 84, 94, 119
IF 14, 26, 27, 31, 32, 40, 51, 83, 89, 94, 95
IG 61, 65, 88, 90, 101, 118
IH 16, 23, 32, 33, 42, 45, 52, 55, 56, 59, 65, 79, 95
II 32, 45, 67, 77, 124
IJ 12, 15, 16, 18, 19, 20, 22, 23, 25, 27, 30, 32, 36, 38, 40, 43, 44, 46, 48, 83, 92, 101, 121
IK 13, 14, 15, 16, 25, 32, 35, 77, 82, 89, 114
IL 14, 15, 16, 23, 27, 41, 61, 63, 83, 103, 118

JA 19, 22, 24, 26, 28, 42, 43, 72, 88, 96, 120, 131
JB 15, 19, 20, 21, 22, 32, 40, 41, 42, 43, 61, 76, 83, 120, 131
JC 15, 16, 21, 22, 23, 27, 32, 37, 40, 41, 42, 43, 44, 49, 52, 61, 73
JD 15, 16, 17, 23, 27, 40, 41, 42, 43, 44, 53, 61, 88, 94, 99, 101
JE 14, 15, 27, 32, 38, 40, 41, 43, 48, 52, 53, 63, 69, 73, 74, 76
JF 15, 22, 27, 31, 40, 41, 42, 43, 44, 52, 53, 57, 61, 63, 98
JG 12, 23, 40, 41, 43, 56, 59, 61, 95
JH 14, 23, 36, 38, 40, 41, 43, 44, 48, 57, 59, 61, 98
JI 12, 14, 15, 19, 22, 37, 38, 40, 41, 42, 43, 44, 57, 66, 77, 94, 101, 112, 124
JJ 14, 15, 21, 22, 27, 29, 30, 36, 37, 38, 40, 41, 42, 43, 44, 48, 52, 57, 77, 84, 87, 99
JK 15, 29, 35, 36, 37, 40, 41, 43, 44, 50, 57, 62, 74, 76, 80, 88, 89
JL 15, 19, 22, 27, 28, 29, 31, 34, 36, 37, 40, 43, 44, 54, 59, 61

KA 21, 34, 40, 42, 48, 50, 60, 81, 89, 120, 122, 131
KB 21, 34, 40, 51, 61, 70, 89, 96, 97, 120, 131
KC 20, 29, 89, 110, 131
KD 14, 32, 42, 45, 58, 65, 76, 89, 113, 119
KE 28, 31, 33, 35, 61, 72, 81, 88, 89, 94, 95, 98, 101, 125
KF 12, 14, 33, 42, 89, 127
KG 14, 42, 46, 52, 56, 81, 88, 89
KH 14, 30, 36, 40, 42, 61, 88, 89, 118
KI 12, 14, 35, 70, 88, 89
KJ 12, 19, 22, 26, 33, 35, 38, 42, 46, 50, 77, 89
KK 14, 20, 25, 27, 33, 35, 55, 64, 83, 89, 100, 111, 118
KL 14, 19, 27, 45, 64, 80, 89, 128

LA 19, 20, 27, 35, 48, 77, 88, 93, 109, 131
LB 18, 19, 29, 40, 63, 88, 94, 120, 121, 127, 128, 131
LC 22, 32, 51, 64, 78, 88, 113
LD 12, 18, 29, 32, 35, 47, 75, 76, 78, 88, 97, 107, 121

LE 19, 21, 23, 43, 54, 56, 61, 75, 77, 85, 88, 101, 106, 121
LF 18, 23, 33, 37, 56, 83, 100, 121
LG 15, 33, 40, 51, 56, 67, 74, 88, 98
LH 18, 34, 46, 63, 74, 79, 84, 88, 90
LI 14, 18, 22, 26, 56, 77, 92, 99, 131
LJ 12, 14, 15, 18, 21, 22, 27, 33, 34, 36, 38, 41, 42, 43, 46, 72, 77, 84, 97, 99, 115
LK 14, 15, 17, 18, 41, 46, 61, 75, 80, 83, 85, 87, 89, 98, 131
LL 14, 15, 21, 27, 34, 76, 94

MA 14, 21, 27, 28, 34, 37, 39, 45, 63, 76, 78, 88, 93, 96, 97, 102, 120, 124, 131
MB 13, 14, 17, 18, 77, 101, 102, 120, 131
MC 15, 18, 21, 23, 32, 41, 45, 46, 51, 56, 59, 64, 115, 119
MD 14, 18, 28, 32, 42, 49, 71, 77, 88, 100, 102, 103, 121
ME 15, 18, 33, 37, 66, 81, 88, 99, 131
MF 18, 35, 70, 88, 94, 121
MG 86, 88, 99
MH 13, 14, 15, 33, 40, 45, 56, 60, 80, 88, 90, 119, 124
MI 14, 20, 40, 51, 60, 98
MJ 12, 14, 15, 17, 18, 19, 22, 24, 26, 27, 28, 34, 35, 37, 38, 39, 40, 43, 49, 61, 70, 71, 96, 99
MK 14, 15, 33, 37, 49, 55, 61, 64, 67, 85, 87, 89, 94, 98, 120
ML 13, 16, 20, 21, 27, 68, 76, 117

NA 16, 19, 20, 41, 50, 53, 57, 77, 88, 93, 95, 97, 101, 122, 131
NB 13, 18, 19, 53, 57, 61, 97, 111, 120, 131
NC 14, 18, 20, 26, 37, 53, 57, 93
ND 15, 18, 19, 20, 21, 53, 57, 94, 95, 122
NE 13, 18, 32, 45, 53, 57, 76
NF 36, 46, 53, 57, 69, 75, 90, 94, 95, 100, 121
NG 13, 19, 29, 32, 57, 60, 84, 87, 88, 128
NH 15, 19, 20, 29, 32, 34, 49, 57, 81, 84, 88, 98, 105
NI 19, 23, 48, 57, 90, 112
NJ 12, 15, 18, 19, 22, 27, 32, 35, 36, 38, 40, 43, 48, 51, 54, 57, 93, 97
NK 14, 20, 34, 37, 52, 57, 61, 82, 89, 120
NL 14, 20, 32, 36, 40, 47, 48, 54, 57, 120

OA 12, 14, 16, 19, 57, 70, 88, 89, 93, 122, 131
OB 14, 17, 18, 57, 73, 78, 91, 98, 102, 119, 131
OC 12, 14, 15, 18, 33, 45, 57, 82, 84, 103, 106
OD 14, 15, 16, 19, 24, 35, 48, 57, 88, 94, 101, 102, 127
OE 12, 14, 15, 16, 18, 19, 32, 35, 49, 88, 94, 100
OF 15, 17, 23, 28, 33, 34, 49, 66, 76, 83, 88, 94, 98
OG 13, 14, 17, 18, 33, 34, 76, 88, 94
OH 14, 15, 16, 17, 18, 19, 20, 21, 31, 32, 33, 36, 37, 49, 57, 88, 114, 120
OI 14, 15, 18, 19, 20, 31, 32, 33, 38, 57, 77, 88, 94, 98
OJ 12, 14, 17, 18, 19, 21, 22, 26, 27, 32, 33, 36, 38, 43, 44, 48, 63, 64, 88, 120
OK 14, 16, 19, 20, 28, 32, 33, 34, 37, 40, 52, 57, 60, 76, 88, 89, 113, 120
OL 14, 17, 19, 21, 27, 28, 32, 50, 57, 76, 88, 120, 129

PA 12, 15, 28, 33, 34, 40, 43, 72, 88, 92, 93, 98, 100, 120, 122, 131
PB 17, 19, 27, 28, 33, 34, 40, 56, 61, 76, 102, 112, 121, 129, 131
PC 16, 17, 19, 20, 28, 35, 40, 75, 88
PD 17, 28, 33, 40, 42, 43, 57, 98, 122
PE 17, 35, 36, 40, 46, 76, 97
PF 14, 15, 16, 30, 40, 62, 93, 128
PG 15, 18, 21, 23, 32, 36, 43, 48, 85, 102, 113
PH 12, 13, 15, 16, 23, 28, 39, 48, 80, 98, 121
PI 12, 13, 14, 15, 16, 18, 19, 21, 23, 28, 35, 38, 42, 46, 50, 53, 56, 86, 96, 120
PJ 13, 15, 16, 18, 19, 22, 23, 27, 34, 35, 37, 38, 41, 43, 44, 63, 76, 90, 94, 104, 131
PK 19, 23, 31, 37, 38, 56, 89, 95
PL 13, 19, 20, 21, 27, 38, 41, 48, 55, 94, 100

QA 16, 17, 18, 19, 21, 33, 34, 39, 41, 42, 43, 52, 76, 88, 95, 118, 121, 122, 131
QB 13, 14, 16, 17, 18, 19, 21, 22, 34, 39, 41, 47, 58, 60, 118, 121, 131
QC 17, 18, 19, 21, 28, 34, 36, 39, 41, 65, 76, 78, 94, 112
QD 13, 17, 18, 19, 20, 28, 39, 41, 54, 66, 94, 96, 101, 116, 119, 121
QE 12, 15, 18, 28, 33, 39, 41, 75, 116, 121
QF 12, 15, 18, 36, 39, 41, 43, 62, 76, 77, 120
QG 12, 15, 16, 17, 18, 19, 36, 39, 41, 62, 75, 81, 108
QH 12, 14, 15, 18, 28, 36, 39, 41, 43, 48, 66, 119
QI 14, 15, 17, 18, 19, 20, 36, 39, 41, 49, 51, 56, 66
QJ 14, 15, 18, 19, 22, 26, 27, 28, 35, 37, 38, 39, 41, 43, 44, 63, 88, 120
QK 13, 18, 19, 32, 37, 39, 41, 72, 77, 89, 93
QL 12, 18, 19, 27, 41, 52, 75, 88, 94

RA 17, 18, 19, 21, 25, 30, 31, 33, 34, 36, 41, 57, 60, 75, 81, 83, 86, 87, 88, 97, 118, 127, 131
RB 13, 14, 18, 21, 25, 30, 31, 32, 33, 34, 41, 46, 73, 77, 83, 86, 87, 118, 121, 122, 131
RC 13, 14, 18, 25, 30, 31, 33, 34, 41, 83, 86, 87, 94, 100, 114
RD 18, 30, 31, 33, 41, 54, 77, 83, 86, 87, 94, 121
RE 13, 15, 17, 18, 25, 30, 31, 33, 41, 66, 75, 77, 83, 86, 87, 113
RF 13, 16, 17, 18, 26, 30, 31, 32, 33, 41, 62, 83, 86, 87, 114, 116
RG 14, 16, 18, 30, 31, 33, 38, 41, 83, 86, 87, 113
RH 13, 18, 30, 31, 33, 38, 40, 41, 49, 66, 71, 83, 86, 87, 109, 117
RI 14, 16, 17, 18, 30, 31, 32, 33, 38, 41, 51, 66, 78, 83, 86, 87, 116
RJ 13, 14, 15, 16, 18, 19, 20, 22, 23, 27, 30, 31, 33, 36, 37, 41, 51, 66, 77, 83, 86, 87, 97, 99
RK 16, 18, 26, 30, 31, 33, 37, 41, 42, 59, 81, 83, 86, 87, 89
RL 12, 14, 15, 17, 18, 21, 25, 27, 30, 31, 33, 41, 75, 83, 86, 87, 106, 116, 120, 129

SA 13, 17, 18, 21, 25, 29, 34, 38, 40, 41, 78, 88, 101, 105, 107, 120, 131
SB 17, 18, 19, 21, 25, 29, 30, 34, 41, 58, 68, 78, 105, 107, 121, 124, 131
SC 15, 18, 19, 25, 29, 34, 39, 41, 77, 78, 79, 98, 105, 107, 122
SD 14, 18, 19, 20, 21, 29, 31, 32, 34, 41, 50, 53, 77, 78, 88, 98, 105, 107, 109, 119, 121
SE 14, 17, 18, 21, 29, 30, 33, 34, 41, 50, 55, 69, 77, 78, 101, 104, 105, 107
SF 18, 29, 33, 35, 41, 51, 56, 77, 78, 85, 99, 105, 107, 121
SG 14, 18, 29, 41, 62, 71, 74, 78, 105, 107, 109
SH 23, 29, 34, 35, 36, 41, 54, 55, 56, 58, 77, 78, 82, 84, 98, 105, 107, 119
SI 14, 16, 17, 18, 29, 32, 34, 35, 37, 41, 44, 47, 49, 54, 61, 78, 96, 105, 107, 108
SJ 12, 14, 16, 18, 19, 20, 21, 22, 29, 35, 36, 37, 38, 41, 51, 66, 78, 99, 105, 107
SK 12, 16, 20, 29, 33, 36, 37, 41, 49, 52, 78, 84, 89, 95, 97, 105, 107, 109, 121, 124
SL 14, 16, 19, 21, 27, 29, 38, 41, 60, 68, 78, 105, 107, 128

TA 14, 15, 19, 22, 25, 30, 33, 34, 38, 41, 45, 48, 60, 63, 84, 85, 88, 91, 93, 95, 96, 120, 121, 131
TB 12, 15, 16, 18, 19, 25, 33, 34, 36, 38, 40, 41, 48, 60, 90, 96, 101, 121, 131
TC 15, 16, 18, 19, 25, 29, 34, 35, 38, 40, 41, 48, 72, 77, 119, 122
TD 13, 14, 15, 16, 17, 18, 19, 20, 25, 34, 36, 37, 38, 41, 48, 49, 53, 71, 75, 85, 95, 113, 121
TE 14, 15, 16, 18, 19, 26, 34, 38, 40, 41, 48, 49, 53, 57, 77, 84, 95, 113, 121
TF 15, 17, 18, 19, 20, 28, 33, 34, 36, 40, 41, 48, 49, 54, 59, 60, 82, 114
TG 12, 14, 15, 16, 18, 19, 28, 30, 33, 34, 35, 38, 41, 48, 51, 54, 71, 98, 106, 118
TH 12, 14, 15, 16, 17, 18, 19, 28, 33, 34, 36, 39, 40, 41, 48, 49, 75, 84, 98, 126, 127
TI 12, 14, 15, 16, 18, 19, 28, 33, 35, 38, 39, 40, 41, 45, 48, 49, 79, 81, 84, 88
TJ 12, 14, 15, 16, 18, 19, 21, 22, 28, 33, 36, 38, 39, 41, 43, 48, 49, 62, 66, 82, 84, 91, 112
TK 12, 14, 15, 16, 17, 18, 19, 20, 27, 28, 33, 37, 38, 39, 40, 41, 48, 62, 72, 80, 89, 119
TL 17, 19, 21, 26, 27, 28, 33, 38, 39, 40, 41, 48, 77, 88, 93, 100, 110, 117, 124, 127

SECTION BB

One Penny Red, Type A1, Imperforate, Die I, Alphabet II (Plates 132 to 177)

These plates, the first to show Alphabet II, were registered between 6 February 1852 and 20 July 1853. They were laid down with care and regularity so that little in the way of plate or group characteristics can be found. All corner squares were recut. The second type of selvedge star ornament appeared, from Plate 132 onwards, for the first time, being engraved before the plates were used. The thicker, lavender-tinted paper continued to be used with early plates of this group.

Plates of this group were still in use when official perforating began and Plates 155, 157 and 162 to 177 are known to have been issued both imperforate and perforated. Plates 175/7 are rare imperf.

It is stamps of this group which are known with the so-called *Treasury Roulette:* an unauthorized variety which resulted in stamps with serpentine edges. The "Roulette" was produced by a revolving cutter producing approximately four "waves" to the length of the stamp. See B2a, aa below. These should be purchased with certificates of genuineness. The Government Trial perforation of 1853–54 was also on Alphabet II stamps. See Section CA.

The used prices are for stamps with contemporary cancellations. These were the 1844 numeral types at first and from 1853 the duplex types were introduced, occurring on the later plates.

Repaired Impressions—Prices for Original States

The note on page 96 also applies to this Section.

1852 (6 February)–1853. Introduction of Alphabet II. Die I. Wmk Small Crown. Imperf.

B2	(1)	1d. red-brown	£425	32·00
	(2)	1d. lake-red	£3800	£675
	(3)	1d. orange-brown	£1300	£175
		Block of four	£2500	£325
		Used on cover	†	45·00
	a.	With Treasury Roulette (on cover)	†	£12500
	aa.	With Treasury Roulette (off cover)	†	£4500
	c.	Watermark inverted	—	£300
	d.	Re-entry (Major)	—	75·00
	e.	Double letter	—	40·00
	f.	Inverted "S": Plates 140, SA, SB and 143, SA	—	£200
	g.	Broken frame below "PENNY"	—	45·00
	h.	Badly misplaced letter	—	35·00
	i.	Recut frame	—	35·00
	j.	Ivory head ... *from*	£450	35·00
	k.	On thicker, lavender-tinted paper (Plates 132 to 136) ... *from*	£1000	£225
	l.	Constant varieties ... *from*	—	40·00
	m.	Second states from unhardened plates 155 to 175 ... *from*		

The "Treasury Roulette", B2a *tied on cover*

Imprimaturs, Plates 132–175, *each* £650. Stamps removed from the imprimatur sheets are: Plate 132: AA to AL, PF to PL, QF, TL; Plate 133: AA to AL, RF to RL, SL, TL; Plate 134: AA to AL, QF to QL, RL, TL; Plate 135: AA to AL, QL, RF to RL, TL; Plate 136: AA to AL, RF to RL, SL, TL; Plate 137: AA to AL, PF to PL, QF, TL; Plate 138: AA to AL, RF to RL, SL, TL; Plate 139: AA to AL, RF to RL, SL, TL; Plate 140: AA to AL, HK, HL, IG to IL, TL; Plate 141, AA to AL, IK, IL, JG to JL, TL; Plate 142; AA to AL, GK, GL, HG to HL, TL; Plate 143: AA to AL, HK, HL, IG to IL, TL; Plate 144: AA to AL, HK, HL, IG to IL, TL; Plate 145: AA to AL, HK, HL, IG to IL, TL; Plate 146: AA to AL, HK, HL, IG to IL, TL; Plate 147: AA to AL, GK to GL, HG to HL, TL; Plate 148: AA to AL, IK, IL, JG to JL, TL; Plate 149: AA to AL, HK, HL, IG to IL, TL; Plate 150: AA to AL, GK, GL, HG to HL, TL; Plate 151: AA to AL, HL, IG to IL, JL, TL; Plate 152: AA to AL, GK, GL, HG to HL, TL; Plate 153: AA to AL, HK, HL, IG to IL, TL; Plate 154: AA to AL, HK, HL, IG to IL, TL; Plate 155: AA to AL, RF to RL, SL, TL; Plate 156: AA to AL, RF to RL, SL, TL; Plate 157: AA to AL, HL, IF to IL, TL; Plate 158: AA to AL, HL, IF to IL, TL; Plate 159: AA to AL, GF to GL, HL, TL; Plate 160: AA to AL, QF to QL, RH, TL; Plate 161: AA to AL, IK, IL, JG to JL, TL; Plate 162: AA to AL, IK, IL, JG to JL, TL; Plate 163: AA to AL, IK, IL, JG to JL, TL; Plate 164: AA to AL, IL, JL, KG to KL, TL; Plate 165: AA to AL, BJ, KA to KF, LA, TL; Plate 166: AA to AL, IK, IL, JG to JL, TL; Plate 167: AA to AL, HK, HL, IG to IL, TL; Plate 168: AA to AL, FK, FL, GG to GL, TL; Plate 169: AL, HK, HL, IG to IL, TA to TL; Plate 170: AL, HK, HL, IG to IL, TA to TL; Plate 171: AL, SE to SL, TA to TL; Plate 172: AA to AL, FL, GG to GL, HL, TL; Plate 173: AA to AL, GK, GL, HG to HL, TL; Plate 174: AA to AL, JK, JL, KG to KL, TL; Plate 175: AA to AL, HK, HL, IG to IL, TL.

Plates registered: Plates 132 to 137, 6 February 1852; Plates 138 to 143, 17 April 1852; Plates 144 to 148, 4 June 1852; Plates 149 to 154, 27 July 1852; Plates 155 to 160, 16 September 1852; Plates 161 to 166, 14 January 1853; Plates 167 to 172, 18 April 1853; Plates 173 to 175, 1853. Plates 176 and 177 20 July 1853.

Plated Used Examples

Plate 132	38·00	Plate 143	38·00
Plate 133	38·00	Plate 144	32·00
Plate 134	38·00	Plate 145	38·00
Plate 135	32·00	Plate 146	32·00
Plate 136	40·00	Plate 147	32·00
Plate 137	38·00	Plate 148	32·00
Plate 138	32·00	Plate 149	32·00
Plate 139	38·00	Plate 150	32·00
Plate 140	38·00	Plate 151	32·00
Plate 141	40·00	Plate 152	32·00
Plate 142	32·00	Plate 153	32·00

Plate 154	32·00	Plate 166	40·00
Plate 155	40·00	Plate 167	45·00
Plate 156	32·00	Plate 168	45·00
Plate 157	40·00	Plate 169	45·00
Plate 158	32·00	Plate 170	50·00
Plate 159	38·00	Plate 171	45·00
Plate 160	40·00	Plate 172	50·00
Plate 161	40·00	Plate 173	90·00
Plate 162	40·00	Plate 174	£250
Plate 163	40·00	Plate 175	£750
Plate 164	40·00	Plate 176	£1900
Plate 165	40·00	Plate 177	£2500

Plating Aids

While space does not permit anything approaching a full plating guide, the information below will undoubtedly be of considerable assistance to collectors.

As a group these plates are identifiable by the use of Alphabet II in imperforate state and a further classification is by reference to the papers.

In the listing below the following abbreviations have been used: ***R***, re-entry; ***D***, double letter; ***M***, corner letter badly misplaced; ***B***, baseline broken below PE of PENNY; ***RC***, right frameline partly recut, more usually at lower right; ***LC***, left frameline partly recut; ***FS***, a constant flaw or mark in or near a "star" corner; ***FL***, a constant flaw or mark in or near a letter corner, often in the form of a short extra line below the corner square; ***CV***, constant variety in some other position. Such flaws are generally very small and of interest only for plating purposes. Other features are more fully described when necessary. The date given in brackets against each plate is the put to press date.

Plate 132 (19 February 1852): ***R***: OI. ***B***: AA, JA. ***RC***: AD, CD, DH, OF. ***LC***: FG, JE, JI. ***FL***: GK, *K*E, M*C*, *M*H, *N*H, R*F*. The Gs in the vertical G row and on GC, GD are small. There are heavy burrs on left of AE to AK, BE to BK, CE to CK, DE to DK, EE to EK, and all stamps of the vertical G row.

Plate 133 (21 February 1852): ***CV***: AI, *PH*. ***B***: BE. ***RC***: AD, ***FS***: ED. ***FL***: *A*E, *C*C, *G*C, I*B*. All Gs in the horizontal G row are large.

Plate 134 (23 February 1852): ***R***: AI. ***D***: E*K*. ***RC***: AH, ED, JA. ***FL***: *D*D. The top frame on BI is broken above AGE; NF has a tall N; MH a weak H bar; there are no burrs.

Plate 135 (28 February 1852): ***CV***: KA, NA, SA. ***B***: AA, AC, AI, BA, BK, CA, FC, FG, FH, FK, FL, GH, GI, GK, GL, HE, IE, IG, IH, II, IJ, JA, JE, JI, LC, LI, LK, MA, MB, MC, ME, OC, QE. The top is broken above AGE on JJ. The right frame is wholly recut on AA, BE, JA, KE, and the left frame wholly recut on IB, JB, MC, OB. There is a heavy burr between the A and B vertical rows and down the left of the C vert. row. Q of QH is faint. Partial recutting of frames is too prevalent to allow of listing. ***FS***: NL. ***FL***: A*B*, E*E*, *H*H, *L*A, S*H*.

Plate 136 (8 March 1852): ***D***: A*J*; ***FL***: *I*G, *L*I. ***M***: S*H*. The K is large on TK.

Plate 137 (30 March 1852): ***RC***: AB, AD, AH, BD, CA, CH, DA, EE, EJ, FH, GC, HG, IA, JD, JH, LH, ME, ND, OC, RH, TA, TC. ***FS***: MK. ***FL***: *A*B, *A*D, *T*I.

Plate 138 (17 April 1852): ***D***: C*I*. ***RC***: AD, BC, EH, FA, FB, LB, MH, NJ, PB, RB, TA, TB, TC, TH. ***FL***: B*H*, *B*I, *C*E, I*H*, *J*F, *L*D, *M*K, SF. There is a roller flaw extending across LJ, MJ, NJ, OJ and PJ.

Plate 139 (17 April 1852): ***FL***: C*H*, C*I*, F*D*, I*K*, L*C*, N*B*, *S*G, T*H*. ***RC***: BB, NF, OD. All Ps are blind.

Plate 140 (19 April 1852): SA, SB have inverted S. ***D***: E*J*. ***RC***: AH, BH, EF, OB, SH. ***FS***: ED, FA, HD, JL. ***FL***: *CA*, *DA*, *E*K, F*C*, *I*F, *Q*A, *QD*. ***CV***: LI. The J of HJ is large, recut.

Plate 141 (27 April 1852): ***RC***: AH, AJ, BB, BH, DA, FB, IH, LB, MA, MB, ME, MI, ND, OD, OF, PH, QA, QB, RB, RI, SB, TJ, TK. ***FL***: A*F*, *F*D, *F*I, R*B*, R*E*.

Plate 142 (20 May 1852): ***R***: AG. ***D***: A*K*. ***RC***: AH, BB, GA, JC, JD, JK, KC, PD, QD, RD, TA, TB, TJ. ***FL***: *A*E, *EA*, *H*D, *LH*, L*I*. ***CV***: RK. It is probable that the S on SB is inverted.

Plate 143 (22 May 1852): Inverted S, SA. ***B***: AC, BA, BB, EE, HG, KA, MA, OA, PA, RA, SA. ***RC***: AA, DA, EA, FA, GA, IA. ***FL***: *D*F, *E*F, *N*J, O*H*, *R*B.

Plate 144 (11 June 1852): ***R***: Marks in one or both top squares, KD, KE, LF. ***RC***: AD, AF, BA, BC, CA, DA, EA, EG, GL, ID, JC, MC, NA, NB, NH, OB, QA, QF, SH. ***LC***: AE, JL, PG. ***FL***: A*H*, *D*D, *I*L, *T*A,

Plate 145 (11 June 1852): ***R***: JJ, TA. ***D***: A*I*. ***RC***: AB, AC, BD, CA, CB, CD, FB, GC, GF, JF, JI, JJ, KF, LF, OH, QF, RF, SE, SF, SH. ***LC***: LG. ***FL***: *Q*A, R*I*.

Plate 146 (11 June 1852): ***D***: A*D*. ***FS***: MC, ME–MF. ***FL***: E*G*, *MC*, *SK*.

Plate 147 (15 June 1852): ***R***: AA. ***LC***: DD, DF, EF, EL, HH, IA, IB, MD, OB, OI, QG. ***RC***: AH, AI, CC, CF, DE, EE, FA, LD, LH, MD, NF, NI, OB, PF, QF, QI, QJ, RH, SB, SC, SH, SJ, SK, TE, TL. ***FL***: A*D*, G*E*, G*I*, *M*H, *MJ*, *M*L, *PC*, *R*C.

Plate 148 (16 June 1852): ***M***: S*J*. ***FL***: K*B*, *K*G, *K*J, *M*A, *M*K. ***CV***: AL. On FB, FD, HJ, IF, OF, the stop after PENNY runs into the S.E. corner square.

Plate 149 (27 July 1852): ***RC***: MC, SE. ***FL***: D*I*, *F*F, *G*D, *L*E, *M*F, *M*G, *M*H, *M*K, Q*H*, R*J*, *S*E, T*D*. There is a large flaw on the diadem on CI.

Plate 150 (28 July 1852): ***D***: A*D*. ***FS***: SK. ***LC***: MC. ***FL***: *A*G, B*C*, *BI*, *I*A, *J*A, L*I*, *M*B, *M*C, *M*F, *M*J, *N*A, O*H*, *SG*, *TA*.

Plate 151 (28 July 1852): ***FS***: BK. ***FL***: K*D*–*K*E, *L*F, *L*L, *O*I, *Q*C, *S*B.

Plate 152 (28 July 1852): ***RC***: AA, AB, AI, AL ***FL***: F*L*, K*L*, M*A*, *M*F, *R*H, *S*A, *S*K, T*F*.

Plate 153 (10 August 1852): ***R***: NJ. ***CV***: *SB*. ***FL***: A*E*, L*C*, T*E*, T*H*. The K on TK is large, slim, recut.

Plate 154 (14 August 1852): ***D***: D*D*, E*J* ***FL***: E*J*, *E*K, *J*G, *M*I–*M*J, P*C*, R*J*, S*B*, SC; there is a flaw below the first N of NNY on OJ.

Plate 155 (30 August 1852): ***R***: AG, BB, BD, HA, MJ, RF, RJ, ***D***: J*D*. ***FL***: B*J*, EF, F*H*, *G*1, KC, P*C*, P*D*, P*G*, ***FS***: (2nd State) EF, PL. Stamp PD has the letter D weak in 2nd State, retouched in 3rd State, ***LC***: (top left) QG. As a general rule the first repair (State 2) resulted in the stamps having thinner or fainter corner letters and the engraving remained weak. After the second repair on perforated stamps the letters are stronger, after retouching, and the engraving noticeably improved (State 3). MJ (State 3 perf.) shows a larger J than States 1 and 2.

Plate 156 (17 September 1852): ***D***: *E*D. ***CV***: AL. ***RC***: AB, AD, AE, AF, BF, CF, DF, IF, SA. ***FL***: B*A*, E*C*, H*I*, *I*C, *M*D, T*B*. Large retouched letters are seen on B*J*, *K*A, *R*F.

Plate 157 (17 September 1852): ***R***: AA, AB, AC, BA, MJ, MK, SJ, TF, TI. ***D***: *D*F, *D*G. ***FL***: B*H*, *B*K, B*L*, C*D*, *C*G, CH, E*K*, *HG*, *I*J, *I*K, *J*I, *Q*B, TA, T*B*, *T*L. ***FS***: DD, NJ, PL. ***CV***: LK. There is a square flaw below the ear on PB. The flaws on CD and DD are a late state plate crack joining the two stamps.

Plate 158 (3 November 1852): ***R***: RD (State 1) and BG, RD (State 2). BG is known in first state without re-entry. ***CV***: TD. ***LC***: DG. ***FL***: *E*K, *H*G, M*G*, *R*F, *T*K. There are sizeable flaws in the vertical gutters between DI–DJ, JJ–JK, OF–OG, and a flaw on the left margin of KA.

Plate 159 (30 November 1852): ***R***: HA, IA, JA. ***RC***: AC. ***LC***: BA. ***FL***: *A*E, *A*F, *A*G, *B*A, CH, *L*F, M*F*, *M*K, Q*F*–*Q*G, SE. ***FS***: EG, FE, HE. On CF the frame is broken above AGE.

Plate 160 (9 December 1852): ***R***: AA, BA, BG. ***CV***: TB. ***LC***: CA. ***B***: PG. ***FS***: GF, HE, JB. ***FL***: *B*B, *E*H, F*K*, *I*H, *I*I, *J*F, *J*I, L*L*, *TD*, T*I*.

Plate 161 (17 January 1853): ***R***: QA 2nd State. ***CV***: TB. ***RC***: BF, JD, KB, LG, SF, *TH*. ***FL***: B*J*, C*A*, *G*B, H*I*, *I*A, *J*K, *J*L, *M*B, *M*K, N*H*, S*I*. ***FS***: OG. There is a large dot near the eye on EK. LL, OJ, OK, PK, PL, all show a break below the O of ONE.

Plate 162 (27 January 1853): ***R***: KB, PB, RC, RD, SC, TJ. ***RC***: AH, CD. ***LC***: CE, HI. ***FL***: D*H*, *E*G–*E*H, K*J*, *O*K, R*K*, S*I*, *T*L. In later prints a crack extended from OC into OD. Second states reported on IC, JB, MB, NB, QA, QC to QE, RE, SA, SB, SD, TA to TD, TH.

Plate 163 (5 February 1853): 50 per cent of the stamps had partially recut frames at top or bottom right or bottom left; only PF had recutting at top left. ***R***: AD, AE and AF (both two states), AH, TG. ***FL***: *A*F, *E*G, P*J*, *R*F, SJ, T*A*. ***FS***: BD (two states). Stamp FJ has broken frame above AGE. Second states reported on AB, AG, AI, BC, BH, BI, BK, BL, TB, TE, TH, TK.

Plate 164 (17 February 1853): ***R***: TH, TI. ***RC***: OF, PF, QF, RE, SE. ***LC***: RF, RG. ***FL***: *C*I, D*C*, F*I*, G*C*, H*E*, I*C*, K*E*, *M*E. ***FS***: TG. There is a flaw to right of the mouth on EL. Second states reported on AJ to AL, BJ, BL, CK, SA, SK, TF.

Plate 165 (12 March 1853); ***R***: BB, ML. ***CV***: NA. ***RC***: AF, BF, FF, HF, NF. ***LC***: CD, FG. ***FL***: A*I*, *E*G, *G*L, L*G*, *M*I. *M*J, Q*A*. On late prints a flaw stretched from the neck on TK diagonally upwards to the top of TL. Second states reported on AB, AE, BA.

Plate 166 (15 April 1853): ***RC***: AB, BD, CD, CF, DB, LF, OD, PB, PF. ***FL***: A*C*, *I*I, *K*D, *M*G. *N*C. DC has a flaw on headband of crown.

Plate 167 (18 April 1853): ***R***: HF, SH–TH (SH also lacks bottom frame line). ***CV***: HI. ***RC***: AH, LF, PD. ***FL***: A*I*, B*I*, *M*F, M*I*, N*A*, *S*B. T*I*, T*J* (second state). ***FS***: AK. The top frame is broken on IF.

Plate 168 (19 April 1853): ***CV***: HA. ***RC***: DC. ***FL***: B*A*, *F*I, *M*E, *M*F. ***FS***: MJ and MB in second state (re-entry).

Plate 169 (30 April 1853); ***R***: in none of the imperforates but AJ–BJ in second state (perforated stamps only). ***RC***: LD, PA. ***FL***: *F*I, *G*E, H*D*, *J*J, L*K*, *M*E, M*G*, *M*H, *O*F, *O*K, Q*H*, *S*K, T*L*.

Plate 170 (4 May 1853): ***R***: TA. ***FL***: *B*I, CA, *H*J, MF, R*I*. Second states on TA, TJ.

Plate 171 (24 May 1853): ***R***: SC. ***D***: E*H*. ***CV***: BB. ***FL***: *F*K, *M*K. *Q*L, T*I* (second state). There are marks above POST on AH. Flaws on chin on FD. Second states reported on OB, SB, SD, TB.

Plate 172 (25 May 1853): Very few varieties. ***RC***: JC. ***FL***: *P*B, *Q*K, TC. Second states on AF. AJ, GA, RA, SA, SC to SE, TG.

Plate 173 (19 August 1853): ***RC***: AB, AD, BB, BD, BG, BH, BJ, CB. CH, DH, EH, EI, FB, GD, HH, ID, IH, JB, KA, KD, KH, LD, LF, MD, NA, ND, PA, QD. ***LC***: CE, CK, DI, ME, NE. ***FL***: *G*D, *P*H. The following exist in two states. State 1 can be found imperf. and/or perf., but State 2 is perf. only. It is probable that re-entering was made using a worn transfer roller because the background and the Queen's head are frequently worn on State 2 examples. Second states, AH to AK, BK, DB, DD to DF, HA, LB, OD, OH, RC to RE, RG, RJ, SH, TA to TC, TF to TH. These all are coincident re-entries except HA and TG which show some doubling at the corner and are non-coincident re-entries.

Plate 174 (27 August 1853): ***R***: DA, HA. ***D***: *M*C. ***FL***: *C*L, *H*K, *M*D, *O*D. ***RC***: BH. ***FS***: QH. Second state reported on TB.

Plate 175 (15 December 1853): ***RC***: BH, BI, BJ, DK, GE, QC, RB, RF, SB. ***LC***: NI, NK, PK. ***FL***: J*B*, *M*A, M*E*, N*B*. ***CV***: LE. Second state reported on PL.

The Unhardened Plates. Plates 155 to 176 include the Unhardened Plates, which were the subject of an experiment by Perkins Bacon & Co. in 1853. The experiment was abandoned as extensive re-entering became necessary due to plate wear.

Plate Repairs. Plate 155 was twice repaired throughout giving rise to 2nd and 3rd states. Plates 173 and 176 were also re-entered, probably throughout. Plates 162, 163 and 164 were extensively repaired while repaired second states from plate 170, perforated 16, are very scarce. In most cases re-entering was coincident, i.e. without duplication, but with weakened corner letters, which were sometimes re-cut, strengthened side lines. Transfer Roller Lines in margin and thinner letters of "POSTAGE" and "ONE PENNY". It should be noted that these are true re-entries; not to be confused with fresh entries which are sometimes described as re-entries (see Line-Engraved Notes). For further details see the articles by R. G. Folkard and the late F. M. Johnson in *Gibbons Stamp Monthly* of February and March 1992.

Introduction of Perforation 16. Plates 176 and 177 are both very scarce imperforate, but were issued in the normal way. Plating notes and varieties are given following C2 in Section CB. Of the plates tabulated above, Plates 155, 157 and 162 to 177 are known both officially imperforate (priced under B2) and perforated (priced under C2).

RE-ENTRIES

Plate 132

Plate 134

Plate 135, *base line broken*

Plate 145

Plate 145

Plate 155

Plate 155

Plate 157

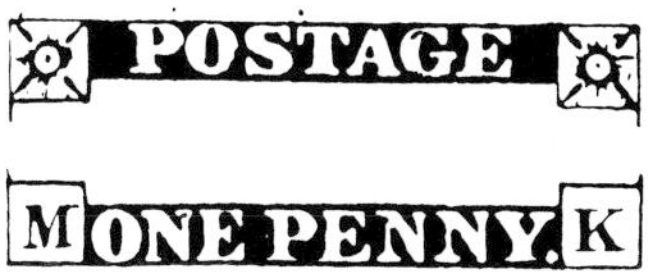

Plate 157

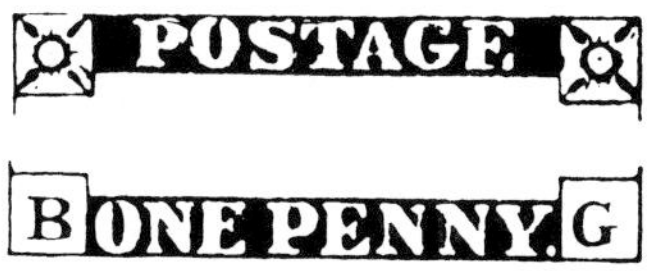

Plate 158, *second state*

First state

Plate 158

Second state

QA, *Plate* 161, *second state*

TA, *Plate* 170, *second state*

Plate 167

Plate 174

DOUBLE LETTERS AND CONSTANT VARIETIES

GK

KE

MC

NH

RF

Plate 132

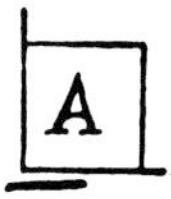

AE

AI

ED

PH

Plate 133

EE

HH

KA

NA

NL

SA

Plate 135

IG LI SH MK

Plate 136 — *Plate* 137

BI JF LD MK SF

Plate 138

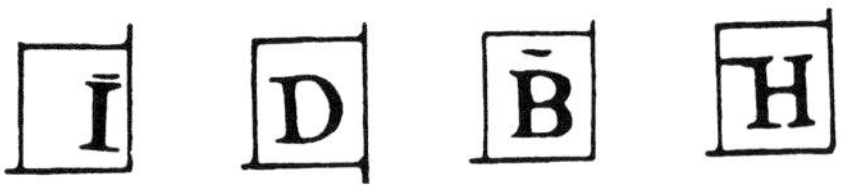

CI FD NB TH

Plate 139

CA EJ EK LI QD SA SB

Plate 140

FD FI EA LI RK

Plate 141 — *Plate* 142

DF EF NJ SA SB IL TA

Plate 143 — *Plate* 144

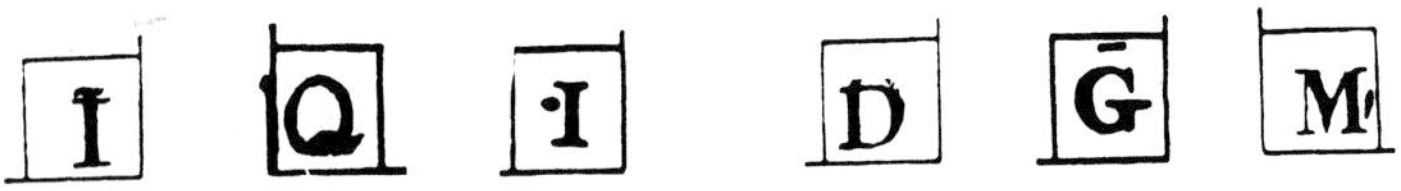

AI QA RI AD EG MC

Plate 145 — *Plate* 146

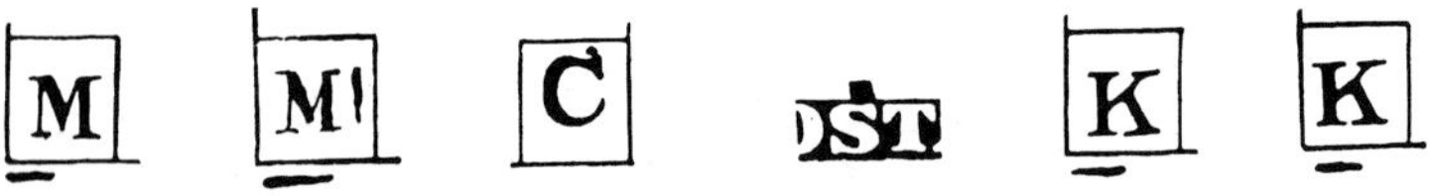

MJ ML PC AL KG KJ

Plate 147 — *Plate* 148

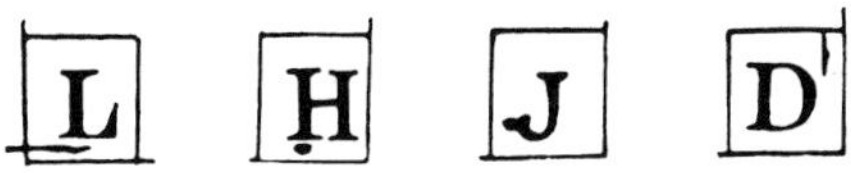

LE QH RJ TD

Plate 149

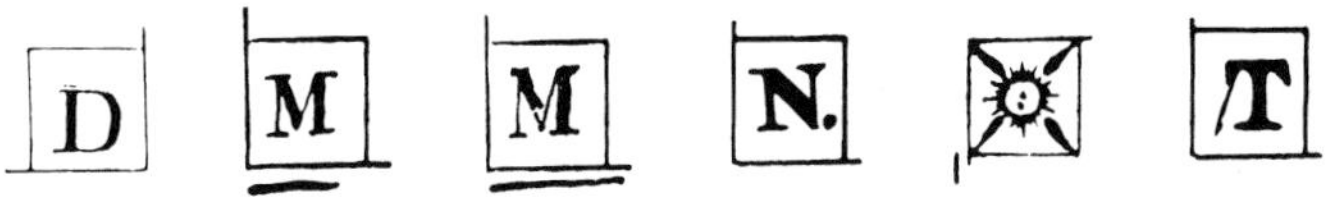

AD MC MF NA SK TA

Plate 150

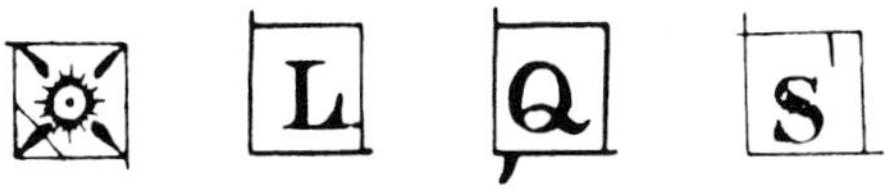

BK LF QC SB

Plate 151

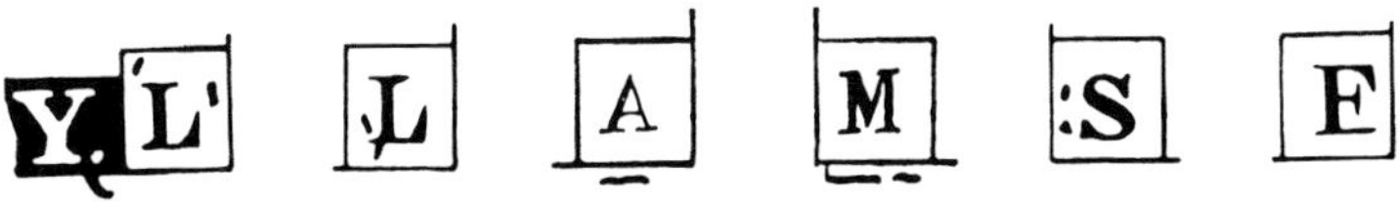

FL KL MA MF SK TF

Plate 152

AE SB

Plate 153

EJ EK

Plate 154

JG OJ PC RJ SC

Plate 154

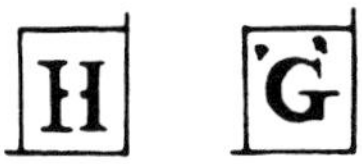

FH PG

Plate 155

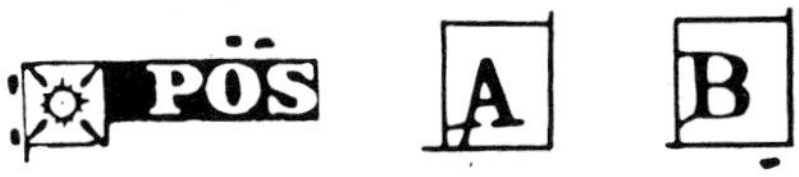

AL BA TB

Plate 156

EK JI LK QB TB

Plate 157

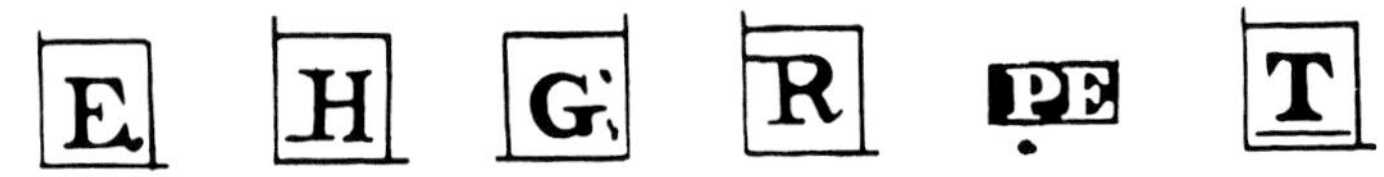

EK HG MG RF TD TK

Plate 158

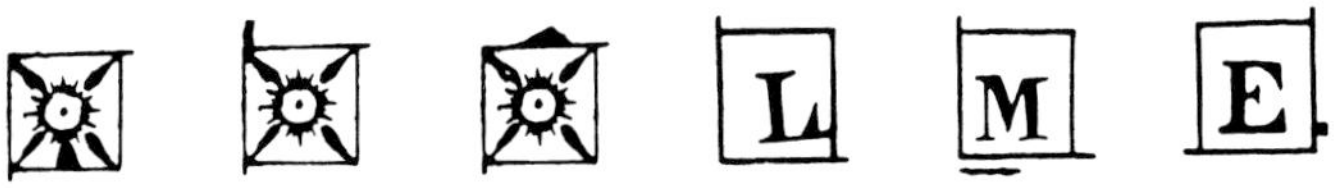

EG FE HE LF MK SE

Plate 159

FK IH II JF JI

LL TB TD TI

Plate 160

HI IA MK NH OG TB

Plate 161

KJ OK RK SI

Plate 162

BD EG PJ SJ TA

Plate 163

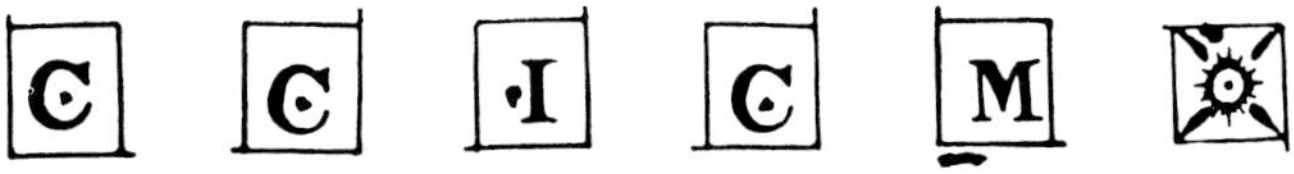

CI DC FI IC ME TG

Plate 164

BB *(second state)* GL LG NA QA
Plate 165

AC DC *(flaw on headband)* II NC
Plate 166

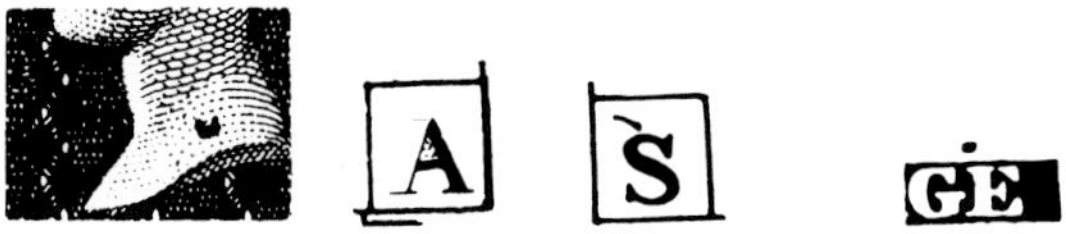

HI *(semi-circular flaw)* NA SB HA, *Plate* 168
Plate 167

FI HD JJ ME QH
Plate 169

BI CA HJ MF RI
Plate 170

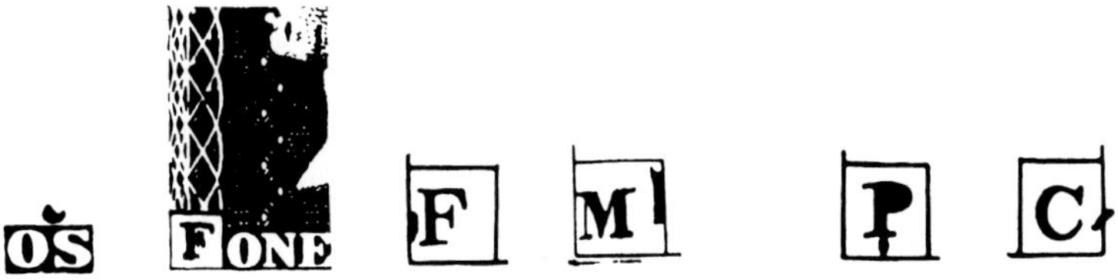

BB FD *(flaws on chin)* FK MK PB TC
Plate 171 *Plate* 172

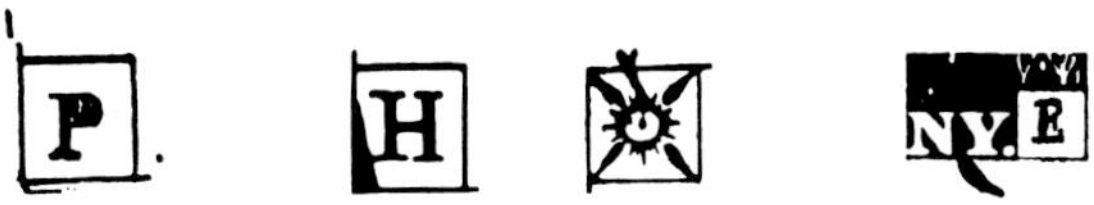

PH, *Plate* 173 HK QH LE, *Plate* 175
Plate 174

Index to Catalogued Varieties in Section BB

This index covers all the stamps, whether imperforate or perforated, of the Die I Plates 132 to 175. These plates, either always imperforate or more commonly imperforate, are listed in Section BB; Plates 176 to 204 and six Reserve plates, being normally found only in perforated form, are listed in Section CB.

AA 132, 135, 143, 147, 152, 157, 160
AB 135, 137, 145, 152, 156, 157, 163, 165, 166, 173
AC 135, 143, 145, 157, 159, 166
AD 132, 133, 137, 138, 144, 146, 147, 150, 156, 163, 173
AE 132, 133, 142, 144, 153, 156, 159, 163, 165
AF 132, 141, 144, 156, 159, 163, 165, 172
AG 132, 142, 150, 155, 159, 163
AH 132, 134, 137, 140, 141, 142, 144, 147, 162, 163, 167, 171, 173
AI 132, 133, 134, 135, 145, 147, 152, 163, 165, 167, 173
AJ 132, 136, 141, 152, 164, 169, 173
AK 132, 142, 164, 167, 173
AL 148, 156, 164

BA 135, 143, 144, 156, 157, 159, 160, 165, 168
BB 139, 141, 142, 143, 155, 160, 165, 171, 173
BC 138, 144, 150, 163
BD 137, 145, 155, 163, 166, 173
BE 132, 133, 135
BF 132, 156, 161, 165
BG 132, 158, 160,173
BH 132, 138, 140, 141, 157, 163, 173, 174, 175
BI 132, 134, 138, 150, 163, 167, 170, 175
BJ 132, 155, 156, 161, 164, 169, 173, 175
BK 132, 135, 151, 157, 163, 173
BL 157, 163, 164

CA 135, 137, 140, 144, 145, 160, 161, 170
CB 145, 173
CC 133, 147
CD 132, 145, 157, 162, 165, 166
CE 132, 138, 162, 173
CF 132, 147, 156, 159, 166
CG 132, 157
CH 132, 137, 139, 157, 159, 173
CI 132, 138, 139, 149, 164
CJ 132
CK 132, 164, 173
CL 174

DA 137, 140, 141, 143, 144, 174
DB 166, 173
DC 164, 166, 168
DD 134, 144, 147, 154, 157, 173
DE 132, 147, 173
DF 132, 143, 147, 156, 157, 173
DG 132, 157, 158
DH 132, 162, 173
DI 132, 149, 158, 173
DJ 132, 158
DK 132, 175

EA 142, 143, 144
EC 156
ED 133, 134, 140, 156
EE 132, 135, 137, 143, 147
EF 132, 140, 143, 147, 155
EG 132, 144, 146, 159, 162, 163, 165
EH 132, 138, 160, 162, 171, 173
EI 132, 173
EJ 132, 137, 140, 154
EK 132, 134, 140, 154, 157, 158, 161
EL 147, 164

FA 138, 140, 143, 147
FB 138, 141, 145, 148, 173
FC 135, 140
FD 139, 141, 148, 171
FE 159
FF 149, 165
FG 132, 135, 148, 165
FH 135, 137, 155
FI 141, 164, 168, 169
FJ 163
FK 135, 160, 171
FL 135, 152

GA 133, 142, 143
GB 133, 161
GC 132, 133, 137, 145, 164
GD 132, 133, 149, 173
GE 133, 147, 169, 175
GF 133, 145, 160
GG 132, 133
GH 133, 135
GI 133, 135, 147, 155
GJ 133
GK 132, 133, 135
GL 133, 135, 144, 165

HA 155, 159, 168, 173, 174
HD 140, 142, 169
HE 135, 159, 160, 164
HF 165, 167
HG 132, 137, 143, 157, 158
HH 135, 147, 173
HI 156, 161, 162, 167
HJ 140, 148, 170
HK 174

IA 137, 143, 147, 150, 159, 161
IB 133, 135, 147
IC 156, 162, 164
ID 144, 173
IE 135
IF 140, 148, 156, 167
IG 132, 135, 136
IH 135, 138, 141, 160, 173
II 135, 160, 166
IJ 135, 157
IK 139, 157
IL 144

JA 132, 134, 135, 150, 159
JB 135, 160, 162, 173, 175
JC 142, 144, 172
JD 137, 142, 155, 161
JE 132, 135
JF 138, 145, 160
JG 132, 154
JH 137
JI 132, 135, 145, 157, 160
JJ 135, 145, 158, 169
JK 142, 158, 161
JL 140, 144, 161

KA 135, 143, 156, 158, 173
KB 148, 161, 162

KC 142, 155
KD 144, 151, 166, 173
KE 132, 135, 144, 151, 164
KF 145
KG 132, 148
KH 173
KJ 162
KL 152

LA 135
LB 138, 141, 173
LC 135, 139, 153
LD 138, 147, 169, 173
LE 149, 175
LF 144, 145, 151, 159, 166, 167, 173
LG 132, 145, 161, 165
LH 137, 142, 147
LI 135, 136, 140, 142, 150
LJ 138
LK 135, 157, 169
LL 151, 160, 161

MA 135, 141, 143, 148, 152, 175
MB 135, 141, 150, 161, 162, 168
MC 132, 135, 144, 146, 149, 150, 174
MD 147, 156, 173, 174
ME 135, 137, 141, 146, 164, 168, 169, 173, 175
MF 146, 149, 150, 152, 159, 167, 168, 170
MG 132, 149, 158, 166, 169
MH 132, 134, 138, 147, 149, 169
MI 141, 154, 165, 167
MJ 138, 147, 150, 154, 155, 157, 165, 168
MK 137, 138, 148, 149, 157, 159, 161, 171
ML 147, 165

NA 135, 144, 150, 165, 167, 173
NB 139, 144, 162, 175
NC 166
ND 137, 141, 173
NE 173
NF 134, 139, 147, 165
NG 132
NH 132, 144, 161
NI 147, 175
NJ 138, 143, 153, 157
NK 175
NL 135

OA 143
OB 135, 140, 144, 147, 171
OC 135, 137, 162
OD 139, 141, 162, 166, 173, 174
OF 132, 141, 148, 158, 164, 169
OG 132, 158, 161
OH 143, 145, 150, 173
OI 132, 147, 151
OJ 138, 154, 161
OK 161, 162, 169

PA 139, 143, 169, 173
PB 138, 139, 157, 162, 166, 172
PC 139, 147, 154, 155
PD 139, 142, 155, 167
PE 139
PF 139, 147, 163, 164, 166
PG 132, 139, 144, 155, 160
PH 133, 139, 141, 173
PI 139
PJ 138, 139, 163
PK 139, 161, 175
PL 139, 155, 157, 161, 175

QA 140, 141, 144, 145, 161, 162, 165
QB 141, 157
QC 151, 162, 175
QD 140, 142, 162, 173
QE 135, 162
QF 144, 145, 147, 159, 164
QG 132, 147, 155, 159
QH 145, 149, 169, 174
QI 147
QJ 147
QK 172
QL 171

RA 143, 172
RB 138, 141, 143, 175
RC 147, 162, 173
RD 142, 158, 162, 173
RE 141, 162, 164, 173
RF 132, 145 155, 156, 158, 163, 164, 175
RG 132, 164, 173
RH 137, 147, 152
RI 141, 145, 170
RJ 149, 154, 155, 173
RK 142, 162

SA 135, 140, 143, 152, 156, 162, 164, 172
SB 140, 141, 142, 147, 151, 153, 154, 162, 167, 171, 175
SC 147, 154, 162, 171, 172
SD 162, 171, 172
SE 145, 149, 159, 164, 172
SF 138, 145, 161
SG 132, 139, 150
SH 135, 136, 140, 144, 145, 147, 167, 173
SI 161, 162
SJ 147, 148, 157, 163
SK 146, 147, 150, 152, 164, 169

TA 137, 138, 142, 144, 145, 150, 157, 162, 163, 170, 173
TB 138, 142, 156, 157, 160, 161, 162, 163, 171, 173, 174
TC 137, 138, 162, 172, 173
TD 149, 158, 160, 162
TE 147, 153, 163
TF 152, 157, 164, 173
TG 132, 163, 164, 172, 173
TH 138, 139, 153, 161, 162, 163, 164, 167, 173
TI 137, 144, 157, 160, 164, 167, 171
TJ 141, 142, 162, 167, 170
TK 136, 141, 153, 158, 163, 165
TL 147, 157, 162, 165, 169

SECTION CA

One Penny Red, Type A1, Experimental Forms of Separation

The advantages of having an easy method of separating stamps were first brought to the notice of the Government by Henry Archer, an Irish-born London businessman. He submitted his plan to the Postmaster-General by whom it was passed on through various channels and experiments until finally approved. Archer's patents were purchased in June 1853 and new machines, initially equipped with two 16 gauge punch sets, were constructed by David Napier & Sons. Examples of Archer's rouletting and perforating trials are well authenticated. There is no evidence to support claims that trials of the Napier machine were conducted before official perforation began in January 1854.

Archer Roulette

Both Henry Archer's early experiments with two rouletting machines were failures, but of one a few stamps have survived. They are rouletted approximately 11½ though this is generally referred to as a gauge 12 roulette.

1848. Die I. Alphabet I. Wmk Small Crown. Rouletted approx. 11½ by Henry Archer.

CE1 (=S.G.16a)	1d. red-brown	. . . .	£9500	†

Stamps from Plates 70 and 71 were used.

Archer Roulette

Archer Trial Perforation

Henry Archer's third machine was the first to be based on perforating, as distinct from rouletting. This machine proved very unsatisfactory at first but after extensive repairs and alteration it was finally approved. The stamps which resulted from these trials were generally issued and are known used in different parts of the country; many went to the West of England.

"Archer" covers used after the issue of officially perforated stamps are no less rare than the earlier ones but are not so keenly sought. Claims for the use of earlier plates and for Plate 107 are suspect. Archer's machine utilised a double comb that perforated two batches of 5 sheets side by side. It is clear from Archer's evidence to the Select Committee that only one comb was used in his trials which were concluded by May 1850.

For other trials by Henry Archer see DP71 under "Line-Engraved Essays, Proofs, etc.".

1850—January 1854. Die I. Alphabet I. Wmk Small Crown. Perforated 16 by Henry Archer.

CE2 (= S.G.16b)		1d. red-brown	£1500	£475
		Block of four	£8000	£3000
		Used on cover, dated prior to February 1854	†	£1750
		Used on cover, dated February 1854 or after	†	£1200
		Used on cover, blue Ashburton "29" numeral	†	£1500
	d.	Watermark inverted	—	£1700

Plated Examples

	Unused single	*Used single*	*Used on cover dated 1850–51*	*Used on cover dated 1853*
Plate 90	—	—	—	—
Plate 91	—	—	—	—
Plate 92	—	£625	£1400	£1300
Plate 93	—	£500	£1100	£1075
Plate 94	—	£450	£1050	£1025
Plate 95	—	£450	£1050	£1025
Plate 96	—	£425	£1050	£800
Plate 97	—	£425	£1050	£800
Plate 98	—	£425	£1050	£800
Plate 99	—	£450	£1150	£1000
Plate 100	—	£450	£1150	£1000
Plate 101	—	£500	£1200	£1050

Examples from other plates previously recorded here have been deleted. Apart from singles from plates 90 and 91 the stamps and covers listed are from the plates accepted as being given to Archer for his perforating experiments.

Plating aids and registration dates for these plates are listed in Section BA.

Government Trial Perforations

Stamps from Die I, Alphabet II, perforation 16, apparently used on cover prior to 27 January (the date on which official perforation began), have previously been attributed to trials of the Napier machine conducted in 1853. There is, however, no supporting evidence for such trials, and it is unlikely that Napier had produced a punch set for the postage stamps (as opposed to the revenue stamps) by the autumn of that year. If these stamps are genuine, it seems more likely that they were produced on the Archer machine after the financial settlement with Archer was concluded in June 1853.

Die I, Alphabet I, stamps from Plates 74 and 113 perforated 14 have been recorded for many years, but it is now generally recognised that the type of machine used, producing one extension hole in the side margins, cannot be contemporary with other trials of this period.

1853. Die I. Alphabet II. Wmk Small Crown. Government trial perf 16.

CE3 (=S.G.16c)	1d. red-brown	*used on cover*	£13000

For the so-called *"Treasury Roulette"* see No, B2a in Section BB,

SECTION CB

One Penny Red, Type A1, Officially Perforated

The stamps dealt with in this Section are divided into five groups as follows:

	Cat Nos.	Page
Group 1: Die I, blued paper	Cl–2	180
Group 2: Die II, blued paper	C3–8	187
Group 3: Die II, red-brown on white paper	C8A	200
Group 4: Die II, transitional issues on yellowish to cream-toned paper	C9	200
Group 5: Die II, rose-red on white paper	C10–13	201

Prices for Stamps in Used Condition

As the perforating of stamps was a new invention applied to imprecise printing technology, it stands to reason that many of the Line-Engraved stamps were issued in sheets containing badly centred examples. The "used" prices quoted are for average examples. Inferior grade stamps and those with very heavy or smudged postmarks are worth less.

On the other hand there is a premium for well centred lightly used stamps. Prices for these in this Section can be calculated by adding **125%** to the prices quoted.

Repaired Impressions—Prices for Original States

Although they are not separately listed, it must be understood that wherever impressions are repaired, creating second states, the prices for the letterings in original states may be higher than those for normal unrepaired letterings that exist in only one state. This applies throughout the Line-Engraved issues.

Group 1: Die I, Blued Paper

A perforation machine equipped with two gauge 16 punch sets began work on 27 January 1854 when 50 sheets of stamps were perforated. A second machine, similarly equipped, started work on 22 February. The machines were designed by James Murdoch Napier, and constructed by the family firm, David Napier & Son.

Instructions were sent to postmasters on 12 March 1854 not to issue the perforated stamps until stocks of the imperforate stamps were exhausted. Nevertheless, some of the perforated stamps were issued in the latter part of February 1854. The earliest recorded cover is dated 24 February 1854. Covers dated before 12 March are rare.

The earliest officially perforated stamps came from plates which were already in use and from which imperforate sheets had already emanated. The plates from which stamps both imperforate and perforated are known fall within the group 155 to 177. Plates employed for perf. 16 and 14 are identified below Nos. Cl and C2. Stamps existing with both perforations are priced below No. C2.

The group here dealt with is apparently of manageable size and differs from all other groups in the major features of being Die I perforated; probably due to the high proportion of poorly centred examples and the uniform check letters in their squares, this group has not been widely studied. At this stage there is little information on record for the guidance of would-be platers, apart from the opportunity of inspecting the imprimaturs at The Post Office Heritage Services and of purchasing actual-size photos of them; nevertheless the group contains many hidden rarities and will repay any collector who turns his attention to it even at this late date.

Frank Ives Scudamore. Stamps in this group exist handstamped "Frank Ives Scudamore Chief Examiner" in script. Scudamore was appointed as the chief examiner by the Post Office when the posts of accountant-general and receiver-general were combined at Somerset House in 1852. The handstamp, which was in use between February 1854 and March 1855, can be found complete on vertical strips of 3 or on a horizontal strip of 4. It was designed to render stamps so cancelled unusable for letters. The handstamp has been seen on the following: Nos. Cl, plates 166, 174, 194, 200; C3, plates 2, 6, 8, 9, 12; C4, plates 6, 7, 9; 2d., Nos. Fl and F2 both plate 4, also ls. embossed No. H1, die 2 (1854). (*Price for a strip of four showing complete handstamp from* £950.)

1854 (24 February–March). First Official Perforated Issue. Die I. Alphabet II. Blued Paper. Wmk Small Crown. Perf 16.

C1 (=S.G.17/18)	(1)	1d. red-brown	£275	22·00
	(2)	1d. yellow-brown	£325	45·00
	(3)	1d. brick-red	£425	45·00
	(4)	1d. plum	£2500	£750
	(5)	1d. orange-red	£1250	£300
		Block of four	£1750	£275
		Used on cover	†	45·00
	c.	Very blue paper	—	22·00
	d.	Watermark inverted	—	£180
	e.	Major re-entry	—	£100
	f.	Minor re-entry	—	30·00
	g.	Double letter	—	30·00
	h.	Imperforate three sides (horiz. pair from J or N rows)	†	—
	i.	Double perforation	—	95·00
	j.	Constant varieties	—	35·00
	k.	Imperforate (Plates 200 and 203)	†	
	l.	Recut frame	—	32·00

Plates used for this issue were 155, 157, 162 to 204 and R1 to R6. Prices for plated used examples are given in the table below C2.

Similar 1d. stamps with Alphabet I corner letters are Archer trials. See Section CA.

Imprimaturs (imperf), Plates 176–204, *prices from* £650, R1–14, £700. Stamps removed from the imprimatur sheets are: Plate 176: AA to AL, IK, IL, JG to JL, TL; Plate 177: AA to AL, JL, KF to KL, TL; Plate 178: AA to AL, SE to SL, TL; Plate 179: AA to AL, SF to SL, TK, TL; Plate 180: AA to AL, BE to BL, TL; Plate 181: AA to AL, BA to BG, BI, TL; Plate 182: AA to AL, GK, GL, HG to HL, TL; Plate 183: AA to AL, IG to IL, JK, JL, TL; Plate 184: AA to AL, HK, HL, IG to IL, TL; Plate 185: AA to AL, HK, HL, IG to IL, TL; Plate 186: AA to AL, HK, HL, IG to IL, TL; Plate 187: AA to AL, HK, HL, IG to IL, TL; Plate 188: AA to AL, HK, HL, IG to IL, TL; Plate 189: AA to AL, FL, GG to GL, HL, TL; Plate 190: AL, FK, FL, GG to GL, TL; Plate 191: AL, GK, GL, HG to HL, TA to TL; Plate 192: AA to AL, FK, FL, GG to GL, TL; Plate 193: AL, GK, GL, HG to HL, TA to TL; Plate 194: AL, SE to SL, TA to TL; Plate 195: AL, SE to SL, TA to TL; Plate 196: AL, SE to SL, TA to TL; Plate 197: AL, SE to SL, TA to TL; Plate 198: AA to AL, QG to QL, RH, RL, TL; Plate 199: AA to AL, SF to SL, TK, TL; Plate 200: AA to AL GG to GL, HK, HL, TL; Plate 201: AA to AL, RH, SF to SL, TL; Plate 202: AA to AL, SF to SL, TK, TL; Plate 203: AA to AL, HL, QF to QL, TL; Plate 204: AA to AL, RG, SF to SL, TL; Plate R1: AA to AL, IK, IL, JG to JL, TL; Plate R2: AA to AL, IK, IL, JG to JL, TL; Plate R3: AA to AL, IK, IL, JG to JL, TL; Plate R4: AA to AL, IK, IL, JG to JL, TL; Plate R5: AA to AL, HK, HL, IG to IL, TL; Plate R6: AA to AL, GK, GL, HG to HL, TL; Plate R7: AA to AL, GK, GL, HG to HL, TL; Plate R8: AA to AL, HK, HL, IG to IL, TL; Plate R9: AA to AL, HK, HL, IG to IL, TL; Plate R10: AA to AL, HK, HL, IG to IL, TL; Plate R11: AA to AL, KK, KL, LG to LL, TL; Plate R12: AL, SE to SL, TA to TL; Plate R13: AA to AL, QF to QL, RF, TL; Plate R14: AA to AL, RE to RL, TL.

Plates registered: Plates 178 to 183, 13 February 1854; Plates 184 to 189, 12 July 1854; Plates 190 to 193, 11 August 1854; Plates 194 to 197, 21 September 1854; Plates 198 to 201, 8 November 1854; Plates 202 to 204, 30 November 1854; Reserve Plates R1 to R3, 4 June 1852; R4 to R6, 27 July 1852; R7, 16 September 1852; R8 to R10, 14 January 1853; R11, 18 April 1853; R12, R13, 20 July 1853; R14, 13 February 1854.

Prices for Distinctive and Coloured Cancellations

The following listing applies to all groups of the offically perforated One Penny Red (SG. Spec C1–13).

Prices quoted for coloured cancellations are for fine clearly coloured examples, uncontaminated by black ink. Contaminated 'mixed ink pad' examples, are worth less. Superb complete strikes are worth a premium **+50%.**

From December 1852 intentionally coloured inks were issued as an experiment to help to distinguish town datestamps from different GPO Surveyors districts. They were not intended for obliterating (ie cancelling) stamps, for which black ink was provided. Misuse of *datestamping* inks for *obliteration* accounts for most coloured cancellations on stamps. Blue inks of the period vary widely in hue and depth and encompass blue-green shades. 'Violet' inks are in fact distinctive shades of violet-blue ink. True green cancellations are most often encountered from Irish offices. Examples from Scottish and English offices are worth a premium. By 1857 the experiment had effectively ceased with most provincial offices reverting to blue or black ink for datestamping. C10–13 issues are rarely seen with coloured cancellations other than blue.

Prices for Town and Namestamp cancellations are those not additionally obliterated by other means.

Maltese Cross Cancellations (Late Use)

		Large portion of p/m on stamp	*Complete p/m on stamp on piece*	*On stamp on cover*
ta.	Black . . . *from*	£500	£650	£1800
tb.	Blue	£750	£1000	£2500

1844-Type numeral Cancellations

ua.	Black . . . *from*	10·00	15·00	20·00
ub.	Blue	£125	£150	£425
uc.	Green	£250	£300	£750
ud.	Red	£550	£900	£4000
ue.	Violet	£500	£800	£3500
uf.	Brown*	£500	£800	£3000

Spoon and Duplex Cancellations

		Complete p/m on stamp on piece	*On stamp on cover*
va.	Black . . . *from*	25·00	35·00
vb.	Blue	£250	£500
vc.	Green	£375	£850
vd.	Red	£1500	£4500

Town Cancellations (on Stamps)

		Large portion of p/m on stamp	*Complete p/m on stamp on piece*	*On stamp on cover*
wa.	Black	95·00	£125	£250
wb.	Blue	£175	£225	£700
wc.	Green	£400	£500	£1800
wd.	Red	£2000	—	—
we.	Violet	£2000	£2500	—

English and Irish Undated Name Stamps (on Stamps)

xa.	Black . . . *from*	£175	£300	£900
xb.	Blue	£275	£450	£1600
xc.	Green	£375	£650	£2000

Scots Local Name Stamp Cancellations (on Stamps)

		Large portion of p/m on stamp	*Complete p/m on stamp on piece*	*On stamp on cover*
ya.	Black . . . . . *from*	25·00	35·00	60·00
yb.	Blue	£150	£250	£600
yc.	Green	£250	£500	£1250

*True Brown datestamping ink was supplied to the 'Home District' GPO Surveyor of England and certain PO Surveyors in Ireland. Brown cancellations on stamps are known from Bagshot, Wimborne, Cuckfield, Winchester, Southampton and Banbridge. Brown Irish numerals are worth a premium. The issue of brown ink effectively ceased during 1856. Hence 'brown' cancellations on later C9–13 issues should be viewed with caution.

Apparently 'Olive' cancellations can be found from offices in the 'Western' district of England, particularly during 1855–56, but are believed to be due to excessively oiled blue inks. Prices are similar to those of blue cancellations.

1855 (January). Second Official Perforation. Die I. Alphabet II. Blued Paper. Wmk Small Crown. Perf 14.

C2 (=S.G.22)	(1)	1d. red-brown	£500	70·00
	(2)	1d. yellow-brown	£500	70·00
	(3)	1d. brick-red	£900	£200
	(4)	1d. plum	£2500	£900
	(5)	1d. orange-brown	£1200	£325
		Block of four	£3000	£450
		Used on cover	†	£125
	c.	Very blue paper	—	80·00
	d.	Watermark inverted	—	£225
	e.	Major re-entry	—	£140
	f.	Minor re-entry	—	85·00
	g.	Double letter	—	75·00
	h.	Double perforation	—	£125
	i.	Constant varieties	—	75·00

Plates used for this issue were 194 to 198, 200 to 204 and R1 to R6.

Plated Used Examples

	C1
Plate 155	32·00
Plate 157	85·00
Plate 162	45·00
Plate 163	£100
Plate 164	38·00
Plate 165	£140
Plate 166	32·00
Plate 167	32·00
Plate 168	£2800
Plate 169	35·00
Plate 170	£240
Plate 171	35·00
Plate 172	32·00
Plate 173	32·00
Plate 174	35·00
Plate 175	35·00
Plate 176	32·00
Plate 177	32·00
Plate 178	32·00
Plate 179	32·00
Plate 180	32·00
Plate 181	32·00
Plate 182	35·00
Plate 183	35·00
Plate 184	35·00

	C1	*C2*
Plate 185	35·00	†
Plate 186	45·00	†
Plate 187	40·00	†
Plate 188	32·00	†
Plate 189	35·00	†
Plate 190	35·00	†
Plate 191	35·00	†
Plate 192	35·00	†
Plate 193	35·00	†
Plate 194	32·00	£140
Plate 195	35·00	£400
Plate 196	32·00	£140
Plate 197	35·00	£175
Plate 198	35·00	£110
Plate 199	£110	†
Plate 200	45·00	95·00
Plate 201	50·00	80·00
Plate 202	35·00	75·00
Plate 203	45·00	80·00
Plate 204	£110	80·00
Plate R1	35·00	75·00
Plate R2	32·00	75·00
Plate R3	35·00	75·00
Plate R4	45·00	75·00
Plate R5	35·00	75·00
Plate R6	35·00	75·00

Plates 155, 157 and 162 to 177 are also known imperforate. See Section BB and the notes there.

The existence of plated examples from plates 160 and 161 perforated 16 and plates 192 and 193 perforated 14 is doubtful and we have accordingly deleted these from the above table, Examples from plate 168 are rare (16 examples known).

Plating Aids

For Plating aids for Plates 155, 157 and 162 to 175 see the list below B2.

The date given in brackets against each plate is the date on which it was put to press.

Plate 176 (12 January 1854): The bottom of the D square on ID is missing as are the bottom lines on both letter squares on IH and LD. Many stamps from this plate can be found in a very worn state with either the top lines of N.W. and N.E. squares missing, or the bottom lines of the letter squares either very faint or sometimes missing. ***R***: AA, AB, EB, ED, EH, FC, GF, GG, GH, JD, JE, KD, KE, KH (three states), LC, LF, LG, NG, NH–NL; OG, QA, QD, RA, RF, RG, SG–SJ, TD. All except AA and KD are coincident re-entries with corner letters recut. MC exists in two states with recut corner letters and worn impression, but no obvious signs of re-entry.

Plate 177 (12 January 1854): There is a blur above the (blind) A on TA. Mark on PO of POSTAGE on ML. There are dots below PENNY on KK.

Plate 178 (17 February 1854): Badly misplaced letters occur on *JD*, J*F*, K*B*, *MH*, P*H*. Mark on F*H*.

Plate 179 (17 February 1854): On NG the N extends below. Marks appear in the top loop of the B on each of CB, DB, FB, GB. Mark in E of POSTAGE on SE.

Plate 180 (22 February 1854): A flaw appears by the top serif of the L on LE.

Plate 181 (17 March 1854): There is a mark on the G of CG. Two marks to left of S square on SH.

Plate 182 (24 April 1854); Nothing reported.

Plate 183 (26 April 1854): Marks occur in the N.E. corner of AG, over the I of FI and near the G on PG. Horizontal line under M square on MI.

Plate 184 (13 July 1854): There is a minor re-entry on PF, mainly notable in the thinning of the letters of POSTAGE. The L is double on LA. Many stamps have extensively recut sides, either one or both, most frequently from the top half of the sheet. Marks occur on *A*H and *S*L.

Plate 185 (18 July 1854): SE shows a minor re-entry. AA, AB have lower right frame recut, with burrs; on FF and NG (N blind) there is recutting of the left side.

Plate 186 (13 July 1854): A re-entry occurs on QB in the letters ONE PENNY and below. Horizontal line under M square on MH.

Plate 187 (13 July 1854): A re-entry occurs on CJ in top squares, and on FL in upper portion. An extra line occurs below the M square on MI. The I is central.

Plate 188 (18 July 1854): A good re-entry on BI. Prominent marks appear on GK above POSTAGE and the N.E. square. There are traces of re-entry to the left of JF and the J square lacks a bottom line on the same stamp.

Plate 189 (18 July 1854): Re-entry: BA–CA. There is a slight re-entry on IK and on TK and prominent doubling of the top line of the N.W. square on HA.

Plate 190 (11 August 1854): Re-entry on KA. On QK, QL, the Qs are wholly or partly blind. On BD the D is extremely low and to the left. On RF the F is possibly double. There is a flaw in the A square of LA.

Plate 191 (12 August 1854): Re-entry SG, upper portion. Many of the Js are low and to the left of their squares. There is a vertical stroke to the left of K on RK,

Plate 192 (12 August 1854): AI shows a good re-entry. The top loop of the Bs in the B row is blind (except BE, recut, high in square). On HL the L is probably doubled upwards.

Plate 193 (12 August 1854): On EG and OE the Es are double. The Q of QI is partly blind and the Fs are blind on HF, QF. The T on TH is double, Prominent mark on L of EL.

Plate 194 (23 September 1854): On BA there is a mark on the bust above P of PENNY. KG and PA show re-entries and KI has the I recut. MK and ML both have strong recutting to the lower quarter of the left frame, SI, TF and TH also have recut frames, MI has double M, Horizontal line beneath M square on MG.

Plate 195 (23 September 1854): D*H* and *LC* are probably double letters, NI shows re-entry. Blob in lower left frame of CK and in middle left frame of LJ. Horizontal mark under L square on KL.

Plate 196 (23 September 1854): There is a flaw on the crown of each of KB, LB and MB. Constant varieties on *M*K, NK and *P*E (illustrated).

Plate 197 (29 September 1854): There is a blob over the N.W. star of DC; an apparent doubling of E in EK and a mark over the eye in FA. The I is possibly double on IH, a prominent mark in J of JD and a prominent doubling below the M square of MF. On QF there is a thick line through T of POSTAGE.

Plate 198 (9 November 1854): The L appears double on LI. The lower third of the right frame is strongly recut on EF. There is a mark from NY to the B square of TB.

Plate 199 (9 November 1854): Re-entry on IG. The Qs tend to be blurred inside. There is a diagonal line extending from forehead to N.E. square on later printings of CG and on DH there are marks below H square.

Plate 200 (9 November 1854): Re-entries: AG–BG, EA–FA, FD–GD, MG–NJ, The lower left frame is recut on KI.
Plate 201 (10 November 1854): There is a possible double letter (B) on BJ; a probable re-entry on later printings of OA; the Q on QH is blind and set high. There is a mark in S.E. corner of T square on TG and TH.
Plate 202 (2 December 1854).
Plate 203 (20 December 1854): AB recut right side; AC re-entry; DA–EA re-entry; OA has line below O square in later printings; PL bottom of P square weak or missing.
Plate 204 (11 January 1855): An extra line under the M square in MI. I is well to the left.
Plate R1 (22 November 1854): AE, mark on back of neck; QA, line under Y of PENNY.
Plate R2 (22 November 1854): AA, re-entry; SB, notable blob under B square.
Plate R3 (22 November 1854): OF, irregular marks on F square. Horizontal line under M square on MJ and MK.
Plate R4 (22 November 1854): A slightly doubled on TA; G on NG recut larger; marks in left frame of RL.
Plate R5 (22 November 1854): A notable flaw joins ND to NE; there are lines under the M squares on MB, MJ; line below S square in SD.
Plate R6 (22 November 1854): GB, possible re-entry marks in B square.

RE-ENTRIES

Plate 188

Plate 188 (GK)

Plate 189 (BA–CA)

Plate 192

Plate 194

Plate 195

Plate 200 (EA–FA)

Plate 200 (FD–GD)

Plate 201

Plate 203

Plate 203

Plate R2

FLAWS, ETC.

ML, *Plate* 177

FH, *Plate* 178

AH SL
Plate 184

HA, *Plate* 189

RK,
Plate 191

HL, *Plate* 192

EG

EL

OE

TH

Plate 193

KI

MI

Plate 194

CK

DH

LC

Plate 195

LJ,
Plate 195

Plate 196, *flaw on front of diadem*
(KB, LB, MB)

MK

NK

PE

Plate 196

DC EK FA IH JD–KD MF
Plate 197

LI TB
Plate 198

CG DH
Plate 199

QH TG & TH
Plate 201

OA, *Plate* 203 SB, *Plate* R2

RL TA
Plate R4

ND–NE SD
Plate R5

GB, *Plate* R6

Group 2: Die II, Blued Paper

A new series of plate numbers commenced with the new die. Plates numbered 1 to 21, having the Die II head and Alphabet II letters, form a distinct group as all plates thereafter had Alphabet III letters. Plates 1 to 21 appeared in both perforations with both Small Crown and Large Crown watermarks so that this is a particularly interesting group. Some re-entries exist, PL–QL of Plate 13 being particularly outstanding, and there are a number of double letters and constant varieties recorded.

Stamps from these plates are occasionally found on toned or pale grey papers as well as on the usual blued paper.

The plum shade, previously listed (Nos. C3/4), is now known to be from printings in deep red-brown on very blue paper and sometimes darkened by a deposit of sulphide accumulated over the years. It resulted from excessive sulphur dioxide in the air (prior to the Clean Air Act) reacting with certain chemical ingredients present on the stamp. It is possible to remove this with an oxidizing agent to restore the original red-brown shade.

1855 (February). Introduction of New Die II. Alphabet II. Blued Paper. Wmk Small Crown.
(a) Perf 14

C3 (=S.G.24/25)	(1)	1d. red-brown (27.2.55)*	£450	50·00
	(2)	1d. deep red-brown (very blue paper)	£575	90·00
	(3)	1d. orange-brown	£1400	£140
	(4)	1d. lake-brown		
		Block of four	£3000	£400
		Used on cover	†	90·00
	d.	Watermark inverted	£1250	£180
	e.	Major re-entry	—	£180
	f.	Minor re-entry	—	65·00
	g.	Double letter	—	65·00
	h.	Constant varieties *from*	—	65·00
	i.	Inverted S (Plate 5)	—	£150
	j.	Minute G (Plates 5, 6)	—	£125
	k.	Double perforation	—	£125

Plates 1 to 21 were used for this issue.
* The date is the earliest known use.

1855 (February).
(b) Perf 16

C4 (=S.G.21)	(1)	1d. red-brown (22.2.55)*	£325	60·00
	(2)	1d. yellow-brown	£375	65·00
	(3)	1d. brick-red	£475	70·00
		Block of four	£2400	£400
		Used on cover	†	£100
	c.	Watermark inverted	£650	£180
	d.	Major re-entry	—	£180
	e.	Minor re-entry	—	65·00
	f.	Double letter	—	65·00
	g.	Constant varieties *from*	—	65·00
	h.	Inverted S (Plate 5)	—	£160
	i.	Minute G (Plates 5, 6)	—	£125
	j.	Imperforate (Plate 2, 14)		

Plates 1 to 15 were used for this issue.
* The date is the earliest known use.

Imprimaturs (imperf), Plates 1 *to* 21 *from* £600. The Plate 8 imprimatur sheet has the watermark inverted. Stamps removed from the imprimatur sheets are: Plate 1: AA to AL, HL, IG to IL, JL, TL; Plate 2: AA to AL, HK, HL, IG to IL, TL; Plate 3: AA to AL, HK, HL, IG to IL, TL; Plate 4: AA to AL, GK, GL, HG to HL, TL; Plate 5: AA to AL, RF to RL, SK, TA; Plate 6: AA to AL, RH, SF to SL, TL; Plate 7: AA to AL GG to GL, HK, HL, TL; Plate 8: AA to AL, IG to IL, JK, JL, TL; Plate 9: AA to AL, FG to FL, GK, GL, TL; Plate 10: AA to AL, GK, GL, HG to HL, TL; Plate 11: AA to AL, IK, IL, JG to JL, TL; Plate 12: AA to AL, IK, IL, JG to JL, TL; Plate 13: AA to AL, IK, IL, JG to JL, TL; Plate 14: AA to AL, IA, IB, JA to JF, TL; Plate 15: AA to AL, IA, IB JA to JF TL; Plate 16: AA to AL, IA, IB, JA to JF, TL; Plate 17: AA to AL, IA, IB, JA to JF, TL; Plate 18: AA to AL, HA, HB, IA to IF, TL; Plate 19: AA to AL, IA, IB, JA to JF, TL; Plate 20: AA to AL, IA, IB, JA to JF, TL; Plate 21: AA to AL, IA, IB, JA to JF, TA.

Plates registered: Plates 1 to 4, 15 January 1855; Plates 5 to 7, 1 February 1855; Plates 8 to 13, 19 March 1855; Plates 14 to 20, 12 May 1855; Plate 21, 8 June 1855.

1855 (May). Introduction of Large Crown watermark, Type I. Die II. Alphabet II. Blued Paper.
(a) Perf 16

C5 (=S.G.26)	(1)	1d. red-brown (15.5.55)	£800	95·00
	(2)	1d. very deep red-brown	£950	£120
		Block of four	£5000	£500
		Used on cover	†	£180
	c.	Watermark inverted	—	£250
	d.	Major re-entry	—	£200
	e.	Minor re-entry	—	£110
	f.	Double letter	—	£110
	g.	Constant varieties *from*	—	£110
	h.	Inverted S (Plate 5)	—	£180
	i.	Minute G (Plates 5, 6)	—	£140

Plates 1 to 15 were used for this issue.

1855 (June). Large Crown watermark, Type I. Die II. Alphabet II. Blued Paper.
(b) Perf 14

C6	(1)	1d. red-brown	£425	25·00
	(2)	1d. yellow-brown	£450	35·00
	(3)	1d. plum (February 1856)	£2500	£750
	(4)	1d. brown-rose	£500	45·00
	(5)	1d. orange-brown	£1200	£125
		Block of four	£3000	£275
		Used on cover	†	60·00
	c.	Watermark inverted	—	£140
	d.	Major re-entry	—	90·00
	e.	Minor re-entry	—	35·00
	f.	Double letter	—	35·00
	g.	Constant varieties *from*	—	35·00
	h.	Inverted S (Plate 5)	—	£175
	i.	Minute G (Plates 5, 6)	—	£120
	j.	Imperforate (Plates 7, 10, 13, 14, 15, 18)		
	k.	Double perforation		

Plates 1 to 21 were used.

A used imperforate single from plate 18 is known with inverted watermark.

Transitional Period. The destruction of plates 16 to 18 took place on 22 June 1857. Very small printings were probably the result of the late use of the plates in Spring 1857. The stamps have Alphabet II letters, are known in red-brown on toned paper, also rose-red and similar to the shade (5) listed under No. C10, but on paper which is slightly blued or toned. These are scarce to very rare and so far are only known used (*price* £1200). See notes under Nos. C8 and C9.

Plated Used Examples

	C3	*C4*	*C5*	*C6*
Plate 1	55·00	60·00	95·00	25·00
Plate 2	55·00	60·00	95·00	25·00
Plate 3	£100	£110	—	£750
Plate 4	50·00	60·00	95·00	25·00
Plate 5	50·00	60·00	95·00	25·00
Plate 6	50·00	60·00	£100	25·00
Plate 7	65·00	65·00	95·00	25·00
Plate 8	50·00	65·00	£100	25·00
Plate 9	50·00	65·00	95·00	25·00
Plate 10	70·00	70·00	95·00	25·00
Plate 11	70·00	90·00	£100	25·00
Plate 12	65·00	70·00	95·00	25·00
Plate 13	£140	£325	£350	25·00
Plate 14	70·00	90·00	95·00	25·00
Plate 15	£140	£375	£400	25·00
Plate 16	£325	†	†	25·00
Plate 17	£550	†	†	25·00
Plate 18	£380	†	†	£110
Plate 19	£110	†	†	90·00
Plate 20	£110	†	†	70·00
Plate 21	£325	†	†	80·00

A single example has been recorded of No. C5 from plate 3.

Prices for Varieties

Prices for varieties listed under "Plating Aids" are naturally governed by the scarcity of the plate. The prices quoted in the catalogue lists apply to the cheapest form of varieties, and the price for a variety on a "plated" stamp will be greater than that for an item bought "plate unknown".

So although items listed under "Plating Aids" may be evaluated by reference to the prices listed under C3 to C11, these valuations must often be increased to take account of the prices quoted under "Plated Used Examples".

Plating Aids

This list covers Die II Plates 1 to 21.

The date in brackets against each plate is the date on which it was put to press. Abbreviations used are as follows: ***R***, re-entry; ***D***, double letter; ***CV***, constant variety.

Plate 1 (16 January 1855): ***CV***: F*B*, H*H*, *L*A, *M*H, Q*B*. ***D***: A*K*.
Plate 2 (20 January 1855): ***CV***: BI, CI, FG, QB, QF.
Plate 3 (20 January 1855): ***R***: QK. ***CV***: NI–OI.
Plate 4 (20 January 1855): ***CV***: BD, *I*L.
Plate 5 (3 February 1855): ***R***: LJ, MJ, TD. ***CV***: *B*L, CK, CL, E*G*, E*K*, *LL*, *M*G. ***D***: A*D*, H*B*, SD to SL have inverted S.
Plate 6 (3 February 1855): ***R***: EH, ***CV***: AL, *D*D, *D*L, *F*B, I*L*, *T*J.
Plate 7 (7 February 1855): ***CV***: *F*G, *J*A, *J*G, M*B*, QD, R*E*, SB, SG.
Plate 8 (24 March 1855): ***CV***: C*G*, *F*C, *H*K, LC, OE, Q*B*.
Plate 9 (24 March 1855): ***R***: IG. ***D***: *P*L. ***CV***: *F*F.
Plate 10 (11 April 1855): ***R***: KK, KL, ***D***: H*H*. ***CV***: NL, OF, R*A*.
Plate 11 (16 April 1855): ***CV***: *T*E.
Plate 12 (19 April 1855): ***CV***: D*K*, HB, *Q*A.
Plate 13 (23 April 1855): ***R***: PL–QL, QE. ***CV***: AI, AJ, BJ, CJ, R*L*.
Plate 14 (22 May 1855): ***R***: OE, TD. ***CV***: NE.
Plate 15 (26 May 1855): ***CV***: OD.
Plate 16 (15 May 1855): ***R***: OE. ***CV***: C*E*, CL, DE, Q*G*.
Plate 17 (15 May 1855): ***R***: TD. ***CV***: SI, TI.
Plate 18 (1 June 1855):
Plate 19 (16 October 1855): ***CV***: *D*L, *J*L, SJ.
Plate 20 (19 October 1855):
Plate 21 (8 June 1855): ***CV***: G*G*.

RE-ENTRIES, ETC.

Plate 2

Plate 4

TD
Plate 5

EH
Plate 6

Plate 7

Plate 9

Plate 10

Plate 13

Plate 14

Plate 16

CONSTANT VARIETIES AND DOUBLE LETTERS

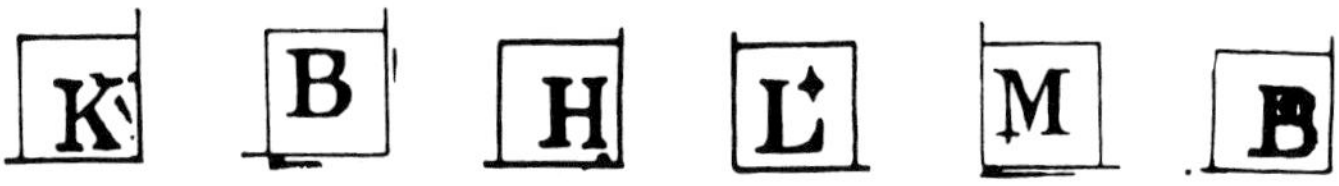

AK FB HH LA MH QB

Plate 1

CI FG QB QF

Plate 2

NI–OI, *Plate* 3 IL, *Plate* 4 AD BL CK

Plate 5

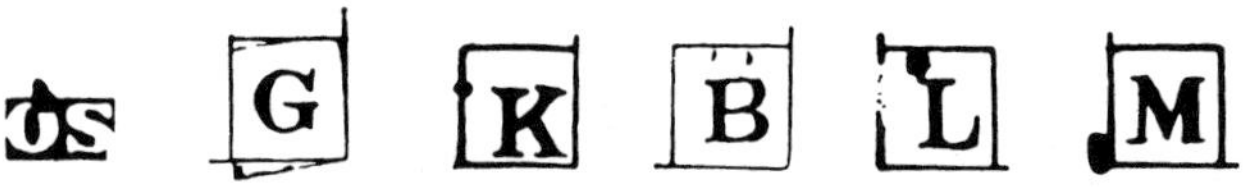

CL EG EK HB LL MG

Plate 5

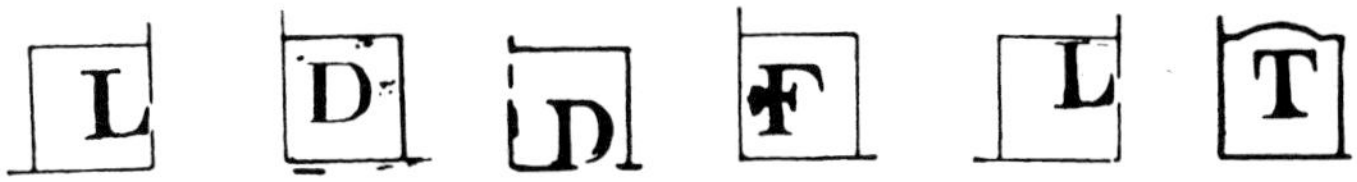

AL DD DL FB IL TJ

Plate 6

FG JA JG MB QD RE (*large* E) SG

Plate 7

CG FC HK LC OE QB

Plate 8

FF PL HH KK (*re-entry*) NL OF RA

Plate 9 *Plate* 10

TE, *Plate* 11 DK HB QA AI, AJ, BJ, CJ RL

Plate 12 *Plate* 13

NE, *Plate* 14 OD, *Plate* 15

CE CL DE QG (*large* G)

Plate 16

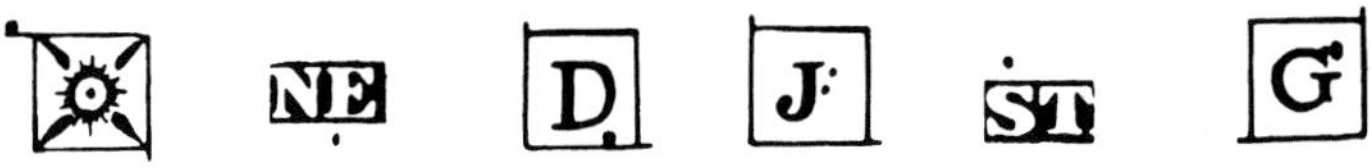

SI TI DL JL SJ GG, *Plate* 21

Plate 17 *Plate* 19

1855 (August). Introduction of Alphabet III. Die II. Blued Paper. Wmk Small Crown. Perf 14.

C7		1d. red-brown	£2750	£650
		Block of four	£16000	£5000
		Used on cover	†	£1500
	c.	Watermark inverted	—	£1750
	d.	Re-entry CE, Plate 22	—	£850
	e.	Re-entries, Plates 24, 25 *from*	—	£700
	f.	Re-entry AD–BD, Plate 27		
	g.	Other re-entries, Plate 27		
	h.	Constant varieties *from*	—	£700
	i.	Characteristic letters *from*	—	£700

Plates 22 to 27 are known to have been used for this issue.

Imprimaturs (*imperf*), *Plates* 22, 24: £750; *Plate R*20; £725. Stamps removed from the imprimatur sheets are: Plate 22: AL, RA, SA to SG, TA to TL; Plate 24: AA to AL, HL, IL, JG to JL, TL; Plate R20: AA to AL, IK, IL, JG to JL, TL.

No. C7 arose when a few remaining sheets of paper with Small Crown watermark were used in the first few months of the printings from the first plates with Alphabet III (Plates 22 to 27). Plated used examples are priced below C8. Plating aids are similarly listed below C8.

Characteristic letters found in Alphabet III plates are illustrated below C10.

1856 (10 January). Die II. Alphabet III. More or less Blued Paper. Wmk Large Crown, Type I. Perf 14.

C8 (=S.G.29/33)	(1)	1d. red-brown	£200	18·00
	(2)	1d. brick-red	£275	40·00
	(3)	1d. plum	£2000	£650
	(4)	1d. brown-rose	£275	40·00
	(5)	1d. orange-brown (March 1857)	£425	45·00
	(6)	1d. deep claret on deep blue paper	£1600	£350
	(7)	1d. orange-red	£550	£110
		Block of four	£1250	£250
		Used on cover	†	35·00
	c.	Watermark inverted	£750	£100
	e.	Major re-entry	£275	40·00
	f.	Minor re-entry	£240	18·00
	g.	Double letter	£225	18·00
	h.	Imperforate (red-brown)*	£3000	£2500
	i.	Constant varieties *from*	£225	25·00
	j.	Gothic K, Plates 23–31 *from*	£275	30·00
	k.	Characteristic letters, Plate 22 *each*	£1000	£400
	l.	Double perforation		
	s.	"Specimen", Type 2 (Plate 35) horiz.	£550	
	t.	Do. but vert.	£450	

Plates known to have been used are Nos. 22 to 38, 40 and 42 to 49.

*Plates 22, 24, 25, 32 and 43 have been recorded imperforate, and of these, Plate 22 was used for an experiment on Neale's steam press and was ungummed. Imperforate stamps from Plate 25 in a different shade to those of Plate 22 exist, but this plate was put to press after the experiment had failed.

Imprimaturs (imperf), Plates 23, 25–49, 52, 53, 55–60: £500. *Plate* R17, £550. *Plates* R18, R19, £525. The Plate 29 imprimatur sheet has the watermark inverted. Stamps removed from the imprimatur sheets are: Plate 23: AA to AL, GL, HL, IG to IL, TL; Plate 24: AA to AL, HL, IL, JG to JL, TL; Plate 25: AA to AL, IK, IL, JG to JL, TL; Plate 26: AA to AL, IK, IL, JG to JL, TL; Plate 27: AA to AL, GK, GL, HG to HL, TL; Plate 28: AA to AL, HK, HL, IG to IL, TL; Plate 29: AA to AL, JG to JL, KK, KL, TL; Plate 30: AA to AL, JG to JL, KK, KL, TL; Plate 31: AA to AL, HI, HL, IG to IL, TL; Plate 32: AA to AL, HK, HL, IG to IL, TL; Plate 33: AA to AL, GL, HL, IG to IL, TL; Plate 34: AA to AL, HK, HL, IG to IL, TL; Plate 35: AA to AL, HK, HL, IG to IL, TL; Plate 36: AA to AL, HK, HL, IG to IL, TL; Plate 37: AA to AL, GK, GL, HG to HL, TL; Plate 38: AA to AL, HK, HL, IG to IL, TL; Plate 39: AA to AL, HK, HL, IG to IL, TL; Plate 40: AA to AL, IL, JF to JL, TL; Plate 41: AA to AL, HK, HL, IG to IL, TL; Plate 42: AA to AL, IL, JF to JL, TL; Plate 43: AA to AL, GK, GL, HG to HL, TL; Plate 44: AA to AL, HK, HL, IG to IL, TL; Plate 45: AA to AL, JE to JL, TL; Plate 46: AA to AL, HK, HL, IG to IL, TL; Plate 47: AA to AL, IL, JF to JL, TL; Plate 48: AL, HK, HL, IG to IL, TA to TL; Plate 49: AL, HK, HL, IG to IL, TA to TL; Plate 52: AA to AL, IG to

IL, JK, JL, TL; Plate 53: AA to AL, HK, HL, IG to IL, TL; Plate 55: AA to AL, GK, GL, HG to HL, TL; Plate 56: AA to AL, IK, IL, JG to JL, TL; Plate 57: AA to AL, HK, HL, IG to IL, TL; Plate 58: AA to AL, HK, HL, IG to IL, TL; Plate 59: AA to AL, HK, HL, IG to IL, TL; Plate 60: AA to AL, HK, HL, IG to IL, TL; Plate R17: AL, SE to SL, TA to TL; Plate R18: AA to AL, GK, GL, HG to HL, TL; Plate R19: AA to AL, IK, IL, JG to JL, TL.

Plates registered: Plate 22, 8 June 1855; Plates 23 to 26, 12 November 1855; Plates 27 to 31, 27 December 1855; Plates 32 to 36, 16 January 1856; Plates 37, 38, 2 April 1856; Plate 39, 7 April 1856; Plates 40 to 44, 2 April 1856; Plates 45 to 49, 25 June 1856; Plates 52, 53, 11 February 1857 Plate 54 was defective and was never registered; Plates 55 to 60, 11 February 1857; Plates 61 to 68, 18 January 1858; Reserve Plates R17 to R20, 12 November 1855.

Plated Used Examples

	C7	*C8*		*C8*
Plate 22	£1500	£400	Plate 35	18·00
Plate 23	£650	45·00	Plate 36	18·00
Plate 24	£650	45·00	Plate 37	18·00
Plate 25	£700	70·00	Plate 38	18·00
Plate 26	£900	60·00	Plate 40	20·00
Plate 27	£2000	18·00	Plate 42	20·00
Plate 28	†	22·00	Plate 43	22·00
Plate 29	†	20·00	Plate 44	22·00
Plate 30	†	20·00	Plate 45	20·00
Plate 31	†	18·00	Plate 46	70·00
Plate 32	†	18·00	Plate 47	60·00
Plate 33	†	18·00	Plate 48	£850
Plate 34	†	18·00	Plate 49	—

Plating Aids

Abbreviations used are: ***R***, re-entry; ***C***, special characteristics; ***D***, double letter; ***CV***, constant variety. The date given in brackets against each plate is the date when it was put to press.

Plate 22 (1 August 1855): ***R***: CE. ***C***: small E, broad H, tall L and S, K semi-Gothic (all similar to Plate R17).

Plate 23 (17 November 1855): ***D***: *O*D. ***C***: all Ls tall, all Ss tall, all Ks Gothic.

Plate 24 (24 November 1855): ***R***: EK–FK. ***C***: tall L in horizontal row except LJ; constant variety and short L in *LJ*; LL, first L tall, second L short: all Ks Gothic.

Plate 25 (12 November 1855): ***R***: IE, TD. ***C***: Gothic K.

Plate 26 (12 November 1855): ***C***: Gothic K. ***D***: *S*E.

Plate 27 (27 December 1855): ***R***: AD–BD. ***C***: Letters hand-retouched (larger): *FJ*, *FK*. Gothic K. ***CV***: DI.

Plate 28 (27 December 1855): ***R***: GL–HL, KI, MF, NL. ***C***: Gothic K.

Plate 29 (27 December 1855): ***R***: NI–OI, PK–QK. ***C***: Gothic K. ***CV***: *BJ*, *SE*.

Plate 30 (27 December 1855): ***R***: AA, AC. **D***: CE*, *NF*, R*D*. ***C***: Gothic K.

Plate 31 (27 December 1855): ***R***: FG, GI. ***D***: G*F*, N*K*; Recut K on RK. ***C***: Gothic K. ***CV***: MA.

Plate 32 (8 February 1856): ***R***: BG, SL. ***CV***: B*L*, FL, LF.

Plate 33 (? February 1856: ***R***: KC. ***D****:* R*K*, S*K*. ***CV****:* J*A*, SA.

Plate 34 (22 January 1856): ***R***: (TRLs): MJ, OB. ***CV***: DF, *L*F. Stamps IK–IL, JK–JL, KK–KL, LK–LL, MK–ML laid down very close together. ***C***: Enlarged D on GD. Base of D weak on JD.

Plate 35 (23 January 1856): ***D***: B*I*.

Plate 36 (20 February 1856): ***CV***, D*A*, *T*B.

Plate 37 (19 April 1856): ***R***: BI. **D***:* B*L*, *O*G, S*B*.

Plate 38 (24 May 1856): ***CV***: Q*K*.

Plate 40 (3 May 1856): ***R***: HD. ***D***: F*J*. A printing in orange on very blue paper was mostly from this plate.

Plate 42 (23 June 1856): ***R***: AA. ***D****:* T*L*. ***CV****:* A*I*, *T*B.

Plate 43 (5 July 1856): ***R***: RC, RJ. ***CV***: *E*B, *E*I, L*L*, TH–TI.

Plate 44 (19 July 1856): ***D****:* *M*I, R*J*. ***CV****:* AB, *C*I, FI, SC.

Plate 45 (26 August 1856): ***D***: P*H*. ***CV***: QH.

Plate 46 (27 August 1856): ***R***: BH, LI. ***D***: *G*E.

Plate 47 (15 December 1856): ***D****:* A*H*, E*C*.

Plate 48 (2 February 1857): ***R***: BG. ***D****:* A*L*, *G*D. ***CV****:* OI. TL repaired.

Plate 49 (3 April 1857): Only one example recorded.

Plate 27 was printed in black for the South Kensington Exhibition.

Plates 39 and 41 though laid down in their correct sequence are known only in rose-red shades on the later white paper. For the data which made it possible to compile the above tabulation we are indebted to the late specialists Dr. W. R. D. Wiggins and C. W. Meredith. It follows that the above varieties exist in white or cream-toned paper from plates not discarded before the change from blue paper. See after No. C11.

Plate 43 has been recorded postmarked 8 June 1856, Plate 44, 7 May, and Plate 46, 17 August, all prior to the recorded dates for putting these plates to press. The evidence does not point to incorrectly set date stamps. One explanation could be that spare imprimatur sheets were perforated and put into use before the main supplies were printed.

RE-ENTRIES, ETC.

Plate 22

Plate 24 (EK–FK)

Letter characteristics, Plate 24

Plate 25

Plate 25

Plate 27 (AD–BD)

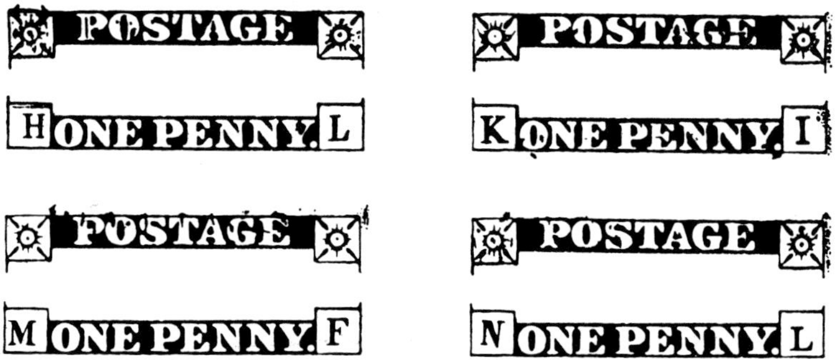

Plate 28

Plate 29

Plate 30

Plate 31

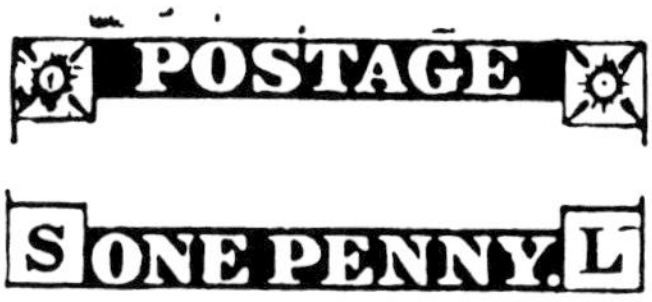

Plate 32

Plate 33

Plate 37

Plate 40

Plate 42

Plate 46

Plate 46

Plate 48

CONSTANT VARIETIES, CHARACTERISTIC AND DOUBLE LETTERS

Gothic

Semi-Gothic

OD, *Plate* 23

LJ, *Plate* 24

SE, *Plate* 26

DI

FJ

FK

Plate 27

BJ

SE

CE

Plate 29

NF

Plate 30

RD

Plate 30

NK, *Plate* 31

MA

RK (*non-Gothic* K)

Plate 31

BG (*re-entry*)

BL

Plate 32

LF

Plate 32

Plate 33

JA

RK

Plate 33

SK

DF

GD

Plate 34

JD

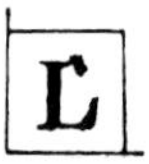

LF

Plate 34

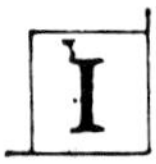

BI, *Plate* 35

DA

TB

Plate 36

BL, *Plate* 37

OG

SB

Plate 37

QK, *Plate* 38

FJ, *Plate* 40

AI

TB

Plate 42

TL, *Plate* 42

EB

EI

LL

Plate 43

RJ

AB, *Plate* 44

TH–TI, *Plate* 43

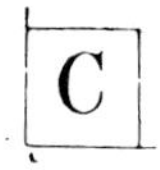

CI

FI

Plate 44

MI

RJ

Plate 44

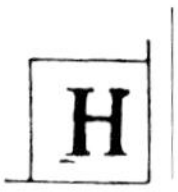

PH, *Plate* 45

QH, *Plate* 45

GE, *Plate* 46

AH

EC

Plate 47

AL

GD

Plate 48

THE CHANGE FROM BLUED PAPER TO CREAM-TONED AND WHITE PAPERS

The printings of No. C8 made between about October 1856 and March 1857 are extremely interesting as they can be regarded as marking the first phase of the attempts made by the printers to eliminate the blueing of the paper to obtain a constant shade of colour for the stamps. With the exception of No. C8A the experiment was only partially successful in that many stamps show blotched areas of blue still remaining.

As the combination of variations between the colour of the stamp and the blueing of the paper (including blued paper with yellowish or toned areas) is variable, it is not practical to make a separate listing of them. Almost any of the shades of No. C8, particularly (5) to (7) and also shades resembling those listed under No. C10 (2 and 3) may be found in this first transitional condition. *(Prices range from* £325 *unused and* £60 *used.)*

The printings listed below No. C9 on paper completely free of blueing are also known as the "transitional" shades; they may be the old inks without prussiate of potash or possibly had a neutralizing agent added. This latter may be the cause of the cream-toning which is typical of the paper at this time. Later, the inks were changed to a fairly consistent rose-red colour, some of the late prints on cream-toned paper being in shades of pale rose like the first issues on purely white paper. The early shades on cream-toned paper are scarce but the later rose shades on the same paper are commoner. The whole "transitional" period lasted only about six months; from January to June 1857.

The transitional period coincided with a major fire at Perkins, Bacon's Whitefriars premises on the night of 11/12 March 1857. The stamp printing area was badly damaged and much stock was lost. Perkins, Bacon resumed printing in temporary premises in the Strand as supplies were needed urgently. Both the public and the Inland Revenue noted that the stamps appeared pink rather than red-brown. On 21 April Ormond Hill attributed this to two causes. The stamps were reaching the public sooner so that colour changes, which normally occurred while the stamps were in stock, had not had time to take place and, additionally, Perkins, Bacon, in their haste to resume production, had been less careful than normal in their preparation of the ink, which Hill described as "to be thin and gritty and very difficult to work satisfactorily". It is possible to establish that this unintentional ink change resulted in at least one of the recognised transitional shades (orange-brown).

The ideal towards which the printer had been working was not really achieved until the consistent rose-red on white paper appeared in September 1857. This group listed as No. C10 was to set the standard until check letters were introduced in each of the four corners on the ld. in 1864.

Group 3: Die II, Red-brown on White Paper

1856 (November). Red-brown on White Paper. Die II. Alphabet III. Wmk Large Crown, Type I. Perf. 14.

C8A (=S.G.37)	1d. red-brown	£850	£250
	Used on cover	†	£600

A small number of covers are known with November 1856 postmarks and these have been accepted as being the first use on the white paper. Examples of No. C8A are known from plates 23 to 26, 28, 29, 32, 38, 40 and 43 to 45. It has not been possible from the quantities known of each plate to form a priced table for plated stamps. It is sufficient to record that these stamps on genuinely white paper are scarce and should be purchased with certificate stating provenance.

Group 4: Die II, Transitional Issues on Yellowish to Cream-Toned Paper

1857 (January). Yellowish to Cream Paper. Die II. Alphabet III. Wmk Large Crown, Type I. Perf. 14.

C9	(1)	1d. orange-brown	£550	£150
	(2)	1d. red-orange (shades)	£450	£100
	(3)	1d pale red (shades)	£325	55·00
	(4)	1d. pale rose (shades)	£325	55·00

	Block of four	£1800	£350
	Used on cover	†	£110
c.	Major re-entry	—	£120
d.	Minor re-entry	—	60·00
e.	Double letter	—	60·00
f.	Constant varieties *from*	—	60·00
g.	Imperforate	£2000	
h.	Watermark inverted	—	£225

Plates used are as in the tabulated list below C11. Differentiation between C9 and C10 is not so much a matter of the toning of the paper (though that is helpful) as of the shades of the stamps. Except perhaps for the pale red shades, none of the C9 colours is likely to be mistaken for any in C10. With the pale stamps assistance is obtainable from the cream toning of the paper. The toned paper is rough and occasionally thicker.

Group 5: Die 11, Rose-red on White Paper

1857–63. Die II. Alphabet III. White Paper. Wmk Large Crown, Type I. Perf 14.

C10 (=S.G.38/41)	(1)	1d. bright-rose-red (March–April 1857)	—	85·00
	(2)	1d. pale red (9.4.57)	80·00	18·00
	(3)	1d. pale rose (March 1857)	80·00	28·00
	(4)	1d. deep rose-red (July 1857)	£100	15·00
	(5)	1d. rose-red (September 1857)	45·00	10·00
	(6)	1d. pale rose-pink (1863)	£475	45·00
		Block of four	£250	90·00
		Used on cover	†	20·00
	c.	Wmk Large Crown Type II	55·00	15·00
	d.	Error of watemark, MA (ML); TA (TL) (Types I or II)	£4000	£475
	e.	Watermark inverted (Type I)	£120	60·00
	ea.	Watermark inverted (Type II)	£150	70·00
	f.	Major re-entry	90·00	30·00
	g.	Minor re-entry	55·00	15·00
	h.	Double letter	55·00	15·00
	i.	Double perforations	£175	55·00
	j.	Constant varieties *from*	55·00	12·00
	k.	Imperforate (rose-red)	£2000	£1700
	l.	Imperforate (pale red)	£2000	£1700
	m.	Imperforate vert. (horiz. pair)	†	—
	s.	"Specimen", Type 7 (Plate 55)		
	t.	"Specimen", Type 10 (Plates 43, 44, 55) *from*	£180	
	u.	"Specimen", Type 6 (Plate 55)		
	v.	Bisected on cover*	†	£17500

*Examples are known bisected on cover to pre-pay the 10½d. rate to Denmark and the 1 shilling 2½d. rate to California.

Imprimaturs. Plates 61 *to* 68, *each* £425. The Plate 66 imprimatur sheet has the watermark inverted. Stamps removed from the imprimatur sheets are: Plate 61: AA to AL, IG to IL, JJ to JL, TL; Plate 62: AA to AL, IG to IL, JJ to JL, TL; Plate 63: AA to AL, IG to IL, JK, JL, TL; Plate 64, AA to AL, IG to IL, JK, JL, TL; Plate 65: AA to AL, HK, HL, IG to IL, TL; Plate 66: AA to AL, HK, HL, IG to IL, TL; Plate 67: AA to AL, HK, HL, IG to IL, TL; Plate 68: AA to AL, HK, HL, IG to IL, TL.

Imperforates are known from Plates 41, 42, 43, 45, 46, 47, 48, 49, 50, 51, 52, 55 to 57, 60, 62, 66, R17. The watermark errors and types are described in the General Notes. *Imperforate stamps in black or carmine-rose from Plate* 66 *are the so-called Royal Reprint.*

Plates as given in the tabulated list after No. C11 were used. This group of plates has received more specialist study than some of the earlier groups probably because the stamps are more readily available and because some striking characteristics in the corner letters provide good aids to identification.

About March 1861 Type II of the Large Crown watermark was introduced and it is believed to have been in concurrent use with Type I until April 1862, when the stock of the Type I paper became exhausted. All the plates issued for No. C10 on white paper exist with Type I watermark, Plate R17 being rare, and all are known on Type II paper except Plates 33, 37, 38, 45 and 53.

As a general rule, the stamps of Plates 22 to 36, 52, 53, 55 to 57, 61 to 65, 67, 68, have an unbroken right side line, whereas those of Plates 37 to 49, 58 to 60 and 66 show a break, variable in size, in the same line about one-third of the way up from the bottom.

No plater of the "rose-reds" can fail to appreciate the importance as plating guides of the series of recognizable letters which occurs within the group. The letters of special importance are E, H, K, L, M and P. Our list below shows that these letters of readily identifiable shape and size were brought into use over a period. They serve to narrow the field in enough cases to justify the statement that they are the prime feature of the group here under consideration.

E	*H*	*K*	*L*	*M*	*P* (loop)	*Plates*
Tall	Large	Gothic	Short	Large	Large	27, 31 (but 31 R*K* recut).
Tall	Large	Normal	Short	Large	Large	33 to 36, 37 (MA to MI).
Tall	Large	Normal	Short	Small	Large	37 (MJ to ML), 38 to 45, 46 (PA to PI).
Tall	Large	Normal	Short	Small	Small	46 (PJ to PL), 47 to 49.
Broad	Large	Normal	Short	Small	Small	52, 53.
Broad	Large	Normal	Tall	Small	Small	55, 56 (HA to HD).
Broad	Small	Normal	Tall	Small	Small	56 (HE to HL) and all vertical H row stamps, Plates 57 to 68.

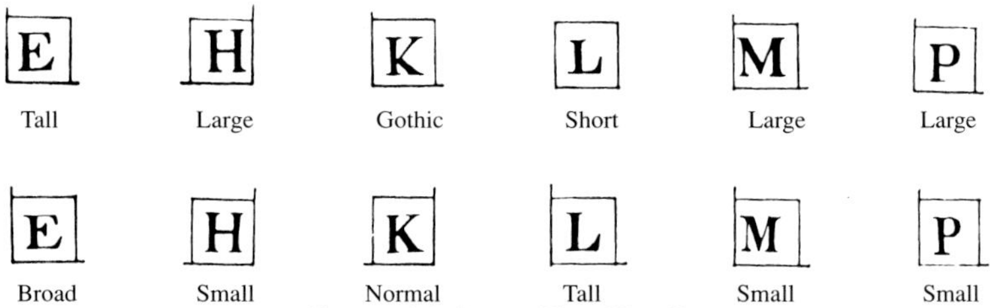

Characteristic Letters, Plates 27 *to* 68

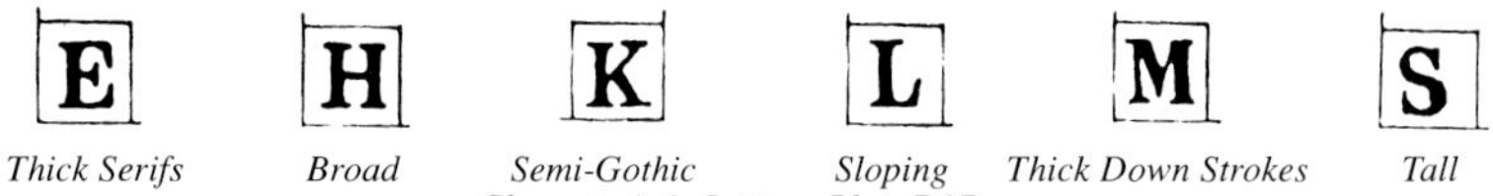

Characteristic Letters, Plate R17

See under "Plating Aids" for characteristic letters on Plates 22 to 27.

From Plate 52 onwards the upper loop of the B becomes more obviously smaller than the lower loop. Reserve Plate 17, which also comes within the "rose-red" group, has several distinctive letters; they are similar to those of Plate 22 as the two plates were laid down at the same time, R17 being originally numbered 23. We illustrate the R17 characteristic letters as well as those of the main group. Note the "semi-Gothic" K, the broad H and the notably large S.

It will be noticed that a stamp with a broad E cannot be from a plate earlier than 52; similarly, a large M indicates a plate in the small group 27, 31 and 33 to 37 (omitting MJ to ML in the last). These are but two of the obvious deductions to be made from a study of the above tabulation.

Dates can be of assistance in cases where they can be read since they allow of the elimination from consideration of those plates which were not at that time in use. All the plates up to Plate 47 were in use during 1856; Plates 48, 49 and 52 to 60 came into use before October of 1857; Plate 61 was put to press in May 1858 and 62 in December 1859. Plate 63 (March 1860) and the rare Plates 64 (November 1860) and 65 (January 1861) come in a period when few new plates were being put to press and here the dates can be really useful even if usually in a negative sense. The last plates of the group were 66 (February 1861), 67 (13 February 1862), 68 (January 1862) and R17 (4 August 1862).

"O.U.S." Overprints. Between 1858 and 1860 the Oxford Union Society adopted the practice of overprinting current 1d. stamps with their initials, between two wavy lines. A fuller description of these overprints and their usage is given in Appendix 2. See Nos. PP148 etc.

1857 (26 December). Provisional use of the perf 16 gauge. Die II. Alphabet III. Wmk Large Crown, Type I.

C11 (=S.G.36)		1d. rose-red	£1500	65·00
		Block of four	£8000	£475
		Used on cover	†	£140
	c.	Inverted watermark	—	£250
	e.	Error of watermark MA (ML); TA (TL) (Type I)	—	£800
	f.	Major re-entry	—	£100
	g.	Minor re-entry	—	70·00
	h.	Double letter	—	70·00
	i.	Constant varieties *from*	£1750	70·00
	j.	Double perforation		

Plates 27, 34, 36 to 38, 42 to 49, 52 and 55 to 60 were used.

Plated Used Examples

	C9	*C10*	*C11*
Plate 27	75·00	15·00	85·00
Plate 31	75·00	†	†
Plate 32	£550	†	†
Plate 33	65·00	£450	†
Plate 34	65·00	15·00	75·00
Plate 35	£120	—	†
Plate 36	55·00	20·00	75·00
Plate 37	55·00	25·00	75·00
Plate 38	55·00	25·00	75·00
Plate 39	†	20·00	†
Plate 40	£280	†	†
Plate 41	†	20·00	†
Plate 42	65·00	15·00	70·00
Plate 43	55·00	15·00	70·00
Plate 44	55·00	15·00	70·00
Plate 45	£300	£450	£550
Plate 46	75·00	15·00	70·00
Plate 47	65·00	15·00	70·00
Plate 48	75·00	15·00	70·00
Plate 49*	£300	15·00	£350
Plate 52*	£300	15·00	70·00
Plate 53	£2000	—	†
Plate 55	£550	15·00	70·00
Plate 56	†	15·00	70·00
Plate 57	†	15·00	70·00
Plate 58	†	15·00	£180
Plate 59	†	15·00	70·00
Plate 60	†	15·00	90·00
Plate 61	†	20·00	†
Plate 62	†	15·00	†
Plate 63	†	45·00	†
Plate 64	†	£225	†
Plate 65	†	£450	†
Plate 66	†	15·00	†
Plate 67	†	15·00	†
Plate 68	†	20·00	†
Plate R17	†	22·00	†

* Printings from Plates 49 and 52 perforated 14, on white paper, in the pale rose shade, C10(3), are exceedingly scarce.

Plating Aids

Information on Plates 39, 41, 49, 52 to 68 and R17 is included below. For information on Plates. 23, 25 to 27, 29, 31 to 38, 40 and 42 to 48 see the list of Plating Aids below C8.

The following abbreviations are used below: ***R***, re-entries; ***C***, special characteristics; ***D***, double letters; ***CV***, constant varieties. The date in brackets against each plate is the date on which it was put to press; it should be understood that this date refers to the *original* use of the plate.

Plate 39 (7 April 1856): ***D***: E*F*. ***CV***: *R*I, *T*L.

Plate 41 (7 April 1856): ***CV***: C*K*, FF, PC.

Plate 49 (3 April 1857): ***R***: AD. ***D***: *K*K. ***CV***: IB, *J*D, *LG*, OB, and many others; plate was badly corroded, PC illustrated.

Plate 52 (7 May 1857): All Qs smudged or blind. ***R***: TG. ***CV***: A*J*, *A*K, B*G*, D*D*, GJ, JG, *Q*G, and many others; plate was badly corroded, TF illustrated. TA repaired. LB scratch across forehead.

Plate 53 (12 February 1857): Rare; a very few unused and fifteen used in pale rose and two in rose-red are recorded.

Plate 55 (21 May 1857): ***R***: many, notably AA, BA, CA, DA, DB, FB, MB, OC, PC, RA, RD, TA. ***D***: *H*J. In fact all stamps in the first four columns show some trace of re-entering. Repair: TL.

Plate 56 (14 July 1857): ***R***: DG, GJ. ***D***: C*L*, G*F*, *L*B, R*E*. TA, TB, TC were repaired. NI, OA and OI were also repaired. ***CV***: EF, F*F* and many others.

Plate 57 (14 July 1857): ***R***: BJ **D**: E*H*, H*K*, *M*L. Left L shorter than right L on LL. G displaced on NG.

Plate 58 (14 July 1857): Repair re-entry TI. ***CV***: AK, FB. Mark in D on CD.

Plate 59 (14 July 1857): ***R***: CI, QG–RG, TF. ***D***: S*C*. Recut letter *B*K.
Plate 60 (14 July 1857): ***R***: BI, FB, OC. ***D***: F*C*, *F*D. ***CV***: KJ. Recut letter E*B*. Mark in H square on RH.
Plate 61 (8 May 1858): Numerous misplaced letters occur. ***CV***: A*E*, MH.
Plate 62 (5 December 1859): ***R***: AE (from BE), LK, PJ, QJ, RC, RJ, SF, SJ, SL, TJ, TK, TL. Letter varieties: N*D*, *P*F. Flaw on neck KH.
Plate 63 (5 March 1860): Most copies show a cameo-like appearance of the head. ***CV***: GE.
Plate 64 (5 November 1860): ***R***: TB, TC, TD, TL. MF damaged impression.
Plate 65 (14 January 1861): ***R***: MI, RL, TL.
Plate 66 (13 February 1861): ***CV***: AC. Misplaced letter *E*L.
Plate 67 (13 February 1862): DB, EB, FB, GB all show flaw at top left of O of ONE. JA, LA, RA, SA show NE of ONE joined. ***CV***: *B*F, *I*H, TA.
Plate 68 (9 January 1862): ***R***: AG, IE–JE, IF–JF, KL, NC. Shades are always pale.
Plate R17 (4 August 1862): ***R***: JF, RI, SI. ***D***: D*J*, *O*E, *O*G. ***C***: tall E, big H, semi-Gothic K, tall narrow L and M, big S. ***CV***: mark in T square on TF.

Plates 28 and 30 had been defaced before the advent of the transitional and rose-red inks which resulted in the elimination of the blueing of the paper. Hence they do not appear in the above group. Plate 33 had little use during the white paper period although the records state that it was not defaced until 29 October 1861. Plate 45 (defaced on the same date) likewise seems to have been little used for the white paper printings. Plate 54 was spoiled in the making. Printings from Plate 63 were rather restricted and from Plate 64 very small indeed. Both were defaced on 29 October 1861, after a short life of under sixteen months for Plate 63 and under one year for Plate 64. Plate 65 had an even shorter life (nine months) and is exceedingly rare. (Compare Plate 27 which had a life of over five years and provided over 1,000,000 sheets but was still in good order after this heavy usage.) Reserve Plate R17 was laid down originally as Plate 23 which accounts for the similarity of its peculiar check letters to those of Plate 22 (q.v., Blued Paper Issues). Would-be platers are referred to the notes about the various characteristic letters which appear before No. C11. These will be found to be of great assistance in the narrowing down of the field when plating single stamps and blocks. Unused blocks of Plate 38 are peculiarly rare.

RE-ENTRIES

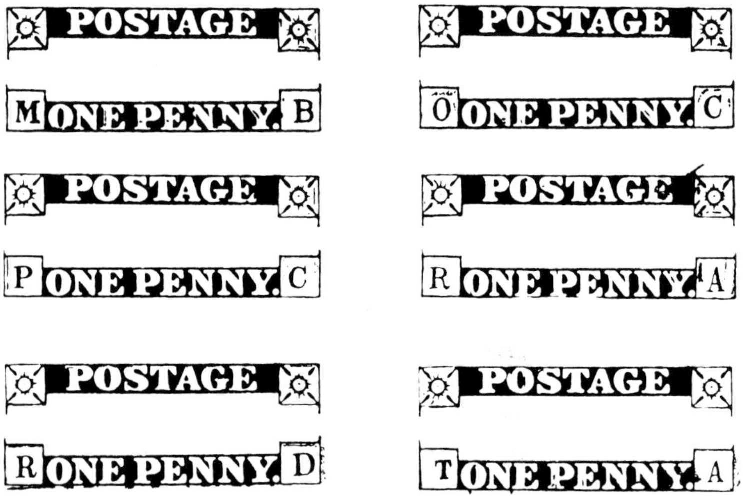

Plate 55

DG

GJ

Plate 56

Plate 57

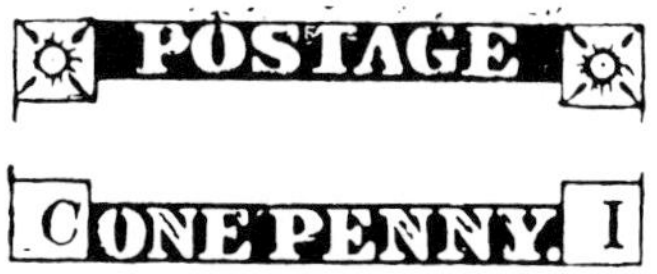

Plate 59

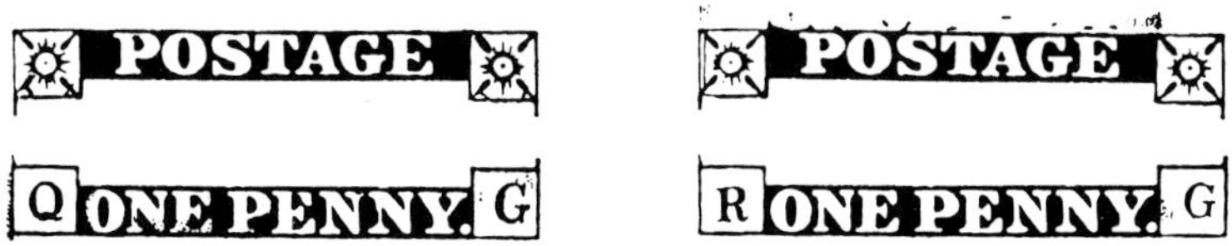

Plate 59

Plate 59

Plate 60

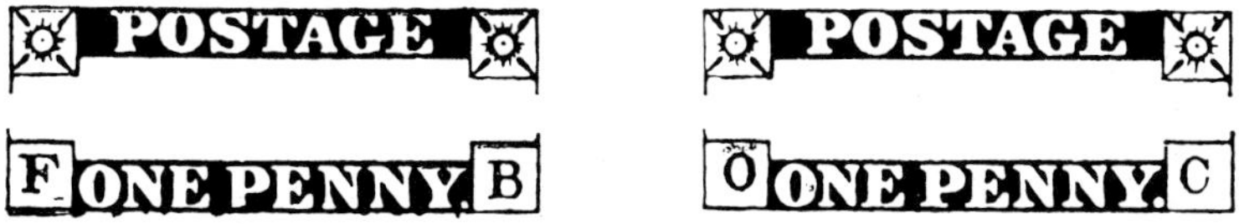

Plate 60

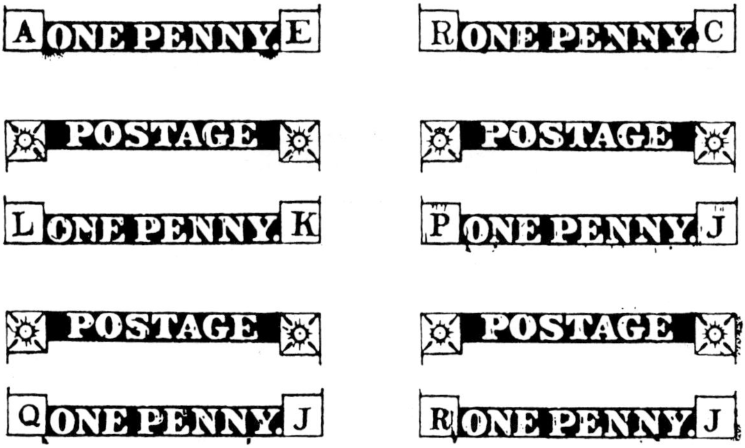

Plate 62

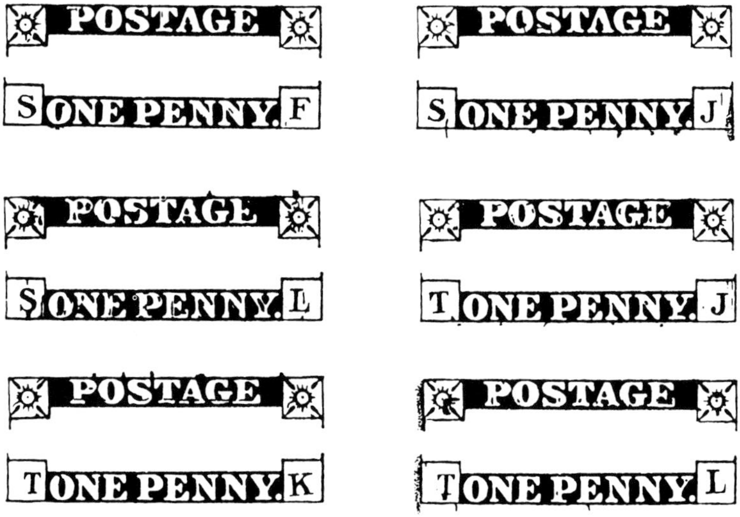

Plate 62

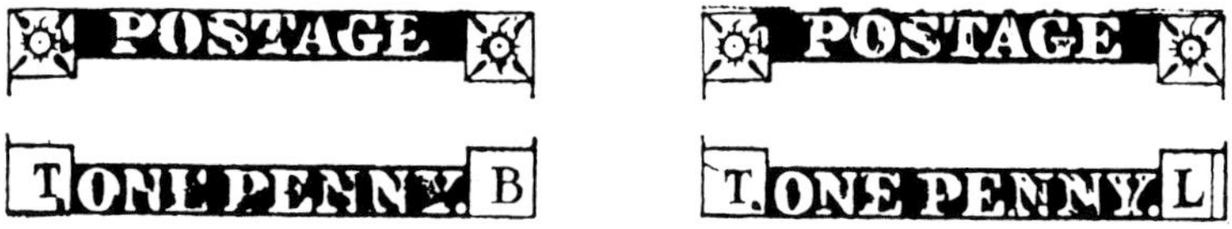

Plate 64

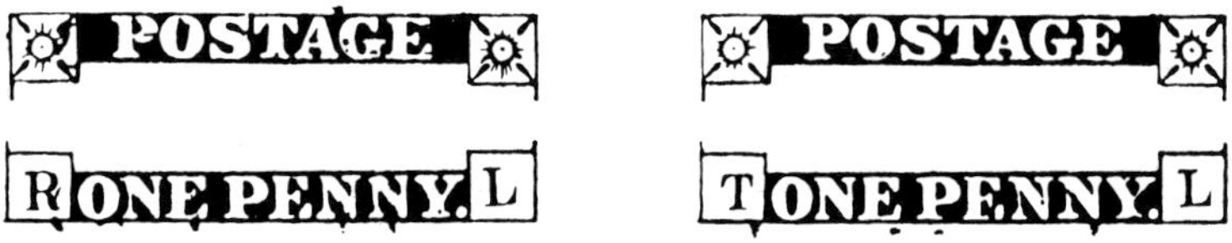

Plate 65

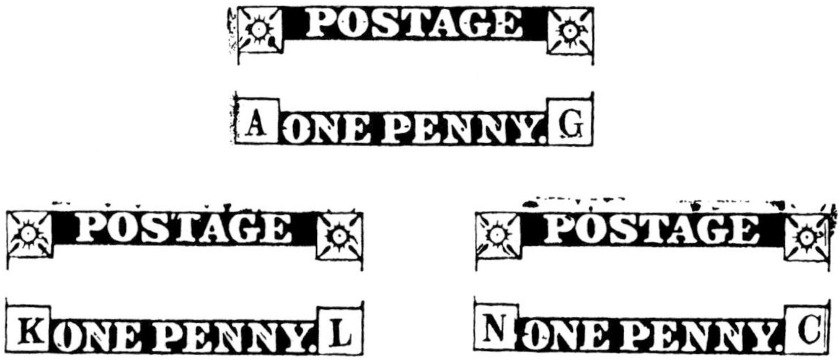

Plate 68

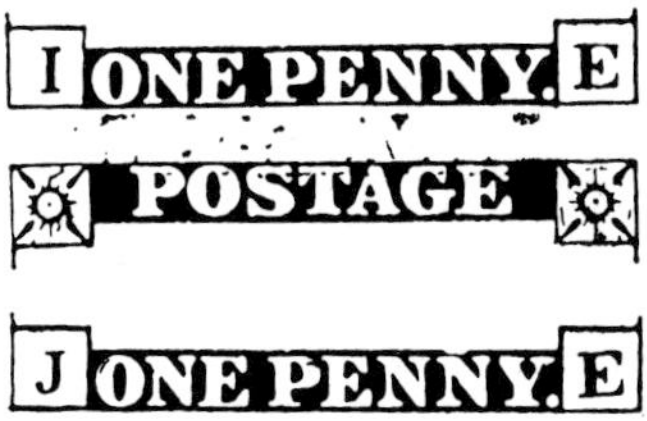

Plate 68 (IE–JE)

Plate 68 (IF–JF)

Plate R17 (JF)

RI

SI

Plate R17

CORROSION MARKS

Plate 49

Plate 52

CONSTANT VARIETIES

EF

RI

TL

CK

Plate 39

FF

PC

Plate 41

IB

JD

KK

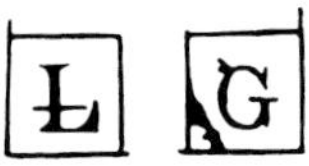
LG

OB

Plate 49

AJ

AK

BG

DD

GJ

JG

QG

Plate 52

HJ, *Plate* 55 — CL — EF — FF — GF, *Plate* 56 — LB — RE

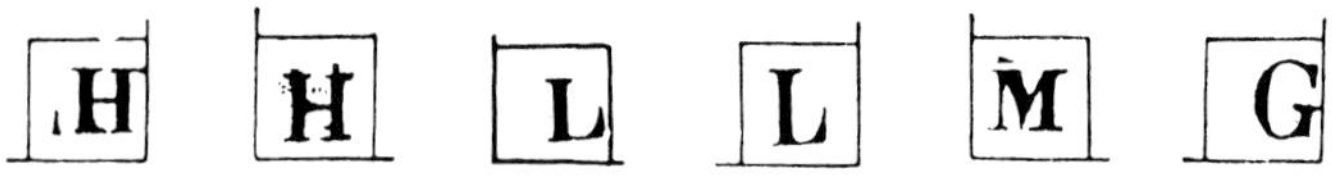

EH — HK — LL, *Plate* 57 — ML — NG

AK — CD, *Plate* 58 — FB — BK — SC, *Plate* 59 — EB — FC, *Plate* 60

FD — KJ, *Plate* 60 — RH — AE — MH, *Plate* 61 — ND — PF, *Plate* 62

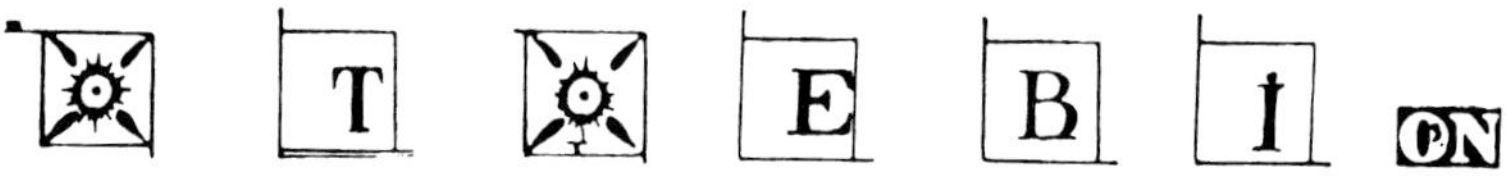

GE, *Plate* 63 — TC (*re-entry*), *Plate* 64 — AC — EL, *Plate* 66 — BF — IH — TA, *Plate* 67

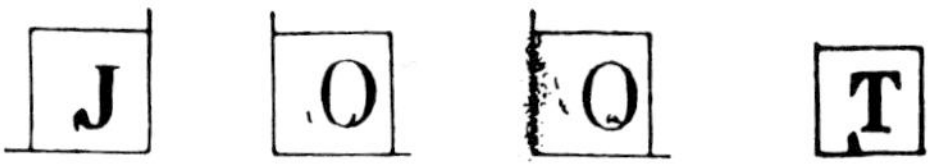

DJ — OE — OG, *Plate* R17 — TF

1861. Experimental Engraving of Corner Letters. Plates 50 and 51. Die II. Alphabet IV. Wmk Large Crown, Type II. Perf 14.

C12 (=S.G.42)	(1)	1d. rose-red, Plate 50	£225	35·00
	(2)	1d. pale rose-red, Plate 50	£225	35·00
	(3)	1d. rose-red, Plate 51	£250	40·00
	(4)	1d. pale rose-red, Plate 51	£250	40·00
		Block of four, Plate 50	£1000	£200
		Block of four, Plate 51	£1200	£225
		Used on cover, Plate 50	†	60·00
		Used on cover, Plate 51	†	70·00
	c.	Wmk. Large Crown, Type I, Plate 50	£250	40·00
	d.	Wmk Large Crown, Type I, Plate 51	£275	45·00
	e.	Watermark inverted, Plate 50	£350	85·00
	f.	Watermark inverted, Plate 51	£375	90·00
	g.	Error of watermark, TA(TL) (Plate 50) (Type II)	£2750	£750
	h.	Plate 51; KB, first state		
	ha.	Plate 51, KB, second state	—	£325
	hb.	Plate 51, K.B, third state	—	80·00
	j.	Constant varieties, Plate 51: *AA*, AJ, BA, BB, *CI*, GB, GE, *IJ*, *JD*, K*D*, L*A*, LB, LD, LE, MD, QC, RG ... *from*	£275	45·00
	k.	Imperforate, Plate 50	†	—
	l.	Imperforate, Plate 51	—	£3500

Imprimaturs (Imperf Plates 50, 51): *each* £500. Stamps removed from each imprimatur sheet are AL, HK, HL, IG to IL, TA to TL.

Plates registered: 25 June 1856.

These stamps were from Plates 50 and 51 which were experimental in that all the corner letters were engraved by hand. (From Plate 52 onwards the old method of entering by punching was resumed.)

There being but two plates in this group and the corner letters usually larger than on any other plates, they form an interesting study. Again we refer collectors to Part II of *The Postage Stamps of Great Britain* where considerable information is given. It should be remembered that since each letter was engraved by hand no two are exactly alike on either plate.

Stamps from Plate 50 show the characteristic frame break about a third of the way up the right-hand side which occurred on Plates 37 to 49 and some later plates.

Plate 51 is particularly interesting in that it shows extensive recutting of side and base lines. In addition to the various states of KB as illustrated, many second states of letterings exist, notably on AA, AB, AD, AE, AF, AH, AJ, BD, BE, BG, CD, CE, CG, JD, JJ, KC, KH, KJ, OJ, PH, SG and TI. The repairs were done by hand recutting and not by the re-entering of a roller impression.

The Three States of Stamp KB, Plate 51

First state. The N.E. square is weak and the contained dot is weak and central. The curved white lines at right are also weak. Only three examples of this state are known.

Second state. First repair: The N.E. square has been recut slightly larger and the dot placed too low. The inner curved lines at right have been pared and thinned except the two bottom segments.

Third state. Second repair: As State 2 but the two lower segments have been pared and thinned.

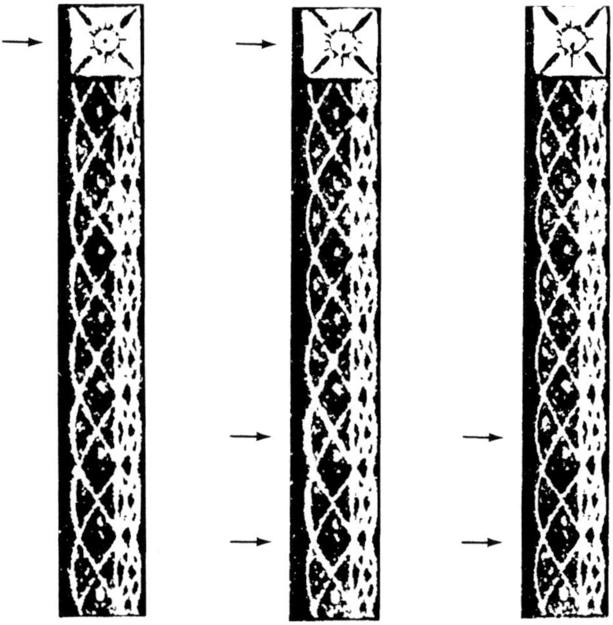

First state with N.E. dot central *Second state with N.E. dot low* *Third state as second state but curved lines thinned*

The three states of Stamp KB, *Plate* 51

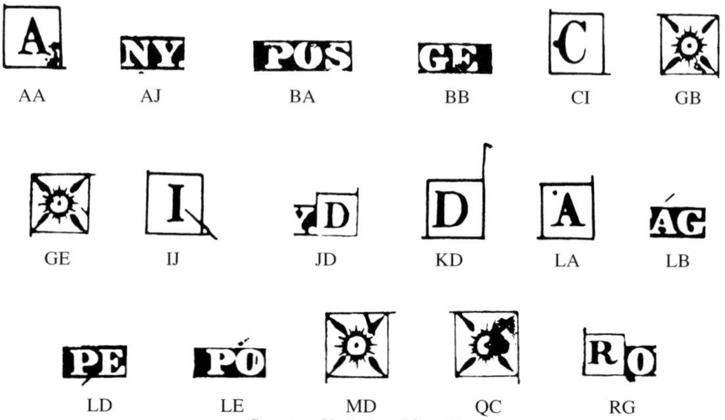

Constant Varieties, Plate 51

1862. Provisional use of Reserve Plates 15 and 16. Die II. Alphabet II. Wmk Large Crown, Type II. Perf. 14.

C13	(1)	1d. rose-red, Plate R15	£200	30·00
	(2)	1d. pale rose-red, Plate R15	£175	30·00
	(3)	1d. rose-red, Plate R16	£200	30·00
	(4)	1d. pale rose-red, Plate R16	£175	30·00
		Block of four	£900	£180
		Used on cover	†	60·00
	c.	Watermark inverted	—	95·00
	d.	Watermark Type I, Plate R15	—	35·00
	e.	Do Plate R16	—	35·00
	f.	Re-entries (Plate R15 only), CE, JA, QA, RD, TD	—	50·00
	g.	Double letters: Plate R15, R*L*; Plate R16, A*E*, *L*C, *M*B, *M*D, *O*F, *T*H	—	40·00
	h.	Constant varieties (Plate R15); *A*G, A*K*, BG, E*F*, H*C*, *L*E, *M*E, *O*I, R*K*	£210	35·00
	i.	Constant varieties (Plate R16): BI, *B*J, DF, E*G*, IL, *S*H	£200	35·00
	j.	Imperforate, Plate R15	†	£2000
	k.	Error of watermark, ML (Plate R15)	†	£800

*Imprimaturs (Plates R*15, *R*16, *Imperf. S.C. Wmk): each* £500. Stamps removed from each imprimatur sheet are AA to AL, HK, HL, IG to IL, TL.

Plates registered: 15 January 1855.

Owing to a shortage of the penny plates with stars in the upper corners, and the delay in preparing the new plates with letters in those corners, Reserve Plates 15, 16 and 17 were brought into use from April 1862 until 1 March 1864. As R17 had Alphabet III corner letters its products are listed under C10. Plates R15 and R16 had Alphabet II letters with the consequence that their use provides the only Alphabet II stamps on white paper and in the rose-red shades.

The letters being generally distinctive in their Alphabet II characteristics, the identification of stamps of this group is not difficult.

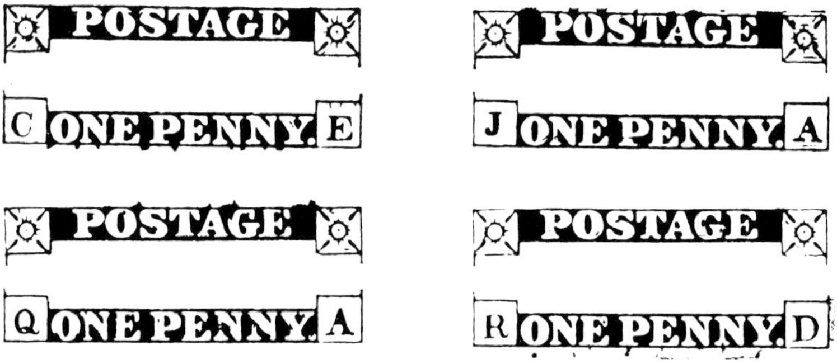

Re-entries, Plate R15

Re-entry, Plate R15

AG AK BG EF HC

LE ME RK RL OI

Double letters and constant varieties, Plate R15

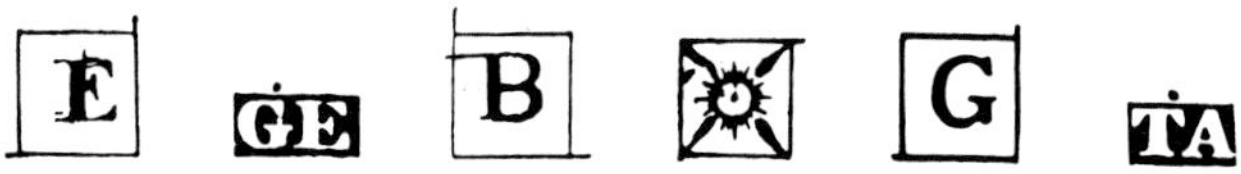

AE BI BJ DF EG IL

LC MB MD SH TH

Double letters and constant varieties, Plate R16

Index to Catalogued Varieties in Section CB

Die I, Plates 176 to 204 and R1 to R6

AA 176, 185, R2
AB 176, 185, 203
AC 203
AE R1
AG 183, 200
AH 184
AI 192

BA 189, 192, 194
BB 192
BC 192
BD 190, 192
BE 192
BF 192
BG 192, 200
BH 192
BI 188, 192
BJ 192, 201
BK 192
BL 192

CA 189
CB 179
CG 181, 199
CJ 187
CK 195

DA 203
DB 179
DC 197
DH 195, 199

EA 200, 203
EB 176
ED 176
EF 198
EG 193
EH 176
EK 197
EL 193

FA 197, 200
FB 179
FC 176
FD 200
FF 185
FH 178
FI 183
FL 187

GB 179, R6
GD 200
GF 176
GG 176
GH 176
GK 188

HA 189
HF 193
HL 192

ID 176
IG 199
IH 176, 197
IK 189

JD 176, 178, 197
JE 176
JF 178, 188

KA 190
KB 178, 196
KD 176, 197
KE 176
KG 194
KH 176
KI 194, 200
KK 177
KL 195

LA 184, 190
LB 196
LC 176, 195
LD 176
LE 180
LF 176
LG 176
LI 198
LJ 195

MB 196, R5
MC 176
MF 197
MG 194
MH 178, 186
MI 183, 187, 194, 204
MJ 200, R3, R5
MK 194, R3
ML 177, 194

ND R5
NE R5
NG 176, 179, 185, R4
NH 176
NI 176
NJ 176, 200
NK 176, 196
NL 176, 195

OA 201, 203
OE 193
OF R3
OG 176

PA 194
PE 196
PF 184
PG 183
PH 178
PL 203

QA 176, 199, R1
QB 186, 199
QC 199
QD 176, 199
QE 199
QF 193, 197, 199
QG 199
QH 199, 201
QI 193, 199
QJ 199
QK 190, 199
QL 190, 199

RA 176
RF 176, 190
RG 176
RK 191
RL R4

SB R2
SD R5
SE 179, 185
SG 176, 191
SH 176, 181
SI 176, 194
SJ 176
SL 184

TA 177, R4
TB 198
TD 176
TF 194
TG 201
TH 193, 194, 201
TK 189

Die II, Plates 1 to 68 and R15 to R17

AA 30, 42, 51, 55
AB 44, 51
AC 30, 66
AD 5, 27, 49, 51
AE 22, 51, 61, 62, R16, R17
AG 68, R15
AH 22, 47, 51, R17
AI 13, 42
AJ 13, 51, 52
AK 1, 22 to 31, 52, 58, R15, R17
AL 6, 22, 23, 25, 48, R17

BA 51, 55
BB 51
BD 4, 27, 51
BE 22, 51, 62, R17
BF 67
BG 32, 48, 51, 52, R15
BH 22, 46, R17
BI 2, 35, 37, 60, R16
BJ 13, 29, 57, R16
BK 22 to 31, 59, R17
BL 5, 22, 23, 32, 37, R17

CA 55
CD 51, 52, 58
CE 16, 22, 30, 51, R15, R17
CG 8
CH 22, R17
CI 2, 44, 51, 59
CJ 13
CK 5, 22 to 31, 41, R17
CL 5, 16, 22, 23, 56, R17

DA 36, 55
DB 55, 67
DD 6, 52
DE 16, 22, R17
DF 34, R16
DG 56
DH 22, R17
DI 27
DJ 17
DK 12, 22 to 31, R17
DL 6, 19, 22, 23, R17

EA 22, R17
EB 22, 43, 60, 67, R17
EC 22, 47, R17
ED 22, R17
EE 22, R17

EF 22, 39, 56, R15, R17
EG 5, 22, R16,. R17
EH 22, 57, R17
EI 22, 43, R17
EJ 22, R17
EK 5, 22 to 31, R17
EL 22, 23, 66, R17

FB 1, 6, 55, 58, 60, 67
FC 8, 60
FD 60
FE 22, R17
FF 9, 41, 56
FG 2, 7, 31
FH 22, R17
FI 44
FJ 27, 40
FK 22 to 31, R17
FL 22, 23, 32, R17

GB 51, 67
GC 21
GD 34, 48
GE 22, 46, 51, 63, R17
GF 31, 56
GG 21
GH 22, R17
GI 31
GJ 52, 56
GK 22 to 31, R17
GL 22, 23, 28, R17

HA 22, R17
HB 5, 12, 22, R17
HC 22, R15, R17
HD 22, 40, R17
HE 22, R17
HF 22, R17
HG 22, R17
HH 1, 10, 22, R17
HI 22, R17
HJ 22, 55, R17
HK 8, 22 to 31, 57, R17
HL 22, 23, 28, R17

IB 49
IE 22, 25, 68, R17
IF 68
IG 9
IH 22, 67, R17
IJ 51
IK 22 to 31, R17
IL 4, 6, 22, 23, R16, R17

JA 7, 33, 67, R15
JD 34, 49, 51
JE 22, 68, R17
JF 68, R17
JG 7, 52
JH 22, R17
JK 22 to 31, R17
JL 19, 22, 23, 61, R17

KA 22 to 31, R17
KB 22 to 31, 51, R17
KC 22 to 31, 33, R17
KD 22 to 31, 51, R17
KE 22 to 31, R17
KF 22 to 31, R17
KG 22 to 31, R17
KH 22 to 31, 51, 62, R17
KI 22 to 31, R17
KJ 22 to 31, 51, 60, R17
KK 10, 22 to 31, 49, R17
KL 10, 22 to 31, 68, R17

LA 1, 22, 23, 24, 51, 67, R17
LB 22, 23, 34, 51, 52, 56, R17
LC 8, 22, 23, 24, R16, R17
LD 22, 23, 24, 51, R17
LE 22, 23, 24, 51, R15, R17
LF 22, 23, 24, 32, 34, R17
LG 22, 23, 24, 49, R17
LH 22, 23, 24, R17
LI 22, 23, 24, 46, R17
LJ 5, 22, 23, 24, R17
LK 5, 22 to 31, 62, R17
LL 5, 22, 23, 24, 43, 57, R17

MA 31, R17
MB 7, 55, R16, R17
MC R17
MD 51, R16, R17
ME 22, R15, R17
MF 28, 64, R17
MG 5, R17
MH 1, 22, 61, R17
MI 44, R 17
MJ 5, 34, R17
MK 22 to 31, R17
ML 22, 23, 57, R17

NC 68
ND 62
NE 14, 22, R17
NF 30
NG 57
NH 22, R17
NI 3, 29, 56
NK 22 to 31, R17
NL 10, 22, 23, 28, R17

OA 56
OB 34, 49
OC 55, 60
OD 15, 23
OE 8, 14, 16, 22, R17
OF 10, R16
OG 37, R17
OH 22, R17
OI 3, 29. 48, 56, R15
OJ 51
OK 22 to 31, R17
OL 22, 23, R 17

PC 41, 49, 55
PE 22, R17
PF 62
PH 22, 45, 51, R17
PJ 62
PK 22 to 31, R17
PL 9, 13, 22, 23, R17

QA 12, 52, R15
QB 1, 2, 8, 52
QC 51, 52
QD 7, 52
QE 13, 22, 52, R17
QF 2, 52
QG 16, 52
QH 22, 45, 52, R17
QI 52
QJ 52, 62
QK 3, 22 to 31, 38, 52, R17
QL 13, 22, 23, 52, R17

RA 10, 55, 67
RC 43, 62
RD 30, 55, R15
RE 7, 22, 56, R17
RG 51, 59
RH 22, 60. R17
RI 39, R17
RJ 43, 44, 62
RK 22 to 31, 33, R15, R17
RL 13, 22, 23, 65, R15, R17

SA 22, 23, 33, 67, R17
SB 7, 22, 23, 37, R17
SC 22, 23, 44, 59, R17
SD 5, 22, 23, R17
SE 5, 22, 23, 26, 29, R17
SF 5, 22, 23, 62. R17
SG 5, 7, 22, 23, 51, R17
SH 5, 22, 23, R16, R17
SI 5, 17, 22, 23, R17
SJ 5, 19, 22, 23, 62, R17
SK 5, 22 to 31, 33, R17
SL 5, 19, 22, 23, 62, R17

TA 52, 55, 56, 67
TB 6, 42, 56, 64
TC 56, 64
TD 5, 14, 17, 25, 64, R15
TE 11, 22, R17
TF 52, 59, R17
TH 22, 43, R16, R17
TI 17, 43, 51, 58
TJ 6, 62
TK 22 to 31, 62, R17
TL 22, 23, 39, 42, 48, 55, 62, 64, 65, R17

SECTION D

Twopence Blue, Type D1 (No Lines), Imperforate

This issue was contemporary with the 1d. black and therefore shares the distinction of being one of the world's first two postage stamps. The die for these first 2d. stamps was taken, indirectly, from the Original Die of the One Penny so that details of designer, printer, etc., are all as given in the Essays, Die Proofs, etc., and the General Notes to the Line-Engraved Issues.

Initially the printers had problems in gumming the 2d. sheets, but by 6 May 1840 a total of 619 sheets had been delivered to the Commissioners of Stamps and Taxes. From this supply it is likely that sales to the public in London would have been made by the 6 May. The 1d. black was distributed several days earlier. Both values were valid from Wednesday 6 May 1840.

This first 2d. stamp differs from all subsequent 2d. issues in having no white lines above the value and below "POSTAGE".

Two plates only were used and these are dealt with in detail below the basic listing.

D1

1840 (6 May). Introduction of Postage Stamps. Die I. Alphabet I. Wmk Small Crown. Imperf.

D1 (=S.G.4/6)	(1)	2d. deep full blue	£22000	£825
	(2)	2d. blue	£16000	£650
	(3)	2d. pale blue	£22000	£700
	(4)	2d. milky blue	£24000	£2000
	(5)	2d. steel-blue	£22000	£1400
	(6)	2d. bright blue	£22000	£850
	(7)	2d. deep blue	£24000	£850
	(8)	2d. violet-blue	—	£4000
		Pair	£60000	£1500
		Block of four	£140000	£20000
		Used on cover	†	£1700
	d.	Watermark inverted	£35000	£3000
	e.	Re-entry	—	£750
	f.	Double letter	—	£700
	g.	Guide line in corner	—	£675
	h.	Guide line through value	—	£675

Twopenny stamps bisected and used to pay the 1d. rate are known on cover. However the practice was unauthorised by the Post Office and covers are not listed.

Early Usage: 2d. Blue used on cover during May 1840

ta.	Used before 8 May	£125000
tb.	8 May	£85000
tc.	9 May	—
td.	10 May (Sunday)	—
te.	17, 24, 31 May (Sundays)	£18000
tf.	Other May dates	£8500

A 2d. blue cancelled by a red Maltese Cross is known on a lettersheet with 6 May 1840 Morning duty circular datestamp. It was sent from London to Louth, Lincolnshire. One cover with 7 May 1840 date is known sent from Liverpool to Leicester. It is probable that the Postmasters's Notice of 7 May was the source of the adhesive.

Coloured Maltese Cross Cancellations

		Off Cover	*On Cover*
ua.	Red (on Plate 1)	£700	£2000
ub.	Red (on Plate 2)	£1000	£3000
uc.	Black	£650	£1700
ud.	Blue	£7500	£22000
ue.	Magenta (*shades*)	£6500	£16000
uf.	Ruby (Aberdeen)	£4000	£8500
ug.	Red + black	—	—
uh.	Brown	£6000	

Distinctive Maltese Cross Cancellations

va.	Greenock	£1800	£5000
vb.	Kelso	£2500	£6000
vc.	Kilmarnock	£4500	£12000
vd.	Leeds	£1750	£4500
ve.	Manchester	£1250	£4750
vf.	Mullingar	£7000	£25000
vg.	Plymouth	£2750	£8000
vh.	Wotton-under-Edge (Pl. 1)	£7000	£18000
vi.	York (Pl. 2 only)	£3500	£9000
vj.	Dublin	£1800	£3500
vk.	Stonehaven	£5500	£15000
vl.	Norwich	£2500	£7000
vm.	Welshpool		
vn.	Stirling		
vo.	Leamington	£3000	

For illustrations of these cancellations see after Line-Engraved General Notes.

"Numbers in Maltese Cross" Cancellations

wa.	No. 1 in Cross ... *from*	£6750
wb.	No. 2 in Cross	£6750
wc.	No. 3 in Cross	£6750
wd.	No. 4 in Cross	£6750
we.	No. 5 in Cross	£6750
wf.	No. 6 in Cross	£6750
wg.	No. 7 in Cross	£6750
wh.	No. 8 in Cross	£6750
wi.	No. 9 in Cross	£6750
wj.	No. 10 in Cross	£6750
wk.	No. 11 in Cross	£6750
wl.	No. 12 in Cross	£5500

Various Other Cancellations (on the stamps), In Black Unless Stated

		Off Cover	*On Cover*
xa.	"Penny Post" postmark	£4800	£12000
xb.	Town dated postmark	£3800	£13000
xc.	1844-type postmark	£1500	£3000
xd.	1844-type postmark in blue	£10000	£10000

For 2d. proof see under DP41 in "Line Engraved Essays, Proofs etc.".

There were only two plates of the Twopence "without white lines", namely Plates 1 and 2. The stamps from these two plates can, in nearly all cases, be differentiated easily by plate characteristics without reference to check letter positions. The first distinguishing feature is the weakness of the left side of the left upper corner of the stamps from Plate 1; the thicker line seen on Plate 2 stamps is suggestive of retouching. In most cases, the distinction between the two is easy. Another important clue, which definitely distinguishes all stamps from the upper nine-tenths of each plate, is found in the upper segment of the right "corner star". In every one of the 240 stamps of Plate 2, the upper segment of the right star has two of its three rays (left and middle) broken off short. As the remaining

N.W. corner, weak left side, Plate 1

N.E. corner, "shorn off" top rays, Plate 2

(right) ray is never very long, this gives a "shorn off" appearance to the rays of the upper part of Plate 2. In Plate 1, on the other hand, there are only 23 stamps (SB to TL) that have a right star identical with the above. In all of the remaining 217 impressions (AA to SA) of Plate 1, the upper segment of the right star shows the middle ray intact and this vertical ray is usually a pronounced feature. In the remainder, the check letters S and T are generally distinctly lower on Plate 2 than on Plate 1, and further there are the thinner outer lines of the left upper corner of Plate 1 stamps to help in the distinction.

"TW joined" and indented O", Plate 1

An additional distinguishing feature is the "TW of TWOPENCE joined" roller flaw which is found on Plate 1 only, and is limited to the A, B, C, D, E, M, N, O and P horizontal rows. Very worn impressions come from Plate 1, as this plate, unlike Plate 2, was not hardened. Plate 1, having printed 16,962 sheets of stamps, was discarded as soon as Plate 2 was ready (18 July 1840). As Plate 2 supplied only 10,600 sheets, stamps from this plate are the rarer.

Horizontal guide-lines and shifted transfers occur normally on Plate 2 at the base of the impressions in both upper and lower parts of the plate. In the 2d. Plate 1, on the other hand, the arrangement of these is abnormal and bears a striking resemblance to that of the 1d. Plate 2, in which horizontal guide-lines and shifts are to be found at the base of the impression in the upper part of the sheet, and at the upper border in the lower part of the sheet.

Repairs of plate: in the 2d. Plate 1, the stamp DJ exists in two states, the impression having been repaired by re-entry at an early date; the original unrepaired state is much the rarer of the two.

Repaired Impressions—Prices for Original States

Although they are not separately listed, it must be understood that wherever impressions are repaired, creating second states, the prices for the letterings in original states may be higher than those for normal unrepaired letterings that exist in only one state. This applies throughout the Line-Engraved issues.

Twopence, Plate 1

Plate 1 was not ready until 1 May 1840 and was registered on the following day.

DS1	2d. deep full blue	£22000	£825
DS2	2d. violet-blue	—	£4000
DS3	2d. milky blue	£24000	£2000
DS4	2d. steel-blue	£22000	£1400
DS5	2d. blue	£16000	£650
DS6	2d. pale blue	£22000	£700
DS6A	2d. bright blue	£22000	£850
	Pair	£60000	£1500
	Block of four	£140000	£20000
	Used on cover	†	£1700
a.	Watermark inverted	£35000	£3000
b.	Re-entries (not prominent): AH, ED, NC	—	£750
c.	Shifted transfers (basal): AJ, AK, BI, CF, DK	—	£700
d.	Shifted transfers (upper border): OA, OC, OK, RI, TD	—	£700
e.	Guide line in corner	—	£675
f.	Guide line through value	—	£675
g.	Left lower corner lines recut PI	—	£750
h.	DJ State 1, without re-entry	—	£2800
i.	DJ State 2, with re-entry	—	£1500
j.	Double letters: A*L*, B*A*, B*L*, C*D*, D*F*, E*K*, *F*B, *F*C, *J*L, K*I*, L*C* *from*	—	£700
k.	Constant varieties: CK, L*H*, NB, PE, *P*L, TH	—	£700

No imprimaturs of this plate have ever been reported.

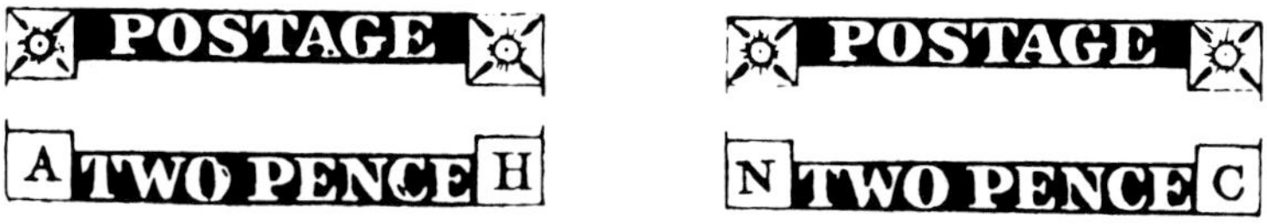

Plate 1, *re-entries*

Plate 1, *second state re-entry*

EK FB FC JL LC

Plate 1, *double letters*

CK LH NB PE PI TH

Plate 1, *constant varieties*

Twopence, Plate 2

Plate 2 was put to press in July 1840 and the earliest known used examples are dated 18 August.

DS7		2d. deep blue	£22000	£825
DS8		2d. blue	£20000	£700
DS9		2d. pale blue	£22000	£800
		Pair	£65000	£1750
		Block of four	£160000	£22000
		Used on cover	†	£2000
	a.	Watermark inverted	†	£3000
	b.	Re-entries QL, TA	—	£850
	c.	Shifted transfers (basal): GJ, ME, RB, RI, RJ, SD	—	£800
	d.	Double letters: A*D*, B*B*, *C*A, D*E*, *F*A, F*K*, *G*A, G*B*, *HJ*, *K*A, *K*G, *K*J, *L*A, *N*A, *N*B, *N*L, *OA*, O*E*, *P*A, *Q*A *from*	—	£800
	e.	Constant varieties: *A*D, JK, *K*L, RH, *S*A	—	£800
	f.	Cancelled with red Maltese Cross	—	£1000

The used prices quoted for DS7–9 are for stamps with *black* Maltese Cross cancellations.
No imprimaturs of this plate have ever been reported.

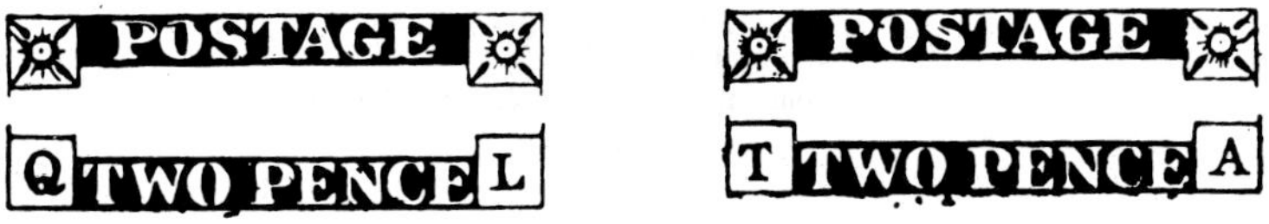

Plate 2, re-entries

CA DE GA KA KJ QA

Plate 2, double letters

AD JK KL RH SA

Plate 2, constant varieties

SECTION E

Twopence Blue, Type E1 (White Lines Added), Imperforate

The special new type of ink, first employed for the Penny Red printings from Plate 1, was used for the Twopence from Plate 3 onwards (see notes above No. AS6). According to the Treasury Minute dated 17 December 1840, it had proved to be impracticable to change the colour of the Twopence Blue to another light colour, and in compliance with the instructions: ". . . as it may be important, hereafter, to have the means of distinguishing the new Twopenny Labels from the old ones, to make some alteration in the plate used for printing them", the white lines were added. It is therefore often termed "the 2d. with lines".

E1

1841 (13 March). First Issue with White Lines, on Blued Paper. Die I. Alphabet I. Wmk Small Crown. Imperf.

E1 (=S.G.13/15aa)	(1)	2d. pale blue	£3500	85·00
	(2)	2d. blue	£3000	75·00
	(3)	2d. deep full blue	£4000	85·00
	(4)	2d. "violet-blue" (1851)	£14000	£1000
		Block of four	£20000	£1000
		Block of four (black Maltese Cross canc.)	†	£2500
		Used on cover	†	£275
	c.	Watermark inverted	£7000	£550
	d.	Ivory head	£3250	85·00
	e.	Re-entry	£4250	£140
	f.	Double letter in corner	—	95·00
	g.	Guide line in corner (Plate 3 only)	—	90·00
	h.	Guide line through value (Plate 3 only)	£3250	90·00
	s.	"Specimen". Type 1 (Plates 3, 4) *from*	£5000	

Imprimaturs (Plate 3 or 4), £10000.

Coloured or Distinctive Maltese Cross Cancellations

		Stamp off cover	*Stamp on cover*
ua.	Red Cross	£16000	—
ub.	Black Cross	£225	£550
uc.	Blue Cross	£3250	£7000
ud.	Channel Is.	—	—
ue.	Kelso.	£1000	£3500
uf.	Kilmarnock	£2000	£5000
ug.	Leeds	£1200	£3500
uh.	Norwich	£900	£2500
ui.	York	£1000	£3200
uj.	Belfast	£500	£1500
uk.	Cork	£900	£2500

ul. Dublin	£450	£1200
um. Greenock	£450	£1200
un. Scottish I or II	£300	£700
uo. Coventry	—	—
up. Mullingar	£8000	£20000
uq. Welshpool	—	†
ur. Stirling		

For illustrations of these cancellations see after Line-engraved General Notes.

"Numbers in Maltese Cross" Cancellations

	Stamp off cover	*Stamp on cover*
va. No. 1 in Cross	£450	£1600
vb. No. 2 in Cross	£450	£1600
vc. No. 3 in Cross	£450	£1600
vd. No. 4 in Cross	£425	£1500
ve. No. 5 in Cross	£550	£2000
vf. No. 6 in Cross	£425	£1500
vg. No. 7 in Cross	£750	£2200
vh. No. 8 in Cross	£600	£2000
vi. No. 9 in Cross	£750	£2500
vj. No. 10 in Cross	£875	£2500
vk. No. 11 in Cross	£550	£2200
vl. No. 12 in Cross	£350	£1200

Various other Cancellations (on the stamps), in black unless stated

wa. 1844-type postmark	75·00	£275
wb. As wa, in blue	£650	£2000
wc. As wa, in red	£12000	—
wd. As wa, in green	£2500	£8500
we. Town dated postmark	£1250	£4200
wf. As we, in blue	£2000	£7500

For 2d. Essays, Trials etc. see under "Line-Engraved Essays, etc.", Nos. DP42 to 44.

Plates 3 and 4 of the twopence may be distinguished as follows:

1. The earlier issues of Twopence Plate 3 were normally cancelled with a black Maltese Cross. Examples from Plate 4 cancelled in this manner are extremely rare.

2. Perforated stamps of Plate 3 are unknown. The later issues of Plate 4 were perforated 16 or 14.

Open *Narrow* *Square-footed Plate 3* *Narrow* *Open*

Blind *Broad* *Rounded Plate 4* *Broad* *Blind*

3. The check letters of both plates belong to Alphabet I, but those of Plate 4 are of a later type, resembling those of the later Alphabet I plates of the ld. red. In Plate 3 the J is square-footed, D and O are narrow, A and P open. In Plate 4 the J is rounded, D and O broad, A and P blind.

4. A large number of the stamps from Plate 3 show prominent guide-lines, running either horizontally through the basal portion, or vertically on the right; such are not seen on Plate 4.

5. Plate 3 impressions show a marked difference in the strength of the engraving on the two sides, the left being much firmer; this difference is not nearly so pronounced on Plate 4.

6. Many of the side-lines (particularly on the right) were partially recut in Plate 4; not so in Plate 3.

7. A large number of Plate 3 impressions show thickened base-line, sometimes with duplication, and frequently the white letters of the value appear thinned and distorted towards their tops. In Plate 4, the base-lines of the stamps are not unduly thickened, nor is there distortion of the white letters "TWOPENCE'.

Repaired Impressions—Prices for Original States

Although they are not separately listed, it must be understood that wherever impressions are repaired, creating second states, the prices for the letterings in original states may be higher than those for normal unrepaired letterings that exist in only one state. This applies throughout the Line-Engraved issues.

Twopence "With Lines", Plate 3

The Twopence Plate 3 was finished on 25 February 1841, and printing from it commenced two days later. The imprimatur sheet is dated 25 February 1841. The stamps were printed on Small Crown watermarked paper which often shows considerable blueing. All sheets from this plate were issued imperforate. The earliest known used example is 17 March 1841. The plate was in use until December 1849, a period of nearly nine years, during which time 191,000 sheets were printed.

During the first three years of issue, the stamps were cancelled with the *black* Maltese Cross, after which the 1844 type of obliteration was used. The early use of the Maltese Cross postmark facilitates the separation of early and later printings.

Plate characteristics: The stamps show a marked firmness of the left border as compared with the right. There is a remarkable tendency to distortion of the white letters of "TWOPENCE", particularly in their upper parts; also the tendency to thickened baseline, or to basal duplications or to elongation of the lower part of the impression, all of which tendencies may be attributed to "Shifted Transfer", a happening favoured by hurried production of the plate. Another interesting character is the extraordinary number of visible guide-lines, the layout of which provides an informative study. The "J" flaw, which appeared on the 1d. value and is illustrated in the General Notes to the Line-Engraved Issues, appears on this plate in varying degrees. The plate apparently acquired a number of corrosion blemishes, some of which caused disfigurement of impression, so calling for removal of the blemishes, and repair of the affected subjects. A diagonal smear across the Queen's eyebrow on LE and a similar mark across the northwest corner of LF are notable. During 1844 corrosion cleaning on LE, PB and QC was followed by re-entering to restore shading on the Queen's neck. A further re-entry on QC shows the C with lower elongated serif and transfer roller lines at both sides. For further information about these the reader is referred to Dr. H. Osborne's *British Line Engraved Stamps, Twopence Blue, Studies of Plates* 1 *to* 15 and *Gibbons Stamp Monthly* for October 1991.

ES10		2d. pale blue	£3500	£100
ES11		2d. blue	£3000	85·00
ES12		2d. deep full blue	£4000	95·00
		Block of four	£20000	£1000
		Used on cover	†	£275
	a.	Watermark inverted	£7000	£550
	b.	Re-entry: OG	—	£140
	c.	Shifted tranfer, elongation of stamp: OL, PA, RL, SJ	—	£100
	d.	Shifted transfer, distorted white letters of value and basal duplication: EK, HA, HB, NL, PB, PC, PE, PK, QF, QK, RG, RI, SG, SL plus "J" flaw on P*J*	—	95·00
	e.	Repaired impressions (2nd & 3rd states): LE, PB, QC *from*	—	£250
	ea.	Fourth repair: QC with left and right transfer roller lines and recut C.	—	£200
	f.	Guide line in corner	—	95·00
	g.	Guide line through value	£3250	95·00

h.	Double letters: G*D*, *H*K, J*D*, *K*D, S*D* plus "J" flaw on *JJ*	—	£100
i.	"J" flaw: D*J*, H*J*, *J*G, *J*H, *J*I, *J*L, K*J*, L*J*, M*J*, N*J*, O*J*, Q*J*, R*J*	£3250	95·00
j.	Constant variety: MD	—	£100

Imprimatur: £10000. Stamps removed from the imprimatur sheet are AL, SC to SL, TA to TL.

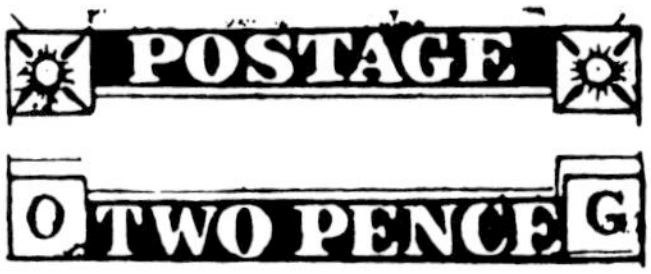

Plate 3, *re-entry*

MD
Plate 3, *constant variety*

GD HK JD KD SD
Plate 3, *double letters*

Twopence "With Lines", Plate 4

Plate 4 was finished on 29 November 1849, and printing from it commenced early the following month. The imprimatur sheet is dated 6 December 1849. For just over four years the sheets of stamps from this plate were issued in the imperforate condition. Official perforation came into operation on 31 January 1854, and from that time onwards the stamps were issued in perforated sheets. Plate 4 is the only Twopence plate from which stamps were issued both imperforate and perforated; thus in a collection embracing both conditions will be represented the earlier and the later states of the plate respectively. A total of 250,000 sheets of stamps was printed from the 2d. Plate 4. Small Crown watermarked paper was used for all the 2d. Plate 4 issues, both imperforate and perforated.

Recent work has shown that the so-called "violet-blue" shade was due to the chemical reaction of a bleaching agent with the printing ink and other constituents present in the process. This gives a whitish paper effect with some lavender tint and it is present on the ld. values of the same period, listed under Nos. BS32e and B2k. On medium paper with marked ivory head there is only a slight tint of lavender. For further details see article by F. M. Johnson and M. R. Fox in *The GB Journal* Volume 14 for October and November 1976.

This stamp has always been known as "violet-blue" but the actual colour is nearest to deep turquoise-blue in the S.G. Colour Key.

Alterations and additions to the marginal inscriptions and markings were made shortly after printing of the stamps had begun but the alterations were not all effected simultaneously. The first to be made was the alteration of the words "£2 Per Sheet" to "£1 Per Sheet", along with the addition of a fan-like ornament at the centre of each of the side margins to show the correct spot where to divide the sheet into two equal parts of the value of one pound. Other alterations include the marks introduced in 1849 for pinning the 1d. sheets, for the Archer perforation trials, which were also added to plate 4 of the 2d. These took the form of a centrally placed small dot above the inscription, between the sixth and seventh stamps. A vertical line was placed in a similar position on the bottom selvedge. Later a cross and a vertical line were used on the upper and lower sheet margins.

This plate was apparently inadequately hardened, and soon after the erasure of the marginal "£2" (above AC and below TC), wear appeared on the upper parts of AB, AC and AD and on the lower parts of TB, TC and TD. The plate also suffered an attack of corrosion very soon after printing commenced, also due to the failure of the hardened skin. Although the effects of corrosion can be found on most letterings, it was the top and bottom of the plate which suffered most, affecting particularly the A and T rows. Several attempts to clear this corrosion by burnishing were made during the lifetime of Plate 4, but as more of the hardening was removed at each operation, further corrosion and wear occurred on the affected areas.

Late in the imperforate printings (probably October 1853), the first attempt at plate cleaning was made, it being necessary to re-enter the worn units AB, AC, AD, TB and TC, although not always successfully, for TC retained its worn appearance of the bottom network, etc. All these letterings received much firmer side lines, and TB received a blue transfer roller line in its right vertical gutter. The other letterings re-entered at the same time were AE, AF, AI, TF, TG and TH which probably had been weakened by the corrosion cleaning, all of which now show a strong blue transfer roller line in their left vertical gutters and much firmer left side lines.

Further wear and corrosion appeared during the perforated stamp printings. Extreme wear led to the second repair by re-entry of AB, AC, AD, TB, and TC, whilst AA and TD were re-entered for the first time. The most striking repair was on TC where the extremely worn lower parts were completely restored and there is marked thinning of the check-letter C (see F11 and F2j).

ES13		2d. pale blue	£3750	85·00
ES14		2d. blue	£3500	75·00
ES15		2d. deep full blue	£4250	85·00
ES16		2d. "violet-blue", thicker, lavender tinted paper (1851)	£14000	£1000
ES17		2d. "violet-blue", marked ivory head with slight sign of lavender tint (early stage)	£5000	£225
		Block of four	£22000	£1100
		Used on cover	†	£275
	a.	Watermark inverted	—	£550
	b.	Re-entries: CE, HK	—	£125
	c.	Re-entry: TH first state (fresh entry)	—	£180
	d.	Re-entry: TH second state (after further re-entry)	—	£300
	e.	Shifted transfers: upper shifts: CA, GK, IK, JK, KH, KI, KK, KL, LK, MK, NA, NB, NK, OK, RA, SA, TA, TL	—	80·00
	f.	Double letter: P*C*	—	85·00
	g.	Retouched check letter L: IL	—	85·00
	h.	Recut side line: PG	—	80·00
	i.	Worn plate (upper corners of "A" row stamps)	—	85·00
	j.	Worn plate (base of TC)	—	90·00
	k.	First repair: AB, AC, AD, TC with firmer side lines	—	£200
	l.	First repair: TB with right-hand transfer roller lines and firmer side lines	—	£200
	m.	First repair: AE, AF, AI, TF, TG with left-hand transfer roller lines and firmer side lines	—	£200
	n.	BH without Spectacle variety (early printings)	—	£1000
	o.	Spectacle variety: BH (later printings)	—	£650
	p.	Constant varieties under POSTAGE: JF, JL	—	85·00
	q.	Thin paper	—	£150

Imprimatur: £10000. Stamps removed from the imprimatur sheet are AA to AL, HE to HL, IK and TL.

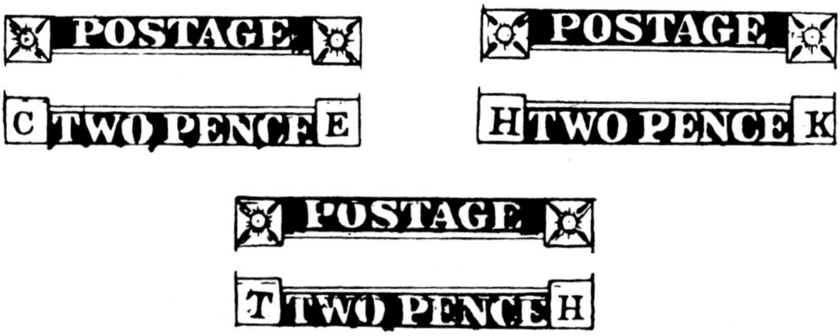

Plate 4, *re-entries*

BH (*spectacles flaw, plate scratch from eye to ear)*

JF

JL

Plate 4, *constant varieties*

SECTION F

Twopence Blue, Type E1, Perforated

Listed as F1 to F8 in this section are eight basic stamps. They are from three different plates, and share two watermarks and two gauges of perforation.

The notes provided will aid recognition of the three plates, which depends upon the corner letters and the thickness of the white lines. In addition the boldface heading above each basic stamp gives its watermark and perforation.

Prices for Stamps in Used Condition

The notes about condition at the beginning of Section CB also apply to this Section. Prices for well centred lightly used examples can be calculated by adding **125%** to the prices quoted.

Repaired Impressions—Prices for Original States

Although they are not separately listed, it must be understood that wherever impressions are repaired, creating second states, the prices for the letterings in original states may be higher than those for normal unrepaired letterings that exist in only one state. This applies throughout the Line-Engraved issues.

Twopence, Plate 4

F1 and F2 were printed from the same Plate 4 already described in Section E together with descriptions and illustrations of the varieties. These stamps can be fairly readily distinguished from the Plate 5 issue (see F3 and F4 below) by the fact that while Plate 4 has Alphabet I corner letters Plate 5 has Alphabet II.

1854 (1 March). Plate 4 (Die I, Alphabet I). Wmk Small Crown. Perf 16.

F1 (=S.G.19/20)	(1)	2d. deep blue	£2750	90·00
	(2)	2d. pale blue	£2750	£100
		Block of four	£18000	£1500
		Used on cover	†	£175
	b.	Imperforate three sides (horiz. pair)	†	—
	c.	Watermark inverted	—	£250
	d.	Imperforate horizontally (M and N rows)	—	£3000
	e.	Double perforation	—	£225
	f.	Re-entries: CE, HK	—	£120
	g.	Re-entry: TH second state	—	£250
	h.	Repaired stamps (from first repair): AB, AC, AD, AE, AF, AI, TB, TC, TF, TG	—	£200
	i.	Worn plate (second wear): AB, AC, AD, TB	—	£120
	j.	Worn plate (extreme wear): base of TC	—	£120
	k.	First repair of AA, TD and second repair of AB, AC, AD, TB	—	£250
	l.	Second repair of TC (third state; thin C, repaired value tablet)	£3500	£550
	m.	Shifted transfers, upper shifts: CA, GK, etc.	—	£110
	n.	Double letter: PC	—	£120
	o.	Retouched check-letter L: IL	—	£110
	p.	Recut side line PG	—	£100
	q.	Spectacles variety: BH	—	£400
	r.	Constant varieties under POSTAGE: JF, JL	—	£110
	s.	"Specimen", Type 2	£1200	

1855 (22 February). Plate 4 (Die I, Alphabet I). Wmk Small Crown. Perf 14.

F2 (=S.G.23)		2d. blue	£5000	£200
		Block of four	—	£1900
		Used on cover	†	£300
	c.	Watermark inverted	—	£450
	d.	Re-entries: CE, HK	—	£250
	e.	Re-entry: TH second state	—	£300
	f.	Repaired stamps (from first repair): AB, AC, AD, AE, AF, AI, TB, TC, TF, TG	—	£275
	g.	Worn plate (second wear): AB, AC, AD, TB	—	£250
	h.	Worn plate (extreme wear): base of TC	—	£275
	i.	First repair of AA, TD and second repair of AB, AC, AD, TB	—	£380
	j.	Second repair of TC (third state; thin C, repaired value tablet)	—	£900
	k.	Shifted transfers, upper shifts: CA, GK etc.	—	£250
	l.	Double letter: P*C*	—	£225
	m.	Retouched check letter L: IL	—	£225
	n.	Recut side line: PG	—	£225
	o.	Spectacles variety: BH	—	£600
	p.	Constant varieties under POSTAGE: JF, JL	—	£225
	s.	"Specimen", Type 2	£1200	

TC, *Plate* 4 *(third state: thin* C *and repaired value tablet)*

For note on the Frank Ives Scudamore handstamp, see below Section CB, Group 1.

Twopence, Plate 5

This plate was registered on 8 June 1855. It differed from Plate 4 in that the corner letters were of Alphabet II, Plate 4 letters having been of the late form, of Alphabet I, i.e., rather larger than the early Alphabet I letters (as seen on the One Penny Black and early One Penny Red) but smaller than Alphabet II.

Stamps of Plate 5 are found with both the perfs 14 and 16 and both watermarks, Small Crown and Large Crown. The paper is generally blued in some degree. The letter A is "blind" except on MA. A particularly fine re-entry shows between stamps CB and DB, an earlier impression of DB having been placed much too high, necessitating fresh entering. The only definite double letters are *P*K and T*L*.

There is a ray flaw consisting of the absence or extreme weakness of the "8 o'clock" ray of the top left corner "star" on every impression of Plate 5. As this peculiarity is also present throughout Plate 4 it cannot serve to assist in differentiation between stamps of these two plates; there is however no sign of this flaw on Plate 6 and so it does in a negative sense serve to identify Plate 6 stamps.

It will be noticed from the dates of issue of F3, F4, F5 and F6 that in July/August 1855 there were two different watermarks and two different perforations in concurrent use.

1855 (4 July). Plate 5 (Die I, Alphabet II). Wmk Small Crown. Perf 14.

F3 (=S.G.23a)		2d. blue	£6000	£275
		Block of four	—	£2500
		Used on cover	†	£400
	c.	Watermark inverted	—	£500
	d.	Major re-entry DB	—	£425
	e.	Double letters, *P*K, T*L*	—	£300
	f.	Constant varieties CA, L*K*, *P*J, SH*	—	£300
	g.	Imperforate		

Imprimatur: £8000. Stamps removed from the imprimatur sheet are AA to AL, BA to BH and TA.

1855 (18 August). Plate 5 (Die I, Alphabet II). Wmk Small Crown. Perf 16.

F4 (=S.G.20a)		2d. blue	£5000	£275
		Block of four		
		Used on cover	†	£425
	c.	Major re-entry DB	—	£600
	d.	Double letters *P*K, T*L*	—	£300
	e.	Constant varieties CA, L*K*, *P*J, SH*	—	£300
	f.	Watermark inverted	—	£600

1855 (20 July). Plate 5 (Die I, Alphabet II). Wmk Large Crown, Type I. Perf 16.

F5 (=S.G.27)		2d. blue	£6500	£350
		Block of four	—	£2500
		Used on cover	†	£450
	c.	Watermark inverted	—	£600
	d.	Imperforate	—	£5500
	e.	Major re-entry DB	—	£550
	f.	Imperforate between vertical pair IL–JL		
	g.	Double letters *P*K, T*L*	—	£375
	h.	Constant varieties CA, L*K*, *P*J, SH*	—	£375
	i.	Double perforation		

1855 (20 July). Plate 5 (Die I, Alphabet II). Wmk Large Crown, Type I. Perf 14.

F6 (=S.G.34)	(1)	2d. blue	£1900	55·00
	(2)	2d. greenish blue	£2500	£100
		Block of four	£12000	£700
		Used on cover	†	£140
	c.	Watermark inverted	—	£225
	d.	Major re-entry DB	—	£125
	e.	Double letters *P*K, T*L*	—	75·00
	f.	Constant varieties CA, L*K*, *P*J, SH*	—	75·00
	g.	Double perforation		

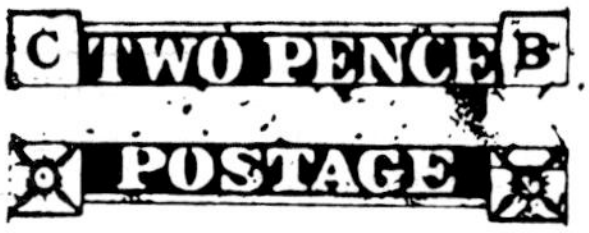

Plate 5, re-entry (CB–DB)

PK

TL

Plate 5, double letters

CA

LK

PJ

SH

Plate 5, constant varieites

*A coloured roller flaw (shown as SH) is also found on eight more letterings in G and H columns, namely RG, SG, TG plus OH, PH, QH, RH and TH.

Twopence, Plate 6

Registered 11 February 1857. This plate is found used with both perforations but with only the Large Crown watermark. The letters were of Alphabet III and therefore usually readily distinguishable from those of Plate 5 (Alph. II). The white lines below POSTAGE and above the value are thinner than on Plate 5. The paper is generally without blueing.

Plate 6 does not show the top left corner "8 o'clock" flaw previously noted on Plate 5 but it does have a similar flaw; this taking the form of an absence or extreme weakness of the "11 o'clock" ray of the top right corner "star".

Double letters exist on *FL* and *GD* but are not outstanding examples. A number of re-entries (fresh entries) occur, the majority being in the E vertical column; they are AF, JH, KE, LE, ME, NE, OE, PE, QE, RE, SE. There may be traces of re-entry on IH. Recutting of corners was done on numerous impressions.

1857 (2 July). Plate 6 (Die I, Alphabet III). Wmk Large Crown, Type I. Perf 14.

F7 (=S.G.35)		2d. deep blue	£2200	55·00
		Block of four	£12000	£700
		Used on cover	†	£140
	c.	Watermark inverted	—	£225
	d.	Re-entries: KE to SE *from*	—	90·00
	de.	Re-entry and constant variety: JH	—	£100
	e.	Double letters *FL*, *GD*	—	75·00
	f.	AF State 1, without re-entry		
	g.	AF State 2, with re-entry	—	£125
	h.	Constant varieties A*K*, GB, LG, RA	—	65·00
	i.	Imperforate	—	£5500
	j.	Imperforate between vertical pair RD–SD	†	£18000
	k.	Double perforation		

Imprimatur: £8000. Stamps removed from the imprimatur sheet are AA to AL, GK, GL, HG to HL, TL.

1858 (1 February). Plate 6 (Die I, Alphabet III). Wmk Large Crown, Type I. Perf 16.

F8 (=S.G.36a)		2d. deep blue	£6750	£325
		Block of four	—	£2500
		Used on cover	†	£450
	c.	Re-entries: AF, KE to SF *from*	—	£375
	ca.	Re-entry and constant variety: JH	—	£400
	d.	Double letters *FL*, *GD*	—	£350
	e.	Constant varieties A*K*, GB, LG, RA	—	£350
	f.	Watermark inverted	—	£650

AF, *State* 2

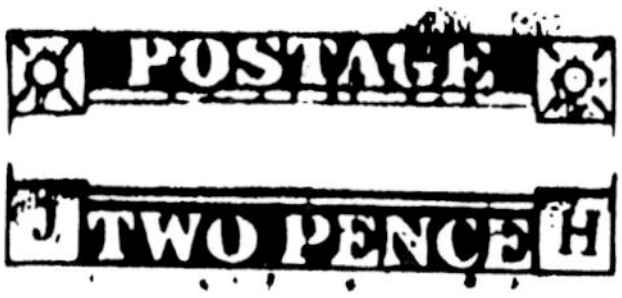

Plate 6

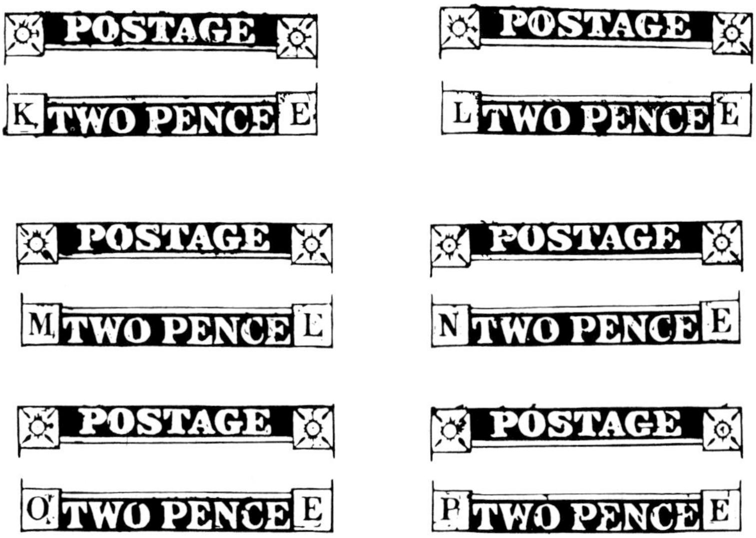

Plate 6, *re-entries*

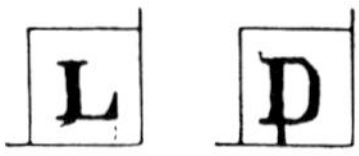

FL GD

Plate 6, *double letters*

AK GB LG RA

Plate 6, *constant varieties*

SECTION G

Line-Engraved Stamps with Letters in all Four Corners and with Plate Numbers incorporated in the Design

The order followed for the stamps in this Section (Types **G1** to **G4** below) is: 1d., 2d., ½d., 1½d.

The most important feature is that the plate numbers are now incorporated in the design, and the illustrations below show where these numbers are located.

The stamps with letters in all four corners have the same letters at the top as at the bottom but in the reverse order. In identifying these stamps the *bottom* corner letters are always quoted. Stamps with the names of firms printed on the backs are listed in Appendix 2.

A significant development in perforation technology occurred while these stamps were in production. Thomas Peacock, Superintendent of the Perforating Room, invented a feed mechanism that greatly improved productivity from 3200 to 5500 sheets a day per machine. At least one of the three Napier machines used for the low value stamps may have been adapted to take Peacock's invention before the end of 1874, with trials satisfactorily concluded by August 1875. Problems of design or workmanship resulted in an approach to Napier who further developed the principle of continuous feed. The process of equipping the three machines with the new Napier feed mechanism (and of fully overhauling them) began in November 1876 and was completed a year or so later.

Sheets of the standard format stamps (1d., 1½d. and 2d.) from the adapted machines were perforated through both the top and bottom margins, and this was the normal pattern from early 1878 onwards, although some exceptions are known. Previously the top margin had been imperforate. The ½d. stamps perforated after 1877 also show the margin of the leading edge perforated. It is suggested that the new equipment also permitted the final row of stamps to be fully perforated.

G1

G2

G3

G4

LOCATION OF PLATE NUMBERS

1d. *and* 2d (170 *shown*)

½d. (9 *shown*)

1½d. (3 *shown*)

Prices for Stamps in Used Condition

The notes about condition at the beginning of Section CB also apply to this Section. Prices for well centred lightly used examples can be calculated by adding the following percentages to the prices quoted: **125%** G1/3, G6; **200%** G4.

Repaired Impressions—Prices for Original States

Although they are not separately listed, it must be understood that wherever impressions are repaired, creating second states, the prices for the letterings in original states may be higher than those for normal unrepaired letterings that exist in only one state. This applies throughout the Line-Engraved issues.

One Penny, Type G1

The numbering of this series of plates follows on from that of the previous 1d. *(see* Section CB), last printed from Plate 68. Although the first roller dies were prepared in 1858 it was not until 1864 that the stamps appeared. Plates 69, 70, 75, 77, 126 and 128 were rejected and of these no stamps exist save for a very few from Plate 77 which somehow reached the public. Collectors should be wary of stamps from Plate 177 which by accident or design have the small figures "1" of the plate numbers obscured; so making them appear to be from Plate 77.

Re-entries are very few, the best being MK and TK of Plate 71; SL and TL of Plate 83 are also noteworthy. Considering the number of plates, varieties are remarkably few and it is evident that great care and skill were exercised in the laying down. However, recent research has revealed details of repairs on some letterings in early plates including Plates 73, 80, 81, 85, 88, 90 and 100. Fresh entries, i.e. repaired impressions made prior to the " put-to-press" date, exist on Plates 71 and 83. Dr. W. R. D. Wiggins has written about the repairs on Plate 88 in *The Philatelic Journal of Great Britain* of December 1974 and subsequent correspondence appears in the issues of March and September 1975. A very detailed study of all the plates has been carried out by members of the Great Britain Philatelic Society and the findings have been co-ordinated by Mr. G. C. Akerman and published in *The GB Journal* in the issues from January 1974 to May 1977.

According to the day-to-day records of Perkins, Bacon & Petch a number of repairs were made to plates 146/8, 152, 156/8, 160, 166, 170, 179, 181, 187, 190, 192/3, 197 and 201 before they were withdrawn from press. The letterings were not identified in the records but it is possible that certain stamps printed from the repaired plates may exist showing second or even third states. For further details see an article by F. M. Johnson in the *Gibbons Stamp Monthly* of March 1981.

The MA (or ML) error of watermark occurs on plates up to about Plate 96. See under "Watermarks" in the General Notes to the Line-Engraved Issues.

The presence of plate numbers and corner letters makes the plating of these stamps a simple matter and many complete platings are formed.

Inverted watermarks exist on every plate, except plates 77 and 93; the average number of inverted against normal is about 1 in 700, scarcity is not pro rata of normal. Among the scarcest/rarest are those from Plates 93, 102, 103, 110, 124, 125, 132, 143, 145, 147, 168, 172, 175, 181, 183, 191, 206, 211, 213, 215, 217, 219, 220, 222, 223 and 224. Among the more common are those from Plates 71, 74, 83, 84, 99, 101, 117, 118, 136, 141, 157, 158, 190, 201 and 208.

Examples with reversed watermark exist, but these can only be confirmed when attached to selvedge showing part of the marginal watermark letter, which when reversed and viewed from the back of the stamp, will be the right way round. When normal, such letters appear as a mirror image when viewed from the back of the stamp. A study of mint blocks from different plates showed that reversed watermarks were almost five times more common than normal watermarks for this issue.

Plate 103. Proof Sheets were taken from this plate on soft white card imperforate for the Paris Exhibition of 1867 (see No. DP38).

Unused blocks from Plate 225 are notably scarce and blocks from any plate showing plate number or inscription are much sought after. Sheets were, as before, of 240 stamps.

From Plate 98 onwards a serial number was added on the selvedge and the plate numbers on the corners of the sheets were enclosed in circles.

1864 (1 April). Original Issue. Wmk Large Crown, Type II. Perf 14.

G1 (=S.G.43/44)	(1)	1d. rose-red	18·00	2·50
	(2)	1d. lake-red	18·00	2·50
		Block of four	85·00	20·00
		Used on cover	†	6·00
	c.	Error of watermark MA (or ML) *from*	—	£300
	d.	Watermark inverted *from*	75·00	25·00
	e.	Re-entry MK, TK Plate 71	£125	40·00
	f.	Re-entry SL, TL Plate 83	£280	50·00
	g.	Imperforate "Cardiff Penny" (Plate 116)	£5000	£2500
	h.	Imperforate other plates *from*	£5000	£2500
	i.	Imperforate, Dr Perkins paper (blued) (Plate 121)	£2000	
	j.	Repaired states (Plates 73, 80, 81, 85, 88, 90, 100) *from*	—	70·00
	k.	Double perforation	—	£100
	s.	Imperforate "Specimen" Type 2 (Plate 121)	£400	
	t.	Specimen", Type 6 (Plate 121)	£250	
	u.	"Specimen", Type 8 (Plate 164)	£225	
	v.	Specimen", Type 9 (Plates 146, 183, 198, 207, 224) *from*	£175	
	w.	Dr Perkins paper (Plate 121) Perforated 14 "Specimen"	£2000	
	x.	Do. Imperforate		
	y.	"Specimen", Type 1 (Plate 133)	£450	

Imprimaturs: Plates 71–225 *except* 75, 77, 126, 128, 158. *From* £350 *each.*

List of Plates

Plate No.	*Regd.*	*Put to press*		
71	14. 3.61	1. 3.64	40·00	3·50
72	14. 3.61	1. 3.64	45·00	4·50
73	14. 3.61	1. 3.64	45·00	3·50
74	14. 3.61	1. 3.64	45·00	2·50
76	7. 2.63	1. 3.64	40·00	2·50
77	—	—	—	£160000
78	7. 2.63	1. 3.64	£100	2·50
79	7. 2.63	1. 3.64	35·00	2·50
80	7. 2.63	1. 3.64	50·00	2·50
81	7. 2.63	1. 3.64	50·00	2·75
82	1. 3.64	1. 3.64	£100	4·50
83	1. 3.64	1. 3.64	£125	8·00
84	1. 3.64	1. 3.64	65·00	2·75
85	1. 3.64	1. 3.64	45·00	3·75
86	1. 3.64	1. 3.64	55·00	4·50
87	7. 3.64	7. 3.64	35·00	2·50
88	17. 3.64	17. 3.64	£150	8·50
89	22. 3.64	22. 3.64	45·00	2·50
90	30. 3.64	30. 3.64	45·00	2·50
91	5. 4.64	5. 4.64	60·00	6·50
92	12. 4.64	12. 4.64	40·00	2·50
93	19. 4.64	19. 4.64	55·00	2·50
94	26. 4.64	26. 4.64	50·00	5·50
95	14. 4.64	4. 7.64	45·00	2·50
96	5.10.64	11.10.64	50·00	2·50
97	5.10.64	7. 3.65	45·00	4·00
98	10. 3.65	20. 3.65	55·00	6·50
99	5. 1.66	6. 1.66	60·00	5·50
100	5. 1.66	19. 1.66	65·00	2·75
101	5. 1.66	12. 4.66	65·00	10·00
102	4. 4.66	16. 4.66	50·00	2·50
103	4. 4.66	8. 8.66	55·00	4·00
104	4. 4.66	22. 1.68	80·00	5·50
105	4. 4.66	31. 1.68	£100	8·00
106	4. 4.66	29. 2.68	60·00	2·50
107	4. 4.66	18. 3.68	65·00	8·00
108	23. 3.68	23. 3.68	85·00	2·75
109	23. 3.68	23. 3.68	90·00	4·00
110	23. 3.68	23. 3.68	65·00	10·00
111	23. 3.68	23. 3.68	55·00	2·75
112	12. 5.68	12. 5.68	75·00	2·75
113	12. 5.68	12. 5.68	55·00	14·00
114	12. 5.68	12. 5.68	£280	14·00
115	12. 5.68	12. 5.68	£100	2·75
116	12. 5.68	12. 5.68	80·00	10·00
117	9. 6.68	9. 6.68	50·00	2·50
118	9. 6.68	9. 6.68	55·00	2·50
119	15. 8.68	15. 8.68	50·00	2·50
120	15. 8.68	8. 9.68	18·00	2·50
121	15. 8.68	17.12.68	45·00	10·00
122	15. 8.68	16. 1.69	18·00	2·50
123	15. 8.68	18. 1.69	45·00	2·50
124	15. 8.68	18. 1.69	32·00	2·50
125	5. 2.69	15. 2.69	45·00	2·50
127	5. 2.69	3. 5.69	60·00	2·75
129	5. 2.69	10. 5.69	45·00	9·00
130	5. 2.69	5. 6.69	60·00	2·75
131	5. 2.69	3. 8.69	70·00	18·00
132	5. 2.69	4. 9.69	£150	25·00
133	31. 3.69	1.10.69	£125	10·00
134	31. 3.69	8.10.69	18·00	2·50
135	31. 3.69	13.12.69	£100	28·00
136	1. 3.69	6. 1.70	£100	22·00
137	31. 3.69	5. 3.70	32·00	2·75

Plate No.	*Regd.*	*Put to press*				*Plate No.*	*Regd.*	*Put to press*			
138	31. 3.69	10. 3.70	..	22·00	2·50	182	13. 4.74	19. 6.75	..	£100	5·50
139	2. 2.70	19. 3.70	..	65·00	18·00	183	13. 4.74	9. 8.75	..	60·00	3·50
140	2. 2.70	9. 4.70	..	22·00	2·50	184	13. 4.74	20.10.75	..	35·00	2·75
141	2. 2.70	7. 5.70	..	£125	10·00	185	13. 4.74	4.12.75	..	55·00	3·50
142	2. 2.70	13. 7.70	..	75·00	28·00	186	13. 4.74	18.12.75	..	70·00	2·75
143	2. 2.70	7.10.70	..	65·00	16·00	187	20. 4.75	3. 1.76	..	55·00	2·50
144	2. 2.70	3. 1.71	..	£100	22·00	188	20. 4.75	8. 1.76	..	75·00	11·00
145	23.12.70	16. 1.71	..	35·00	2·75	189	20. 4.75	8. 1.76	..	75·00	7·50
146	23.12.70	23. 1.71	..	45·00	6·50	190	20. 4.75	31. 1.76	..	55·00	6·50
147	23.12.70	4. 2.71	..	55·00	3·50	191	3. 9.75	19. 2.76	..	35·00	8·00
148	23.12.70	29. 4.71	..	45·00	3·50	192	3. 9.75	19. 2.76	..	55·00	2·50
149	23.12.70	15. 5.71	..	45·00	6·50	193	3. 9.75	2. 9.76	..	35·00	2·50
150	24. 4.71	30. 5.71	..	18·00	2·50	194	3. 9.75	13.11.76	..	55·00	9·00
151	24. 4.71	14.11.71	..	65·00	10·00	195	9. 3.76	18.11.76	..	55·00	9·00
152	24. 4.71	14.11.71	..	65·00	6·00	196	9. 3.76	15. 1.77	..	55·00	5·50
153	24. 4.71	27.12.71	..	£110	10·00	197	9. 3.76	20. 1.77	..	60·00	10·00
154	24. 4.71	30. 1.72	..	55·00	2·50	198	9. 3.76	27. 1.77	..	45·00	6·50
155	24. 4.71	20. 4.72	..	55·00	2·75	199	9. 3.76	5. 2.77	..	60·00	6·50
156	12. 1.72	22. 4.72	..	50·00	2·50	200	9. 3.76	3. 3.77	..	65·00	2·50
157	12. 1.72	22. 4.72	..	55·00	2·50	201	16.11.76	21. 4.77	..	35·00	5·50
158	12. 1.72	4. 5.72	..	35·00	2·50	202	16.11.76	19. 5.77	..	65·00	9·00
159	12. 1.72	17. 8.72	..	35·00	2·50	203	16.11.76	19. 5.77	..	35·00	18·00
160	12. 1.72	17. 8.72	..	35·00	2·50	204	16.11.76	23. 6.77	..	60·00	2·75
161	12. 1.72	17. 9.72	..	65·00	8·00	205	16.11.76	8. 9.77	..	60·00	3·50
162	24.10.72	26.10.72	..	55·00	8·00	206	10. 5.77	8. 9.77	..	60·00	10·00
163	24.10.72	5.11.72	..	55·00	3·50	207	10. 5.77	12.11.77	..	65·00	10·00
164	24.10.72	30.11.72	..	55·00	3·50	208	10. 5.77	17.11.77	..	60·00	18·00
165	24.10.72	17. 1.73	..	50·00	2·50	209	10. 5.77	24.11.77	..	55·00	10·00
166	24.10.72	18. 1.73	..	50·00	6·50	210	16.11.77	8.12.77	..	70·00	13·00
167	24.10.72	8. 2.73	..	50·00	2·50	211	16.11.77	16. 3.78	..	75·00	22·00
168	9. 4.73	8. 5.73	..	55·00	9·00	212	16.11.77	20. 5.78	..	65·00	12·00
169	9. 4.73	21. 6.73	..	65·00	8·00	213	25. 2.78	1. 7.78	..	65·00	12·00
170	9. 4.73	11.10.73	..	40·00	2·50	214	25. 2.78	6. 8.78	..	70·00	20·00
171	9. 4.73	27.10.73	..	18·00	2·50	215	25. 2.78	6. 8.78	..	70·00	20·00
172	9. 4.73	27.10.73	..	35·00	2·50	216	25. 2.78	2. 9.78	..	75·00	20·00
173	9. 4.73	2. 4.74	..	75·00	10·00	217	14. 8.78	23.11.78	..	75·00	8·00
174	14.10.73	20. 4.74	..	35·00	2·50	218	14. 8.78	30.11.78	..	70·00	9·00
175	14.10.73	5. 9.74	..	65·00	4·00	219	14. 8.78	11. 1.79	..	£100	75·00
176	14.10.73	12.12.74	..	65·00	2·75	220	14. 8.78	11. 1.79	..	45·00	8·00
177	14.10.73	29.12.74	..	45·00	2·50	221	31.12.78	3. 4.79	..	75·00	18·00
178	14.10.73	1. 2.75	..	65·00	4·00	222	31.12.78	6. 5.79	..	85·00	45·00
179	14.10.73	15. 5.75	..	55·00	2·75	223	31.12.78	21. 6.79	..	£100	65·00
180	14.10.73	22. 5.75	..	65·00	5·50	224	31.12.78	23. 6.79	..	£125	55·00
181	14.10.73	26. 5.75	..	50·00	2·50	225	31.12.78	27.10.79	..	£2500	£700

Imperforates known to exist used are from Plates 72, 79, 80, 81, 82, 83, 84, 85, 86, 87, 88, 90, 91, 92, 93, 96, 97, 98, 100, 101, 102, 103, 104, 105, 107, 108, 109, 111, 112, 113, 114, 116, 117, 120, 121, 122, 136, 137, 142, 146, 148, 158, 162, 164, 166, 171, 174, 191, 198, 202. Cancelled proofs from Plates 146 and 191 should not be mistaken for issued imperfs. Known unused imperforates are from Plates 107, 116, 120, 122, 136. To aid identification of true imperforates we give a list of the stamps removed from the imprimatur sheets of these plates: Plate 107, AA to AL, BA to BH, TA; Plates 116, 120, 122, 136 each, AA to AL, BE to BL, TA.

An example from Plate 190 with "Specimen" Type 10 exists in the Royal Collection.

For 1d. Essays, Proofs, Trials see "Line-Engraved Essays, Proofs, etc.", Nos. DP 37 to 40.

Twopence, Type G2

These 2d. stamps were the companion issue to the 1d. of similar form. The fact that the 2d. preceded the 1d. by some six years was solely the result of delays in the production of the 1d. plates. The first moves towards having both 1d. and 2d. in the new form were taken in the same year, 1858.

The 2d. die was produced by the modification of an impression taken from the ld. Die II. In due course two different series of roller impressions were taken from this new 2d. die; in the first the white lines below POSTAGE and above TWOPENCE were thicker than in the second. The series with thicker lines was used to lay down Plates 7, 8, 9 and 12; the series with thinner white lines was used for Plates 13, 14 and 15.

For fuller details than it is possible to give in this Catalogue readers are referred to Dr. H. Osborne's *British Line Engraved Stamps: Twopence Blue* and the same author's *Twopence Plate Nine.*

1858 (July). With Thick White Lines. Wmk Large Crown, Type I or II (see "List of Plates" below). Perf. 14.

G2 (=S.G.45)		2d. blue	£300	12·00
		Block of four	£1900	£150
		Used on cover	†	40·00
	c.	Error of watermark (Plates 8 or 9)	£800	£300
	d.	Watermark inverted *from*	£800	£160
	e.	Re-entry HG, Plate 7		
	f.	Re-entries *from*	—	90·00
	g.	Bisected (Plate 9) on piece	—	£2200
	h.	Double letter *from*	—	35·00
	i.	Repaired impressions		
		Plate 8	—	70·00
		Do. (3rd & 4th states)	—	£160
		Plate 9 (1866)	—	50·00
		Plate 9 (1868)	—	£175
	j.	Imperforates (Plate 9)	—	£5000
	k.	Double perforation		
	s.	"Specimen", Type 1 (Plate 12)	£450	
	t.	"Specimen", Type 7 (Plate 9)		

Imprimaturs: each, £3000.

List of Plates

Wmk Type I					*Wmk Type II*				
Plate No.	*Regd.*	*Put to press*			*Plate No.*	*Regd.*	*Put to press*		
7	11. 6.58	19. 7.58 ..	£1200	50·00	9	—	— ..	£380	12·00
8	7. 7.59	21. 9.59 ..	£1100	35·00	12	1. 1.68	28.10.68 ..	£1800	£120
9	14. 3.61	14. 3.61 ..	£300	12·00					

Plates 10 and 11 were defective and were rejected. Only Plate 12 was given a serial number (123).

For 2d. Die Proofs, Trials, etc., see under "Line-Engraved Essays, Proofs, etc.", Nos. DP49 and 50.

For notes on the error of watermark, see under "Watermark" in the General Notes on the Line-Engraved Issues.

The paper is normally white but in some sheets blueing occurred and "Ivory Heads" are known. Imperforate examples are known from Plates 9 and 13; the latter being liable to confusion with a printing on experimental paper.

Plate 7. Eight excellent re-entries occur on this plate, these stamps being AH, CB, DC–EC, FB, HG–IG, JB–KB and NB–OB. Recut sidelines are common and some suggestion of doubling of letters occurs on about 16 stamps.

Plate 8. One of the error watermarks has been found, though rarely, on this plate, stamps TA and TL being known with it. Re-entries have been noted on CE, DA and TH and recutting of corners is prevalent. Repairing of impressions was extensive and Dr. Osborne has recorded over fifty stamps as occurring in two and even three or four different states. All but two (AK and AL) are in the O to T horizontal rows.

Plate 9. Both the error watermarks have been seen on Plate 9 stamps. Doubling of letters has been recorded on over 30 stamps but as corrosion blemishes are common it is not easy to say which are true double letters. Repairing was effected in 1866 and in 1868, the stamps so dealt with being restricted almost entirely to the K and L vertical columns in 1866 and to the J, K and L vertical columns in 1868.

Plate 12. Stamps AA, AB and possibly CB show re-entries, the first two being pronounced. The only noteworthy double letter is the lower B on BG.

"ST" (part) of "POSTAGE"

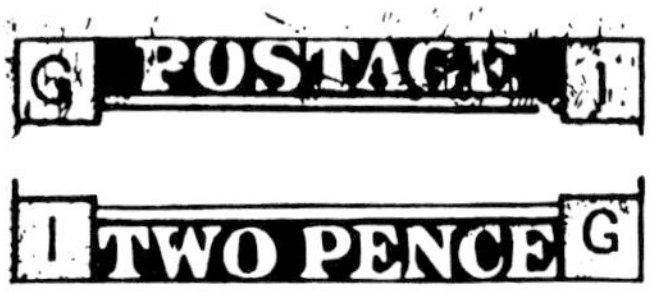

Re-entries, Plate 7

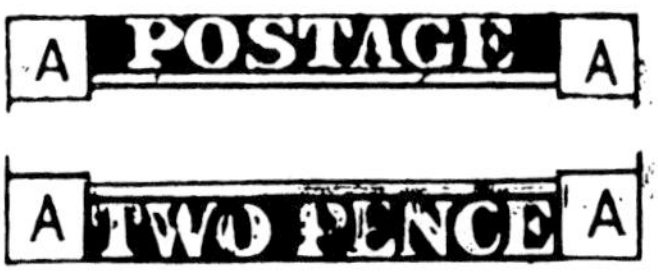

Re-entries, Plate 12

1869 (7 July). With Thin White Lines. Wmk Large Crown, Type II. Perf 14.

G3 (=S.G.46/47)	(1)	2d. blue	£325	22·00
	(2)	2d. deep blue	£325	22·00
		Block of four	£1900	£250
		Used on cover	†	60·00
	c.	Watermark inverted *from*	£1250	£160
	d.	Re-entry	—	85·00
	e.	Imperforate (Plate 13)	£5000	
	f.	Imperforate Dr. Perkins paper (blued) (Plates 9, 13) *from*	£6000	
	s.	Imperforate "Specimen", Type 2 (Plate 13)	£4000	
	t.	"Specimen", Type 6 (Plates 14, 15) *from*	£500	
	u.	"Specimen", Type 8 (Plate 14)	£500	
	v.	"Specimen", Type 9 (Plate 15)	£200	
	w.	"Specimen", Type 10 (Plate 15)		
	x.	Dr. Perkin's paper (Plate 13) Perforated 14 "Specimen"	£2250	

Imprimaturs: each, £3000. To aid identification of the true imperforates from Plate 13 we give a list of the stamps removed from the imprimatur sheet: AA to AL, BF to BL, CK, TA.

List of Plates

Plate No.	*Regd.*	*Put to press*			*Plate No.*	*Regd.*	*Put to press*		
13	31. 3.69	13. 4.69	£325	22·00	15	3. 9.75	14. 3.76	£400	30·00
14	24. 4.71	16. 9.71	£425	30·00					

These three plates were carefully laid down and show few varieties of special interest. There are a few double letters on Plate 13 and the stamps AA and BA of the same plate are possible re-entries. Plate 14 was repaired prior to final withdrawal from press and some letterings may show evidence of a second state repair.

POSTAGE
ONE POUND
TEN PENCE
ONE PENNY
FIVE POUNDS
England

Halfpenny, Type G3

The sheets of the ½d. were of 480 stamps in 20 horizontal rows of 24. The lettering (of the lower corners) ran from AA to AX in the top row and so on to the bottom row, TA to TX. The top corners of the stamps merely repeated the lettering of the lower corners, in reverse. The watermark "halfpenny", Type **W3**, extended over three stamps.

Because of their size the sheets were perforated from side to side, not top to bottom, with the A column normally inserted first. Stamps imperforate on the right or left side from the A or X vertical rows occurred because the final strike of the perforating comb was not made, probably because the overall length of the sheet prevented it. Partially imperforate A row stamps result from the sheets being inserted into the machines in the inverted position and are therefore scarcer than the equivalent stamps from the X row. Stamps from A and X rows are also known perforated all round and this became increasingly common due to the use of the continuous feed apparatus.

Unused blocks with selvedge are scarce. "No watermark" stamps are known, due to faulty registration or badly cut paper. The sheet margin inscription was transferred to the plate by means of two rollers which were hardened on 14 June 1870.

W3

For ½d. Essays, Die Proofs, Trials see under "Line-Engraved Essays, Proofs, etc." Nos. DP58A to 69. Essays were also prepared in 1865 by De La Rue and in 1868 by Somerset House. De La Rue also prepared further essays in 1870.

A Die Proof of the legend or sheet margin inscription around the sheet exists on soft card in three lines "PRICE ½d. Per Label 1/- Per Row of 24. £1 Per Sheet. Place the Labels ABOVE and at the RIGHT HAND SIDE of the Address. In Wetting the Back be careful not to remove the Cement", *Price* £2500.

1870 (1 October). First Halfpenny Stamp. Wmk W3. Perf 14.

G4 (=S.G.48/49)	(1)	½d. rose-red	90·00	18·00
	(2)	½d. rose	90·00	18·00
		Block of four	£450	£150
		Used on cover	†	60·00
	c.	Watermark inverted	—	£125
	d.	Watermark reversed	—	£125
	e.	Watermark inverted and reversed	£225	75·00
	f.	No watermark	—	£750
	g.	Imperforate one side (with selvedge)	£140	50·00
	h.	Imperforate *from*	£2750	£1800
	s.	"Specimen", Type 2 (Plates 3, 9) *from*	£250	
	t.	"Specimen", Type 8 (Plates 10, 11) *from*	£210	
	u.	"Specimen", Type 9 (Plates 10, 13, 19) *from*	£175	
	v.	"Specimen", Type 10 (Plate 11)		

Imprimaturs: from £750.

List of Plates

Plate No.	*Regd.*	*Put to press*			*Plate No.*	*Regd.*	*Put to press*		
1	20. 6.70	20. 6.70	£225	75·00	11	24.10.72	21. 1.74	£100	18·00
3	28. 6.70	28. 6.70	£150	40·00	12	13. 4.74	29. 6.74	£100	18·00
4	4. 7.70	4. 7.70	£130	30·00	13	20. 4.75	6. 5.76	£100	18·00
5	19. 7.70	12. 7.70	90·00	18·00	14	30. 4.75	16.11.76	£100	18·00
6	19. 7.70	19. 7.70	£100	18·00	15	16.11.76	6. 5.78	£150	40·00
8	26. 7.70	?	£300	95·00	19	16.11.77	18. 7.78	£175	55·00
9	23.12.70	9.10.71	£4500	£700	20	31.12.78	27. 6.79	£250	75·00
10	24.10.70	2.10.73	£110	18·00					

The Head on the die was engraved by Frederick Heath.

Imperforates, used, are known from Plates 1, 3, 4, 5, 6, 8, 10 and 14. Plates 2, 7, 16, 17, 18, were not completed and Plates 21 and 22 though laid down were not used. Plate 9 was held as a Reserve plate and consequently was not greatly used.

Plates 5 *and* 6. Repaired states may exist. For a general note on "Later States of the Plates" see under Line Engraved Notes, Section A.

Plate 8. Earliest date of use 13 October 1870. It was later removed from press on 8 December 1870 and kept as a reserve plate until 4 April 1872.

Plates 12 *and* 15. Both plates were re-entered before putting to press, but after registration.

Three Halfpence, Type G4

1860. Prepared for use but not issued. Blued Paper. Wmk Large Crown, Type I. Perf 14.

G5 (=S.G.53a)		1½d. rosy mauve	£5000	
	a.	Error of lettering: OP–PC for CP–PC	—	†
	s.	"Specimen", Types 2, 6 *from*	£1250	
	t.	Imperforate "Specimen", Type 2	£4000	

Imprimatur: Plate (1), £6000. The sheet is dated 22 March 1860. Stamps removed from the imprimatur sheet are as follows: Plate (1), AA–AL, BA–BL, CA–CH, CK, CL, DA, DL, EA, TL.

This 1½d. stamp in rosy mauve is from supplies prepared for use but not issued. The preparation of this stamp in 1860 was in anticipation of a change in postal rates. This did not eventuate but some 10,000 sheets had already been printed and in 1867 8,962 sheets were destroyed and only a few stamps survive in unused condition. Postally used examples in rosy mauve also exist.

A few examples exist of the OP–PC error, one of which is in the Royal Collection.

The plate was registered on 22 March 1860 and put to press on the same day.

No. G5 overwritten "Specimen" exists and should be purchased with a certificate of genuineness. See also Line-Engraved Essays, Proofs, No. DP54.

1870 (1 October). First Issued Three Halfpence Stamp. Wmk Large Crown, Type II. Perf 14.

G6 (=S.G.51/52)	(1)	1½d. rose-red	£375	50·00
	(2)	1½d. lake-red	£375	50·00
		Block of four	£1900	£450
		Used on cover	†	£250
(=S.G.53)	*c.*	Error of lettering: OP–PC for CP–PC (Plate 1)	£13000	£1300
	d.	Watermark inverted	—	£300
	e.	Imperforate (Plate 1)	£4000	†
	f.	Imperforte (Plate 3)	£4000	†
	g.	Imperforate, Dr. Perkins paper (blued) (Plate 1)	£4000	
	s.	"Specimen", Types 2, 6 (Plate 1) *from*	£350	
	t.	Imperforate, "Specimen", Type 1 (Plate 3)	£2000	
	u.	"Specimen", Types 8, 9, 10 (Plate 3) *from*	£225	
	v.	Dr. Perkins paper (Plate 1), Perforated 14 "Specimen"	£2000	

Imprimatur: Plate (1) see under No. G5. These are on blued paper. *Plate* 3, £3000. Stamps removed from the imprimatur sheet are as follows: Plate 3, AA–AL, BG–BL, CI–CL, TL.

List of Plates

Plate (1)	£550	70·00
Plate 3	£375	50·00

Plate 2 was defective and was not completed so no stamps exist from it.

The error OP–PC instead of CP–PC occurred on all printings from Plate (1). It was not apparently noticed by anyone until 1894 when it was recorded in an American journal.

Plate (1), without the plate number incorporated in the design, was put to press for the second time in the issued colour on 6 June 1870; Plate 3 was registered on 13 April 1874 and put to press on 10 August 1874.

For 1½d. Essays, Die Proofs and Trials see under "Line-Engraved Essays, Proofs, etc." Nos. DP51 to 58.

SECTION H

The Embossed Issues

General Notes

Introduction. These issues embody at least three features unique among British adhesive postage stamps. These are: (a) the method of production of the Dies, (b) the "one by one" method of printing and (c) the use of the Dickinson silk thread paper for two of the values. Another peculiarity was the use of tinted gum on later printings of the 6d. value.

Embossing. In "working" dies prepared for this type of printing the raised ("embossed") portions of the design are sunk into the metal. Colourless details, such as are seen here in the diadem, hair, eye, ear and plate number, are achieved by variations in the depth of the engraving.

When an impression is to be printed, ink is first spread over the flat unrecessed parts of the die. Then the paper is pressed on the die (by a comparatively soft material, leather or gutta percha) and that part of the paper which is forced into the recessed parts of the design remains uncoloured though not lacking in detail; at the same time the parts of the paper that contact the unrecessed parts of the die pick up the ink and form the coloured portions of the stamp.

The Dies. The primary die was engraved by William Wyon, using as his model his own City Medal of 1837. This primary die, which did not show the pendant curl at the back of the hair, was used, probably in the coining presses at the Royal Mint where Wyon was employed, to strike "original" dies. To these were later added the curl which was slightly different in each value. At the same time the ground was engraved with the reticulated framework but the inscription was added on the "punch"; an intermediate stage between the original and the working dies. This latter work was done by Thomas Moss at Somerset House. The working dies bore at the base of the bust the uncoloured letters W. W. (William Wyon) and the die number. Of the 6d. only Die I (1WW) was used for the postage stamps.

Position of the die number

In the 10d. the number and letters on stamps from Die 1 are seldom clear and many specimens are known without any trace of them. Because of this the stamp we previously listed as "No die number" has been deleted. That they are from Die 1 is proved by the existence of blocks showing stamps with and without the die number.

The 10d. Die 5 was confirmed by Wright and Creeke. It is on paper with Dickinson silk threads and the only reported example is without gum. From 1889 Die 5 was used for postal stationery, but without the silk threads.

Other dies of all values have been used, with or without data plugs, on postal stationery, for stamping paper at Somerset House and on telegraph forms. Great care should be taken in identifying any indistinct die numbers as being postal issues. Only the postal issues have silk threads but the 1s. value exists without silk threads from the edge of the sheet.

The Paper. The "Dickinson silk thread" (actually a twisted cotton yarn) paper was used for the 1s. and 10d. values. In this paper threads, blue in colour, were embedded during manufacture. The threads were so placed as to ensure that two threads, approximately 5 mm. apart, would cross each stamp vertically. Examples with misplaced threads 20 mm. apart, one thread at side or omitted due to misplacement are listed. Such varieties should be purchased with a certificate showing that they are genuine. Although the 10d. was not issued until 14 months after the 1s. an interesting case has been made out for the belief that the mill sheets (later cut up into printing sheets) were each intended to provide six printing sheets: four for the 1s. stamp, each to bear 20 impressions, and two for the 10d. stamp, each to bear 24 impressions. It seems likely that the mill sheets were in fact cut up and used in this manner, though it is difficult to understand the gap of 14 months between the dates of issue of the two values.

The paper used for the 6d. was hand made and of stout quality, varying somewhat in thickness. It was watermarked VR (Type **W4**) so arranged that each stamp would have the complete watermark.

Following an incident when some sheets of the 6d. were printed over the (colourless) gum the latter was tinted pale green.

W4

The Printing. The presses available allowed of only one impression at a time being struck. This resulted in poor spacing so that not only were impressions uncomfortably close together, but in many instances they overlapped. This makes it difficult to find stamps with good margins. The stamps were printed (embossed) at Somerset House.

Embossed Proofs and Essays

Essay (no frame)

Essay (no pendant curl)

EP1. **1847.** Proofs of the head taken before the pendant curl was added. No frame or value inscription. Embossed on paper with blue and red horizontal lines to simulate Dickinson paper previously gummed.
(a) In white on pale green. *Price* £15000.
(b) In white on yellow. *Price* £15000.
Nos. EP1a/b can be found with additional inscriptions in manuscript.

EP2. **1847.** Essays of the head without pendant curl but with frames. Embossed on Dickinson paper previously gummed.
(a) One shilling pale green with or without trial cancellation Nos. 14 or 67. *Price* £7000.
(b) One shilling brown with or without trial cancellation Nos. 14 or 67. *Price* £7500.

EP3. **1866.** Proof of one shilling Die 2 (without date plugs) on white, cream, blue, pink, green or lilac paper.

EP4. **1866.** As last on white or cream paper overprinted "Specimen" similar to Type 4.

The above were prepared for the 1867 Paris Exhibition together with a similar range of proofs of the one shilling Die 3 with date plugs "16.3.66" but these have not been seen with "Specimen" overprint. Similar proofs are also known of the Sixpence purple from Die 4 without date plugs. No more than one of each of the above items has so far been reported.

H1

H2

H3

Condition

The prices quoted in the Section are for cut-square examples with average to fine embossing. Stamps with exceptionally clear embossing are worth more.

1s. Green, Type H1

1847 (11 September). On Dickinson "silk" thread paper (two threads 5 mm apart). No wmk. Imperf.

H1 (=S.G.54/56)	(1)		1s. pale green	£8750	£750
	(2)		1s. green	£8750	£800
	(3)		1s. deep green	£9500	£800
			Die W.W.1 (1847)	£8750	£750
			Die W.W.2 (1854)	£9500	£825
			Block of four	£60000	£5000
			Used on cover	†	£1000
		c.	Two threads 20 mm apart	—	£1300
		ca.	One thread		
		cb.	Thread omitted		
		d.	Double impression	—	£10000
		s.	"Specimen", Type 1 in red (Die W.W.1)	£1900	
		t.	"Specimen", Type 1 in black (Die W.W.1)	£1900	
		u.	"Specimen", Type 2 (Die W.W.2)	£4000	

For note on the Frank Ives Scudamore handstamp see below Section CB, Group 1. This is known on examples of No. H1 Die 2 (1854).

10d. Brown, Type H2

1848 (6 November). On Dickinson "silk" thread paper (two threads 5 mm apart). No wmk. Imperf.

H2 (=S.G.57)	(1)		10d. brown	£6000	£1000
	(2)		10d. deep brown	£8000	£1500
			Die W.W.1 (1848)	£6500	£1000
			Die 2.W.W. (1850)	£6000	£1000
			Die 3.W.W. (1853)	£6000	£1000
			Die 4.W.W. (1854)	£6500	£1000
			Die 5.W.W.		
			Block of four	£45000	£6500
			Used on cover	†	£1900
		c.	Two threads 20 mm apart	—	£1800
		ca.	One thread		
		d.	Double impression	—	£10000
		s.	"Specimen", Type 1 (Die W.W.1)	£1900	
		t.	"Specimen", Type 2 (Die 4.W.W.)	£7000	

6d. Violet, Type H3

1854 (1 March). Wmk W4 reversed. Imperf.

H3 (=S.G.58/61)	(1)	6d. mauve	£7500	£800
	(2)	6d. dull lilac	£7500	£800
	(3)	6d. purple	£7500	£800
	(4)	6d. violet	£10000	£2200
		Block of four	£60000	£7500
		Used on cover	†	£1250
	c.	Watermark upright	—	£800
	e.	Watermark inverted	—	£800
	f.	Watermark inverted and reversed	£7500	£800
	g.	Greenish gum	£7500	
	h.	Double impression	—	£7000
	i.	Printed on the gummed side		
	j.	On thick cartridge paper with silk threads	—	£3000
	s.	"Specimen", Type 1	£2200	
	t.	"Specimen", Type 2	£2200	

Only one die was used for the 6d., expressed as 1WW without stops.

The 6d. and 1s. exist with private pin-perf 11–11½ on covers from Taunton dated 1855.

Invalidation. Along with the line-engraved issues these three embossed values were declared invalid from 1 June 1901 by which time they were worth well in excess of their face value to dealers and collectors.

SECTION J

The Surface-Printed Issues

1855–83 Surface-Printed Issues

General Notes

Introduction. The "Embossed" issues were found to be unsatisfactory, being cumbersome to produce and unsuited for perforating. Accordingly it was decided to produce stamps by the surface-printed method. Thomas De La Rue & Co., London, were chosen to print the values over 2d. while Perkins, Bacon & Co. continued to produce the (line-engraved) ½d. to 2d. until 1880.

De La Rue & Co. continued to print all the surface-printed stamps until the latter part of the reign of King Edward VII. Unless otherwise stated all the listed items and illustrations are those of De La Rue & Co.

Arrangement. This section is arranged in order of value, and in chronological order within each value. There is no satisfactory way of producing a solely chronological classification, since at no time were these stamps issued as a "set" in the philatelic meaning of the term.

Plates and Printing. The method adopted was the invention of Anatole Hulot, at that time producing stamps for the French Government. His method was to have the original die cut in reverse on steel. The design was then transferred by pressure to lead blocks the size of the stamp. The required number of these would be locked in a frame and the whole placed in an electro-chemical bath, there to receive a thin coating of copper. This in turn was backed by type metal and used as a printing plate. Later, as demand increased, master plates were made by an intermediate process and from these any number of electrotypes could be made. Two or more of these electrotypes, known as panes, would be used to form a plate. The number of panes to each plate differed between the various values. In 1858 M. Joubert, a Frenchman employed by De La Rue, invented a process for coating the plates with steel, thereby greatly increasing their life and making the surface-printed method more economical.

Dates of Issue. Throughout this section the official date of "putting to press" is given where known. The date of issue or earliest known date of use is given in the headings.

Paper. The papers with Garter or Emblems watermarks were at first hand-made and in consequence vary considerably in thickness, but from December 1864 all the paper was machine-made by Turner & Co., Chafford Mills, Fordcombe. The watermark "bits" were supplied by De La Rue. They were struck from sheet brass and attached with brass wire to the moulds and (later) the dandy rolls.

Perforation. Comb perforation, gauging 14 all round, was the rule throughout these issues (including "Abnormals"), except for the 15½ × 15 gauge used for the 1867–78 High Values (5s., 10s., £1) with the Maltese Cross watermark. All perforating up to 1880 was done at Somerset House, thereafter by the contractors themselves. A single line perforation also gauging 14 was used on occasion at Somerset House for part sheets and for perforating stamps which were not officially issued, such as those mounted in the souvenir album presented to Queen Victoria, members of the Stamp Committee of 1884 and other senior officials. The book contained only three pages and a note describing the contents will be found in Section KD Part III.

Double perforation varieties are listed. These appear to be rouletted at the sides due to two, instead of one, downward strokes of the comb perforator. This perforated the top and two sides of the stamp with the sheet moving forward. If the movement was only half a perforation forward then the sides will show perforations similar to rouletting but the top of the stamp will be normal.

Imperforates. The imperforates that are listed do not come from the imprimatur sheets. They either bear check-letters that are still present in the imprimatur sheets, differ from the imprimaturs in having the watermark inverted or else belong to an issue for which no imprimatur sheet was registered.

Wing margin

Wing Margins. The vertical gutters (spaces) between the panes, into which sheets of stamps of most values were divided until the introduction of the Imperial Crown watermark, were perforated through the centre of the gutter with a single row of holes, instead of each vertical row of stamps on either side of the gutter having its own line of perforation as is now usual; accordingly a proportion of the stamps in each sheet have what is called a "wing margin" about 5 mm. wide on one or other side.

The stamps with "wing margins" are the watermarked Emblems and Spray of Rose series (3d., 6d., 9d., 10d., 1s. and 2s.) with letters D, E, H or I in S.E. corner, and the watermark Garter series (4d. and 8d.) with letters F or G in S.E. corner. Knowledge of this lettering will enable collectors to guard against stamps with wing margin cut down and reperforated. It should be noted, however, that the first 4d., 6d. and 1s. stamps, without letters in the corners, also exist with wing margins. When these have been cut away and reperforated they form dangerous fakes owing to the absence of letters to aid in their detection. See also the note under "Alteration of Plates" on page 248.

Imprimaturs and "Abnormals". It was apparently usual for De La Rue & Co. to submit six imperforate sheets to Somerset House for approval when a new plate was ready for use. In the great majority of cases these sheets were gummed. There seems to be no clear knowledge of what was usually done with the five extra sheets when one had been selected as the imprimatur (officially approved) sheet and placed in the archives. Nor is it certain that in every case there was more than one sheet submitted. Certainly in some cases more than one sheet was submitted, for perforated specimens are known, both unused and used, and these cannot be from the imprimatur sheets, which were always imperforate. Prices for imprimaturs are for normal marginal examples. Stamps with sheet margins showing plate numbers (as illustrated) or current numbers are worth very much more.

Usually the perforating and issuing of the "five extra sheets", when such existed, would have no philatelic consequences since the resultant stamps would not be distinguishable from the general issue. However, in cases where there is some delay between registration and putting to press, instances have come to light where stamps have been found with genuine earlier postmarks than the putting to press dates and which were also very clear impressions showing no signs of plate wear; such items must have been put to stock before the main supply was printed. Moreover, as happened in a number of cases, if after registration no general issue was made from a new plate, or if such general issue was long delayed, the issuing of the stamps of "the extra five sheets" resulted in the existence of "abnormals", different in some major respect from the general issue and always of considerable rarity.

The abnormal stamps of this class listed in the Catalogue and distinguished, where not priced, by a star (*) are:

Spec. No.		
J27	3d.	Plate 3 (with white dots)
J63	4d.	vermilion, Plate 16
J66	4d.	sage-green, Plate 17
J78	6d.	mauve, Plate 10
J80	6d.	pale chestnut and 6d. chestnut, Plate 12
J82	6d.	pale buff, Plate 13
J93	9d.	Plate 3 (hair lines)
J95	9d.	Plate 5 (see footnote to No. J95)
J98	10d.	Plate 2
J102	1s.	Plate 3 (Plate No. "2")
J114	1s.	green, Plate 14
J119	2s.	blue, Plate 3

Those which may have been issued, but of which no specimens are known, are $2\frac{1}{2}$d., wmk Anchor, Plates 4 and 5; 3d., wmk Emblems, Plate 5; 3d., wmk Spray, Plate 21; 6d. grey, wmk Spray, Plate 18; 8d. orange, Plate 2; 1s., wmk Emblems, Plate 5; 5s., wmk Maltese Cross, Plate 4.

No. J99, the 10d., Plate 1, on Emblems paper, is sometimes reckoned among the "abnormals", but was probably an error, due to the use of the wrong paper.

Artists' drawings

Two experimental essays of 1861. Left, by Bradbury, Wilkinson, using a female head. Right, by De La Rue, using the head of the King of Portugal.

Artists' Drawings. No attempt has been made to list artists' drawings, experimental essays and similar pre-die material, except for essays released from the De La Rue archives. Only occasionally has a known pencil marking been noted as such are presumed not to appear on all examples of the same proof.

Corner Letters. With the exception of the 4d., 6d. and 1s. of 1855–57, and the £5 (which had letters in lower corners only, and in reverse order to the normal), all the surface-printed stamps included in this Section had letters in all four corners, as in the later line-engraved stamps. The arrangement is the same, the letters running in sequence right across and down the sheets, whether these were divided into panes or not. The corner letters existing naturally depend on the number of stamps in the sheet and their arrangement.

Throughout this Section, when reference is made to corner letters, those of the lower corners only are quoted since those of the upper corners merely repeat those of the lower, in reverse order.

Imprimaturs from the 1855–83 Surface-Printed issues. From left to right: no corner letters, small uncoloured corner letters, large uncoloured corner letters, large coloured corner letters

The change from uncoloured to coloured corner letters was made to facilitate a quicker method of plate making after a proposal from Messrs. De La Rue in 1872. Interesting evidence of this is to be found in the Die Proofs inscribed "OLD" and those inscribed "NEW", in the text.

Plate Numbers. All stamps in this Section except the first design 4d., 6d. and 1s. issues bear in their designs either the plate number or, in one or two earlier instances, some other indication by which one plate can be distinguished from another. With the aid of these and of the corner letters it is possible to "reconstruct" a sheet of stamps from any plate of any issue or denomination; a task undertaken by many collectors.

Die Proofs. During the various stages of the engraving of a die, it was necessary to take proofs to check the work. These are referred to as progressive die proofs. Upon completion of the die, proofs were taken before it was hardened; these were generally in black on white glazed cards and were usually stamped with the date and inscription "BEFORE HARDENING" or "AFTER HARDENING". Proofs were also taken before and after the die had been used for striking moulds to see if it had become damaged and these were correspondingly inscribed (*see illustrations*). Occasionally proofs from the die have been taken after the insertion of plate numbers and corner letters in the appropriate spaces; the numbers and letters are often arbitrary and are not necessarily the actual plate used for the issued stamps; in most instances the corner letters are of a different size from those of the issued stamps. Proofs were sometimes taken in colour for exhibition and various other purposes. Die proofs are to be found with additional markings often in manuscript; some are initialled by various persons, including Ormond Hill, after the proofs had been approved. Abbreviations used in the listings: "B/H" = BEFORE HARDENING; "A/H" = AFTER HARDENING; B/S" = BEFORE STRIKING; "A/S" = AFTER STRIKING; "M/S" = in manuscript.

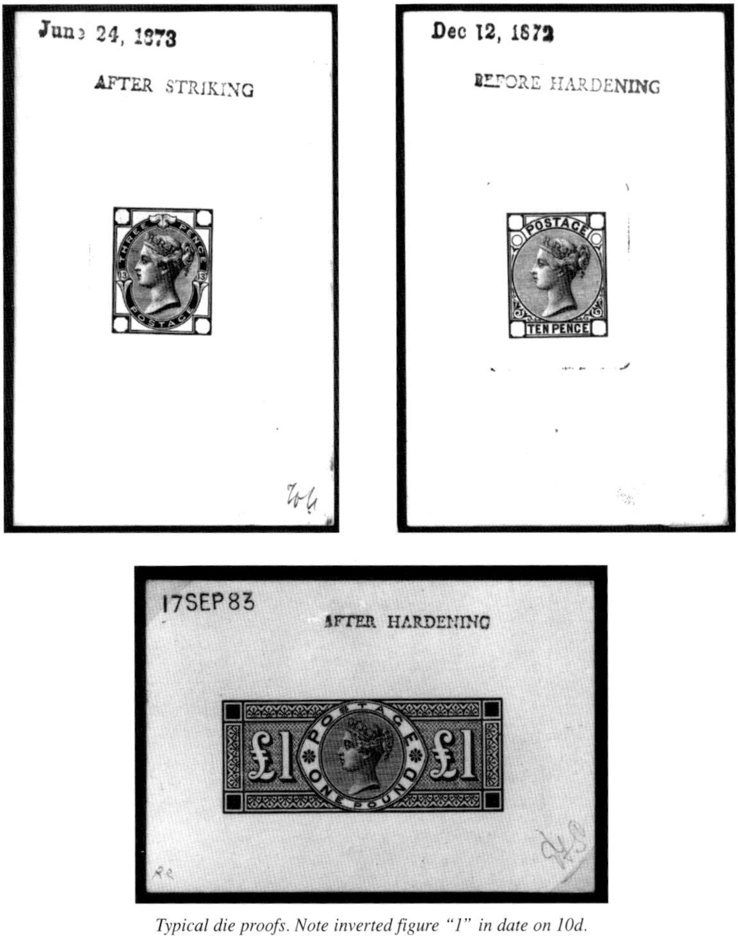

Typical die proofs. Note inverted figure "1" in date on 10d.

Die Proofs for the 1867 Paris and 1871 London Exhibitions. Hitherto it has been believed that the die proofs with uncleared corner letters and plate numbers and without inscription that were printed on the normal glazed card were for the 1867 Paris Exhibition, and that those on matt card (sometimes cut down) were for the 1871 London Exhibition. The existence in a private collection of an original exhibition sheet with headings in French containing cut down die proofs on matt card suggests, however, that this was for the Paris Exhibition. If this is so the listing of these in this volume should be revised to show that the die proofs on glazed card were in fact for the 1871 (London) exhibition and that those on matt card were for the 1867 exhibition. The Editor would be glad to receive any information on the subject, so that the necessary alterations can be made. It is possible that some die proofs in the same colours listed now for both exhibitions may be duplicates, that is, on the same type of card.

The De La Rue Archives. After they lost the printing contract in 1910, De La Rue were allowed to keep their essays, proofs and colour trials which had been prepared over the years, provided that they were defaced with the word "Cancelled" written across the face (although some items escaped and received only an ink cross).

These archives were stored at Bunhill Row in the City and suffered considerable damage during the Second World War, some being destroyed. An archivist was employed to sort through the material and remount it, and he copied some of the original manuscript writing which had become almost illegible.

Mounted die proof

Unmounted die proof

Original extract from Striking Book

Re-backed impression from Striking Book

Amongst this material were the Striking Books containing impressions from the dies with manuscript dates and references to plate numbers and other technical information. Striking Books Nos. 5 and 6, covering the period from about July 1893 until 1910, survived almost intact but there were only fragments of the earlier books. Only a few of the die impressions were defaced by the original compiler and none as a result of losing the contract.

A few essays for the $2\frac{1}{2}$d. and 8d. values were placed on the market by De La Rue in 1976 and are listed under those values in this section. Others related to the 1879 and 1880 tenders are recorded in Section K.

During 1975 and 1976 De La Rue placed on the market a quantity of spare die proofs, which are listed in this catalogue. These are of two forms; (a) cut down die proofs in black, either mounted in small sunken frames or unmounted with traces of gum or paper (or both) on the reverse; (b) die proofs from the Striking

Books, listed in abbreviated form, no distinction being made between items cut from the original Striking Books and those that have been re-backed with details written on the mount.

Alteration of Plates. When the Crown watermarked paper, on which the watermarks were arranged in two panes of 120 stamps, superseded the Orb, Spray and Garter papers in 1880–81 it became necessary to alter to this form all the existing plates which had been laid down for use with the 2-pane Orb paper, the 12-pane Spray paper or the 4-pane Garter paper. The alternative would have been to discard them. The exact method used to make the alteration is not clear.

The plates so rearranged that each now consisted of two panes of 120 impressions were the 3d., Plates 20 and 21; the 4d., Plate 17; the 6d., Plates 17 and 18; the 1s., Plates 13 and 14. All these plates had been used or had been registered on paper with the earlier watermarks and all were subsequently used with the Crown paper. It has been suggested elsewhere that Plate 21 of the 2½d. was likewise modified, but since it was neither used nor registered on anything but Crown paper this would be necessary only if the plate had been just (or nearly) finished in "2 panes of 96" form yet still unregistered at the moment when the decision to change to Crown paper was taken.

Wing margin examples from the first state of any of these modified plates are of considerable interest when matched with similarly lettered stamps of the second state on Crown paper, without wing margins.

"Specimen" and "Cancelled" Stamps. From time to time for various reasons such as circularization of information to postmasters or the presentation of sets to foreign governments, certain stamps were overprinted "Specimen". In 1879 supplies of current stamps, and thereafter of all new stamps, were sent to the U.P.U. for distribution to member countries. Stamps overprinted "Cancelled" are very much scarcer and come from official records. We have not listed varieties which have only been seen in official archives. For further information and illustrations of the numerous types see Appendix 3.

Protective Underprints. With or without official co-operation some firms adopted the practice of printing their names on the backs of their stocks of certain values. Stamps so treated are dealt with in Appendix 2.

Presentation Album. In recognition of the work of the 1884 Stamp Committee De La Rue issued a special album is described in Section KD.

Invalidation. The early surface-printed stamps issued before 1 January 1887 were invalidated on 1 June 1901, with the exception of the 1d. lilac (1881) and £5 orange (1882). This was followed by the ½d., 1d. (lilac), 2½d. and 6d. "Jubilee" values on 1 January 1902 when stamps with the head of the new King appeared on these four values.

Watermarks of the Surface-Printed issues. The illustrations show the watermarks in the upright position unless otherwise stated.

ALL AS SEEN FROM THE PRINTED SIDE OF THE STAMP

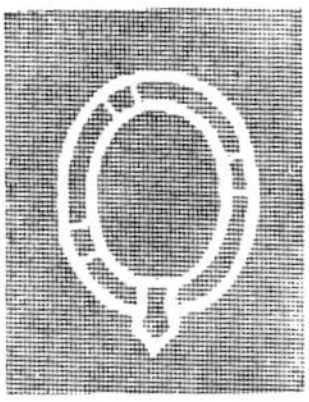

W5a *Small Garter*

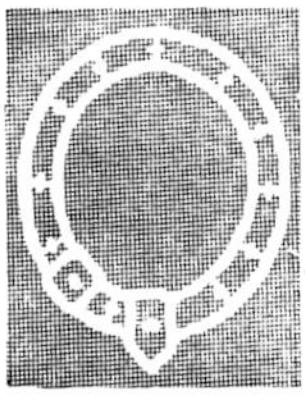

W5b *Medium Garter*

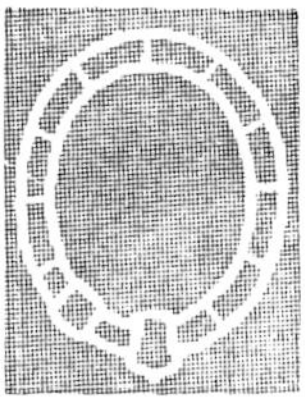

W5c *Large Garter*

W6 *Emblems*

W6a *Emblems error (three roses and a shamrock)*

W6b *Emblems error (three roses and a thistle)*

W7 *Spray (of Rose)*

W8 *Maltese Cross*

W9 *Large Anchor*

W10 *Small Anchor*

W11 *Orb*

W12 *(Imperial) Crown*

The watermark errors. It is not known exactly when the above errors occurred. They are due to "bits" having become detached from the dandy roll and being incorrectly replaced. Type **W6a** resulted from the thistle being replaced by a rose and is known on stamp TA of the 3d. Plate 4; 6d. Plates 1, 5 and 6; 9d. Plate 4 and 1s. Plate 4. Type **W6b** resulted from the shamrock being replaced by a rose and is known on stamp TF of the 6d. Plate 3 and the 9d. Plate 4.

Key to the 1855–83 Surface-Printed Issues. The table below is intended to give the reader a condensed view of these issues, including the frequent changes of type, watermark and colour. The asterisks in the column headed *Plates* indicate "abnormals". The page numbers in the extreme right-hand column indicate the relevant part of the catalogue listing.

Spec. Nos.	*SG Nos.*	*Description*	*Watermark*	*Date of Issue*	*Plates*	*Page No.*
		No Corner Letters				
J47	62	4d. carmine	Small Garter	31.7.55	1, 2	263
J48/50	63/5	4d. carmine	Medium Garter	25.2.56	1	263
J51	66/a	4d. carmine	Large Garter	Jan. '57	1, 2	264
J70	69/70	6d. lilac	Emblems	21.10.56	1	270
J100	71/3	1s. green	Emblems	1.11.56	1	284
		Small White Corner Letters				
J25A/26	75/7	3d. carmine	Emblems	1.5.62	2	257
J27	78	3d. carmine (dots)	Emblems	Aug. '62	3*	258
J52/53	79/82	4d. red	Large Garter	15.1.62	3, 4	265
J71/72	83/85	6d. lilac	Emblems	1.12.62	3, 4	271
J92/93	86/88	9d. bistre	Emblems	15.1.62	2, 3*	279
J101/2	89/91	1s. green	Emblems	1.12.62	2 = (1), 3 = (2)*	285
		Large White Corner Letters				
J28	92	3d. rose	Emblems	1.3.65	4	258
J29/35	102/3	3d. rose	Spray	July '67	4–10	258
J54/61	93/4	4d. vermilion	Large Garter	4.7.65	7–14	266
J73/4	96/7	6d. lilac	Emblems	7.3.65	(Hyphen) 5, 6	272
J75	104/7	6d. lilac	Spray	21.6.67	(Hyphen) 6	272
J76/8	108/9	6d. lilac	Spray	8.3.69	(No Hyphen) 8, 9, 10*	273
J79/80	122/4	6d. chestnut	Spray	12.4.72	11, 12, 12*	274
J81	125	6d. grey	Spray	24.4.73	12	275
J94/5	98	9d. straw	Emblems	30.10.65	4, 5*	280
J96	110/11	9d. straw	Spray	3.10.67	4	280
J97/98	112/4	10d. brown	Spray	1.7.67	1, 2*	282
J99	99	10d. brown	Emblems	11.11.67	(Error) 1	283
J103	101	1s. green	Emblems	26.1.65	4	286
J104/7	115/7	1s. green	Spray	13.7.67	4–7	286
J118/9	118/20b	2s. blue	Spray	1.7.67	1, 3*	291
J120	121	2s. brown	Spray	27.2.80	1	291
J121/2	126/7	5s. rose	Cross	1.7.67	1, 2	293
J123	130, 134	5s. rose	Anchor	25.11.82	4	293
J124	128	10s. grey	Cross	26.9.78	1	294
J125	131, 135	10s. grey-green	Anchor	Feb. '83	1	294
J126	129	£1 brown-lilac	Cross	26.9.78	1	296
J127	132, 136	£1 brown-lilac	Anchor	Dec. '82	1	296
J128	133, 137	£5 orange	Anchor	21.3.82	1	297
		Large Coloured Corner Letters				
J1/3	138/9	$2\frac{1}{2}$d. rosy mauve	Anchor	1.7.75	1–3	252
J4/18	141	$2\frac{1}{2}$d. rosy mauve	Orb	1.5.76	3–17	253
J19/22	142	$2\frac{1}{2}$d. blue	Orb	5.2.80	17–20	254
J23/5	157	$2\frac{1}{2}$d. blue	Crown	23.3.81	21–23	254
J36/44	143/4	3d. rose	Spray	5.7.73	11, 12, 14–20	260
J45/A	158	3d. rose	Crown	Mar. '81	20, 21	261
J62/3	152	4d. vermilion	Large Garter	1.3.76	15, 16*	267
J64/6	153	4d. sage-green	Large Garter	12.3.77	15, 16, 17*	268
J67	154	4d. brown	Large Garter	15.8.80	17	268
J68/9	160	4d. brown	Crown	8.12.80	17, 18	268
J82	145	6d. buff	Spray	15.3.73	13*	275
J83/7	146/7	6d. grey	Spray	20.3.74	13–17	275
J88/9	161	6d. grey	Crown	1.1.81	17, 18	276
J91	156a	8d. purple brown	Large Garter	July '76	1	278

Spec. Nos.	*SG Nos.*	*Description*	*Watermark*	*Date of Issue*	*Plates*	*Page No.*
J91A	156	8d. orange	Large Garter	11.9.76	1	278
J108/14	148/50	1s. green	Spray	1.9.73	8–13, 14*	288
J115	151	1s. brown	Spray	14.10.80	13	289
J116/7	163	1s. brown	Crown	29.5.81	13, 14	289

Former Nos. J46 (3d. on 3d.) and J90 (6d. on 6d.) are relisted as Nos. K8A, K8B.

Prices for Stamps in Used Condition

Most British issues of the nineteenth century were subjected to heavy cancelling with "killer" postmarks. In no group more than the Surface-Printed are the results more destructive of value. The "used" prices in this catalogue are for fine used; inferior examples with very heavy or smudged postmarks are of reduced value. On the other hand there is a premium for well centred lightly used stamps. Prices can be calculated by adding the following percentages to the prices quoted:

50%	75%	100%	125%
J79/81	J23/25, J29/35, J45/45A, J68/69, J75/78, J88/89 J96/J98, J104/107, J116/128	J1/22, J28, J36/44, J54/67, J73/74, J82/87, J91A, J94/95, J99, J103, J108/115	J25A/27, J47/53, J70/72, J92/93, J100/102

2½d, Type J1 (1875–81)

The 2½d. plates (Nos. 1 to 20) used with Anchor or Orb watermark papers had 192 impressions arranged in two panes (one above the other) of 96 stamps each in 8 horizontal rows of 12. The corner letters (quoting lower corners only) ran from AA–AL, BA–BL and so on down the plate to PA–PL. Plates 21 to 23, used only with the Crown watermark paper, comprised two panes (one above the other) each of 120 impressions in 10 horizontal rows of 12. The lettering ran from AA–AL down to TA–TL (quoting lower corner lettters only). Plate numbers appeared on both top and bottom selvede, as did "Current Numbers", in both the Anchor and Orb watermarked issues. There were no selvedge numbers in the Crown watermarked issue. The perforation 14 remained unchanged throughout.

Chemical blueing in greater or lesser degree occurred with the Anchor watermark paper. In many cases this blueing is so slight as to be negligible; on the other hand Plate 1 stamps quite deeply blued are not uncommon. Prices for blued stamps are for those with unmistakable blue coloration. Collectors are warned to be on their guard against stamps fraudulently blued. Printings began in the same ink as used on the Orb paper. As this proved unsuitable a new ink was formulated for use with plates 22 and 23, which were put to press as a pair, printing onto the 480 set mill sheet with plate 22 printing right sheets and 23 printing left.

J1

1875 (1 July). 2½d. Rosy Mauve, Type J1. Wmk Anchor (W10). Perf 14.

J1 (=S.G.138/139)	2½d. rosy mauve, Plate 1	£500	80·00
	Block of four	£3250	£675
	Used on cover	†	£140
	a. Blued paper	£700	£120
	b. Watermark inverted (blued)	£1250	£250
	c. Watermark inverted (white)	£850	£180
	d. Imperforate (blued)		
	s. "Specimen", Type 8 (blued)	£200	
J2 (=S.G.138/140)	2½d. rosy mauve, Plate 2	£500	80·00
	Block of four	£2750	£675
	Used on cover	†	£140
	a. Blued paper	£6000	£1350
	b. Error of lettering: LH–FL (for LH–HL)	£15000	£2000
	c. Ditto on blued paper		

	d. Watermark inverted (white)	£850	£180
	e. Watermark inverted (blued)	†	—
J3 (=S.G.138/139)	2½d. rosy mauve, Plate 3	£775	£120
	Block of four	£4500	£800
	Used on cover	†	£200
	a. Blued paper	—	£4250
	b. Watermark inverted (white)	£1500	£250

Imprimaturs: Plates 1, 2, 3, *each* £1500; *Plates* 4, 5, *each* £1800. Stamps removed from the Plate 1 imprimatur sheet: AA–AL, BB–BL, PA–PB.

Put to press date: Plate 1, 30.3.75; Plate 2, 18.6.75; Plate 3, 12.6.75.

1876 (1 May). 2½d. Rosy Mauve, Type J1. Wmk Orb (W11). Perf 14.

J4 (S.G.141)	2½d. rosy mauve, Plate 3	£925	£100
	Block of four	£5500	£950
	Used on cover	†	£200
	a. Watermark inverted	£1800	£225
	s. "Specimen", Type 10		
J5 (=S.G.141)	2½d. rosy mauve, Plate 4	£425	50·00
	Block of four	£2750	£425
	Used on cover	†	90·00
	a. Watermark inverted	£650	£100
J6 (=S.G.141)	2½d. rosy mauve, Plate 5	£425	50·00
	Block of four	£2750	£425
	Used on cover	†	90·00
	a. Watermark inverted	£650	£100
	s. "Specimen", Type 9	£180	
J7 (=S.G.141)	2½d. rosy mauve, Plate 6	£425	50·00
	Block of four	£2750	£425
	Used on cover	†	90·00
	a. Watermark inverted	£650	£100
	s. "Specimen", Types 8, 9	£180	
J8 (=S.G.141)	2½d. rosy mauve, Plate 7	£425	50·00
	Block of four	£2750	£425
	Used on cover	†	90·00
	a. Watermark inverted	£650	£100
	s. "Specimen", Type 9	£180	
J9 (=S.G.141)	2½d. rosy mauve, Plate 8	£425	50·00
	Block of four	£2750	£425
	Used on cover	†	95·00
	a. Watermark inverted	£650	£100
	s. Imperforate "Specimen", Type 9	£250	
J10 (=S.G.141)	2½d. rosy mauve, Plate 9	£425	50·00
	Block of four	£2750	£425
	Used on cover	†	90·00
	a. Watermark inverted	£650	£100
J11 (=S.G.141)	2½d. rosy mauve, Plate 10	£475	65·00
	Block of four	£3000	£525
	Used on cover	†	£120
	a. Watermark inverted	£650	£125
	s. "Specimen", Type 9	£180	
J12 (=S.G.141)	2½d. rosy mauve, Plate 11	£425	50·00
	Block of four	£2750	£425
	Used on cover	†	90·00
	a. Watermark inverted	£650	£100
J13 (=S.G.141)	2½d. rosy mauve, Plate 12	£425	50·00
	Block of four	£2750	£425
	Used on cover	†	95·00
	a. Watermark inverted	£650	£100

J14 (=S.G.141)	2½d. rosy mauve, Plate 13	£425	50·00
	Block of four	£2750	£425
	Used on cover	†	95·00
	a. Watermark inverted	£650	£100
J15 (=S.G.141)	2½d. rosy mauve, Plate 14	£425	50·00
	Block of four	£2750	£425
	Used on cover	†	90·00
	a. Watermark inverted	£650	£100
J16 (=S.G.141)	2½d. rosy mauve, Plate 15	£425	50·00
	Block of four	£2750	£425
	Used on cover	†	90·00
	a. Watermark inverted	£650	£100
J17 (=S.G.141)	2½d. rosy mauve, Plate 16	£425	50·00
	Block of four	£2750	£425
	Used on cover	†	90·00
	a. Watermark inverted	£650	£100
	s. "Specimen", Type 9	£180	
J18 (=S.G.141)	2½d. rosy mauve, Plate 17	£1250	£240
	Block of four	£6800	£1750
	Used on cover	†	£425
	a. Watermark inverted	£3000	£500

Imprimaturs: Plates 6 to 17, *each* £1500.

Of the above plates, Nos. 4 and 5 were registered on the Anchor watermark paper though put to press only on the Orb paper. No perforated examples, either unused or used, have ever been found on the Anchor paper.

Put to press dates: Plate 4, 21.4.76; Plate 5, 3.7.76; Plate 6, 7.9.76; Plate 7, 16.2.77; Plate 8, 4.6.77; Plate 9, 14.9.77; Plate 10, 7.12.77; Plate 11, 19.3.78; Plate 12, 25.7.78; Plate 13, 30.9.78; Plate 14, 11.2.79; Plate 15, 8.5.79; Plate 16, 15.8.79; Plate 17, 23.12.79.

1880 (5 February). 2½d. Blue, Type J1. Wmk Orb (W11). Perf 14.

J19 (=S.G.142)	2½d. blue, Plate 17	£375	55·00
	Block of four	£2200	£375
	Used on cover	†	75·00
	a. Watermark inverted	£850	£175
	s. "Specimen", Type 9	£140	
J20 (=S.G.142)	2½d. blue, Plate 18	£400	40·00
	Block of four	£2200	£375
	Used on cover	†	75·00
	a. Watermark inverted	£850	£175
J21 (=S.G.142)	2½d. blue, Plate 19	£375	40·00
	Block of four	£2200	£375
	Used on cover	†	75·00
	a. Watermark inverted	£850	£175
J22 (=S.G.142)	2½d. blue, Plate 20	£375	40·00
	Block of four	£2200	£375
	Used on cover	†	75·00
	a. Watermark inverted	£850	£175

Imprimaturs: Plates 18 *to* 20, *each* £1400.

Put to press dates: Plate 17 (in blue), 1880; Plate 18, 11.2.80; Plate 19, 6.4.80; Plate 22, 11.10.80.

1881 (23 March). 2½d. Blue, Type J1. Wmk Crown (W12). Perf 14.

J23 (=S.G.157)	2½d. blue, Plate 21	£375	35·00
	Block of four	£2200	£250
	Used on cover	†	60·00
	a. Watermark inverted		

J24 (=S.G.157)		2½d. blue, Plate 22	£350	35·00
		Block of four	£2200	£250
		Used on cover	†	60·00
	a.	Watermark inverted		
J25 (=S.G.157)		2½d. blue, Plate 23	£350	28·00
		Block of four	£2200	£250
		Used on cover	†	45·00
	a.	Watermark inverted	—	£325
	s.	"Specimen", Type 9	£160	

Imprimaturs: Plates 21 to 23, *each* £1500.
Put to press dates: Plate 21 3.2.81; Plates 22, 23, 9.6.81.

Essays from the De La Rue Archives. Submitted in October 1874 in various designs with head printed and frame hand painted with lettering of "POSTAGE" and value in white. Lettered JI. Plate 5. These exist with date in m/s "27 Oct 74", "9 Nov 74" and undated.

On thick card in various colours . . . . . *from* £6000

Die Proofs of 2½d. Type J1. In black on white glazed card (unless otherwise stated):

Date	*Plate No.*	*Corner Letters*	*Inscr.*	*Additional Inscriptions or Notes*	
26 Jan 75	—	—	—	Solid black in place of ornaments . . . *from*	£1400
29 Jan 75	6	—	—	In Venetian red	£4500
9 Feb 75	—	—	—		
10 Feb 75	—	—	B/H		£1100
10 Feb 75	—	—	B/H	Endorsed "Duplicate Proof" (M/S)	£1100
11 Feb 75	"16"	—	—	"proof with plugs" (M/S)	£1100
11 Feb 75	"16"	AD–MN	—	The plate number figures are larger than normal	£1100
—	—	—	A/S		£1100
2 Mar 75	2	—	A/S		£1100
—	3	—	—	Plate number at right only. Initialled "G.E.I." (M/S)	£1100
—	3	—	—	Plate number at both sides	£1100
26 Apr 75	3	—	B/S	Initialled "S.E.J. 26.4.75" (M/S)	£1100
18 June 75	5	—	A/S		£1100
5 Apr 76	6	—	A/S		£1100
—	7	—	—	Plate number figures heavy, initialled "F.I." (M/S)	£1100
—	7	—	—	Plate number figures thinner	£1100
18 Aug. 76	7	—	A/S		£1100
—	7	CG–GC	—	Endorsed "Figures after striking 48–F.I." (M/S)	£1100
(M/S)	8	—	(M/S)	Endorsed "12 Mar 77 After striking" (M/S)	£1100
(M/S)	9	—	(M/S)	Endorsed "31 Mar 77 After striking" (M/S)	£1100
31 May 77	9	KB–BK	A/S	Initialled "F.I."	£1100
(M/S)	10	—	(M/S)	Endorsed "25 Aug 77 after striking" (M/S)	£1100
29 Aug 77	10	—	A/S		£1100
—	11	—	B/S		£1100
10 Nov 77	11	—	B/S		£1100
19 Nov 77	11	—	A/S		£1100
(M/S)	11	—	(M/S)	Endorsed "19 Nov 77 After striking" (M/S)	£1100
22 Mar 78	12	—	B/S		£1100
(M/S)	12	CB–BC	(M/S)	Endorsed "22 Mar 78 After striking 30 Leads" (M/S)	£1100
10 July 78	13	—	—		£1100
(M/S)	13	—	(M/S)	Endorsed "10 July 78 After striking" (M/S)	£1100
(M/S)	13	AH–HA	(M/S)	Endorsed "10 July 78 After striking 12 Leads" (M/S)	£1100
—	14	—	—		£1100
—	14	—	(M/S)	Endorsed "After striking 9 Leads C.P.K." (M/S)	£1100
24 Oct 78	14	—	A/S		£1100
(M/S)	14	—	(M/S)	Endorsed "24 Oct 78 After striking" (M/S)	£1100
19 Feb 79	15	AN–NA	—	Endorsed "After striking 12 Leads W.G." (M/S)	£1100
21 Feb 79	15	—	A/S		£1100
(M/S)	16	BH–HB	(M/S)	Endorsed "29 May 79 After striking 15 Leads" (M/S)	£1100

Date	Plate No.	Corner Letters	Inscr.	Additional Inscriptions or Notes	
(M/S)	17	BH–HB	(M/S)	Endorsed "8 Aug 79 After striking 24 Leads G.H.E." (M/S)	£1100
20 Nov 79	18	BC–CB	—	Endorsed "15 Leads" (M/S)	£1100
(M/S)	19	—	(M/S)	Endorsed "3 Mar 80 Before striking W.G." (M/S)	£1100
3 Mar 80	19	—	(M/S)	Endorsed "before Striking W.G." (M/S)	£1100
6 Mar 80	19	EC–CE	—	Date-stamped twice both inverted and 7 April 80 right way up	£1100
28 Apr 80	20	—	A/S	Stamped twice A/S, and once B/S, initialled "W.G." (M/S)	£1100
28 Apr 80	20	—	A/S		£1100
15 Nov 80	21	CS–SC	(M/S)	Endorsed "After striking 60" (M/S)	£1100
(M/S)	21	—	(M/S)	Endorsed "12 Nov 82 Before striking" (M/S)	£1100
Mar 80	22	—	—		£1100
7 Mar 80	22	—	—	Date is probably an error	£1100
10 Mar 81	22	EG–GE	(M/S)	Endorsed "After striking 90 Leads W.G." (M/S)	£1100
18 Mar 81	22	—	—	Initialled "W.P." (M/S)	£1100
28 Jan 81	23	AT–TA	(M/S)	Endorsed "After striking 10" (M/S)	£1100

Die proofs from the De La Rue Archives. Cut down die proofs mounted or unmounted:

With corner squares and plate numbers void . . . . . *from* £950

Die Proofs from the Striking Books:

Plate 1 (corner letters BB), Plate 3 (corner letters BP–PB), Plate 10 (corner letters BA–AB) . . . . . *from* £950

Plates 2 to 7, 9 to 18, 20, 21 and 23 with letter tablets void . . . . . *from* £950

Plate Proofs. In black on white wove paper:

Plates 7, 9, 16, 17 . . . . . *each* £1000

Colour Trials. Watermark Orbs. Imperforate:

Plates 15, 16 in various blues . . . . . *each* £2500

Watermark Orb (inverted) Imperforate:

Plates 15 . . . . . £2500

3d., Types J2 to J5 (1862–83)

Plate 1 of the 3d. was defective and was never registered.

Plate 2 (Type **J2**) originally had reticulated shading in the spandrels and examples exist in this form from the imprimatur sheet and from other sheets; these are nearly always oveprinted "Specimen". In the Second State of Plate 2 (Type **J3**) the shading was removed and the plate re-registered. The re-registered Plate 2 imprimatur is one of the few De La Rue imprimatur sheets to be registered in ungummed condition.

Plate 3 is distinguishable from Plate 2 by a small white dot at either end of the word "Postage" just below the foliate ornament (Type **J3a**). This plate was registered but was never put to press. Extra sheets must have been printed at the time of registration as a few officially perforated stamps, both unused and used, are known. Also known are unused stamps with the unofficial line perf 14 of Somerset House. The usual imprimatur examples exist of Plate 3. They are gummed as was usual, with De La Rue imprimaturs.

The above plates were composed of 240 impressions in 12 panes of 20 stamps, the panes arranged in four horizontal rows of three panes each. Each pane of 20 comprised five horizontal rows of four. Two adjoining vertical panes consitituted a "Post Office sheet". The plate number appeared only twice on the full sheet of 240; on left top and left bottom selvedges. The corner letters ran from AA–AL down to TA–TL (quoting bottom corners only) as if the sheet consisted of a single pane of 240.

J2 *Small white corner letters; with shaded spandrels*

J3 *Small white corner letters; without dots*

J3A *With dots (illustration enlarged)*

1861 (October). 3d. Rose, Type J2. Without dots, Plate 2, State 1, with shaded spandrels. Wmk Emblems (W6). Perf 14. Not issued.

J25A		3d. rose	£10000	£12000
	s.	"Specimen", Types 2, 6 . . . *each*	£700	

Imprimatur: Plate 2 (*State* 1), £4500.
Put to press: 17.10.61.

Die Proof. In black on white glazed card:

Unfinished, with shaded spandrels endorsed "6 JUN 61" . . . £3500

This was considered to resemble too closely the 4d. value and so the stamp was not officially issued.

1862 (1 May). 3d. Rose, Type J3. Without dots, Plate 2, State 2, with clear spandrels. Wmk Emblems (W6). Perf 14.

J26 (=S.G.75/77)	(1)	3d. deep carmine-rose	£3250	£425
	(2)	3d. bright carmine-rose	£1500	£250
	(3)	3d. pale carmine-rose	£1500	£250
		Block of four	£7500	£2500
		Used on cover	†	£450
	c.	Thick paper	—	£350
	d.	Watermark inverted	—	£700
	e.	Watermark reversed		
	s.	"Specimen", Types 2, 5, 6, 8 . . . *from*	£300	
	t.	"Specimen", Types 2, 6 (reading up) . . . *from*	£300	
	u.	"Specimen", Types 2, 6 (reading down) . *from*	£300	

Imprimatur: Plate 2 (*State* 2), £3000.
Put to press: 19.3.62.

1862 (August). 3d. Rose, Type J3A. With dots, Plate 3. Wmk Emblems (W6). Perf 14.

J27 (=S.G.78)	3d. rose	£20000	£8000
	a. With unofficial line perf 14	£9000	
	b. Imperforate	£4000	
	c. Imperforate "Specimen", Type 2	£1000	

Imprimatur: Plate 3, £3500. Stamps removed from the imprimatur sheet, AA–AL, BC–BL, TA, TB.

J27 is an "abnormal". Plate 3 was registered on 25 August 1862, but never put to press. The usual "five extra sheets" were printed and at least eighteen perforated used stamps and several unused are known.

Die Proof. In black on white glazed card:

Dated "8 Jul 62" with number "3" in oval and number "218" in frame, marked "After Striking" £2500

Die Proof from the De La Rue Archives. Cut down and mounted:

With white dots and uncleared corner letter circles £2200

Plate Proof. In black on white wove paper:

Plate 3 . . . . £2200

J4 *Large white corner letters*

1865 (1 March). 3d. Rose, Type J4. Wmk Emblems (W6). Perf 14.

J28 (=S.G.92)	3d. rose, Plate 4	£1350	£180
	Block of four	£7500	£1200
	Used on cover	†	£350
	c. Watermark error **W6a:** three roses and shamrock (stamp TA)	£3500	£900
	d. Thick paper	£1350	£200
	e. Watermark inverted	—	£350
	f. Watermark reversed		
	g. Watermark inverted and reversed		
	s. "Specimen" Type 2, in blue	£3500	

Imprimatur: Plate 4, £1500, *Plate* 5, £1800.

Put to press: Plate 4, 19.12.64.

The layout of the sheets was as with J2. Plate 5 was registered on Emblems paper but put to press only on Spray paper.

1867 (12 July). 3d. Rose, Type J4. Wmk Spray (W7). Perf 14.

J29 (=S.G.102/103)	3d. rose, Plate 4	£825	£190
	Block of four	£4500	£950
	Used on cover	†	£300
	a. Watermark inverted	£2000	£400
J30 (=S.G.102/103)	3d. rose, Plate 5	£450	55·00
	Block of four	£2750	£375
	Used on cover	†	90·00
	a. Imperforate	£3000	
	b. Imperforate, on Dr. Perkins paper (blued)	£3000	
	c. Double perforation		

	c. Watermark inverted	£950	£180
	s. Imperforate "Specimen", Types 2, 6 . . . . *from*	£400	
	t. "Specimen", Type 8	£200	
	u. Dr. Perkins paper, perf 14, "Specimen"	£1200	
J31 (=S.G.102/103)	3d. rose, Plate 6	£475	55·00
	Block of four	£3000	£350
	Used on cover	†	90·00
	a. Imperforate	£3000	
	b. Watermark inverted	£950	£180
	s. "Specimen", Types 2, 8 . . . . *from*	£220	
J32 (=S.G.102/103)	3d. rose, Plate 7	£550	60·00
	Block of four	£3250	£400
	Used on cover	†	90·00
	a. Watermark inverted	£950	£180
	s. "Specimen", Types 2, 6 . . . . *from*	£220	
J33 (=S.G.102/103)	3d. rose, Plate 8	£525	55·00
	Block of four	£3000	£350
	Used on cover	†	90·00
	a. Imperforate	£3000	
	b. Watermark inverted	£950	£180
	s. "Specimen", Type 8	£220	
J34 (=S.G.102/103)	3d. rose, Plate 9	£525	60·00
	Block of four	£3000	£400
	Used on cover	†	90·00
	a. Watermark inverted	£950	£180
J35 (=S.G.102/103)	3d. rose, Plate 10	£650	£110
	Block of four	£4000	£650
	Used on cover	†	£175
	a. Watermark inverted	£1500	£275
	b. Double perforation		
	s. "Specimen", Types 2, 8, 9 . . . . *from*	£220	
	t. "Cancelled", Type 14A		

Imprimaturs: Plates 6 *to* 10, *each* £1500. Stamps removed from the imprimatur sheets are: Plate 6: AA–AL, BE–BL, TA, TB; Plate 8: AK, AL, SE–SL, TA–TL.

Put to press dates: Plate 5, 18.12.67; Plate 6, 22.6.69; Plate 7, 19.10.71; Plate 8, 29.2.72; Plate 9, 31.7.72; Plate 10, 1.1.73.

The layout of the plates was as before. Imperforates of Plate 10 have been reported but these would be indistinguishable from imprimatur examples unless they duplicated the letterings of known imprimaturs, or are of the same letters as those still intact on the imprimatur sheet.

The colour name "rose" covers a range of shades from rose to deep rose. There is little difference in scarcity.

Die Proofs of 3d. Type J4. In black on white glazed card (unless otherwise stated):

Date	*Plate No.*	*Corner Letters*	*Inscr.*	*Additional Inscriptions or Notes*	
—	—	—	—	There are three progressive proofs (The Post Office)	
	—	—		Basic Die Proof	£1100
—	—	—	—	On thick glazed card for 1867 Paris Exhibition	£1100
—	—	—	—	Ditto, in pale carmine	£4500
—	—	—	—	Ditto, in pale yellow	£4500
—	—	—	—	Circa 1870 on matt card, in rose (cut close)	£3000
—	—	—	—	Ditto in brown, yellow or mauve (cut close) . *each*	£3000
—	—	—	—	On matt card 1871 London Exhibition (cut close)	£1000
—	5	BC–CB	"OLD"	In rose	£4500
26 Oct 71	—	—	—		
31 Oct 71	—	—	"B/H"	Endorsed with a figure "2" on right	£1100
1 Nov 71	—	—	"A/H"	Initialled	£1100
16 Nov 71	—	—	B/S	Initialled "W.G." (M/S)	
20 Nov 71	—	—	"A/S"	Probably made for Plate 8	£1100
1 Oct 72	—	—	"B/S"	Initialled	£1100
3 Oct 72	—	—	"A/S"	Initialled	£1100
3 Nov 72	—	—	"A/S"	Initialled in pencil	£1100

Die Proofs from the De La Rue Archives. Cut down and mounted:

Plate 4 with uncleared corner squares and plate number circles, endorsed "No. 2" . . . £950

Die Proofs from the Striking Books:
With uncleared corner squares and plate number circles . . . . *from* £900

Plate proof

In rose on white unwatermarked paper (Plate 4) £1250

Colour Trials. Watermark Spray. Plate 8. Imperforate:

In deep rose, bright orange, green, olive-brown, red-brown . . . . *each* £1250

J5 *Large coloured corner letters*

1873 (5 July). 3d. Rose, Type J5. Wmk Spray (W7). Perf 14.

J36 (=S.G.143/144)		3d. rose, Plate 11	£350	45·00
		Block of four	£2250	£350
		Used on cover	†	60·00
	a.	Watermark inverted	£850	£225
	b.	Double perforation		
J37 (=S.G.143/144)		3d. rose, Plate 12	£400	45·00
		Block of four	£2500	£350
		Used on cover	†	60·00
	a.	Watermark inverted	£850	£225
J38 (=S.G.143/144)		3d. rose, Plate 14	£425	45·00
		Block of four	£2750	£350
		Used on cover	†	60·00
	a.	Watermark inverted	£850	£225
	s.	"Specimen", Type 2	£250	
J39 (=S.G.143/144)		3d. rose, Plate 15	£350	45·00
		Block of four	£2250	£350
		Used on cover	†	60·00
	a.	Watermark inverted	£850	£225
J40 (=S.G.143/144)		3d. rose, Plate 16	£350	45·00
		Block of four	£2250	£350
		Used on cover	†	60·00
	a.	Watermark inverted	£850	£225
J41 (=S.G.143/144)		3d. rose, Plate 17	£400	45·00
		Block of four	£2500	£350
		Used on cover	†	60·00
	s.	"Specimen", Types 8, 9 . . . *from*	£220	
J42 (=S.G.143/144)		3d. rose, Plate 18	£400	45·00
		Block of four	£2500	£350
		Used on cover	†	60·00
	a.	Watermark inverted	£850	£225
	s.	"Specimen", Types 8, 9, 10 . . . *from*	£220	

J43 (=S.G.143/144)	3d. rose, Plate 19	£350	45·00
	Block of four	£2250	£350
	Used on cover	†	60·00
	a. Watermark inverted	£850	£225
	s. "Specimen", Types 9, 10 *from*	£220	
J44 (=S.G.143/144)	3d. rose, Plate 20	£480	85·00
	Block of four	£3000	£550
	Used on cover	†	£140
	a. Watermark inverted	£850	£225
	b. With wing margin (see footnote)	£480	85·00

Imprimaturs: Plates 11 *to* 20, *each* £1500. *Plate* 21, £1800.

Put to press dates: Plate 11, 17.4.73; Plate 12, 4.9.73; Plate 14, 12.1.74; Plate 15, 9.6.74; Plate 16, 29.10.74; Plate 17, 20.2.75; Plate 18, 13.7.75; Plate 19, 8.3.76; Plate 20, 29.11.78.

The layout was as before. Plate 13 was defective and was neither registered nor put to press.

The colour name "rose" covers a range of shades from pale to quite deep. There is little difference in value between the shades; the palest being perhaps a little scarcer than the others.

In order that they should conform to the layout of the Crown paper, plates 20 and 21 were altered from their Spray 12-pane form to the Crown 2-pane form. The Crown paper bore no plate or current numbers on the selvedge.

Examples of J44 with wing margins are of considerable interest when matched with those of J45 similarly lettered on Crown paper. These, being from the same plate after modification, have no wing margins.

1881 (March). 3d. Rose, Type J5. Wmk Crown (W12). Perf 14.

J45 (=S.G.158)	3d. rose, Plate 20	£550	£130
	Block of four	£3000	£675
	Used on cover	†	£220
	a. Watermark inverted	—	£380
J45A (=S.G.158)	3d. rose, Plate 21	£400	80·00
	Block of four	£2500	£450
	Used on cover	†	£140
	a. Watermark inverted	—	£380
	s. "Specimen", Type 9	£220	

Imprimaturs: Plates 20 *and* 21 *re-registered, each* £1500.

Put to press: Plate 21, 15.7.80.

The Crown watermarks were arranged in two panes each of 120 stamps in 10 horizontal rows of 12.

Die Proofs of 3d. Type J5. In black on white glazed card (unless otherwise stated):

Date	*Plate No.*	*Corner Letters*	*Inscr.*	*Additional Inscriptions or Notes*	
(M/S)	5	BC–CB	"NEW"	In rose. "Approved 11 Mar 1872 2280/72"	£5000
—	7	NN—MM	—	Pencilled around the design "121212"	£1100
—	8	KK-KK	—	Pencilled around the design "3421"	£1100
—	8	LL-LL	—	Pencilled around the design "3421"	£1100
3 Oct 72	—	—	B/H		£1100
1 Nov 72	—	—	B/H		£1100
22 Nov 72	—	—	A/S	The date is inverted	£1100
22 Nov 72	—	—	A/S	Initialled "A.C." (M/S)	£1100
—	—	—	—	Basic Die Proof	£1100
—	—	—	—	In rose	£4500
21 Apr 73	12	—	B/S		£1100
13 June 73	13	—	A/S	Unregistered Plate	£1100
(M/S)	13	—	(M/S)	Endorsed "June 24, 1873" and "A/S" (M/S)	£1100
24 June 72	13	—	A/S	Initialled	£1100
21 July	14	—	B/S	The "2" in date is inverted	£1100
15 Oct 73	15	—	B/S		£1100
22 Oct 73	15	—	A/S		£1100
17 Apr 74	16	—	B/S	"Plugs 16 Approved O.H." (M/S) "18 APR 74" violet	£1100
20 Apr. 74	16	MA	A/S	"13 Leads" (M/S) and initialled	
24 Apr 74	16	—	A/S	Initialled	£1100

Date	Plate No.	Corner Letters	Inscr.	Additional Inscriptions or Notes	
21 Aug 74	17	MA	A/S	Initialled	£1100
27 Aug 74	17	—	A/S		£1100
27 Aug 74	17	—	—		£1100
16 Dec 74	18	—	A/S	"19 Leads" (M/S)	£1100
(M/S)	18	—	A/S	Endorsed "Dec 24 1874" and initialled "A.G.W." in pencil	£1100
6 Apr (M/S)	19	—	(M/S)	No year indicated, "After Striking" (M/S)	£1100
7 May 75	—	—	—		£1100
—	20	FA–AF	A/S	"105 Leads" (M/S) "A/S" is also (M/S)	£1100
3 June 80	21	QB	A/S	"36 Leads" (M/S) "A/S" is also (M/S)	£1100
(M/S)	21	—	(M/S)	Endorsed "240 Leads" and "June 17 1880"	£1100

Die Proofs from the De La Rue Archives. Cut down and unmounted:

With letter tablets and plate number circles void £950

Die Proofs from the Striking Books:

Plate 19 with corner letters AT–TA, unmounted £950
Plate 12, 14/21 with letter tablets void . . . . . *from* £950

Plate Proofs

Plate 19 in black on thick white wove paper £1100
Plate 20 in black on thick white wove paper £1100

Colour Trials. Plate 20. Without watermark, imperforate:

In pink, orange, green, buff, rose on pink, orange-yellow on yellowish, green on greenish, blue on bluish . . . . . *each* £3000

Plate 20. Without watermark, perf. 14:

In red-brown on buff £3000

Plate 20. Watermark Crown, perf 14:

In carmine-pink, orange, yellow, dull green, blue, Prussian blue, purple, mauve, purple-brown, red-brown . . . . . *each* £3000

4d., Types J7 to J11 (1855–82)

The 4d. value was first introduced to prepay letters to France. The first issues are somewhat confusing owing to the almost simultaneous use of three different Garter watermarks and three different papers. It is considered expedient to follow the order adopted in other publications, dealing first with the Small Garter issues, then the Medium and finally the Large. It should be noted, however, that some issues on the Small Garter paper were made later than the last on the Medium Garter paper.

Plates Nos. 1 and 2, Type **J7** without letters in the corners, were each of 240 stamps arranged in four panes, two and two, each of 60 stamps in 10 horizontal rows of six. The plate numbers appeared on the selvedge at the four corners of the sheets but were trimmed off from the issued sheets, existing only on the imprimatur sheets. There is, therefore, no definite characteristic by which stamps can be identified as to plate. However, there are many frame breaks in this issue and quite a number of these have been recorded as to position and plate by Mr. J. Perkins and published in *The GB Journal* for January and March 1972, with additional notes in July 1972.

All subsequent 4d. plates up to and including Plate 17 were in details of layout the same as Plates 1 and 2. Plate 17 (after modification) and Plate 18 were in two panes of 120 arranged in 10 horizontal rows of 12. The printings from Plates 17 and 18 on Crown paper were without plate or current numbers on the selvedge.

J7 *No corner letters*

1855 (31 July). 4d. Carmine, Type J7. Thick, highly glazed, deeply blued upper. Wmk Small Garter (W5a). Perf 14.

J47 (=S.G.62)	(1)	4d. deep bright carmine	£6500	£450
	(2)	4d. pale bright carmine	£5000	£375
	(3)	4d. deep carmine	£6500	£425
	(4)	4d. pale carmine	£5000	£375
		Block of four	£40000	
		Used on cover	†	£650
	c.	Paper slightly blued	£5250	£375
	e.	White paper	—	£750
	f.	Watermark inverted	—	£900
	g.	Double perforation	—	£900
	s.	"Specimen", Types 2, 3 *from*	£700	

Imprimaturs: On deeply blued paper, Plates 1 *or* 2, £4500.

Plates 1 and 2 were used, and were put to press on 13.7.55.

1856 (25 February). 4d. Carmine, Type J7. Thick, highly glazed paper, normally more or less deeply blued. Wmk Medium Garter (W5b). Perf 14.

J48 (=S.G.63)	(1)	4d. pale carmine	£5750	£425
	(2)	4d. carmine	£5750	£425
	(3)	4d. deep carmine	£6250	£450
		Block of four	£40000	£2800
		Used on cover	†	£650
	c.	White paper	£4750	
	d.	Watermark inverted	—	£900
	s.	"Specimen", Type 2 (hor.)	£650	
	t.	"Specimen", Type 2 (vert.)	£650	

1856 (September). 4d. Carmine, Type J7. Thin, ordinary white paper. Wmk Medium Garter (W5b). Perf 14.

J49 (=S.G.64)		4d. pale carmine	£4500	£350
		Block of four	£28000	
		Used on cover	†	£550
	a.	Stamp printed double	†	—
	c.	Watermark inverted	—	£750
	s.	"Specimen", Type 2	£650	

1856 (1 November). 4d. Rose, Type J7. Ordinary white wove paper, specially prepared ink. Wmk Medium Garter (W5b). Perf 14.

J50 (=S.G.65)	(1)	4d. rose	£4250	£350
	(2)	4d. deep rose	£4250	£350
		Block of four	£26000	
		Used on cover	†	£500
	s.	"Specimen", Type 4	£1200	

Plate 1 was used for J48–50.

The Postage Stamps of Great Britain, Part III, emphasizes that the late 1856 Medium Garter issues here listed as J49 and J50 differ entirely as to paper, ink and colour. It is also stated that no fully authenticated examples of these two issues are known with blueing of the paper or with the paper thick and glazed. Ordinary paper can be blued without difficulty.

1857 (January). 4d. Rose, Type J7. Ordinary white paper. Wmk Large Garter (W5c). Perf 14.

J51 (=S.G.66/66a)	(1)		4d. rose-carmine	£1400	£100
	(2)		4d. rose	£1100	£100
	(3)		4d. deep rose (1858)	£2000	£150
			Block of four	£7500	£600
			Used on cover	†	£175
		c.	Thick glazed paper	£3000	£275
		ca.	As J51c but watermark inverted		
		d.	Watermark inverted	—	£280
		e.	Watermark inverted and reversed		
		s.	"Specimen", Types 2, 7 *from*	£350	

Plates 1 and 2 were used for J51; again it is not possible to distinguish between them.

Die Proofs of 4d. Type J7. In black on white glazed card (unless otherwise stated):

Date	*Plate No.*	*Corner Letters*	*Inscr.*	*Additional Inscriptions or Notes*	
Head Die Only					
30 Apr 55	—	—	"No 3"	With pencilled marks showing work to be done	£3000
3 May 55	—	—	"No 2"	From circular punch	£3000
3 May 55	—	—	—	From circular punch	£3000
4 May 55	—	—	"No 3"	Inscribed "Before Hardening" (M/S). The Head in a solid rectangular frame	£3000
Complete Die					
15 June 55	—	—	—	Basic Die Proof	£3000
18 June 55	—	—	"B/H"	Inscribed "Duplicate No. 5" (M/S)	£3000
21 June 55	—	—	(M/S)	Ditto but inscribed "After Striking 1st Form G.H.S." (M/S)	£3000
23 June 55	—	—	(M/S)	Ditto but inscirbed "After Striking 2nd Form G.H.S." (M/S)	£3000
(M/S)	—	—	(M/S)	Inscribed "23 June 1855" and "A/S" (M/S)	£3000
23 June 55	—	—	A/H		£3000
25 June 55	—	—	A/H		£3000

Die Proofs from the De La Rue Archives. Cut down and mounted:

In black £2500

Colour Trial. Watermark Large Garter:

In mauve with trial obliteration . . . .

J8 *Small white corner letters, no hair lines, Roman "I"*

1862 (15 January). 4d. Red, Type J8. (Plate 3, without hair lines). Wmk Large Garter (W5c). Perf 14.

J52 (=S.G.79/80)	(1)	4d. bright red	£1350	£110
	(2)	4d. pale red	£1100	90·00
		Block of four	£6500	£650
		Used on cover	†	£200
	c.	Watermark inverted	—	£240
	d.	Defective letter K (stamp CK)	—	£400
	e.	Lower case corner letter (stamp BA)	—	£400
	t.	"Specimen", Types 2, 5, 6, 8 *from*	£275	

Imprimatur: £2500
Put to press: 30.11.61.

J52e

No. J52e is not a plate flaw, nevertheless a number of examples are known.

J9 *Small white corner letters, hair lines, Roman "II"*

J9 *Enlarged illustration showing hair lines and Roman "II"*

1863 (16 October). 4d. Red, Type J9. (Plate 4, with hair lines). Wmk Large Garter (W5c). Perf 14.

J53 (=S.G.81/82)	(1)	4d. bright red	£1500	£110
	(2)	4d. pale red	£1350	90·00
		Block of four	£7000	£650
		Used on cover	†	£200
	c.	Watermark inverted	—	£250
	d.	Imperforate	£3250	
	s.	"Specimen", Type 2	£325	

Imprimatur: £2500. Stamps removed from the imprimatur sheet are AA–AL, BE–BL, TA, TB and are in much deeper shade than No. J53d.

Put to press: 7.9.63.

Plates 3 and 4 were laid down in the same form as Plates 1 and 2 except that in the later plates the selvedge plate numbers appeared above the top row of stamps to the right and below the bottom row to the left. Plate 4 can be distinguished from Plate 3 by the "hair lines" across the four corner squares; in addition, Plate 4 has the Roman numeral "II" beside the S.W. and S.E. corner squares. In Plate 3 the numeral is "I" and there are no hair lines. Plates 5 and 6 were neither registered nor put to press. All subsequent 4d. plates up to and including Plate 17 were in form similar to Plates 3 and 4 and the sheet markings followed the same plan.

Die Proofs. In black on white glazed card:

No hair lines. Without corner letters or plate number £2500
No hair lines. Without "POSTAGE" and value, endorsed "29 JUN 61" . . . .
With hair lines. Dated "9 Apr 62 After Striking". The Plate number "4" and serial number "216" are both printed on the card £2500

Die Proofs from the De La Rue Archives. Cut down and mounted:

With hair lines and uncleared corner letter squares £2500

Plate Proof. In black on white wove paper:

Plate 4, with hair lines £1200

Colour Trial. Watermark Large Garter, Imperforate, Plate 3:

In deep red, overprinted "Specimen", Type 2 . . . . £2000

J10 *Large white corner letters*

J11 *Large coloured corner letters*

1865 (4 July). 4d. Vermilion, Type J10. Wmk Large Garter (W5c), inverted on J57 and J58. Perf 14.

J54 (=S.G.93/94)	4d. dull vermilion, Plate 7	£550	£100
	Block of four	£3000	£525
	Used on cover	†	£180
J55 (=S.G.93/94)	4d. dull vermilion (shades), Plate 8	£500	60·00
	Block of four	£2800	£450
	Used on cover	†	£130
	a. Watermark inverted	£525	70·00
J56 (=S.G.93/94)	4d. vermilion (shades), Plate 9	£500	60·00
	Block of four	£2800	£450
	Used on cover	†	£130
	a. Watermark inverted	£525	70·00
J57 (=S.G.93/94)	4d. dull vermilion (shades), Plate 10	£550	£110
	Block of four	£3000	£550
	Used on cover	†	£200
J58 (=S.G.93/94)	4d. vermilion (shades), Plate 11	£500	60·00
	Block of four	£2800	£450
	Used on cover	†	£130
	a. Imperforate (inverted wmk)	£1900	
	b. Watermark upright		
	s. Imperforate "Specimen", Type 2		
J59 (=S.G.93/94)	4d. vermilion (shades), Plate 12	£475	55·00
	Block of four	£2700	£425
	Used on cover	†	£125
	a. Imperforate (inverted wmk)	£1900	
	b. Imperforate. Dr. Perkins paper (blued)	£2250	
	c. Watermark inverted	£475	55·00

	s. Imperforate "Specimen", Type 6 over two stamps	£850	
	t. "Specimen", Type 6	£350	
	u. Dr. Perkins paper, perf 14 "Specimen"	£2250	
J60 (=S.G.93/94)	4d. vermilion (shades), Plate 13	£500	55·00
	Block of four	£2800	£450
	Used on cover	†	£125
	s. "Cancelled", Type 14A		
J61 (=S.G.93/94)	4d. vermilion (shades), Plate 14	£550	85·00
	Block of four	£3000	£500
	Used on cover	†	£175
	s. "Specimen", Type 8	£300	

Imprimaturs: Plates 7 *to* 14 *(with upright watermark), each* £1500.

Put to press dates: Plate 7, 5.6.65; Plate 8, 23.1.66; Plate 9, 16.5.67; Plate 10, 17.3.68; Plate 11, late 1868; Plate 12, 21.3.70; Plate 13, 11.10.72; Plate 14, 8.5.73.

The layout of Plates 7 to 14 (Type **J10**), with large white letters in the corners, was the same as for Type **J8**.

The colour name "vermilion" is to be taken as a general term covering shades from dull vermilion to deep vermilion. None is notably scarcer than another except perhaps the deepest shade, for which a premium of 10 per cent is charged.

In 1872, during the currency of Plate 12, a new paper was introduced with thicker lines to the Garter watermark. Printings on the new paper from Plate 12 and subsequent plates were generally paler than earlier printings.

Die Proofs of 4d. Type J10. In black on white glazed card (unless otherwise stated):

Date	*Plate No.*	*Corner Letters*	*Inscr.*	*Additional Inscriptions or Notes*	
—	—	—	—	Small size cards only seen, uncleared	
—	—	—	—	In vermilion for 1867 Paris Exhibition	£4500
10 June 68	—	—	B/S	Said to be Plate 10	£1100
9 Oct 68	—	—	A/S	Said to be Plate 11	£1100
—	—	—	—	In blue or rose "Taken for experiment Aug 68"	£4500
30 Oct 68	—	—	B/S	With cross at N.W. corner, endorsed "To show injured corner of die H.J.E." and "recd 3 Nov 68" and initials	£1400
—	—	—	—	On matt card circa 1870, in vermilion, brown, yellow, mauve, lilac	£4500
—	—	—	—	On matt card in black for 1871 London International Exhibition	£1100
(M/S)	"I"	FG–GF	—	In bistre. Inscribed (M/S) "22 Feb 72 Pulled in wrong colour by mistake"	£5000
—	"I"	FG–GF	"OLD"	In vermilion	£4500

Die Proofs from the De La Rue Archives. Cut down and mounted:

With uncleared corner squares and plate number circles £950

Die Proofs from the Striking Books:

With uncleared corner squares and plate number circles .... *from* £950

Plate Proof

Plate 8 in vermilion on unwatermarked and ungummed paper £1250

1876 (1 March). 4d. Vermilion, Type J11. Wmk Large Garter (W5c). Perf 14.

J62 (=S.G.152)	4d. vermilion, Plate 15	£1750	£425
	Block of four	£8500	
	Used on cover	†	£850
	c. Watermark inverted	—	£700
	d. Large "5" in "15" (AA and TK)	—	£750
	t. "Specimen", Type 9	£325	
J63 (=S.G.152)	4d. vermilion, Plate 16	*	£22000

Imprimatur: Plate 15, £1800; *Plate* 16, £8500.

Put to press dates: Plate 15, 17.11.75; Plate 16, 23.10.77.

J63 is an "abnormal" resulting from the perforating and issuing of one or more sheets which had been run off the plate at the same time as the imprimatur sheet. Eleven used examples are known. This stamp is not known to exist with wing margins although two of the extant stamps are from "wing margin" positions. See note after J67.

1877 (12 March). 4d. Sage-green, Type J11. Wmk Large Garter (W5c). Perf 14.

J64 (=S.G.153)		4d. sage-green, Plate 15	£1000	£275
		Block of four	£6000	
		Used on cover	†	£500
	c.	Watermark inverted	—	£500
	d.	Large "5" in "15" (AA and TK)	—	£650
	s.	Imperforate "Specimen", Type 9	£475	
	t.	"Specimen", Type 9	£280	
J65 (=S.G.153)		4d. sage-green, Plate 16	£900	£250
		Block of four	£5500	
		Used on cover	†	£475
	c.	Watermark inverted	—	£500
	s.	"Specimen", Type 9	£275	
J66 (=S.G.153)		4d. sage-green, Plate 17	*	£15000

Imprimatur: Plate 15, *re-registered,* £1800; *Plate* 17, £8000.

Put to press dates: Plate 15, 27.2.77; Plate 16, 23.10.77.

J66 is an "abnormal". At least twenty-three examples are known, many of which are postmarked with one or both parts of the Bradford duplex cancellation number 107.

(15 August). 4d. Grey-brown, Type J11. Wmk Large Garter (W5c). Perf 14.

J67 (=S.G.154)		4d. grey-brown, Plate 17	£1500	£450
		Block of four	£8500	
		Used on cover	†	£1200
	c.	With wing margin	£1500	£450
	d.	Watermark inverted	—	£900
	e.	Imperforate	£7500	
	s.	"Specimen", Type 9	£280	

Put to press: 10.6.80.

As the imprimatur sheet is in sage-green there should be no difficulty in identifying the imperforate J67*e*.

The first supplies of this stamp were perforated at Somerset House and the F and G column stamps display the characteristic wing margin. A later supply of stamps was perforated by De La Rue using their own machine and punch set which perforated the F and G column stamps close to the design, thus eliminating the wing margin effect. Examples of J67 exist with "Specimen" Type 9 partly on the stamp and partly on the gutter margin. This punch set was not adopted but is known in connection with some "abnormal" issues.

With the introduction of the Crown paper, with its watermarks arranged in two panes of 120, it became necessary to modify Plate 17 from its earlier 4-pane Garter form to the 2-plane Crown form. No new imprimatur of this plate appears to have been registered. Plate 18 was laid down in 2-pane form and required no modification. The Crown paper bore no plate or current numbers on the selvedge. Examples of J67 with wing margin (Somerset House perforation) matched with identically lettered stamps without the wing margin (De La Rue perforation) are of interest. They may also be matched with similarly lettered examples of J68 without wing margins.

1880 (8 December). 4d. Grey-brown, Type J11. Wmk Crown (W12). Perf 14.

J68 (=S.G.160)	(1)	4d. grey-brown, Plate 17	£350	60·00
	(2)	4d. pale grey-brown, Plate 17	£350	60·00
		Block of four	£2250	£425
		Used on cover	†	£140
	c.	Watermark inverted	—	£550
	s.	"Specimen", Type 9	£220	
J69 (=S.G.160)		4d. grey-brown, Plate 18	£350	60·00
		Block of four	£2250	£425
		Used on cover	†	£140
	c.	Watermark inverted	—	£550
	s.	"Specimen", Type 9	£240	

Imprimatur: Plate 18, £750.
Put to press: Plate 18, 15.8.82.

Die Proofs of 4d., Type J11. In black on white glazed card (unless otherwise stated):

Date	*Plate No.*	*Corner Letters*	*Inscr.*	*Additional Inscriptions or Notes*	
(M/S)	"1"	FG–GF	"NEW"	In vermilion. "Approved 11 March 1872 2280/72" (M/S)	£4750
—	"2"	OD–DC	—		£1100
—	"2"	AB–BA	—		£1100
—	—	—	—	Basic Die Proof	£1100
19 Nov 72	—	—	B/H		£1100
6 Feb 74	15	AB–CD	B/H	"Old Plug (15)" (M/S)	£1100
13 Apr 74	—	—	A/H		£1100
17 June 74	16	AM–MA	A/S	"12 Leads" (M/S)	£1100
19 June 74	16	—	B/S		£1100
19 June 77	17	—	B/S		£1100
27 June 77	17	—	A/S	The date and A/S are in (M/S)	£1100

Die Proofs from the De La Rue Archives. Cut down and mounted or unmounted:

With corner squares and plate number circles void . . . . *from* £950

Die Proof from the Striking Books:

With plate number circles and corner squares void £950
Plates 16, 17, 18 with corner squares void . . . . *from* £950

Plate Proof

Plate 16. In black on white wove paper £1100

Colour Trials. Watermark Large Garter, Imperf, Plate 15 (1876):

In light sage, sage-grey, turquoise-blue, grey-lilac, pale red-brown, chestnut, pale orange-brown, pale olive-bistre . . . . *each* £200
Ditto, overprinted "Specimen", Types 8, 9, 11 . . . . *each* £375

Watermark Large Garter, Plate 17 (1883):

Imperforate in blue, lilac . . . .
Perf 14 in purple, purple-brown, grey, slate and also on coloured papers . . . . *from* £1800

Watermark Crown, Perf 14, Plate 17:

In carmine-pink, orange, yellow, yellow-green, dull green, blue-green, blue, Prussian blue, mauve, purple-brown, red-brown, grey-brown (issued colour), olive-bistre, slate-grey . . . . *each* £1800

No Watermark, Perf 14, Plate 17:

In purple-brown on buff, purple on pale purple, blue-green on pale green . . . . *from* £3000

6d., Types J12 to J17 (1856–83)

The 6d. stamp was first issued to replace the Embossed issue. The first plate was registered on 29 March 1856, the imprimatur sheet being of blue "Safety" paper, thick and highly glazed. The plate numbers appeared at each of the four corners of the plate which was of 240 stamps in twelve panes, each of 20 stamps; the panes were arranged in four horizontal rows of three and the stamps in each pane were in five horizontal rows of four. Each pane of 20 comprised five horizontal rows of four. Two adjoining vertical panes constituted a "Post Office sheet". Plate 2 was neither registered nor put to press. Plates 3 and 4, with small white corner letters, followed the same layout as Plate 1 but in their case the selvedge plate numbers appeared on the top selvedge, to the left, and on the bottom selvedge, to the right. The corner letters followed the usual course, with the top row lettered AA to AL and so on to the bottom row, TA–AL (mentioning lower corners only). All subsequent issues followed the same layout until the printings in 2 panes of 120 on Crown paper. These had no plate or current numbers on the selvedge. Plate 7 was not registered or put to press. A die proof from the De La Rue archive exists with uncleared squares, plate number circles and (M/S) "No. 7" showing "SIX PENCE" without hyphen.

J12 *No corner letters*

J13 *Small white corner letters*

J13A *Hair lines (illustration enlarged)*

1856 (21 October). 6d. Lilac, Type J12. Wmk Emblems (W6). Perf 14.

J70 (=S.G.69/70)	(1)	6d. deep lilac, Plate 1	£1100	£120
	(2)	6d. pale lilac, Plate 1	£900	95·00
	(3)	6d. lilac, Plate 1	£900	95·00
		Block of four	£5500	£575
		Used on cover	†	£190
	d.	On thick white paper	£2200	£275
	e.	On ordinary paper, blued ("azure")	£4500	£700
	f.	Watermark inverted	—	£250
	g.	Watermark inverted and reversed		
	h.	Watermark reversed		
	i.	Watermark error **W6a**: three roses and shamrock (R. 20/1)		
	j.	Double perforation	†	—
	s.	"Specimen", Types 2, 4, 7, 8 *from*	£350	
	t.	Azure paper. "Specimen", Type 4	£750	

Imprimatur: on thick highly glazed, blued paper, £3250.
Put to press: 29.3.56.
Examples of J70*e* should be purchased only if accompanied by an expert committee's certificate.

A

Die Proofs. On white glazed card:

In black endorsed "3 Jan 56" (M/S) with hyphen between "SIX" and "PENCE", being an essay as the hyphen was not used until the next issue . . . £2000
In black endorsed "28 JAN 56" . . . £1800
In black endorsed (M/S) "Jany 30/56" . . . £1800
In black endorsed (M/S) "After Hardening Feby 2/56" and with hyphen removed £1800
In lilac (Type A) unadopted essay endorsed (M/S) "Approved by me as to design but colour not full enough. O.H. 12 Oct 1858" . . . £5000

Die Proof from the De La Rue Archives. Cut down and mounted:

In black . . . £1500

Plate Proofs. On wove paper, watermark Emblems, imperforate:

In deep mauve on "azure" paper with trial cancellation . . . £2000

On unwatermarked wove paper, imperforate:

In green on white paper	£1800
In green on white paper with trial cancellation	£2000

1862 (1 December). 6d. Lilac, Type J13. Plate 3 (without hair lines across the corners). Wmk Emblems (W6). Perf 14.

J71 (=S.G.83/84)	(1)	6d. deep lilac	£1450	£110
	(2)	6d. lilac	£1400	90·00
		Block of four	£7750	£500
		Used on cover	†	£170
	c.	Thick, highly glazed paper	—	£225
	d.	Azure (blued) paper	—	£1000
	e.	Watermark inverted	£3000	£280
	f.	Watermark error **W6b**: three roses and thistle (stamp TF)	—	£6000
	g.	Watermark inverted and reversed		
	h.	Watermark reversed		
	i.	Shamrock missing from watermark		
	s.	"Specimen", Types 2, 5, 8 *from*	£350	

Imprimatur: £2000.
Put to press: 9.9.62.
Variety No. J71*i* came from different sheet positions including stamp TF.

Die Proof. In black on white glazed card:

Without corner letters endorsed "July 12–61 A/S," also with number "2" in circle and number "199" in box printed on the card	£2000

1864 (20 April). 6d. Lilac, Type J13A. Plate 4 (with hair lines). Wmk Emblems (W6). Perf 14.

J72 (=S.G.85)		6d. lilac	£1800	£180
		Block of four	£8500	£975
		Used on cover	†	£275
	c.	Thick paper	£2200	£225
	d.	Watermark inverted	—	£350
	e.	Watermark inverted and reversed		
	f.	Imperforate and watermark inverted	£3000	
	g.	Imperforate and watermark upright	£3500	
	h.	Watermark error **W6b**; three roses and thistle (stamp TF)		
	s.	"Specimen", Type 2	£350	

Imprimatur: (watermark upright), £2500. Stamps removed from the imprimatur sheet are AA–AL, BE–BL, TA, TB.
Put to press: 11.4.64.
Examples of J72*g* imperforate with watermark upright should be purchased only if accompanied by an expert committee's certificate. Examples from the imprimatur are in a bright shade and have no gum.

Die Proofs. In black on white glazed card:

Without corner letters endorsed "18 JUN 61"	£2000
Without corner letters endorsed "Jan 6-62" B/S	£2000
Ditto but in lilac, no endorsement	£4500

Die Proof from the De La Rue Archives. Cut down and mounted:

With hair lines and uncleared corner letter squares	£1800

Plate Proofs. In black on thick white card:

Endorsed "Specimen"	£1500

J14 *Large white corner letters;* "SIX-PENCE" *with hyphen*

J15 *Large white corner letters;* "SIX PENCE" *without hyphen*

1865 (7 March). 6d. Lilac, Type J14. Wmk Emblems (W6). Perf 14.

J73 (=S.G.96/97)	(1)	6d. deep lilac, Plate 5	£1100	£130
	(2)	6d. lilac, Plate 5	£725	80·00
		Block of four	£4500	£450
		Used on cover	†	£150
	c.	Watermark error **W6a**: three roses and a shamrock (stamp TA)	—	£750
	d.	Watermark inverted	—	£175
	e.	Watermark inverted		
	f.	Thick paper	£825	£110
	g.	Watermark error **W6b**: three roses and thistle (stamp TF)		
	h.	Watermark inverted and reversed	†	—
	s.	"Specimen", Type 2, in blue	£3800	
J74 (=S.G.96/97)	(1)	6d. deep lilac, Plate 6	£2200	£150
	(2)	6d. lilac, Plate 6	£2200	£150
		Block of four	£13000	
		Used on cover	†	£300
	c.	Watermark error **W6a**: three roses and a shamrock (stamp TA)	—	£1500
	d.	Watermark inverted	—	£300
	e.	Double print, stamp RD	—	£12000

Imprimaturs: Plate 5, £1800; *Plate* 6, £2000.
Put to press: Plate 5, 4.1.65; Plate 6, 22.11.66.

1867 (21 June). 6d. Lilac, Type J14. Wmk Spray (W7). Perf 14.

J75 (=S.G.104/107)	(1)	6d. lilac, Plate 6	£1100	80·00
	(2)	6d. deep lilac, Plate 6	£1100	80·00
	(3)	6d. purple, Plate 6	£1100	£110
	(4)	6d. bright violet, Plate 6 (22 July 1868)	£950	90·00
		Block of four	£6250	£450
		Used on cover	†	£160
	c.	Imperforate (lilac)		
	d.	Watermark inverted	—	£225
	e.	Double perforation (vertical sides appear rouletted)	†	—
	s.	Imperforate "Specimen", Type 2, in brown	£4000	

No. J75*c* is known used lettered FD.

Die Proofs

In black on white glazed card without corner letters or plate numbers endorsed (M/S) "Aug 8th/64 5694" and signature £1200
In blue or lilac £5000

Die Proof from the De La Rue Archives. Cut down and mounted:

With uncleared corner squares and plate number circles £1000

Plate Proof

Plate 6 in deep lilac, ungummed unwatermarked paper £1100

Colour Trials. On thin unwatermarked wove paper gummed or ungummed:

In rose, orange,-red, green, blue, lilac, brown-lilac, straw .... *from* £3000

1869 (8 March). 6d. Mauve, Type J15. Wmk Spray (W7). Perf 14.

J76 (=S.G.108/109)	(1)	6d. dull violet, Plate 8		£550	80·00
	(2)	6d. mauve, Plate 8		£500	£110
			Block of four	£2750	£425
			Used on cover	†	£120
		c.	Imperforate	£4750	£3250
		d.	Watermark inverted	—	£225
		e.	Double perforation (vert. sides appear rouletted)		
		s.	Imperforate "Specimen", Type 2	£4250	
		t.	"Specimen", Types 1, 8 ... *from*	£300	
J77 (=S.G.109)		6d. mauve, Plate 9		£500	80·00
			Block of four	£2750	£400
			Used on cover	†	£120
		c.	Imperforate	£4750	£3250
		d.	Imperforate, Dr. Perkins paper (blued)	£1750	
		e.	Watermark inverted	—	£200
		f.	Double perforation		
		s.	Imperforate "Specimen", Type 6	£400	
		t.	"Specimen", Types 6, 8 ... *from*	£300	
		u.	Dr. Perkins paper, perf 14. "Specimen"	£1200	
J78 (=S.G.109)		6d. mauve, Plate 10		*	£22000

Imprimaturs: Plates 8, 9, *each* £2000; *Plate* 10, £10000. Stamps removed from the imprimatur sheets are: Plate 8: AK, AL, SE–SL, TA–TL; Plate 9: AA–AL, BC–BL, TA, TB.

Put to press: 8, 18.12.68; Plate 9, 3.5.70.

J78 is an "abnormal". Plate 10 was never put to press. The few existing perforated stamps are apparently from a few sheets run off at the same time as the imprimatur sheet and later perforated and issued. Ten examples have been recorded.

Die Proofs of 6d. Type J15. In black on white glazed card (unless otherwise stated):

Date	*Plate No.*	*Corner Letters*	*Inscr.*	*Additional Inscriptions or Notes*	
51 Feb 69	—	—	B/S	Date reads "51 Feb" for "15 Feb"	£1500
16 Feb 69	—	—	A/S		£1500
—	—	—	—	On matt card circa 1870 in brown, yellow, mauve, lilac ... *each*	£4500
—	—	—	—	Ditto in black for 1871 London International Exhibition	£1500

Die Proof from the De La Rue Archives. Cut down and mounted:

With uncleared corner squares and plate number circles £1500
As last but mount endorsed "No. 2" £1500

Die Proofs from the Striking Books:

With uncleared corner squares and plate number circles .... *from* £1200

Colour Trials. Imperf:

In brown, red-brown, orange .... *from* £3000

J16 *Hexagonal type; large white corner letters*

J17 *Hexagonal type; large coloured corner letters*

1872 (12 April). 6d. Chestnut, Type J16. Plate 11. Wmk Spray (W7). Perf 14.

J79 (=S.G.122/123)	(1)	6d. very deep chestnut		£1250	£150
	(2)	6d. deep chestnut		£875	90·00
	(3)	6d. chestnut (22 May 1872)		£650	50·00
	(4)	6d. pale chestnut (1872)		£550	50·00
	(5)	6d. pale buff (19 October 1872)		£600	85·00
			Block of four	£3800	£325
			Used on cover	†	£120
			Used on cover (Shade (5))	†	£250
		c.	Watermark inverted (Shade (3))	—	£200
		d.	Figure "11" on left damaged (stamp NF)	—	£300
		s.	Imperforate "Specimen", Type 6	£350	
		t.	"Specimen", Types 2, 6, 8 *from*	£275	

Imprimatur: £2000.
Put to press: 25.1.72.

J79d

J80/81c

J80/81d

1872. 6d. Buff, Type J16. Plate 12. Wmk Spray (W7). Perf 14.

J80 (=S.G.123/124a)	(1)	6d. pale buff		£2000	£250
	(2)	6d. pale chestnut		*	£2750
	(3)	6d. chestnut		*	£2750
			Block of four (buff)	£10000	
			Used on cover (buff)	†	£450
		c.	Figure "12" on left doubled (stamp DE)	—	£400
		d.	Ditto (stamp DF)	—	£400
		e.	Watermark inverted (Shade (1))	—	£750

Imprimatur: (pale chestnut). £4000.

The chestnut shades of J80 are "abnormals" (from sheets printed with the imprimatur, registered 22 April 1872). The stamp was put to press in buff on 30 October 1872. Used examples dated prior to this must be chestnut or pale chestnut.

1873 (24 April). 6d. Grey, Type J16. Plate 12. Wmk Spray (W7). Perf 14.

J81 (=S.G.125)	6d. grey	£1400	£225
	Block of four	£8000	£1600
	Used on cover	†	£250
	c. Figure "12" on left doubled (stamp DE)	—	£400
	d. Ditto (stamp DF)	—	£400
	e. Imperforate	£4000	
	f. Watermark inverted	£3250	£475
	s. "Specimen", Types 6, 8, 9 *from*	£325	
	t. "Cancelled", Type 14A		

As there is no imprimatur sheet in grey there should be no difficulty in identifying J81*e*.

Die Proofs of 6d. Type J16. In black on white glazed card (unless otherwise stated):

Date	*Plate No.*	*Corner Letters*	*Inscr.*	*Additional Inscriptions or Notes*	
—	—	—	"A"	(M/S) "Selected by P.M.G. letter 23 June 71" in Ormond Hill's writing. This is in fact an Essay made from the 1865 type with alterations made in Indian ink	
26 Oct 71	—	—	—	Said to be a rejected die	£1500
27 Oct 71	—	—	—		£1500
31 Oct 71	—	—	—		£1500
31 Oct 71	11	—	B/H		
1 Nov 71	—	—	—	In brown	£4500
—	—	—	—	In chestnut	£4500
16 Nov 71	11	—	A/S		£1500
11 Jan 72	12	—	B/S		£1500
—	"6"	HL–LH	"OLD"	In pale chestnut	£5000

Die Proofs from the De La Rue Archives. From the Striking Books:

With uncleared corner squares and plate number circles . . . *from* £1200

1873 (15 March). 6d. Pale Buff, Type J17. Plate 13. Wmk Spray (W7). Perf 14.

J82 (=S.G.145)	(1)	6d. pale buff	*	£15000

Imprimatur: (pale buff). £8000.

J82 is an "abnormal". Plate 13 was never put to press other than in grey so that examples are from the extra sheets run off at the same time as the imprimatur and later perforated.

1874 (20 March). 6d. Grey, Type J17. Wmk Spray (W7). Perf 14.

J83 (=S.G.146/147)	6d. grey (to deep), Plate 13	£400	60·00
	Block of four	£2250	£325
	Used on cover	†	£110
	a. Watermark inverted	£850	£225
J84 (=S.G.146/147)	6d. grey (to deep), Plate 14	£400	60·00
	Block of four	£2250	£325
	Used on cover	†	£110
	a. Watermark inverted	£850	£225
	b. Double perforation		
	s. "Specimen", Types 8, 10 *from*	£250	
J85 (=S.G.146/147)	6d. grey (to deep), Plate 15	£400	60·00
	Block of four	£2250	£325
	Used on cover	†	£110
	a. Watermark inverted	£850	£225
	s. "Specimen", Types 8, 9 *from*	£250	

J86 (=S.G.146/147)		6d. grey (to deep), Plate 16	£400	60·00
		Block of four	£2250	£325
		Used on cover	†	£110
	a.	Watermark inverted	£850	£225
	s.	Imperforate "Specimen", Type 9	£350	
	t.	"Specimen", Type 9	£250	
J87 (=S.G.146/147)		6d. grey (to deep), Plate 17	£675	£140
		Block of four	£3750	£700
		Used on cover	†	£250
	a.	With wing margin	—	£140
	b.	Watermark inverted	£1500	£350

Imprimaturs: Plates. 14 *to* 17, *each* £1600; *Plate* 18, £2000.

Put to press: Plate 13, 11.12.73; Plate 14, 16.10.74; Plate 15, 26.11.75; Plate 16, 2.11.77; Plate 17, 21.4.80.

Plate 18 was registered on Spray paper, but was only issued with the Crown watermark.

Shades range from deep grey to grey (no difference in value). With the introduction of the 2-pane Cross watermarked paper. Plates 17 and 18 required modification, having been laid down in the 12-pane form suitable for the Spray paper. Interest attaches to wing margin examples of J87 matched with similarly lettered stamps of J88. The latter, being from the modified second state of the plate, have no wing margins.

1881 (1 January). 6d. Grey, Type J17. Wmk Crown (W12). Perf 14.

J88 (=S.G.161)		6d. grey, Plate 17	£400	65·00
		Block of four	£2250	£325
		Used on cover	†	£120
	a.	Watermark inverted	—	£550
J89 (=S.G.161)		6d. grey, Plate 18	£350	65·00
		Block of four	£2000	£325
		Used on cover	†	£120
	s.	"Specimen", Type 9	£250	

Imprimaturs: Plates. 17 *and* 18, *re-registered, each* £1500.

Put to press: Plate 18, 11.1.81.

A

Die Proofs of 6d., Type J17. In black on white glazed card (unless otherwise stated):

Date	*Plate No.*	*Corner Letters*	*Inscr.*	*Additional Inscriptions or Notes*	
(M/S)	"3"	HL–LH	"NEW"	In pale chestnut. "Approved 11 March 1872. 2280/72" (M/S)	£5000
—	"3"	HL–LH	—	In pale chestnut, Cut down	£3000
—	1	AB–BA	—	This is an essay. The plate number lugs are at the foot of the design (Type A)	
—	—	—	—	Basic Die Proof	£1250
8 Nov 72	—	—	B/H		£1250
—	11	HH–HH	—	Inscribed in pencil around the design "112243"	£1250
—	13	IE–EI	—	Ditto but "112245"	£1250
1 July 73	14	—	A/S	Initialled (M/S)	£1250
—	15	—	—		£1250
21 Mar 74	15	—	—	Initialled (M/S)	£1250
11 Apr 74	15	—	B/S		£1250

Date	Plate No.	Corner Letters	Inscr.	Additional Inscriptions or Notes	
11 Apr 74	15	—	B/S	Endorsed "Alteration of figure 5 very satisfactory" and initialled (M/S), additionally stamped "11 APR 74" in blue	£5000
14 Apr 74	15	AP–PA	—	"After striking 20 Leads" and initials (M/S)	£1250
—	16	—	—		£1250
19 Aug 75	16	—	B/S	Initialled (M/S)	£1250
19 Aug 75	16	BK–KB	—	"after striking 16 Leads" and initials (M/S)	£1250
14 Nov 77	"11"	—	A/H		£1250
14 Nov 77	17	—	A/S		£1250
14 Nov 77	17	—	A/S	Additional "A/S" over "A/H"	£1250
—	18	—	B/S		£1250
—	18	BG–GB	—		£1250
—	—	—	—	Numbered in pencil on reverse, pulled in 1873 in olive-green, orange-yellow, orange, magenta, bright lilac, deep brown, ultramarine, deep blue-green, deep grey, burnt umber, greenish grey, lilac-rose	£4500
—	—	—	—	In mauve (not cut down)	£4500

Die Proofs from the De La Rue Archives. Cut down and mounted or unmounted:

With corner squares and plate number circles void . . . . *from* £950

Die Proofs from the Striking Books:

With plate number circles and corner squares void £950
Plates 15/18 with corner squares void . . . . *from* £950

Plate Proofs

In black. Plates 15, 16, 18 . . . . *each* £1100

Colour Trials. Plate 17. Watermarked Crown, Perf. 14:

In carmine-pink, orange, yellow, yellow-green, dull green, blue-green, blue, Prussian blue, purple-brown, red-brown, olive-bistre, slate-grey £3500
In grey-blue on light blue £3500

8d., Type J19 (1876)

This value was first issued to prepay the then rate of postage to India via Marseilles and to Australia via Brindisi. Plates 1 and 2 were prepared and registered but Plate 2 was never put to press. Plate 1 was used for a printing of 10,000 sheets in purple-brown which were later almost all destroyed. The only regular issue was therefore that in orange from Plate 1.

Both plates were of 240 stamps in four panes of 60 arranged two and two, the stamps in each pane being in ten horizontal rows of six. The large coloured corner letters ran from AA–AL in the top row to TA–TL in the bottom row (quoting lower letters only).

The inscriptions at top and bottom of the sheet and repeated over and under each pane read "PRICE 8 Pence per Label 4 Shillings per Row of 6 1 Pound per Sheet of 30". These are repeated twice in the central horizontal gutter margin between each pane, i.e. four times. The intention, therefore, was to make the stamps available in half panes of 30, each containing an inscription.

There had been delay in preparing this value, which was urgently needed, and Somerset House were faced with the problem of perforating the sheets so as to produce half panes of 30.

By design, the four-pane layout for the 8d. was identical to that for the 4d., enabling the same perforation punch set to be used for both. As with the 4d., the complete sheets were divided in half horizontally using a guillotine. As regards vertical separation of the panes, the wing margins were sometimes perforated and sometimes left imperforate (imperforate wing margins are unique to the 8d.). Earlier claims that the first supplies had perforated wing margins and that the pins were later removed are not substantiated by a recent review of dated pieces.

The imperforate wing margin panes were separated by guillotine. As the cut was often off-centre the size of the imperforate right margins of the vertical F row and the left margin of the vertical G row varies significantly. When the wing margins were perforated, some were clearly severed by the guillotine, but others appear to have been severed in the normal way, that is by tearing through the perforations.

The ratio of imperforate to perforated wing margin stamps is about 1:1, but this, of course, is only evident when the wing margin is intact over 50% or more of its width. These findings are the result of an examination of examples either on cover or else bearing a dated postmark. See the article by Ray Simpson and Peter Sargent in the December 2005 issue of *Gibbons Stamp Monthly.*

All the surviving examples of J91 are from the top left quarter of the sheet of 240 stamps, i.e. from letterings AA–AF down to JA–JF and their centering indicates that they can be traced to one of three panes that were issued. The "Specimen" stamps known to exist come from rows A, B, H, I or J from one of these sheets. All the remainder of the printing was destroyed. See the article by Malcolm Burnett in the September 1977 issue of *The Philatelic Journal of Great Britain.*

J19

1876 (July). 8d. Purple-brown, Type J19. Wmk Large Garter (W5c). Perf 14. Unissued.

J91 (=S.G.156a)	8d. purple-brown, Plate 1		£6500
	s. "Specimen", Types 8, 9	*from*	£2500

Imprimatur: Plate. 1 *(watermark inverted),* £5500.

1876 (11 September). 8d. Orange, Type J19. Wmk Large Garter (W5c). Perf 14.

J91A (=S.G.156)	8d. orange, Plate 1		£1100	£300
	Block of four		£7000	
	Used on cover		†	£500
	c. Watermark inverted		—	£650
	s. "Specimen", Types 8, 9	*from*	£250	

Imprimatur: Plate. 2, £3000.

There is no convincing evidence of the existence of examples of the 8d. stamps, J91A from the wing margin positions with perforations close to the frames. Such examples as are found are thought to be reperforated.

Essay from the De La Rue Archives. Submitted with others on 6 April 1876. Octagonal design with head printed and frame hand painted in red-brown and white. Plate 5. Lettered HN

On card size 29 × 32 mm £6000

Die Proofs of 8d., Type J19. In black on white glazed card (unless otherwise stated):

Date	*Plate No.*	*Corner Letters*	*Inscr.*	*Additional Inscriptions or Notes*	
13 June 75	—	—	B/H		£1500
—	13	NH–MD	—		£1500
—	—	—	—	Basic Die Proof	£1500
12 June 76	13	NH–MD	—		£1500
13 June 76	—	—	—		£1500
13 June 76	—	—	B/H		£1500
14 June 76	—	—	—		£1500
14 June 76	—	—	B/H		£1500
—	1	AK–KA	—	"FI" initials (M/S)	£1500
2 Aug 76	2	—	B/S		£1500
3 Aug 76	2	AF–FA	A/S	"6 Leads" (M/S)	£1500
(M/S)	2	—	A/S	Inscribed "Aug 14, 1876" and "FI" (M/S)	£1500

Die Proofs from the De La Rue Archives. Cut down and mounted or unmounted:

With corner squares and plate number circles void . . . . *from* £1250

Plate Proofs

In black on white wove paper £1500

Colour Trials. Wmk. Large Garter, imperf:

In orange, pale orange-yellow, brown-orange, overprinted "Specimen", Type 11 . . . . *from* £325
In yellow . . . .

9d., Types J20 and J21 (1862–67)

This value was issued for use as the then rate to India, Australia and Brazil. Plate 1 was not registered or put to press. Plate 2 was of 240 stamps arranged in 12 panes, each pane of 20 stamps in five horizontal rows of four. The letters were as usual, AA to AL in the top row and so on down to TA to TL in the bottom row (quoting lower corner letters only).

J20 *Small white corner letters*

J21 *Large white corner letters*

1862 (15 January). 9d. Bistre, Type J20. Plate 2 (without hair lines). Wmk Emblems (W6). Perf 14.

J92 (=S.G.86/87)	(1)	9d. bistre	£3250	£400
	(2)	9d. straw	£2750	£350
		Block of four	£15000	
		Used on cover	†	£750
	c.	Azure paper		
	d.	Thick paper	£3500	£425
	e.	Watermark inverted	—	£525
	f.	Watermark reversed	—	£600
	g.	Watermark error **W6b**: three roses and thistle (stamp TF)	†	—
	h.	Watermark inverted and reversed		
	s.	"Specimen", Types 2, 6 *from*	£425	

Imprimatur: £3500.
Put to press: 14.11.61
The 9d. on azure paper (No. J92c) is very rare, only one confirmed example being known.

Die Proof. In black on white glazed card:

Endorsed "June 21–61" and with "2" printed on the card £3000

Plate Proof

In black on white wove paper £2000

1862 (May). 9d. Bistre, Type J20. Plate 3 (with hair lines across the corners). Wmk Emblems (W6). Perf 14.

J93 (=S.G.88)	9d. bistre	£13500	£7500

Imprimatur: £8500.

J93 is an "abnormal" as the plate was never put to press. The existing perforated stamps total 57 of which 11 are unused and undoubtedly from sheets run off at the same time as the imprimatur sheet and later perforated.

Die Proof. In black on white glazed card:

Endorsed "27 JUN 61" £3000

Die Proof from the De La Rue Archives. Cut down and mounted:

With hair lines and uncleared corner letter squares £3000

1865 (30 October). 9d. Straw, Type J21. Wmk Emblems (W6). Perf 14.

J94 (=S.G.98)		9d. straw, Plate 4	£2200	£500
		Block of four	£9500	
		Used on cover	†	£1000
	c.	Watermark error **W6a**: three roses and shamrock (stamp TA)	—	£1200
	d.	Thick paper	£2500	£625
	e.	Watermark inverted	—	£700
	f.	Watermark error **W6b**: three roses and thistle (stamp TF)		
	s.	Imperforate "Specimen", Type 2	£4000	
	t.	"Specimen", Type 2	£675	
J95		9d. straw, Plate 5	£15000	*

Imprimaturs: Plate 4, £2200; *Plate* 5, £8000.
Put to press: Plate 4, 24.5.65

Stamps from this plate 5 were never issued. AA, AI–AL, BK, BL, SI–SL, TA–TL were removed imperforate from the registration sheet and TL has been given fake perforations. In 1886 KA–NL were line perforated 14, but 12 stamps were replaced and 36 (KA–KD, KF–KL, LA–LL, MA, MC, ME–ML, NJ–NL) used for Stamp Committee Books.

1867 (3 October). 9d. Straw, Type J21. Plate 4. Wmk Spray (W7). Perf 14.

J96 (=S.G.110/111)	(1)	9d. straw	£1700	£275
	(2)	9d. pale straw	£1600	£250
	(3)	9d. deep straw	£2000	£350
		Block of four	£8500	£1500
		Used on cover	†	£500
	c.	Imperforate	£5500	
	d.	Watermark inverted	—	£500
	s.	Imperforate "Specimen" Type 2	£4000	
	t.	"Specimen", Types 2, 8, 9, 10, 11 ..... *from*	£325	
	u.	"Cancelled", Type 14A		

The imprimatur sheet has watermark Emblems so there should be no difficulty in identifying J96*c*. The 9d. stamp was withdrawn in 1877.

Die Proofs of 9d., Type J21. In black on white glazed card (unless otherwise stated):

Date	*Plate No.*	*Corner Letters*	*Inscr.*	*Additional Inscriptions or Notes*	
—	—	—	—	There are 6 cut down progressive die proofs (The Post Office)	
—	—	—	—	Basic Die Proof	£2000
—	—	—	—	In straw for the 1867 Paris Exhibition	£4500
—	—	—	—	On matt card, circa 1870 in brown, yellow, mauve, straw ..... *from*	£4500
—	—	—	—	On matt card, for the 1871 London International Exhibition	£2000
—	2	KD–DK	"OLD"	In bistre	£5000

Die Proof from the De La Rue Archives. Cut down and mounted:

With uncleared corner squares and plate number circles £1500

Plate Proof

Plate 4 in straw on ungummed and unwatermarked paper £1800

A

B

Die Proofs for the Proposed 9d. Design with Coloured Corner Letters. The die was never used as this value was withdrawn. In black on white glazed card (unless otherwise stated):

Date	*Plate No.*	*Corner Letters*	*Inscr.*	*Additional Inscriptions or Notes*	
(M/S)	2	KD–DK	"NEW"	In bistre "Approved 11 March 1872 2280/72" (M/S)	£6000
	2	KD–DK	—	In bistre. Cut down	£3500
—	3	EF–FE	—	Circles for plate numbers at foot (Type A)	£1500
—	3	EF–FE	—	Circles at upper part, plate numbers very small and frame around the head is thick	£1500
19 Dec 72	—	—	B/H	Circles at upper part, and of normal size (Type B) .	£1500
—	—	—	—	Numbered in pencil on reverse, pulled in 1873 in olive-green, orange-yellow, orange, magenta, bright lilac, deep brown, ultramarine, deep blue-green, deep grey, burnt umber, greenish grey, lilac-rose (Type B) . . . . *from*	£4500
31 Jan 73	—	—	—	Ditto in lilac-rose "No. 12 maroon" on reverse (M/S)	£4500

Die Proof from the De La Rue Archives. Cut down and mounted:

Type B with corner squares and plate number circles void . . . . *from* £1250

10d., Type J22 (1867)

This value was introduced for prepayment of postage to India, Mauritius and Australia via Marseilles. When the rate was changed in 1870 there was little demand and the value was withdrawn in 1877.

Two plates were produced in 1867. Plate 2 was never put to press but "abnormals" reached the public, these being from extra sheets produced with the imprimatur sheet and later perforated. It seems probable that the perforating (of one sheet at least) was not done on the normal machine at Somerset House, but on some other machine; perhaps the same one used for perforating the 9d. Plate 5 (J95 in this Catalogue). Both plates consisted of 240 stamps in 12 panes arranged in four horizontal rows of three each containing 20 stamps in five horizontal rows of four. The lettering was as usual AA to AL in the top row and so on down to TA to TL in the bottom row. Selvedge plate numbers appeared towards the right end of the top selvedge and the left end of the bottom selvedge.

Forgeries. Used forgeries have been recorded lettered "LK" with wing margin on forged spray watermarked paper. They are in a deep shade and have a crude appearance when compared to the issued stamp.

J22

1867 (1 July). 10d. Red-brown, Type J22. Wmk Spray (W7). Perf 14.

J97 (=S.G.112/114)	(1)	10d. red-brown, Plate 1	£2300	£300
	(2)	10d. pale red-brown, Plate 1	£2300	£325
	(3)	10d. deep red-brown, Plate 1	£3250	£475
		Block of four	£15000	£2000
		Used on cover	†	£700
	c.	Smaller figures "1" (stamp AA)	—	£600
	d.	Imperforate	£5000	
	e.	Watermark inverted	—	£650
	s.	"Specimen", Types 2, 5, 6, 8, 9, 10,11 .. *from*	£375	
	t.	"Specimen", Type 2, in blue	£1500	
	u.	"Cancelled", Type 14A		
J98 (=S.G.113)		10d. pale red-brown, Plate 2	£22000	£8500

Imprimaturs: Plate 1, £2500; *Plate* 2, £8000. Stamps removed from the Plate 1 imprimatur sheet are: AK, AL, SA–SD, SF–SL, TA–TL.

Put to press: Plate 1, 22.3.67.

J98 is an "abnormal" and is not known with wing margins. Five examples are known mint or unused. Plate 2 was never put to press.

Die Proofs of 10d., Type J22. In black on white glazed card (unless otherwise stated):

Date	*Plate No.*	*Corner Letters*	*Inscr.*	*Additional Inscriptions or Notes*	
Head Proof only					
8 Apr 64	—	—	—	Head only on black surround "50,41.JB" (M/S)	£2000
8 Apr 64	—	—	—	Ditto but "5038 JB" (M/S)	
Complete Design					
—	—	—	—	Basic Die Proof	£1800
18 Dec 66	—	—	—		£1800
1 Jan 67	—	—	A/H		£1800
—	—	—	—	For 1867 Paris Exhibition in issued colour	£4500
—	—	—	—	Ditto, in straw, olive-green, blue, purple, black, rose, orange *each*	£4500
—	—	—	—	On matt card, circa 1870 in brown, yellow, mauve, green *from*	£4500
—	—	—	—	On matt card for 1871 London International Exhibition	£1800
—	4	DE–ED	"OLD"	In brown	£5000

Die Proofs from the De La Rue Archives. Cut down and mounted:

With uncleared corner squares and plate number circles £1000

From the Striking Books:

With uncleared corner squares and plate number circles .... *from* £1000

A

B

C

Die Proofs for the Proposed 10d. Design with Coloured Corner Letters. The die was never used as this value was withdrawn. In black on white glazed card (unless otherwise stated):

Date	*Plate No.*	*Corner Letters*	*Inscr.*	*Additional Inscriptions or Notes*	
—	4	DE–ED	"NEW"	In brown. No endorsement	£5000
—	4	DE–ED	"NEW"	In brown. "Superseded"	£5000
—	4	DE–ED	"NEW"	In brown. "Approved 11 March 2280/72"	£5000
—	4	GH–HG	"A"	In red-brown."(Submitted 30/10/72)" (Type A) . . .	£5000
—	4	GH–HG	—	In red-brown M/S date "Oct 72" (Type A)	£5000
—	4	GH–HG	—	(Type A)	£2200
12 Dec 72	—	—	B/H	Plate number circles at top "(submitted 12/12/72)" (Type B)	£2200
—	4	GH–HG	—	In red-brown. Plate number circles painted by hand at top and the bottom plate number circles erased (Type C)	£5000

Die Proofs from the De La Rue Archives. Cut down and mounted or unmounted:

Type B with corner squares and plate number circles void . . . . *from* £1000

1867 (11 November). 10d. Red-brown, Type J22, Plate 1. Printed in error on paper with wmk Emblems (W6). Perf 14

J99 (=S.G.99) 10d. red-brown . . . . † £25000

Some fourteen examples of J99 have been recorded, all used, nine of them in Constantinople.

1s., Types J23 to J26 (1856–81)

This value was introduced to replace the Embossed issue. The imprimatur sheet from Plate 1 (with no corner letters) was in bright green on thick, highly surfaced, deeply blued paper. A trial printing on this paper was rejected but used examples are known. Some blueing is also seen on stamps printed on normal thin paper. These were probably experimental. Examples should not be accepted without a satisfactory guarantee.

The layout of the first plate was of 240 stamps in 12 panes of 20, the panes lying in four horizontal rows of three, and the stamps of each pane in five rows of four. The plate number appeared in a circle at each of the four corners of the full sheet. Later plates up to the issues in brown on Spray paper followed the same layout but the with Plate numbers towards the right end of the top selvedge and towards the left end of the bottom selvedge. The lettering on the stamps followed the usual course of AA to AL for the top row and so on to TA to TL for the bottom row (quoting the lower corner letters only). The Crown watermark printings, made after Plates 13 and 14 had been modified for 12-pane to 2-pane form, bore no Plate or current numbers on the selvedge.

J23 *No corner letters*

J24 *Small white corner letters*

1856 (1 November). 1s. Green, Type J23. Plate 1. Wmk Emblems (W6). Perf 14.

J100 (=S.G.71/73)	(1)	1s. deep green	£2200	£375
	(2)	1s. green	£1250	£260
	(3)	1s. pale green	£1250	£260
		Block of four	£7500	£1700
		Used on cover	†	£350
	c.	Thick paper	—	£300
	d.	Ordinary thin paper, blued (azure)	—	£1500
	e.	Watermark inverted	—	£425
	f.	Watermark reversed	—	£1000
	g.	Watermark inverted and reversed		
	h.	Imperforate (Shade 3)	†	—
	i.	Double perforation		
	s.	"Specimen", Types 2, 4, 7	£600	

Imprimatur: on blue glazed paper, £3500.
Put to press: Plate 1, 12.10.56.
The listing of No. J100*h* is based on an example with a Glasgow postmark.

Die Proofs

Essay in red in a slightly different design endorsed "This is the form approved by the Board 12 March, 1856. O.H. But the colour is to be green" £6000
Essay in blue with corner ornaments (The Post Office) . . . .
In black in the issued design on unglazed paper £3000
In black. Endorsed (M/S) "Before Hardening April 30/56" £3000

Die Proof from the De La Rue Archives. Cut down and mounted:

In black £2500

Plate Proofs

In carmine and blue on glazed paper with trial cancellations . . . . *each* £2000
In green on white wove pelure paper, pen-cancelled £1800

Imperforate colour trial with cross marked on plate

Colour Trials

On white glazed wove paper, imperf, with white cross below chin in carmine-red, green, blue . . . . *each* £2500
With trial cancellation in M/S or by "39" in diamond obliterator . . . . *each* £2500

1862 (1 December). 1s. Green, Type J24. Plate 2 (but each stamp bears the number "1"). Wmk Emblems (W6). Perf 14.

J101 (=S.G.89/90)	(1)	1s. deep green	£2500	£350
	(2)	1s. green	£1700	£200
		Block of four	£9500	£1200
		Used on cover	†	£325
	c.	Letter "K" normal (stamp KD)	—	£1250
	d.	"K" in circle (stamp KD)	£5500	£950
	e.	Defective S.W. corner letter "A" (stamp AL)	—	£400
	f.	Azure paper		
	g.	Thick paper	—	£275
	h.	Thick paper, "K" in circle (stamp KD)	—	£2100
	i.	Watermark inverted	—	£275
	j.	Watermark inverted and reversed	—	£275
	k.	Watermark reversed		
	l.	Double perforation		
	s.	"Specimen", Types 2, 5, 8 *from*	£325	

Imprimatur: £2000.
Put to press: 8.10.62.

The variety "K" in circle (J101*d*, J101*h*) is believed to be due to a damaged letter having to be cut out and replaced, since it is not present on the imprimatur sheet and is known without the circle (J101*c*), presumably from the first printing. It is probable that the punch was driven in too deeply, causing the flange of the punch to penetrate the surface to produce a circular indentation which showed as an uncoloured line on the stamps.

Die Proofs. In black on white glazed card:

Without corner letters or plate numbers	£3500
Ditto, but endorsed "Feb. 11–62 Before Hardening"	£3500
Ditto, but endorsed "Feb. 13–62" only	£3500

"K" *in circle (illustration enlarged)*

1862 1s. Green, Type J24. Plate 3 (but each stamp bears the number "2"). Wmk Emblems (W6). Perf 14.

J102 (=S.G.91)		1s. deep green	£20000
	a.	Imperforate	£4000
	b.	Imperforate, watermark inverted	£3000
	s.	Imperforate "Specimen", Type 2	£2500

Imprimatur: £6000. Stamps removed from the imprimatur sheet: AK, AL, SE–SL, TA–TL.

The above is an "abnormal" as the plate was never put to press. Existing stamps, unofficially perforated 14 or imperforate, are from extra sheets run off with the imprimatur sheet. The stamps show corner hair lines. The plate was registered on 16 June 1862.

Die Proof from the De La Rue Archives. Cut down and mounted:

With hair lines and uncleared corners and plate number squares . . . . *from* £1800

J25 *Large white corner letters*

J26 *Large coloured corner letters*

1865 (19 January). 1s. Green, Type J25. Wmk Emblems (W6). Perf 14.

J103 (=S.G.101)	1s. green, Plate 4	£1450	£200
	Block of four	£8000	£1000
	Used on cover	†	£350
	c. Thick paper	£1600	£275
	d. Watermark error **W6a**: three roses and a shamrock (stamp TA)	—	£1100
	da. Watermark error **W6b**: three roses and a thistle (stamp TF)	—	
	e. Imperforate between (vertical pair)	—	£10000
	f. Watermark inverted	—	£400
	g. Imperforate, watermark inverted		
	s. Imperforate "Specimen", Type 2, in blue	£1500	
	t. "Specimen", Type 2	£450	

Imprimaturs: Plate 4, £2000: *Plate* 5, £3000.
Put to press: 8.12.64.

Plate 5 was registered on Emblems watermark, but was put to press only on Spray paper.

The green ink used for some printings of J104/114 contained an unstable yellow element which could be removed to produce a blue colour changeling. Plates 4, 12 and 13 in "blue" exist with "Specimen", Type 9 and are considered to be normal green stamps that were used for tests and may be regarded as official colour changelings, and as such we do not list them.

1867 (13 July). 1s. Green, Type J25. Wmk Spray (W7). Perf 14.

J104 (=S.G.115/117)(1)	1s. deep green, Plate 4	£900	60·00
(2)	1s. pale green to green, Plate 4	£825	50·00
	Block of four	£5000	£200
	Used on cover	†	90·00
	a. Imperforate	£3250	£1800
	b. Imperforate, Dr. Perkins paper (blued)	£2500	
	c. Watermark inverted	£1500	£150
	d. Double perforation (vertical sides appear rouletted)		
	s. Imperforate "Specimen", Types 2, 6 ... *from*	£350	
	t. "Specimen", Types 1, 8, 9 ... *from*	£275	
	u. Dr. Perkins paper, perf 14, "Specimen"	£2000	
J105 (=S.G.115/117)(1)	1s. deep green, Plate 5	£650	40·00
(2)	1s. pale green to green, Plate 5	£650	35·00
	Block of four	£4250	£175
	Used on cover	†	75·00
	a. Watermark inverted	—	£140
	b. Extended tail to 5 at right (stamp EC)	—	£300
	s. "Specimen", Types 2, 6, 8, 9 ... *from*	£300	
J106 (=S.G.115/117)(1)	1s. deep green, Plate 6	£1000	40·00
(2)	1s. pale green to green, Plate 6	£1000	35·00
	Block of four	£5500	£175
	Used on cover	†	75·00
	a. Double plate number: JC (left), KB (right)	—	£300
	b. Watermark inverted	—	£140
	s. "Specimen", Types 8, 9 ... *from*	£300	

J107 (=S.G.115/117)		1s. pale green to green, Plate 7	£1000	60·00
		Block of four	£5500	£300
		Used on cover	†	£125
	a.	Imperforate between (horizontal pair)		
	ab.	Watermark inverted	—	£225
	b.	Broken "O" in "ONE" (stamp SK)		
	s.	"Specimen", Type 9	£300	
	t.	"Cancelled", Type 14A		

Imprimaturs: Plates 6 *and* 7, *each* £1800.

Put to press: Plate 4 (J104), 1867; Plate 5, 20.2.71; Plate 6, 20.3.72; Plate 7, 11.11.72.

The pale green and green shades of Plates 4 to 7 are of about equal value.

As the Plate 4 imprimatur sheet has the Emblems watermark there should be no difficulty in identifying J104*a*.

Although the "put to press" date for plate 6 is quoted as 20 March 1872, covers exist with genuine postmarks dated 29 March, 17 April 1869 and 14 June 1871 on a block of four. This may be due to a spare perforated imprimatur sheet being used before the main supply was printed.

J105*b*

Die Proofs of 1s., Type J25. In black on white glazed card (unless otherwise stated):

Date	*Plate No.*	*Corner Letters*	*Inscr.*	*Additional Inscriptions or Notes*	
Head Proof only					
—	—	—	—	There are 3 progressive Die Proofs (The Post Office)	
Complete Design					
—	—	—	—	There are 6 stages of the design (The Post Office)	
—	—	—	—	Basic Die Proof	£1500
—	—	—	—	Made for the 1867 Paris Exhibition in olive-bistre	£4500
—	—	—	—	In green	£4500
—	—	—	—	On matt card, circa 1870 in yellow, brown, mauve, green ... *from*	£4500
—	—	—	—	On matt card for the 1871 London International Exhibition ... *from*	£1500
2 Mar 72	—	—	B/S		£1500
2 Mar 72	—	—	B/S	"(Plate 6)"	£1500
25 Apr 72	—	—	B/H		£1500
1 July 72	—	—	B/H	Initialled and endorsed "Intended for Plate 7"	£1500
11 July 72	—	—	B/S	"(Plate 7)" Initialled "A.C." (M/S)	£1500
—	7	LN–NL	"OLD"	In green	£5000

Die Proofs from the De La Rue Archives. From the Striking Books:

With uncleared corner and plate number squares ... *from* £1200

Plate Proof

Plate 4. In green on unwatermarked wove paper ... £1200

Colour Trial. No watermark. Imperf:

Plate 5. In blue ... £1500

The "Stock Exchange" Forgery

In 1898 supplies of used 1s. Type **J25**, from old telegraph forms originally used at the Stock Exchange Post Office, came on the market. That a proportion of these were skilful forgeries was noticed by the well-known philatelist, Mr. Charles Nissen. They were evidence of a successful and lucrative fraud perpetrated 26 years earlier.

Although the culprit was never identified it is fair to assume that one of the counter clerks must have been using the forged stamps; when telegrams were handed in he would take the cash from the sender, as was the custom, and would affix the equivalent amount in stamps. Whenever he used his forged stamps his genuine stock would not be depleted and he could pocket the money. The great success of this fraud was made possible mainly because no one apart from the perpetrator handled the forgeries; at least until after they had been affixed to the telegram forms and genuinely cancelled.

The forgeries have no watermark and are not as finely produced as the genuine stamps, nevertheless, they are skilful. Several different letterings are found, some of which are impossible in the sense that no such combination of letters occurred on genuine sheets. Both Plates 5 and 6 which were in current use at the time were forged. Plate 6 is the scarcer and the better produced of the two. These forgeries are popular with collectors and are priced as follows:

Stamp with "impossible" lettering, Plate 5	£1300
Stamp with "impossible" lettering, Plate 6	£3500
Stamp with normal lettering, Plate 5	£800
Stamp with normal lettering, Plate 6	£2200

1873 (1 September). 1s. Green, Type J26. Wmk Spray (W7). Perf 14.

J108 (=S.G.148/150)		1s. green, Plate 8	£575	£120
		Block of four	£3250	£550
		Used on cover	†	£200
	a.	Watermark inverted	£1000	£225
J109 (=S.G.148/150)		1s. green, Plate 9	£575	£120
		Block of four	£3250	£550
		Used on cover	†	£200
	a.	Watermark inverted		
J110 (=S.G.148/150)		1s. green, Plate 10	£575	£140
		Block of four	£3250	£575
		Used on cover	†	£225
	a.	Watermark inverted		
J111 (=S.G.148/150)		1s. green, Plate 11	£575	£120
		Block of four	£3250	£550
		Used on cover	†	£200
	s.	"Specimen", Type 8	£250	
J112 (=S.G.148/150)		1s. green, Plate 12	£500	£100
		Block of four	£3000	£500
		Used on cover	†	£190
	a.	Watermark inverted		
	s.	"Specimen", Types 8, 9, 10 . . . . *from*	£250	
	t.	"Cancelled", Type 14A	£1500	
J113 (=S.G.148/150)		1s. green, Plate 13	£500	£100
		Block of four	£3000	£500
		Used on cover	†	£190
	a.	Watermark inverted	£1000	£250
	s.	"Specimen", Type 9	£250	
J114 (=S.G.148/150)		1s. green, Plate 14	*	£22000

Imprimaturs: Plates 8 *to* 13, *each* £1800; *Plate* 14, £7500.

Put to press: Plate 8, 10.6.73; Plate 9, 21.11.73; Plate 10, 14.7.74; Plate 11, 14.12.74; Plate 12, 24.6.75; Plate 13, 17.1.76.

J114 is an "abnormal". Plate 14 was registered in green on Spray paper, being then a plate of 12 panes. It was never put to press in this form other than for the Imprimatur sheet and at least one extra sheet. The latter was evidently perforated officially and five used stamps are known. When in 1881 the plate was eventually put to use in brown with Crown watermark, it was re-registered as a two-pane plate, having been modified to fit the Crown paper. Wing margin examples of J114, if ever found (a trimmed wing margin example is known), would be of considerable interest and extreme rarity. Examples of J114 were first discovered as late as 1915.

The other 1s. plate that was altered in form at the time of the introduction of the Crown paper, Plate 13, is also interesting. Matched trios can be found, all from Plate 13 and all with the same lettering; the first (J113) in green with wing margin; the second (J115) in orange-brown with the wing margin; the third (J116) in orange-brown without wing margin.

Colour Change. A Post Office circular of 21 September 1880 gave notice that the colour of the one shilling green would be changed to brown. The reason was to avoid possible confusion, in artificial light, with the halfpenny of 14 October 1880 issued in green. This replaced the $\frac{1}{2}$d. rose printed by Perkins, Bacon & Co.

1880 (14 October). 1s. Orange-brown, Type J26. Wmk Spray (W7). Perf 14.

J115 (=S.G.151)		1s. orange-brown, Plate 13	£3250	£575
		Block of four	£17000	£3250
		Used on cover	†	£1250
	c.	Watermark inverted	£6000	£1000
	d.	With wing margin	—	£575
	e.	No watermark (stamp LA)	—	£3500
	s.	"Specimen", Type 9	£350	

1881 (24 May) 1s. Orange-brown, Type J26. Wmk Crown (W12). Perf 14.

J116 (=S.G.163)		1s. orange-brown, Plate 13	£625	£140
		Block of four	£3500	£700
		Used on cover	†	£450
	c.	Watermark inverted	£1400	£600
	s.	"Specimen", Type 9	£225	
J117 (=S.G.163)		1s. orange-brown, Plate 14	£500	£140
		Block of four	£3000	£700
		Used on cover	†	£450
	c.	Watermark inverted	£4500	£600
	s.	"Specimen", Type 9	£225	

Imprimaturs: Plate 13 (1881) *in orange-brown (re-registered after alteration)*, £2000; *Plate* 14 (1881) *in orange-brown (re-registered after alteration)*, £2000.

Put to press: Plate 13, May 1881 (registered 4.1.81), plate 14, 21.10.81 (registered same day).

For 1 shilling purple see Section KC, "Unification" No. K8C.

A

Die Proofs of 1s. ,Type J26. In black on white glazed card (unless otherwise stated):

Date	*Plate No.*	*Corner Letters*	*Inscr.*	*Additional Inscriptions or Notes*	
(M/S)	7	LN–NL	"NEW"	In green. Endorsed. "Approved 11 March 1872 2280/72"	£5000
25 Apr 72	—	—	B/H		£1500
14 May 72	—	—	B/H		£1500
17 May 72	—	—	B/H	"2" Printed on card	£1500
17 July 72	—	—	—	"After taking proofs from plugs, A.C." (M/S)	£1500
—	—	AA–AA	—		£1500
—	—	FF–FF	—		£1500
—	—	HH–HH	—		£1500

Date	Plate No.	Corner Letters	Inscr.	Additional Inscriptions or Notes	
—	—	KK–KK	—	. . . .	£1500
—	—	QR–ST	—	. . . .	£1500
—	7	HH–HH	—	The Plate numbers are placed in a square box (Type A)	£1500
—	7	KL–LK	—	. . . .	
9 June 73	9	—	B/S	Initialled (M/S)	£1500
18 June 73	9	—	A/S	Initialled (M/S)	£1500
21 Oct 73	10	AE–EA	B/S	"After 6 Leads and plugs re-adjust" (M/S)	£1500
5 Nov 73	10	—	A/S	The date "NVO" is an error for "NOV". Initialled "F.I." (M/S)	£1500
6 Feb 72	11	—	B/S	Initialled "F.I." (M/S)	£1500
31 Aug 74	12	A-–B	A/S	The only corner letters are "A" top left, "B" bottom right "17 Leads F.C." (M/S)	£1500
5 Sep 74	12	—	A/S	Initialled "F.C." (M/S)	£1500
24 Mar 75	13	—	A/S	Initialled "F.C." (M/S)	£1500
22 Nov 75	14	—	B/S	Initialled (M/S)	£1500
26 Nov 75	14	—	A/S	Initialled (M/S)	£1500

Die Proofs from the De La Rue Archives. Cut down and mounted or unmounted:

With corner squares and plate number circles void . . . . *from* £1500

Die Proofs from the Striking Books:
Plate 8/9, 11/12, 14 with corner squares void. . . . . *from* £1200
Plate 13 with corner letters AD–DA £1200

Plate Proof

Plate 13 in black on card or white wove paper . . . . *from* £1500

Colour Trials

Plate 13 on white paper watermarked Crown in green (issued colour), orange, purple-brown, red-brown, slate-grey . . . . *from* £3000
Plate 13 on unwatermarked coloured papers . . . . *from* £3000
Plate 13 in double fugitive purple, watermarked Crown, perforated and overprinted "Specimen", Type 9 . . . . £3500
Plate 14 in doubly fugitive purple, watermarked Crown, imperf £3500

2s., Type J27 (1867–80)

Plates 1 and 2 were both of 240 stamps in the usual form for use with the Spray paper: twelve panes in four horizontal rows of three, each pane having 20 stamps in five horizontal rows of four. The lettering was as usual in a 240 unit plate. AA to AL in the top row and so on down to TA to TL in the bottom row. The selvedge Plate Numbers were on the top selvedge to the right and the bottom selvedge to the left. Plate 2 was never registered or used. This value was withdrawn in 1880.

J27

1867 (1 July). 2s. Blue, Type J27. Wmk Spray (W7). Perf 14.

J118 (=S.G.118/120*b*)	(1)	2s. dull blue, Plate 1	£2200	£175
	(2)	2s. deep blue, Plate 1	£2750	£175
	(3)	2s. pale blue, Plate 1	£2750	£200
	(4)	2s. cobalt, Plate 1	£11000	£2200
	(5)	2s. milky blue, Plate 1	£9250	£1400
		Block of four	£12000	£1000
		Used on cover	†	£675
	c.	Imperforate (deep blue)	£7000	
	d.	Imperforate (pale blue)	£7000	
	e.	Watermark inverted	—	£450
	s.	Imperforate "Specimen", Type 2, in blue	£5000	
	t.	Imperforate "Specimen", Type 6	£500	
	u.	"Specimen", Types 2, 5, 8, 9, 10,11 . . . *from*	£425	
	v.	"Specimen", Type 2, in blue	£1500	
	w.	"Cancelled". Type 14A		
J119 (=S.G.120)		2s. pale blue, Plate 3	*	£7000

Imprimaturs: Plate 1 (*first or second registration sheet*), *each* £2500; *Plate* 3, £8000.

Plate 1 was put to press on 10.4.67. Plate 3 was registered on 23.1.67.

Plate 1 as originally laid down was out of square. It was registered on 5 April 1867 (lightly inked). It was cut up, put together properly and re-registered on 5 July 1867 (heavily inked). There are thus two imprimatur sheets.

From the original imprimatur sheet the stamps missing are AK, AL, SB–SL, TA–TL. From the second Plate 1 imprimatur sheet the stamps missing are AA–AL, BE–BL, TA, TB.

A few used examples are known of J119. This is an "abnormal" in that the plate was never put to press. Existing stamps have the unofficial Somerset House perf 14.

1880 (27 February). 2s. Brown, Type J27. Wmk Spray (W7). Perf 14.

J120 (=S.G.121)		2s. brown, Plate 1	£16000	£2800
		Block of four		
		Used on cover	†	—
	c.	Watermark inverted	—	£3800
	d.	Imperforate	£18000	
	e.	No watermark	†	—
	s.	"Specimen", Type 9	£2200	

Imperforate and partly perforated blocks exist in a slightly different shade from the normal. They may be colour trials or perforation tests. Forgeries of this stamp are known. In the Royal Collection there is a large imperforate block in a shade slightly lighter than the issued stamp.

Die Proofs of 2s., Type J27. In black on white glazed card (unless otherwise stated):

Date	*Plate No.*	*Corner Letters*	*Inscr.*	*Additional Inscriptions or Notes*	
13 Dec 66	—	—	—	Unfinished Die Proof	£2000
—	—	—	—	Basic Die Proof	£2000
18 Dec 66	—	—	—		£2000
31 Dec 66	—	—	A/H		£2000
23 Feb 67	—	—	—		£2000
—	—	—	—	For the 1867 Paris Exhibition in blue close to the issued colour	£4500
—	—	—	—	Ditto but in yellow, brown, green, mauve . . . *from*	£4500
—	—	—	—	On matt card, circa 1870 in blue, brown, yellow, orange, green, mauve . . . *from*	£4500
—	—	—	—	On matt card for the 1871 London International Exhibition	£2000
—	8	AM–MA	"OLD"	In blue	£2000

Die Proofs from the De La Rue Archives. Cut down and mounted:

With uncleared corner squares and plate number circles . . . *from* £1500

Die Proofs from the Striking Books:

With uncleared corner squares and plate number circles . . . *from* £1500

Plate Proof

In black £1800

A

B

Die Proofs for the Proposed 2s. Design with Coloured Corner Letters. The die was never used as this value was withdrawn. In black on white glazed card (unless otherwise stated):

Date	*Plate No.*	*Corner Letters*	*Inscr.*	*Additional Inscriptions or Notes*	
(M/S)	8	AM–MA	"NEW"	In blue. "Approved 11 March 1872, 2280/72" (M/S)	£6000
—	8	FM–MF	—	The date is not certain, (around Oct 72) (Type A) .	£2200
—	8	FM–MF	—	Ditto in blue (Pencilled "Oct 72" (M/S)	£5500
(M/S)	—	—	—	"Approved 30 Oct 72" (M/S). The circles for the plate number are small and at the centre of design	£2200
11 Dec 72	7	EH–MR	—	Circles for the plate numbers are in the centre of design and the letters of the value and "POSTAGE" are of different shape from the issued stamp (Type B) . . . .*each*	£2200
11 Dec 72	7	MR–EH	—		
11 Dec 72	7	HE–RM	—		
11 Dec 72	7	RH–HE	—		
19 Dec 72	—	—	B/H		

Die Proofs from the De La Rue Archives. From the Striking Books:

Type B with corner squares and value tablets void . . . . *from* £2000

5s., Type J28 (1867–82)

Plates 1, 2 and 4 were used. Plate 3 was never registered or put to press. Plates 1 and 2 were each of 80 stamps in four panes of 20; in each pane the stamps were in four horizontal rows of five each. The corner lettering ran from AA to AJ in the top row down to HA to HJ in the bottom row. The marginal Plate Numbers lay at the top right and bottom left corners of the sheet. Plate 4 (from a slightly different die) was first registered in the same layout as Plates 1 and 2 but was then altered so that it consisted of 56 stamps in a single pane of seven horizontal rows of eight, lettered AA–AH down to GA–GH. It was re-registered thus on Large Anchor paper, slightly blued. There were no selvedge plate or current numbers on the Anchor sheets.

J28

1867 (1 July). 5s. Rose, Type J28. Wmk Maltese Cross (W8). Perf $15\frac{1}{2} \times 15$.

J121 (=S.G.126/127)	(1)	5s. rose, Plate 1	£5000	£600
	(2)	5s. pale rose, Plate 1	£5000	£600
		Block of four	—	£4000
	a.	Imperforate	£10000	
	s.	Imperforate "Specimen", Types 2, 6 .. *from*	£2500	
	t.	"Specimen", Types 2, 6 *from*	£750	
	u.	"Specimen", Type 2, in blue	£3000	
	v.	"Cancelled", Type 14A		
J122 (=S.G.126/127)		5s. pale rose, Plate 2	£7500	£950
	s.	"Specimen", Types 8, 9 *from*	£800	

Imprimaturs: Plate 1 (*Deep rose*); *Plate* 2 (*Pale rose); Plate* 4 *(Carmine-pink),* from £12000.
Stamps removed from the Plate 1 imprimatur sheet: AE–AJ, BH–BJ, CJ–EJ, FH–FJ, GH–GJ, HA, HF–HJ.
Put to press: Plate 1, 18.4.67; Plate 2, 25.3.74.

1882 (25 November). 5s. Rose, Type J28. Blued Paper. Wmk Large Anchor (W9). Perf 14.

J123 (=S.G.130, 134)		5s. rose, Plate 4	£18000	£3750
	a	White paper	£14000	£2700
	b.	Watermark inverted (blued)	—	£7000
	s.	"Specimen", Type 9	£2500	

Imprimatur: (re-registered after alteration, carmine-pink on slightly blued paper), £14000.
The blueing characteristic of the printing on Anchor paper was chemical and variable. Pure white paper in unused stamps is rare. Used stamps can be bleached white and caution is necessary in buying.

Die Proofs of 5s., Type J28. In black on white glazed card (unless otherwise stated):

Date	*Plate No.*	*Corner Letters*	*Inscr.*	*Additional Inscriptions or Notes*	
1st Die. (a) Plates 1 and 2					
21 Dec 66	—	—	—	Sunken on card	£3000
28 Dec 66	—	—	A/H	Sunken on card	£3000
—	—	—	—	For the 1867 Paris Exhibition	£3000
—	—	—	—	Ditto in yellow, green, lilac, carmine *from*	£10000
—	—	—	—	On matt card, circa 1870, in carmine, brown, yellow, mauve, blue *from*	£10000
—	—	—	—	On matt card for 1871 London International Exhibition	£3000
20 Feb 73	—	—	—		£3000
8 May 73	—	—	B/H		£3000
(b) Intended for Plate 3					
(M/S)	—	—	(M/S)	"Before Striking F.I. 23/4/74" (M/S)	£3000
23 Apr 74	—	—	B/S		£3000
1 May 74	—	—	A/S		£3000
(M/S)	—	—	B/H	"For Approval 9 Apr 73". "Not satisfactory O.H. Augt 74" (M/S)	£3000
2nd Die. Plate 4					
12 Aug 74	—	—	—	"Approved after alteration 13/8/74 O.H." (M/S)	£3000
14 Aug 74	—	—	B/H	Stamped "Before re-hardening" "re" in m/s, initialled "FJ" (M/S)	£3000
22 Aug 74	—	—	A/S		£3000

Die Proofs from the De La Rue Archives. (All with uncleared corner squares and plate number circle.) Cut down and mounted:

Two impressions on the same card (for Plates 2 and 4) inscribed in pencil "After recutting Aug 18th 74" £4000
One impression for Plate 4 with card dated "Aug 14th/74" in manuscript £2500

Cut down and unmounted:
In pale brown or green .... *from* £3000

Die Proofs from the Striking Books:
For Plates 1, 2 or 4 . . . . *from* £2000

Plate Proofs

Plate 2 in black on card £1800
Plate 4 in black on white wove paper £1800

Colour Trials. Plate 2, Perf 14

On white paper watermarked Maltese Cross, in carmine-pink, Venetian red, orange, yellow, yellow-olive, olive-green, yellow-green, dull green, blue-green, light blue, Prussian blue, grey-blue, mauve, purple, reddish purple, purple-brown, red-brown, olive-bistre, slate-grey . . . . *from* —
Without watermark, in brown-lake on buff, rose on lilac, green on green, blue on green, brown on yellow . . . . *from* —

10s., Type J29 (1878–83)

Only one plate (Plate 1) was used for this value. The plate was laid down in the same four-pane Maltese Cross watermark form as the 5s. Plates 1 and 2 (see J121 notes above) and with similarly placed selvedge markings. With the introduction of the Large Anchor watermarked paper the plate was altered to the same "single pane of 56" form as had been the 5s. Plate 4. There was no selvedge plate numbers or current numbers on the Anchor sheets. An official reproduction was made of this stamp.

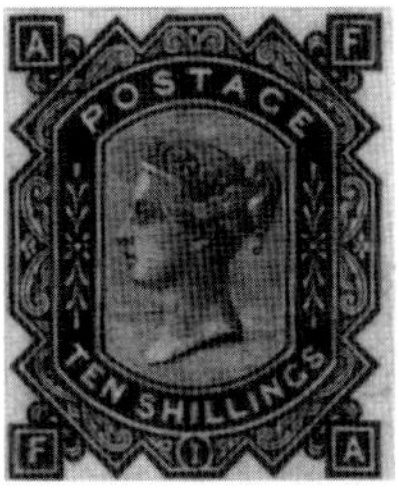

J29

1878 (26 September). 10s. Greenish Grey, Type J29. Wmk Maltese Cross (W8). Perf $15\frac{1}{2} \times 15$.

J124 (=S.G.128) 10s. greenish grey, Plate 1 . . . . £38000 £2500
t. "Specimen", Types 8, 9 . . . . *from* £2500

Imprimatur: £20000.
Put to press: 6.8.78.

1883 (February). 10s. Grey-green, Type J29. Blued Paper. Wmk Large Anchor (W9). Perf 14.

J125 (=S.G.131, 135) 10s. grey-green, Plate 1 . . . . £60000 £4500
a. Greenish grey on white paper £60000 £3500
t. "Specimen", Type 9 (blued) £5500

Imprimatur (re-registered after alteration): £28000. Overprinted "Specimen". Type 9 (formerly listed as No. J125*s*), £30000.

The blueing of the paper is very slight

Die Proofs of 10s., Type J29. In black on white glazed card (unless otherwise stated):

Date	*Plate No.*	*Corner Letters*	*Inscr.*	*Additional Inscriptions or Notes*	
—	—	—	—	Progressive Die Proof (probably 16 to 18 April 1878)	£2000
25 Apr 78	—	—	—	Progressive Die Proof showing minor differences .	£2000
26 Apr 78	—	—	—	Ditto	£2000
29 Apr 78	—	—	—	Ditto	£2000
30 Apr 78	—	—	—	Ditto but with pencil markings showing work to be done	£2000
30 Apr 78	—	—	—	Ditto but without markings	£2000
1 May 78	—	—	—	Ditto but with pencil markings showing work to be done	£2000
1 May 78	—	—	—	Ditto but without markings	£2000
2 May 78	—	—	—	Ditto but with pencil markings showing work to be done	£2000
2 May 78	—	—	—	Ditto but without markings	£2000
3 May 78	—	—	—	Ditto	£2000
4 May 78	—	—	B/H	Ditto	£2000
6 May 78	—	—	B/H	Ditto	£2000

Die Proofs from the De La Rue Archives. Cut down and mounted or unmounted:

With uncleared corner squares and plate number circle . . . . *from* £1800

Die Proof from the Striking Books:
With uncleared corner squares and plate number circles . . . . *from* £1800

Plate Proof

In black on thick white wove paper £1800

Colour Trials

Imperforate on white paper, watermarked Maltese Cross, in orange, blue, mauve, brown, bistre, greenish grey, all overprinted "Specimen", Type 9 . . . . . . *from* £1800

Perforated 14 on white paper watermarked Maltese Cross, in brown-lake, carmine-pink, Venetian red, orange, yellow, yellow-olive, olive-green, yellow-green, dull green, blue-green, light blue, blue, Prussian blue, grey-blue, mauve, purple, purple-brown, brown-purple, red-brown, olive-bistre, bistre . . . . *from* —

Perf 14 on coloured paper without watermark in brown-lake on buff, lake on rose, red on orange, red on yellow, green on green, bistre on lemon, olive-brown on buff, greenish grey on greyish . . . . *from* —

£1, Type J30 (1878–82)

One plate only (Plate 1) was used. The features of the plate were similar to the J121 and J124 5s. and 10s. plates and like those plates the £1 plate was altered at the time of the change to Large Anchor watermarked paper.

J30

1878 (26 September). £1. Brown-lilac, Type J30. Wmk Maltese Cross (W8). Perf $15\frac{1}{2} \times 15$.

J126 (=S.G.129)	£1 brown-lilac, Plate 1	£50000	£3750
	t. "Specimen", Types 9	£4500	

Imprimatur: £28000.
Put to press: 6.8.78.

1882 (December). £1 Brown-lilac, Type J30. Blued paper. Wmk Large Anchor (W9). Perf 14.

J127 (=S.G.132, 136)	£1 brown-lilac, Plate 1	£80000	£8000
	a White paper	£90000	£7000
	t. "Specimen", Type 9 (blued)	£7500	
	u. "Specimen", Types 6, 9 (white) .... *from*	£7000	

Imprimatur (re-registered after alteration): £35000. Overprinted "Specimen", Type 9 (formerly listed as No. J127s), £28000.

The blueing of the paper is very slight.

Die Proofs of £1., Type J30. In black on white glazed card (unless otherwise stated):

Date	*Plate No.*	*Corner Letters*	*Inscr.*	*Additional Inscriptions or Notes*	
—	—	—	—	Progressive Die Proof with outer frame lines (probably 16 April 1878)	£3000
16 Apr 78	—	—	—	Ditto	£3000
17 Apr 78	—	—	—	Ditto	£3000
18 Apr 78	—	—	—	Ditto	£3000
23 Apr 78	—	—	—	Ditto	£3000
25 Apr 78	—	—	—	Ditto but with outer frame lines removed	£3000
26 Apr 78	—	—	—	Ditto	£3000
27 Apr 78	—	—	—	Ditto	£3000
29 Apr 78	—	—	—	Ditto	£3000
30 Apr 78	—	—	B/H	In finished state	£3000
11 May 78	—	—	A/S	Initialled "W.G." (M/S)	

Die Proofs from the De La Rue Archives. Cut down and mounted or unmounted:

With uncleared corner squares and plate number circle .... *from* £2000

Die Proofs from the Striking Books:
With uncleared corner squares and plate number circles £2000

Plate Proof

In black, no watermark, imperforate £2500
In black on unsurfaced paper, perf $15\frac{1}{2} \times 15$ £2500

Colour Trials

Imperforate on white paper watermarked Maltese Cross, in orange, blue, mauve, purple, brown-lilac, bistre, greenish grey, deep grey-black all overprinted "Specimen", Type 9 .... *from* £2200

Perf 14 on white paper watermarked Maltese Cross, in brown-lake, carmine-pink, Venetian red (shades), orange, yellow, yellow-olive, olive-green, yellow-green, dull green, blue-green, light blue, blue, Prussian blue, grey-blue, mauve, purple, purple-brown, red-brown, olive-bistre, slate-grey .... *from* —

Perf 14 on coloured paper without watermark in lake on buff, rose on lemon, rose on lilac, red on yellow, green on green, greenish grey on buff ..... *from* —

Essay of Prince Consort

An essay of Prince Albert in blue was prepared but not adopted .... —

£5, Type J31 (1882)

Essays for the design of this stamp are shown and described under "Essays for the Unified Series and High Values".

One plate only (Plate 1) was used. This was originally the "Telegraphs" £5 plate. Type **L31**, and was altered by the substitution of the word "Postage". "POSTAGE" was printed in a separate operation so it is possible for it to be out of register with the rest of the design.

The plate was of 56 stamps disposed in two panes of 28 in seven horizontal rows of four. No selvedge numbers appeared. Each stamp bore two Large Anchor watermarks. The corner letters ran from AA to DN, the reverse of the usual, for here the letter D in the lower left square (for example) denotes the fourth vertical row, not the fourth horizontal row. Shades varied with more orange and less vermilion on the first printing and less orange in the subsequent printings.

The paper was at first blued and varied from one sheet to another. Our prices are for markedly blued paper, stamps only slightly blued being worth rather less.

This stamp was printed on white paper from March 1889.

Hand-painted £5 essays were created for the 1883 issue (see Section KC).

J31

1882 (21 March). £5 Orange, Type J31. Blued paper. Wmk Large Anchor (W9). Perf 14.

J128 (=S.G.133, 137)		£5 orange, Plate 1	£45000	£11000
	a	White paper	£9000	£4000
	s.	"Specimen", Type 9, 11 (blued paper) ... *from*	£2400	
	t.	"Specimen", Types 9, 11, 16 (white paper) ... *from*	£2800	
	u.	"Specimen", Types 9 and 11 (white paper) on one stamp	£4500	
	v.	"Cancelled", Types 14, 18 ... *from*	£4500	

Imprimatur: blued paper, £20000.

Put to press: Jan./Feb. 1882.

There are many frame break varieties which are not as prominent as those found on the £1 Type **K10**, stamps JC and TA, but they are of interest to the specialist.

Die Proofs

Telegraph stamp with upper and lower tablets partially overprinted "POST" and "FIVE P" endorsed "10 NOV 76" ... £9500

The die proofs and plate proofs of the unaltered Telegraph design formerly listed here will now be found in Section LC.

SECTIONS KA–KE

1880–1900 Surface-Printed Issues

General Notes

Introduction. The 1880–1900 Surface-Printed issues are listed in Sections KA to KE, in the following order: KA The "Provisional" Issue, 1 January 1880; KB 1d. Lilac 12 July 1881; KC The Unfied Issue, 1 January 1883; KD Before and After the Stamp Committee, 1884–85; KE The "Jubilee" Issue, 1 January 1887.

Termination of the Perkins, Bacon Contract. In 1878 the Board of Inland Revenue were negotiating with Perkins, Bacon & Co. for the renewal of their contract to print the $\frac{1}{2}$d., 1d., $1\frac{1}{2}$d. and 2d. postage stamps when the Post Office intimated that the current low values were unsafe in that the cancellations could easily be removed without damage to the stamps and recommended that they be printed "in precisely the same way as the Stamps of higher value, both as regards the mode of manufacture and the printing in fugitive colours".

There were also other objections to the line-engraved process and the change in artistic tastes in the late Victorian period also contributed to the feeling that it was time to have some new designs. Hence on 23 December 1878 the Inland Revenue gave Perkins, Bacon & Co. six months notice of termination of the contracts for printing the low values.

The 1879 Tender. In due course, on 3 April 1879, the Board of Inland Revenue invited seven firms to submit tenders to print the 1d. value only, the closing date being 17 May. The firms were Perkins, Bacon, De La Rue, McCorquodale, Charles Skipper & East, James Truscott, Waterlow, and Bradbury, Wilkinson. In the event six tenders were received by the closing date as James Truscott did not tender.

Each firm was provided with ten sheets of thin wove paper, size $20\frac{1}{4} \times 10\frac{7}{8}$ in. (514 × 276 mm) with Anchor watermark, Type **W10**. Most of the printed stamps actually submitted were on this paper, every sheet of which had to be accounted for. Stamps on the market come from proofs retained by the printers, which are on unwatermarked paper.

The final decision was made by the Board of Inland Revenue on the basis of a report from Mr. George B. Robertson, then controller of the Stamping Department of the Inland Revenue. The report is in Post Office Archives and references are made to it under the illustrations of the designs submitted, which appear below under "Essays for the 1879 Tender for the 1d Value".

However, it was a foregone conclusion that the contract should be awarded to De La Rue since the report of the Government Chemist showed that only De La Rue's work satisfied all the requirements which had been specified, particularly with regard to the use of fugitive inks which prevented the removal of cancellations without damage to the stamps. Accordingly, their tender was accepted on 27 June 1879. The contract was for a period of seven years.

Paper. De La Rue revolutionised British stamp production. Imperial Crown watermarked paper was to be used for values up to and including the 1s. It was set as two panes of 120, ten horizontal rows of 12, one above the other with an exact one-stamp high unwatermarked and unprinted gutter in between rows 10(J) and 11(K).

W12 *(Imperial) Crown*

The paper, machine-made off white wove, came from R. D. Turner & Company of Roughway Mill, Malling, Kent in 480 set "mill" sheets approx. 22 × 22 inches, in one ream (500 sheet) packets.

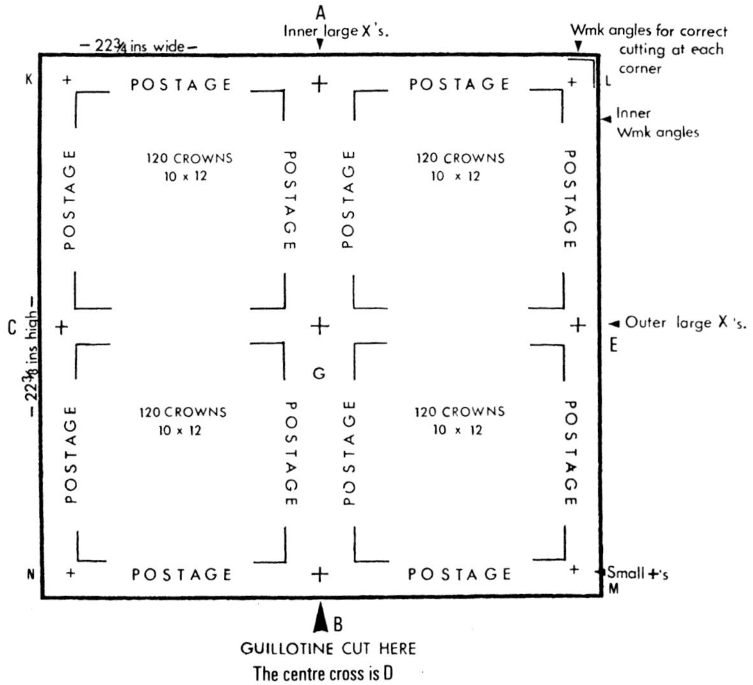

Diagram of 480 Crown Mill Sheet
(Everything within the outer rectangle is part of the watermark
except the references to the number of crowns)

For 240 set printing and for the issue of ½d., 1d., and 1½d. values in 240 set "issue" sheets the mill sheet was divided down the centre, as shown ("cut 1"). Further cuts "2", "3" and "4" were made to produce issue sheets for other values as below:

2d., 2½d.	120 set, pane size ("cut 2", 10 rows of 12)
3d., 4d., 6d.	40 set ("cut 3", 10 rows of 4)
5d.	60 set ("cut 3a", 10 rows of 6)
1s.	20 set ("cut 4", 5 rows of 4)

Around the Imperial Crown "bits" were other "bits" e.g. corner pieces of the watermark which enable left and right halves of the mill sheets to be recognised from most corner pieces.

Diagram X shows the crosses on left sheets and diagram Y those on right sheets. They are mirror images of each other. Cross K shows to the left above row 1, while cross N shows to the left below row 20 on left sheets. Cross L shows to the right above row 1 and cross M to the right below row 20 on right sheets.

Cross C to the left of the centre gutter indicates a left sheet and cross E to the right, a right sheet. Both lie closer to the stamps than the crosses, A, D and B, down the centre of the mill sheet which are almost never seen complete. They appear to the right of left sheets and the left of right sheets.

The 480 set mill sheet arrangement was unchanged to 1911 except for the addition of "papermaker's" letters in the middle (Section KE). These identified dandy rolls from which mill sheets came. The dandy roll had "bits" for two mill sheets side by side.

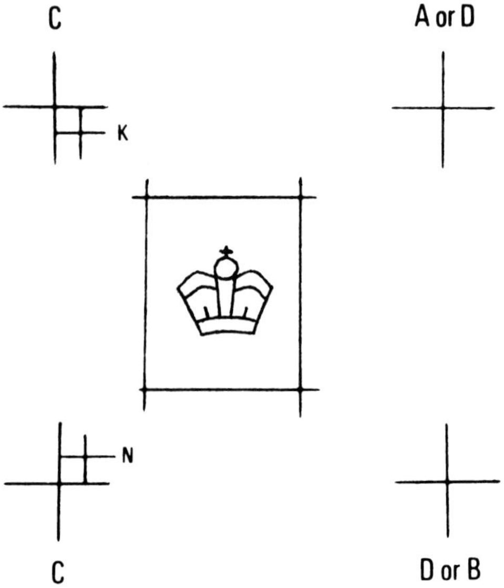

Diagram X. Left Sheet Corner Crosses
(*Actual size*)

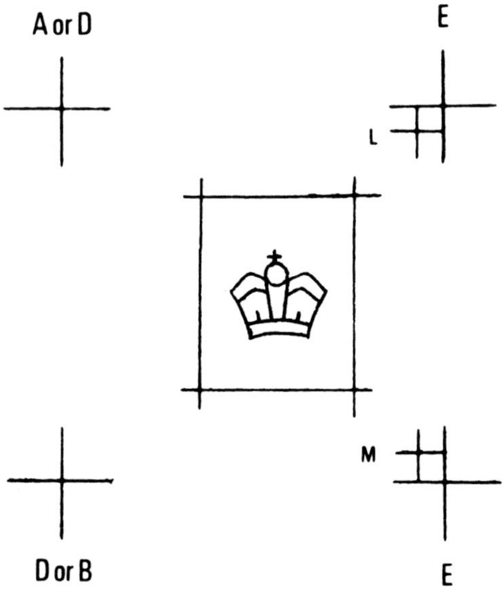

Diagram Y. Right Sheet Corner Crosses
(*Actual size*)

Few watermark varieties, except inverted, are known with the most significant being inverted "POSTAGE" at the bottom, but placed in the margin inverted "POSTAGE" is normal. Other faults exist such as damaged "POSTAGE" and misplaced Imperial Crown.

Some paper is found with a ribbed appearance, previously called "repp paper". It was probably caused by ribbed wrapping paper during storage in stacks and is only seen on sheet selvedges.

The high values were printed on new Anchor watermark paper in two panes of 56, seven horizontal rows of eight, one above the other, again with an unprinted centre gutter between rows 7(G) and 8(H). The paper was the same quality as the Imperial Crown, mill sheets being 224 set.

Blue Paper. Anchor paper was already blued by the addition of small quantities of Prussian blue to the pulp vat to prevent the removal of cancellation ink. It reacted with the ink to leave an indelible mark when attempts were made to remove it. In the absence of new instructions Turners continued to add Prussian blue to the new paper causing early printings of high values to appear on blued paper. In 1884, following public comment, it became clear that at least one low value stamp would have to be printed on blue paper. The practice of adding Prussian blue to Anchor paper ceased in 1884.

Perforation. A failure of communications at Somerset House resulted in the perforation implications of the De La Rue proposals being not fully understood until after their tender had been accepted. The dimensions of De La Rue's mill sheets produced component stamp sheets which were both too wide and too long for two of the three machines on which they would have to be perforated. As the size of the mill sheets could not be altered, De La Rue offered to pay the costs of adapting the machines. Even if this was possible, it would have been both expensive and time consuming. As Somerset House was unwilling to be without the machines at a particularly busy time of year Robertson proposed a simple solution. The mill sheets, on which two sheets of stamps were printed side by side, were to be divided in half with both the remaining side margins, and those at the top and bottom, trimmed to a size suitable for the machines. Final instructions to this effect were issued to De La Rue a few days before production of the new 1d. stamp (No. K3) began.

All issued stamps in Sections KA to KE are comb perf 14. Stamps with line perf 12 are trial perforations made for the 1884 Stamp Committee.

The Consolidated Contract. Is proposing the contract, De La Rue provided a series of convincing arguments in favour of consolidation, but failed to mention perforation. This matter was only raised much later by the Inland Revenue who indicated their willingness to agree a consolidated contract subject to certain conditions, among which was that De La Rue should assume responsibility for stamp perforation without any additional charge. The firm immediately agreed to this, and proposed that they should acquire Somerset House's perforating machinery. The transfer began on 7 June 1880 and was completed by the end of August. De La Rue assumed full responsibility for perforation from 1 September.

Die Proofs. The listing of die proofs follows the style used in Section J and the remarks in the General Notes to Section J relating to die proofs and to the De La Rue archives also apply here.

The listing of the conventional die proofs on glazed card is followed by the cut down die proofs on sunken card from the archives and then the material from the Striking Books. From this period the Striking Books are generally undamaged, so most of the impressions cut from them are in fine condition. The low values usually comprise a single impression with records of leads taken over a series of dates.

De La Rue Head Dies. De La Rue made a large number of head dies. The exact relationship of these, one to another, and to those used for the issued stamps is currently obscure. Many bear close relationship to the head dies of issued stamps but are not those actually used. Care should therefore be exercised in purchasing head die proofs purporting to be those of the issued stamps. Later head dies are listed in Sections KC–KE.

Plate Proofs. These were generally taken in black on white wove paper or card. Just before printing, when working up the colour, they were also taken in the colours in which the stamps were printed on rough buff paper, but these were generally destroyed as printers' waste. They also exist in colour on other coloured papers, mainly in the 1887 "Jubilee" issue.

Plate and Current Numbers. Every plate with the Sovereign's head on it received two numbers in sequence, one denoting the plate number of the particular design and the other a current number in a sequential series. All plates (postage, fiscal, revenue) were recorded in the stock book kept at Somerset House for the purpose. Other plates, e.g. duty plates, were numbered in their own series, but record was kept in the same book.

Two small deformed "T"s appear in the top and bottom centres of every sheet above and below the perforation gutter between 6th(F) and 7th(G) stamps on Crown paper and 4th(D) and 5th(E) on Anchor paper. They served to locate the sheets on the "lay" table for correct perforation.

Dies and Plates. All dies and plates were the property of the Inland Revenue. Stock books were kept and regularly signed by the senior official at the Inland Revenue. Up to 1889 any creation or destruction required a Warrant and thereafter a Secretarial letter.

Colour Trials. The De La Rue designs submitted for the 1879 tender were in black on card bearing the statement: "It is suggested that the colour should not be determined upon until the plates are completed and proof-sheets, in a variety of colours, can be submitted." It then became standard practice to wait until new designs had been approved before proceeding to make dies and plates and then to submit colour trials from the plates. These were usually in sheets of 120 from which samples were sent to the Post Office, Inland Revenue, etc., and the remainder of the sheets were eventually sent to the Inland Revenue.

Colour trials from 1880 were related to single values as listed below or were created in connection with the 1884 Stamp Committee when current plates and dies were used on a large scale (see Section KD).

Imprimaturs. A registration sheet continued to be taken from new plates at the time they were put to press, or shortly after, until 1889 when the procedure was confined to the first plate of a new design. It was generally imperforate. At the same time other imperforate sheets were taken and are the source of "imperforate" stamps which cannot be matched to the registration sheets.

"Specimen" and "Cancelled" Stamps and Protective Underprints. The notes in the General Notes to Section J also apply to stamps listed in Sections KA to KE and reference is made to Appendixes 3 and 2 respectively.

Essays and Die Proofs of the 1880–1900 Surface-Printed Issues

Essays for the 1879 Tender for the 1d. Value

Perkins, Bacon. Perkins, Bacon had little experience in making dies for surface-printing. Although Robertson commended the head he criticised the frames, owing to the fineness of the lines. The illustration (*Fig.* 1) is taken from stamps without watermark which are on the market.

Fig. 1. *Essay submitted by Perkins, Bacon, engraved by Ridgway and known in deep brown (illustration reduced)*

Bradbury, Wilkinson. Bradbury, Wilkinson submitted seven designs, of which No. 2 is illustrated in *Fig.* 2. Robertson liked these and they were returned to the printers whose property they remain. However, they are now on loan to Post Office Heritage Services. There was also an eighth design (not numbered), of a 5s. stamp similar to the Falkland Islands stamps which Bradbury, Wilkinson had printed by line-engraving. Apparently Robertson thought that this design had been submitted as part of the tender; he considered it to be inferior, and unsuitable for surface-printing. There is a copy of this eighth design in the R. M. Phillips collection held by Post Office Heritage Services, so that it is possible that others exist. Other examples of surface-printed designs were supplied, including the Cape of Good Hope style dummy design illustrated in *Fig.* 3.

Fig. 2 *Submitted design*

Fig. 3. *Dummy stamp*

Waterlow. Waterlow submitted nineteen essays in various colours similar to *Fig.* 4, together with a recommendation in favour of the line-engraved process, which naturally ruled them out of order (in fact Robertson made no mention of them in his report). The essays are inscribed "QUEENSLAND" and were connected with this tender.

Fig. 4 *Waterlow essay inscribed "QUEENSLAND" (illustration reduced)*

Charles Skipper & East. Charles Skipper & East submitted the two designs shown in *Fig.* 5. The head of Queen Victoria was identical to that struck on medals for the Maori Wars and the Abyssinia Expedition of 1868–69, which were the work of Alfred Benjamin Wyon, a close relative of William Wyon. Robertson was unimpressed by these and in any case the St. George design was inadmissible.

The dummy stamp with right-facing profile of Ceres instead of Queen Victoria, illustrated in *Fig.* 6 was among those submitted on the watermarked paper as examples of surface-printing which Robertson considered to be very good. Similar examples (unwatermarked) and perforated exist with head facing left.

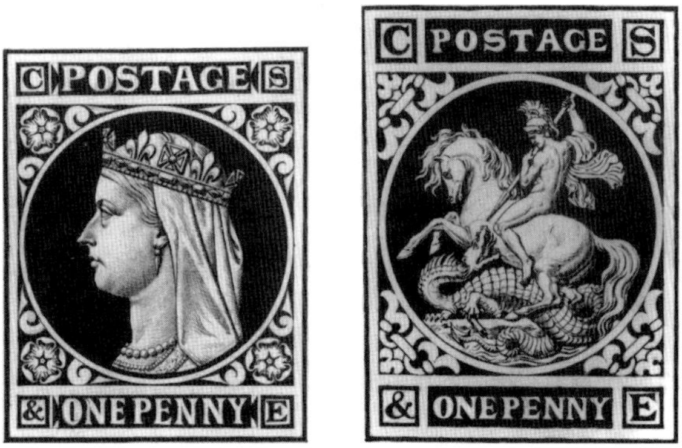

Fig. 5. *Two essays submitted by Charles Skipper & East*

Fig. 6. *Dummy stamp by Charles Skipper & East*

McCorquodale. McCorquodale submitted six designs, two of which are shown in *Fig.* 7. They were pesented in two colours, the heads being cut from existing stamps and only the borders being new designs. Robertson did not like them as they were unsuitable for monocolour printing; nor did he like the quality of McCorquodale's surface-printing or inks. Dummy stamps (*Fig.* 8), engraved by Hooper, may or may not have been submitted as samples of McCorquodale's work. Several examples of the design exist, lettered JA, printed in rosy mauve on blued paper with small anchor watermark.

Fig. 7. *Two designs submitted by McCorquodale*

Fig. 8. *Dummy stamps by McCorquodale*

De La Rue. De La Rue submitted four cards of die proofs. The cards were lettered A to D and each had a different head set in the same six frame designs. The heads in particular were engraved with all the requirements of surface-printing in mind. Robertson was very impressed by these and he particularly recommended the head and frame lettered D on Card A as shown in *Fig.* 9. This was the one accepted by the Board.

The original Card A was acquired by R. M. Phillips and Cards B and D are also in Post Office Heritage Services, but the original Card C was missing. However, De La Rue put their duplicate set on the market, on which each design is marked "Cancelled" in manuscript, and Card C was purchased by the National Postal Museum (now Post Office Heritage Services) to complete their set. The other three duplicate cards and the original Card C are in private collections. They bear no letters above the designs and each card is dated "MAY 17th 79".

Fig. 9. De La Rue's design lettered D on card A was the one selected (illustration reduced)

De La Rue also submitted five hand-painted essays in red-brown and white on card size 25 × 28 mm, similar to the one illustrated in *Fig.* 10. They were placed on the market and all except the one illustrated were purchased by the Post Office. They are lettered KK or KM–MK.

It is believed that the die proof shown in *Fig.* 11, an adaption of the Inland Revenue design (Type **L20**) introduced in 1868, was submitted at the same time. These die proofs are on the market and an unmounted example was sold from the De La Rue archives, but a small sheet exists with a manuscript inscription stating that it was from the firm of Charles Skipper & East. Essays in various colours also exist in the design. Both imperforate examples and others line perforated 14 × $12\frac{1}{2}$ are known, each on thin paper with traces of a paper-makers watermark. The precise origin of these essays and their purpose has not been established. Postally used examples, perforated and printed in pale blue or dull rose are known, both on and off cover.

Fig. 10. *Hand painted De La Rue essay*

Fig. 11. *Die proof adapted from the Inland Revenue Type* **L20**

Individual Head and composite die proofs by De La Rue on white glazed card are also on the market and these are listed and priced below (and see *Fig.* 12).

Head A is with diadem and chignon ribbon; Head B is with diadem but no ribbon; Head C is with Imperial Crown and chignon ribbon; Head D is with Imperial Crown but without ribbon.

Head Dies only, in various stages	*from*	£1500
Composite Die Proofs of Heads A to D with Frames 1 to 6 . .	*from*	£1800

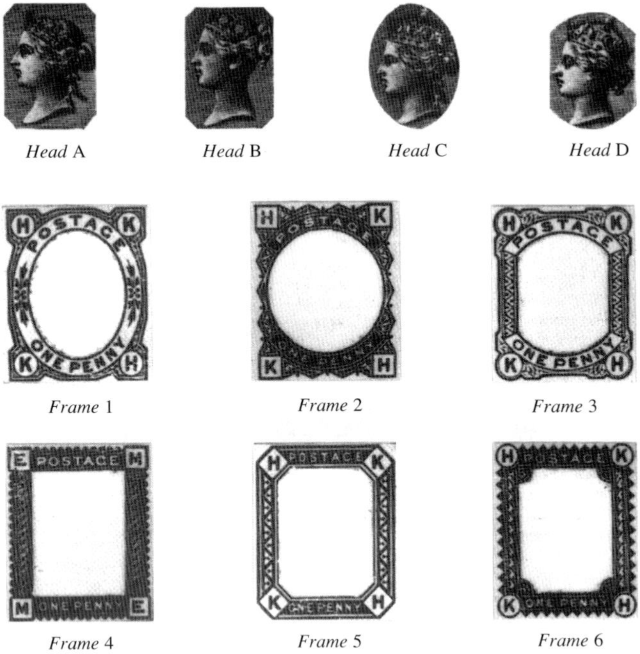

Fig. 12. *De La Rue die proofs*

Essays for the 1880 Tender for the ½d., 1½d. and 2d. Values

Details of the 1880 Tender are obscure, but tender documents were sent out on 7 January 1880. Perkins, Bacon and De La Rue were invited to submit designs although it appeared a foregone conclusion that De La Rue would secure the new contract. The Perkins Bacon inks did not meet with the approval of the Post Office and De La Rue were advised that they had been successful on 19 February 1880.

Perkins, Bacon. Perkins, Bacon submitted designs similar to those they had produced for the 1d. value and these are in the R. M. Phillips collection. Those that are on the market come from printer's trials. All were engraved by William Ridgway.

The three 2d. essays of those in *Fig.* 13 exist in pale brown in a block of nine (three of each design), imperforate. It is not known how the ½d. and 1½d. were made up, although they are known in a vertical strip of five comprising ½d., 2d., 1½d., 2d. and 2d., and block (6 × 6) of the 1d in *Fig.* 1 in deep dull blue, imperforate. The paper used for these essays was cream, gummed and unwatermarked.

The designs shown in *Fig.* 14 exist in two forms: (a) imperforate in a block of twenty-four comprising three rows, each containing ½d., ½d., 2d., 1½d., 1½d., 2d., ½d., ½d., in brown-red; (b) perforated in a block of twenty-four comprising four rows, the first two each having two 4½d., three 1½d. and one 2d. and the second two having four ½d. and two 2d., in black, grey-blue and also on lilac. All eight designs exist as a composite die proof in red-brown on thin paper. Single perforated examples of the ½d. are known in grey-blue, salmon, red-brown and turquoise-green, which may be colour trials.

Fig. 13. *Perkins, Bacon essays*

Fig. 14. *Perkins, Bacon die proofs*

Essays for the 1880 $1\frac{1}{2}$d. and 2d.

De La Rue. Although De La Rue did not formally tender under the terms and conditions of the invitation it appears that they were quite confident of obtaining a consolidated contract to print all classes of stamps on their own terms as previously stated.

Designs were not submitted until 7 February 1880, but before a decision was taken it was decided to dispense with the corner letters.

Fig. 15 *Typical De La Rue* $1\frac{1}{2}$*d. and 2d. essays (illustrations reduced)*

Fig. 16. De La Rue Frame 7

On 27 and 31 May, two new essays were submitted but were rejected. The essays for accepted designs of both values were submitted on 25 June 1880.

In 1976, De La Rue put on the market eleven essays for the $1\frac{1}{2}$d. and six for the 2d.; of these the then National Postal Museum acquired four of each (two are shown in *Fig.* 15).
Essays hand-painted on card 24 × 28 mm in pink, red and white, lettered IJ–JI:

Various designs for $1\frac{1}{2}$d.	*from*	£5000
Two different designs for 2d.	*from*	£9000

The following die proofs are on the market and were presumably made at about the same time as the essays described above.
Die Proofs combining Head D with some of the frames used for the 1879 tender and an additional Frame 7 (see *Fig.* 16):

$\frac{1}{2}$d. in green with Frame 2	*each from* £1800
$1\frac{1}{2}$d. in black with Frame 1	
$1\frac{1}{2}$d. in rose with Frame 1	
$1\frac{1}{2}$d. in black with Frame 3	
2d. in brown with Frame 7	

Key to 1880–1900 Surface-Printed Issues. The table below is intended to give the user of this catalogue a condensed view of the surface-printed issues in Sections KA to KE. The page numbers in the extreme right-hand column aid rapid location of the relevant part of the catalogue listing.

Spec. Nos.	*S.G. Nos.*	*Description*	*Date of Issue*	*Page No.*
K1	164/5	½d. green	14.10.80	311
K17A	187	½d. slate-blue	1.4.84	331
K27	197/e	½d. vermilion	1.1.87	350
K28	213	½d. blue-green	17.4.1900	354
K3	166	1d. Venetian red	1.1.80	311
K7	170/1	1d. lilac, Die I	12.7.81	316
K8	172/4	1d. lilac, Die II	13.12.81	316
K4	167	1½d. Venetian red	14.10.80	312
K18	188	1½d. lilac	1.4.84	331
K29	198	1½d. purple and green	1.1.87	355
K5	168/a	2d. rose	8.12.80	313
K19	189	2d. lilac	1.4.84	332
K30	199/200	2d. green and red	1.1.87	357
K20	190	2½d. lilac	1.4.84	332
K31	201	2½d. purple on blue paper	1.1.87	359
K8A	159	3d. on 3d. lilac	1.1.83	321
K21	191	3d. lilac	1.4.84	333
K32	202/4	3d. purple on yellow paper	1.1.87	361
K22	192	4d. dull green	1.4.84	333
K33	205/a	4d. green and brown	1.1.87	363
K34	206a	4½d. green and carmine	15.9.92	365
K6	169	5d. indigo	15.3.81	314
K23	193	5d. dull green	1.4.84	334
K35	207	5d. purple and blue, Die I	1.1.87	367
K36	207a	5d. purple and blue, Die II	1888	367
K8B	162	6d. on 6d. lilac	1.1.83	321
K24	194	6d. dull green	1.4.84	334
K37	208/a	6d. purple on rose-red paper	1.1.87	370
K25	195	9d. dull green	1.8.83	335
K38	209	9d. purple and blue	1.1.87	371
K39	210b	10d. purple and carmine	24.2.90	372
K8C	—	1s. purple	1.1.82	321
K26	196	1s. dull green	1.4.84	335
K40	211	1s. green	1.1.87	376
K41	214	1s. green and carmine	11.7.1900	377
K9	175	2s. 6d. lilac on blued paper	2.7.83	326
K10	178/9	2s. 6d. lilac	1884	327
K11	176	5s. rose on blued paper	1.4.84	327
K12	180/1	5s. rose	1884	327
K13	177/a	10s. ultramarine on blued paper	1.4.84	328
K14	182/3a	10s. ultramarine	1884	328
K15	185	£1 brown-lilac, wmk Crowns	1.4.84	328
K16	186	£1 brown-lilac, wmk Orbs	1.2.88	329
K17	212	£1 green	28.1.91	329

Note that the £5 value with the above series is listed as J128.

SECTION KA

The "Provisional" Issue, 1 January 1880

The ½d., 1d., 1½d. and 2d. stamps replaced the corresponding values of the Line-Engraved stamps at the termination of the contract with Perkins, Bacon & Co. In the case of the 1d. and 2d. this meant the disappearance of designs which had done service for nearly 40 years.

Only the 1d. stamp carried corner lettering; this being on the usual plan of AA–AL down to TA–TL. No plate numbers appeared on any value and indeed were never again shown in the design of British stamps.

The designs of the ½d. and 1d. followed from those submitted for the 1d. contract, but new ones were created for the 1½d. and 2d. The 5d. was required for correspondence with India and China paying double rate (1 ounce). A hand-painted essay in the issued design, except that it had corner letters and was for a 9d., was amongst those submitted on 31 May 1880. It now became the issued 5d. Printing was delayed while the colour was decided. Colour trials in shades of blue (following U.P.U. guidelines) and in yellow were submitted on 30 October, but were rejected as the former was too similar to the 2½d., and yellow was too weak.

Apart from those listed below, the other designs in use at the end of 1879 continued unchanged, except that they were printed on either Imperial Crown or Anchor paper. The stamps involved are: 2½d. J23/25, 3d. J45/45A, 4d. J68/69, 6d. J88/89, 1s. J116/117, 5s. J123, 10s. J125, £1 J127.

Prices for Stamps in Unused Condition

Prices are for lightly hinged examples. Unmounted prices are also provided for No. K17 (£1 green, 1891) and Nos. K27 to K41 (½d. to 1 shilling ("Jubilee" Issue)).

Prices for Stamps in Used Condition

The notes about condition given at the end of the General Notes to Section J also apply to Sections KA to KE. The prices for well centred lightly used stamps can be calculated by adding the following percentages to the prices quoted: **50%** for K7/17 and K27/41, **75%** for K1 and K3/6, **100%** for K17A–26.

K1

K2

K3

K4

K5

1880 (14 October). ½d. Green, Type K1. Wmk Crown. Perf 14.

K1 (=S.G.164/5)	(1)	½d. deep green	45·00	12·00
	(2)	½d. pale green	45·00	18·00
		Block of four	£225	70·00
		Used on cover	†	22·00
	a.	Imperforate (shade 1)	£1800	
	b.	No watermark)	£5500	
	c.	Watermark inverted	—	£325
	s.	"Specimen", Type 9	55·00	

Imprimaturs: Plates 1, 2, 3, 6, 7 (*all pale green*), *each* £220; *Plate* 8 (*deep green*), £300.

Plates 2 and 3 were registered 18 August 1880 and Plate 1 not until 23 August.

Plates used were as indicated by the imprimaturs; Plates 4 and 5 were spoiled.

There are two imprimatur sheets of Plate 8 in deep green and stamps removed were from the top of the sheets. A pair is known of No. K1a from the bottom of the sheet.

Die Proofs. In black on thick glazed card:

Endorsed "16 JUL 80" in blue and "BEFORE HARDENING" in red	£1000
Endorsed "16 JUL 80 BEFORE HARDENING" all in black	£1000
Endorsed "16 JUL 80 BEFORE HARDENING"	£1000
Endorsed "3 NOV 80 AFTER STRIKING"	£1000
Basic Die Proof. No endorsements	£1000

Die Proofs from the De La Rue Archives

Cut down and mounted	£1000
From the Striking Books	£900

Plate Proof

In black on thick white wove paper	£550

Trial Cancellations. Watermark Crown, perf 13½ × 14

In pale green shade close to the issued colour and cancelled with squared circle "LONDON, E.C., H Au 11,80" on unaddressed envelope	£3500
As before but dated 12 August 1880	£3500

From 1879 controlled experiments using the first squared circle postmarks were carried out at the London E.C. and Inland Branch offices. It is likely that the above were colour trials used in this experiment.

This stamp is known cancelled "BO1" (Alexandria type). This was probably from cancellation removal trials conducted by De La Rue.

For ½d. slate-blue (formerly No. K2), see No. K17A in Sections KC.

1880 (1 January). 1d. Venetian Red, Type K2. Wmk Crown. Perf 14.

K3 (=S.G.166)		1d. Venetian red (shades)	22·00	12·00
		Block of four	90·00	70·00
		Used on cover	†	25·00
	a.	Imperforate	£1800	
	b.	Watermark inverted	—	£250
	c.	Deeply blued paper		
	d.	S joined to frame above, damage above this and spot ater T (AB)	—	75·00
	e.	Line below G broken (QD)	—	60·00
	s.	"Specimen", Type 9	90·00	

Imprimaturs: Plates 1, 2, 4 *to* 10, 12 *to* 33, *each* £200. The first was registered 28 October 1879. Imperforate stamps lettered other than AA to AL, BA to BL, CA, CB, CJ to CL or DL do not come from any of the imprimatur sheets.

The first and later another example of this stamp was reported in 1968 to exist with watermark Orb (Fiscal Orb), but until we have evidence of further examples or more information is forthcoming we will defer listing.

This issue contains many frame breaks and constant varieties but they are mostly of minor significance.

Die Proofs. In black on white glazed card (unless otherwise stated):

Date	Corner Letters	Inscr.	Additional Inscriptions or Notes	
Head Die only, used in the production of the other values as well				
2 May 79	—	B/H		£1000
11 July 79	—	B/H		£1000
14 July 79	—	B/H		£1000
18 July 79	—	A/H		£1000
Complete Design				
14 Aug 79	—	B/H		£1000
19 Aug 79	—	B/H		£1000
19 Aug 79	ME–H/R	B/S		£1000
20 Aug 79	—	B/H	Could be Die I	£1000
1 Sep 79	—	B/H	Also endorsed "2" (presumably the die number)	£1000
1 Sep 79	—	B/H	Also endorsed "3" (presumably the die number)	£1000
13 Oct 79	—	B/S		£1000
24 Nov 79	—	(M/S)	"After Striking" (M/S)	£1000
24 Dec 79	—	A/S		£1000
3 Nov 80	—	B/S		£1000

Die Proofs from the De La Rue Archives

Cut down and mounted, with corner squares void .... *from* £1000
From the Striking Books, with corner squares void .... *from* £900

Plate Proof

In black on thick white wove paper £550
Block of ten with manuscript "specimen" twice £2200
Overprinted specimen Type 10 .... £1200

Colour Trials

Sheet of paper with three marginal pairs in different shades of Venetian red, perforated 14 on gummed, crown watermarked paper inscribed "A, B and C" (M/S). Shade "B" was the accepted colour. Additionally inscribed "Three specimens of colour submitted for the 1d. Postage Stamp. R. 6659/79 S. 20th Octr. 1879" (M/S) ....

These were to decide the colour of this stamp.

Watermark Crown, perf 14:
On white paper in orange-red, yellow-orange, slate-blue, orange-brown, mauve, purple, greenish grey .... *from* £2500
On coloured paper in Venetian red on orange, Venetian red on blue ...... *each* £2500

Without watermark, perf 14:
On coloured paper in brown on orange, red-brown on orange, brown on yellow, lake on greenish, lake on bluish, Venetian red on blue, Venetian red on orange .... *from* £2500

The above were taken in obscure conditions; some were in connection with the 1884 Committee (Section KD).

Trial Cancellation. Perf 14:

In mauve on white paper with London trial cancel of February 1881 on piece . . . £2500
In mauve on white paper with London trial cancel 16 March 1881, AH, KA, KB on separate piece ....

KB shows attempts of cancellation removal.

1880 (14 October). 1½d. Venetian Red, Type K3. Wmk Crown. Perf 14.

K4 (=S.G.167)		1½d. Venetian red	£175	45·00
		Block of four	£800	£275
		Used on cover	†	£130
	s.	"Specimen", Type 9	70·00	

Imprimaturs: Plates 1 *and* 2, *each* £400.

Die Proofs. In black on thick glazed card. Head proof only:

Endorsed "Punch P. 238" and "1½d. and 5d." (M/S) £1200

Complete design:
Endorsed "27 JUL 80" in blue and "BEFORE HARDENING" in red £1000
Endorsed "27 JUL 80 BEFORE HARDENING" all in black £1000
Endorsed "28 JUL 80 AFTER HARDENING" £1000
Endorsed "3 NOV 80" with "After Striking" in M/S £1000
Endorsed "4 AUG 83 BEFORE HARDENING" £1000

Die Proofs from the De La Rue Archives

Cut down and mounted £1000
From the Striking Books . . . . *from* £900

Plate Proof

In black on thick white wove paper £550

Colour Trials. Watermark Crown, perf 14:

On white paper in carmine-pink, rose, Venetian red, orange, orange-yellow, yellow, blue-green, blue Prussian blue, slate-blue, mauve, purple, maroon, red-brown, olive-brown, olive-bistre, slate-grey . . . . *from* £2000

Without watermark, perf 14:
On coloured paper in various colours . . . . *from* £2000

The context of these trials is unknown, but they were not produced to decide the colour of this stamp.

Trial Cancellation. Perf 14:

In rose on white paper with London trial cancel of 18 February 1881 on piece . . £2500

1880 (8 December). 2d. Rose, Type K4. Wmk Crown. Perf 14.

K5 (=S.G.168–168a)	(1) 2d. pale rose	£225	90·00
	(2) 2d. deep rose	£250	90·00
	(3) 2d. rose	£225	90·00
	Block of four	£1250	£450
	Used on cover	†	£225
	a. Watermark inverted	£1100	£500
	t. "Specimen", Type 9	95·00	

Imprimaturs: Plates 1 *and* 2, *each* £400.

Imprimatur overprinted "Specimen" Type 9 (formerly No. K5s). Seven examples were taken from the plate 1 imprimatur sheet in January 1885.

Die Proofs. In black on thick glazed card:

Endorsed "27 JUL 80" in blue and "BEFORE HARDENING" in red £1000
Endorsed "27 JUL 80 BEFORE HARDENING" all in black £1000
Endorsed "14 AUG 80 AFTER HARDENING" £1000
Endorsed "3 NOV 80" with "After Striking" in M/S £1000

Die Proofs from the De La Rose Archives:

Cut down and mounted . . . . *from* £1000
From the Striking Books £900

Plate Proof

In black on thick white wove paper £550

Colour Trials. Watermark Crown, perf 14:

On white paper in carmine-pink, pink, red-brown, orange, orange-yellow, yellow, yellow-green, blue-green, blue, Prussian blue, mauve, purple, purple-brown, maroon, olive-bistre, olive-brown . . . . *from* £2800

Without watermark, perf 14:
On coloured paper in various colours . . . . *from* £2800

The context of these trials is unknown, but they were not produced to decide the colour of this stamp.

Trial Cancellations. Perf 14:

In rose on white paper with London trial cancel of February 1881 on piece £2500
In orange-yellow with London trial cancel of 18 February 1881 . . . .

Imperf:
In pale green on white paper with London trial cancel of February 1881 on piece £2500
In pale green on piece with London trial cancel of 4 February 1881 with "2½" (M/S) . . . .

1881 (15 March). 5d. Indigo, Type K5. Wmk Crown. Perf. 14.

K6 (=S.G.169)		5d. indigo	£625	£110
		Block of four	£3500	£600
		Used on cover	†	£225
	a.	Imperforate (showing bottom margins)	£3250	£2750
	b.	Watermark inverted	—	£3250
	c.	Line below O of POSTAGE broken	—	
	s.	"Specimen", Types 9, 12, 13 . . . *from*	£140	
	t.	Imperforate "Cancelled", Type 14A	£1500	

Imprimaturs: Plates 1, 2, 3, *each* £1250. The first was registered 26 February 1881. Plate 3 was never put to press.

Die Proofs. In black on thick glazed card:

Endorsed "5 Aug 80" in blue £1000
Endorsed "10 Aug 80 AFTER HARDENING" £1000

Die Proofs from the De La Rue Archives

Cut down and mounted . . . . *from* £1000
From the Striking Books £900

Plate Proof

In black on thick white wove paper £575

Colour Trials. Watermark Crown, perf 14:

On white paper in carmine-pink, rose, yellow, yellow-green, dull green, blue-green, blue, Prussian blue, purple, purple-brown, red-brown, yellow-brown, olive-bistre, slate-grey . . . . *from* £3000

Without watermark, perf 14:
On coloured paper in various colours . . . . *each* £3000

Trial Cancellation. Watermark Crown, Perf 14:

The issued stamp with London trial cancel of 17 February 1881 on piece £2500

SECTION KB

The First Unified Stamp, 1d. Lilac, 12 July 1881

Unification. This major change in policy influenced the design of stamps to 1911. It came from a desire to unify the functions of Postage and Revenue stamps.

When the Customs and Revenue Act came into force on 1 June 1881, 1d. Venetian red postage stamps could be used on receipts and 1d. receipt stamps could be used for postage. Production of the 1d. receipt stamp ceased with stocks at Somerset House being sent out in response to orders for postage stamps. They amounted to about a fortnight's total usage, after which the new unified 1d. was available.

Essays. Only one essay (hand-painted, dated 7 Apr. 1881) is known which is in the Royal Collection. The colour trials of the 1880 1d. in mauve, the subject of experiments including the removal of a London trial cancel, are tests of the double fugitive ink.

Inks. All previous De La Rue stamps were printed in single fugitive ink, i.e. the colour ran when washed with organic solvents. Revenue stamps were printed in double fugitive ink which would run if washed with all organic solvents or water.

The first ink ("950") used for the 1881 1d. was the same as that used for the 1d. receipt stamp, but after production began this proved to be unsatisfactory. A new ink ("951") was introduced from 22 June, giving a slight bluish look to the stamps. This also was found to be unsatisfactory, so a third ink ("952") was introduced from 1 January 1882. Stocks of "951" ink continued to be used and "952" remained in use until about April 1887, when a fourth ink "2078", was introduced.

Dies. There were two dies of this stamp. The second was created as the writing on the first was too cramped. Only 8 plates and 2,300,000 sheets were created from die 1.

Colour standards. These were held by De La Rue and Inland Revenue officers in the print room for recognition purposes. They were not standards of quality or of colour. Such standards had been taken from De La Rue's earliest days, but with the increase in workload from January 1880, they became essential. In 1881, die 1 stamps handstamped "Specimen" types 9 and 12 were used. Six such stamps were held by De La Rue and six by the Inland Revenue, whose officers would usually deface unwanted examples with manuscript "Superseded". In 1887, a new procedure was introduced and two lots of six stamps were handstamped "Cancelled" type 14. In 1888, for obscure reasons, the procedure was modified and 24 stamps were so handstamped and divided into two blocks of 12, one for each party. All identifiable surviving colour standards are now listed.

K6 *(Die* II *shown)*

Die I *(fourteen complete dots or pearls)*

Die II *(sixteen complete dots or pearls)*

Identification between Dies I and II. In die I the white letters are small and the "O" of "One" is a horizontal oblong and in die II it is a vertical oblong.

1881 (12 July). 1d. Lilac, Type K6, Die I (14 dots). Wmk Crown. Perf 14.

K7 (=S.G.170/171)	(1)	1d. lilac	£200	30·00
	(2)	1d. bluish lilac (December 1881)	£500	£130
	(3)	1d. pale lilac	£200	30·00
		Block of four	£1000	£175
		Used on cover	†	50·00
	a.	Watermark inverted	—	£500
	b.	Partial double impression	†	—
	s.	"Specimen", Type 9	60·00	
	t.	Do. Bluish lilac, Type 9	£120	

Imprimaturs: Plates 1 *to* 8, *each* £350. The first was registered on 23 May 1881. Pencil numbers on the back are not reliable as plate numbers.

Die Proofs. In black on glazed card.

Endorsed "4 MAY 81 BEFORE HARDENING" and "United Die 252" £1000
Endorsed "5 May 81" £1000
Endorsed "6 May 81 BEFORE HARDENING" £1000

Die Proofs from the De La Rue Archives

Cut down and mounted, inscribed "No 252" in manuscript £1500
From the Striking Books struck in 1881 with dates £1200

Colour standards: Specimen type 12, shade K7(1)

A block of 4 and two singles known, all but one with m/s "superseded" . . . .

Die II, with 16 dots in each corner

During the twenty years this stamp was in production 129 plates were put to press. There are many shades; those listed below are group names only. In 1884, De La Rue introduced "Controls" in the form of a letter beneath stamp 11 in the bottom row starting with A and changing at irregular intervals up to X.

Bisected stamps are to be found but these were unofficial although there are commercial usages (*Prices range from* £150).

This issue is treated very fully in *The Penny Lilac, Parts I and II,* by R. A. G. LEE, RDP, FRPS, L.

1881 (13 December). 1d. Lilac, Type K6. Die II (16 dots). Wmk Crown. Perf 14.

K8 (=S.G.172/174)	(1)	1d. lilac	2·50	2·00
	(2)	1d. bluish lilac	£375	£125
	(3)	1d. deep purple	2·50	2·00
	(4)	1d. mauve	2·50	1·50
		Block of four	12·00	7·00
		Used on cover	†	3·00
	a.	On blued paper (shade 3)	£4000	
	c.	No watermark	£3250	
	d.	Watermark inverted	40·00	25·00
	e.	Imperforate (pair). Mauve*	£2750	
	f.	Imperforate three sides (pair)	£5000	†
	g.	Printed on gummed side	£700	†
	ga.	Do. Watermark inverted		
	h.	Printed both sides	£750	†
	ha.	Do. Watermark inverted		
	i.	Printed both sides, back print inverted	£800	†
	j.	Frame broken at bottom (R. 1/2, Sheet Control S, upper pane)	£800	£300
	k.	Frame break, right side broken	—	£100
	l.	"Pears Soap," advertisement on back in orange, blue or mauve *from*	£600	
	m.	Do. "Specimen", Type 9	£1500	
	n.	"One Penny" on back	£1000	
	o.	Line perforated 14	£1200	
	p.	Double perforation		
	t.	"Specimen", Type 9, 12 *from*	50·00	
	u.	"Cancelled", Type 14	£700	

Imprimaturs: Plates 9 *to* 18, 25 *to* 28, 33 *to* 52, 54 *to* 69, 72 *to* 80, *each* £200. Plate 9 was first registered 14 October 1881.

Plate 80 was put to press on 4 January 1889, control J; a further 57 plates were put to press but none registered.

*Genuine imperforate stamps have been confirmed with Control E or L and M control is known totally imperforate as a single. No imperforate control examples have been removed from imprimatur sheets of the 59 plates.

No. K8j, shows the bottom frame-line broken away from the vertical frame at left and right. A narrow white space shows, from left to right, across the stamp and the oval frame is broken below "E" of "ONE" and "PEN" of "PENNY". Many other frame breaks show the oval complete or distorted at this point.

On K8n, "One Penny" was printed in two lines in black on the back on the gum as an experiment for the "Pears Soap" advertisement.

No. K8o comes from the imprimatur sheet, plate 28 taken in 1886. Although this stamp was current several line perf 14 examples exist from the Presentation Album, "Before and After the Stamp Committee".

A block of six with Crowns watermark upright exists with the bottom selvedge showing "AGE" of "POSTAGE" inverted in error instead of upright, and a bottom right corner piece from the same sheet showing no control is also known. Other examples exist in the former National Postal Museum. It is possible that other pieces may exist for this stamp and also for other stamps of this period.

Repp paper. Formerly listed as No. K8b this variety is believed to have been due to the storage of sheets of stamps in brown laid or ribbed paper.

Die Proofs. In black on white glazed card (unless otherwise stated):

Date	*Inscr.*	*Additional Inscriptions or Notes*	
1 Jun 81	B/H		£1000
—	B/H	Endorsed "Background has been opened out and the legend is new and bolder-hand engraved"	£1000
2 Jun 81	A/H		£1000
3 Jun 81	B/H		£1000
22 Aug 81	—	Initialled "R.K." (M/S)	£1000
1 Nov 83	B/S		£1000
22 Feb 84	—	Initialled "N.G."	£1000
23 Feb 84	—	Initialled (M/S)	£1000
23 Feb 84	A/S	Initialled "G.F.S." (M/S)	£1000
—	—	In lilac	£4500

Die Proofs from the De La Rue Archives

Cut down and mounted, inscribed "No 253" in manuscript . . . £1500
14 dots and 16 dots cut down and mounted on same card, inscribed "Old" and "New" respectively in manuscript . . . £4500
From the Striking Books struck between 1881 and 1901, each with various dates . . . *from* £900
1d. and ½d. of 1887 struck on same card inscribed "Aug 16/12 leads from each die" in manuscript . . . £2000

Plate Proofs

In black on thick white wove paper . . . £400
In lilac on buff or black on green . . . *from* £175

Colour Trials. Watermark Crown:

White paper trials were taken in 1885 in connection with the 1884 Stamp Committee, see Section KD.

Perf 14, on coloured papers, in purple on pink, lilac on pink, greenish slate on pink, purple on blue, purple on green, purple on yellow, black on green . *from* £1800

The trial cancellations on this stamp were in connection with the 1884 Stamp Committee, see Section KD.

Booklets

The earliest "Booklets" were not sold by the Post Office but were distributed by the concessionaries, The Stamp Distribution Syndicate Ltd. The first booklet of 64 pages consisted of advertisements and blank memo pages. It had a stiff red linen cover with the word "Memoranda" across the front. On the back there was a slit in which was inserted an example of the 1d. Lilac bearing the initials of the Company perforated through "SDS". The second booklet with similar content was distributed by a new company and contains advertisements on both sides of the red card cover with the same stamp inset in the back but with initials "SDC" (Stamp Distribution Parent Company Ltd.). *Price (each)* £8500.

1d. Lilac Controls

Unless otherwise stated prices are given for unused single stamps with a piece of selvedge attached bearing the control letter. They are priced for examples with *imperforate* selvedge (abbreviated to "*I*"), *perforated through* (abbreviated to "*P*") both from horizontal comb perforators. Examples with selvedge with *one extension hole* (abbreviated to "*E*") were from vertical comb perforators. Starting with "A" and progressing in alphabetical order the controls were changed about twice a year.

The lists are sub-divided into examples with and without marginal rules extending round the pane outside the stamps. Both the items illustrated below have marginal rules. Where the rules are unbroken they are described as *continuous* (though in some plates the rules have occasional breaks). Where the rules are composed of short pieces with gaps exactly opposite the spaces between the stamps they are termed *coextensive*.

Perf (P) selvedge with continuous rule

O *and* N *control with imperf (I) and continuous rule*

Prices. For controls in marginal corner pairs, add 50% to the prices shown.

Cat. No.	*Control*	*I.*	*P.*
	(a) Marginal Setting (1A), (1B)		
KC24*	no control (1A)		
	Strip of 4	†	£600
KC25	A (1B)	†	£250
KC26	B	†	£100
KC27	C	†	90·00
KC28	D	†	30·00
KC29	E	†	30·00
KC30	F	†	30·00
KC31	G	†	30·00
KC32	H	†	15·00
KC33	I	†	50·00
KC34	J	†	40·00
	(b) Marginal Setting (2)		
KC34a*	no control *Strip of* 4	†	—
KC35	G	†	25·00
KC36	H	†	15·00

Cat. No.	*Control*	*I.*	*P.*
KC37	I	†	15·00
KC38	J	£150	10·00
KC39	K	£150	10·00
KC40	L	25·00	10·00
KC41	M	25·00	10·00
KC42	N	10·00	10·00
KC43	O	10·00	10·00
KC44	O over N	£2500	£2500
KC45	P	50·00	10·00
KC46	Q	15·00	10·00
KC47	R	15·00	10·00
KC48	S	10·00	10·00
KC49	T	10·00	10·00
KC50	U	10·00	10·00
KC51	V	10·00	10·00
KC52	W	10·00	10·00
KC53	X	10·00	10·00
KC53a	X inverted	£150	—

*Nos. KC24 and KC34a must be in corner strips of 4 stamps, sufficient to show part of the "POSTAGE" watermark in the bottom margin.

Marginal Settings. (1A) No marginal rule, no control; (1B) as (1A) but with control; (2) with marginal rules, blank interpane gutter; (3) as (2) but with interpane "pillars".

Marginal setting (2). In 1887, during the G control period, marginal rules (continuous purple lines known as "Jubilee lines", were added round each pane of plates 65 and 66 as an experiment to improve printing and plate durability. These were approved and incorporated into all subsequent plates for all values.

In October 1899 (W control period) permission was granted to include 48 short "ladders" or "pillars" in the interpane gutter to improve printing (*marginal setting* (3)).

Marginal setting (3), as (2) but with interpane "pillars" and prices are the same as quoted for setting (2).

Vertical comb perforator (a single extension hole in bottom margin). Perf. Type E.

Cat No.	*Control*	*E.*
KC54	V *Setting* (2) . . . . (*pair*)	—
KC55	W *Settings* (2) or (3). . .	10·00
KC56	X *Settings* (2) or (3) . . .	10·00
KC56a	X inverted. *Setting* (2) or (3)	£100

Control Periods. The following relates to the 1887 and 1900 ½d., and the 1d. lilac, Die II (16 dots). The no-control period ran from October 1881 to January 1884 after which the control letter was changed every six months or so. The following table is therefore of use in providing an approximate date of issue for marginal stamps with a control letter. The issues are described fully in "*Great Britain: The De La Rue Years 1878–1910*", *Volumes 1 and 2*, by W. A. Wiseman, FRPS, L.

1887 ½d.	*1881* 1d.	*Period*
—	A	February 1884 to June 1884
—	B	July 1884 to January 1885
—	C	February 1885 to July 1885
—	D	August 1885 to February 1886
—	E	March 1886 to August 1886
None	F	September 1886 to February 1887
A	G	March 1887 to August 1887
B	H	September 1887 to February 1888
C	I	March 1888 to August 1888
D	J	September 1888 to February 1889
E	K	March 1889 to August 1889
F	L	September 1889 to June 1890
G	M	July 1890 to January 1891
H	N	February 1891 to September 1891
I	O	October 1891 to May 1892
J	P	Jun. 1892 to January 1893
K	Q	February 1883 to November 1893
L	R	December 1893 to May 1894
M	S	June 1894 to March 1895
N	T	April 1895 to January 1896
O	U	February 1896 to April 1897
P	V	May 1897 to August 1898
Q	—	September 1898 to December 1899
—	W	September 1898 to April 1900
—	X	May 1900 to January 1902

1900 ½d. (No. K28)		
R	—	January 1900 to November 1901

During 1898 vertical perforators were introduced which gave a single extension hole below the bottom horizontal row of holes. This took place during the V control period. Perforation was from left to right or right to left according to feed direction. Later a line of pins was added to the vertical comb which gave a perforated bottom or top margin depending on which end had the extension to the comb. This had the same end result as the horizontal combs in use from 1884. Controls V (rare), W and X are known with a single extension hole (Perf. Type E) in the bottom margin from the vertical comb perforator.

SECTION KC

The Unified Issue, 1 January 1883

From the day the Consolidated Contract was won, the authorities and De La Rue wanted a series of stamps, recognisable in poor lighting even when cancelled. The 1883 Unified issue was intended to be that new series, but it did not succeed. Nothing like it had been attempted before so the time required for such a huge enterprise was unknown. In any case, new criteria were introduced which disrupted work on the new issue. The new factors included; parcel post, telegraph stamps and unification. There was pressure to introduce a Parcel Post during the early 1880's. Special stamps were proposed in early 1881, but were not pursued and the service commenced on 1 August 1883. On 15 October 1881, the Post Office, without reference to the Inland Revenue, decided to discontinue use of Telegraph stamps and revert to postage stamps for this purpose. The success of the 1881 1d. lilac required that the 2d., 3d., 6d., 9d., 1s. and 2s. 6d. Inland Revenue stamps also be unified.

The most widely used were the 3d., 6d. and 1s. printed in double fugitive lilac ink like the 1881 1d. The others were embossed stamps, little used and expensive to produce. The enabling Act was passed on 18 August to come into force on 1 January 1883. It was realised early in 1882 that an issue of new stamps to conform with the Act would be impossible to produce by that date. On 4 May 1882. De La Rue created a series (½d., to 1s.) of existing designs (as Type Nos. **K1** (½d.), **K6** (1d.), **K3** (1½d.), **K4** (2d.), **J1** (2½d.), **K8A** (3d. as issued), **J11** (4d.), **K5** (5d.), **K8B** (6d. as issued), **J26** (1s.)) in double fugitive ink overprinted in black with the same figure of value as temporary unified stamps. It was decided to issue the 3d., 6d. and 1s. Inland Revenue values surcharged on existing designs (*Fig.* 20). It was also clear that a black surcharge would clash with cancellations. So, in September 1882, essays of 1881 one penny stamps from stock with overprints of "3d.", "6d." and "1s." in red and blue were created. Red was chosen and printing in lilac from existing plates of those three values began. At the last moment the Telegraph Branch was shown the proposed stamps and objected to the 1s. Most of the stock of 1s. stamps in purple, without the intended surcharge, was destroyed. Eight complete sets of temporary unified stamps are known to have existed, but some have been broken up. The sets are recognised by the lettering on the 1s. stamp from plate 14 and each surcharged with its own face value in large black type.

Sets AD, AB, AC, BC sets of 10 trials	£25000
Set of 10 trials *without* surcharges (½d. 4d., and 1s. TL, are imperf	£25000
Pair of 181 1d. surcharged "1d." in black	—
2d. 1880 surcharged "2d." in black	—

Fig. 20. *Surcharged essays*

Essays submitted 25 September 1882

1d. Lilac in strip of 3, surch "3d.", "6d." and "1s." as in *Fig.* 20, in blue or red .£15000

K8A *Surcharged "3d."*

K8B *Surcharged "6d."*

1883 (1 January). 3d. Lilac, Type K8A (surcharged "3d." in carmine). Wmk Crown (W12). Perf 14.

K8A (=S.G.159)		3d. lilac, Plate 21	£450	£130
		Block of four	£2200	£750
		Used on cover	†	£350
	a.	Watermark inverted		
	s.	"Specimen", Type 9	£220	

Imprimatur: Plate 21, £1500.

The layout remained the same as the previous issue.

This stamp is companion to the 6d. lilac listed below. They resulted from the 1882 trials of stamps in lilac fugitive ink surcharged in black with their own face value.

1883 (1 January). 6d. Lilac, Type K8B (surcharged "6d." in carmine). Wmk Crown (W12). Perf 14.

K8B (=S.G.162)		6d. lilac, Plate 18	£500	£130
		Block of four	£2500	£750
		Used on cover	†	£350
	c.	Overprint double	—	£9000
	d.	Watermark inverted	£1400	£550
	e.	Slanting dots (stamps AF, DC, MG, MH, MI, PJ, SJ; also OI and PH in part of the printing) *from*	£950	£350
	f.	MH, late state, first dot very small	£550	£250
	g.	OI, second state, left dot only	£550	£250
	h.	TF, right dot in two halves	£550	£250
	s.	"Specimen", Type 9	£220	

Imprimatur: Plate 18, £800.

1882 (Nov). 1s. Purple, Type J26, Wmk Crown (W12). Line Perf 14. Intended for Surcharge and Unissued.

K8C		1s. purple, Plate 14	£9000
	s.	"Specimen", Type 9 (Plate 13, comb perf 14)	£5500

Imprimaturs: Plates 13 *and* 14, *each* £4000. Stamps removed from the imprimatur sheets are: Plate 13: AA–AL, BL, HE, HF–JL, TL; Plate 14; AA–FL, KB, LA–LG, TL. Of these 81 stamps, 24 were replaced, all perf 14 line; BA–BL, CC, CJ–CL, DA, DJ–DL, EK–FL. The B row is imperforate at top. The top row (AA–AL) were removed prior to perforation and are imperforate as are KB, LA–LG, TL. The G row is perforated top only and the remaining stamps are line perf 14 namely CA, CB, CD–CI, DB–DI, EA–FJ, 36 examples and these are all imprimaturs.

The source of examples of No. K8C was a printing of 23,555 sheets which was aborted. These are comb perforated 14 and it is believed that no genuine unoverprinted examples from plates 13 and 14 survive. Collectors should be wary of faked perforations on stamps taken from the imprimatur sheets.

The Designs of the 1883 Issue

On 10 March 1881 T. Jeffrey, Head of the London Postal Service wrote suggesting that stamps could be distinguished by the three primary colours (red, blue and yellow) and by shape. On 19

March 1881 De La Rue submitted three copies of their interpretations of Jeffrey's ideas. Each had ten lithographed essays, mostly of "Two Pence" value. Four were "normal" stamps and three each upright, oblong and hexagonal. One copy is in the Royal Collection, one in the Phillips Collection in The Post Office Heritage Services and the third, from the De La Rue archives, in private hands.

A single sheet inscribed "Jeffrey's Scheme" and stamped "19 MAR 81" with impressions of the above designs, all inscribed "TWO PENCE" (including Type C), headed "Postage" in manuscript with the intended face values written above them, arranged as follows: first row, Type A in green for $\frac{1}{2}$d.; second row, Types A to C in lilac for 1d., 1$\frac{1}{2}$d. and 2d. respectively; third row, Types A to C in blue for 2$\frac{1}{2}$d., 3d. and 4d. respectively; fourth row, Types A to C in red for 5d., 6d. and 1s. respectively. See *Fig*. 21.

Price for sheet £12000

Type A

Type B

Type C

Fig. 21. *Jeffrey's scheme*

Jeffrey's ideas dominated contemporary Post Office thinking on design. Both De La Rue and the Inland Revenue saw defects as the former had only two colours of double fugitive ink, green and purple, and the Inland Revenue realised there were difficulties with watemark and perforation.

Fig. 22. *Some designs from De La Rue's First Scheme*

De La Rue's First Scheme. On 29 November 1881 De La Rue submitted their "First Scheme" of 14 hand-painted essays for all relevant values, $\frac{1}{2}$, 1d. lilac (as issued), $1\frac{1}{2}$, 2, $2\frac{1}{2}$, 3, 4, 5, 6d., 1, 3, 5, 10s., £1 and £5 (*Fig.* 22). They combined acknowledgement of Jeffrey's ideas with the need for the 3, 6d., and 1s. values in fugitive ink. Those three were inscribed "Postage and (&) Revenue", while others were inscribed "Postage Revenue". The 3s. was required by the Telegraph Department. Two such sets were created. One is now in the Phillips Collection (Post Office Heritage Services) and the second from the De La Rue archives was broken up and sold:

Small horiz. $\frac{1}{2}$d. green; hexagon 2d. blue, 6d. purple, 3s. red; normal stamps $2\frac{1}{2}$d. blue, 4d. red; upright oblong $1\frac{1}{2}$d. blue, 3d. purple, 5d. red; horiz oblong 1s. purple and 5s., 10s., £1, £5 in brown. All inscribed "Postage Revenue", except 3d., 6d., 1s. with "Postage & Revenue" . . . . *from* £5000 each

Fig. 23. *De La Rue's Second Scheme*

De La Rue's Second Scheme. There is no surviving comment on the First Scheme. Much time had been lost when the Second Scheme was created on 18 July 1882. There are now 15 hand-painted essays (*Fig*. 23), values as before but a 9d. added for Parcel Post. The $1\frac{1}{2}$, 9d., and 3s. are large, the size of the 5s. Two copies were created, one for De La Rue records and the other for the Inland Revenue; the latter is in the Post Office Heritage Services. On 17 November De La Rue's file copy was sent to the Inland Revenue. De La Rue's copy was sold at auction in 1989. All were defaced with an m/s ink cross or wavy line.

The $\frac{1}{2}$, $1\frac{1}{2}$, 3, 6d., 1s. purple essays were offered separately, while the 2, $2\frac{1}{2}$, 4, 5, 9d., essays in green were offered in a strip with m/s "colour" in Warren William De La Rue's handwriting at left. All have "Postage & Revenue". The $\frac{1}{2}$d., has m/s "purple" over it. . . . . *from* £5000 each

De La Rue's Third Scheme. On 8 December just one copy of this Scheme with 20 hand-painted essays from $\frac{1}{2}$d. to £5 was created. No accompanying letter has survived. Part is now in the Post Office Heritage Services. It has 13 hand-painted essays of new 1, $1\frac{1}{2}$, 2 (two), $2\frac{1}{2}$, 3 (close to accepted design), 4 (two), 5, 6 (two), 9d., and 1s. (close to accepted design); all are inscribed "Postage and (&) Revenue", all have corner letters (except 4d.) and defaced with ink crosses (except for the 2d.). There is a 1d. lilac with "cancelled" (m/s) diagonally across the stamp. The Scheme was broken into five pieces at the De La Rue archive sales. It is understood that the following are on the market.

$\frac{1}{2}$d. green, without corner letters, defaced with cross £5000
$\frac{1}{2}$d. green, AB/BA defaced with cross £5000
3s., 5s., 10s., £1, £5 inscribed "Postage Revenue" in red and defaced with ink on piece with m/s note by WWD below . . . .

The Accepted Designs

Revised Designs for the High Values. On 8 December 1882 De La Rue submitted revised designs for the high values, including a 3s. value for use on telegrams, all inscribed "POSTAGE REVENUE", together with a reminder that the use of corner letters would add considerably to the expense.

Essays from the De La Rue archives, hand-painted on card:

3s.in blue, 5s. in carmine, 10s. and £1 in brown and £5 in orange, all crossed through in ink by wavy lines . . . . £5000 each

De La Rue's Fourth Scheme. This Scheme, submitted on 12 December, was in the form of lithographed essays on separate pieces of paper. As Schemes, full sets of all values were affixed on squared paper. Four sets are known including one each in the Royal and Phillips collections. A third,

De La Rue's own set, with ink defacements, and the fourth on two leaves are in private hands. Each set comprises the 16 values from ½d. to £5, including the ½d. (in slate), the issued 1d. lilac, 1½, 2 in adopted design but without corner letters and the rest in the issued design and colours. The corner letters used were AB/BA. The 1½d. to 2s. 6d. were inscribed "Postage and (&) Revenue" while the ½d. and 5s. to £5 had only "Postage". Individual essays not affixed to paper are also on the market.

Essays from the De La Rue archives, crudely printed on card:

An impression of the ½d. of 1880 in slate, the issued 1d. lilac with"Cancelled" in manuscript, ½d., 2d., 2½d. and 3d. in lilac, 4d., 5d., 6d., 9d. and 1s. in green, 2s. 6d. in lilac, 5s. in carmine, 10s. in ultramarine, £1 in lilac and £5 in orange, with pen cancellations £12500

On 13 December 1882 W. C. Cousins, Controller of Stamps at the Inland Revenue wrote to S. A. Blackwood, Secretary to the Post Office, enclosing the Third Scheme and virtually giving a final approved decision. This was confirmed the next day when a Warrant was sent to De La Rue to create the dies and plates for the complete issue. One change was made in the £1 value and that was to have the corner letters in colour on white to be uniform with the other values instead of being in white on coloured ground. The £5 was issued on 21 March 1882 and is listed under J128.

Die proof from the De La Rue archives, comprising designs cut down and mounted in sunken frames on one card:

1½d., 2d., 2½d., 3d., 4d., 5d., 6d., 9d. and 1s. without corner letters £12500

Unmounted die proofs of the high values are listed under each value.

The Small Head Die. A new, small head die was needed. Such dies had been created before, e.g. in 1881 for Natal telegraph stamps. On this occasion, work had begun unofficially but eventually the new die became no. 269.

A/H 7 Jan 1883 . . . .£1000
B/H 7 Jan 1883 . . . .£1000
B/H 15 Jan 1883 . . . .£1000
(M/S) "269" undated £1000
(M/S) "New original die no. 269" undated £1000

The 2s. 6d. Value. After 1 January 1883 a 2s. 6d. stamp was urgently required for legal purposes. The 3s. design was therefore hurriedly modified and used as a 2s. 6d. on 2 July 1883 printed on blued Anchor watermark paper.

The 9d. Value. This was needed for the new Parcel Post service from 1 August 1883. The first plates were made as vertical stamps and not horizontal ones.

Low Values Issued on 1 April 1884. The first die to be engraved was that of the 5d. value. It had a line under the "d." (die no. 271–die 1), but when it was put to press, the plates were "condemned as defective". The new designs had large areas of white compared to previous ones. Paper fell into them, picking up stray ink and ruining the print. A new die (no. 283–die 2) was made.

The 5s. and 10s. Values. The last printing of the 5s. on blued paper was in January 1884 and of the 10s. in November 1884.

The £1 Stamp. These were printed on 240 set Imperial Crown paper in two panes of 40, each stamp having three watermark Crowns (or Obs). The printing on Orbs paper in December 1887 was an error. The change in colour in 1891 was caused by fears that brown-lilac stamps could be reproduced photographically.

The £5 Stamp. In 1900, new colour standards ("Cancelled" type 18) were taken, because a new and brighter ink had been in use for some time without any. The final issue was made on 28 February 1903.

Colour Trials. An immense number of colour trials of the low values of this issue exist. None was taken to decide the colours of the stamps; all were taken in connection with events after 1 April 1884 and will be detailed in Section KD.

Perf 12 Stamps. A few of these stamps exist line perf 12. They were created in connection with 1887 stamps with fringes in the perforation gutter, e.g. the 4d., but they will be listed here. This is because some were used as colour standards.

Colour standards. These were stamps held in the print room in equal numbers by the Inland Revenue and De La Rue to help officials and printers to see the nature of the stamps to be printed.

For the particular issue, stamps, some perf 12, handstamped "Specimen" type 9, were used; identifiable examples are listed under the basic stamp since these were not colour trials. Others were handstamped "Cancelled", type 14.

The following was created after 17 August 1883 but its purpose is unknown.

Die proofs of $\frac{1}{2}$d. to 1s. (5d. die 2), without corner letters all cut down on single card

Issued colours created in 1886:

1$\frac{1}{2}$d. to 1s. overprinted "Cancelled" type 14 on card . . . .

Postmasters were supplied with interleaves showing the new stamps. These were printed by De La Rue in lithography using the Fourth Scheme as their model. On 25 February 1884, the deletion of the letters AB at the top of the £5 image was approved by W. C. Cousins. The issued interleaves of which 16,000 were produced have this alteration thereby distinguishing them from the proofs. These, together with the interleaves are outside the scope of this catalogue.

2s. 6d., 5s., 10s., £1, 2 July 1883

Sheet Format. The 2s. 6d., 5s. and 10s. were printed from plates arranged in two panes, one above the other, each of 56, in 7 horizontal rows of 8, and without marginal inscriptions. The stamps were at first normally blued, the blueing varying from deep to light. The first printings of these values on white Anchor paper was in 1885. The lettering was AA–AH down to NA–NH.

The £1 value was printed from plates of 80 stamps in two panes each of 40 impressions in ten horizontal rows of four. There were no marginal inscriptions. The corner lettering in the £1 ran from AA–AD in the top row to TA–TD in the bottom row (quoting lower corner letters only). Plate 2 (with the JC, TA varieties) and Plate 3 were used for the printings in brown-lilac. Plate 3 was re-registered, and used with Plate 2 for the £1 green.

K9

K10

K11

K12

1883 (2 July). 2s. 6d. Lilac, Type K9. Blued paper. Wmk Anchor (W9). Perf 14.

K9 (=S.G.175) 2s. 6d. lilac £4000 £1200

s. "Specimen", Type 9 . . . . £425

u. "Specimen", Type 9 (paper blued, deep lilac) £4000

Imprimaturs: (*2 plates*), *each* £3000.

1884 2s. 6d. Lilac, Type K9. White paper. Wmk Anchor (W9). Perf 14.

K10 (=S.G.178/179) (1)		2s. 6d. lilac	£450	£140
(2)		2s. 6d. deep lilac	£550	£175
		Block of four	£2800	£875
	a.	Paper blued (from "white paper" period), deep lilac	£6000	£2500
	b.	Watermark inverted	—	£6000
	s.	"Specimen", Types 9, 11, 12, 13 .... *from*	£350	
	t.	"Cancelled", Type 14	£2800	
	u.	"Specimen", Type 11 and "R & A.G.O." datestamp	£2500	

Two examples of No. K10b are known, (ME and NB).

Colour standards: Blue paper standards were handstamped specimen type 9, probably AE–CH. White paper standards were taken in 1887 AA–CD and in 1888 HA–JH all handstamped "Cancelled" type 14. Two blocks of six, AA–CB and HC–JD are in the Post Office Heritage Services. Those known outside the Post Office are AG, AH, HG, IG, JF, JG.

Die Proofs. In black on white glazed card (unless otherwise stated):

Date	*Corner Letters*	*Inscr.*	*Additional Inscriptions or Notes*	
5 Apr 83	—	B/H		£2000
11 Apr 83	—	B/H		£2000
11 Apr 83	—	A/H	Initialled "W.G." (M/S)	£2000
13 Apr 83	—	B/S		£2000
25 Apr 83	—	(M/S)	Inscribed "After Striking W.G." (M/S)	£2000
—	BF–FB	—	Endorsed "30 Leads" (M/S) and initialled (M/S)	£2000
11 May 83	—	B/H		£2000

There was one 2s. 6d. die.

Die Proofs from the De La Rue Archives

Cut down and unmounted with corner squares void £1750
From the Striking Books with corner letters AE–EA £1750

Plate Proof

In black on thick white wove paper £2000

1884 (1 April). 5s. Rose, Type K10. Blued paper. Wmk Anchor (W9). Perf 14.

K11 (=S.G.176)		5s. rose	£10000	£3500
	s.	"Specimen", Types 9, 11 .... *from*	£1000	
	t.	"Specimen", perf 12, Type 9	£1800	
	u.	Imperforate "Specimen", Type 9	£3000	

Imprimaturs: (2 *Plates*), *each* £3500.

Colour standards: Perf 12 stamps MA, NA–NC are in the P.O. Heritage Services but none recognised to date elsewhere.

1884 5s. Rose, Type K10. White paper. Wmk Anchor (W9). Perf 14.

K12 (=S.G.180/181) (1)		5s. rose	£875	£200
(2)		5s. crimson (1890?)	£775	£200
		Block of four	£4500	£1200
	a.	Watermark inverted	†	£7000
	s.	Imperforate "Specimen", Type 9	£3000	
	t.	"Specimen", Types 9, 11, 12, 13 .... *from*	£375	
	u.	"Specimen", perf 12, Type 9	£800	
	v.	"Cancelled", Type 14	£3000	
	w.	"Specimen", Type 11 and "R & A.G.O." datestamp	£2750	

Two examples of No. K12a are known (AD and CC).

Colour standards: In February 1888. AA–CH were handstamped "Cancelled" type 14, AA–CB except CA are in the P.O. Heritage Services; AF–AH, BG are known elsewhere.

Die Proofs. In black on white glazed card:

Without endorsement or date £2500
Endorsed "11 July 83 BEFORE HARDENING" £2500
Endorsed "30 July 83 AFTER HARDENING" and initialled. Date is stamped twice £2500

Die Proofs from the De La Rue Archives

Cut down and unmounted with corner squares void £2000
From the Striking Books with corner letters AE–EA £2000

Plate Proof

In black on thick white wove paper £2000

1884 (1 April). 10s. Ultramarine, Type K11. Blued paper. Wmk Anchor (W9). Perf 14.

K13 (=S.G.177/177a)	(1)	10s. ultramarine	£32000	£7500
	(2)	10s. cobalt (May 1884)	£38000	£11000
	s..	"Specimen", Type 9 (ultramarine)	£1300	
	t.	"Specimen", Type 9 (cobalt)	£2500	
	u.	"Specimen", Type 9 and "R & A.G.O." datestamp	£3000	

Imprimaturs: (*2 plates*), *each* £4000.

1884. 10s. Ultramarine, Type K11. White paper. Wmk Anchor (W9). Perf 14.

K14 (=S.G.182/183a)	(1)	10s. cobalt	£25000	£6500
	(2)	10s. ultramarine	£1700	£475
	(3)	10s. pale ultramarine (1887?)	£1900	£475
		Block of four	£10000	£2750
	s.	"Specimen", Types 9, 11, 13 (ultramarine) . . . *from*	£400	
	t.	"Cancelled", Type 14 (ultramarine)	£4000	
	u.	"Specimen", Type 9 (two shades of cobalt)	£1500	

Colour standards: In June 1888, AA–CH were taken and handstamped Cancelled type 14, AA–CD are in the P.O. Heritage Services and CC, AG, BG are known elsewhere.

Die Proofs. In black on white glazed card (unless otherwise stated):

Endorsed "19 June 83 BEFORE HARDENING" £2750
Endorsed "25 June 83 AFTER HARDENING" and initialled "GFS" £2750
Endorsed "26 June 83 AFTER STRIKING" and (M/S) "JV Leads GFS" £2750
Endorsed "2 July 83" and (M/S) "After striking" £2750

Die Proofs from the De La Rue Archives

Cut down and unmounted with corner squares void £2200
From the Striking Books with corner letters AN–NA £2200

Plate Proof

In black on thick white wove paper £2000

1884 (1 April). £1 Brown-lilac, Type K12. Wmk Three Crowns (W12). Perf 14.

K15 (=S.G.185)		£1 brown-lilac	£22000	£2200
	a.	Frame broken, stamps JC or TA (Plate 2)	£35000	£3800
	b.	Watermark inverted	—	£10000
	s.	Imperforate "Specimen", Type 9	£6500	
	t.	"Specimen", Types 9, 11, 12 . . . *from*	£1600	
	ta.	Do. frame broken JC or TA . . . *from*	£2250	
	u.	"Cancelled" Type 14	£5500	

Imprimaturs: (*Plates* 2 *and* 3), each £9000.

Colour standards: In November 1888, AA–DF were handstamped "Cancelled" type 14; AD, AE are known outside the P.O. Heritage Services.

Plate 2, broken frames

1888 (February). £1 Brown-lilac, Type K12. Wmk Three Orbs (W10). Perf 14.

K16 (=S.G.186)	£1 brown-lilac	£50000	£3500
	a. Frame broken, stamps JC or TA (Plate 2)	£60000	£6000
	s. "Specimen", Type 11	£4000	
	sa. Do. broken frame JC or TA	£6000	
	t. "Specimen", Type 11 and "R & A.G.O." datestamp	£6000	

The December 1887 printing of 997 sheets of this stamp was on Orbs paper in error. It was easier to let it be issued than try to call back the paperwork and accounts. The precise issue date is unknown.

1891 (28 January). £1 Green, Type K12. Wmk Three Crowns (W12). Perf 14.

		Unmtd mint	Mtd mint	Used
K17 (=S.G.212)	£1 green	£5000	£3000	£650
	Block of four	—	—	—
	a. Frame broken, stamps JC or TA (Plate 2)	£10000	£6000	£1750
	aa. Frame unbroken JC or TA (Plate 3)	£7500	£5000	£1100
	b. Watermark inverted	—	£60000	£6000
	s. Imperforate "Specimen", Type 9		£4500	
	sa. Do. lettered AA, initialled "H.C.R." in margin		£10000	
	sb. Do. marginal copy with part (m/s) inscription (see below)			
	t. "Specimen", Types 9, 11, 13, 15, 16 *from*		£700	
	ta. Do. broken frame JC or TA *from*		£1000	

Imprimatur: (Plate 2 in green), each from £25000.

Imprimaturs: Plate 2: ND, OD, PD; OD was taken separately with Authority E5864/90 "New Colour (green) for £1 Postage Stamps".

Eleven stamps have been removed from the imprimatur sheet but four of these were subsequently returned after being on exhibition. One is in the Royal Collection, three in the P.O. Heritage Services of which two are in the R. M. Phillips Collection. There remain three examples in private hands, ND, OD (marginal) and PD.

No. K17s/sb. As a result of concern about photographic forgery of the £1 brown-lilac around the middle of 1890, it was decided to change the colour of this stamp to green. A Warrant for a new printing was issued about October 1890. When the first sheet was printed in the new colour, every stamp was handstamped specimen type 9 and sent to the P.O. Secretary S. A. Blackwood. P.O. Minute 15501/90 states "H.C.R. marked the sheet I have approved". H. C. Raikes was the P.M.G. and he wrote in the top left corner of the sheet adjacent to stamp AA "App'd Nov 18 1890" and initialled it. Elsewhere on the sheet there are m/s annotations on the selvedge which read "Selected sheet/18 Nov 1890". Those words cover several rows and can only be seen if adjacent marginal examples can be put together. These items are listed under K17s above.

Colour standards: Imperf QD–TD handstamped specimen type 9 exist in the P.O. Heritage Services but nothing else can be recognised.

Die Proofs. In black on white glazed card (unless otherwise stated):

Date	*Corner Letters*	*Inscr.*	*Additional Inscriptions or Notes*	
15 Apr 83	—	B/H		£3000
13 Sep 83	—	A/H		£3000
17 Sep 83		A/H		£3000
30 Oct 83	—	A/S		£3000
—	—	—	In lilac	£10000
—	—	—	In black	£3000

Die Proofs from the De La Rue Archives

Cut down and unmounted with corner squares uncleared £2500
From the Striking Books with corner squares uncleared £2500

Plate Proof

In black on thick white wove paper £2800

Colour trial. See, K17s and relevant description.

The Stamps of the Unified issue ½d. to 1s. 1 August 1883 to 1 April 1884
The "Lilac and Green" Issue

Plate layout and letterings. The temporary unified 3d. and 6d. stamps were printed on Imperial Crown Type **W12** watermark paper from existing 240 set plates. The ½d. continued as before but in the new colour. The remainder were printed 480 set from 240 set plates arranged in two panes. Those in upright format (the ½d., 1½d., 3d., 4d., 5d. and 1s.) were the same as the 1880 1d. including the letterings. Those in horizontal format (the 2d., 2½d., 6d. and 9d.) had left and right panes, each 120 set, 12 rows of 10, divided by a vertical blank gutter one stamp wide; hence the watermark was sideways. The normal arrangement was for the top of the Crown to point right when viewed from the back. It is regarded as inverted when the top of the Crown points left.

The lettering of the left pane was AA–AJ in row 1, BA–BJ in row 2 and so on down to LA–LJ in row 12. The right pane was lettered AK–AT in row 1 and so on down to LK–LT. None of these letterings, however read, match in position any on stamps in vertical format.

Unissued Five Pence. The original die used for the 5d. value had a line under the "d" of the value instead of the dot as seen on the issued stamps. Two plates were made and from them sheets were printed. The die having cracked it was decided to destroy these plates and the printed sheets; however, a few examples have survived and are much prized.

Sheet issue sizes. These continued from the 1880 issue except:

2d., 2½d. were 120 set (pane size, 12 rows of 10)
6d., 9d. were 40 set (4 rows of 10)

The places where cuts were to be made continued to be shown by pentagonal sheet dividing marks in the selvedge, and never seen complete.

Colour trials and Trial cancellations. See Section KD for these which were taken in connection with the work of the 1884 Stamp Committee.

K13

K14

K15

K16

K17

K19

K20

K20A

K18

K18A *Unissued type with line under "d"*

1884 (1 April). $\frac{1}{2}$d. Slate-blue, Type K1. Wmk Crown. Perf 14.

K17A (=S.G.187)		$\frac{1}{2}$d. slate-blue	25·00	8·00
		Block of four	£125	40·00
		Used on cover	†	15·00
	a.	Watermark inverted	—	£250
	b.	Imperforate (showing bottom margin)	£2000	
	s.	"Specimen", Type 9 (two shades) *from*	45·00	
	t.	"Cancelled", Type 14	£500	
	w.	Line perf 12	£1200	

Imprimaturs: Plates 7 *to* 14, *each* £250. No stamps were removed from the bottom margin of the imprimatur sheets.

Plate 7 was re-registered in slate-blue on 20 February 1884.

Die Proofs from the De La Rue Archives

From the Striking Books . . . . *from* £900

1884 (1 April). 1$\frac{1}{2}$d. Lilac, Type K13. Wmk Crown (W12). Perf 14.

K18 (=S.G.188)		1$\frac{1}{2}$d. lilac	95·00	38·00
		Block of four	£475	£170
		Used on cover	†	£100
	a.	Watermark inverted	—	£200
	b.	Imperforate	£2000	
	s.	Imperforate "Specimen", Type 9	£600	
	t.	"Specimen", Type 9	75·00	
	u.	Perforated 12. "Specimen", Type 9	£350	
	v.	"Cancelled", Type 14	£850	
	w.	Line perf 12	£2500	

Imprimaturs: (*Plates* 1 *and* 2), *each* £450. Stamps removed from the imprimatur sheets are: Plate 1: AF–AL, BG–BL, CG–CL, DG–DL; Plate 2: AG–AL, BG–BL, CF–CL, DH–DL.

Die Proofs. In black on white glazed card:

Date	*Corner Letters*	*Inscr.*	*Additional Inscriptions or Notes*	
—	—	—	Basic Die Proof	£1000
2 Aug 83	—	B/H		£1000
4 Aug 83	—	B/H		£1000
7 Aug 83	—	A/H		£1000

Die Proof from the De La Rue Archives

From the Striking Books £900

Plate Proof

In black on thick white wove paper £900

1884 (1 April). 2d. Lilac, Type K13. Wmk Crown (W12), sideways. Perf 14.

K19 (=S.G.189)	2d. lilac	£175	70·00
	Block of four	£800	£325
	Used on cover	†	£125
	a. Watermark sideways-inverted (crown points left from gummed side)		
	b. Imperforate	£2500	
	s. "Specimen", Type 9	75·00	
	t. Perf 12. "Specimen", Type 9	£350	
	u. "Cancelled", Type 14	£850	
	w. Line perf 12	£2500	

Imprimaturs: (*Plates* 1 *and* 2), *each* £450. Stamps removed from the imprimatur sheets are: Plate 1: IN, IO, JN–JT, KM–KT, LM–LT; Plate 2: HF–HJ, ID–IJ, JD–JJ, KD–KJ.

Die Proofs. In black on white glazed card:

Date	*Corner Letters*	*Inscr.*	*Additional Inscriptions or Notes*	
7 July 83	LB–BL	(M/S)	"After Striking 36 Leads" (M/S). Two date stamps, one inverted	£1000
27 July 83	—	B/H		£1000
31 July 83	—	(M/S)	"After Hardening" (M/S)	£1000
7 Aug 83	—	A/H	Initialled in pencil	£1000
23 Aug 83	—	A/H		£1000
23 Aug 83	—	A/S	Initialled in pencil	£1000

Die Proof from the De La Rue Archives

From the Striking Books with corner letters DN–ND £900

Plate Proof

In black on thick white wove paper £900

1884 (1 April). 2½d. Lilac, Type K15. Wmk Crown (W12), sideways. Perf 14.

K20 (=S.G.190)	2½d. lilac	75·00	15·00
	Block of four	£375	70·00
	Used on cover	†	25·00
	a. Watermark sideways-inverted (crown points left from gummed side)	£400	
	b. Imperforate	£2500	
	s. Imperforate "Specimen", Type 9	£600	
	t. "Specimen", Type 9	75·00	
	u. Perf 12. "Specimen", Type 9	£350	
	v. "Cancelled", Type 14	£850	
	w. Line perf 12	£2500	

Imprimaturs: Plate 1 (*Purple*) £450; *Plate* 2 (*Pale Purple*), £450. Stamps removed from the imprimatur sheets are: Plate 1: GQ–GT, HQ–HT, IQ–IT, JQ–JT, KQ–KT, LA, LQ–LT; Plate 2: GQ–GT, HR–HT, IQ–IT, JQ–JT, KQ–KT, LA, LQ–LT.

Die Proofs. In black on white glazed card:

Date	*Corner Letters*	*Inscr.*	*Additional Inscriptions or Notes*	
28 July 83	—	B/H		£1000
31 July 83	—	(M/S)	"After Hardening" (M/S)	£1000
7 Aug 83	—	A/H	Initialled in pencil	£1000
—	JA–AJ	(M/S)	"After Striking 1 doz Leads" (M/S)	£1000

Die Proof from the De La Rue Archives

From the Striking Books with corner letters £900
From the Striking Books with corner letters DN–ND £900

Plate Proof

In black on thick white wove paper £900

1884 (1 April). 3d. Lilac, Type K16. Wmk Crown (W12). Perf 14.

K21 (=S.G.191)		3d. lilac	£190	90·00
		Block of four	£950	£450
		Used on cover	†	£150
	a.	Imperforate	£2500	
	b.	Watermark inverted	†	£800
	s.	"Specimen", Type 9	75·00	
	t.	"Cancelled", Type 14	£850	
	w.	Line perf 12	£2500	

Imprimaturs: Plate 1 (*Purple*), £450; *Plate* 2 (*Pale Purple*), £450. Stamps removed from the imprimatur sheets are: Plate 1: AG–AL, BG–BL, CG–CL, DG–DL; Plate 2; AG–AL, BG–BL, CG–CL, DH, DJ–DL.

Die Proofs. In black on white glazed card:

Date	*Corner Letters*	*Inscr.*	*Additional Inscriptions or Notes*	
13 June 83	—	B/H		£1000
19 June 83	—	B/H		£1000

Die Proofs from the De La Rue Archives

From the Striking Books without corner letters £900
From the Striking Books with corner letters AE–EA £900

Plate Proof

In black on thick white wove paper £900

1884 (1 April). 4d. Dull green, Type K17. Wmk Crown (W12). Perf 14.

K22 (=S.G.192)		4d. dull green	£425	£185
		Block of four	£2200	£850
		Used on cover	†	£275
	a.	Imperforate	£2500	
	s.	"Specimen", Type 9	£160	
	t.	Perforated 12. "Specimen", Type 9	£450	
	u.	"Cancelled", Type 14	£850	
	w.	Line perf 12	£2750	

Imprimaturs: (*Plates* 1 *and* 2), *each* £500. Stamps removed from the imprimatur sheets are: Plate 1: AF–AL, BF–BL, CG–CL, DK, DL; Plate 2: AG–AL, BG–BL, CG–CL, DI–DL.

Die Proofs. In black on white glazed card:

Date	*Corner Letters*	*Inscr.*	*Additional Inscriptions or Notes*	
13 July 83	—	B/H		£1100
18 July 83	—	A/H		£1100
23 Aug 83	—	A/S	Also has additional "A/S" over "B/S" put on originally in error initialled "W.G." (M/S)	£1100
(M/S)	AI–IA	A/S	"27 Leads July 21st 1893" (M/S) also pencilled initials	£1100

Die Proof from the De La Rue Archives

From the Striking Books with corner letters AE–EA £950

Plate Proof

In black on thick white wove paper £950

1884 (1 April). 5d. Dull green, Type K18. Wmk Crown (W12). Perf 14.

K23 (=S.G.193)	5d. dull green (die 2)	£425	£185
	Block of four	£2250	£850
	Used on cover	†	£275
	a. With line under "d" (unissued), Type **K18A** (die 1)	£25000	
	b. Imperforate	£2800	
	s. "Specimen", Type 9	£160	
	t. Do. line under "d" (die 1)	£5000	
	v. Perforated 12. "Specimen", Type 9	£475	
	w. Line perf 12	£2750	
	y. "Cancelled", Type 14	£900	

Die 1 has a line below d and die 2 a dot; there are other differences. Plates 1, 2 were from die 1 and plates 3, 4 from die 2. No die 1 stamps were issued, but these letterings are known: SA, SC–SF, TA, TH, TI, TL. TH is in the Phillips Collection and SF in the Royal Collection.

Plates 1 and 2 were registered and put to press on 5.4.83, but the registration sheets, nearly all printed sheets, and the plates were destroyed as they were far below De La Rue's standards.

Imprimaturs: (*Plates* 3 *and* 4), *each* £500. Stamps removed from the imprimatur sheets are: Plate 3: KF–KL, LG–LL, MG–ML, NH–NL; Plate 4: AG–AL, BG–BL, CG–CL, DI–DL.

Die Proofs. In black on white glazed card:

Date	*Corner Letters*	*Inscr.*	*Additional Inscriptions or Notes*	
Type **K18A** (with line under "d", unissued)				
26 Feb 83	—	B/H		£2500
28 Feb 83	—	B/H		
2 Mar 83	BK–KB	(M/S)	"After Striking 1st forme" (M/S)	£2500
7 Mar 83	—	A/S	"Endorsed 2 Forms" (M/S)	£2500

Both February proofs usually show rings or parts of rings around the letter holes revealing the unsatisfactory nature of the die.

Type **K18** (with line under "d", issued)				
15 Aug 83	—	B/H		£1100
23 Aug 83	—	A/H		£1100
—	LM–ML	—	With pencilled initials "GFS"	£1100

Die Proof from the De La Rue Archives

From the Striking Books without corner letters £950

Plate Proof

In black on thick white wove paper £950

1884 (1 April). 6d. Dull green, Type K19. Wmk Crown (W12), sideways. Perf 14.

K24 (=S.G.194)	6d. dull green	£450	£200
	Block of four	£2200	£900
	Used on cover	†	£300
	a. Imperforate	£2800	
	b. Watermark sideways-inverted (crown points left from gummed side)	£700	
	s. "Specimen", Type 9	£190	
	t. Perf 12. "Specimen", Type 9	£475	
	u. "Cancelled", Type 14	£950	
	w. Line perf 12	£2750	

Imprimaturs: (*Plates* 1 *and* 2), *each* £550. Stamps removed from the imprimatur sheets are: Plate 1: GQ–GT, HQ–HT, IQ–IT, JQ–JT, KQ–KT, LQ–LT; Plate 2: FS, FT, GR–GT, HR–HT, IR–IT, JR–JT, KQ–KT.

Die Proofs. In black on white glazed card:

Endorsed "10 Aug 83 BEFORE HARDENING" £1100
Endorsed "28 Sep 83 AFTER STRIKING" £1100

Die Proof from the De La Rue Archives

From the Striking Books without corner letters £950

Plate Proof

In black on thick white wove paper £950

1883 (1 August). 9d. Dull green, Type K20. Wmk Crown (W12), sideways. Perf 14.

K25 (=S.G.195)		9d. dull green	£875	£400
		Block of four	£4000	£1800
		Used on cover	†	£2000
	b.	Watermark sideways-inverted (crown points left from gummed side)	£1400	£650
	s.	"Specimen", Type 9	£300	
	t.	"Cancelled", Type 14	£950	
	w.	Line perf 12	£2800	

Imprimaturs: Plate 3 (*Green*), £1500; *Plate* 4 (*Pale Green*), £1500. Plates 1 and 2 were never registered or put to press. Stamps removed from the imprimatur sheets are: Plate 3: GQ–GT, HQ–HT, IQ–IT, JQ–JT, KQ–KT, LQ–LT; Plate 4: GR–GT, HQ–HT, IQ–HT, IQ–IT, JQ–JT, KQ–KT, LQ–LT.

Die Proofs. In black on white glazed card:

Date	*Corner Letters*	*Inscr.*	*Additional Inscriptions or Notes*	
13 June 83	—	B/H	Was stamped "13 Jun 83" but altered to "18" (M/S)	£1300
18 June 83	—	B/H	Faint circles in three letter corners	£1300
26 June 83	—	A/S	With pencilled initials "GFS"	£1300
6 Jul 83	—	—	Initialled	£1300
6 Jul 83	—	—	Shows plugs in place of corner letters	£1300
—	BN/NB	(M/S)	"After Striking 30 Leads" and pencilled initials "C.S."	£1300
—	LS–SL	—	With pencilled initials "GFS"	£1300
—	—	—	Basic Die Proof	£1300

Die Proof from the De La Rue Archives

From the Striking Books with corner letters AE–EA £1100

Plate Proof

In black on thick white wove paper £1100

1884 (1 April). 1s. Dull green, Type K20A. Wmk Crown (W12). Perf 14.

K26 (=S.G.196)		1s. dull green	£950	£225
		Block of four	£4750	£1100
		Used on cover	†	£475
	a.	Imperforate	£4250	
	b.	Watermark inverted		
	s.	"Specimen", Type 9	£250	
	t.	Perforated 12. "Specimen", Type 9	£475	
	u.	"Cancelled", Type 14	£950	
	w.	Line perf 12	£2800	

Imprimaturs: (*Plates* 1 *and* 2), *each* £1100. Stamps removed from the imprimatur sheets are: Plate 1: AG–AL, BG–BL, CG–CL, DG–DL; Plate 2: AG–AL, BG–BL, CG–CL, DI–DL.

Die Proofs. In black on white glazed card:

Date	*Corner Letters*	*Inscr.*	*Additional Inscriptions or Notes*	
15 Aug 83	—	B/H		£1300
23 Aug 83	—	A/H	Pencilled initials "W.G."	£1300
23 Aug 83	—	A/H		£1300
30 Oct 83	—	A/H		£1300
30 Oct 83	—	A/S	Initialled	£1300

Die Proof from the De La Rue Archives

From the Striking Books without corner letters . . . . *from* £1100

Plate Proof

In black on thick white wove paper £1100

SECTION KD

Before and After the 1884 Stamp Committee

(Contributed by W. A. Wiseman, F.R.P.S.L.)

Sources: *The De La Rue Years* 1878–1910 *Vols 1 and 2* by W. A. Wiseman, B.A.(Oxon) F.R.P.S.L. and *Great Britain, Hand Painted Essays for the* 1884–1892 *Stamp Committee, sale* 13 *January* 1976, *Robson Lowe Ltd., London.*

I. 1 April 1884–30 October 1884

When the 1884 stamps appeared there was a public outcry which the Government was minded to ignore, but when it was pointed out that the Revenue might suffer from inability to check the correct value of stamps used, reaction was immediate. Warren William De La Rue was given virtually *carte blanche* to remedy the situation. The Inland Revenue's concern was to safeguard its revenue, in the shape of taxes raised by unified stamps. The 1d. receipt stamp brought in annually between £0.5 and £1 million out of a total Revenue of about £80 million which, in modern times, is around £2 billion. They wanted every stamp up to 2s. 6d., except the ½d., to have the Queen's Head in double fugitive ink to prevent removal of pen cancellations.

The Post Office had the practical task of checking frankings under sometimes very difficult conditions; hence Jeffrey's commitment to the three primary colours, red, blue and yellow. They were seeking brightly coloured stamps, cheap to produce and easily recognised.

De La Rue wanted their expensive fugitive, especially double fugitive, inks to be used as much as possible and they realised that this was an opportunity not to be missed. Designs, papers, printing qualities of inks, bicoloured stamps could all be explored.

De La Rue had been experimenting with coloured papers before 1 April 1884, as earlier issues show. Their first efforts were colour trials, mostly in purple and green, from production plates of Nos. K18 to K21, 1½d., 2d., 2½d. and 3d. values onto coloured papers. These were made by dyeing just a few or even single sheets, giving a lack of uniformity.

Colour trials on coloured unwatermarked paper. Colours are grouped into red, orange, yellow, buff(brown), green, blue, lilac and grey. Imperforate trials are incomplete and not distinguished. Comb perf 14:

1½d. purple on all above papers except lilac	£425
1½d. green on white, grey, orange, blue	£425
2d. purple on buff, orange, pink, blue	£450
2d. green on red	£525
2½d. purple on all above except grey, orange	£450
2½d.. green on white, buff yellow	£425
3d. purple on yellow, green, blue, lilac	£425
3d. green on green	£425

Prices are for single stamps not stuck down.

Once they had authority to proceed, colour trials were produced of the same values on white watermarked Crown paper in the following colour groups:

1½d. purple, red/orange/brown, yellow, green, blue, black/grey	*from* £1500
2d. purple, red/orange/brown, green, blue, black/grey	*from* £1500
2½d. As 1½d.	*from* £1500
3d. As 2d.	*from* £1500

Trials in other colour inks on coloured papers. Two pieces of squared paper existed to which were stuck a total of 120 trials (63 + 57) of the 1884 2d. and 2½d. on various coloured unwatermarked papers, printed in various coloured inks and mostly lettered LJ or LT. Arranged neatly in columns of 4 to 14 stamps in each. These were subsequently broken up. (*From* £250 *each stamp*).

"Coloured Paper" Scheme 13 June 1884. Produced formally to show what could be achieved by printing existing designs on coloured papers. Four copies were made:

No. 1 is in the Phillips Collection, the whereabouts of No. 2 is unknown and No's 3 and 4 (De La Rue's own copy, all stamps defaced) are in private hands. Each comprises a copy of the issued 1d. and 4d. with two colour trials or unwatermarked paper of each of the 1½d., 2d., 2½d. and 3d. stamps. Arranged in two rows of five, the top row of trials represented their face values:

1½d., (purple/orange), 2d. (purple/yellow), 2½d. (purple/pink), 3d. (purple/pale blue shades): and the lower row of those values represented:

5d. (1½d., purple/grey), 6d. (2d., purple/pink), 9d. (2½d. green/buff) and 1s. (3d. purple/deep blue) as indicated in m/s above each.

Price (for complete Schemes) . . . .

The following are based on the Scheme:

All ten stamps on piece, annotated but no date . . . .

1½d. purple on pink, purple on grey . . . . *from* £1200
2d. purple on yellow, purple on pink . . . . *from* £1200
2½d. purple on pink, green on buff . . . . *from* £1200
3d. purple on pale blue, purple on deep blue . . . . *from* £1200

The Scheme was favourably received by the Post Office. On 25 June 1884, it was decided to send 6 to 12 examples of each of the same colour trials to various officials for their opinions and for "experiments".

Trial cancellations are known from this exercise, mostly on piece (other letterings exist):

Probably from W. H. Mulock, Confidential Enquiry Branch:

Octagonal LONDON/8 (or a) B/30 Ju/84:

1½d. purple/orange (BF); purple/grey (AF) . . . .
2d. purple/pink (FB) . . . .
2½d. purple/pink (IB); green/buff (HA) . . . .
3d. purple/pale blue (DC); purple/deep blue (BF) . . . .
4d. (No. K22 as issued) (LH) . . . .

Probably from G. Richardson, Accountant General's Office.

London squared circle 3/JY/84:

1d.. (No. K8 as issued) . . . .
1½d. purple/orange (BD); purple/grey (BD, BB) . . . .
2d. purple/yellow (IB); purple/pink (BB) . . . .
2½d. purple/pink (KC); green/buff (IB) . . . .
3d. purple/pale blue (DB); purple/deep blue (BD) . . . .
4d. (No. K22 as issued) (LI) . . . .
1d. 1½d. (BD) and 2½d. (IB) are on one piece.

London squared circle 4/JY/84:

1d.. (No. K8 as issued) . . . .
1½d. purple/orange (BC); purple/grey (BC) . . . .
2½d. green/buff (JB) . . . .
3d. purple/pale blue (CB) . . . .
4d. (No. K22 as issued) (LF, DA)

Undated London squared:

1d.. (No. K8 as issued) . . . .
1½d. purple/orange (AD) . . . .
2½d. green/buff (IA) . . . .

From T. Jeffrey, Head London Postal Service:

L.P.S., Controllers office 22/JY/84:

1½d. purple/grey (AC) . . . . *from* £800
2d. purple/yellow (CB) . . . . *from* £800
2½d. green/buff (AD, JA) . . . . *from* £800
3d. purple/pale blue (CA); purple/deep blue (AD) . . . . *from* £800

From Mr. Cunynghame, Postmaster, Edinburgh;

2K/EDINBURGH/3/JY/84 duplex (131 rarely seen):

1½d. purple/orange (IE); purple/grey (EC) . . . .
2d. purple/yellow (JE); purple/pink (CH) . . . .
2½d. purple/pink (JE); green/buff (IG) . . . .
3d. purple/pale blue (GD); purple/deep blue (EC) . . . .
4d. (No. K22 as issued) (OK) . . . .
Piece with issued 1d., colour trials of 1½d. (×2), 2d. (×2), 2½d., 3d., issued 4d.,
all letterings unknown, all cancelled as above with 131 in bars . . . . *the sheet* £12000

6K/EDINBURGH/29/JY/84:

1½d. purple/orange (IB, ID); purple/grey (GC, HC) . . . . *from* £900
2d. purple/yellow (JF/JH) . . . . *from* £900
2½d. purple/pink (JG, JH); green/buff (JF–JH) . . . . *from* £900
3d. purple/pale blue (ID, JH); purple/deep blue (GC, HC) . . . . *from* £900
4d. (No. K22 as issued) (PK–RK on piece) . . . . *from* £900
This cancel also known on issued 1½d. lettering unknown.

From W. J. Beaufort, Postmaster Manchester:

Manchester squared circle Y6/JU30/84:

1½d. lilac/grey (lettering unknown) . . . . *from* £900
3d. purple/pale blue (DF); purple/deep blue (HD) . . . . *from* £900

Manchester 498 duplex JY8/84:

1d. (No. K8 as issued) . . . . *from* £900
1½d. purple/orange; purple/buff (lettering unknown) . . . .
2d. purple/pink (DE) and others*; purple/yellow (JA) and others* . . . . *from* £900
2½d. purple/pink (GG, HE); green/buff (JA) and others* . . . . *from* £900
3d. purple/pale blue (CE) others* . . . . *from* £900
* letterings unknown.

R. Cornwall, Postmaster of Dublin, examples on unaddressed covers cancelled Dublin, 14C 7 JY 84. Some are in the Post Office Heritage Services, but some may be on the market.

The Postmasters of Liverpool, Birmingham and Glasgow also received copies but nothing is known of them.

Stamp Committee Proposal. Coloured papers were an improvement, but they were not the complete answer. New designs could not be avoided so the 1884 Stamp Committee was set up. Its purpose was to recommend new designs, but it was also to restore relations between the Post Office and Inland Revenue. Its establishment took time so De La Rue and others continued to evolve their ideas.

Jeffrey's Ideas. On 2 August 1884 T. Jeffrey sent pieces of gummed, unwatermarked paper with five crude lithographed impractical designs to the Secretary's Office, as Types D and E. Known in red, yellow-orange, green, blue and purple.

Type D

Type E

Essays by Jeffrey

Essays for Biocoloured Stamps. The earliest seen, a dummy stamp on card dated 6 August 1884. It is inscribed "De La Rue London Four Pence" and large "4d." each side of the Queen's Head. The corner letters are BH/HB and frame lines printed in green and the remainder hand painted in deep pink. It demonstrated that unsupported frame lines were undesirable in bicoloured design.

There are also die proofs of the head and red parts of the above in black, and of the latter in both green and red, in the Phillips Collection. There is a striking book piece with the same die proofs and die proofs of two otherwise unknown dummy stamps, lettered HB. The same letter combination is used on later De La Rue essays.

Only two types of bicoloured stamps were practical – the "patch of colour" type, as the 1887 2d. and 5d. stamps and the "fringe" type, as the 4d. and 9d.

The "fringe" type. A piece of paper is in the Royal Collection with two perf 12 1s. stamps handstamped "SPECIMEN" Type 9, FI, FJ, FI is cancelled with three POSTAL-STAMP-BRANCH/A/250C/84/INLAND REVENUE circular date stamps. The perforations are coloured red on both stamps (this is the only dated piece with perf 12 stamps). In the Phillips Collection there is a letter dated 23 Oct. 1884 from Warren William De La Rue to T. A. Colls with an issued 1s. and a hexagonal hand painted 3d. essay, both also with red borders.

Inleave Border Essays:

De La Rue inleave cut outs with stamp borders in red and defaced (two examples known) . . . .

1884 Striking Book Pieces:

(1) Die proof essays of duty designs with (m/s) "Aug 20" (later used for Siam stamps) . . . .
(2) As (1) but blank head (no head) and duty (no duty) "fringe" designs similar to 4d., dated in (m/s) "Aug 28" . . . .
(3) As (2), but duty only and dated "Sept 26" . . . .
(4) As (3), dated "Oct 9/10" . . . .
(5) As (2), but head and duty, dated 1884 "Oct 30", "Nov. 2" . . . .

II. 31 October 1884–11 June 1885

The members of the Committee, which sat from 31 October 1884 to 13 April 1885 were: T. Jeffrey, Head of the London Postal Service, Chairman: J. S. Purcell, Controller of Stamps, Inland Revenue Stamping Department; Henry R. Page, P.O. employee, artistic adviser; W. H. Mulock, Head of the Confidential Enquiry Branch of the P.O.; T. C. Bokenham, Assistant Controller of Stamps, Inland Revenue Stamping Department.

Their terms of reference were set out by S. A. Blackwood, Secretary to the P.O., on 29 October 1884. They formally met 24 times and interviewed 32 witnesses. Their Report was issued in April 1885.

Warren De La Rue was not a member of the Committee, having declined an invitation. He was, however, the key witness on whom everything depended and who nudged the Committee forward to an acceptable conclusion. The witnesses called before the Committee were a cross section of officials from those Departments with an interest in the outcome.

If a witness such as Carey, a Clerk in the P.O. Secretary's Department, came forward with ideas, Warren De La Rue produced essays to illustrate them. Carey's comment on seeing such essays is revealing; he liked them very much, but they were not what he had in mind. The only major contribution to design came from Committee Member H. R. Page who suggested the Queen's Head on white background which was immediately adopted by De La Rue despite its technical difficulty.

The Work of the Committee. An early decision was that the Committee should concern itself only with the 1½d. to 1s, values. The ½d., 1d., 2s. 6d., 5s., 10s., £1 and £5 designs were considered satisfactory. The decision remained unchanged for the high values, but towards the end, both the ½d. and 1d. came under scrutiny. The 1d. was always included as a standard, but the ½d. was ignored. Some copies of early Schemes have ½d. stamps on them, but they were added later.

On 20 November, printing by typography and double fugitive inks were confirmed. On 8 December, it was decided corner letters were unnecessary as Circular cancels almost invariably left at least one corner of a stamp clear.

Handpainted essays. These were vital to the Committee's work. Some 350 were produced of which about 200 have survived. Two major types exist: on tracing paper which ages to a pink or yellow tone, and on white paper which does not suffer so much from ageing. The former were used to save time in ensuring heads were the correct size and in the correct place.

Essays for single colour on coloured papers are usually described as if they were for bicoloured. Essays for bicoloured have been described as three colours and so on. Recognising which type is involved is not easy: For example, a lined feature on the finished stamp is shown in a light wash, easily mistaken for a new colour. White, i.e. to be unprinted, is either unpainted (when age can give it a colour) or the area is painted white. Perforations are normally in pencil.

The Committee decided by 21 November that three values, the 2½, 3 and 6d., were to be in purple on paper in one of the three primary colours. Most hand painted essays of those values are purple on a coloured wash.

In addition to essays for intended stamps, some with "impossible" designs, such as exaggerated figures of value, were created to wean the Committee away from various impracticable ideas.

Mixed Scheme. Created 21 November 1884 showing 2½d. on blue, 3d. on yellow, 6d. on pink all on a page and signed by J. S. Purcell . . . . —

3 December 1884. Envelopes with duplicate stamps from the Mixed Scheme (above) were sent to be cancelled at a working office as normal mail. Whereabouts of this material, each cover signed by J. S. Purcell, is unknown.

On 12 December Warren De La Rue produced designs close to those finally accepted. The Committee generally agreed with them, but more work on design and production problems was needed.

On 5 January 1885 the Committee re-assembled. Warren De La Rue returned with improved designs, cancelled and uncancelled. The 5 January Portsmouth squared circle, new and unissued without additional date plugs, was provided for this meeting. The ½d. and 1d. values now came into the discussion.

The lilac and green issue with PORTSMOUTH squared circle IL/JA 5/85:

½d. (No. K17A)	£900
1½d. (No. K18)	
2d. (No. K19)	£900
2½d.(No. K20)	£900
3d. (No. K21)	£900
4d. (No. K22)	£900
5d. (No. K23)	£900
6d. (No. K24)	£900
9d. (No. K25)	£900
1s. (No. K26)	£900

The First ½d. Essays. Handpainted essays of ½d. with "POSTAGE" and "ONE HALFPENNY" in orange-red. *Price from* £2500.

1881 1d. Colour Trials. As No. K8 on white watermarked paper perf 14 (imperf are incomplete and not listed separately, prices are the same as perforated examples). Shades are by broad colour groups:

Brown (6 shades); Orange (2 shades); Red (2 shades); Blue (4 shades); Grey (2 shades); Green (2 shades) . . . . *from* £2000

Lilac and mauve trials are reported, but perf examples could be production stamps and imperforate from imprimatur sheets.

Colour Trials Without Corner Letters.
As Nos. K20, K21, K26 Without watermark, line perf 14:

2½d.: purple on blue	£2500
3d.: purple on pink, blue, yellow	£2500
1s.: purple on orange, yellow	£2800

The 2½d., 3d. and 1s. are those from the dies of which 18 leads were struck (2½d., 1s. on 13 and 3d. on 15 December 1884).

Trial Small Head Dies on White Background. Created early December 1884:

Striking Book piece with small head in circle with square hatched surround and (m/s) "Dec 24/1884/10 leads" . . . .

Striking Book piece with die proofs of stamp die with preceding head on white and two matching 2d. duty dies, one with lined and one with speckled tablet and (m/s) "1885 (1885 incorrectly altered to 1886)/Jan 31/18 leads off each" .

Die proof of same stamp die . . . .

A 2d. essay from stamp and duty die (lined tablet) above, printed in green and red . . . .

As last, but from die proofs and with tinted red highlights in leaves to left and right of head . . . .

Proper comparison of the head on the 2d. stamp essays above with the small head die itself has not been made, but they appear to be the same. A small head die on white ground is said to have been created on 11 December 1884.

$1\frac{1}{2}$d. Hand-painted Essays. The $1\frac{1}{2}$d was originally a "patch of colour" design changed after 16 March 1885.

Hand-painted essay, as accepted design, but leaves in purple, head in green. Defaced with pen cross . . . .

Later essays for minor adjustments:

As issued, "POSTAGE & REVENUE" highlighted in white £5500
As issued, blue leaves and tablet £5000

A

B

The 6d. Embossing Essays

(1) Striking book piece with die proof in accepted design except 6d. white on coloured, and blank circle where head should be (m/s) "Jan 2nd/18 leads" Type B £2500
(2) As (1), but 6d. as issued but with line under d. Type A £2500
(3) As die proof from (1), but parts of design embossed £2500
(4) As die proof from (2), but parts of design embossed £2500
(5) Stamp as (4) in pale green with large top selvedge line perf 14 and part design embossed £4750
(1) and (2) were once joined.

1884 $\frac{1}{2}$d. Colour Trials. On watermarked white paper, perf 14; imperf trials are incomplete:

Venetian red, Orange-red, Orange, Orange-brown . . . . *from* £2000

Four trials possibly the above, were sent to Jeffrey by Warren De La Rue on 10 January 1885. The context for the following is not known:

Greenish grey £2000

At the 5 January meeting, J. S. Purcell announced that he and others would visit Foreign Stamping Departments. The next Committee meeting was on 12 March when Arliss and Warren De La Rue gave further evidence, much of it unrecorded. The 1s. essays were shown to the Committee who chose the accepted design.

1s. Hand Painted Essays.

In green . . . . *from* £5000

At the 16 March meeting Warren De La Rue recommended "orange" for the $\frac{1}{2}$d., and the following day it was decided that the 1d. would not be changed, the 2d. to "adjust", the 6d. would not be embossed and the $\frac{1}{2}$d. agreed should be "orange-red". Warren de La Rue was asked to produce yet more $\frac{1}{2}$d. design with "Postage and Revenue".

$\frac{1}{2}$d. Hand-painted in orange-red Essays with "Postage & Revenue":

Value in words . . . . *from* £5000
Value "$\frac{1}{2}$d." repeated four times . . . . *from* £5000

At the final recorded meeting on 13 April 1885, a $\frac{1}{2}$d. design with "$\frac{1}{2}$d." in each corner was accepted, provided the corner $\frac{1}{2}$d.'s were removed. It is not known when the final selections were sent to the Post Master General, but he accepted all the designs, except for $2\frac{1}{2}$d. More $2\frac{1}{2}$d. essays had to be prepared

Choosing the 2½d. Design.

Eleven new hand-painted essays, including the finally accepted design, were created and sent to the Post Master General with the rejected design, making 12 in all. The 11 rejected designs were mounted on a sheet, with five hand-painted very large figure essays of 1½d., 2d., 4d., 5d., 9d. values, behind sunk card. Warren De La Rue added an (m/s) note. It is dated 12 June 1885. . . . . £60000

Other Hand-painted Essays from this Period.

These divide broadly into 5 groups.

(a) Before the Committee had been given guidelines. These are from the De La Rue archives and show corner letters BH/HB. Before 31 October 1884:

2d. pale green and white; 2½d. (horiz.); red; 2½d. same design slate-lilac; 4d. green and pink; 5d. yellow and grey-lilac; 6d. red-brown; 6d. deep blue, yellow and green . . . . *from* £5000

(b) For illustrative purposes, with very large figures of value. Submitted 21 November 1884.

Square design with large uncoloured numeral:

9d. in dull lilac and orange £5000

Extra large figure scheme:

3d., 4d. and 5d. in various colours . . . . *from* £5000

G. R. Smith's designs with quite large figures and the Queen's head off-centre on a solid background:

1½d. (horiz.) and 1½d. (vert.) in lilac and blue; 2½d. (horiz.) and 2½d. (vert.) in purple on blue; 3d. in purple on buff; 1s. in green on buff . . . . *from* £5000

(c) Trial designs of "patch-of-colour" type (as 1887 2d. and 5d.) Queen's head on solid background with numerals uncoloured and outlined:

1½d. (9) in lilac and blue, green or carmine (each differs) . . . . *from* £5000
1½d. lilac and green (Queen's head on a circular blank surround) . . . .
2d. (8) in various colours . . . . *from* £5000
2d. grey-green and mauve (Queen's head on a circular blank surround) . . . .
4d. (2) in grey-green and rose, one showing 5d. converted to 4d. . . . . *from* £5000
5d. in green and purple in design of 6d. £5000
1s. orange, greenish blue and white . . . . *from* £5000

(d) Trial designs of "fringe" type (as 1887 4d. and 9d.)

1½d. blue, dull lilac and white £5000
2d. blue, pale blue, grey-lilac and white £5000
4d. red, green and white £5000
5d. deep blue, grey-violet and white £5000
9d. (5) in various colours . . . . *from* £5000
9d. in rosy mauve and green in issued design £6000
9d. in purple in issued design £6000

Combination of G. R. Smith's design with Carey's borders:

1½d. (2), 9d. in various colours on buff paper . . . . *from* £5000

Queen's head on solid background with solid numerals:

5d., 9d. each bicoloured . . . . *from* £5000

5d. essays generally based on Carey's ideas with Queen's head on solid background:

5d. (5) in brown and grey-green with uncoloured numerals . . . . *from* £5000
5d. (5) in brown and grey-green with solid numerals . . . . *from* £5000

(e) Single colour essays.

Queen's head on a circular blank surround; numerals vary:
3d. grey-green . . . .
6d. in red-purple on buff in design of 3d. £6000
6d. in purple on buff in design of 5d. £6000

6d. in purple and pink in design of 5d. £6000
6d. in green in the issued design £6000

The colours of some have changed over time. Thus the two 6d. essays in the design of the issued 5d. were not intended originally as bicolours as the tolerances are too small; compare bicolour essays.

The Approved Designs, 11 June 1885
Piece, with hand painted essays on white paper of approved 1887 designs, ½d., 1½d., 2d., 2½d., 3d., 4d., 5d., 6d., 9d. and 1s. values plus 1881 1d. signed and dated by W. C. Cousins £55000

Trial Cancellation London 1844 type, 3 in Diamond.
Probably from 1886: no known context therefore included here:

Cancel on blocks of four of the issued 1884 2½d. . . . .

EK–FL, EM–FN, LD–ME, known, EM–FN is in the Phillips Collection in the Post Office Heritage Services.

III. 12 June 1885–26 January 1888

Major technical problems remained after the Committee members had disbanded. They affected design, especially details of the 1½d., 2d. and 4d. duty plates.

On 25 May 1885 the Board of Inland Revenue authorised work on the new stamps to start, beginning with the small head dies.

Die Proofs. The Small Head Dies

In black on white glazed card.

Date	*Inscr*	*Additional Inscriptions or Notes*	
—	—	Die "288", on solid ground	£1000
8 May 85	—	Date in unusual style, head in small circle	£1000
2 Jul 85	B/H	On card, surrounded by black ring with two slots	£1000
2 Jul 85	B/H	With "288 for solid ground" (m/s)	£1000
2 Jul 85	B/H	With "288" in S.W. corner	£1000
—	B/H		£1000
—	—	Cut down to stamp size	£1000
—	—	Head in large black circle	£1000
—	—	Die "289" on white ground and head outlined with fine white line	
3 Jul 85	B/H	"3" altered to "2" (m/s)	£1000
3 Jul 85	B/H	"289 for white ground" (m/s)	£1000
3 Jul 85	B/H	"289" in S.W. corner	£1000
—	—	Cut down to stamp size	£1000

The new 320 Set Mill Sheet. A new mill sheet was required for "fringe" type stamps. Originally intended to have 200 stamps per plate, 400 per mill sheet, it was finally (February 1896) to have 160 stamps per plate and 320 per mill sheet.

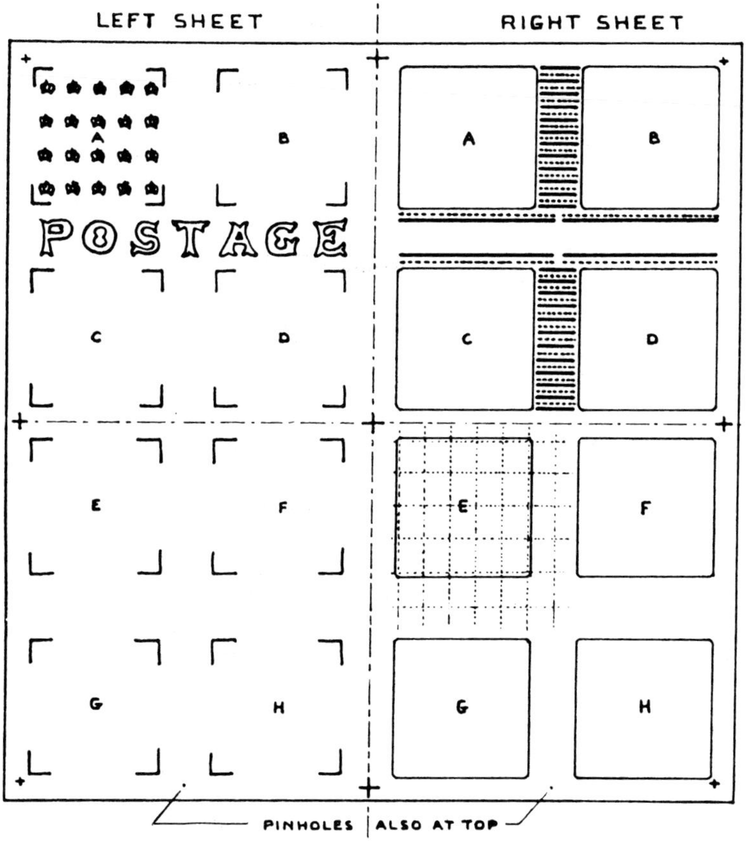

The 320 set Crown sheet for the 4d., 4½d., 9d. and 10d. values with philatelic identifying letters in centre of the panes; the lined blocks, top right, were introduced in 1888, marginal rules in 1889. The illustration does not include the watermark angles (45°) at each corner. These were usually trimmed off.

The Design of the Duty Tablets. The hand painted essays of the accepted design of the 2d. duty tablet had the "2d." in white on solid colour. The 1½d. and 4d. tablets had figures on pale wash backgrounds, implying lined (or similar) tablets. The authorities wanted "engine-turned" backgrounds, that is "speckled".

Duty dies were numbered in their own series: 1½d. – no. 3; 2d. – no. 2; 4d. – no. 1; 5d. – no's 5, 6; 9d. – no. 4. Although not recorded, there were two 1½d., three 2d. and two 4d. dies, distinguished by collectors with "a", "b" and "c" suffixes. The first created (a) all had speckled tablets as did the 9d.

Rejected Duty Dies

1½d. value, die 3a, speckled tablet:

Undated proof . . . .

One copy is in the Phillips Collection.

2d. value, die 2a, speckled tablet:

Die proof: 31 Mar 86, B/H £1500
Striking book piece with 2d. head plate die proof with (m/s) date "Mar 11" and "1886 2d. die" . . . . *from* £1000

A corresponding striking book piece dated 2nd April with proofs of die 2a duty plate and head plate 3/753 is in the Post Office Heritage Services.

A small printing convinced the authorities that engine turned backgrounds were unsuitable. Several uncancelled copies have survived. Tablet in carmine. Perf 14:

Uncancelled single £2000

2d. value, die 2b, tablet in solid colour, white 2:

Undated proof . . . .

Printings were also made using die 2b. A few copies survive. Tablet in carmine. Perf 14:

Uncancelled single £2000
One piece, cancelled Portsmouth squared circle 5.1.85 . . . . £1500
One piece, cancelled BO1 (Alexandria type) in bars . . . .
One piece, three copies, and three copies of the issued stamp in two vertical columns, top pair uncancelled, second pair cancelled . . . .
Portsmouth as above and third pair cancelled BO1 as above . . . .

2d. accepted die was 2c; proofs are listed in Section KE 2d. value.

4d. value: Die 1a; 4d.'s on speckled background.

21 Jan 86	A/H	£1000	17 Mar 86	A/H	£1000
17 Feb 86	B/H	£1000	18 Mar 86	A/H	£1000
17 Mar 86	B/H	£1000	20 Mar 86		£1000

Many of the above show the die upside down.

An original plate of 20 (plate no. 01) was made from this die and completed 14 April 1886, but never used. The accepted die was die 1b, see Section KE, 4d. value.

The letter of 11 November 1886 is relevant; there were three appendices:

"A": All 11 values ½d.–1s. in issue on April 1st 1884 and all 11 values of imminent 1887 issue, none cancelled . . . .
"B": As A, but all cancelled Portsmouth squared circle 5.1.85 . . . .
"C": Stamps of imminent 1887 issue showing attempts to remove normal or abnormal cancellations, including ink . . . .

It is likely three copies of these appendices were made. They are the main, though not the only, source of stamps of the 1883 and 1887 issue cancelled with Portsmouth 5.1.85 trial cancel (see list below **The Work of the Committee** 5 Jan 85). It is uncertain whether complete pages or half pages still exist:

Appendix A, complete as above . . . .
Appendix B, complete as above . . . .
piece from B, 1883 issue . . . .
piece from B, 1887 issue . . . .
Appendix C, complete as above . . . .
piece from C, 1883 issue . . . .
piece from C, 1887 issue . . . .
Any stamp from these appendices cancelled with Portsmouth trial cancellation . . £1500

Leads Struck for Gauging Purposes 16 November 1886.

Striking book pieces with date and (m/s) "For gauging purposes".

Die proofs of ½d., 1d., 1½d. (head and duty), 2d. (head and duty) 2½d.;
As before, but proofs of 3d., 4d. (head and duty), 5d., head, duty dies 1, 2, 6d., 9d. head only
As before, with proofs of 9d. duty only, 1s. . . . .

"Cancelled" Type 14,

All 11 values to 1s. in use after January 1 1887 "cancelled", Type 14 . . . .

De La Rue Presentation Books. To commemorate the introduction of the new stamps, De La Rue created 36 Presentation books for officials and others deemed of importance in connection with their creation. Entitled "*Before and After the Stamp Committee*" each had three pages with stamps. The first had the $\frac{1}{2}$d.–1s. in use before 1883, mostly those of the 1880 Provisional issue. The second had the stamps in use after 1 April 1884 and the third had those to be issued on 1 January 1887.

To create the first page, stamps from registration sheets were line perforated, including the 1866 9d. plate 5 and the 1880 1s. in brown and in purple. The 1s. purple was never issued and the 9d. was not in use in 1882. Most books have been broken up, but occasionally the 9d. and 1s. line perforated were replaced by comb perf.

Not all books had the 1s. purple, but they all had 9d. plate 5. Stamps taken from registration sheets can be recognised by their plate numbers and letterings, and by the fact that they are line perforated. In particular a few books contained line perforated 1s. brown plate 14, being much rarer than the 1s. purple. Replacement 1s. brown tend to be plate 13 and are comb perforated. Most of the stamps without corner letters on the first page were also line perf. 14.

Complete, as created, Presentation books are very rare. In the list below, all first page stamps are line perf 14 unless stated.

Complete books are identified by the lettering of the 6d.:

1. QL: complete as presented . . . .
2. OC: complete as presented . . . .
3. PC: complete but dismantled . . . .

Still bound, complete books, but missing original 9d. and 1s.

4. PH: with replacement pl. 4 9d., pl. 13 1s. . . . .
5. QI: no replacement (i.e. empty spaces) . . . .
6. RL with line perf pl. 14 1s. brown and replacement pl. 4 9d... . . . .

Complete book with ALL comb per stamps:

7. NI (plate 18) . . . .

Additional three books were made with comb perf. stamps on the first page handstamped "Specimen", Type 9:

8. CI (plate 18) . . . .
9. DL (plate 18) . . . .

Other books are believed to exist. There are also examples in the Royal Collection (Queen Victoria received a copy) and in the Post Office Heritage Services.

Line Perf 14 1866 9d. plate 5 Imprimaturs: Those known are: KA–KC, KF–KJ, KL, LA–LK, MA, MC, ME, MI, MK, ML, NJ–NL, 29 out of 36 stamps removed and listed under No. J95.

TL perf is a fake, (removed imperf).

Line Perf 14 1s. purple plate 14 Imprimaturs: Those known are: CB, CD, CE, CH, DB, DG–DI, EB, EE–EH, EJ, FB, FC, FE, FG–FI, 20 out of 36 stamps removed and listed under No. K8C.

Line Perf examples of the other Imprimaturs:

1880	$\frac{1}{2}$d. plate 8		1880 3d., plate 21	
1881	1d., plate 28 (No. K80)	£600	1880 4d., plate 18	£3000
1880	1$\frac{1}{2}$d. plate 1		1880 5d., plate 1	
1880	2d., plate 2		1880 6d., plate 18	
1880	2$\frac{1}{2}$d. plate 22		1881 1s., brown, plate 14	

Illustrative Cards for T. A. Colls. In August 1887, Warren De La Rue arranged for T. A. Colls, Head of the Postal Stamp Branch at Somerset House, to receive cards made from die proofs of dies in use showing how the marginal rules were incorporated onto the plates of bicoloureds. The interpane gutters on all plates had to be accurately made for correct register in printing, perforation etc. Unstruck leads were smaller than struck ones and so blank "division" leads also were struck. They were incorporated into the chase before electroplating. Normally, they did not print, but new dies for rules were made. These Cards are listed under the relevant stamps.

1890 Essays for Postage Stamp Jubilee

The year 1890 was the Golden Jubilee of the introduction of the first adhesive postage stamp. It was thought appropriate to mark the event with a new stamp but the idea was dropped when it was pointed out that De La Rue would not only have to be paid for dics and new plates but also for throwing out of use large numbers of usuable 1881 1d. plates. Two designs with the recommended head based on the portrait by Sir Edgar Boehm was submitted. However, the printers suggested the Queen Victoria portrait by Professor von Angeli would be preferable and later essays using the three-quarter portrait were submitted. The eight different basic designs are referred to below as Types A to H.

The pen-cancelled essays are all from the De La Rue archives.
Hand-painted on card and pen-cancelled.
Dated "Dec. 17th. 89".
Essays inscribed "Postage and Inland Revenue".

Type A (Boehm head in Type C frame) in lilac and white £5500
Type B (Boehm head in frame similar to Type F) in lilac and white £5500

Type C

Type D

(*Angeli Head*)

Type E

Type F

(*Boehm Head*)

Dated "Dec. 23rd. 89".
Essays inscribed "Postage and Revenue".

Type C in lilac and white, inscr. "No. 2" £5500
Type E in lilac and white, inscr. "No. 4" £5500
Type F in lilac and white, inscr. "No. 5" £5500
Type G (Boehm head in Type C frame) in red and white, inscr. "No. 6" £5500

Dated "Dec. 27th. 89".

Type E in lilac, red and white, inscr. "No. 9" £5500

This essay with the head in lilac, frame in red, was submitted on 27 December 1889 together with Type H showing the Boehm head in an oval frame. This was hand-painted in red, green and white and inscribed "No. 8". This was the final incident in the proposed Postage Stamp Jubilee issue. At this date what would have been the first commemorative stamp passed into oblivion.

Essays from the De La Rue archives with pen-cancellation which were acquired by the National Postal Museum were "No. 1" as Type C but with Boehm head in lilac and white; "No. 3" Type D in lilac and white; "No. 7" Type C in red and "No. 8" Type H in red, green and white.

Essays on card, hand-painted and *without* pen-cancellation.

Type D in lilac and white, inscr. "No. 3". The best I think" and initials £5500
Type E in lilac and white, inscr. "No. 4" £5500
Type F in lilac and white, inscr. "No. 5" £5500
Type C in red and white, inscr. "No. 7" £5500

SECTION KE

The "Jubilee" Issue, Types K21 to K32 (1887–1900)

This issue has always been known as the "Jubilee" Issue as it happened to appear during the year when the Queen celebrated the 50th Anniversary of her Accession.

Paper and Watermark. New Imperial Crown watermark paper had to be produced for those stamps printed in panes of 20 (4d., 4½d., 9d., 10d.). The mill sheet was 320 set as shown in Section KD. The same features shown separately for clarity are on both halves and all appropriate parts of the mill sheet. The dotted lines joining the watermark crosses (virtually in the same places as on the 480 crown mill sheet) show how sheets were cut before issue. Identification of left and right sheets is the same as for 480 sheets. The letters on each pane (A, B, C, D; E, F, G, H) are philatelic identifying letters. The 2½d., 3d. and 6d. were printed on coloured 480 set mill sheets.

From 1892, letters in the watermark were introduced on 480 set mill sheets on the centre line below central cross D between rows 11/12, i.e. to the right of those rows on left sheets and to the left on right sheets. Letters A–C were joined about 1896 by D–F and G came later.

Imperial Crown watermark Type **W12** paper remained unchanged, except for the new 320 set mill sheets, see Section KD, and all stamps were comb perf 14.

Marginal Rules. These were adopted in mid-1887 so that the first plates were constructed without them. Bicoloured printing involved not only accurate perforation but also correct register between the two colours. Plates divide into fixed and movable plates. Fixed plates printed the frame lines of the stamps and provided the register for perforation by correct positioning of pinning points. They could be head plates ("patch of colour" type), duty plates ("fringe" type) or, in the case of the 1900 1s., "frame" plates. On head and frame plates pinning points were created as for single coloured stamps. On "fringe" plates for panes of 20, the pinning points are dots top and bottom in duty plate colours on the centre lines of 160 set sheets. Since each pane was made separately from 20 set master plates they were positioned by measurement when assembling a group of plates ready for printing. The movable plates could be adjusted to ensure proper colour registration across sheets. When marginal rules were introduced, 240 set "patch of colour" duty plates were made with continuous rules round each pane. Before printing the plates and rules were broken up to create movable units.

Sheet Issue Sizes. The 2d., 2½d., 5d., 6d. and 1s. were as the 1884 issue. The 3d. was issued 120 set; the 4d. and 4½d. 80 set; the 9d. and 10d. 20 set, pane size. All, except the 4½d., were changed during the period, as noted below. The 5d., 6d. and 1s. sheets continued to have sheet dividing marks in the selvedges.

Printing Inks. Head plate green is very fugitive to water, first turning blue then yellow. Stamps with signs of water damage are worthless. The purple is also easily damaged. Duty or frame inks are fast in water. One of the three inks used for the 1900 ½d. was also highly sensitive to water leaving stamps in various shades of blue.

All single coloured values were printed direct onto 480 set mill sheets. The bicoloureds were first printed on half mill sheets (240 or 160 set) or smaller, but as printers became more proficient, they also were printed directly onto mill sheets.

Colour Standards ("Cancelled" Type 14). In 1887 twelve stamps, handstamped "Cancelled" type 14, were taken as colour standards for use in the print room, divided equally between De La Rue and the Inland Revenue. In 1888 the number taken was increased to 24, in the form of two top or bottom marginal rows where possible.

Departmental Overprints. These stamps appear with I.R./Official, Govt./Parcels, O.W./Official, Army/Telegraphs, Army/Official and Board/of/Education overprints for use in Head and local offices of relevant Departments. Substantial numbers were created to meet rises in taxation and administration, see Section LA.

Invalidation. The ½d., 1d., 2½d. and 6d. were invalidated on 1 January 1902 when these values were issued showing King Edward VII. Other values were replaced from March to July 1902. The £5 orange was not included and was reported to be still available into the early 1920's. Examples of late use exist but are philatelic and without authority.

Change of Colour ½d. and 1 shilling. In 1900 the colour of the ½d. was changed from vermilion to blue-green to confirm with the U.P.U. colour scheme and the 1 shilling was subsequently changed from a monocoloured to a bicoloured design to avoid confusion with the new colour of the ½d.

Only the ½d. value had "Controls" and these are listed. In all values marginal rules were used and form a study in themselves. Coloured "pillars" between the panes were also introduced. It is not possible satisfactorily to catalogue such plate-marking variations since each sheet with marginal markings would provide a considerable number of positional blocks differing in size and in philatelic desirability.

A note describing the numerous De La Rue head dies is included in the general notes on page 286.

K21

K22

K23

K24

K25

K26

K27

K28

K29

K30

K31

K32

1887 (1 January). ½d. Vermilion, Type K21. Wmk Crown (W12). Perf 14.

			Unmtd mint	Mtd mint	Used
K27 (=S.G.197,197e)	(1)	½d. deep vermilion	18·00	10·00	5·00
	(2)	½d. vermilion	2·25	1·50	1·00
	(3)	½d. orange-vermilion	2·25	1·50	1·00
	(4)	½d. pale-vermilion	2·25	1·50	1·00
		Block of four	12·00	7·00	5·00
		Used on cover	†	†	6·00
	a.	Watermark inverted	45·00	30·00	25·00
	c.	Printed on the gummed side	£2250	£1400	†
	d.	Do. Watermark inverted	£2800	£2000	
	e.	Printed both sides			
	f.	Doubly printed	—	£12000	
	g.	Imperforate (showing bottom margins)		£2200	

h. Imperforate top margin		£2800	
i. Split frame . . . . . *from*	25·00	15·00	8·00
j. Cracked plate (Control Q)	50·00	30·00	15·00
k. Dot in oval under H (Controls O and P)	25·00	15·00	8·00
l. Join in inner oval VE (Control P)	25·00	15·00	8·00
m. "Pears Soap" advert on back in outline letters in blue, orange or mauve" . . . . . *from*		£550	
n. Do. "Specimen", Type 9	£1500	£1000	
o. "Use Pears Soap" advert on back in solid letters in red	—	£900	
p. "Half-penny" on back		£3000	
s. "Specimen" Types 9, 10, 12 . *from*	45·00	32·00	
t. "Cancelled", Type 14		£750	

1887 ½d. The only 1887 value issued with a control letter (for De La Rue's own purpose) as for the 1d. lilac of 1881. The first printings were without control.

Essays. For hand painted essays, see Section KD Part II.

Printing. Printing was 480 set onto the mill sheet, using two plates side by side. The dates of putting to press and removal are known for all but one plate from official records. Only plates 7 to 10 are known with both plate number and control.

Imprimaturs: Plates 1 *to* 6 (*no marginal rules*), *each* £250; *Plates* 7 *to* 10 (*with marginal rules*), *each* £250. No stamps were removed from the bottom rows of the imprimatur sheets, but 134 examples were taken from plates 1–6 without rules; 28 from plates 7–10 with rules.

Registration sheets were taken from plates 11 and 12 but the system was changed and they were not retained.

The first plate was registered on 9 April 1886.

The bottom sheet marginal watermark of K27*a* is known with the word "POSTAGE" inverted and reversed.

On K27p, "Half-penny" was printed in two lines in black on the back under the gum. This is similar to K8*n* and was probably a trial for the "Pears Soap" advertisement. Examples may show damage by pinholes caused when the underprint was positioned for printing.

K27*j*

K27*k*

K27*l*

Die Proofs. Die "292". In black on white glazed card:

Date	*Inscr.*	*Additional Inscriptions or Notes*	
5 Feb 86	B/H		£1000
22 Mar 86	—		£1000
28 Jun 89	A/S	Initialled "G.F.S." (M/S) (The year should be 1898)	£1000
2 Feb 98	A/S		£1000
(M/S)	—	Dated "28–6–98" in pencil	£1000
28 Jun 98	B/H		£1000
28 Jun 98	→	"BEFORE REHARDENING". "Re" in (M/S)	£1000

Date	*Inscr.*	*Additional Inscriptions or Notes*	
30 Jun 98	→	"AFTER REHARDENING". "Re" in (M/S) also pencilled initials	£1000
2 Feb 98	A/S	Also pencilled initials	£1000
—	B/S	Also pencilled initials	£1000
30 Mar 00	A/S	Also pencilled initials "G.F.S."	£1000
5 May	A/S	Initialled "G.F.S." (M/S)	£1000

Die Proofs from De La Rue Striking Books

½d. struck between 1886 and 1900 . . . . *from* £900
½d. struck with 1d. Lilac in 1887 . . . . £1000

Dates on piece	*Plates and other details*
23, 26 Feb 1886	plates 1, 2, "2 formes";
6 May 1886	plate 3;
14 May	repairs (1886);
21, 29 July	plates 4–6 (1886);
19, 22 Aug	plates 7, 8 (1887);
1888	plates 9–12;
23, 31 May	plates 13, 14 (1889);
17 Sep	repairs (1889);
1891	plates 19–24;
20, 25 Oct	plates 25, 26 (1893);
26 July	repairs (1894);
12 Mar–10 Jul	plates 27–30 (1895);
20 Apr	repairs (1896);
25 Feb	repairs (1897);

The remaining six pieces have plate numbers (31–70); those (2) for plates 35–52 are poor quality. Piece for plates 15–18 is lost.

Plates. Plates 1–6 were without rules (setting 1), Plates 7–70 had marginal rules (setting 2). 14 and 15 were reserves at Somerset House, 56 was faulty and 67–70 were never used. Plate 4, created and used without rules, had rules added so is also known as plate 4A (setting 3). Therefore 57 plates with rule were used.

Marginal Settings. (1A) No marginal rule, without control; (1B) No marginal rule, with controls A to E; (2(a, b)). With continuous vermilion rule (rounded at corners) round each pane, with controls B to Q; (3) As (2) but with squared corners, with controls D to F.

Plate Usage with Controls.

Control letters were under stamp 11 in the bottom row.

I. Setting (1A), no rules, no control:

Plates 1, 4, 6 printed left and 2, 3, 5 right sheets.

Pieces MUST show either watermark cross M (Section KA) or watermark "E" under stamp 9 and at least two stamps (10, 11) to the right.

II. Setting (1B), no rules, with controls. All controls are Perf (P).

Control	Plates: Left	Right
A	4, 6	3, 5
B	4	5
C	6	3, 5
D	6	3
E	6	3

B control, plates 4, 5 were overprinted I.R. Official. Controls A–D known with no perf extension hole in side selvedge.

III. Setting (2) (a) with rules and controls Perf (P).

B	8	7
C	8	7
D	4A	7
E	4A, 10	7, 9

IV. Setting (2) (b) with rules and controls Perf (P) and imperf (I).

F	4A, 10, 12, 16	7, 9, 11, 13
G	12, 16	11, 13

G control: Plates 11, 12 overprinted I.R. Official.

H	12, 16	11, 13
I	16, 18	11, 17

I control: Plates 13, 16 overprinted I.R. Official.

J	16, 18	11, 17
K	19	13, 17, 20
L	18, 19, 22	13, 20, 21
M	18, 19, 22, 26	13, 19, 20, 21, 25
N	22–24, 26–28	19–21, 23, 25

Plate 25 overprinted I.R. Official.

O	19, 22, 27, 28	21, 23, 24, 26, 29, 30

Plate 27 overprinted I.R. Official; plate 24 overprinted O.W. Official; plates 24, 26, 27 overprinted Army Official; plate 26 overprinted Army Telegraphs.

P	21, 22, 24, 27, 28 30, 32, 33, 36, 40	23, 27, 29–31, 33–35 37–39

Plates 33 (L), 34 overprinted I.R. Official; plates 24, 28, 30 (L & R), 33 (L), 34, 38, 39 overprinted Army Official.

Q	32, 36, 37, 40–43 47–50, 52, 53, 55	37, 39, 43–46, 48 49, 51, 54, 57*

Plates 46, 50, 54 overprinted I.R. Official; plate 40 overprinted O.W. Official; plates 32, 43, 44, 48 (×2) overprinted Army Official.

* Plate 57 was the last plate to be put to press in vermilion (Q control), about 14 days before the changeover to green.

V. Setting (3), rules with "square" corners.

D.E.F.	Plate 4A	Left sheet only

Prices. For controls in marginal corner pairs, add 50% to the prices shown.

½d. Vermilion, Controls

Cat. No.	*Control*	*I.*	*P.*
	(a) Marginal Setting 1A, 1B		
KC1	no control (1A)		
	Strip of 4	†	£130
KC2	A (1B)	†	20·00
KC3	B	†	40·00
KC4	C	†	25·00
KC5	D	†	25·00
KC6	E	†	£220
	(b) Marginal Setting 2(a)		
KC7	B	†	£180
KC8	C	†	20·00
KC9	D	—	20·00
KC10	E	—	10·00
	(c) Marginal Setting 2(b)		
KC11	F	90·00	10·00
KC12	G	£160	10·00
KC13	H	10·00	10·00
KC14	I	15·00	10·00
KC15	J	40·00	10·00
KC16	K	25·00	10·00
KC17	L	25·00	10·00
KC18	M	10·00	10·00

Cat. No.	*Control*	*I.*	*P.*
	(c) Marginal Setting 2(b)		
KC19	N	10·00	10·00
KC20	O	10·00	10·00
KC20a	"C" for "0" . . .	£100	†
KC21	P	10·00	10·00
KC20	Q	10·00	10·00
	. . . .	*E*	
KC22a	Q (vert. comb.)	—	

Cat. No.	*Control*	*I.*	*P.*
	(d) Marginal Setting 3		
KC22b	D	†	£160
KC22c	E	†	20·00
KC22d	F	†	25·00

For further information see the boxed notes on "Controls" in Section KB.

The price above for KC1 is for a bottom right-hand corner strip of four sufficient to show part of the "POSTAGE" watermark in the bottom margin.

Controls D, E and F with marginal rules had a rule (i) rounded at corners, (ii) square at corners and (iii) square and bevelled at corners. (ii) and (iii) are scarce with control E. Control Q is known with a single extension hole in the bottom margin from a vertical comb perforator.

Trial Cancellation

Issued stamp with squared "PORTSMOUTH IL/JA5/85" cancel on piece £1800

From appendix "B" dated 11 November 1886, see Section KD Part III.

1900 ½d. The colour was changed to green to conform to U.P.U. guidelines. Three inks were used, but they can only be distinguished under ultra-violet light. During its currency, interpane ladders (pillars) were introduced.

1900 (17 April). ½d. Blue-green, Type K21. Wmk Crown (W12). Perf 14.

			Unmtd mint	Mtd mint	Used
K28 (=S.G.213)	(1)	½d. dull blue-green	2·25	1·75	2·00
	(2)	½d. bright blue-green	4·00	3·25	2·25
		Block of four	9·00	8·00	9·00
		Used on cover	†	†	6·00
	a.	Watermark inverted	45·00	30·00	30·00
	b.	Imperforate (with bottom or right-hand marginal rule)	—	£4000	
	c.	Printed on the gummed side	—	—	†
	s.	"Specimen", Types 11, 15 . . . . *from*	£375	£275	
	t.	"Cancelled", Type 18		£850	

Imprimaturs are known from the two imprimatur sheets from plate 55 but only three examples were taken from each sheet, all from the top right-hand corner. They are of great rarity. The first plate was registered 8 January 1900.

The ink used for early printings of K28 contained lead chromate. This compound is poisonous and so was replaced by a mixture of Prussian blue and zinc chromate. The yellow zinc chromate pigment is soluble in water and is the cause of the examples of this stamp known in various shades of blue due to exposure to moisture. Finally the unstable colouring was eliminated by the use of a non-soluble pigment. These three inks can be distinguished under long wave ultra-violet light.

Plate Proof. Imperf. No gum:

In green on buff £175

Colour Trials. Perf 14, without watermark:

In lime green, dull blue-green, blue-green (issued colour) . . . . *from* £2000

Marginal Settings. (2) With continuous green rule (rounded at corners) round each pane; (3) As (2) but with "pillars" added between panes.

A few plates were initially produced with ladders, but most had them added at various times.

Plates. The printing continued unchanged from 1887 until 6 January 1900. At that time twelve Q plates had not been formally removed from use. At the present nine plates are recognised: plates 43, 47, 48, 51–55 and 57. Plates 46, 49 and 50 are unlikely but possible.

Controls. These follow on from the 1887 ½d. No. K27:

Control	Plates: left	Right
R	47, 48b, 51a, 52b, 53b 55a, 58, 59a, 63a, 64	43b, 51a, 53b, 54a, b 57a, b, 60a, 62a

Plates 65, 66 were put to press but not recognised to date.

Plate 48 can exist only with chromate ink and plates 61–66 only with organic ink. The rest may exist with all three.

½d. Blue-Green, Controls

Cat. No.	*Control*	*I.*	*P.*	*E.*
KC23	R (with marginal role)	12·00	12·00	—

For further information see the boxed notes on "Controls" in Section KB.

1887 (1 January). 1½d. Purple and Green, Type K22. Wmk Crown (W12). Perf 14.

			Unmtd mint	Mtd mint	Used
K29 (=S.G.198)	(1)	1½d. pale dull purple and pale green	22·00	15·00	7·00
	(2)	1½d. dull purple and pale green	22·00	15·00	7·00
	(3)	1½d. deep purple and pale green	40·00	28·00	12·00
		Block of four	£110	75·00	32·00
		Used on cover	†	†	22·00
	a.	Purple print double	—	—	£6500
	b.	Watermark inverted	£850	£600	£350
	c.	"Horns" variety (Duty Pl. 4, R. 16/7)	£250	£125	70·00
	d.	Frame breaks *from*	45·00	28·00	20·00
	e.	Deformed leaf (Duty Pl. 4, R. 19/1)	£800		
	f.	Retouch left of tablet and around large figure 1 (Duty Pl. 4, R. 10/2)	£800	£600	£325
	s.	"Specimen", Types 6, 9, 12 *from*	70·00	45·00	
	t.	"Cancelled", Type 14		£850	

Imprimatur: £550.

Imprimaturs. From registration sheets: H3, 4D1, no rules 1st setting, 32 taken, 14 marginal; H5, 6D3, with rules 2nd setting, 14 taken, 11 marginal.

Some margins have been removed. There are also imperforate stamps from spare registration sheets.

This stamp exists from the top right with the Queen's head and most of the frame omitted, caused by a paper fold. It is separated from the left-hand stamp, which shows a triangular patch of missing purple. The green printing is complete on both examples.

K29*c*

Three examples of K29*d*

K29*e*

K29*f*

Reply Paid Essays

Imperforate and part perforated proofs in blue on watermarked paper from head plate. Used for reply paid stamp experiments in 1894 with and without various overprints in blue, black, green and brown . . . . *from* £350

Marginal paper with strikes of the duty die exist £600

Essay from the De La Rue Archives

In issued design in green and lilac (laurel sprigs also in lilac) with pen cancellation. Hand-painted £6500

For other hand painted essays, see Section KD Part III.

Type A Head Plate Die

Type B Duty Die

Die Proofs. In black on white glazed card:

Date	*Inscr.*	*Additional Inscriptions or Notes*	
Head Plate only (Type A)			
2 Apr 86	B/H		£1000
12 Apr 86	—		£1000
12 Apr 86	B/H		£1000
17 Sep 86	A/S		£1000
19 Aug 87	—		£1000
17 Sep 87	A/S	Initialled "G.F.S." (M/S) in ink	£1000
23 Jan 90	A/S	Initialled "G.F.S." (M/S) in ink	£1000
24 Aug 99	A/S	Initialled "G.F.S." (M/S) in ink	£1000
Duty Plate only (Type B)			
5 Feb 86	B/H		£1100
8 June 86	B/H		£1100
19 Aug 87	—		£1100

Die Proofs for the setting of the marginal rules. Sunk into protective covers into which a window has been cut out and covered with thin transparent protective material. Dated and initialled "N.R.N." with instructions in M/S.

Head Plate in black with thin red and black at top and left side dated "AUGUST 19TH, 87" and endorsed "DIVISION LEAD OF THE INNER LINE" (set close) . . . .
Duty Plate as last but endorsed "DIVISION LEAD OF THE OUTER LINE" (set wide) . } £2500

Die Proofs from the De La Rue Striking Books

Head and duty plates . . . . *from* £900
Head plate only . . . . *from* £900
Duty plate only . . . . *from* £900

Date on price	*Plates and other details*
22 Apr 86	H3/754,
May 19	Head repairs (1886)
1 Jul 86	D1,
20 Oct 86	H4/773, very poor quality,
April 19	Head repairs (1887)
16, 28 May 87	H5/819, D5, on one piece,
Feb 3	H8/914 (1890)
April 29	D6 (1890)
Sept 20	H9/934 (1894)
Jan 19	H10/959 (1897)
Aug 30	H11/1006 (1899)

Pieces for D3, D4 and D5 have been lost. Plate numbers for head plates 10, 11 were cut off.

Plates and Printings. 11 head, prefixed with "H" throughout and 6 duty, prefixed with "D" throughout, plates were created, of which 10 head and 4 duty were used. Head plate numbering was from H3 (from 1884 $1\frac{1}{2}$d.); duty plates from D1. Plates H3, 4 and D1, 2 were without rules; D2 was not used. In 1888, H5D3, both with rules, were put to press. H6 replaced H5 in October 1888.

Printing was 240 set until 7th printing late 1889, when 480 set printing began. H6D3 printed right sheets and H7D4 printed left. Once a duty plate had been placed on the left or right, it was never changed. The duty plate rule above applied to all bicoloureds with 240 set duty plates, i.e. 1½d., 2d. and 5d.

Marginal Settings

Setting 1. No rules. Plates H3, 4; D1.

Setting 2. Head and duty rules round each plane, head no breaks, green breaks every three stamps horizontally. Plates H5, 6; D3.

Setting 3. As 2, but horizontal green rules removed.

Setting 3 only, 480 set printing (ptg), plates used:

1889, ptg 7	Right sheets H6D3	Left sheets H7D4
1895, ptg 13	H6D5	H8D4
1896, ptg 14	H8D5	H9D4
1898, ptg 16 to end	H10D5	H9D4

T. A. Colls Presentation Cards

Head die proof mounted behind film on card dated 19.8.87, initialled Warren De La Rue with added continuous rule. As last, but die proof of the duty die. These were made by J. S. Turner, De La Rue's print room manager.

Trial Cancellation

The issued stamp with squared "PORTSMOUTH/IL/JA5/85" cancel on piece . . . £1800

1887 (1 January). 2d. Green and Red, Type K23. Wmk Crown (W12). Perf 14.

				Unmtd mint	Mtd mint	Used
K30 (=S.G.199/200)	(1)		2d. green and scarlet	£450	£350	£225
	(2)		2d. yellow-green and carmine	40·00	28·00	12·00
	(3)		2d. grey-green and carmine	40·00	28·00	12·00
	(4)		2d. deep grey-green and carmine	£100	70·00	30·00
			Block of four	£180	£125	60·00
			Used on cover	†	†	24·00
		a.	Watermark inverted	£850	£600	£375
		b.	Double frame line at left (Head Pl. 5, R. 20/12)	£300	£200	£100
		c.	Irregular shading on right side of tablet (Duty Pl. 3, R. 9/3)	90·00	50·00	45·00
		d.	Various damage to duty tablet frame *from*	90·00	50·00	45·00
		e.	Retouched right frame (Head Pl. 6, R. 11/12)	90·00	50·00	45·00
		f.	Bottom right tablet corner raised (Pl. D4, R. 3/12)	90·00	50·00	45·00
		s.	"Specimen", Types 9, 10, 12 *from*	80·00	50·00	—
		sa.	"Specimen", Types 9 + 12	£250	£150	
		t.	"Cancelled", Type 14		£850	

Imprimatur: £550.

Imprimaturs. From registration sheets: H4D1, no rules, 1st setting, 24 taken, 8 marginal; H5D3, with rules, setting 3, 6 taken, 3 marginal.

Some margins have been removed; there are also imperforate stamps from spare registration sheets.

Many of the frame break varieties are to be found on the Edward VII issue.

K30*b*

K30*c*

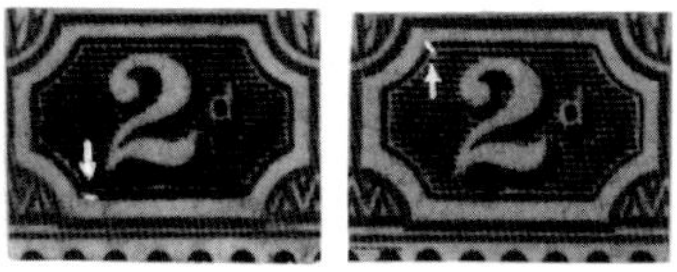

Two examples of K30*d*

K30*e*

K30*f*

Nos. K30*c* and K30*f* also occur on the K.E. VII issue

A

B

Die Proof Essays. On white card:

In black (Type A) £3500
In green with side ornaments in pink (Type B) £5000

Die Proofs. Head die "296". In black on white glazed card:

Date	*Inscr.*	*Additional Inscriptions or Notes*	
Head Plate only			
5 Mar 86	B/H		£1000
5 Mar 86	B/H	Endorsed "2d." (M/S)	£1000
5 Mar 86	B/H	Endorsed (M/S) "Die chgd (charged) 17 Mar" and in the value tablet in M/S "2d."	£2000
20 Mar 86	—		£1000
20 Mar 86	A/H		£1000
Duty Plate only			
31 Mar 86	B/H	With solid background (unadopted)	£2000
23 May 86	B/H		£1000
25 May 86	B/H	Adopted design	£1000
4 Jun 86	A/H		£1000

Die proofs for the setting of the marginal rules

Head Plate as for the $1\frac{1}{2}$d. value . . . .
Duty Plate as for the $1\frac{1}{2}$d. value . . . . } £2500

Die Proofs from the De La Rue Striking Books

Head and duty plates . . . . *from* £900

Date on piece	*Plates and other details*
Aug 83	D2, duty die proof originally attached to larger piece with "1886" on it.
May 14, July 16	H4/758 May 14; repairs.
Dec 13, 16 (1887), Jan 2 1888	D3, D4, D5.

Striking book pieces for H5, H6, H7 and D1 are lost.

For head and duty essays, see Section KD Parts II and III.

Plates and Printings. 5 head plates (prefixed "H" throughout) and 5 duty plates (prefixed "D" throughout) were created; numbered from H3 (from 1884 2d.) and D1, H3, 4 and D1, 2 were without rules; H3 was used only for April 1886 essays, see Section KD Part II; D2 and H7 were never used. H4D1 printed setting 1. H5, 6 and D3, 4 had rules. H5D3 were put to press in 1889 (ptg 4), printing 240 set setting 2. During printing 4, the red rules were broken into short bars (ptg 4b, setting 3). At ptg. 5 (1890) 480 set printing (setting 3) was introduced with H5D3 printing right and H6D4 left sheets to 1902.

Marginal Settings

Setting 1, no rules;

Setting 2, continuous green and red rules round each pane; red rules broken every three stamps horizontally and five vertically.

Setting 3, red rules now short bars.

T. A. Colls Preentation Cards

Head and duty proofs on cards as for the 1½d. value exist for the 2d.

Colour Trials. Taken under Warrant 79/99 for 50 sheets in connection with the 1900 1s., 37 trials were submitted on 21 August 1899. There are 13 different duty colours with green heads and 17 different with purple heads. Those from this Warrant are watermarked.

Perf 14, Watermark Crown: Head in green, duty tablet in:

Violet, blue, orange-yellow, blue-green, black, purple, brown, deep blue, pale brown, olive, deep brown, grey-brown, grey-green . . . . *from* £750

Head in purple, duty tablet in:

Orange, black, blue, sage-green, violet, yellow, carmine-red, scarlet, pale brown, blue-green, olive or ochre, bright purple, pale blue-green, brown, bottle green, purple-brown, deep blue . . . . *from* £750

These were prepared in 1899 for the 1s. green and carmine of 1900.

Trial Cancellations

Issued stamp with squared "PORTSMOUTH/1 L/JA5/85" cancel on piece £1500
Issued stamp with "BO1" (Alexandria type) cancel on piece £1500

1844 London oval horizontal bar cancel "3 or B" in diamond exists but its purpose is unknown. See also 1884 2½d. Section KD approved design 11 June 1885, and 1884 6d. and 1s. in Section KC. BO1 trial cancel, see Section KD, Part III.

1887 (1 January). 2½d. Purple on Blue Paper, Type K24. Wmk Crown (W12). Perf 14.

			Unmtd mint	Mtd mint	Used
K31 (=S.G.201)	(1)	2½d. pale purple on blue paper	35·00	22·00	3·00
	(2)	2½d. purple on blue paper	35·00	22·00	3·00
	(3)	2½d. deep purple on blue paper	70·00	50·00	10·00

	Block of four	£160	£100	18·00
	Used on cover	†	†	6·00
aa.	Imperforate (pair)*		£12000	
ab.	Imperforate (single)		£6000	
a.	Watermark inverted	£1400	£900	£700
b.	Imperforate top margin	£2500		
c.	Imperforate three sides		£3500	
d.	Printed on the gummed side	£5500	£4500	†
e.	Missing "d" in value	†	†	£5500
f.	Damaged bottom frame . . . . *from*	£110	55·00	35·00
g.	Minor damage to frame . . . . *from*	60·00	35·00	15·00
h.	Double top frame	£200	£140	50·00
i.	Split left-hand frame (R. 1/10, upper pane, setting (1))	75·00	40·00	20·00
j.	Damaged right-hand frame (R. 9/10, upper pane)	£100	55·00	35·00
s.	"Specimen", Types 6, 9, 12, 13 . . . . *from*	95·00	60·00	
t.	"Cancelled", Type 14		£850	

Imprimatur: £550.

Imprimaturs. Plates 3, 4, 46 stamps taken. Imperforate stamps from spare registration sheets also exist e.g. K31*aa*, *ab*.

*K31*aa* exists from the top left-hand corner of a lower pane and has the selvedge containing the marginal rules intact. The listed pair may come from another registration sheet and singles are listed as K31*ab*. The shade differs from the shade of the imprimaturs but K31*ab* should be purchased with an expert committee's certificate. In 1886, registration sheets were not taken under Warrant as in 1900, so more than one is likely.

Probably due to a fortuitous inking flaw No. K31 is known with the "d" omitted and used with Throgmorton Street postmark, see K31*e*.

K31*f*

K31*h*

K31*i*

K31*j*

Die Proofs. Die "294". In black on white glazed card:

Date	*Inscr.*	*Additional Inscriptions or Notes*	
5 Mar 86	B/H		£1000
17 Mar 86	A/H		£1000
17 Mar 86	A/S		£1000
22 Mar 86	—		£1000
—	—	With red (M/S) "Broken in neck"	£1000
5 Apr 00	B/H	(M/S) "Re" between "BEFORE" and "HARDENING"	£1000
11 Apr 00	A/H	(M/S) "Re" between "AFTER" and "HARDENING"	£1000
13 May	—	(M/S) "After Striking" and initialled (no year given)	£1000
(M/S)	(M/S)	"After Striking April 21, 1900" and initialled	£1000

Die Proofs from the De La Rue Striking Books

With various dates . . . . *from* £900

Striking book pieces from De La Rue archives.

Dates on piece	*Plates and other details*
May 18	3/751 (1886)
June 22 (1886)	4/760, (m/s) "1886" not contemporary.
Aug 17	5/770; writing removed from piece; original, not an "improvement" that went wrong (1886).
April 4, June 27	6/930, 7/931 (1894).
May 9, 14	6/894, 9/985 (1898).
April 10, May 3	10/1029, 11/1030 (1900).

Pieces relating to repairs lost.

Plate Proofs. Imperf:

In black on white card £450
In purple on green on thin paper £450

Plates and Printings. 11 plates were created, 9 used. Plates 3–5 (from 1884 2½d.) had no rules (setting 1) and 6–9 had rules round each pane (setting 2). 10, 11 were created with ladders (pillars) in the interpane gutter, but not put to press. Ladders were added to plates 6–9 to create setting 3, so they exist both with and without them. Printing was 480 set.

Marginal Settings

Printing	Setting	Plates: left	Right
1–15a (1897)	1A	3	4
15b	2A	6	7
16, 17 (1898–9)	1A, 1B, 2A	4, 6	5, 7
18 (1899/1900)	1C, 2C	4, 6	7, 8
19–22 (end)	3	6, 9	7, 8

Setting 1A No rules, 120 set issue;
1B As 1A but added interpane dots*;
1C As 1B? 240 set issue.
Setting 2A Rules, 120 set issue;
2B As 2A but added interpane dots*;
2C As 2A but 240 issue.
Setting 3 Rules and interpane ladders.

*1B, 2B settings: 2½d. and 3d. (below) had two dots added centre, interpane gutter, just above and below the middle of the two panes, probably for 120 set perforation. Pieces showing them are very rare as are setting 1C, 2C pieces with joined upper and lower panes.

Colour Trials. Perf 14, watermark Crown:

In green on blue, green on yellow . . . . *each* £4000

Trials formerly listed imperf are incomplete, prices as for perforated examples.

On 23 November 1887, De La Rue's attention was drawn to the problems caused by the new "art" of photography. They prepared a Report (copy in Post Office Heritage Services) on the subject dated 26 January 1888 which included line perf 14 colour trials of the 2½d., 3d. and 6d. values on coloured papers different from those then in use. Nothing came of this. The trials are listed under those three stamps.

Trial Cancellation

Issued stamp with squared "PORTSMOUTH IL/JA5/85" cancel on piece £1800

1887 (1 January). 3d. Purple on Yellow Paper, Type K25. Wmk Crown (W12). Perf 14.

			Unmtd mint	Mtd mint	Used
K32 (=S.G.202/204)	(1)	3d. purple on yellow paper	35·00	22·00	3·25
	(2)	3d. deep purple on yellow paper	35·00	22·00	3·25
	(3)	3d. purple on orange paper (1890)	£900	£500	
		Block of four	£160	£100	16·00
		Used on cover	†	†	30·00
	a.	Watermark inverted	—	—	£550

b.	Imperforate (watermark inverted)	—	£6000	
c.	Split bottom frame . . . . *from*	£110	55·00	30·00
d.	Major damage to bottom frame (R. 20/12)		—	£140
e.	Bottom frame damage			
ea.	Various frame damage . . . . *from*	70·00	40·00	25·00
f.	Split top frame	70·00	40·00	25·00
g.	Damaged S.E. ornament (Pl. 4, R. 20/11)			
ga.	Do later stage (worn print)			
h.	Displaced cliche (left sheet, Pl. 3, R. 20/1)			
s.	"Specimen", Types 6, 9, 12 *from*	65·00	45·00	
t.	"Cancelled", Type 14		£850	

Paper. Pigment lead chromate; colour fast, but chromate can be oxidised to orange dichromate, the likely cause of orange paper shade K32(3). The use of lead compound in the paper was not in breach of De La Rue's contract, which only refers to inks.

No K32*b* also exists with normal watermark from top left corner of the sheet, this being present on the imprimatur sheet.

Imprimatur: (*Plate* 4), £550.

Imprimaturs. According to official records, plates 3 and 4 were put to press 29 Sept 1886, but only one imperf registration sheet, from plate 4, has survived. A second perforated sheet is marked plate "5/769" (correct numbers, but not put to press until 24 Dec 1897). Stamps from it cannot be recognised out of context. 24 imperf imprimaturs (four right marginal) were taken from plate 4 sheet. Other imperf stamps come from spare registration sheets, probably from plate 3.

Plate 5 also exists but is perforated and specimens cannot be distinguished from the issued stamps.

K32*c*

K32*d*

K32*f*

K332*e*

K32*g*

K32*ga*

K32*h*

Nos. K32*d* and K32*ga* are both late states and can be found as a pair.

Die Proofs. Die "295". In black on white glazed card:

Date	*Inscr.*	*Additional Inscriptions or Notes*	
5 Mar 86	B/H	. . . .	£1000
(M/S)	(M/S)	Endorsed "March 8 After Striking" and initialled	£1000
18 Mar 86	B/S	. . . .	£1000
20 Mar 86	—	. . . .	£1000
7 Mar 98	A/S	Endorsed with initials "G.F.S."	£1000
24 Aug 00	A/S	. . . .	£1000
—	A/S	. . . .	£1000

Die Proofs from the De La Rue Striking Books

With various dates . . . . *from* £900

Date on piece	*Plates and other details*
Mar 23	3/752 (1886).
July 13 1886	4/762.
Aug 14 1886	5/769, same fault as 2½d plate 5/770 piece.

Pieces (4) for plates 6, 7; 8, 9; 10; 11–13 all have plate numbers written on them. Pieces for repairs are lost.

Plate Proofs. Imperf:

In black on green, dark green on green . . . . *each* £250

Plates and Printings. 13 plates were created, only 7 used. Numbering from plate 3 (from 1884 (3d). Plates 3–5 had no rules (setting 1) and plates 6–8, 10 had rules round each pane (setting 2), all used. Plates 10–13 had ladders (only 10 used) from new while plates 6–8 had them added later (setting 3) therefore they can be found both without and with them.

Marginal Settings

Printing	Setting	Plates: left	Right
1–12 (1896)	1A	3	4
13, 14 (1897, 8)	1A, 1B, 2A	3, (?) 4, 6	(?) 3, 4, 7
15 (1898)	1B, 2B	5, 6	7, 8
16 (1899)	1C, 2B	6, 7	5, 8
17–20	3	6, 10	7, 8

Setting 1A No rules, 120 set issue;
1B As 1A but added interpane dots;
1C As 1A, but 240 set issue;
Setting 2A continuous rules, 120 set issue;
2B As 2A but 240 set issue;
Setting 3 Rules and interpane ladders.

Colour Trials. Perf 14, watermark Crown:

In green on blue, green on yellow . . . . *from* £3500

For a note on these see 2½d. under colour trials. See also Section KD, Part III.
Trials formerly listed imperf are incomplete, prices as for perforated examples.

Trial Cancellation

Issued stamp with squared "PORTSMOUTH IL/JA5/85" cancel on piece £1800

1887 (1 January). 4d. Green and Brown, Type K26. Wmk Crown (W12). Perf 14.

			Unmtd mint	Mtd mint	Used
K33 (=S.G.205/205a)	(1)	4d. green and purple-brown	50·00	30·00	13·00
	(2)	4d. green and deep brown	50·00	30·00	13·00
	(3)	4d. green and deep chocolate-brown	95·00	60·00	18·00
		Block of four	£200	£140	60·00
		Used on cover	†	†	35·00
		a. Imperforate		£6000	
		b. Watermark inverted	£800	£550	£350
		c. "White 4" in 4 corners	£180	90·00	45·00
		d. "White 4" in 3 corners	£120	60·00	30·00
		e. "White 4" in 2 corners	£120	60·00	30·00
		f. "White 4" in 1 corner	£120	60·00	30·00
		g. Major break in frame	£150	80·00	40·00
		h. Split frame and bulge (S.W. corner) (pane P, R. 1/5)			
		s. "Specimen", Types 6, 9, 10, 12 *from*	65·00	45·00	
		t. "Cancelled", Type 14		£850	

Imprimatur: £550.

Imprimaturs. From registration sheets: No rules (6.12.86 and 19.8.87) 46 stamps taken; Rules (24.10.88) 28 stamps taken. Some imprimaturs can be assigned to sheets, but there are also imperforate stamps from spare registration sheets.

K33*c/f*

K33*g*

K33*h*

Die Proof Essays from De La Rue Archives. Each bearing instructions about the number of leads and "Exp" in red:

Frame with lined values circles only £1000
As above with two other dies of a design similar to that used in the Malayan States £1000
As above with head die lacking head and inscriptions . . . . . *from* £1000

Die Proofs. Die "293". In black on white glazed card:

Date	*Inscr.*	*Additional Inscriptions or Notes*	
Head Plate only			
16 Feb 86	B/H		£1000
18 Mar 86	A/H		£1000
20 Mar 86	—		£1000
6 Sep 87	A/S	Initialled "C.S." (M/S)	£1000
28 Nov 89	A/S	Initialled "G.F.S." (M/S)	£1000
Duty Die 1b proofs			
8 Jun 86	B/H		£1500
—	—	Value omitted. Background with straight lines (Essay)	£1500

Accepted head cut down to fit into space for head on duty die 1a proof (Section KD Part III) believed created to show that tolerances in die 1a were inadequate; hence new die 1b with accepted lined duty tablets.

Die Proofs for the setting of the marginal rules prepared in the style of the 1½d. value

Head Plate as for the 1½d.value . . . . .
Duty Plate in black with hand-painted red thick rule at top and left side (set close) together with issued stamp with hand-painted brown thin rule at top and left side (set close), endorsed "THE RED TO BE MADE UP BY CUTTING THE EDGE ON THE DIVISION LEADS OF THE INNER LINE DOWN TO THE SAME PLANE AS THE LINE" } £2800

Die Proofs from the De La Rue Striking Books

Head and duty plates £900
Head plate only . . . . . *from* £900
Duty plate only £900
4d. duty plate and 9d. duty plate on single card . . . . . *from* £1000

Dates on piece	*Plates and other details*
May 25	Duty master plate O1.
Undated	H3/755, no writing; separated from 2d. piece of 3 April 1886 (plate 3/753); presently lost, from about 20 April.
May 19	H4/777 (1886).
Jun 2 1886	H5–7.
July 7, 16*	Duty master plates O2, O3 (1886).

Dates on piece	*Plates and other details*
Nov 22 1886	H8–11.
Dec 23	H12–14 (1886).
Aug 29	Duty master plates O4 and 9d. O2 (1887).
Oct 17	Duty master plates O5 and 9d. O3 (1887).
Dec† 4, 11, 16 1889	Repairs (4.12), 35/909 (11.12), 36/910 (16.12).
May 23	37/917 (1890).

* "16" looks like "11", which was a Sunday.
† "Dec" has been read as "Oct".

Plates and Printings. 34 20 set and 3 160 set head plates (prefixed "H" throughout) were created. H3–14 (numbered from 1884 4d.) were without rules, all except H3 used. H15–22 with rules were put to press but no sheets were issued. H23–34 and H36 (160 set) with rules were used. Issue size was 80 set to 1899; then 160 set.

Duty plates (prefixed "D" throughout) were made, via "matrices", from 20 set master plates, of which five were created. O1 was made from die 1a (see Section KD Part III) and the remainder from die 1b (below). O2 created D1–16 without rules (D1–12 used) and O5 D17–41 with rules; D17–19, 23, 24, 26–30 and 41 used.

Marginal Settings

Setting 1A No rules, no lined blocks, 80 set printing and perforation (extra pinning points below C, D and above E, F panes as well as normal ones above A, B and below G, H panes; for panes, see Introduction to 1887 issue above.
1B No rules, no lined blocks, 160 set printing and perforation but from only 4 pairs of plates (80 set).
2 Added lined blocks, partly printed from four pairs and partly from 8 pairs of plates (160 set).
3 Rules, head panes without breaks, 320 set printing.
4A As 3, but thin lines between two halves of mill sheet; i.e. they are on right side of L. sheets and left side of R. sheets.
4B As 4A, but head plate rules cut away at corners.
5A As 4B, but thin lines removed; 80 set issue, so C, D panes are not joined to E, F panes.
5B As 5A, but 160 set issue so C, D panes joined to E, F panes; such pieces are rare.

T. A. Colls Presentation Cards

Head and duty cards as for the 1½d. value exist for the 4d.

Trial Cancellation

Issued stamp with squared "PORTSMOUTH IL/JA5/85" cancel, on piece £1800

1892 (15 September). 4½d. Green and Carmine, Type K27. Wmk Crown (W12). Perf 14.

			Unmtd mint	Mtd mint	Used
K34 (=S.G.206/206a)	(1)	4½d. green and carmine	15·00	10·00	40·00
	(2)	4½d. deep green and carmine	18·00	15·00	40·00
	(3)	4½d. green and deep bright carmine	£750	£500	£425
	(4)	4½d. green and dull scarlet	22·00	18·00	45·00
		Block of four	70·00	45·00	£175
		Used on cover	†	†	75·00
	aa.	Watermark inverted			
	a.	Dot between 4 and ½ (S.E. value) (Pane G, R. 4/5)	£125	60·00	70·00
	b.	Broken bar to 1 of ½ (N.E. value) Pane B, R. 2/4 and Pane C R. 4/5)	£125	60·00	70·00
	c.	Break in top of N.E. value tablet (Pane B, R. 1/1)	£125	60·00	70·00
	d.	Damage to frame .... *from*	75·00	40·00	70·00
	e.	Damage to value tablet ... *from*	75·00	40·00	70·00
	f.	Dot between 4 and ½ (N.W. value)	£125	60·00	70·00

g.	Damage to inner frame lines (Pane A, R. 3/2)	90·00	45·00	70·00
h.	Broken bar to fraction (Pane F, R. 2/4)	90·00	45·00	70·00
s.	"Specimen", Types 9, 13 .. *from*	£400	£300	
t.	"Cancelled", Type 14		£1100	

Imprimatur: (*Plates* 4, 5 *and* 6), *each* £600.
Imprimaturs, From the registration sheet 29 stamps were taken.
It is not possible to differentiate between the three plates.

K34*b*

K34*d*

K34*e*

K34*g*

K34*h*

Essays from the De La Rue Archives. The 10 essays submitted 1 Feb. 1892, each on dated white card, lettered A–J. Two sets created; De La Rue's copy has pen cancelled essays on tracing paper; other set direct onto card. F was selected.

Different designs in various colours, lettered A to E, G to J	*from* £5000
As last but pen-cancelled, lettered A, B, E to G and J	*from* £5000
As last but pen-cancelled	£5000
The issued design lettered F	

The designs lettered C, D and I with pen cancellations were acquired by Post Office Heritage Services.

Die Proofs. Die "313". In black on white glazed card:

Date	*Inscr.*	*Additional Inscriptions or Notes*	
Head Plate only			
25 May 92	B/H		£1250
28 May 92	A/H	Initialled	£1250
28 Jun 92	A/S		£1250
15 Aug 92	—	Initialled	£1250
20 Oct 92	A/S	Initialled "G.F.S."	£1250
Duty Plate die 8			
10 May 92	B/H		£1250
15 Aug 92	—	Initialled	£1250

Die Proofs from the De La Rue Striking Books

Head plate only	*from* £1000
Duty plate only	£1000

All from 1892: June 23, H1/925,
Nov 1, H3/927,
Aug 11, For repairs (head),
May 17, Duty plate O1.
Piece for H2 is lost.

Plates. Three head plates (prefixed "H" throughout) were created 160 set, 24 duty plates (prefixed "D" throughout) were made from 20 set master plate O1. Two head, H1 printing right and H2 left sheets, and 23 duty plates were used. One setting, rules all round every pane with head corners cut away. Issue size 80 set.

Plate recognition	Left sheets	Right sheets
Head plates:	H2	H1
Duty panes	A D9; B D13	A D1; B D5
	C D10; D D14	C D2; D D6
	E D11; F D15	E D3; F D7
	G D12; H D16	G D4; H D8

Duty plate assignments: left sheets from known right sheets. For panes, see Introduction to this issue.

D17 replaced D7 6.7.95; D18 (7.3.95), D19 (13.3.95), D20 (31.1.96) replaced D3, D8, D16 but which replacement unknown. D21–23 were put to press on 15.12.96, but which retired unknown.

Inks. The 4½d. Ink 1 printed 1st and 2nd ptgs (e.g. specimen type 9) in carmine and scarlet consistently weakly fluorescing carmine. 3rd printing (1895) is uncertain with inks producing the rarer shades followed by the 4th and 5th (last, Jun 1897) ptgs in duty ink 3, a light carmine, which weakly fluoresces scarlet.

Colour Trials. Taken to decide colours of this stamp, following problems with the 10d. First, 10d. colour trials in the place cited were taken in early 1892. In July, a Warrant was issued for 12 sheets of 160. The trials are watermark Crown, line perf 14. Imperf and part perforate trials are incomplete and prices are as for perforated examples.

On 6 July, De La Rue submitted a set of 12 trials in two matching columns of 6, one cancelled BO1 in bars:

Head plate in green, duty in purple, red, blue;
Head plate in purple, duty in green, brown, orange.

Uncancelled (except issued colours) . . . . *each*
Cancelled BO1 (includes issued colours) . . . . *each*

Perf 14, watermark Crown:

Head plate in grey-green

Value plate in carmine, rose, orange red, orange, deep blue, mauve, dark brown, bistre . . . . *each* £2800
The same colours handstamped "Specimen", Type 13 . . . . *each* £2800

Head plate in mauve

Value plate in carmine, emerald, grey-green, blue, deep blue, brown, orange *each* £2800
The same colours handstamped "Specimen", Type 13 . . . . *each* £2800

Die Proofs for the setting of the "Jubilee" lines. Dated "AUGUST 16th 92"

Head Plate as for the 1½d. value . . . . }
Duty Plate as for the 1½d. value . . . . } £2800

T. A. Colls Presentation Cards

Head and duty proofs on cards, as 1½d. value, exist dated 16.8.92 and initialled "T.A.C."

1887 (1 January). 5d. Purple and Blue, Type K28. Wmk Crown (W12). Perf 14.

			Unmtd mint	Mtd mint	Used
K35 (=S.G.207)		5d. dull purple and blue, Die I	£700	£500	85·00
		Block of four	£4000	£3000	£475
		Used on cover	†	†	£175
	s.	"Specimen", Types 9, 12 . . . *from*	£130	90·00	
	t.	"Cancelled", Type 14			
K36 (=S.G.207a)	(1)	5d. dull purple and blue, Die II (1888) . . .	50·00	35·00	11·00
	(2)	5d. dull purple and bright blue, Die II	50·00	35·00	11·00

	Block of four	£225	£175	55·00
	Used on cover	†	†	40·00
a.	Watermark inverted	—	£8000	£600
b.	Damaged lion (R, 1/8)	£140	75·00	55·00
c.	Damaged value tablet . . . . . . *from*	£130	60·00	45·00
d.	Sliced spandrel above leaf (Head pl. 9, R. 1/1)	£130	60·00	45·00
e.	Buckled frame top left (Head pl. 9, R. 1/2)	£130	60·00	45·00
s.	"Specimen", Types 9, 12 . . . *from*	75·00	50·00	
t.	"Cancelled", Type 14		£850	

Imprimatur (*Die* I): £600. There are two imprimatur sheets of Die I endorsed; HP5/772—DP1—2.11.86 and HP6/776—DP "Not known"—2.2.87. *Imprimatur* (*Die* II): £1500. The Die II imprimatur sheet is endorsed HP9/872—DP3—10.8.88.

H5D1	2.11.86,	24 stamps removed
H6D1	2.2.87,	6 stamps removed
H9D3	(see below) setting 2, 10.8.88,	6 stamps removed

Also imperforate stamps from spare registration sheets.

H9D3 sheet recorded on sheet as "H7D3" is incorrect, H7 was not proofed, plate number misread.

Left Right

Die I (*square dots to right of* "d" *and value centred to left on the left-hand tablet*)
(from duty die No. 5)

Left Right

Die II (*thin vertical lines to right of* "d" *and value centred to right on the left-hand tablet*)
(from duty die No. 6)

K36*b*

Typical damage to value tablet

K 36*d*/*e*

Type A Head Plate Die

Type B Duty Die

Die Proofs. In black on white glazed card:

Date	*Inscr.*	*Additional Inscriptions or Notes*	
Head Plate Die "303" (Type A)			
12 Aug 86	B/H		£1200
13 Aug 86	A/H		£1200
20 Nov 87	A/S	Initialled "G.F.S." (M/S)	£1200
Duty die No. 5 only (Type B)			
12 Aug 86	B/H	(Duty Plate 1)	£1200
13 Aug 86	B/H		£1200
Duty die No. 6			
9 Nov 86	B/H	"2nd Die" (M/S) (Duty Plate 2)	£1200
9 Nov 86	B/H		£1200

Die Proofs for the setting of the marginal rules

Head Plate as for the 1½d. value
Duty Plate as for the 1½d. value } £300

Die Proofs from the De La Rue Striking Books

Head plate and two duty plates, one marked "2nd die"	£2500
Head plate only	*from* £900
Duty plate only, Die I	£900
Both duty plates marked respectively "1st Die" and "2nd Die"	£1100

Date on piece	*Plates and other details*
Oct 1886	D1;
Oct 27 1886	H6/776, (m/s) 5d. in tablet slots;
Dec 16	D2, (m/s) "2nd die" (1886)
Feb 1 1887	Repairs, proofs of dies 5, 6, (m/s) "1st die" and "2nd die"; initialled G.F.S.;
Jan 10, 16, 21	D3, D4, D5 (1888);
Jan 21, Feb 7, 13	H7/871, 8/872, 9/872 and (m/s) 5d. (1888);
May	H10/916 (1890).

Pieces for H5, D6 and repairs missing.

Plates and Printings. 6 head plates (prefixed "H" throughout) numbered from H5, (from 1884 5d.) and 6 duty plates (prefixed "D" throughout) from D1, were created. H5, 6 were without rules, both used and H7–10 with rules, H8, 9 being used. D1 was from duty die 5 (die "1") without rules; D2–6 from duty die 6 (die "2") with rules. D2 was never used and D5, 6 not used in QV times. It is not known why duty 5 was replaced. Issue size 60 set 1887, 120 set 1888–1899, then 240 set.

Marginal Settings

Setting 1. No rules, H5 (printing 1), 6 (printing 2) D1; 240 set printing; sheet dividers (see 6d.) in centre of interpane gutter; H6 failed Feb 1887. Printing 2 interrupted for new head, no new plate available; printing 2 resumed Aug 1887. Records show this was the only substitution during the whole 1887 issue.

Setting 2. Rules, head and duty round each pane, blue rules broken every three stamps horizontally, head 9 duty 3240 set printing 3, 120 set issue (no room in gutter for sheet dividers).

Setting 3A. Blue rules short bars, 480 set printing, H9D3 R., H8D4 L. sheets (printing 4, 1889), 120 set issue.

Setting 3B. As 3A, but 240 set issue (printing 12 1899), upper and lower panes joined. H8a cut under 1st row 20 (printing 13, 1900). H9a cut under 2nd row 20 (printing 13, 1900).

T. A. Colls Presentation Cards

Head and duty proofs on cards, 1½d. value exist.

Trial Cancellation

Issued stamp with squared "PORTSMOUTH IL/JA5/85" cancel on piece £1500

1887 (1 January). 6d. Purple on Rose-red Paper, Type K29. Wmk Crown (W12). Perf 14.

			Unmtd mint	Mtd mint	Used
K37 (=S.G.208/208a)	(1)	6d. purple on rose-red paper	50·00	30·00	10·00
	(2)	6d. deep purple on rose-red paper	50·00	30·00	11·00
	(3)	6d. slate-purple on rose-red paper	55·00	35·00	15·00
		Block of four	£225	£140	45·00
		Used on cover	†	†	75·00
	a.	Watermark inverted	£2800	£1500	£750
	e.	"Specimen", Types 9, 10, 12 *from*	65·00	50·00	
	t.	"Cancelled", Type 14		£850	

Imprimatur: £650. From registration sheets, plates 3, 4; 47 stamps taken and from imperforate spare registration sheets.

Essays. For essays (for embossing), see Section KD Part II.
Essays have unadorned stalks at bottom of thistles top left and right; on issued stamps the stalks have "bows" on them.

Die Proofs. No. "299". In black on white glazed card:

Date	*Inscr*	*Additional Inscriptions or Notes*	
17 May 86	B/H	Card 60 × 35 mm with date close to proof due to shortage of card	£1200
19 May 86	A/H		£1200
(M/S)	(M/s)	"Aug 5 1896 After Striking" and initialled	£1200
26 July 60	A/S	Card 92 × 41 mm	£1200

Die Proofs from the De La Rue Striking Books

With various dates . . . . *from* £1000

Date on piece	*Plates and other details*
May 25	3/759 and repairs (1886)
Aug 25 1886	5/771.

Pieces (3) have plate numbers on them, 6/949, 7/950; 8/974, 9/975; 10/1037, 11/1038.

Plates and Printings. 11 plates were created, numbered 3-11 from 1884 6d. Plates 3–5 were without rules (setting 1), plates 6–9 were with rules (setting 2) and all used. In 1990, ladders (pillars) were added (setting 3). Plates 10, 11 were made but not used. Printing was always 480 set. Issue size was 40 set to 1894 necessitating sheet pentagonal dividing marks "shield", then 120 set, followed by 240 set (1899).

Marginal Settings

Printing	*Setting*	Plates: Left	Right
1–11 (1896)	1	3	4
12, 13	1, 2A	5, 6	4, 7
14	2A	6, 8	7, 9
15 (1899)	2B	6, 8	7, 9
16–19 (1901)	3	6, 8	7, 9

Setting 1A. No rules, 40 set issue (*dividers "shield" type always cut);
1B. As 1A, but 120 set issue (dividers not cut on issue).

Setting 2A. Rules, 120 set issue, interpane gutter cut.
2B. As 2A, but 240 set issue, upper, lower panes joined.
Setting 3. As 2A, but with ladders in interpane gutter.
Pieces showing setting 2B are very rare.
*Every 4th stamp horizontally-above row 1, in interpane, gutter and below row 20; added by printers whether needed or not, i.e. beyond 1894.

Colour Trials

Perf 14, watermark Crown:

In green on rose-red (shades), purple on rose-red (shades) . . . . *each* £3800

Perf 14, without watermark:

In green on orange (shades), green on red (shades) . . . . *each* £3800

Only 1888 papers have line perf trials but some comb perf 14 stamps have been incorrectly described as "colour trials". The above were not on production papers, therefore the colours were uneven.

The imperforate trials are incomplete and prices for these are the same as shown for perforated examples.

The note below the 2½d. colour trials applies to the 6d.

Trial Cancellation

Issued stamp with squared "PORTSMOUTH IL/JA5/85" cancel on piece £1500

1887 (1 January). 9d.Purple and Blue, Type K30. Wmk Crown (W12). Perf 14.

			Unmtd mint	Mtd mint	Used
K38 (=S.G.209)	(1)	9d. dull purple and blue	90·00	60·00	40·00
	(2)	9d. dull purple and bright blue	£170	£100	65·00
	(3)	9d. slate-purple and blue	£100	75·00	45·00
		Block of four	£375	£260	£190
		Used on cover	†	†	£200
	a.	Watermark inverted	£3000	£2000	£750
	b.	Without crown watermark			
	s.	"Specimen", Types 6, 9, 12 . *from*	75·00	55·00	
	t.	"Cancelled", Type 14		£900	

Imprimatur: £650. From registration sheets: 22.11.86 sheet, 34 stamps taken; 10.4.88 sheet, 27 stamps taken.

Most taken without selvedge, only 10.4.88 F pane R. 2/5, G pane R. 4/1 known to have selvedge; no imperforate stamps from spare registration sheets recognised.

No. K38*b* was due to a shift as the line watermark was present.

Type A Head Plate Die

Type B Duty Die

Die Proofs. Die "288". In black on white glazed card. There were two dies of the head plate but there is no evidence that any plate was made from the first die.

Date	*Inscr.*	*Additional Inscriptions or Notes*	
Head Plate only (Type A)			
10 Jun 86	B/H		£1200
18 Aug 86	—		£1200
6 Sep 86	A/S		£1200
6 Sep 86	A/S	Initialled "C.S." (m/s)	£1200
—	—	Card 57 × 62 mm (approx) and initialled "G (or A).H."	
Head die "311"			
5 July 90	B/H	Larger pendant curl than die "288"	£1400
Duty Plate die "4" (Type B)			
29 Jun 86	B/H		£1400

Die Proofs for the setting of the marginal rules

Head Plate as for the 4d. value .... } £3000
Duty Plate as for the 4d. value but rule round the issued stamp is in blue .... }

Die Proofs from the De La Rue Striking Books

Head plate only	*from* £1000
Duty plate only	£1200
Duty plate and two head plates marked "Die I" and "Die II" respectively	£2800

Date on piece	*Plates and other details*
July 7, 11	Duty master plate O1 (1886).
July 16, 29, Aug 24	H5/781–12/788 and repairs (1886).
Jan 29	20 leads, one unidentified plate (H13–15).
Sept 1, 22 Oct 12	H16/825–H35844 (1889).
Apr 10 1890	H36/915.

Duty master plates O2, O3 pieces, see 4d. value.

See under 4d. value for Die Proof combining 4d. and 9d. duty plates.

Plates and Printing. The 20 set head plates 5–15 (prefixed "H" throughout and numbered from 1884 9d.) were without rules and used. Duty plates (prefixed "D" throughout) were created from 20 set master plate O1 without rules: D1–16, D5, 12, 15, 16 not being used. 20 set H16–35 with rules were from die 288; H36 from die 311 in 1890, H33–36 were not used. D17–49 (from master plate O3) were with rules; D21, 22, 26, 47, 49 were not used, while D39–46, 48 were not used in the Queen Victoria period. Printing was 80 set to 1888, 160 set to 1889 and 320 set from 1890. Issue size was 20 set to 1899, then 80 set.

Marginal Settings

Setting 1.	No rules, no lined blocks (printings 1–3a), 20 set issue.
Setting 2.	No rules, lined blocks (printings 3b, 4), 20 set issue.
Setting 3A.	Rules round all panes, head and duty head cut away at corners, 20 set issue.
Setting 3B.	As 3A, but 80 issue: A, B, C, D panes joined; E, F, G, H panes joined (printings 11, 12-end).

T. A. Colls Presentation Cards

Head and duty proofs on cards, as 1½d. value exist.

Trial Cancellations

Issued stamp with squared "PORTSMOUTH IL/JA5/85" cancel on piece	£2000
Issued stamp with "BO1" (Alexandria type) cancel on piece	£2000

BO1 (Alexandria type) was created in connection with 10d. colour trials.

1890 (24 February). 10d. Purple and Carmine, Type K31. Wmk Crown (W12). Perf 14.

			Unmtd mint	Mtd mint	Used
K39 (=S.G.210/210b)	(1)	10d. dull purple and carmine	70·00	45·00	38·00
	(2)	10d. dull purple and deep dull carmine	£600	£450	£225
	(3)	10d. dull purple and scarlet	£140	80·00	50·00
		Block of four	£325	£200	£190
		Used on cover	†	†	£225

a.	Watermark inverted	£3500	£2500	£750
b.	Imperforate		£9000	
c.	Damaged left tablet (Pane C, R. 1/4)	£250	£120	
d.	Damaged lower ornament (Pane D. R. 1/1)	£250	£120	
e.	Clipped S.W. corner to right value tablet and cracked plate (Pane D, R. 4/1)	£250	£120	
f.	Cracked plate below right value tablet (Pane C, R. 4/4)	£220	£100	
fa.	As above but crack above right value tablet (Pane C, R. 4/5)	£220	£100	
g.	Damage to left tablet and break to left of 1 at right (Pane H, R. 4/1)	£220	£100	
s.	"Specimen", Types 9, 13, 15 *from*	£110	80·00	
t.	"Cancelled", Type 14		£1000	

The carmine ink used by De La Rue on the 10d. shows different reactions under long wave u.v. light. These can be categorised as:

1. Non-reactive range. Frame of stamp shows no fluorescent reaction under the lamp.
2. Carmine range. Frame of stamp fluoresces brightly but in the same colour as is visible under normal light.
3. Lake range. Frame of stamp shows significant fluorescence in shades of lake ranging from bright and pale to very deep. All examples show a characteristic and distinctive purplish cast.
4. Scarlet range. Frame of stamp shows significant fluroescence in shades of scarlet, ranging from bright orange-red to deep scarlet. All examples show a distinctive scarlet/vermilion cast.

Nos. K39(1) and (3) occur with all four categories of ink but shade (2) only with 3 and 4.

Imprimaturs. Registration sheet, dated 7.2.90, setting 2, from which 8 stamps taken; also imperforate stamps from spare registration sheets, including No. K39*b*. No separate price can be quoted for imprimaturs.

K39*c*

K39*d*

↑ K39*e*

K39*f*

K39*g*

No. K39*fa* has the crack above the value tablet at right.
Nos. K39*f*/*fa* can be found as a pair from Pane C.

Essays from the De La Rue Archives. On 15 March 1889 ten hand painted essays (numbered 1 to 10) were sent to Somerset House. Another set on tracing paper was retained by De La Rue. On 19 March another essay, similar to card 3 (close to accepted design in purple and blue with smaller lettering) was submitted. On 22 March four more cards A, B, C, D were produced, each with a tablet in each corner. A and B are missing. H. C. Raikes (P.M.G.) initialled design 3 on 4 June. De La Rue's copies are pen cancelled, of which 1–3, 8–10 are in Post Office Heritage Services. The Raikes card is in the Phillips Collection.

Hand painted and each pen cancelled:

Dated "MARCH. 15.89." and numbered 4 to 7 . . . . *from* £5000
Accepted design marked "3 ALTERNATIVE DESIGN", "MARCH. 19/89" £5500
Dated "MARCH. 22.89." and lettered C and D . . . . *from* £5000

Hand painted without cancel:

Dated "MARCH. 15.89." numbered 9 . . . . *from* £5500

Type A Head Plate Die

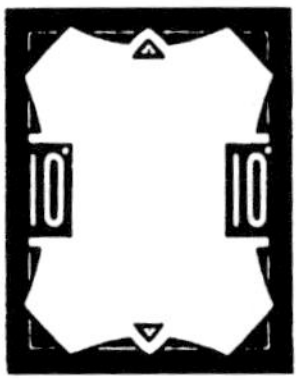

Type B Duty Die

Die Proofs. No. "310". In black on white glazed card:

Date	*Inscr.*	*Additional Inscriptions or Notes*	
Head Plate only (Type A)			
14 Aug 89	B/H		£1500
15 Aug 89	A/H	Initialled "G.F.S." and (m/s) "10d."	£1500
20 Dec 89	A/S	Initialled "G.F.S." (M/S)	£1500
Duty die "7" only (Type B)			
14 Aug 89	B/H		£2000
15 Aug 89	A/H	(M/S)	£2000

Die Proofs for the setting of the marginal rules. Dated "FEBRUARY 28 90"
Head Plate as for the 4d. value . . . . }
Duty Plate as for the 4d. value but rule round the issued stamp is in carmine . . . . } £3000

Die Proofs from the De La Rue Striking Books

Head plate only . . . . *from* £1000
Duty plate only £1250

Date on piece	*Plates and other details*
Sep 2, 5	H1/897, H2/898 (1889),
Jan 24	H3/913 (1890).
Aug 23	O1 (1889).

Piece dated about May 5 1893 for repairs is lost.

Plates and Printings. Two 160 set head plates (prefixed "H" throughout) H1, H2 and duty plates (prefixed "D" throughout) D1–3 from 20 set master plate O1, all with rules, were quickly made so colour trials could be taken. Later, H3 (not used) and D4–33 were created. Printing 1 (H1/D1, 2, 4, 5, 80 set) was in setting 2. Due to pressure on De La Rue from changes in stock levels at Somerset House, printing 2 (April 1890) was from only two head and two duty plates (40 set) in setting 1; also perforated 40 set probably on an experimental perforator not normally used for production.

A 160 set printing began September 1890 (printing 3) from H1/D1, 2, 4, 5, 14–17. Printing 15 (1900) H2/D18–25 were put to press for 320 set. Issue size 20 set probably to 1894, but possibly to 1900 after which 80 set issue began.

Marginal Settings

Setting 1.	Printing and perforation 40 set; head plate corners cut away and vertical lined blocks (printing 2).
Setting 2A.	As setting 1 but horizontal, not vertical lined blocks (paintings 1, 3–15), 20 set issue.
Setting 2B.	As 2A, but 80 issue, A, B, C, D and E, F, G, H panes joined, possibly from 1894.

Colour Trials

I. For colours of 10d. value.

On white paper, watermark Crown, line perf 14:

Submitted 24.1.90 in two matching columns of 8 with issued 9d. at head of both, left column cancelled BO1 in bars, right uncancelled. Two copies produced; De La Rue's now have pen cancels on right column.

10d. trials reading down (head colour/duty colour) were: purple/blue; green/red; purple/brown; green/blue; green/purple; purple/red; green/brown.

De La Rue's copy, as above . . . . *from*
Trials, including in issued colours, cancelled BO1 on piece . . . . . . *each* £4500
Trials, excluding issued colours, uncancelled . . . . *each* £4500

Pieces:

1. 9d., 10d. purple/blue, one pair cancelled BO1, other not, (m/s) "1", "2" right of each pair . . . . *from*
2. As 1, but no 9d.; 10d. green/purple, purple/red and (m/s) "6" "7" at right . . . .

Both have contemporary (m/s).
Trials 3, 4, 5 and 8 may also exist either in similar pairs or singles.

Trials, cancelled Bedford St S.O. W.C./JA/6/90:

Purple/blue, purple/brown, purple/red (selected), green/red . . . . . . *each* £3000

II. For colour of 1892 4½d. value

On coloured papers, submitted 3 February 1892. Inks on white paper appear different when on coloured paper; head plate green often appears black on red paper. Heads had to be either green or purple so head colours are ink colours.

The 36 trials, 12 each on blue, yellow, and red production papers as for the 2½d. 3d., 6d. watermark Crown, line perf 14, were submitted. Trials with green heads have inverted watermark; purple heads upright watermark.

1. On blue paper:

Head plate in green: duty plate in: orange, red brown, blue, violet, green, purple . . . . *each* £3500
Head plate in purple: duty plate in: blue-green, blue, red, green, ultramarine, orange, brown . . . . *each* £3500

2. On yellow paper:

Head plate in green: duty plate in: red, purple, blue, orange, brown, green . *each* £3500
Head plate in purple: duty plate in: yellow-green, green, red, purple, blue-green orange, brown, blue .... *each* £3500

3. On red paper:

Head plate in green: duty plate in: red-orange, red, brown, violet, blue .... *each* £3500
Head plate in purple: duty plate in: orange-red, red, brown, green, violet, magenta .... *each* £3500

The above do not cover all recorded trials, even allowing for subjective variation.

Perf. × imperforate at left and right on thick white card

Head plate in purple, value plate in brown £4000

T. A. Colls Presentation Cards

Head and duty proofs on cards, as 1½d. value exist.

1887 (1 January). 1s. Green, Type K32. Wmk Crown (W12). Perf 14.

			Unmtd mint	Mtd mint	Used
K40 (=S.G.211)	(1)	1s. dull green	£300	£200	60·00
	(2)	1s. grey-green	£325	£250	80·00
		Block of four	£1500	£900	£300
		Used on cover	†	†	£125
		a. Watermark inverted	£900	£575	£375
		s. "Specimen", Types 9, 10, 12 .. *from*	75·00	55·00	
		t. "Cancelled", Type 14		£1000	

Imprimatur: £550. From registration sheets, plates 3, 4; 46 stamps taken, also imperf stamps from spare registration sheets.

No. K40*t* refers to colour standards and the 1887 examples are in yellowish green, as damp affected stamps which are rgarded as damaged. The 1888 standards are in shade (1).

Plates. Plates 3 to 7. Plate 8 was not put to press.

Die Proofs. Die No. "297". In black on white glazed card:

Date	*Inscr.*	*Additional Inscriptions or Notes*	
23 Mar 86	B/H	....	£1500
24 Mar 86	B/H	....	£1500
27 Mar 86	—	....	£1500
30 May 99	A/S	Initialled "G.F.S." (M/S)	£1500

Die Proofs from the De La Rue Striking Books

With various dates .... *from* £1100

Dates on piece	*Plates and other details*
July 8, 14	3/761, 4/762, repairs (1886)
Aug 11 1886	5/768 (on piece).

Remaining pieces (2) have plate numbers on them.

Plates and Printings. 8 plates were made, numbered from 3 (1884 1s.). Plates 3–5 were without rules. Plate 3 printed left sheet and plate 4 right from printing 1 (1886) to printing 12 (1898) when plate 5 was used; not known which plate was withdrawn. At printing 13, plates 6 and 7 with rules were put to press, plate 6 on left and 7 on right sheets. Plate 8 was never used.

Issue size 20 set (from 1884 1s.) but changed at printing 8 (Aug 1893) to 120 set, then unchanged to end. All sheets had sheet dividers as for the 6d. above, plus one each side of rows 5, 6 and 15, 16 perforated gutters.

Marginal Settings.

Setting 1A. No rules, 20 set issue (printings 1–7);
1B. As 1A, but 120 set issue, complete sheet dividers, (printings 8–12).
2. Rules (printing 13), 120 set issue.

Colour Trials. Taken to decide colour of 1900 1 shilling, No. K41.

Warrant 109/99 was issued 27.10.99 for 60 sheets, from which De La Rue printed many trials including head plate green and purple. Heads were cut from those sheets to fit into holes left by cutting out the heads in other sheets. Composite trials were submitted. Remainders were returned to Somerset House to satisfy the Warrant; from there, many leaked out. Complete stamps in various colours are without significance but popular. Since they have been dispersed, no listing is complete, but the following are known.

Perf 14, watermark Crown:

In crimson, carmine, brown-red, yellow, deep olive, olive-green, grey-green, emerald, blue, bright blue, violet, mauve, deep lilac, purple, yellow-brown, brown, slate . . . . . *each* £1800

For submitted trials, see 1900 1 shilling below.

1900 (11 July). 1s. Green and Carmine, Type K32. Wmk Crown (W12). Perf. 14.

		Unmtd mint	Mtd mint	Used
K41 (=S.G.214)	1s. green and carmine	80·00	50·00	£125
	Block of four	£350	£250	£600
	Used on cover	†	†	£850
	a. Watermark inverted	£1500	£850	£750
	b. Frame broken at left (Pl. F3a, R. 19/1)	£500	£400	£275
	s. "Specimen", Type 15	£600	£400	
	t. "Cancelled", Type 18		£1000	

No. K41*t* with Type 14 is a fake.

Imprimatur: £18000. From registration sheet, two stamps taken (there were no spare registration sheets).

K41*b*

The frame break No. K41*b* can be found on the Edward VII 1 shilling Nos. M45/6*e*.

Die Proofs. Die No. "317". In black on white glazed card:

Date	*Inscr..*	*Additional Inscriptions or Notes*	
Head plate only			
6 Feb 00	B/H		£1100
—	B/S		£1100
—	B/S	Initialled "G.F.S." (M/S)	£1100
15 Feb 00	—		£1100
17 Feb 00	—		£1100
9 Mar 00	A/S		£1100

Date	*Inscr*	*Additional Inscriptions or Notes*	
Frame plate only			
6 Feb 00	B/H	Duty die "9"	£1100
16 Feb 00	B/H		£1100
16 Feb 00	—		£1100
25 Feb 00	B/H		£1100
25 Feb 00	A/H		£1100

Date	*Inscr*	*Additional Inscriptions or Notes*	
26 Jul 00	—	Duty die "10"	£1100
26 Jul 00	—		£1100
26 Jul 00	B/H		£1100
25 Sep 00	—	"Die No. 10" (M/S)	£1100

Die Proofs from the De La Rue Archives

M/S dates on left side: 24.1.00; 25.1.00; 26.1.00; 29.1.00; 30.1.00; 31.1.00; 3.2.00; 5.2.00; no other markings, except tick in north-east corner. Dates are of preceding proofs on way to completion of die.

From the Striking Books

One piece only, with strikings for all plates, head, frame and repairs between 19 Feb and 26 March 1900; except plate F5 .... £3500

Plates and Printing. Head plates 9–12 (from 1887 1s., prefixed H throughout) with rules and frame plates 1–5 (prefixed "F" throughout) also with rules, were created. H9, 10 with rules cut away at corners were used with F2, 3, H9F2 printed right sheets and H10F3 left (the only setting). F1 was faulty, possibly due to one or more frames being inserted inverted. None of the plates used showed such inverted frames.

Colour Trials. A bicolour 1 shilling stamp became mandatory once the ½d. was changed to green. On 9 November 1899 a set of 1s. colour trials was submitted with different coloured duty plates and either purple or green centres superimposed. Marked with the numbers shown below, on card with "9 Nov 99" and without watermark:

Head in purple (cards 1–9), frame plate in (card order):
Dark green; Mauve; Bistre; Pale olive-green*; Violet; Prussian blue; Emerald-green*; Brown; Scarlet .... *each* £8500

Head in green (cards A1–9A), frame plate in (card order):
Dark green; Mauve; Pale olive-green*; Violet; Bright blue; Emerald-green*; Brown; Carmine .... *each* £8500

* The colours of these are not identical.

SECTION LA

Departmental Official Issues and Government Mail

General Notes

These stamps are overprinted with the name of a Government Department and, in most cases, the word "OFFICIAL". They were for the use of essentially autonomous Government Departments. Those overprinted "GOVT PARCELS" were introduced by the Post Office for use by all Departments on packages over 3 lbs. in weight.

Each Government Department had a Head Office, usually located in London, but sometimes separate Scottish or Irish headquarters in Edinburgh or Dublin also enjoyed the postal privileges of being a "Head Office". Mail to and from Head Offices went essentially free of all charges with the Post Office merely receiving an annual budgetary credit for services provided. This system survived, with minor alterations, into the 1980s. The only exception was that some, but not all, Head Offices were required to purchase stamps to pay for registration fees. Most surviving unstamped Government mail between 1840 and 1914 is from Head Offices. "Local" mail was posted between provincial offices, but for others such mail was very extensive. The largest output was from the Post Office itself; other Departments with large local mails included the Inland Revenue, the Army and the Navy.

The Inland Revenue's local mail was second in quantity only to that of the Post Office. It had a network of local offices each with many tax collectors who were, in the 19th century, mainly private firms and individuals remunerated on a commission basis. Not only the volume of mail, but also the weight of individual packets grew with increasing prosperity. In 1882 the Inland Revenue obtained overprinted stamps for use on such local mail. No payment was made for these, but the Post Office received quarterly returns of the value of stamps actually used and obtained an annual budgetary credit. In essence the Head Office "free" mail privilege had been extended the local mail. This proved in the long run to be a damaging precedent for the Post Office. Other Departments tried, on a number of occasions, to obtain the same concession. The Post Office vigorously refused such requests, but in 1895 both the Office of Works, a tiny Department with a few Provincial Offices, and the Army took their case to the Treasury with the result that stamps overprinted "O W OFFICIAL" and "ARMY OFFICIAL" appeared in 1896. "Head Office" status was not, however, granted as both Departments paid cash for the stamps at the time they were issued from Somerset House. This remained policy until 1904 and other Departments following suit.

In 1903 the Inland Revenue were due to perform a quinquennial (5 yearly) revaluation of property throughout the United Kingdom. In 1898 the forms were delivered by hand, but there had been difficulties. Five years later they decided to use the post, but were daunted by the immense task of attaching the essential 5 million stamps. The Post Office granted permission for the use of a printed postal frank on the forms. Subsequently the franks acquired a crown (1904) and appeared in green, red and finally black (1905). The reforms of the 1906 Liberal administration greatly extended the need for local mail and the printed franks were subsequently used by all Departments on both local and Head Office mail. Accounting was by returns quoting the number of forms used and consequent annual budgetary credit to the Post Office. No payments were involved.

In September 1903, W. Richards, a senior officer in charge of the stamp stock of the Inland Revenue Stamping Department at Somerset House, and A. B. Creeke, a well-known philatelist, pleaded guilty at the Old Bailey to a fraud involving Departmental Overprints. The offence stemmed from the huge premium over face value that unused overprints commanded from stamp collectors. As a direct result all stocks of such stamps were called in on 13 May 1904 and their use on mail ceased. For practical reasons 14 May 1904 can be regarded as the final day of usage of such overprints. Local offices reverted to the use of normal postage stamps paid for in cash on which the Post Office promised a meaningless 25% discount.

Government mail sent overseas during the 19th century from both local or Head Offices seems to show no consistent policy with some apparently going free and some being franked by stamps. There is no clear Departmental pattern either. It is a field for further study.

Registered mail is another inconsistent area with some Departments using the service free and others paying for 2d. fee. Inland Revenue covers with the Official/Crown/Paid black franks (local mail) are commonly found registered, often with printed blue crosses.

Since 1914 most Government mail has used printed franks, but postage stamps were always valid and can be found on overseas mail and paying the registration fee on inland covers. British Government mail is exceptionally complicated. This is due not only to Departmental autonomy up to

1920 when they were all brought formally under Treasury control, but also to the blurred boundaries of "Government", local, central or judicial and "private" business.

The stamps were all printed by Thomas De La Rue & Co., and were perforated 14. Values to the one shilling were on Crown watermarked paper and the high values 2s. 6d. to £1 were on Anchor paper unless otherwise stated.

WARNING. Some values do exist with forged overprints and it is recommended that expert opinion and a certificate be obtained for the higher priced stamps, particularly those in fine condition.

Departmental official stamps were also made by puncturing the outline of a crown with the initials of the government department punctured below but these are not listed. They comprise "H.M.O.W." and "O.W." (Office of Works), "B.T." (Board of Trade), and "S.O." (H.M. Stationery Office).

Prices for Stamps in Used Condition

The notes about condition given at the end of the General Notes to Section J also apply to Section LA. The prices for well centred, lightly used stamps can be calculated by adding **100%** to the prices quoted for L18–30. **35%** to the prices quoted for L1–17 and **25%** to the prices quoted for L31–35.

Inland Revenue

The Inland Revenue descended from the Stamp Office. This body stamped legal documents, contracts, etc., with embossed stamps as still happens today. Up to about 1880 the only places where this took place were Edinburgh and at Somerset House in London, but with the huge growth in the north of England another facility was opened at the Manchester provincial office. The documents involved were bulky and heavy, but sending them by post to Edinburgh and Somerset House was not a problem as they had postal Head Office privileges. On documents sent to Manchester the alternatives were expensive post or slow, uncertain and still expensive private carterage. In 1882 the Inland Revenue requested Head Office postal privileges for the Manchester provincial office, but this was refused. I. R. Official overprints were the finally agreed alternative. Whether the arrangements for accounting for these was deliberate or an aberration on the part of the Post Office is not clear. The effect was, however, that the effective Head Office privilege of free mail was extended to every Inland Revenue and Tax Collector office throughout the land.

At first use of the new overprints was confined, by the Post Circular of 26 September 1882 announcing their issue, to mail between provincial offices within England, outside London, and Wales. The I.R. Official overprints on the 1880 ½d. and 6d. and the 1881 1d. (S.G. 01, 03, 04) are unique in being initially valid in a part of the United Kingdom only. Such a situation could not last and use was extended in Scotland on 17 April 1883 and to London on 29 May 1883. Although the Post Office circular of 26 September 1882 authorised the use of all three values from 1 October 1882, only the 1d. value was in existence by that date. The earliest cover or postal item found so far is from 13 October 1882, but it is impossible to be certain that there was no earlier use than this. The ½d. overprinted stamp became available from 1 November 1882 and the 6d. from 3 November 1882.

In early 1885 the decision was taken to issue the 2½d., 1s., 5s., 10s., and £1 stamps with I.R. Official overprints. Supplies of used examples of high value I.R. Official overprints were haphazard, depending on unauthorised leakages from material intended for destruction. There was also a steady leakage of mint examples to the stamp market. This was not illegal, but did breach the trust expected of Civil Servants. The Chairman of the Board of Inland Revenue attempted to stop this leakage by an internal regulation in 1896, but they continued by fraudulent methods and were only finally stopped in May 1904 when the overprints were withdrawn.

Overprint Type **L1** came from a specially prepared die while Type **L2** was created from type. So far six I.R. Official overprint plates have been recognised. Of these arbitrarily numbered plates Type **L2** came from plates 4 (5s., 10s.) and 5, (£1). Type **L1** came from plates 2 (1887 2½d., 6d., and 1s.) and plate 3 (1883 2½d.). Plates 1 and 6 also of Type **L1** were used for 1880, 1885, 1887 and 1900 ½d.'s and the 1881 1d.

It is understood that Nos. L3 (1d.) 1882, L12 (½d.) 1888, L16 (1s.) 1889 and L11 (£1) 1892 may be found showing worn impressions of the overprints with thicker letters. Later printings reverted to the earlier (thinner) type.

L1

L2

1882–85. Stamps of 1880–84 overprinted in black with Type L1.

L1 (=S.G.O1/O2)	(1) ½d. deep green K1(1) (1.11.82)	85·00	30·00
	(2) ½d. pale green, K1(2)	65·00	25·00
	Block of four	£375	£325
	Used on cover	†	75·00
	s. "Specimen", Type 9	£225	
L2 (=S.G.O5)	½d. slate-blue, K2 (8.5.85)	65·00	25·00
	Block of four	£375	£275
	Used on cover	†	£100
	s. "Specimen", Type 9	£225	
L3 (=S.G.O3)	1d. lilac (Die II), K8 (1.10.82*)	6·00	4·00
	Block of four	40·00	25·00
	Used on cover	†	25·00
	a. Overprinted in blue-black	£200	75·00
	b. "OFFICIAL" omitted	—	£7000
	c. Watermark inverted	—	£1250
	e. Imperforate	£3000	
	f. Imperforate, without watermark (pair)	£5000	
	s. "Specimen", Types 9, 15	£140	
L4 (=S.G.O6)	2½d. lilac K20 (12.3.85)	£325	£110
	Block of four	£2000	£700
	Used on cover	†	£1000
	s. "Specimen", Type 9	£225	
L5 (=S.G.O4)	6d. grey (Plate 18), J89 (3.11.82)	£400	90·00
	Block of four	£2000	£650
	s. "Specimen", Type 9, 15 *from*	£225	
L6 (=S.G.O7)	1s. dull green, K26 (12.3.85)	£4250	£1250
	s. "Specimen", Type 9	£900	

Controls: L3, B, D, F, G, I, K, L, N, P, Q, R, T to X (*Prices* N, W, X £250 *each single. Others from* £300 *each*). Not all are recorded as being extant.

*Although authorised from 1 October 1882 the earliest date is 13 October 1882 at Stoke-on-Trent.

Type A

Type B

Essays for overprint on 1d. Lilac. Mounted on card.

Type A £5000
Type B. As Type A but lettering transposed £5000

Type A is known dated 21 June 1882. In both the above the identical lettering is thinner than on the issued stamps and the letters also differ slightly, particularly the C, A and L.

Die Proof from the De La Rue Striking Books

Type **L1** struck on plain paper cut to size with various endorsements comprising dates, or number of leads.

Dated 31 August 1882, 14 February 1885, 21 May 1897, 29 May1897 . . . . *from* £2000

1885/92. High Value stamps of 1883–91 overprinted in black (L10 in blue-black) with Type L2.

L7 (=S.G.O8/O9)	(1)	5s. rose on blued paper, K11 (12.3.85)	£7500	£2800
	(2)	5s. rose on white paper, K12 (3.90)	£3500	£1200
		Block of four	£18000	£8500
	a.	Raised stop after "R" (white paper)	£4000	£1500
	b.	Overprinted in blue-black (white paper) (1890)	£4500	£1500
	ba.	Do. Raised stop after "R"		
	s.	"Specimen", Type 9, 11 (blued paper) . . . . *from*	£1500	
	t.	"Specimen", Types 9, 11, 13, 16 (white paper) . . . . *from*	£1000	
	u.	"Cancelled", Type 14 (white paper)	£3000	
L8 (=S.G.O9c/O10b)	(1)	10s. ultramarine on blued paper, K13(1) (12.3.85) . .	£12000	£3500
	(2)	10s. cobalt on blued paper, K13(2) (12.3.85)	£16000	£4500
	(3)	10s. cobalt on white paper, K14(1)	£10000	
	(4)	10s. ultramarine on white paper, K14(2) (3.90)	£5500	£1800
		Block of four	£30000	£9000
	a.	Raised stop after "R"	£6000	£2500
	b.	Overprinted in blue-black (white paper) (1890)	£6000	£2500
	ba.	Do. Raised stop after "R"	—	£3500
	s.	"Specimen", Types 9, 10, 11, 16 (ultramarine on white paper) . . . . *from*	£1500	
	t.	"Specimen", Type 11 (cobalt on blued paper)	£2400	
	u.	"Specimen", Type 10, 11 (ultramarine on blue paper) . . . . *from*	£2000	
	v.	"Cancelled", Type 14 (ultramarine on white paper)	£5000	
L9 (=S.G.O11)		£1 brown-lilac (Wmk Crowns), K15 (12.3.85)	£35000	£18000
	a.	Frame broken (JC or TA, Plate 2)	£40000	—
	b.	Overprinted in blue-black		
	s.	"Specimen", Type 11	£3250	
	sa.	Do. with broken frame (JC or TA)	£4500	
L10 (=S.G.O12)		£1 brown-lilac (Wmk Orbs), K16 (3.90)	£55000	£25000
	a.	Frame broken (JC or TA)	£65000	—
	s.	"Specimen", Types 9, 11 . . . . *from*	£6500	
	sa.	Do. with broken frame (JC or TA)	£8000	
	t.	"Cancelled", Type 14	£12000	
L11(S.G.O16)		£1 green, K17 (6.92)	£8000	£1800
		Block of four	£48000	£17000
	a.	Frame broken (JC or TA)	£12000	£3000
	b.	No stop after "R"	—	£2800
	s.	"Specimen", Types 9, 10, 15 . . . . *from*	£1000	
	sa.	Do. with broken frame (JC or TA)	£1500	
	t.	"Cancelled", Type 14	£5000	

The raised stop variety came from plate 4 and exists on the 5s. and 10s. values. The variety occurs on all stamps in the top row of each pane, lettered AA–AH and HA–HH in bottom left-hand corner. No. L11*b* came from plate 5.

Essays. With large overprint with serifs, 32 × 15 mm, overprinted "Specimen", Type 9.

5s. rose (blued paper)	£7000
10s. ultramarine (blued paper)	£9000
£1 brown-lilac (Wmk Crowns)	£12000
£5 orange (blued paper)	£15000

1888–1901. Stamps of 1887–1900 overprinted in black with Type L1.

L12 (S.G.O13)	½d. vermilion, K27 (15.5.88)	10·00	4·00
	Block of four	50·00	20·00
	Used on cover	†	80·00
	a. Without "I.R."	£3800	
	b. Imperforate	£2750	
	c. "Overprint double (imperforate)	£3800	
	s. "Specimen", Types 9, 15 *from*	90·00	
	t. "Cancelled", Type 14	£750	
L13 (=S.G.O17)	½d. blue-green, K28 (4.01)	15·00	10·00
	Block of four	£100	90·00
	Used on cover	†	£250
	s. "Specimen", Type 15	£125	
L14 (=S.G.O14)	2½d. purple on blue paper, K31 (2.92)	£120	15·00
	Block of four	£700	£150
	Used on cover	†	£350
	s. "Specimen", Types 9, 13, 15 *from*	90·00	
	t. "Cancelled", Type 14	£750	
L15 (=S.G.O18)	6d. purple on rose-red paper, K37 (1.7.01)	£300	65·00
	Block of four	£1800	£425
	s. "Specimen", Types 15, 16 *from*	£180	
L16 (=S.G.O15)	1s. dull green, K40 (9.89)	£600	£200
	Block of four	£3500	£1000
	Used on cover	†	£3500
	s. "Specimen", Types 9, 15 *from*	£180	
	t. "Cancelled", Type 14	£850	
L17 (=S.G.O19)	1s. green and carmine, K41 (12.01)	£2500	£900
	s. "Specimen", Type 15	£750	

Controls: L12, B, E, G, I, K, L, N, O, P, Q (*Price* Q £250 *per single, others* £300 *per single*). L13, R (*Price* £250 *per single*).

"*I.R. Specimen*", Stamps overprinted "I R Specimen" in small block type are known. They include the ½d., 1½d., 2d., 2½d., 3d., 4d., 4½d., 5d. (Die II), 6d., 9d., 10d. and 1s. green of the "Jubilee" issue plus the 1d (K8), the 2s. 6d., 5s., 10s. and £1 (Types **K9** to **K12** on white paper, and the £5 (Type **J31**, white paper).

Government Parcels

When the parcel post was introduced on 1 August 1883 it was decided to change the way Government packages were handled. In its negotiations for mail-carrying contracts with the railways the Post Office found itself at a disadvantage because Government Departments with free mail privileges sent heavy items via ordinary letter post. The Post Office and Treasury had tried for many years to diminish this practice by making special arrangements with private carriers, but this largely failed. It was therefore decided to issue, free of charge, to all eligible Government Offices, special stamps to encourage the use of the new Parcel Post service.

Initially approval was given for the use of unappropriated fiscal stamps overprinted "Government Parcels", but De La Rue proposed ordinary stamps overprinted "GOVT PARCELS".

The original Treasury directive was that the new stamps were to be used on parcels weighing between 3 lbs. and 7 lbs. This situation continued until parcel post rates changed on 1 May 1886 when parcels up to 11 lbs. could be sent.

In 1891 registration of parcels was introduced and this necessitated the introduction of a 2d. value.

The minimum authorised weight for use of these overprints was 3 lbs. but it is known that this was ignored, especially by the Inland Revenue, and examples down to the minimum parcel post rate of up to 1 lb are known. Usage on letters was unauthorised.

To produce the overprints, four overprint plates were created, arbitrarily numbered 1 to 4. Plate 1 (in horizontal format) was used to overprint the 1883 6d. and 9d., Plate 2 (in vertical format) was used from 1883 to 1903 for all other values except the $4\frac{1}{2}$d. and 9d. Plate 3 was created in 1888 to overprint the 9d. value which was at that time issued in sheets of 20. It was taken from rows 17/8–20/12 of plate 2 and so incorporates the "open top to S" in position R. 2/1. In 1899 the sheet size of the 9d. was increased to 80 stamps, so a new overprint plate, 4 was created from four transfers of plate 3 so that every pane from plate 4 also has the variety "open top to S" on R. 2/1.

GOVT
PARCELS

L3

1883–86. Stamps of 1881–84 overprinted in black with Type L3 (the overprint is smaller, 14·3 mm long, on L19–20).

L18 (=S.G.O61)	$1\frac{1}{2}$d. lilac, K18 (1.5.86)	£325	70·00
	Block of four	£1750	£550
	a. No dot under "T"	£400	£100
	b. Dot to left of "T"	£380	£100
	s. "Specimen", Type 9	£125	
L19 (=S.G.O62)	6d. dull green, K24 (1.5.86)	£1800	£800
	s. "Specimen", Type 9	£200	
L20 (=S.G.O63)	9d. dull green, K25 (1.8.83)	£1600	£625
	s. "Specimen", Type 9	£200	
	t. "Specimen", Type 9, with trial cancel		
L21 (=S.G.O64)	1s. orange-brown (Plate 13), J116 (1.8.83)	£900	£225
	a. No dot under "T" (stamp LC)	£1250	£300
	b. Dot to left of "T" (stamp BG)	£1250	£300
	s. "Specimen", Type 9	£225	
L22 (=S.G.O64c)	1s. orange-brown (Plate 14), J117 (1.8.83)	£1900	£325
	a. No dot under "T"	£2400	£450
	b. Dot to left of "T"		

Imprimatur: L20 (imperf.), *each* £1000. Stamps removed from the imprimatur sheet are JA, KA–LB, GR–GT, HQ–LT.

An originally constructed, there were a number of faults of type setting which collectors have noticed for many years, i.e. no dot under the T and dot to the left of T. The former occurs three times on the plate (4/2, 12/3, 20/2) and the latter four times (2/7, 6/7, 7/9, 12/9).

1887–1900. Stamps of 1887–1900 and the 1d. Lilac overprinted in black with Type L3.

L23 (=S.G.O69)	1d. lilac (Die II), K8 (18.6.97)	75·00	18·00
	Block of four	£375	90·00
	a. No dot under "T"	£110	40·00
	b. Dot to left of "T"	£110	40·00
	c. Overprint inverted	£3800	£1750
	d. As "c" with dot to left of "T"	£4000	£2200
	e. Watermark inverted	—	£375
	s. "Specimen", Type 15	£300	
	t. "Cancelled", Type 18	£1200	

L24 (=S.G.O65)	1½d. dull purple and pale green, K29 (29.10.87)	85·00	10·00
	Block of four	£475	50·00
	a. No dot under "T"	£130	20·00
	b. Dot to right of "T"	£130	20·00
	c. Dot to left of "T"	£130	20·00
	s. "Specimen", Types 9, 10, 13, 15 *from*	£200	
L25 (=S.G.O70)	2d. green and carmine, K30 (24.10.91)	£170	25·00
	Block of four	£1100	£125
	a. No dot under "T"	£275	50·00
	b. Dot to left of "T"	£275	50·00
	s. "Specimen", Types 9, 11, 13, 15 *from*	£200	
	t. "Cancelled", Type 14	£1000	
L26 (=S.G.O71)	4½d. grey-green and carmine, K34 (29.9.92)	£275	£185
	Block of four	£1700	£1500
	a. Watermark inverted	—	£6500
	b. Dot to right of "T"		
	s. "Specimen", Types 9, 13, 15 *from*	£200	
	t. "Cancelled", Type 14	£1000	
L27 (=S.G.O66)	6d. purple on rose-red paper, K37 (19.12.87)	£160	35·00
	Block of four	£950	£180
	a. No dot under "T"	£220	40·00
	b. Dot to right of "T"	£220	40·00
	c. Dot to left of "T"	£220	40·00
	s. "Specimen", Types 9, 13, 15 *from*	£200	
	t. "Cancelled", Type 14	£850	
L28 (=S.G.O67)	9d. dull purple and blue, K38 (21.8.88)	£250	50·00
	Block of four	£1200	£500
	s. "Specimen", Types 9, 10, 13, 15 *from*	£200	
	t. "Cancelled", Type 14	£950	
L29 (=S.G.O68)	1s. dull green, K40 (25.3.90)	£425	£180
	Block of four	£3750	£1500
	a. No dot under "T"	£500	£250
	b. Dot to right of "T"	£500	£250
	c. Dot to left of "T"	£525	£250
	d. Overprint in blue-black		
	s. "Specimen", Types 9, 13, 15 *from*	£200	
	t. "Cancelled", Type 14	£950	
L30 (=S.G.O72)	1s. green and carmine, K41 (11.00)	£450	£160
	Block of four	£3200	£1400
	a. Overprint inverted	†	£10000
	s. "Specimen", Type 9	£250	
	t. "Cancelled", Type 18	£1200	

Controls: L23, V, W (*Price from* £250 *per single*).

Threepence essay from unapproportiated die

Essays. Essay comprising marginal strip of three printed in lilac from unappropriated die, with "Specimen Type 9 and endorsements as illustrated.

The 3d. strip of three Watermark Orb £20000
The 6d. strip of three. Watermark Orb £20000

Essay struck "2 May 83" in blue on a die proof on glazed white card stamped "May 18, 1872" and "AFTER STRIKING":

3d. black as illustrated but with "GOVERNMENT PARCELS" set in panel in red and endorsed in M/S "The body of the stamps will be green" and "rough sketch" and pencilled initials . . . .

Each of the above are unique.

A

B

C

Government Parcel essays

The "3d." on 3d., No K8A with trial overprint:

With Types A in red £7500
With Types B in red £7500
With Types A in black £7500
With Types B in black £7500
With Types C in black £7500

The "6d." on 6d., No K8B with trial overprint:

With Types A in red £7500
With Types B in red £7500
With Types A in black £7500
With Types B in black £7500
With Types C in black £7500

Six each of the above were prepared and most have survived. Essays with dot after PARCELS exist on 1883 9d. DI and 1881 1s. plate 14 KD.

Office of Works

In 1895 the Office of Works applied to the Post Office for its own overprinted stamps. The Army did so at much the same time and the two applications were dealt with together. They received the usual blank refusal, but then approached the Treasury. The Post Office suggested the use of perforated initials, but the Treasury was willing to extend the Inland Revenue's postal privileges to these two Departments, but hesitated as a considerable sum was involved in the Army application. Finally a compromise was reached by which the Departments paid for overprinted stamps at the time they were issued from Somerset House.

In essence there were two issues of these overprints. The first in March 1896 comprised the $\frac{1}{2}$d. and 1d. values which were officially issued and described in the Post Office circular dated 24 March 1896. These remained in use until May 1904 and were issued to provincial offices as well as being used by Head Office. The second issue was in April–May 1902 when the overprinted 2d., $2\frac{1}{2}$d., 5d. and 10d. values appeared. Their use seems to have been confined to Head Office. The overprints on stamps of 2d. and over were for registration (2d.) or for overseas mail. Since the King Edward VII 5d. and 10d. stamps had not been created when requests for those values came in, the overprints were made on the corresponding Queen Victoria stamps Nos. K36 and K39.

The Office of Works was a very small Department. Its annual usage of overprints in the years between 1899 and 1902 was about £100 face value.

O.W.

OFFICIAL

L4

1896–1902. Stamps of 1887–1900 and the 1d. Lilac overprinted in black with Type L4.

L31 (=S.G.O31)	½d. vermilion, K27 (24.3.96)	£225	£110
	Block of four	£1350	£700
	Used on cover	†	£500
	a. Large stop after "O"	£350	£150
	s. "Specimen", Types 9, 15 *from*	£250	
L32 (=S.G.O32)	½d. blue-green, K28 (2.02)	£325	£160
	Block of four	£2400	£1200
	s. "Specimen", Type 15	£350	
	t. "Cancelled", Type 18	£1200	
L33 (=S.G.O33)	1d. lilac (Die II), K8 (24.3.96)	£375	£110
	Block of four	£2400	£650
	Used on cover	†	£600
	a. Large stop after "O"	£450	£150
	s. "Specimen", Types 9, 15, 16 *from*	£250	
	t. "Cancelled", Type 18	£1200	
L34 (=S.G.O34)	5d. dull purple and blue (Die II), K36 (29.4.02)	£2000	£800
	Block of four	£12000	
	a. "CW" for "OW"	—	£3500
	s. "Specimen", Type 16	£575	
L35 (=S.G.O35)	10d. dull purple and carmine, K39 (28.5.02)	£3500	£1100
	Block of four	£18000	£6500
	s. "Specimen", Type 16	£1250	

Controls: L31, O, Q; L32, R; L33, U, X (*Prices each, per single*, Nos. L31 £1800, L32 £2000, L33 £1250).

C.W.

L34a (R.20/3)

The O.W. official overprint was created from a plate of 120 (12 × 10) so that each sheet of 240 was put through the press twice. The 10d. stamps of 1887 and 1902 were overprinted by masking the unwanted clichés of the plate.

Army

The Army's request to have their own overprinted stamps in 1895 was considered with that of the Office of Works with the same outcome. Their overprints were authorised from 1 September 1896 and were announced in a Post Office circular of that date.

Army Official overprints were produced from a total of four plates of which three were used on the Q.V. stamps. Forme 1 was used from 1896 to 1898 to overprint the ½d. and 1d. stamps. In 1898 the plate became too worn to use and was replaced by forme 2. This plate was more robust and was in use until 1903. The earliest used example so far seen is from March 1899. The 2½d. value was produced from an overprint plate with Type L6 conventionally known as forme 3. In 1901 the Army requested a 6d. value for which forme 3 was also used.

ARMY
OFFICIAL
L5

ARMY
OFFICIAL
L6

1896–1901. Stamps of 1887–1900 and the 1d. Lilac overprinted in black :½d. and 1d. with Type L5; 2½d. and 6d. with Type L6.

L36 (=S.G.O41)	½d. vermilion, K27 (1.9.96)	5·00	2·50
	Block of four	25·00	20·00
	Used on cover	†	50·00
	a. Watermark inverted	£500	£200
	b. Lines of overprint transposed	£2200	
	c. "OFFICIAI" (R. 13/7)	£100	50·00
	e. Long leg to "A" in "ARMY"	40·00	20·00
	g. Stop between legs of "R"	40·00	20·00
	h. Splayed "Y"	40·00	20·00
	i. Short "Y"	40·00	20·00
	k. Short first "I"	40·00	20·00
	l. Long first "I"	40·00	20·00
	m. Tall "L"	40·00	20·00
	n. Short "L"	40·00	20·00
	o. Thick "L"	60·00	30·00
	s. "Specimen", Type 9	£150	
	t. "Cancelled", Type 18	£1200	
L37 (=S.G.O42)	½d. blue-green, K28 (6.00)	5·00	10·00
	Block of four	25·00	60·00
	Used on cover	†	—
	a. Watermark inverted	£500	£175
	e. Long leg to "A" in "ARMY"	40·00	30·00
	g. Stop between legs of "R"	40·00	30·00
	h. Splayed "Y"	40·00	30·00
	i. Short "Y"	40·00	30·00
	j. Long stroke to second "F"	40·00	30·00
	k. Short first "I"	40·00	30·00
	l. Long first "I"	40·00	30·00
	m. Tall "L"	40·00	30·00
	s. "Specimen", Type 15	£200	
L38 (=S.G.O43)	1d. lilac (Die II), K8 (1.9.96)	5·00	4·00
	Block of four	25·00	22·00
	Used on cover	†	75·00
	c. "OFFICIAI" (R. 13/7)	£100	40·00
	e. Long leg to "A" is "ARMY"	40·00	60·00
	g. Stop between legs of "R"	40·00	20·00
	h. Splayed "Y"	40·00	20·00
	i. Short "Y"	40·00	20·00
	j. Long stroke to second "F"	40·00	20·00
	k. Short first "I"	40·00	20·00
	l. Long first "I"	40·00	20·00
	m. Tall "L"	40·00	20·00
	n. Short "L"	40·00	20·00
	o. Thick "L"	60·00	30·00
	s. "Specimen", Type 9	£150	
	t. "Cancelled", Type 18	£1200	

L39 (=S.G.O44)	2½d. purple on blue paper, K31 (1.9.96)	35·00	25·00
	Block of four	£200	£150
	Used on cover	†	£550
	a. Splayed "Y"	60·00	50·00
	s. "Specimen", Type 9	£150	
	t. "Cancelled", Type 18	£1200	
L40 (=S.G.O45)	6d. purple on rose-red paper, K37 (20.9.01)	80·00	45·00
	Block of four	£400	£275
	Used on cover	†	£1200
	a. Splayed "Y"	£150	90·00
	s. "Specimen", Type 15	£275	

Type **L5** was type-set and there were two separate formes. Forme 1 was used in 1896–98 for the ½d. vermilion with Controls O and P and the 1d. lilac with Controls U and V. Forme 2 was introduced early in 1898 and used for the remainder of the printings. For further information see article by Michael Astley in the September 1978 issue of *The Philatelic Journal of Great Britain.*

Controls: L36, O, P, Q; L37, R; L38, U, V, W, X (No. L37, R *price* £250; Nos. L36, L38, *with control prices from*; £200 *per single controls* O *and* U; *others from* £180 *per single).* Control Q exists imperf. and perf., V perf. and all others imperf.

ARMY	**ARMY**	**ARMY**	**ARMY**
L36e–L38e (R. 14/4)	L36g–L38g (R. 5/2)	L36h–L38h (R. 2/3)	L36i–L38i (R. 10/11)
OFFICIAL	**OFFICIAL**	**OFFICIAL**	**OFFICIAL**
L37j, L38j (R. 20/11)	L36k–L38k (R. 18/7)	L36l–L38l (R. 7/5)	L36m–L38m (R. 10/2)
OFFICIAL	**OFFICIAL**	**ARMY**	
L36n, L38n (R. 4/8)	L36o, L38o (R. 13/7). *This is a corrected version of the variety* L36c, L38c. *The thick* "L" *first appeared in* 1897	L39a, L40a (R. 9/11 and 19/11)	

All Type **L5** varieties are from forme 2 except Nos. L36c, L38c, L36n, L38n, L36o and L38o which derive from forme 1, Nos. L39a and L40a Type **L6** are forme 3.

Forgeries. These are not a problem except the "I" for "L" variety of which dangerous forgeries exist, mint and used. The short stroke to the "L" has been faked by scraping away part of the letter but such stamps can be detected by using a philatelic microscope magnifier.

Essays. Dated "May 14.96" on squared paper headed "Appendix." in M/S with the lines of overprint spaced 1¼ mm apart:

½d., 1d., 2½d., 6d. . . . . . . *the sheet*

Dated "May 19 96" on squared paper headed "Appendix." in M/S with the lines of overprint spaced 13 mm apart:

½d., 1d., 2½d . . . . *the sheet*

The ½d. vermilion and 1d. are known unused and overprinted "ARMY OFFICIAL" Type **L6**, with lines spaced 11¼mm. apart. It is probable that these are from a fourth set of essays created about 5 June 1896 as the overprint varies only slightly from the finally adopted type **L6** where the spacing is closer at 9¼ mm. apart. The third set of essays in the De La Rue archives was initialled by J. S. Purcell and returned on 28 May 1896. The overprint again is similar to that actually used.

Board of Education

It was not until after the death of Queen Victoria that stamps were issued for the Board of Education. The 5d. and 1s. Queen Victoria stamps were issued at the same time as $\frac{1}{2}$d., 1d. and 2$\frac{1}{2}$d. King Edward VII stamps on 19 February 1902.

BOARD

OF

EDUCATION

L7

1902 (19 February). Stamps of 1887–1900 overprinted in black with Type L7.

L41 (=S.G.O81)	5d. dull purple and blue (Die II), K36	£2200	£600
	Block of four	£13000	
	s. "Specimen", Type 15	£800	
L42 (=S.G.O82)	1s. grey-green and carmine, K41	£6000	£3500
	Block of four	£30000	
	s. "Specimen", Type 15	£1600	

SECTION LB

The Postal Fiscal Stamps

General Notes

In this Section are listed the fiscal stamps which were authorized and used for postage, following publication of the Customs and Inland Revenue Act of 1881. The 1d. draft and receipt stamps (Nos. L101 to L108) are dealt with in the first part of the listing, followed by the surface-printed and embossed stamps which were inscribed, overprinted or underprinted "INLAND REVENUE" which were authorized for postal use by the Act of 1882 following the delay in issuing the Unified stamps inscribed "POSTAGE AND REVENUE".

The Post Office had the duty of collecting revenue from the issue of licences and adhesive stamps for the purpose began to be issued in 1853. Separate issues of fiscal stamps were made for a wide range of duties. Stamps which were inscribed for a particular purpose, such as bankruptcy, customs, foreign bill etc. were not authorized for postage. However, examples of these stamps do exist on letters, but as the majority bear postmarks with dates after the issue of stamps inscribed "Postage and Revenue", they are outside the scope of this Catalogue. Fiscal stamps used for their intended purpose and cancelled by manuscript are also outside the scope of the lists.

Prior to 1881 the Post Office kept account of all Inland Revenue stamps sold in order that the proceeds could be paid direct to the Inland Revenue Department. The Customs and Inland Revenue Act of 1881 required stamps to be produced which could be used for either postage or revenue purposes. The first such issue was the Penny Lilac of 1881, inscribed "Postage and Inland Revenue". No other British stamp was to have this inscription. The Act of 1881, which came into effect on 1 June, authorized the use for postage "of any penny adhesive stamps not appropriated by any words on the face of them to postage duty, or any particular description of instrument". This may have been intended to cover only Inland Revenue stamps, as Nos. L118/121, or unappropriated general duty stamps, but the Post Office issued a notice in the same month specifically authorizing the use of penny receipt stamps for postal purposes and of postage stamps for use on receipts. There is no doubt that penny draft stamps were accepted for postage since the public were quick to take advantage of the situation in using stamps that the Post Office did not wish to buy back. The Penny Lilac was not available until 12 July 1881.

The financial arrangement between the Inland Revenue and the Post Office from 1 July 1881 called for an annual sum in monthly instalments to be paid to the former department. The figure was based on the sales of unappropriated duty stamps over the previous twenty years.

A further Act of 1882 permitted the use for postage of Inland Revenue stamps up to the face value of 2s. 6d., to take effect from 1 January 1883. At the same time the sale of Inland Revenue stamps up to but not including the 2s. 6d. was discontinued and stocks at post offices were called in and destroyed.

A Post Office Circular of 19 December 1882 ordered that from 1 January 1883 the 2s. 6d. Inland Revenue stamps must be accounted for as postage stamps. The 2s. 6d. fiscal stamps remained in use until 2 July 1883 when they were replaced by the 2s. 6d. "Postage & Revenue" stamp.

It is interesting that the Post Office Guide of 1 April 1883 gives a list of the duties for which postage stamps of 1d., 2d., 3d., 6d., 9d., 1s. and 2s. 6d. could be used and goes on to say that any of the superseded Inland Revenue stamps still in the hands of the public could continue to be used for payment of Inland Revenue duties and *also for the payment of postage*.

Prices for Stamps in Used Condition

In Section LB, the prices in the "used" column are for 1d. stamps with genuine postal cancellations from 1 June 1881 and for other values with genuine postal cancellations from 1 January 1883. Collectors should beware of stamps with fiscal cancellations removed and fraudulent postmarks applied.

Receipt and Draft Stamps (1853–57)

Printing and Arrangement. Surface-printed by De La Rue & Co. in sheets of 240 arranged in 20 horizontal rows of 12 stamps. Most values exist in a number of shades of the basic colour.

The Queen's head in Types **L11/13** was from a wood engraving by W. Thompson and copied by Jean Ferdinand Jonbert de la Ferté.

Plate Numbers. Plate numbers in white on colour within an oval appear above R.1/11 and below R.202/2. They do not occur on the stamps themselves. Current numbers in a rectangular box occur above R.1/2 and below R.20/11.

Perforation. All stamps were perforated $15\frac{1}{2} \times 15$ at Somerset House on two machines specially constructed by Napier for these large format sheets. These were the first perforated stamps to appear, predating the official perforation of the postage issues by nearly four months.

W12A

W12B

The illustrations depict the watermark as seen from the *front* of the stamp.

Watermarks. The Receipt and Draft stamps have the Cabled Anchor watermark, two different types being used. **W12A** has a double-lined stock and **W12B** has a single-lined stock. **W12A** is normally found inverted.

Types **W9** (Anchor), **W10** (Small Anchor) and **W11** (Orb) were used for the Surface-Printed Inland Revenue stamps from 1864.

Dates. Exact dates of issue of the Receipt and Draft stamps are not generally known, nor are the put to press dates. The dates given are registration dates.

Receipt Stamps

→ 

L11 *Die* I (*rectangular buckle*)

→ 

L12 *Die* II (*octagonal buckle*)

1853 (10 October). One Penny Type L11 (Die I). Wmk W12A inverted.

L101 (=S.G.F1)	(1)	1d. light blue (shades)	40·00	50·00
	(2)	1d. pale turquoise-blue (shades)	40·00	50·00
		Block of four	£200	
		Used on cover	†	£180
	a.	Watermark upright	£125	
	b.	Watermark reversed (large loop to right)	£125	
	c.	Thin semi-transparent (pelure) paper	£125	

Imprimaturs: Plates 1 (*unnumbered*) *and* 2, *each* £180.
Registration dates: Pl. 1, 29.9.53; Pl. 2, 5.10.53

Plate Proof

In grey-brown on thick cartridge paper, pen-cancelled £500

1853 (December). One Penny Type L12 (Die II). Wmk W12A inverted.

L102 (=S.G.F3)	(1)	1d. pale turquoise-blue (shades)	30·00	45·00
	(2)	1d. pale turquoise-green (shades)	30·00	90·00
		Block of four	£150	
		Used on cover	†	£275
	c.	Watermark upright	80·00	
	d.	Double perforation		
L103 (=S.G.F4)	(1)	1d. light blue on blue (shades)	75·00	75·00
	(2)	1d. pale dull blue on blue	75·00	75·00
		Block of four	£400	
		Used on cover	†	£450
	c.	Watermark upright	£125	£200

Imprimaturs: Plates 3 *and* 4, *each* £180.
Registration dates: Pl. 3, 11.53; Pl. 4, 1.12.53. Plates 7 and 8 were made but were never registered.
The paper varies from deep to slightly blued and it also occurs in greyish. Stamps on deeply blued are worth more.

Draft Stamps

L13 *Draft*

L14 *Draft or Receipt (die engraved by J. Ferdinand Joubert de la Ferté)*

1853 (late October). One Penny Ochre, Type L13. Wmk W12A inverted.

L104 (=S.G.F2)	(1)	1d. ochre (shades)	£110	£125
	(2)	1d. pale olive-sepia (shades)	£110	£125
		Block of four	£550	
		Used on cover	†	£500
	c.	Error. Téte-běche (in block of four)	£16000	

Imprimaturs: Plates 5 *and* 6 (*both unnumbered*), *each* £180.

Registration dates: Pl. 5 registered 10.10.53 with the penultimate stamp in the fifth row *tête-bêche*; error corrected and plate re-registered 20.10.53.

It is believed that, apart from a strip of three in The Post Office Heritage and another in the Royal Collection, only one example of L104*c* exists and this is in a block of four.

Shade (1) is on thin and shade (2) on thicker opaque paper.

Plate Proof

In pale blue on ungummed paper £500

1855 (25 March). One Penny Lilac, Type L14. Wmk W12A inverted. Blue glazed paper.

L105 (=S.G.F5)	(1)	1d. reddish lilac	£110	£120
	(2)	1d. deep purple	£110	£120
	(3)	1d. grey lilac	£110	£120
		Block of four	£575	
		Used on cover	†	£375
	c.	Watermark upright	£160	£225

Imprimaturs: Plates 9 *and* 10 (*both unnumbered*), *each* £180.
Registration dates: Pl. 9, 25.10.54; Pl. 10, 9.12.54.

Die Proof. In black on white glazed card:

Undated. Basic die proof. Cut to size and countersunk £900

Plate Proof. Imperf. on watermarked paper.

In issued colour and obliterated "Postage Stamps 15 FEB 1855" . . . .

A strip of three is known in private hands.

1856. One Penny Lilac, Type L14. Wmk W12B. White paper.

L106 (=S.G.F6)		1d. reddish lilac (shades)	10·00	8·00
		Block of four	50·00	
		Used on cover	†	£150
	a.	Watermark inverted	£130	
	b.	Watermark reversed	£150	
	s.	"Specimen", Type 2	£125	

Imprimaturs: Plates 11 *to* 16, *each* £180.
Registration dates: Pl. 11, 29.11.55; Pl. 12, 14.12.55; Pls. 13 and 14, 19.3.56; Pls. 15 and 16, 7.11.56.

1857. One Penny Lilac, Type L14. Wmk W12B. Blue paper.

L107 (=S.G.F7)	(1)	1d. reddish lilac on bluish paper (shades)	10·00	8·00
	(2)	1d. lilac on blue paper (shades)	10·00	8·00
		Block of four	50·00	
		Used on cover	†	£150
	a.	Glazed paper	£150	£150
	b.	Watermark reversed	£150	

Imprimaturs: Plates 17 *to* 26, 28 *and* 29, 31 *to* 33, 35 *to* 39, *each* £180.
Registration dates: Pls. 17 and 18, 7.5.57; Pl. 19, 8.7.57; Pl. 20, 17.9.57; Pls. 21 and 22, 2.12.57; Pls. 23 and 24, 6.5.58; Pls. 25 and 26, 29.11.58; Pls. 28 and 29, 21.5.59; Pls. 31 and 32, 12.10.59; Pl. 33, 5.3.60; Pl. 35, 28.3.60; Pls. 36 and 37, 8.8.60; Pls. 38 and 39, 27.2.61.

Paper. In this issue the colour of the paper varies considerably, plates 17/19 and 36/7 being bluish, plates 21/33 more or less bluish and plates 20, 35 and 38/9 distinctly blue.

Surface-Printed Inland Revenue Stamps

Printing and Arrangements. Surface-printed by De La Rue in sheets of 240 arranged in 20 horizontal rows of 12 stamps, except the 6d. Type **L18** which were in sheets of 120 in 20 horizontal rows of 6 stamps.

Exceptionally the 1881 issues, Nos. L123 and L126/7, were rearranged in double panes: the 1d. in sheets of 240 containing panes of 10 horizontal rows of 12 stamps; the 3d. in sheets of 112 containing panes of 7 horizontal rows of 8 stamps; and the 6d. in sheets of 56 containing panes of 7 horizontal rows of 4 stamps.

Plate Numbers. In the 1d. values in both the large and small formats the plate numbers occur in the same positions as the previous issues but are somewhat larger. The current numbers appear in the same style and positions as before. The 3d. and 6d. values each had only one plate.

Paper. This varied from bluish to white and back to bluish again with varying intermediate shades and therefore no attempt is made to list them separately.

W9

W10

W11

Watermarks. Various watermarks were used for the Surface-Printed Inland Revenue stamps. Type **W12B** (Cabled Anchor) (illustrated above No. L101 at the beginning of this section under "Receipt and Draft Stamps"), Types **W9** (Anchor, with the anchor 16 mm, 18 mm or 20 mm high), **W10** (Small Anchor) and **W11** (Orb) as shown above.

Perforation. The stamps were perforated at Somerset House initially using the $15\frac{1}{2} \times 15$ gauge for the large format and 14 for the standard format.

Dates of Issue. The earliest known dates of use as fiscal stamps are quoted and lists of the putting to press dates of the plates are also given.

Die Proofs. These are normally in black on white glazed card as described in the notes to Section J. Only those known to us outside official sources are listed.

"Specimen" Stamps. Stamps overprinted "Specimen" known outside official sources are listed and the different types are illustrated in Appendix 3.

Imprimaturs. Imprimaturs exist for the 1d. values but are not known for the 3d. and 6d. stamps.

L15

L16

L17

L18

1860 (3 April). Provisional Issue: L107 overprinted in red with Type L15.

L108 (=S.G.F8)	1d. dull reddish lilac on bluish paper	£725	£575
	Block of four	£3750	
	Used on cover	†	£1200
	b. Watermark reversed		

It has been confirmed that stamps from plate 28, and possibly others, were overprinted.

Wmk W12B, Perf $15\frac{1}{2} \times 15$

1860 (May). 1d. Lilac, Type L16.

L109 (=S.G.F9)	(1) 1d. reddish lilac (shades)	12·00	12·00
	(2) 1d. reddish purple (shades)		
	Block of four	60·00	
	Used on cover	†	£150
	a. Watermark inverted	£110	
	s. Imperf. "Specimen", Type 2 (wmk inverted)		
	t. "Specimen", Type 2	£140	

Imprimaturs: Plates 1 *to* 22, *each* £175.

Put to press dates: Pl. 1, 26.4.60; Pl. 2, 13.10.61; Pl. 3, 1.6.62; Pl. 4, 26.5.62; Pl. 5, 16.6.62; Pl. 6, 13.8.62; Pl. 7, 3.1.63; Pl. 8, 30.1.63; Pl. 9, 9.2.63; Pl. 10, 4.5.62; Pl. 11, 17.1.63; Pl. 12, 27.8.63; Pl. 13, 21.9.63; Pl. 14, 17.2.64; Pl. 15, 10.11.63; Pls. 16–17, 29.2.64; Pl. 18, 24.3.64; Pl. 19, 14.6.64; Pl. 20, 10.6.64; Pl. 21, 15.8.64; Pl. 22, 4.11.64.

Die Proofs. In black on white glazed card:

Date	*Plate No.*	*Inscr..*	*Additional Inscriptions*	
—	—	—	Basic Die Proof	£850
—	—	—	Undated. Cut to size and mounted	£750
10 July 62	8	A/S	Current No. "219" in rectangle	£850

1860 (June). 3d. Lilac, Type L17.

L110 (=S.G.F10)	(1)	3d. pale reddish lilac	£375	£250
	(2)	3d. reddish purple	£375	£250
		Block of four	£2000	
		Used on cover	†	£425
	s.	"Specimen", Type 2	£180	

Plate 1 was registered on 12 June 1860 and put to press three days later. Imprimaturs are not known.

Die Proof. In black on white glazed card:

Undated Cut to size and mounted £750

Die Proofs from the De La Rue Archives. Cut down to stamp size on white card:

In brown, blue-green, purple .... *from* £1000
Full size in green, purple £2000

Plate Proof. Imperf. On thin card with matt finish

In black £750

1860 (October). 6d. Lilac, Type L18.

L111 (=S.G.F11)		6d. reddish lilac	£175	£150
		Block of four	£850	
		Used on cover	†	£375
	c.	Watermark reversed	£225	£175
	d.	Watermark inverted	£225	£175
	s.	"Specimen", Type 2	£180	

Plate 1 was registered on 26 September 1860 and put to press the following day. Imprimaturs are not known.

Die Proof. In black on white glazed card:

Undated. Cut to size and mounted £750

Die Proof from the De La Rue Archives. Cut down to stamp size and mounted on sunken card.

In red-orange £1000
Full size in red-orange, yellow-orange £2000

Plate Proof. Imperf. On thin card with matt finish

In black £750

Change to Wmk W9 (Anchor 16 mm high), Perf $15\frac{1}{2} \times 15$

1864 (November). 1d. Lilac, Type L16.

L112 (=S.G.F12)	(1)	1d. pale reddish lilac	10·00	10·00
	(2)	1d. rose-lilac	10·00	25·00
	(3)	1d. reddish purple	10·00	10·00
		Block of four	50·00	
		Used on cover	†	£150
	a.	Watermark inverted		

Imprimaturs: Plates 23 *to* 44, *each* £175.

Put to press dates: Pl. 23, 14.11.64; Pl. 24, 15.1.65; Pl. 25, 21.2.65; Pl. 26, 31.3.65; Pl. 27, 5.4.65; Pls. 28–29, 4.7.65; Pl. 30, 2.8.65; Pl. 31, 7.10.65; Pl. 32, 11.12.65; Pl. 33, 18.12.65; Pl. 34, 19.12.65; Pl. 35, 21.2.66; Pl. 36, 5.3.66; Pl. 37, 8.6.66; Pl. 38, 9.6.66; Pl. 39, 12.6.66; Pl. 40, 15.9.66.

1864 (late). 3d. Lilac, Type L17.

L113 (=S.G.F13)	(1)	3d. pale reddish lilac	£220	£150
	(2)	3d. pale reddish purple	£220	£150
		Block of four	£1100	
		Used on cover	†	£425
	s.	"Specimen", Type 9	£150	

Plate 1 was used.

1864 (late). 6d. Lilac, Type L18.

L114 (=S.G.F14)	(1)	6d. pale reddish lilac (shades)	£180	£150
	(2)	6d. pale reddish purple (shades)	£180	£150
		Block of four	£900	
		Used on cover	†	£375
	a.	Watermark inverted	£275	

Plate 1 was used.

Change to Wmk W9 (Anchor 18 mm high), Perf $15\frac{1}{2} \times 15$

1867. 1d. Lilac, Type L16.

L115 (=S.G.F15)	(1)	1d. reddish lilac	20·00	20·00
	(2)	1d. pale reddish purple	20·00	25·00
		Block of four	£100	
		Used on cover	†	£225

Imprimaturs: Plates 43 and 44 were registered on this paper and imprimaturs are known.

Put to press dates: Pl. 43, 22.3.67; Pl. 44, 5.4.67.

1867 3d. Lilac, Type L17.

L116 (=S.G.F16)	(1)	3d. reddish lilac (shades)	£100	95·00
	(2)	3d. pale reddish purple (shades)	£100	95·00
		Block of four	£500	
		Used on cover	†	£375
	s.	"Specimen", Types 9, 10 *from*	£150	
	t.	"Cancelled", Type 14A		

Plate 1 was used.

1867. 6d. Lilac, Type L18.

L117 (=S.G.F17)	(1)	6d. reddish lilac (shades)	90·00	70·00
	(2)	6d. reddish purple (shades)	90·00	70·00
	(3)	6d. dull purple-brown (shades)	90·00	90·00
		Block of four	£425	
		Used on cover	†	£250
	s.	"Specimen", Types 6, 9, 10 *from*	£150	
	t.	"Cancelled", Type 14A		

Plate 1 was used.
See L124–127 for similar stamps perforated 14.

SAMUEL ALLSOPP & SONS LABELS

This Burton brewing firm was authorized by the Inland Revenue to use the 1d. Inland Revenue stamp Type **L16** *se-tenant* with a strip of three Allsopp labels for the purpose of recording excise duties and issuing receipts.

They were supplied in blocks of eight containing two such strips which were perforated vertically down the middle and horizontally through the right-hand block of four, as illustrated. Various gauges were used at different times.

The left-hand pair of the strip was overprinted in black with lines for entering the date, amount received in words and figures, the discount and the name and address of the customer, and this was retained. The corresponding right half was overprinted as a form of receipt and issued to the customer.

Variations exist in the overprint on the different watermarks. Both halves have the same receipt number.

Samuel Allsopp & Sons Labels. Issued examples do not show the hand.

Die proof

	Unused Pane of 8	*Unused Strip of* 4	*Used Pair*
1d. redish lilac, 1863, wmk **W12B** (Cabled Anchor)	£2000	—	£150
1d. redish lilac, 1864, wmk **W9** (Anchor 16 mm high) ...	†	†	£150
1d. redish lilac, 1867, wmk **W9** (Anchor 18 mm high) ...	†	†	£150

Imprimatur: Plate 1 *strip of four, wmk* **W12B**, £1000.

The imprimatur sheet is with overprint. The plate number was printed above stamp 3 (from left) and is white within a solid oval. The imprimatur/proof has no hand or receipt number in the overprint.

The **W9** watermark 18 mm high is known inverted.

Die Proof. In black on white card:

Single label, cut to shape. Imperf. £1000

Plate Proof. In black on white card:

Single label. Perf. . . . . —
Strip of four, Perf . . . . —

L19

L20

(*Engraved by Daniel J. Pound of De La Rue from a bust by Theed*)

Wmk W10 (Small Anchor), Perf 14

1867 (1 September). 1d. Purple, Type L19.

L118 (=S.G.F18)	(1)	1d. pale reddish purple	18·00	18·00
	(2)	3d. dull purple	18·00	18·00
		Block of four	£110	
		Used on cover	†	£120
	a.	Watermark inverted	£110	

Imprimaturs: Plates 1 *to* 12, *each* £100.

Put to press dates: Pl. 1, 6.5.67; Pl. 2, 14.6.67; Pl. 3, 7.7.67; Pl. 4, 22.6.67; Pl. 5, 19.9.67; Pl. 6–7, 21.9.67; Pl. 8, 26.11.67; Pl. 9, 11.12.67; Pl. 10, 19.12.67; Pl. 11, 23.1.68; Pl. 12, 23.12.67.

Die Proof Essays in Colour from the De La Rue Archives. With old head and new frame, each on card, 90 × 60 mm:

Three different styles. . . . . *from* £1250

Three different designs on a single card:

Comprising Type **L19**, Type **L20** without corner ornaments and marked "This middle one is what is suggested 26.3.68" and another £2500
As before but without annotation . . . .
Card with three designs as Type **L19** . . . .
Three designs but central, has hand drawn corner ornaments in purple

Die Proof. In black on white glazed card:

Without date or inscriptions £400
Cut down and mounted with various M/S endorsements. £300
Dated DEC 6 1866 mounted on countersunk card £500
Dated Dec. 8, 1866 A/H and handstamped in purple, "8 Dec. 66 Examined HDLR., In.Rev. Engraver". Inscribed around impression "He who signs must cancel the stamp" . . . .
Cut down in purple (1867 Paris Exhib.) £850

Die Proof from the De La Rue Striking Books. In black on glazed card 32 × 36 mm mounted on paper.

Showing date and number of leads struck £400

Die Proof. Imperforate. Watermark Small Anchor

In black on thin ungummed paper (Plate 1) £300

Dies 1 to 4 of the 1d., Nos. L119–23

Nos. L119/21 show "O" of "ONE" circular. No. L122 (Die 4) shows a horizontal oval and is the only Die to have this plus heavy shading on hair ribbons.

Die 1. *Four lines of shading in left band of ribbon opposite "Y" of "PENNY". Small ornaments and heavy shading under chin*

Die 2. *Two lines of shading in left band of ribbon. Clear lines of shading under chin. Small ornaments*

Die 3. *Mid-size ornaments; line shading under chin extended halfway down neck*

Die 4. *Large size ornaments; straight line of shading continued to bottom of neck*

1868 (June). 1d. Purple, Type L20, Die 1.

L119 (=S.G.F19)	(1)	1d. reddish lilac (shades)	6·00	7·00
	(2)	1d. reddish purple (shades)	6·00	7·00
	(3)	1d. dull purple (pale to deep)	6·00	7·00
		Block of four	30·00	
		Used on cover	†	£120
	a.	Watermark inverted	75·00	
	s.	"Specimen", Type 6, 9, 10 *from*	45·00	
	t.	"Cancelled", Type 14A		

Imprimaturs: Plates 13 *to* 47, 50 *to* 55, 57 to 60, 62 *to* 71, 73 *to* 100, *each* £75.

Put to press dates: Pls. 13–14, 20.5.68; Pl. 15, 30.6.68; Pl. 16, 20.5.68; Pl. 17, 21.7.68; Pl. 18, 20.7.68; Pl. 19, 7.12.68; Pl. 20, 14.12.68; Pl. 21, 18.12.68; Pl. 22, 20.3.69; Pl. 23, 11.5.69; Pl. 24, 26.5.69; Pls. 25–26, 26.8.69; Pl. 27, 25.10.68; Pl. 28, 14.12.69; Pl. 29, 23.12.69; Pl. 30, 6.7.70; Pl. 31, 25.5.70; Pl. 32, 30.5.70; Pl. 33, 29.8.70; Pl. 34, 12.9.70; Pl. 35, 24.11.70; Pl. 36, 19.12.70; Pl. 37, 24.2.71; Pl. 38, 28.2.71; Pl. 39, 27.5.71; Pl. 40, 8.6.71; Pl. 41, 17.6.71; Pl. 42, 8.9.71; Pl. 43, 4.10.71; Pl. 44, 13.10.71; Pl. 45, 18.12.71; Pl. 46, 5.1.72; Pl. 47, 29.2.72; Pl. 50, 15.4.72; Pl. 51, 14.5.72; Pl. 52, 27.5.72; Pl. 53, 19.7.72; Pl. 54, 5.10.72; Pl. 57, 8.10.72; Pl. 58, 4.11.72; Pl. 59, 10.1.73; Pl. 60, 8.1.73; Pl. 62, 27.1.73; Pl. 63, 24.3.73; Pl. 64, 28.3.73; Pl. 65, 26.5.73; Pl. 66, 7.4.73; Pl. 67, 6.6.73; Pl. 68, 19.6.73; Pl. 69, 1.8.73; Pl. 70, 21.8.73; Pl. 71, 2.9.73; Pls. 73–74, 10.11.73; Pl. 75, 13.11.73; Pl. 76, 30.1.74; Pl. 77, 3.2.74; Pl. 78, 19,2,74; Pl. 79, 8.5.74; Pl. 80, 21.5.74; Pl. 81, 1.7.74; Pl. 82, 18.8.74; Pl. 83, 20.8.74; Pl. 84, 28.10.74; Pl. 85, 2.11.74; Pl. 86, 13.11.74; Pl. 87, 11.1.75; Pl. 88, 19.1.75; Pl. 89, 31.1.75; Pl. 90, 19.4.75; Pl. 91, 20.4.75; Pl. 92, 23.6.75; Pl. 93, 9.7.75; Pl. 94, 30.8.75; Pl. 95, 15.11.75; Pl. 96, 7.12.75; Pl. 97, 29.2.76; Pl. 98, 1.3.76; Pl. 99, 22.3.76; Pl. 100, 19.5.76.

Plate 55 was registered on 8 October 1872 but proved to be defective and was not put to press.

Die Proofs. In black on white glazed card:

Date	*Insr.*	*Additional Inscriptions*	
—	—		£400
—	—	Cut down and mounted with various M/S endorsements	£300
25 Apr 68	—		£400
26 Apr 68	A/H		£400
4 June 69	A/S	Initialled (M/S)	£400
6 Aug 69	A/S		£400
21 June 70	A/S	Initialled "R.T." (M/S)	£400
22 July 71	A/S	Initialled (M/S)	£400
6 Apr 72	A/S		£400
15 Jan 73	A/S	Initialled (M/S)	£400
3 Mar 73	A/S	Initialled (M/S)	£400
22 July 73	A/S	Initialled (M/S)	£400
21 Aug 74	A/S	Initialled (M/S)	£400
30 Oct 74	A/S	"6 Leads" and initialled (M/S)	£400
9 Apr 75	A/S	Initialled (M/S)	£400
2 Sept 75	A/S	Initialled (M/S)	£400

Plate Proofs

In black on glazed unwatermarked paper	£300
In black on thick matt, unwatermarked paper	£300
In black on unwatermarked card	£300

1876 (June). 1d. Purple, Type L20, Die 2.

L120 (=S.G.F20)	(1)	1d. reddish lilac	22·00	15·00
	(2)	1d. dull purple	22·00	15·00
		Block of four	£125	
		Used on cover	†	£250
	s.	"Specimen". Type 9	80·00	

Imprimaturs: Plates 101 *to* 105, *each* £150.

Put to press dates: Pl. 101, 8.6.76; Pl. 102, 12.9.76; Pl. 103, 22.9.76; Pl. 104, 2.10.76; Pl. 105, 15.12.76.

Die Proofs. In black on white glazed card:

Date	*Insr.*	*Additional Inscriptions*	
—	—		£400
—	—	Cut down and mounted with various M/S endorsements	£300
6 Mar 76	—		£400
7 Mar 76	—		£400
8 Mar 76	—		£400
9 Mar 76	—		£400
10 Mar 76	—		£400
14 Mar 76	—		£400
15 Mar 76	—		£400
16 Mar 76	—		£400
17 Mar 76	B/H		£400
12 Apr 76	A/S	Initialled (M/S)	£400
2 May 76	—		£400
4 May 76	B/H		£400

1877 (March). 1d. Purple, Type L20, Die 3.

L121 (=S.G.F21)	(1)	1d. reddish purple	12·00	12·00
	(2)	1d. dull purple	12·00	12·00
		Block of four	60·00	
		Used on cover	†	£175
	s.	"Specimen". Type 9	65·00	

Imprimaturs: Plates 106 *to* 116, *each* £150.

Put to press dates: Pl. 106, 12.2.77; Pl. 107, 16.3.77; Pl. 108, 9.5.77; Pls. 109–110, 21.6.77; Pl. 111, 14.9.77; Pl. 112, 26.9.77; Pl. 113, 18.12.77; Pl. 114, 27.12.77; Pl. 115, 11.1.78; Pl. 116, 27.3.78.

Die Proofs. In black on white glazed card:

No plates were created from the die used to strike proofs dated July 1876. A replacement die was used from 3 August 1876.

Date	*Insr.*	*Additional Inscriptions*	
—	—	Cut down and mounted with various M/S endorsements	£300
19 Jul 76	—		£400
20 Jul 76	—		£400
22 Jul 76	—		£400
22 Jul 76	B/H		£400
3 Aug 76	—		£400
4 Aug 76	—		£400
8 Aug 76	B/H	Date in (M/S)	£400
24 Aug 76	A/S	Initialled (M/S)	£400

Plate Proof

In black on thick matt, unwatermarked paper £400

1878 (July). 1d. Purple, Type L20, Die 4.

L122 (=S.G.F22)	(1)	1d. rdull purple	7·00	7·00
	(2)	1d. reddish lilac	7·00	7·00
		Block of four	35·00	
		Used on cover	†	£100
	a.	Watermark inverted		

Imprimaturs: Plates 119 *to* 136 *and* 137 *to* 140, *each* £150.

Put to press dates: Pl. 119, 9.4.78; Pl. 120, 17.6.78; Pl. 121, 5.7.78; Pl. 122, 1.10.78; Pl. 123, 3.12.78; Pl. 124, 27.12.78; Pl. 125, 21.2.79; Pl. 126, 22.2.79; Pl. 127, 20.3.79; Pl. 128, 29.5.79; Pl. 129, 25.8.79; Pl. 130, 27.8.79; Pl. 131, 1.9.79; Pl. 132, 5.12.79; Pl. 133, 14.1.80; Pl. 134. 24.3.80; Pl. 135, 31.3.80; Pl. 137, 22.5.80; Pl. 138, 18.8.80; Pl. 139, 27.9.80; Pl. 140, 16.10.80.

Die Proofs. In black on white glazed card:

No plates were created from the undated die proofs. A replacement die was used from 21 February 1878.

Date	*Insr.*	*Additional Inscriptions*	
—	—	Cut down and mounted with various M/S endorsements ..	£300
—	—	....	£400
21 Feb 78	—	....	£400
22 Feb 78	—	Date (M/S)	£400
23 Feb 78	—	....	£400
27 Feb 78	—	....	£400
1 Mar 78	—	....	
1 Mar 78	B/H	....	£400
20 Mar 78	A/S	Initialled (M/S)	£400
25 Nov 79	B/S	Initialled (M/S)	£400
12 Nov 82	(M/S)	Endorsed "After Striking" (M/S)	£400

Colour Trials. Imperf. Watermark Anchor, Type **W10.**

In brown-purple, light-brown, yellow-ochre, rose-carmine (shades),pale blue, pale emerald .... *from* £200

These were for the 1879 Tender or trials in U.P.U. colours. Plate 127 was used.

Change to Wmk W11 (Orb), Perf 14

1881 (January). 1d. Purple, Type L20, Die 4.

L123 (=S.G.F23)	(1)	1d. reddish lilac	7·00	3·50
	(2)	1d. dull purple	7·00	3·50
	(3)	1d. slate-lilac	7·00	3·50
		Block of four	32·00	
		Used on cover	†	90·00
	a.	Watermark inverted	£110	

Imprimaturs: Plates 141 *to* 144, *each* £180.

Plate 145 had no marginal numbers and cannot be identified. Plate 140 was altered for use on the Orb watermarked paper and plates 141 to 144 were registered on this paper.

Put to press dates: Pl. 140, already at press; Pls. 141–142, 10.1.81; Pl. 143, 20.1.81; Pl. 144, 27.1.81.

After Plates 141 to 144 had been put to press, Plate 140 was re-arranged into two panes, each of 10 horizontal rows of 12 stamps and re-registered on 10 February 1881 and the Imprimatur sheet was endorsed "Proof after alteration of Plate".

Colour Trials. Perf. 14. Watermark Orb.

In grey-blue, claret, dull purple, brown-purple .... *each* £150

Ditto, Endorsed "Cancelled" in manuscript .... *each* £400

Perforated colour trials on Orb watermarked paper were printed from plate 144 in February 1881 as trials for deeper colours for the proposed 5d. postage stamp.

Wmk W9 (Anchor 18 mm high), Perf 14

1881 (January). 3d. Lilac Type L17.

L124 (=S.G.F24)	(1)	3d. reddish lilac	£700	£375
	(2)	3d. pale reddish purple	£700	£375
		Block of four		
		Used on cover	†	£800

The original Plate 1 was used.

1881 (January). 6d. Lilac Type L18.

L125 (=S.G.F25)	6d. reddish lilac	£325	£150
	Block of four	£1700	
	Used on cover	†	£375

The original Plate 1 was used.

Wmk W9 (Anchor 20 mm high), Perf 14

1881 (May). 3d. Lilac Type L17.

L126 (=S.G.F26)		3d. reddish lilac	£525	£300
		Block of four	£2500	
		Used on cover	†	£575
	s.	"Specimen", Type 9	£250	

Plate 1 was later rearranged to provide sheets of 112 containing two panes each of 7 horizontal rows of 8 stamps. It was re-registered on 26 August 1881 and the imprimatur sheet was endorsed "Proof after alteration of Plate".

1881 (May). 6d. Lilac Type L18.

L127 (=S.G.F27)	(1)	6d. pale reddish lilac	£300	£150
	(2)	6d. dull purple	£300	£150
	a.	Block of four	£1500	
	b.	Used on cover	†	£375
	s.	"Specimen", Type 9	£225	

Plate 1 was later re-arranged to provide sheets of 56 containing two panes each of 7 horizontal rows of 4 stamps. It was re-registered on 23 August 1881 and the imprimatur sheet was endorsed "Proof after alteration of Plate". A new current number "628" was used in place of the original "172".

Embossed Inland Revenue Stamps

These embossed stamps were used for provisional values (3d. and 6d. prior to the issue of the surface-printed Inland Revenue stamps) or for the lesser and denominations.

Printing and Arrangement. The stamps were embossed in colour at Somerset House, from dies not appropriated to any particular purpose, on paper already printed with the words "INLAND REVENUE" in green. They thus became available for the payment of any duties for which no special stamps had been provided.

All values were embossed in sheets of 60 arranged in 6 horizontal rows of 10 stamps. The original imperforate issue had thick black horizontal and vertical rules dividing the stamps to assist in separating them.

The press used for the original imperforate issue was not large enough to allow a full sheet to pass under the arm so each sheet was turned round after the impressions had been struck on the upper half and the impressions were then struck on the lower half. Thus each sheet had ten vertical *tête-bêche* pairs, but few of them have survived and we list only those we have seen.

Dies and Date Plugs. The die used is shown by a capital letter which appears in some position in each design.

Three circular holes were drilled for the reception of figure-plugs to indicate the day, month and year when the impression was struck. We record only the dates we have seen, though many others have been reported. Dates shown in italic figures mean that we have only seen them with fiscal cancellations, although there is a strong probability that they also exist unused or with postal obliterations.

Dates of issue quoted are the earliest known dates of use as fiscal stamps.

"Specimen" Stamps. Stamps overprinted "Specimen" known outside official sources are listed and the different types are illustrated in Appendix 3.

L21

L22

L23

L24

L25

L26

L27

INLAND
REVENUE

L28 *Thick Underprint*

Prices

For a given basic stamp, some dates may be much scarcer than others. The prices quoted below are for the commonest dates.

1860–71. Types L21 to L27. Underprint Type L28. Bluish paper. No wmk. Imperf.

L128 (=S.G.F28)	2d. pink, Die A (1.1.71)	£600
	s. "Specimen", Types 2, 9 *from*	£150
L129 (=S.G.F29)	3d. pink, Die C (3.4.60)	£150
	a. *Tête bêche* (vertical pair)	£1200
L130 (=S.G.F30)	3d. pink, Die D	£600
L131 (=S.G.F31)	6d. pink, Die T (27.3.60)	
L132 (=S.G.F32)	6d. pink, Die U (3.4.60)	£300
	a. *Tête bêche* (vertical pair)	
L133 (=S.G.F33)	9d. pink, Die C (1.1.71)	£750
	s. "Specimen", Types 2, 9 *from*	£150
	t. *Tête bêche* (vertical pair) "Specimen", Type 9	
L134 (=S.G.F34)	1s. pink, Die E (28.6.61?)	£600
	a. *Tête bêche* (vertical pair)	
L135 (=S.G.F35)	1s. pink, Die F (28.6.61)	£225
	a. *Tête bêche* (vertical pair)	£850
	b. Albino impression of 3d. (sideways)	£750
	s. "Specimen", Types 2, 9 *from*	£150
L136 (=S.G.F36)	2s. pink, Die K (6.8.61)	£600
	s. "Specimen", Type 2	
L137 (=S.G.F37)	2s. 6d. pink, Die N (28.6.61?)	
L138 (=S.G.F38)	2s. 6d. pink, Die O (28.6.61)	£300
	s. "Specimen", Types 2, 9 *from*	£150

No. L131 is known with the underprint in red (*price each* £450) also with "Specimen" in (M/S) (*price each* £180).

The 3d. pink Die C and D exist with private line perf. 12–12½. They are both rare and date from 1860.

Date plugs known: L128, 8.12.70, 20.12.70; L129, 31.3.60, 1.4.60, 2.4.60, 3.4.60, 4.4.60, 5.4.60, 6.4.60; L130, 14.4.60, 16.4.60; L131, 27.3.60; L132, 31.3.60, 1.4.60, 4.4.60, 10.4.60, 11.4.60, 12.4.60; L133, 8.12.70 (also with "Specimen" overprint), 20.12.70; L134, 29.9.60, 5.4.62, 14.1.63, 6.7.63, 18.10.64, 12.10.65, 11.1.66, 4.2.70, 22.10.70, 20.12.70, 27.1.71; L135, 17.5.61, 2.11.61, 2.7.62, 13.7.62, 13.10.62, 14.1.63, 28.4.63, 11.11.63, 16.1.64, 16.6.64, 20.4.65, 3.5.66, 3.12.67,

17.5.68, 13.7.68, 10.4.69, 4.2.70; L136, 10.9.60, 25.6.60, 27.9.60, 13.10.60, 9.10.61, 10.12.61, 5.4.62, 11.12.62, 16.1.64, 17.6.64, 16.6.65, 11.1.66, 3.5.66, 3.12.67, 12.4.69; L137, 13.10.60; L138, 27.9.60, 31.5.61 (also "Specimen", Type 9), 1.6.61, 3.6.61 (also "Specimen", Type 9), 4.6.61, 5.6.61, 6.6.61, 7.6.61 ("Specimen", Type 2).

Die Proofs

Die proofs of each value are known in sealing wax. Each is unique from Royal Mint or Somerset House archives.

Proofs

Proofs on paper printed Inland Revenue are known:

Unissued 4d. die A with underprint in green, dated 8.10.62 . . . .
6d. die T underprint in red, dated 27.3.60 . . . .
2s. 6d. die T underprint in red, dated 14.10.61 . . . .
Unissued £1 die A with underprint in green, dated 14.10.61. . . . .

Only one example of each is known, except for the 6d. where one is in the Royal Collection and two are in private hands. The 4d. and £1 show an albino impression.

1861–71. As L128–38 but perf 12½.

L139 (=S.G.F39)	2d. pink, Die A (8.71)	£375
	a. *Tête bêche* (vertical pair)	
	s. "Specimen", Type 9	90·00
L142 (=S.G.F42)	9d. pink, Die C (8.71)	£850
	s. "Specimen", Type 9	£150
L143 (=S.G.F43)	1s. pink, Die E (8.71)	£600
L144 (=S.G.F44)	1s. pink, Die F (8.71)	£525
	s. "Specimen", Type 9	£150
L145 (=S.G.F45)	2s. 6d. pink, Die O (8.71)	£300
	s. "Specimen", Type 9	£150

Date plugs known: L139, 26.1.71 (also with "Specimen" overprint); L142, L143, 18.10.72, 7.2.73, 17.4.72, 22.4.73, 28.7.73, 14.10.73, 24.10.73, 14.1.74; L144, 22.2.71, 11.10.71, 15.5.72, 7.2.73, 22.4.73, 28.7.73, 24.4.74, 24.7.74; L145, 5.6.61, 6.6.61, 31.5.62, 11.11.63.

All of the above are from the original imperforate issue and show portions of the printed rules and this accounts for the 1861 printings of the 2s. 6d. appearing perforated in 1871.

L29 *Thin Underprint*

1874 (November). Types L21 to L27. Underprint L29 in green. White paper. Wmk W10 (Small Anchor). Perf 12½.

L146 (=S.G.F46)	2d. pink, Die A	
L147 (=S.G.F47)	9d. pink, Die C	
L148 (=S.G.F48)	1s. pink, Die F	£600
L149 (=S.G.F49)	2s. 6d. pink, Die O	

Date plugs known: L146, L147, L149, ? L148, 26.10.74, 10.3.75, 20.3.75, 27.3.75, 30.3.75, 26.10.75.

It is possible that the 2d. 9d. and 2s. 6d. may not exist with the thin underprint, Type L29, in this shade.

1875–80. Types L21 to L27. Colour changed from pink to vermilion. Underprint Type L29 in green. White or bluish paper. Wmk W10 (Small Anchor). Perf $12\frac{1}{2}$.

L150 (=S.G.F50)	2d. vermilion, Die A (1880)	£450
	s. "Specimen", Type 9	£150
L151 (=S.G.F51)	9d. vermilion, Die C (1876)	£600
	s. "Specimen", Type 9, 10 *from*	£150
L152 (=S.G.F52)	1s. vermilion, Die E (11.75?)	£375
	s. "Specimen", Type 9, 10 *from*	£150
L153 (=S.G.F53)	1s. vermilion, Die F (11.75)	£850
L154 (=S.G.F54)	2s. 6d. vermilion, Die O (1878)	£375
	s. "Specimen", Type 9	£150

Date plugs known: L150, 29.10.80, 14.6.81 (also with "Specimen" overprint), 11.7.82; L151, 18.5.76 (with "Specimen" overprint), 14.5.79, 19.11.81; L152, 12.4.76, 13.4.76, 16.2.77 (with "Specimen" overprint), 8.5.77, 9.5.77, 8.1.78, 13.11.78, 15.4.79, 25.4.79, 19.7.79, 29.1.80, 15.5.80, 12.8.80, 5.10.80, 11.1.81, 12.1.81. 14.6.81, 15.6.81, 3.8.81, 22.10.81, 6.1.82, 7.1.82, 14.1.82; L153, 30.11.76, 12.8.80, 6.1.82; L154, 16.4.78, 13.11.78, 14.5.79, 21.7.79, 8.3.80, 12.8.80, 5.10.80, 3.8.81 (with "Specimen" overprint), 7.1.82.

1882 (October). As L150–154 but wmk W11 (Orb).

L155 (=S.G.F55)	2d. vermilion, Die A		
	s. "Specimen", Type 9	£175	
L156 (=S.G.F56)	9d. vermilion, Die C		
	s. "Specimen", Type 9	£175	
L157 (=S.G.F57)	1s. vermilion, Die E		
	s. "Specimen", Type 9	£175	
L158 (=S.G.F58)	2s. 6d. vermilion, Die O	£750	£600
	s. "Specimen", Type 9	£175	

Date plugs known: L155, L156, 11.7.82 (with "Specimen" overprint), L157, 11.7.82 (with "Specimen" overprint); L158, 11.7.82, 12.10.82 (both with "Specimen" overprint), 24.1.83.

Although specimen overprints of Nos. L155/7 are known there is some doubt if these values were ever issued as with the exception of the 2s. 6d. they were withdrawn on 1 January 1883. The 2s. 6d. was provisonally used as a postage stamp until replaced by the 2s. 6d. lilac (Spec. No. K9) on 2 July 1883.

SECTION LC

The Post Office Telegraph Stamps

General Notes

Introduction. The telegraph service was started and developed by private telegraph companies, of which the Electric Telegraph Company was the most important. With their own capital and research, and by ploughing back much of their profits, the companies spread over a large part of the British Isles. They operated a large number of offices and many issued their own stamps.

The private companies were handicapped in not being allowed to erect telegraph poles on public roads and so they made use of the railway telegraph lines. Many of the railway telegraph offices (or stations) accepted telegrams as agents for the companies or else the railways operated their own services, and both the South Eastern Railways and the London, Chatham and Dover Railway issued stamps.

However, there were still large areas without a telegraph service, especially in Wales, Scotland and Ireland. This led to a demand for nationalization and in 1868 and 1869 Acts were passed giving the Postmaster General and monopoly of inland telegraph business.

The Government made the Post Office a loan for the purchase of the existing companies and the transfer of the properties and undertakings of the private telegraph companies was completed by Saturday, 5 February 1870 when the Post Office took over the service. At that time there were about 1,000 Postal Telegraph Offices and 1,800 railway stations. A uniform 1s. rate came into operation using either forms embossed with the 1s. postal stationery dies or plain forms to which ordinary postage stamps were affixed.

The idea of issuing special Telegraph stamps had been considered in 1868 but rejected on the grounds of the costs of production and distribution and the advantages to the public of using postage stamps which were more easily available.

Within a few years it became evident that the postal telegraph service was running at a loss as no repayments had been made on the Government loan and instead of proper accounts being submitted to the Treasury only estimates of the income were made available.

On 5 October 1874 the Finance Secretary to the Post Office urged the use of special stamps as the only satisfactory means of monitoring the income from the service. Although this was strongly opposed by the head of the telegraph service, the Postmaster General sent a report to the Treasury on 2 January 1875 recommending the introduction of special stamps and on 15 January the Treasury formally authorized him to put the issue in hand.

The first Post Office Telegraph stamps were issued on 1 February 1876 and from 1 May 1876 ordinary postage stamps could no longer be used in payment of telegrams. Forms with special 1s. embossed stamps were also issued.

The first issue, comprising the 1d., 3d., 1s. and 5s. values, was put on sale on 1 February 1876. The intention was to match the colours of the corresponding values of the Postage stamps but this did not apply to the 1d. For this it was decided to go back to the red-brown of the early line-engraved issues as the rose-red of the contemporary 1d. with letters in four corners would have been too close to the carmine of the 3d. Telegraph stamp. Very shortly after the first issue it became evident that additional values were needed, and on 24 March 1876 the Postmaster General gave approval to the issue of new denominations of 4d., 6d., 3s., 10s., £1 and £5, and authorised designs to be obtained. The absence of high values made the payment for expensive telegrams very difficult but action was promptly initiated after the Postmaster General was informed on 10 March 1876 that a telegram by the Anglo-American Company cost £32.2.0, requiring 130 stamps. Despite this problem the Post Office issued a circular on 24 April 1876 to the effect that from 1 May no Postage stamps could be accepted in payment of telegrams, but the new values were not ready for issue until 1 March 1877.

Early in 1880 it was found that ½d. Telegraph stamps were required to meet alterations in some of the foreign rates. To avoid the delays which would attend the preparation of a new design, it was decided to issue the stamp in the same design as the 1d. for which there was only limited use. Accordingly Plate 5 of the 1d., which had never been put to press, was converted by erasing "ONE PENNY" from each cliché and a new duty plate comprising 240 leads was made and this was printed at a separate operation.

In May 1881 consideration was again given to using Postage instead of Telegraph stamps for the telegraph service and the Treasury were satisfied that separate accounts could still be kept. Accordingly on 26 August 1881 the Treasury authorized the Postmaster General to abolish the Telegraph stamps. No further supplies of these were sent to Postmasters after 31 October but considerable stocks remained on hand and large quantities were destroyed. Those still in the hands of the public could not be sold back over the counter but some stamps were used as Postage stamps, although this was never officially authorised.

Printing. All the adhesive Telegraph stamps were surface-printed by De La Rue & Co. The horizontal oblong format was chosen in order to distinguish them from the Postage stamps but initially they were printed in the colours of the corresponding values of the Postage stamps. Check letters appeared in the lower corners only, the upper corners being used for the plate numbers which are shown at each side.

Colours. It had been agreed that where there were Postage stamps of corresponding value the same colours would be used for the Telegraph stamps. The 4d. Postage was changed to sage-green in October 1876 and the 6d. Postage had been changed to grey in 1873. Consequently only one colour trial sheet in each of these colours was submitted for these values. They were dated "15 DEC 1876".

Specimen sheets dated for each of the other four values were submitted in grey-green, slate-blue, dull claret, dull mauve, brown-lilac and pale ultramarine. For the £5 an additional sheet in gold was produced. Grey-green was selected for the 10s.; slate-blue for the 3s.; and brown-lilac for the £1. For the £5 the first choice was gold but this was rejected on ground of cost and the second choice was pale ultramarine, but this was also rejected for fear of confusion with the Probate stamp of the same value in a similar colour. Eventually orange was selected, a colour not originally submitted.

It was natural, therefore, that the colours first adopted for the 10s., £1 and £5. Telegraph stamps were later used for these values when first introduced into the Postage series in 1878 and 1882.

At the end of 1881 the plate of the £5 Telegraph stamp was converted for printing the £5 Postage stamps by drilling out the word "TELEGRAPHS" and substituting "POSTAGE"; this accounts for the 1882 £5 Postage stamps having only two corner letters instead of four. The design of the £1 Telegraph was also adopted for the Postage issue of 1884 but in this case the printers were instructed to prepare a new die and plate.

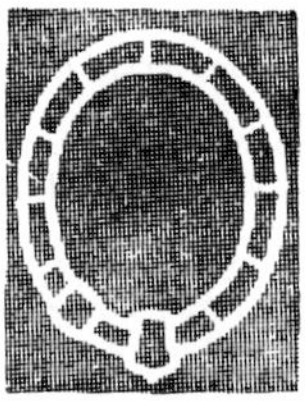

W5C *Large Garter*

W7 Spray (*of Rose*)

W8 *Maltese Cross*

W9 *Larger Anchor*

W12 (*Imperial*) *Crown*

W12C *Shamrock*

As viewed from the printed side of the stamp.

Watermarks. The watermarks used for Post Office Telegraph stamps are shown above. Type **W12C** was not previously used for the surfaced-printed stamps listed in Section J of this Catalogue. The illustrations depict the watermark as seen from the *front* of the stamp.

Watermark Types **W5c, W7, W9** and **W12** occur sideways and of these **W7**, **W12** and **W12C** can also be found with the watermark in the sideways-inverted position. The following illustrations show the watermark *as seen through the back of the stamp.* In order to qualify as the variety sideways-inverted the stamp, when viewed from the gummed side should show the emblem on its side and pointing left.

Sideways

Sideways-inverted

As viewed from the gummed side of the stamp.

Perforation. All the perforating was carried out by the Inland Revenue at Somerset House until the transfer of the machines to De La Rue, starting in June 1880. Gauge 14 punch sets were used on all values except the 5s., 10s. and £5 which were $15\frac{1}{2} \times 15$. Shortly after De La Rue took over the perforating on 1 September 1880, the 5s. values changed to 14. The 10s. and £5 were not affected as sufficient stocks of these were in hand.

Sheet Arrangements. As De La Rue were not printing 1d. Postage stamps at the time, they decided to employ the same paper and layout as they were then using for printing Irish Dog Licence stamps, which were of similar size and watermarked Shamrock. The sheet was of 240 stamps arranged in 12 horizontal rows of 20 stamps lettered AA to TL. The Plate Numbers appeared at AB and TK and the Current Numbers at AK and TB. The inscription "TELEGRAPHS ONE PENNY" appeared in the stop sheet margin.

The 3d., 6d., 1s. and 3s. watermarked Spray of Rose were also in sheets of 240 lettered AA to TL but the sheets were divided into twelve panes (3 rows of 4 panes) each pane containing 20 stamps (4 horizontal rows of 5 stamps). Plate numbers appeared sideways at AA and TL (top left and bottom right corners) and Current Numbers sideways at AL and TA (top right and bottom left corners). The inscription "TELEGRAPHS" and value in words appeared in the left margin reading up and repeated at each pane and similarly in the vertical margins between the panes. Wing margins on these values with Spray of Rose watermark occur on the bottoms of stamps from horizontal rows D and H and on the tops of stamps from horizontal rows E and I. For information about these see General Notes to Section J.

When the 3d. and 1s. changed to the Imperial Crown watermark the sheets also contained 240 stamps but the plate was altered to provide two panes of 120, each having 12 horizontal rows of 10 stamps, with the left pane lettered AA to JL and the right pane KA to TL. No Plate Numbers, Current Numbers or inscriptions appeared in the sheet margins.

The 4d. with Large Garter watermark was printed in sheets of 240 lettered AA to TL and divided into four panes each containing 60 stamps (6 horizontal rows of 10 stamps). Plate Numbers appeared sideways at AA and TL (top left and bottom right corners) and Current Numbers appeared sideways at AL and TL (top right and bottom left corners). The inscription "TELEGRAPHS FOUR PENCE" appeared in the left margin reading up and repeated at each pane, and similarly in the vertical margin between the panes. Wing margins occur on the bottoms of stamps from horizontal row F and on the top from horizontal row G.

The Maltese Cross watermark was used for the 5s. and 10s. values which, being larger, was printed in smaller sheets of 80 stamps lettered AA to HJ and divided into four panes each of 20 stamps (5 horizontal rows of 4 stamps). The Plate Numbers were at HA and AJ (top right and bottom left corners) and the Current Numbers were at AA and HJ (top left and bottom right corners). The inscription "TELEGRAPHS FIVE SHILLINGS" appeared above and below each pane.

With the change to the Anchor watermark the plate used for the 5s. value was altered to produce 56 stamps arranged in 8 horizontal rows of 7 stamps lettered AA to GH. There were no Plate Numbers Current Numbers or inscriptions in the sheet margins.

The £1 with Shamrock watermarks was printed in sheets of 80 stamps arranged in 20 horizontal rows of 4 stamps lettered AA to DT. The Plate Numbers appeared at DA and AT (top right and bottom left corners) and the Current Numbers at AA and DT (top left and bottom right corners). The inscription "TELEGRAPHS ONE POUND" appeared in the top and bottom sheet margins.

The £5 with Shamrock watermarks was printed in sheets of 56 stamps arranged in 14 horizontal rows of 4 stamps lettered AA to DN. The Plate Numbers appeared at DA and AN (top right and bottom left corners) and the Current Numbers at AA and DN (top left and bottom right corners). The inscription "TELEGRAPHS FIVE POUNDS" appeared in the top and bottom sheet margins.

Imperforate Multiples. The following multiples may still exist in private collections and it is believed that they came from the imprimatur sheets: ½d. Plate 5 (pair): 1d. Plate 5 (pair): 3d. Crown wmk. Plate 4 (pair); 4d. Plate 2 (strip of three); 6d. Crown wmk, Plate 2 (pair); 1s. Plate 1 (pair); 1s.

orange-brown, Crown wmk. Plate 12 (pair); 5s. Plate 1 (pair); 5s. Plate 3 (block of four); 10s. Plate 1 (pair and strip of four); £1 Plate 1 (block of four).

Imprimaturs. Although Wright and Creeke inspected the Imprimatur sheets before 1899, their present location is unknown and it is possible that they have been destroyed. It seems certain that all recorded imperforate stamps without "Specimen" overprints, including several pairs and strips, come from the Imprimatur sheets. As evinced by their corner letterings all come from the same general area of the sheets, similar to that form which Imprimaturs of contemporary Postage stamps were removd, the only exception being the 3d. Plate 1, of which very few examples are known.

Dates of Issue. These are given in the headings where known and in addition the recorded "putting to press" dates are quoted for each plate but where this information is not available the date on which the plate was approved is given. This applies mainly where the plate was altered to accommodate a change of watermark.

"Specimen" Stamps. Stamps overprinted "Specimen" known outside official sources are listed and the different types are illustrated in Appendix 3.

Sources of Used Stamps. Although telegraph forms were supposed to be destroyed in due course, the telegraphically used stamps on the market came from forms which escaped destruction. In fact it was as a result of a large supply of telegraph forms that came on the market in 1898 that the "Stock Exchange" forgeries of the 1s. Postage stamps which had occurred in 1872, were first discovered. These are recorded after No. J107.

Essays. On 20 February 1875 Mr Boucher, Controller of the Circulation Department of the Post Office, wrote to the Secretary suggesting that Telegraph stamps be prepared in a horizontal format and he enclosed an essay hand drawn in ink using a head from a current ½d. Postage stamp.

De La Rue prepared two sets of designs in colour, both dated "24 MAR 75", endorsed "Series A" or "Series B" in manuscript.

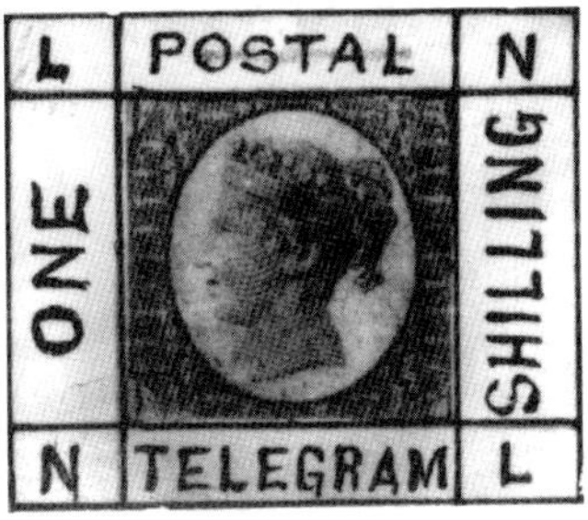

The Boucher Essay

Series A in the horizontal format comprises 1d. purple-brown, 3d. purple-rose and 1s. blue-green. The Queen's head is printed from a die cut out and pasted in and the rest are artist's drawings.

Series B in the vertical format comprises 1d. brown, 3d. purple-brown, 1s. dark green and 5s. magenta. The Queen's head on the three low values is smaller and similar to that actually used. In the 5s. value for example in the Royal Collection shows the head printed from a die but that in Heritage Services shows the head in silhouette.

The designs overleaf have been included as they show the develpment stages in the production of the first Telegraph stamps. Later a number of other essays were prepared.

Between April and June 1876 De La Rue produced various essays for the Second Issue of Telegraph stamps and in 1880 they prepared drawings for Telegraph stamps in various shapes and essays produced lithographically in various colours. In 1881 an essay was prepared for the 3d. stamps, Plate 3, in blue showing the Queen's head against a solid ground, watermarked Imperial Crown and perforated 14. Many of these essays are in the Royal Collection and some from the De La Rue archives were put on the market in 1977.

De La Rue Series A

De La Rue Series B

Die Proofs. Die proofs of each value are included in the lists in accordance with the notes at the beginning of Section J, but we list here the known die proofs of the Queen's head only.

The Small Head. It is possible that this head, measuring 10·4 mm from the top of the crown to the base of the neck, and set in a circle 11 to $11\frac{1}{2}$ mm diameter, was started with the suggested Farthing Postage stamp in mind (see No. DP70 under "Line-Engraved Proofs, etc."), but that its development was continued with a view to using it for the Telegraph stamps.

On 29 February 1875 the Post Office advised the Inland Revenue that the Telegraph stamps were to be the same size as the Postage stamps but in an oblong format. This would obviously entail using a smaller head than that employed on the Postage stamps in order to incorporate the inscriptions at top and bottom. The following die proofs are known on white glazed card, in black except where otherwise stated:

Date	*Inscr.*	*Additional Inscriptions or Notes*	
—	—	Small size head (as illustrated overleaf) in solid circle	£1000
—	—	As last but uncleared square background	£1000
5 Jan 75	—	....	£1000
16 Feb 75	—	....	£1000
31 Mar 75	B/H	....	£1000
29 Apr 75	B/H	....	£1000
29 Apr 75	A/H	....	£1000
29 Apr 75	A/H	"Cancelled" (M/S). Ex De La Rue archives	£1000
—	—	Cut down, with "Sent to In. Rev. see IR 2/58 but retd. in Dec. 1878 to DLR" (M/S)	£1000
—	—	In sepia	£1800
—	—	In pale rose	£1800

On 13 May 1875 De La Rue wrote to the Inland Revenue: "We ... send you the little head Die ... which we prepared some time ago so as to satisfy ourselves that we could, if required, produce postage stamps of the size of the ½d. Postage by the surface process".

It is most probable that the endorsed die proof of 29 April was the one referred to. It is clear that ½d. stamps are referred to and not ¼d. stamps. As the instructions were to produce Telegraph stamps of the same size as Postage stamps, but oblong, it seems likely that De La Rue were working on the idea of producing small stamps of the size of the ½d. Perkins, Bacon line-engraved issue.

The Small Head

The Adopted Head

The Adopted Head. Although there is no corroborating correspondence it seems obvious that at the same time De La Rue were working on a larger head for the values in the same size as the surface-printed stamps in oblong format and the following die proofs have the head, measuring 11·3 mm from the top of the crown to the base of the neck, and set in a 13 mm diameter circle, which was subsequently adopted:

Date	*Inscr*	*Additional Inscriptions or Notes*	
9 Apr 75	—		£1000
12 Apr 75	—		£1000
23 Apr 75	B/H		£1000
27 Apr 75	—	In carmine	£1800
—	—	In sepia	£1800
—	—	In carmine	£1800
—	—	In green	£1800

Cancellations

We illustrate some of the cancellations used by the Post Office on Postage stamps between 1870 and 1876 when the first Telegraph stamps were introduced.

Telegraph Offices. "38" in barred oval was issued to Kensington in May 1844 and its use in the period 1870 to 1876 suggests that it was employed for telegraph purposes. The cancellation appears worn and clogged with ink.

"P.P. 12 PAID" is an old postal cancellation which is sometimes seen in the period 1870 to 1876, again suggesting that this was for telegraphic purposes.

Kensington

Penny Post (Sutton Coldfield)

Concentric Rings

Telegraph Office Date Stamp

The segmented concentric rings had been employed by The British & Irish Magnetic Telegraph Company and also by the Submarine Telegraph Company, with both six or seven rings and the latter cancellation continued in use after the Company was taken over, possibly at Liverpool.

The circular Telegraphs date stamp was introduced by the Post Office in 1870 for use at Telegraph Offices and this continued to be used after Telegraph stamps ceased to be issued.

Railway Telegraph Stations. Numeral cancellations in a circle, numbered 1 to 1569, were used at Railway Telegraph Stations in England and Wales. Numerals in a rectangle, numbered 1 to 270, were used at Scottish Stations and numerals in a diamond, numbered 1 to 28, were used at Irish Stations.

England and Wales

Scotland

Ireland

Great Northern Railway

Railway station-masters were obliged to accept telegraph messages for transmission to the Post Office. In 1892 the Post Office issued an undated oval stamp which bore the name of the station and the initials of the Railway Company. A notice to Postmasters dated January 1892 stated that the oval stamps were intended to replace the numerical type in use at some stations. This followed the introduction, on 1 February 1891, of the Railway Letter Service. By this time the Post Office had erected telephone lines connecting the post offices so that the public telegraph service had virtually by-passed the railway stations except for emergencies. In addition to stamps used on telegraph forms the oval cancellation was frequently used on the 2d. Railway Letter stamp.

Prices for Stamps in Used Condition

The notes about condition given at the end of the General Notes to Section J also apply to Section LC. The prices for well-centred, lightly used stamps can be calculated by adding **50%** to the prices quoted.

L31

1880 (1 April). ½d. Orange, Type L31. Wmk W12C (Shamrock). Perf 14.

L201		½d. orange, Plate 5	10·00	20·00
		Block of four	50·00	£100
	b.	Imperforate (vert. pair)	£1200	
	s.	"Specimen", Type 9	40·00	

Imprimatur: Plate 5 *re-registered,* £250.
No. L201*b* exists with certificate starting that the pair is not from the imprimatur sheet.
Put to press: 13 March 1880.

Essays for ½d. value from the De La Rue Archives

Head painted in black and white £2500

Die Proofs. In black on white glazed card:

Date	*Inscriptions*	
—	1d. die proof with "ONE PENNY" crossed through and endorsed "Halfpenny / this stamp / overprinted (M/S)	
6 Mar 80	Cut down proof of "HALF PENNY" overprint endorsed "Telegraph / March 6th / 240 Leads" in black and later "Temporary ½d Telegraph / May 5. 80 / overprint to fit 1d. forme cut away" in red (M/S)	£1200

L32

1876 (1 February). 1d. Red-brown, Type L32. Wmk W12C (Shamrock). Perf 14.

L202		1d. red-brown, Plate 1	10·00	10·00
		Block of four	50·00	50·00
	a.	Watermark inverted	£150	
	s.	"Specimen", Types 9, 10 *from*	40·00	
L203		1d. red-brown, Plate 2	15·00	7·00
		Block of four	75·00	50·00
	a.	Watermark inverted	£180	£100
	s.	"Specimen", Types 9, 10 *from*	40·00	
L204		1d. red-brown, Plate 3	15·00	10·00
		Block of four	75·00	50·00
	s.	"Specimen", Type 9	50·00	

Imprimatur: Plates 1 *to* 5, *each* £250.

Put to press dates: Plates 1 and 2, 11 August 1875; Plate 3, 17 August 1875.

Plate 4 was put to press on 17 February 1876 but not issued and the stock was destroyed. Plate 5 was approved on 23 September 1875 but not put into use as a 1d. stamp. Instead it was later altered to be used for the ½d. stamp of 1880.

Essays from the De La Rue Archives

Head painted in black and white dated 1875 . . . . . £2500
With crowned head pasted on hand painted frame dated "8. APR. 79." £2500

Die Proofs. In black on white glazed card:

Date	*Plate No.*	*Corner Letters*	*Inscr.*	*Additional Inscriptions or Notes*	
1 July 75	—	—	—	. . . . .	£600
6 July 75	—	—	B/H	. . . . .	£600
—	—	—	—	Basic Die Proof	£600
14 July 75	1	A–A	A/H	"App on 15.7.75/struck 14.7.75 after hardening" in pencil on back	£600
22 July 75	1	A–A	B/S	. . . . .	£600
22 July 75	1	A–A	(M/S)	Endorsed "After Striking" (M/S)	£600
22 July 75	2	A–A	B/S	. . . . .	£600
26 July 75	3	O–L	B/S	. . . . .	£600
26 July 75	3	O–L	B/S	Initialled "J.P.S." in pencil	£600
28 July 75	4	F–C	B/S	. . . . .	£600
6 Aug 75	5	—	A/S	. . . . .	£600

Die Proofs from the De La Rue Archives. Cut down to stamp size and mounted on card in countersunk frame.

With void corner letter squares and no plate number £550

From the striking books:

Plate 1 (unnumbered) £550
Plates 3 to 5 . . . . . *from* £550

L33

1876 (1 February). 3d. Carmine, Type L33. Wmk W7 (Spray) sideways. Perf 14.

L205		3d. carmine, Plate 1	50·00	30·00
		Block of four	£250	£150
	a.	Watermark sideways-inverted	£175	£150
	s.	"Specimen", Types 9, 10	50·00	
	t.	Imperforate "Specimen", Type 10	£100	
L206		3d. carmine, Plate 2	50·00	20·00
		Block of four	£250	£100
	a.	Watermark sideways-inverted	†	£250
	s.	"Specimen", Type 9	50·00	
L207		3d. carmine, Plate 3	60·00	40·00
		Block of four	£300	£200
	a.	Watermark sideways-inverted	£250	
	s.	"Specimen", Type 9	65·00	

Imprimaturs: Plate 1, £600; *Plates* 2 *to* 5, *each* £250.

Put to press dates: Plate 1, 5 August 1875; Plate 2, 23 February 1876; Plate 3, November 1878.

Plate 4 was approved on 9 August 1877 and Plate 5 on 12 January 1878 but no stamps were printed from either of them on Spray of Rose paper other than the registration sheets. There is an example from Plate 4, lettered DB, in the Royal Collection and one other exists, lettered DA.

Die Proofs. In black on white glazed card:

Date	*Plate No.*	*Corner Letters*	*Inscr.*	*Additional Inscriptions or Notes*	
22 June 75	—	—	—		£600
2 July 75	—	—	—		£600
6 July 75	—	—	—		£600
8 July 75	—	—	B/H		£600
14 July 75	—	—	B/H		£600
—	—	—	—	Basic Die Proof	£600
14 July 75	1	A–B	A/H		£600
16 July 75	1	S–B	—		£600
16 Aug 75	2	—	B/S	Initialled "J.P.S." in pencil	£600
16 Aug 75	2	B–B	A/S	Initialled "J.P.S." in pencil	£600
20 Aug 75	2	—	A/S		£600
22 Feb 76	3	—	B/S	Initialled "S.E.J." (M/S)	£600
24 Feb 76	3	D–E	(M/S)	Endorsed "after striking 20 Leads" and date (M/S)	£600
24 Feb 76	3	D–E	(M/S)	As last, initialled "T.R." (M/S)	£600
23 Nov 77	5	—	—	Initialled "S.N.E." in pencil	£650

Essay from the De La Rue Archives

Head painted in black and white, dated 1875 . . . . £2500

Die Proofs from the De La Rue Archives. Cut down to stamp size and mounted on card in countersunk frame:

With void corner letter squares and no plate number £550

From the Striking Books:

Without plate number . . . .
As above, with number "1" inserted in ink in upper squares £550
Plates 3 to 5 . . . . *from* £550

Plate Proofs. In black on white wove unwatermarked paper:

Plates 2, 3, 4 . . . . *each* £350

1881 (8 August?). 3d. Carmine, Type L33. Change to wmk W12 (Crown) sideways. Perf 14.

L208	3d. carmine, Plate 3 (watermark sideways-inverted)	75·00	50·00
	Block of four	£375	£250
L209	3d. carmine, Plate 4	£200	£100
	Block of four	£950	£500
L210	3d. carmine, Plate 5	£200	£100
	Block of four	£900	£475

Imprimaturs: Plates 3 *to* 5 *re-registered, each* £250.

Dates approved: Plate 3, 17 February 1881; Plates 4 and 5, 5 August 1881.

The earliest recorded used example of Plate 3 in 20 March 1881 and a number of examples are known with April 1881 dates. The earliest known date for Plate 4 is 10 September and Plate 5, 1 September 1881 at College Green, Dublin

Colour Trials. Wmk Crown, Plate 3, Perf 14.

In orange, blue, green . . . . *each* £950

The purpose of these colour trials is not known. They were made after the use of Telegraph stamps was abandoned. De La Rue had printed the Telegraph stamps for the United Kingdom Telegraph

Company prior to nationalization and subsequently used the 3d. value as a dummy stamp when demonstrating fugitive colours and tendering for overseas business. It is probable that the Post Office issues were used for similar demonstration purposes.

L34

1877 (1 March). 4d. Sage-green, Type L34. Wmk W5c (Large Garter) sideways-inverted. Perf. 14.

L211	4d. sage-green, Plate 1	75·00	60·00
	Block of four	£400	£350
	a. Watermark sideways		
	b. Imperforate (vert. pair)		
	s. "Specimen", Types 9, 11 *from*	50·00	
	t. Imperforate "Specimen", Type 9	£100	

Imprimaturs: Plates 1 *and* 2, *each* £250.
Put to press: 15 January 1877.
No. L211*b* is not from the imprimatur sheet.
Plate 2 was approved on 18.6.77 but was not put to press.

Essays from the De La Rue Archives

Head painted in black and white, dated 1875 . . . . . £2500

Die Proofs. In black on white glazed card:

Date	*Plate No.*	*Corner Letters*	*Inscr.*	*Additional Inscriptions or Notes*	
30 Oct 76	—	—	—		£600
31 Oct 76	—	—	—		£600
1 Nov 76	—	—	—		£600
2 Nov 76	—	—	—		£600
Nov 76	—	—	—		£600
4 Nov 76	—	—	—		£600
6 Nov 76	—	—	—	One copy initialled (M/S)	£600
7 Nov 76	—	—	B/H		£600
—	—	—	—	Basic Die Proof	£600
17 Nov 76	1	—	A/H	"AFTER" altered in "Before" (M/S) and initialled "F.J."	£650
17 Nov 76	1	—	(M/S)	Endorsed "Before striking" (M/S) and initialled "F.J." and "T.R." in pencil	£650
21 Nov 78	1	—	A/S	Error in year for "1876"	£650
21 Nov 78	1	—	A/S	Do. Initialled "F.J." in pencil	£650
14 May 77	2	E–B	A/S	Initialled "H.A." vert. in pencil	£650
25 May 77	2	—	A/S	Initialled "H.A." in blue crayon	£650

Die Proofs from the De La Rue Archives. Cut down to stamp size and mounted on card in countersunk frame:

With void corner letter squares and no plate number £550

From the Striking Books:

With plate number "1" inserted in ink £550
Plate 2 . . . . . £550

Plate Proofs. In black on white wove unwatermarked paper:

Plate 2 .... £500

Colour Trials. Imperf. wmk Large Garter:

Plate 1 in sage-green (deeper than the issued colour) and overprinted "Specimen", Types 8, 11 .... *from* £100

1883, imperf. wmk Imperial Crown:

Plates 1, 2 in blue-green .... *each*

An example of Plate 2 exists with "Experimental on Crown 15.10.83" endorsed in the margin in manuscript. The purpose of the 1883 trials is not known.

L35

1877 (1 March). 6d. Grey, Type L35. Wmk W7 (Spray) sideways. Perf 14.

L212	6d. grey, Plate 1	50·00	20·00
	Block of four	£250	£100
	s. "Specimen", Types 9, 11 .... *from*	50·00	
	t. Imperforate "Specimen", Type 9	£100	
L213	6d. grey, Plate 2	£150	75·00
	Block of four	£750	£375

Imprimaturs: Plates 1 *and* 2, *each* £300.
Put to press dates: Plate 1, 15 January 1877; Plate 2, 22 June 1880.

Essays from the De La Rue Archives

Head painted in black and white, dated 1875 .... £2500

Die Proofs. In black on white glazed card:

Date	*Plate No.*	*Corner Letters*	*Inscr.*	*Additional Inscriptions or Notes*	
25 Oct 76	—	—	—	Circles in corner letter squares	£600
26 Oct 76	—	—	—	....	£600
27 Oct 76	—	—	—	....	£600
30 Oct 76	—	—	—	Circles in corner squares removed	£600
31 Oct 76	—	—	—	Circles in corner squares removed	£600
2 Nov 76	—	—	—	....	£600
3 Nov 76	—	—	—	....	£600
4 Nov 76	—	—	—	....	£600
6 Nov 76	—	—	—	....	£600
7 Nov 76	—	—	—	....	£600
—	—	—	—	Provisional Basic Die Proof, flowers closed ...	£600
—	—	—	—	Basic Die Proof, flowers opened	£600
9 Nov 76	—	—	B/H	....	£600
20 Nov 76	—	—	(M/S)	Endorsed "After Striking. Nov. 20 1876" (M/S) and initialled "F.J." in pencil	£600
12 May 77	2	—	(M/S)	Endorsed "After Striking. May 12 1877" ..... (M/S). Known initialled "H.A." in pencil ...	£650

Die Proofs from the De La Rue Archives. Cut down to stamp size and mounted on card in countersunk frame:

With void corner letter squares and no plate numbers £550

From the Striking Books:

With plate number "1" inserted in ink £550
Plate 2 . . . . £550

Plate Proofs. In black on white wove unwatermarked paper:

Plate 1, 2 . . . . *each* £500

Colour Trials. Imperf, wmk Spray of Rose:

Plate 1 in grey (slightly deeper than issued colour) and overprinted "Specimen", Types 8, 11 . . . . *from* £100

1881 (January). 6d. Grey, Type L35. Change to wmk W12 (Crown) sideways-inverted (top of crown points to left as seen from the back of stamp). Perf 14.

L214	6d. grey, Plate 2	£100	65·00
	Block of four	£500	£325
	b. Imperforate (vert. pair)		

Imprimaturs: Plate 2 *re-registered,* £300.
Date approved: 29 June 1881.

The imprimatur sheet was endorsed "Proof after alteration of plate" and "Ordered that this altered plate be brought into use". The earliest recorded used example is dated 31 January 1881 and another is known dated 15 February 1881.

No. L214*b* is not from the imprimatur sheet.

Die Proof. In black on white glazed card:

Date	*Plate No.*	*Corner Letters*	*Inscr.*	*Additional Inscriptions or Notes*	
20 Nov 80	—	—	(M/S)	Endorsed "After Striking. Nov. 20 1880" (M/S) and initialled "F.J." in pencil	£700

L36

1876 (1 February). 1s. Green, Type L36. Wmk W7 (Spray) sideways. Perf 14.

L215	1s. deep green, Plate 1	80·00	25·00
	Block of four	£450	£125
	s. "Specimen", Type 10	75·00	
	t. Imperforate "Specimen", Type 10	£125	
L216	1s. deep green, Plate 2	50·00	25·00
	Block of four	£250	£125
	a. Watermark sideways-inverted	£300	
	s. "Specimen", Type 9	75·00	
L217	1s. deep green, Plate 3	50·00	25·00
	Block of four	£250	£125
	s. "Specimen", Type 9	75·00	

L218	1s. green, Plate 4	£100	20·00
	Block of four	£500	£100
	a. Watermark sideways-inverted		
	s. "Specimen", Type 9	£200	
	t. Imperforate "Specimen", Type 9	£100	
L219	1s. green, Plate 5	35·00	15·00
	Block of four	£175	75·00
	a. Watermark sideways-inverted		
	s. "Specimen", Type 9	75·00	
L220	1s. green, Plate 6	35·00	15·00
	Block of four	£175	75·00
	a. Watermark sideways-inverted		
	s. "Specimen", Type 9	75·00	
L221	1s. green, Plate 7	£200	20·00
	Block of four	£1000	£100
	a. Watermark sideways-inverted		
L222	1s. green, Plate 8	80·00	20·00
	Block of four	£475	£100
	a. Watermark sideways-inverted		
	s. "Specimen", Type 9	75·00	
L223	1s. green, Plate 9	80·00	20·00
	Block of four	£475	£100
L224	1s. green, Plate 10	£100	25·00
	Block of four	£500	£125

Imprimaturs: Plates 1 *to* 12, *each* £250.

Put to press dates: Plate 1, 28 July 1875; Plate 2, 22 February 1876; Plate 3, 11 October 1876; Plate 4, 1 May 1877; Plate 5, 23 August 1877; Plate 6, 1 March 1878; Plate 7, 20 August 1878; Plate 8, 9 December 1878; Plate 9, 19 September 1879; Plate 10, 2 February 1880.

Plate 11 was approved on 13.5.80 and Plate 12 on 15.7.80 but these plates were not put to press in green.

Essay from the De La Rue Archives

Hand painted in black and white dated 1875 . . . £2500

Die Proofs. In black on white glazed card:

Date	*Plate No.*	*Corner Letters*	*Inscr.*	*Additional Inscriptions or Notes*	
25 June 75	—	—	—		£550
30 June 75	—	—	—		£550
1 July 75	—	—	—		£550
2 July 75	—	—	—		£550
3 July 75	—	—	—		£550
4 July 75	—	—	—		£550
6 July 75	—	—	B/H		£550
—	—	—	—	Basic Die Proof	£550
14 July 75	1	B–B	A/H		£550
14 July 75	1	R–A	(M/S)	Endorsed "After striking 15 Leads" (M/S)	£600
14 July 75	1	R–A	(M/S)	As last, initialled "J.P.S." in pencil	£600
4 Aug 75	2	L–A	(M/S)	Endorsed "After striking 15 Leads" and date (M/S)	£600
12 Aug 75	3	T–L	B/S		£550
12 Aug 75	3	F–D	(M/S)	As last but before striking erased and endorsed "After striking 81 leads" (M/S) and initialled "J.P.S." in pencil	£600
12 Aug 75	3	T–L	B/S	Initialled "T.R." (M/S)	£600
25 July 76	4	A–B	B/S		£600
25 July 76	4	A–B	B/S	Initialled "F.J." in pencil	£600
25 July 76	4	M–A	(M/S)	Endorsed "After striking 13 Leads" (M/S) and initialled "F.J." in pencil	£600

Date	*Plate No.*	*Corner Letters*	*Inscr.*	*Additional Inscriptions or Notes*	
16 Mar 77	5	—	(M/S)	Endorsed "After Striking" and date (M/S) and initialled "H.H." in pencil	£600
17 Aug 77	6	—	B/S		£600
28 Aug 77	6	—	A/S		£600
2 Apr "(78)"	7	J–B	(M/S)	Endorsed "After Striking 59 Leads" and date in pencil and initialled "S.N.E." in pencil. Vertical format	£600
6 Apr 78	7	—	A/S	Initialled "S.N.E." in blue crayon	£600
26 July 78	8	—	(M/S)	Endorsed "Before Striking" and date (M/S) and initialled "C.P.K." in pencil	£600
27 July 78	8	C–B	(M/S)	Endorsed "After striking 25 leads" and date (M/S) and initialled "C.P.K." in pencil	£600
14 Aug 79	10	—	—	Initialled "W.G." and "J.U.T."(?) (M/S)	£600
—	11	N–C	(M/S)	Endorsed "After Striking 50 Leads" (M/S) and initialled "N.G." in pencil	£600
13 Apr 80	11	—	(M/S)	Endorsed "After Striking (M/S) and initialled "U.G.N." (M/S)	£600
—	12	—	A/S	Initialled "U.G.N." in pencil	£600

Die Proofs from the De La Rue Archives. Cut down to stamp size and mounted on card in countersunk frame:

With void corner letter squares and no plate number £600

From the Striking Books:

Without plate number £600
As above with number "1" inserted in ink in upper squares £600
Plates 2 to 12 . . . . . *from* £600

Plate Proofs. In black on white wove unwatermarked paper:

Plates 2, 3, 4, 8, 9 . . . . . *each* £550

1880 (October). 1s., Type L36. Change of colour to Brown-orange. Wmk W7 (Spray) sideways. Perf 14.

L225		1s. brown-orange, Plate 10	£100	65·00
		Block of four	£500	£350
	s.	"Specimen", Type 9	75·00	
L226		1s. brown-orange, Plate 12	£120	80·00
		Block of four	£600	£400

Imprimatur: Plate 12 *re-registered*, £250.

Put to press dates: Plate 10, 21 September 1880; Plate 12, 14 February 1881.

The Post Office announced the change of colour on 21 September 1880. At that time Plate 10 was at press in green and the colour was changed without re-registering the plate. The earliest recorded used stamp is dated 26 October.

Plate 11 was put to press in brown-orange on 6.12.80 but no examples are known. The original Plate 12 was brought into use on the Spray of Rose watermark after the issue of the reconstructed Plate 11 on the Crown watermark.

Plate 12 was re-registered on 14.2.81 and put to press on the same day. The imprimatur sheet was endorsed "Proof for change of colour" and "Ordered that stamps of this colour be brought into use".

1881 (February ?). 1s. Brown-orange, Type L36. Change to wmk W12 (Crown) sideways (top of crown points to right as seen from back of stamp). Perf 14.

L227		1s. brown-orange, Plate 11	£120	80·00
		Block of four	£600	£500
	b.	Watermark sideways-inverted (top of crown points to left as seen from back)	£120	80·00
	s.	"Specimen", Type 12	£200	
L228		1s. brown-orange, Plate 12	£300	80·00
		Block of four	£1500	£500
	b.	Imperforate (vert. pair)		

Imprimaturs: Plates 11 *and* 12 *re-registered, each* £250.

The imprimatur sheet of Plate 11 was endorsed "Proof after alteration of Plate" and "Ordered that altered Plate be brought into use". Plate 11 must have been taken from press for reconstruction soon after being used on the Spray of Rose watermark and then put to press immediately it was ready as the earliest recorded used example is dated 2 February 1881 at Northern Office, London, eight days before the plate was re-registered.

The imprimatur sheet of Plate 12 was endorsed "Proof after alteration of Plate" and "Ordered that altered Plate be brought into use". The earliest recorded date of use is 10 September 1881.

No. L228*b* is not from the imprimatur sheet.

L37

1877 (1 March). 3s. Slate-blue, Type L37. Wmk W7 (Spray) sideways. Perf 14.

L229	3s. slate-blue, Plate 1	60·00	20·00
	Block of four	£300	£100
	a. Watermark sideways-inverted	—	£300
	s. "Specimen", Types 8, 9, 11 *from*	75·00	

Imprimatur: Plate 1, £125.
Put to press: 15 January 1877.

Die Proofs. In black on white glazed card:

Date	*Plate No.*	*Corner Letters*	*Inscr.*	*Additional Inscriptions or Notes*	
10 Oct 76	—	—	—		£600
14 Oct 76	—	—	—	"4" inverted. Head in circle of horizontal lines	£600
16 Oct 76	—	—	—		£600
17 Oct 76	—	—	—	Head in normal octagon	£600
18 Oct 76	—	—	—		£600
19 Oct 76	—	—	—		£600
20 Oct 76	—	—	—		£600
23 Oct 76	—	—	B/H		£600
24 Oct 76	—	—	—		£600
25 Oct 76	—	—	—		£600
25 Oct 76	—	—	B/H		
26 Oct 76	—	—	—		£600
26 Oct 76	—	—	B/H		£600
—	—	—	—	Basic Die Proof	£600

Die Proofs from the De La Archives. Cut down to stamp size and mounted on card in countersunk frame:

With void corner letter squares and no plate numbers . . . £600

From the Striking Books:

With plate number "1" inserted in ink . . . £600

Plate Proofs. In Black on white wove unwatermarked paper:

Plate 1 . . . £550

Colour Trials. Imperf, wmk Spray of Rose:

Plate 1 in grey-green, slate-blue, dull claret, dull mauve, brown-lilac, pale ultramarine all overprinted "Specimen", Type 8 . . . *each* £100

Plate 1 in slate-blue overprinted "Specimen", Type 11 . . . £750

1881 (August). 3s. Slate-blue, Type L37. Change to wmk W12 (Crown) sideways-inverted (top of crown points to left as seen from the back of the stamp). Perf 14.

L230	3s. slate-blue, Plate 1	£4500	£2500

Imprimatur: Plate 1 *re-registered*, £3500.
Date approved: 29 July 1881.
The Imprimatur sheet was endorsed "Proof after alteration of Plate" and "Ordered that altered Plate be brought into use". The stamps were on sale on 19 August 1881.

L38

1876 (1 February). 5s. Rose, Type L38. Wmk W8 (Maltese Cross). Perf 15 × 15½d

L231	5s. rose, Plate 1	£600	50·00
	Block of four	£3000	£250
	s. "Specimen", Types 8, 9, 10 *from*	£150	
	t. Imperforate "Specimen", Type 9	£300	
L232	5s. rose, Plate 2	£1200	£200
	Block of four	£6000	£1000

Imprimaturs: Plates 1 *and* 2, *each* £600, Plate 3, *each* £1500.
Put to press dates: Plate 1, 9 August 1875; Plate 2, 31 December 1879.
Plate 3 was struck on 4.10.78 and the usual five sheets were printed and perforated 15 × 15½ but not issued. One example is in the Royal Collection.
Two examples of Plate 3 are known perforated 12½ and one of these is in the Royal Collection.

Essays from the De La Rue Archives

Hand painted in black and white, dated 1875 .... *from* £2750

Die Proofs. In black on white glazed card:

Date	*Plate No.*	*Corner Letters*	*Inscr.*	*Additional Inscriptions or Notes*	
16 June 75	—	—	—	Date altered from 19 June (M/S)	£1000
17 June 75	—	—	—		£1000
18 June 75	—	—	—		£1000
25 June 75	—	—	B/H		£1000
—	—	—	—	Basic Die Proof	£1000
2 July 75	—	—	A/S	Initialled "S.E.J." (M/S)	£1000

Die Proofs from the De La Rue Archives. Cut down to stamp size and mounted on card in countersunk frame:

With void corner letter squares and no plate number £750

From the Striking Books:

Two impressions indicated as Dies 1 and 2 .... £1000
Single impression dated 1877 .... £600

Plate Proofs. In black on white wove unwatermarked paper:

Plates 1, 2, 3 .... *each* £550

1880. 5s. Rose, Type L38. Wmk W8 (Maltese Cross). Change to perf 14.

L233	5s. rose, Plate 2	£4000	£250

De La Rue undertook the entire production of stamps including perforation on 1 September 1880. The dates of putting to press and of issue have not been established but the earliest known used example is dated 30 November.

1881 (May). 5s. Rose, Type L38. Change to wmk W9 (Larger Anchor) sideways. Bluish or white paper. Perf 14.

L234	5s, rose, Plate 3	£4000	£600
	s. "Specimen", Types 9, 12 *from*	£650	

Put to press date: 14 May 1881.
The exact date of issue is not known but the earliest recorded used example is dated 20 May 1881.

L39

1877 (1 March). 10s. Grey-green, Type L39. Wmk W8 (Maltese Cross). Perf 15 × 15½.

L235	10s. grey-green, Plate 1	£850	£200
	Block of four	£4000	£1000
	s. "Specimen", Types 8, 9, 11 *from*	£250	
	t. Imperforate "Specimen", Type 9	£400	

Imprimatur: Plate 1, £950.
Put to press: 19 January 1877.

Essay from the De La Rue Archives

Hand-painted in black and white, dated 1875 .... £2800

Die Proofs. In black on white glazed card:

Date	*Plate No.*	*Corner Letters*	*Inscr.*	*Additional Inscriptions or Notes*	
14 Oct 76	—	—	—		£1000
16 Oct 76	—	—	—		£1000
17 Oct 76	—	—	—		£1000
18 Oct 76	—	—	—		£1000
19 Oct 76	—	—	—		£1000
20 Oct 76	—	—	—		£1000
20 Oct 76	—	—	B/H		
—	—	—	—	Basic Die Proof	£1000
1876	—	—	—		£1000

Die Proofs from the De La Rue Archives. Cut down to stamp size and mounted on card in countersunk frame:

With uncleared corner letter and plate number squares £850

From the Striking Books:

With uncleared corner letter and plate number squares £750

Plate Proofs. In black on white wove unwatermarked paper:

Plate 1 . . . . £550

Colour Trials. Imperf, Wmk Maltese Cross:

Plate 1 in grey-green, slate-blue, dull claret, dull mauve, brown-lilac, pale ultramarine all overprinted "Specimen", Type 8 . . . . *each* £250
Plate 1 in grey-green and overprinted "Specimen", Type 11 . . . . £600

L40

1877 (1 March). £1 Brown-lilac, Type L40. Wmk W12C (sideways, three Shamrocks on each stamp). Perf 14.

L236	(1)	£1 pale brown-lilac, Plate 1	£4000	£550
	(2)	£1 brown-lilac, Plate 1	£4000	£550
	s.	"Specimen", Types 8, 9, 11 . . . . *from*	£600	
	t.	Imperforate "Specimen", Type 9	£1000	

Imprimatur: Plate 1: £1800.
Put to press: 15 January 1877.

Easy from the De La Rue Archives. Dated "Jul 24th. 96" (in error for '76):

Hand-painted in pale dull rose, deep claret, lake-brown and Chinese white on buff card £6000

Die Proofs. In black on white glazed card:

Date	*Plate No.*	*Corner Letters*	*Inscr.*	*Additional Inscriptions or Notes*	
20 Oct 76	—	—	—	. . . .	£1500
23 Oct 76	—	—	—	. . . .	£1500
26 Oct 76	—	—	—	. . . .	£1500
26 Oct 76	—	—	—	Endorsed "26 – 10" in pencil	£1500
27 Oct 76	—	—	—	. . . .	£1500
30 Oct 76	—	—	—	. . . .	£1500
31 Oct 76	—	—	B/H	. . . .	£1500
2 Nov 76	—	—	B/H	. . . .	£1500
10 Nov 76	—	—	A/H	Initialled "N.G." in pencil	£1500
—	—	—	—	Basic Die Proof	£1500

Die Proofs from the De La Rue Archives. Cut down to stamp size and mounted on card with countersunk frame:

With uncleared corner letter and plate number squares £1250

From the Striking Books:

With uncleared corner letter and plate number squares £1000

Colour Trials. Imperf. Wmk 3 Shamrocks:

Plate 1 in grey-green, slate-blue, dull claret, dull mauve, brown-lilac, pale ultramarine all overprinted "Specimen", Type 8 . . . . *each* £600
Plate 1 in brown-lilac and overprinted "Specimen", Type 11 . . . . £850

L41

1877 (1 March). £5. Orange, Type L41. Wmk W12C sideways-inverted (see footnote). Perf 15 × 15½.

L237		£5 orange, Plate 1	£12000	£1800
	s.	"Specimen", Types 8, 9, 11 . . . . *from*	£1800	
	t.	"Specimen", Types 8 once *and* 9 four times on one example		

Imprimatur: Plate 1, £6000.
Put to press: 17 January 1877.

Stamps normally have three Shamrock watermarks but they were printed on the same paper used for the £1 value and because of the different size of the stamps many show portions of six Shamrocks.

The plate was subsequently altered by removing "TELEGRAPHS" from each cliché and substituting "POSTAGE" and used for printing the £5 Postage stamp of 1882.

Essay from the De La Rue Archives. Dated "15 Jun 76":

Hand-painted in pale reddish purple, deep claret and Chinese white with head painted in brown-rose £10000

Die Proofs. In black on white glazed card:

Date	*Plate No.*	*Corner Letters*	*Inscr.*	*Additional Inscriptions or Notes*	
8 Nov 76	—	—	—	Dark background to Queen's head	£2500
8 Nov 76	—	—	—	Do. Endorsed "Postage" in pencil	£2500
9 Nov 76	—	—	—	. . . .	£2500
10 Nov 76	—	—	—	. . . .	£2500
14 Nov 76	—	—	—	. . . .	£2500
15 Nov 76	—	—	—	. . . .	£2500
16 Nov 76	—	—	—	. . . .	£2500
17 Nov 76	—	—	—	. . . .	£2500
17 Nov 76	—	—	B/H	. . . .	£2500
—	—	—	—	Basic Die Proof	£2500

Die Proofs from the De La Rue Archives. Cut down to stamp size and mounted on card in countersunk frame:

With uncleared corner letter and plate number squares £2500

From the Striking Books:

With uncleared corner letter and plate number squares £2500

Plate Proof. In black on dull white card:

Plate 1 . . . . £1500

Colour Trials. Imperf, Wmk Shamrocks:

Plate 1 in grey-green, slate-blue, dull claret, dull mauve, brown-lilac, pale ultramarine all overprinted "Specimen", Type 8 . . . . *each* £1000

Plate 1 in pale ultramarine and overprinted "Specimen", Type 11 . . . . £1250

Plate 1 in gold without "Specimen" overprint £3750

Plate 1 in gold and overprinted "Specimen", Type 11 . . . . £3000

Appendixes

APPENDIX 1

Mulready Letter Sheets and Envelopes Printed with Advertisements, etc.

From the beginning, Mulready letter sheets and, in a few instances, envelopes, were recognized as a medium for commercial communications. By the end of May 1840 many advertisers had seized the opportunity. The advertisements, notices, and circular letters are of considerable interest. They provide a glimpse of Victorian life only seen in newspapers or advertising circulars of that period.

The listing is grouped into similar categories: General Advertisers; Insurance Companies; Stamp and Tax Notices; Banking Notices; and Individual Firms and Organizations promoting their own objectives, goods and services.

The listing has been completely revised and renumbered to enable collectors to identify each advertisement or notice. The listings of some advertisers are incomplete and numbers have been omitted to accommodate items reported in the future. The printing on all Mulreadys listed is assumed to be in black, unless another colour is specified, and to be on 1d. letter sheets, unless otherwise indicated. Anyone finding what they believe to be a new item or a variation on one already listed, please contact the Editor. Send photocopies of both sides of the Mulready opened so that the advertisement or message and the postal markings are clear. If in a colour other than black, a colour photocopy would be ideal. All newly reported items will be included in the next edition of the catalogue.

General Advertisers with Various Advertisements

These individuals or firms, generally printers or booksellers, solicited advertisements to be printed on the new "postage covers" much as they had done when publishing their own newspapers or circulars. These covers or letter sheets were then sold to the public, usually at a discount from the post office price. Letter sheets were sent to all parts of the country, achieving a much wider distribution than the printers' own circulars or newspapers. All parties benefited from this innovation. Printers profited from the sale of the advertisements and writing paper, the public from discounted postage, and the advertisers from a greater exposure to potential customers for their wares and services.

MA1 **W. BALLARD** (Bottom Middle)
- a Top Left: W. E. JENKINS,: Top Middle: MOUNTCASTLE'S; Top Right: Important to Gentlemen

MA2 **T. P. CALDWELL'S ENVELOPE CIRCULAR**
- a Details Unknown. No. 1
- b Top Left: No. 2. Main Heading: T. P. CALDWELL'S ENVELOPE CIRCULAR, AUGUST 1840.

MA3 **CHARLTON and MEREDITH** (Bottom Right)
- a Main Heading: REDUCTION OF POSTAGE.—POSTAGE COVERS....Top Left: BUILDERS, PAINTERS,

MA4 **G. CROUCH**
- a Main Heading: CROUCH'S POST OFFICE COVERS for CIRCULARS, &c. Top Left: G. CROUCH... Bottom Right: SATINS and SILKS...

MA5 **A. CUDDY** (Bottom Right)
- a Main Heading: REDUCTION OF POSTAGE....Top Left: York and London Assurance Company. (Printed in Blue)
- b Main Heading: REDUCTION OF POSTAGE....Top Left: BAZAAR BAKER STREET. Third Column, 4th Ad: RICH...PEKOE TEA.
- c Main Heading: REDUCTION OF POSTAGE....Top Left: BAZAAR ... Third Column, 4th Ad: RICH...CONGOU TEA. (Printed in Blue)
- d Main Heading: REDUCTION OF POSTAGE....Top Left: British & Colonial Trust & Assurance Company. (Printed in Blue)
- e Main Heading: Postage Stamps, 9d. Per Dozen....Top Left: NOTICE. - Board of Stamps and Taxes,(Printed in Blue)

f Main Heading: TO ADVERTISERS…July, 55,000!!! Top Left: FAMILY ENDOWMENT SOCIETY, LIFE ASSURANCE(Printed in Blue)
g Main Heading: TO ADVERTISERS…July, 55,000!!! Top Left: HOWQUA'S MIXTURE OF FORTY RARE BLACK
h Main Heading: TO ADVERTISERS…July, 55,000!!! Top Left: York and London Assurance Company. (Printed in Black)
i Main Heading: TO ADVERTISERS…July, 55,000!!! Top Left: To Flute-Players. (Printed in Blue)
j Main Heading: TO ADVERTISERS…July, 55,000!!! Top Left: The New Equitable Life Assurance Company.
k Main Heading: TO ADVERTISERS…August, 75,000!!! Top Left: A MEDICAL GENTLEMAN…
l Main Heading: TO ADVERTISERS…August, 75,000!!! Top Left: A YOUNG LADY accustomed…(Printed in Blue)
m Main Heading: TO ADVERTISERS…August, 75,000!!! Top Left: To Autograph Collectors. (Printed in Blue)
n Main Heading: TO ADVERTISERS…October, 100,000!!! Top Left: Platow's Patent Automaton Coffee Urn. (Printed in Blue)
o Main Heading: TO ADVERTISERS…October, 100,000!!! Top Left: A YOUNG LADY, whose…
p Main Heading: Details Unknown. Top Left: Independent West Middlesex Assurance Co.
q Main Heading: Details Unknown. Top Left: Rigg Brockbank

MA6 THE EAST ANGLIAN ENVELOPE ADVERTISER
a Top Left: No. 1] Top Right: [June 15th, 1840. (Printed in Blue)
b Top Left: No. 1] Top Right: [June 15th, 1840. Bottom Centre: London: Simpkin... (Printed in Black)
c Top Left: No. 1] Top Right: [June 15th, 1840. Bottom Centre: London: Simpkin… Bottom: Prices, 11d & 9d(Printed in Black)
d Top Left: No. 2] Top Right: [July 1st, 1840. (Printed in Black)
e Top Left: NO NUMBER Top Right: NO DATE Further Details Unknown(Printed in Black)
f Contains 12 advertisements for his own books and three other advertisements. Further Details Unknown.

MA7 EDINBURGH ENVELOPE ADVERTISER
a Main Heading: No. I, {AUGUST 12. 1840}…P. 1 Top Left: ABERDEEN ASSURANCE COMPANY…
b Main Heading: No. I, {AUGUST 12. 1840}…P. 2 Top Left: TO AUTHORS, PUBLISHERS,
c Main Heading: No. I, {AUGUST 12, 1840}…P. 3 Top Left: NEW VOLUME.
d Main Heading: No. I, {AUGUST 12. 1840}…P. 4 Top Left: ALBERT DRAB HATS.
e Main Heading: No. I, {AUGUST 12. 1840}…P. 5 Top Left: ???
f Main Heading: No. I, {AUGUST 12. 1840}…P. 6 Top Left: ???
g Main Heading: No. II, {SEPTEMBER 9. 1840.}...P. 1 Top Left: ???
h Main Heading: No. II, {SEPTEMBER 9. 1840.}...P. 2 Top Left: NATIONAL LOAN FUND
i Main Heading: No. II, {SEPTEMBER 9. 1840.}...P. 3 Top Left: Walter Simson,
j Main Heading: No. II, {SEPTEMBER 9. 1840.}...P. 4 Top Left: Just Published, in one…
k Main Heading: No. II, {SEPTEMBER 9. 1840.}...P. 5 Top Left: CHAMBERS'S EDUCATIONAL
l Main Heading: No. II, {SEPTEMBER 9. 1840.}...P. 6 Top Left: NEW VOLUME.
m Main Heading: No. III, {OCTOBER 7. 1840.}…P. 1 Top Left: TO AUTHORS, PUBLISHERS
n Main Heading: No. III, {OCTOBER 7. 1840.}…P. 2 Top Left: Writing, Arithmetic, and Book-
o Main Heading: No. III, {OCTOBER 7. 1840.}…P. 3 Top Left: NOTE-The LAST QUARTER…
p Main Heading: No. III, {OCTOBER 7. 1840.}…P. 4 Top Left: Just Published, Price ONE PENNY.
q Main Heading: No. III, {OCTOBER 7. 1840.}…P. 5 Top Left: Mathematics.
r Main Heading: No. III, {OCTOBER 7. 1840.}…P. 6 Top Left: ???
s Main Heading: No. IV, {NOVEMBER 4. 1840.}…P. 1. Top Left: Caledonian Insurance Company.
t Main Heading: No. IV, {NOVEMBER 4. 1840.}…P. 2. Top Left: ???
u Main Heading: No. IV, {NOVEMBER 4. 1840.}…P. 3. Top Left: NEW ARRIVALS
v Main Heading: No. IV, {NOVEMBER 4. 1840.}…P. 4. Top Left: ???
w Main Heading: No. IV, {NOVEMBER 4. 1840.}…P. 5. Top Left: ???

x Main Heading: No. IV, {NOVEMBER 4. 1840.}...P. 6. Top Left: NEW ARRIVALS???
y Main Heading: No. V, {DECEMBER 2. 1840.}...P. 1. Top Left: ???
z Main Heading: No. V, {DECEMBER 2. 1840.}...P. 2. Top Left: Caledonian Insurance Company.
za Main Heading: No. V, {DECEMBER 2. 1840.}...P. 3. Top Left: Glasgow Insurance Company,
zb Main Heading: No. V, {DECEMBER 2. 1840.}...P.4. Top Left: ???
zc Main Heading: No. V, {DECEMBER 2. 1840.}...P.5. Top Left: ???
zd Main Heading: No. V, {DECEMBER 2. 1840.}...P. 6. Top Left: "New Association for the Fine Arts"????
ze Main Heading: No. VI, {DECEMBER 30. 1840.}...P. 1. Top Left: Scottish (Widows' Fund) Assurance Society
zf Main Heading: No. VI, {DECEMBER 30. 1840.}...P. 2. Top Left: Edinburgh Life Assurance Company,
zg Main Heading: No. VI, {DECEMBER 30. 1840.}...P. 3. Top Left: ???
zh Main Heading: No. VI, {DECEMBER 30. 1840.}...P. 4. Top Left: ???
zi Main Heading: No. VI, {DECEMBER 30. 1840.}...P. 5. Top Left: ???
zj Main Heading: No. VI, {DECEMBER 30. 1840.}...P. 6. Top Left: "Edinburgh Life Insurance Co."????
zk Main Heading: No. III, {OCTOBER 7. 1840.}...P. 1 MISCUT. At Bottom: No. III, {OCTOBER 7. 1840.}...P. 3 ???
zl Main Heading: No. III, {OCTOBER 7. 1840.}...P. 2 MISCUT. At Bottom: No. III, {OCTOBER 7. 1840.}...P. 4 ???
zm Main Heading: NONE, MISCUT. At Bottom: No. III, {OCTOBER 7. 1840.}...P. 5
zn Main Heading: NONE. MISCUT. At Bottom: No. III, {OCTOBER 7. 1840.}...P. 6 ???
zo Main Heading: NONE. Top Left: Mathematics. ???
zp Main Heading: NONE. Top Left: ???

MA8 ENVELOPE ADVERTISER

8a Main Heading: No. 1, JUNE 30TH, 1840. ENVELOPE ADVERTISER. CIRCULATION 2000. (Printed in Blue)

MA9 ENVELOPE OFFICE

a Top Left: Bill of Exchange Found. Top Middle: Total Number...115,000...
b Top Left: PLATOW'S PATENT AUTOMATON COFFEE URN. Top Middle: Total Number...120,000...
c Top Left: PLATOW'S PATENT AUTOMATON COFFEE URN. Top Middle: Total Number...125,000...(Printed in Blue)
d Top Left: TO LET. Top Middle: Total Number...130,000...(Printed in Blue)
e Top Left: BLAND & Co., TAILORS, Top Middle: Total Number...135,000...

MA10 THE ENVELOPE SELECT ADVERTISER

a Main Heading: No. 1,--MAY 30, 1840. (Printed in Blue)
b Main Heading: No. 2,--JUNE 6, 1840. (Printed in Blue)
c Main Heading: No. 3,--JUNE 10, 1840. (Printed in Blue)
d Main Heading: No. 4,--JUNE 13, 1840.
e Main Heading: No. 5,--JUNE 18, 1840. (Printed in Blue)
f Main Heading: No. 6,--JUNE 24, 1840. (Printed in Blue)

MA11 ERREDGE'S POSTAGE ADVERTISER

a Main Heading: No. 1. BRIGHTON, JUNE, 1840.
b Main Heading: No. 2. BRIGHTON, JUNE AND JULY, 1840.
c Main Heading: No. 3. BRIGHTON, JULY AND AUGUST, 1840.

MA12 WILLIAM GILLING

a Details Unknown. Contains Ad: Harle's Improved Supensory bandages.
b Main Heading: POST OFFICE COVERS... Top Right: GRAVESEND, ... Left Column: "r" of reports low(Printed in Blue)
c Main Heading: POST OFFICE COVERS... Top Right: GRAVESEND, ... Left Column: "r" of reports level(Printed in Blue)
d Main Heading: POST OFFICE COVERS... Top Right: DEDICATED BY PERMISSION...(Printed in Blue)
e Main Heading: GILLING'S POSTAGE CIRCULAR. Top Right: Published by HENRY WASHBOURNE...(Printed in Black)

f Main Heading: GILLING'S POSTAGE CIRCULAR. Top Right: CORNS AND BUNIONS. (Printed in Blue)
g Details Unknown. Bottom Right: Intensity of Feeling.

MA13 GRAY'S ROMSEY & HAMPSHIRE POSTAGE COVER GENERAL ADVERTISER
a Main Heading: No. 1.--JULY, 1840.--Guaranteed…(Printed in Blue)

MA14 HALLETT'S POSTAGE ADVERTISER
a Top Left: No. 1.--JUNE 17, 1840.
b Top Left: No. 2.--JUNE 24, 1840.
c Top Left: No. 3.--JULY 4th, 1840.
d Top Left: No. 4.--JULY 27th, 1840.
e Top Left: No. 5.--AUGUST 3rd, 1840.]
f Top Left: No. 6.--AUGUST 10th, 1840.]

MA15 HENEKEY'S COMMERCIAL ENVELOPE
a Top Left: IMPROVED SWEDISH TURNIPS. Top Right: HENEKEY, HUNT & COMPANY,
b Top Left: IMPROVED SWEDISH TURNIPS. Top Right: George(Added in Manuscript) HENEKEY,(HUNT Stricken by Manuscript) & COMPANY,

MA16 JELL'S GENERAL & COMMERCIAL ENVELOPE
a Top Left: ACTIVE LIFE ASSURANCE, LOAN, ENDOWEMENT Top Middle: CALEDONIAN INSURANCE COMPANY,
b Top Left: CALEDONIAN INSURANCE COMPANY, Top Middle: COLLEGE FOR CIVIL ENGINEERS.
c Top Left: CALEDONIAN INSURANCE COMPANY, Top Middle: Contractors to Her Majesty's…
d Top Left: COLLEGE FOR CIVIL ENGINEERS. Top Middle: CALEDONIAN INSURANCE COMPANY,
e Top Left: COLLEGE FOR CIVIL ENGINEERS. Top Middle: Contractors to Her Majesty's Hon. Board of
f Top Left: COLLEGE FOR CIVIL ENGINEERS. Top Middle: University Life Assurance Society,
g Top Left: INDEPENDENT WEST MIDDLESEX ASSURANCE COMPANY, Top Middle: COLLEGE FOR CIVIL ENGINEERS.
h Top Left: London Cemetary Company, Centre Left: IRON FENCES, HURDLES… Bottom Left: FOR CHAPPED HANDS.
i Top Left: London Cemetary Company, Centre Left: IRON FENCES, HURDLES… Bottom Left: Established Forty Years.
j Top Left: London Cemetary Company, Centre Left: THE POMPEIAN HAIR DYE. Bottom Left: Established Forty Years.
k Top Left: MERCANTILE PRESS, Top Middle: CALEDONIAN INSURANCE ... Top Right: VICTORIA LIFE ASSURANCE & LOAN COMPANY
l Top Left: ROYAL HUMANE SOCIETY, Top Middle: Contractors to Her Majesty's Hon. Board of... Bottom Left: O'KELLY'S HAIR DYE.
m Top Left: ROYAL HUMANE SOCIETY, Top Middle: Contractors to Her Majesty's Hon. Board of... Bottom Left: THE POMPEIAN HAIR DYE.
n Top Left: ROYAL HUMANE SOCIETY, Top Middle: The hot baths at the Receiving House…
o Top Left: To Noblemen and Sportsmen… Top Middle: VICTORIA LIFE ASSURANCE & LOAN COMPANY. Top Right: CALEDONIAN …
p Top Left: To Noblemen and Sportsmen... Bottom Left: TO FAMILIES Bottom Right: THAMES TUNNEL OPEN…
q Top Left: To Noblemen and Sportsmen... Bottom Left: TO FAMILIES Bottom Right: Post Office Envelopes…
r Top Left: To Noblemen and Sportsmen... Bottom Left: FOR BEAUTIFYING THE HAIR. Bottom Right: WHITE'S ROYAL ESSENCE …
s Top Left: University Life Assurance Society, Bottom Middle: MERCANTILE PRESS,(Printed in Black)
t Top Left: University Life Assurance Society, Bottom Middle: Thos. Harris & Son's
u Top Left: VICTORIA LIFE ASSURANCE & LOAN COMPANY. Top Middle: CALEDONIAN INSURANCE COMPANY,
v Top Left: VICTORIA LIFE ASSURANCE & LOAN COMPANY. Top Middle: COLLEGE FOR CIVIL ENGINEERS.

w Top Left: VICTORIA LIFE ASSURANCE & LOAN COMPANY. Top Middle: INDEPENDENT WEST MIDDLESEX …

MA17 JELL'S PERIODICAL & ANNUAL ADVERTISER
- a Top Left: To Noblemen and Sportsmen… Top Middle: NEW-ZEALAND COMPANY. Top Right: CALEDONIAN …
- b Top Left: To Noblemen and Sportsmen... Top Middle: VICTORIA LIFE ASSURANCE & LOAN COMPANY. Top Right: ???

MA18 THE LYMINGTON ENVELOPE ADVERTISER
- 18a Top Left: Reduction of Postage. Top Middle: Just Published. Top Right: Music Warehouse. (Printed in Blue)

MA19 F. MAY, (Bottom Right)
- a Top Left: COX, WHITE, AND HARE, Top Left: PRELIMINARY LESSONS,

MA20 THE NEW ENVELOPE SELECT ADVERTISER
- a Top Left: No. 1.--JUNE 27, 1840.
- b Top Left: No. 2.--JULY 4, 1840.
- c Top Left: No. 3.--JULY 11, 1840.
- d Top Left: No. 4.--JULY 18, 1840.
- e Top Left: No. 5.--JULY 25, 1840.
- f Top Left: No. 6.--AUG. 1, 1840.

MA21 PURCELL & SON'S POSTAGE ADVERTISER.
- a Top Left: THE LOVERS OF SUPERIOR COFFEE
- b Top Left: W. J. TOMKINS,

MA22 ORGER AND MERYON (At Bottom)
- a Top Middle: SOUTHAMPTON, HAMPSHIRE.

MA23 RICHARDS & FOX
- a Top Left: Retailed by more than 2,000 Agents

MA24 HENRY SHALDERS
- a Top Left: HENRY SHALDERS, Top Middle: ROBERT MILLER,(Printed in Black)
- b Top Left: HENRY SHALDERS, Top Middle: CROWN AND ANCHOR(Printed in Green)

MA25 SLOPER'S COMMERCIAL POSTAGE ADVERTISER
- a Main Heading: PUBLISHED EVERY MONDAY… Top Left: SLOPER'S SUPERFINE BATH POST 3d.
- b Main Heading: DECEMBER, 1840. PUBLISHED MONTHLY,… Top Left: SLOPER'S POST-OFFICE COVERS,
- c Main Heading: JANUARY, 1841. PUBLISHED MONTHLY,… Top Left: SLOPER'S POST-OFFICE COVERS,
- d Main Heading: FEBRUARY, 1841. PUBLISHED MONTHLY,… Top Left: SLOPER'S
- e Main Heading: No. 4 March, 1841. Top Left: THE MARINER'S CHURCH TEM- Top Right: THE JEWEL; …
- f Main Heading: No. 4 March, 1841. Top Left: THE MARINER'S CHURCH TEM- Top Right: SLOPER'S SUPERFINE BATH
- g Main Heading: No. 5 May, 1841. Top Left: The Complete Guide to the Fine Arts

MA26 SMITH'S ENVELOPE ADVERTISER (Printed in Blue)
- a Top Left: No. I. Top Right: 27th JUNE 1840.
- b Top Left: No II. Top Right: PAGE 1.
- c Top Left: No. II. Top Right: PAGE 2.
- d Top Left: No. III. Top Right: PAGE 1.
- e Top Left: No. III. Top Right: PAGE 2.
- f Top Left: No. III. Top Right: PAGE 3.

MA27 THE SOUTHAMPTON COMMERCIAL ADVERTISER
- a Top: BY SPECIAL APPOINTMENT

MA28 THE SOUTHAMPTON POSTAGE ADVERTISER
- a Top Left: Palk's Eximory Powder, Top Right: HAMPSHIRE PLATE AND LOOKING-GLASS WAREHOUSE,

MA29 TIREBUCK or J. & I. TIREBUCK (At Bottom)
- a Top Left: DRING & FAGE'S IMPROVED SIKES'S HYDROMETER.
- b Top Left: GEO. FOSTER, Top Right: GREEN & CONSTABLE.
- c Top Left: POST OFFICE COVERS Top Right: This useful contrivance...
- d Top Left: The Contriver of this Plan... Top Right: THE ROCHESTER SAUCE
- e Top Left: The Contriver of this Plan... Top Right: W. Gilling, Bookseller...
- f Top Left: The Metropolitan Benefit Societies'... Top Right: W. Gilling, Bookseller...
- g Top Left: TYERS AND COMPYS Top Right: This useful contrivance...
- h Main Heading: HYDROSTATIC OR FLOATING BED, At Bottom: J. & I. TIREBUCK, ...
- i Top Left: L. H. Baigh, ... silver plated goods ... Top Right: This useful contrivance...
- j Top Left: To Public Companies and Societies... Top Right: Details Unknown.

MA30 WATERSTON'S ENVELOPE ADVERTISER (Printed in Blue)
- a Top Left: No. 1. Top Right: JULY 29, 1840. (1d Letter Sheet)
- b Top Left: No. 1. Top Right: JULY 29, 1840. (2d Letter Sheet)

MA31 WEBB'S POSTAGE ADVERTISER
- a Main Heading: No. 1. August 29th, 1840.
- b Main Heading: No. 2. September 25, 1840.

MA32 WEST OF ENGLAND MONTHLY POSTAGE ADVERTISER
- a Top Left: No. 1. MONDAY, AUGUST, 17, 1840.
- b Top Left: No. 2. THURSDAY, OCTOBER 1, 1840.
- c Top Left: No. 3. NOV. 1, 1840.

MA33 UNNAMED
- a Top Left: THE AUSTRALIAN COLONIAL and Top Middle: HODGSON'S EAST INDIA PALE ALE.--

Insurance Companies

MA101 ABERDEEN MARINE INSURANCE COMPANY
- a Main Heading: ABERDEEN MARINE INSURANCE COMPANY. Bottom Left: 59 Marshall Street, Aberdeen 1st September 1840.

MA102 ARGUS LIFE ASSURANCE COMPANY
- a Without an Agent's Information at the Bottom.
- b With Agent's Name at Bottom: Ardrossan: Ardrossan D. S. Mack Agent(Manuscript)
- c With Agent's Name at Bottom: Cupar: Robt Taylor Agent Cupar(Manuscript)
- d With Agent's Name at Bottom: Dundee: Agents, DUNDEE--Messrs C. and J. KERR...

MA103 ATLAS ASSURANCE COMPANY
- a Bottom Left: 92, Cheapside, 21st Dec. 1839. Claims paid table has 9 lines.
- b Bottom Left: 92, Cheapside, 10th Oct. 1840. Claims paid table has 9 lines.
- c Bottom Left: 92, Cheapside, 10th Oct. 1840. Claims paid table has 11 lines.
- d Bottom Left: 92, Cheapside, 10th May 1841. Claims paid table has 11 lines.
- e Bottom Left: 92, Cheapside, 10th Oct. 1841. Claims paid table has 11 lines.
- f Bottom Left: 92, Cheapside, 11th Feb. 1842. Claims paid table has 11 lines.
- g Bottom Left: 92, Cheapside, 7th April, 1842. Claims paid table has 11 lines.
- h Bottom Left: 92, Cheapside, June, 1842. Claims paid table has 11 lines.
- i Bottom Left: 92, Cheapside, Nov. 1842. Claims paid table has 11 lines.
- j Bottom Left: 92, Cheapside, Aug. 1843. Claims paid table has 11 lines.

MA104 BRITISH AND COLONIAL TRUST AND ASSURANCE COMPANY
- a Bottom Right: TABLE OF PREMIUMS. (Printed in Blue)

MA105 CALEDONIAN INSURANCE COMPANY
- a Bottom Middle: Extracts from the Life Tables.

MA106 CLERICAL, MEDICAL, AND GENERAL LIFE ASSURANCE SOCIETY (No Directors At Top)
- a REPORT OF THE DIRECTORS with 4 financial points.
- b REPORT OF THE DIRECTORS with 4 financial points. Bottom Middle: Your perusal... J. S. PIDGEON, Agent, 17, FRIAR STREET, READING.
- c REPORT OF THE DIRECTORS with 4 financial points. Bottom Middle: Office, 78, Great Russell Street, Bloomsbury, London.

MA107 CLERICAL, MEDICAL, AND GENERAL LIFE ASSURANCE SOCIETY (No Directors At Top)
- a REPORT OF THE DIRECTORS with 3 financial points. Bottom Middle: Be pleased to read... Bottom Right: .... Agent, ...

MA108 CLERICAL, MEDICAL, AND GENERAL LIFE ASSURANCE SOCIETY (Directors At Top)
- a REPORT ... with 3 financial points. Bottom Right: GEO. H. PINCKARD, Secretary, 78, Great Russell Street, Bloomsbury, London.
- b REPORT ... with 3 financial points. Bottom Right: ALEXANDER CAVELL, SOLICITOR, Agent, SAXMUNDHAM.
- c REPORT ... with 3 financial points. Bottom Right: James Champion, Agent, Nettlebed.
- d REPORT ... with 3 financial points. Bottom Right: ANNE DEIGHTON, BOOKSELLER, WORCESTER.
- e REPORT ... with 3 financial points. Bottom Right: DOCTOR JOHN EXLEY, Agent, NEW MALTON.
- f REPORT ... with 3 financial points. Bottom Right: ELIAS FORD, Agent, NEWTON ABBOTT.
- g REPORT ... with 3 financial points. Bottom Right: WILLIAM GAISFORD, SOLICITOR, Agent, BERKLEY.
- h REPORT ... with 3 financial points. Bottom Right: HENRY HERBERT, BOOKSELLER, Agent, WIMBOURNE.
- i REPORT ... with 3 financial points. Bottom Right: HENRY HERBERT... WIMBOURNE. (Wimbourne Changed to Ringwood)(Manuscript)
- j REPORT ... with 3 financial points. Bottom Right: JOHN KNAPP, Agent, BRADFORD.
- k REPORT ... with 3 financial points. Bottom Right: CHARLES LAWRENCE, SOLICITOR, Agent, CIRENCESTER.
- l REPORT ... with 3 financial points. Bottom Right: JAMES WILLIAM MACKLIN, Agent, BANK, SHAFTESBURY.
- m REPORT ... with 3 financial points. Bottom Right: J. S. PIDGEON, Agent, 17, FRIAR STREET, READING.
- n REPORT ... with 3 financial points. Bottom Right: WILLIAM RIDLER, Agent, BANK, CHELTENHAM.
- o REPORT ... with 3 financial points. Bottom Right: HENRY THOMPSON, SOLICITOR, Agent, GRANTHAM.
- p REPORT ... with 3 financial points. Bottom Right: T. F. WATLING, SURGEON, Agent, LEOMINSTER.
- q REPORT ... with 3 financial points. Bottom Right: Mr. EALES WHITE, (Family Brewery and Malt House), Agent for TAUNTON.
- r REPORT ... with 3 financial points. Bottom Right: R. T. WYATT, CHEMIST, Agent, TORQUAY.
- s REPORT ... with 3 financial points. Bottom Right: H. S. Young, Agent, Bank, Bury St. Edmunds

MA109 CLERICAL, MEDICAL, AND GENERAL LIFE ASSURANCE SOCIETY (Directors At Top)
- a At Top: PRESENTED TO THE ANNUAL... Bottom Right: William Adams, Agent for Tenbury.
- b At Top: PRESENTED TO THE ANNUAL... Bottom Right: WILLIAM BAKER, CHEMIST, Agent, CHELMSFORD.
- c At Top: PRESENTED TO THE ANNUAL... Bottom Right: Charles F. Bonner, Solicitor, Spaulding.
- d At Top: PRESENTED TO THE ANNUAL... Bottom Right: William Braund, Agent, Bank, Hitchin.
- e At Top: PRESENTED TO THE ANNUAL... Bottom Right: Mr. S. B. CHAPMAN, Agent, CORN HILL, IPSWICH.
- f At Top: PRESENTED TO THE ANNUAL... Bottom Right: William Cranston, Solicitor, Agent, Belfast.
- g At Top: PRESENTED TO THE ANNUAL... Bottom Right: JOSEPH CRANSTONE, Agent, HEMEL HEMPSTEAD.
- h At Top: PRESENTED TO THE ANNUAL... Bottom Right: WILLIAM CRAVEN, SOLICITOR, Agent, HALIFAX.
- i At Top: PRESENTED TO THE ANNUAL... Bottom Right: JOSEPH DOWNIE, Agent, BANK, ABERYSTWITH.
- j At Top: PRESENTED TO THE ANNUAL... Bottom Right: E. G. EDGELL, Agent, BANK, TEWKESBURY.

k At Top: PRESENTED TO THE ANNUAL... Bottom Right: Liddle Elliot, Agent, Newcastle-under-Lyme.
l At Top: PRESENTED TO THE ANNUAL... Bottom Right: WILLIAM HORD, Agent, GAINSBOROUGH.
m At Top: PRESENTED TO THE ANNUAL... Bottom Right: REES HOWELLS, Agent, BANK, HAY.
n At Top: PRESENTED TO THE ANNUAL... Bottom Right: DANIEL JACKSON, Agent, ROMSEY.
o At Top: PRESENTED TO THE ANNUAL... Bottom Right: ??? KING, The Bank, WIGAN.
p At Top: PRESENTED TO THE ANNUAL... Bottom Right: J. MEARS, SOLICITOR, BAGSHOT.
q At Top: PRESENTED TO THE ANNUAL... Bottom Right: JOHN POOLE, Agent, SHREWSBURY.
r At Top: PRESENTED TO THE ANNUAL... Bottom Right: JAMES B. POW, NEWCASTLE CHARE, ... Agent for NEWCASTLE and Vicinity.
s At Top: PRESENTED TO THE ANNUAL... Bottom Right: JAMES B. POW, REWCASTLE CHARE, ... Vicinity. (REWCASTLE Error)
t At Top: PRESENTED TO THE ANNUAL... Bottom Right: William Rees, Agent, Bank, Wigan
u At Top: PRESENTED TO THE ANNUAL... Bottom Right: R. N. Sankey, Postmaster, Agent, Ludlow
v At Top: PRESENTED TO THE ANNUAL... Bottom Right: Sperling & Arden, Agents for Halstead and Clare.
w At Top: PRESENTED TO THE ANNUAL... Bottom Right: A. T. STEAVENSON, SOLICITOR, Agent, DARLINGTON.

MA110 THE CROWN LIFE ASSURANCE COMPANY
a Bottom Middle: TABLE I.--Shewing...
b Bottom Middle: J. Fiddaman, Agent, Newark, Notts.
c Bottom Middle: Mr. WALTER HALL, Agent, KINGTON.
d Bottom Middle: Agent for Wells, Norfolk, Mr. Young, Surgeon.
e Centre: A Table with two parts: BONUSES GIVEN BY THE CROWN LIFE ASSURANCE COMPANY,...IN 1832. IN 1839.

MA111 THE ECONOMIC LIFE ASSURANCE SOCIETY (Middle Left: 9thly)
a Top Right: Directors Are: EDGAR, GORDON, MENDHAM, MEUX, & ROUTH
b Top Right: Directors Are: EDGAR, GORDON, ... Middle: AGENT AT NORWICH.--HORATIO BOLINGBROKE, ESQ.
c Top Right: Directors Are: EDGAR, GORDON, ... Middle: AGENT AT IPSWICH.--MR. CHARLES SILBURN.
d Top Right: Directors Are: EDGAR, GORDON, ... Middle: AGENT AT EXETER.--UNKNOWN

MA112 THE ECONOMIC LIFE ASSURANCE SOCIETY (Middle Left: 9thly)
a Top Right: Directors Are: EDGAR, GORDON, MENDHAM, & ROUTH
b Top Right: Directors Are: EDGAR, GORDON, ... Middle: AGENT AT NORWICH.--HORATIO BOLINGBROKE, ESQ.

MA113 THE ECONOMIC LIFE ASSURANCE SOCIETY (Middle Left: 9thly)
a Top Right: Directors Are: EDGAR, GORDON, HASTIE, MENDHAM, & ROUTH
b Top Right: Directors Are: EDGAR, GORDON, ... Middle: AGENT AT NORWICH.--HORATIO BOLINGBROKE, ESQ.
c Top Right: Directors Are: EDGAR, GORDON, ... Middle: AGENT AT CARLISLE.--Mr. JOSEPH ROME.

MA114 THE ECONOMIC LIFE ASSURANCE SOCIETY (Middle Left: 10thly)
a Top Right: Directors Are: EDGAR, GORDON, HASTIE, MENDHAM, & ROUTH Middle: PHYSICIAN, SURGEON, SOLICITOR...

MA115 THE ECONOMIC LIFE ASSURANCE SOCIETY (Middle Left: 10thly)
a Top Right: Directors Are: EDGAR, GORDON, HASTIE, MENDHAM, & ROUTH Middle Left: SOLICITOR, ACTUARY
b Top Right: Directors Are: EDGAR, GORDON, ... Middle: AGENT AT NORWICH.--HORATIO BOLINGBROKE, ESQ.

c Top Right: Directors Are: EDGAR, GORDON, ... Middle: AGENT AT CARLISLE.--Mr. JOSEPH ROME.

MA116 EDINBURGH LIFE ASSURANCE COMPANY
a Lower Left: HEAD OFFICE, 24, GEORGE STREET, July, 1840.
b Lower Left: HEAD OFFICE, 24, GEORGE STREET, July, 1840. At Bottom: Agent at York Henry Brearey(Manuscript)
c Lower Left: HEAD OFFICE, 24, GEORGE STREET, July, 1840. At Bottom: James Rose, Solicitor, writer, agent in Banff(Manuscript)
d Lower Left: HEAD OFFICE, 24, GEORGE STREET, July, 1840. At Bottom: Tyndall & Son, Solicitors, Agents for Birmingham.
e Lower Left: HEAD OFFICE, 24, GEORGE STREET, March, 1841.
f Lower Left: HEAD OFFICE, 24, GEORGE STREET, March, 1841. At Bottom: AGENTS AT PERTH. MESSRS DUNCAN & M'LEAN, Writers.
g Lower Left: HEAD OFFICE, 24, GEORGE STREET, March, 1841. At Bottom: AGENT AT STRANRAER. MR ALEX. M'NEEL, Banker.
h Lower Left: HEAD OFFICE, 24, GEORGE STREET, March, 1841. At Bottom: AGENT AT STONEHAVEN. MR WILLIAM STEWART, Banker.

MA117 ENGLISH AND SCOTTISH LAW FIRE AND LIFE ASSURANCE
a Top Right: Established 11th October, 1839. Top Right: SANDERS, SHIPPARD... Bottom Left: CROUCH Printer...(Printed in Black)
b Top Right: Established 11th October, 1839. Top Right: McMAHON, RICHARDSON... Bottom Left: J. Wertheimer & Co., Printers....(Printed in Blue)
c Top Right: Established 11th October, 1839. Top Right: McMAHON, PIGOT... Bottom Left: J. Wertheimer & Co., Printers...
d Top Right: Established 11th October, 1839. Top Right: MURRAY, PIGOT... Bottom Left: J. Wertheimer & Co., Printers...
e Top Right: Established ...., 1839. Top Right: MURRAY, ... Bottom Left: J. Wertheimer Bottom: Agent. Wm.Geo. Horder.. (Manuscript)

MA118 ENGLISH AND SCOTTISH LAW FIRE AND LIFE ASSURANCE
a Top Right Directors: MURRAY, PIGOT... Middle Left: Life Department.--The advantages...
b Top Right Directors: MURRAY, PIGOT... Middle Left: Life Department.--Assurances may be...

MA119 ENGLISH AND SCOTTISH LAW FIRE AND LIFE ASSURANCE
a Top Right Directors: MURRAY, PIGOT... Middle Left: IMMEDIATE ANNUITIES "NRAR" for "NEAR" bottom left

MA120 ENGLISH AND SCOTTISH LAW FIRE AND LIFE ASSURANCE
a Top Middle: CAPITAL, ONE MILLION. Top Right Directors: SANDERS, SHIPPARD, STONE, WAY, & WHITMORE
b Top Middle: CAPITAL, ONE MILLION. Top Right Directors: SANDERS, SHIPPARD, STONE, WATERMAN, & WAY

MA121 ENGLISH AND SCOTTISH LAW FIRE AND LIFE ASSURANCE (Printed in Blue)
a Top Middle: SUBSCRIBED CAPITAL, ONE MILLION. Top Right Directors: SANDERS, SHIPPARD, STONE, WATERMAN, & WAY

MA122 EQUITABLE ASSURANCE
a Printed Address: Arthur Morgan, Esq. Equitable Assurance Office, New Bridge St, London.

MA123 FAMILY ENDOWMENT AND LIFE ASSURANCE AND ANNUITY SOCIETY (Printed in Blue)
a Top Left: FAMILY ENDOWMENT... Top Right: Age of the Wife...(A Table)
b Top Left: FAMILY ENDOWMENT... Top Right: Endowments may be...

MA124 FAMILY ENDOWMENT, ANNUITY, LIFE ASSURANCE, & REVERSION INTEREST SOCIETY (Printed in Blue)
a Top Middle: CAPITAL, L500,000.

MA125 GENERAL LIFE ASSURANCE COMPANY
a Details Unknown.

MA126 IMPERIAL FIRE INSURANCE COMPANY

a Main Heading: IMPERIAL FIRE INSURANCE COMPANY, Bottom Centre: AGENT FOR CHELTENHAM … MR. W. LEE, STOCK …

MA127 THE LONDON, EDINBURGH, AND DUBLIN LIFE ASSURANCE COMPANY

a Crest at Top. Top Middle: No. 3, Charlotte Row, Mansion House; Western Branch,... (1d Letter Sheet)
b Crest at Top. Top Middle: No. 3, Charlotte Row, Mansion House; Western Branch,… Mr. Wm. Scott Manager(Manuscript)(1d Letter Sheet)
c Crest at Top. Top Middle: No. 3, Charlotte Row, Mansion House, London. (1d Letter Sheet)
d Crest at Top. Top Middle: No. 3, ..., Mansion … Bottom Right: Agent for Worcester-Mr. Hyld, Holden…(Manuscript)(1d Letter Sheet)
e Crest at Top. Top Middle: No. 3, Charlotte Row, Mansion House, London. (2d Letter Sheet)
f Crown at Top. Top Middle: No. 3, Charlotte-Row, Mansion-House, London. (1d Letter Sheet)
g Crown at Top. Top Middle: No. 3, Charlotte-Row, Mansion-House, London. Bottom Right: Agent for Bristol G. F. FOX ???r. (1d Letter Sheet)
h Main Heading: ASSURANCES.--ANNUITIES.--ENDOWMENTS FOR CHILDREN.--... (1d Letter Sheet)
i Main Heading: ASSURANCES.--ANNUITIES.--ENDOWMENTS … Bottom Middle: Agent for Brighton,--Wm. KENNETT... (1d Letter Sheet)
j Top Left: ASSURANCES. (Vertical Dividing Line) Top Right: ANNUITIES. (1d Letter Sheet)
k Top Left: ASSURANCES. (Vertical …) Top Right: ANNUITIES. Bottom Right: Medical Advisor for Bath,…WINE ... (1d Letter Sheet)

MA128 LONDON AND WESTMINSTER MUTUAL LIFE ASSURANCE SOCIETY

a Main Heading: No. 448, WEST STRAND. At Bottom: Two Premium Tables(Printed in Blue)
b Main Heading: No. 448, WEST STRAND. At Bottom: Two Premium Tables(Printed in Red)

MA129 NATIONAL LOAN FUND SOCIETY

a Middle in Three Columns: Seven Directors Named. Bottom Left: SOCIETY'S OFFICE… Bottom Right: …GEORGE PYE.
b Middle in Three Columns: Each Column Stricken With an X. Bottom Left: Address Stricken. Bottom Right: Name Stricken. (Manuscript)

MA130 NORTH BRITISH FIRE AND LIFE INSURANCE COMPANY

a Details Unknown. John Wilson. Agent for the North British Fire and Life Insurance Company of Edinburgh

MA131 THE SCOTTISH PROVIDENT INSTITUTION FOR ASSURANCES AND ANNUITIES ON LIVES

a Bottom Right: …Manager.
b Bottom Right: …Manager. Bottom Centre: OR TO J. M. KINNELL, AGENT FOR DUMFRIES

MA132 THE SCOTTISH PROVIDENT INSTITUTION FOR ASSURANCES AND ANNUITIES ON LIVES

a Bottom Right: …Manager or Agents.
b Bottom Right: …Manager or Agents. (Printed in Blue)
c Bottom Right: …Manager or Agents. Bottom: Agents,--ABERDEEN…TAIN(Printed in Blue)
d Details Unknown. Bottom Right: …Manager or Agents. Bottom Centre: Aberdeen, Keith, Inverness, Elgin
e Bottom Right: …Manager or Agents. Bottom Centre: Agent for DALKEITH…DUNSE…
f Bottom Right: …Manager or Agents. Bottom Centre: Agent for DUMFRIES…EARLSTON…
g Details Unknown. Bottom Right: …Manager or Agents. Bottom Centre: Andrew Weir, agent and John Crooks, Surgeon(Kilmarnock)
h Bottom Right: …Manager or Agents. Bottom Centre: Agent for KILMARNOCK--ANDREW WEIR, Academy…
i Details Unknown. Bottom Right: …Manager or Agents. Bottom Centre: Agent for Liverpool, Manchester, Newcastle…

j Bottom Right: ...Manager or Agents. Left Margin: + Agent in London--Andrew Turnbull...(Manuscript)
k Bottom Right: ...Manager or Agents. Bottom Centre: Agent for Manchester and Vicinity--...(Printed in Blue)
l Bottom Right: ...Manager or Agents. Bottom Centre: Agents,--NEWCASTLE--...
m Bottom Right: ...Manager or Agents. Bottom Centre: Agent for PAISLEY--...
n Bottom Right: ...Manager or Agents. Bottom Centre: Agent for PERTH--...
o Bottom Right: ...Manager or Agents. The A of Agents is upright versus slanted right.

MA133 THE SCOTTISH PROVIDENT INSTITUTION FOR ASSURANCES AND ANNUITIES ON LIVES (Printed in Blue)
a Top Right: Glasgow, NO. 33 BUCHANAN STREET,... Bottom Left: EDINBURGH, December 1840.
b Top Right: Glasgow, NO. 33 BUCHANAN STREET,... Bottom Left: EDINBURGH, December 1840. Bottom: DUNDEE ... ABERDEEN ...

MA134 THE SCOTTISH PROVIDENT INSTITUTION FOR ASSURANCES AND ANNUITIES ON LIVES
a Top Right: Glasgow, NO. 141 BUCHANAN STREET,... Bottom Left: EDINBURGH, February 1841.
b Top Right: Glasgow, NO. 141 BUCHANAN STREET,... Bottom Left: EDINBURGH, February 1841. Bottom Centre: AGENT for DALKEITH.--...
c Top Right: Glasgow, NO. 141 BUCHANAN STREET,... Bottom Left: EDINBURGH, March 1841.
d Top Right: Glasgow, NO. 141 BUCHANAN STREET,... Bottom Left: EDINBURGH, March 1841. Bottom: LIVERPOOL ...MANCHESTER ...
e Details Unknown.
f Top Right: Glasgow, NO. 141 BUCHANAN STREET,... Bottom Left: EDINBURGH, Nov. 1841.
g Top Right: Glasgow, NO. 141 BUCHANAN STREET,... Bottom Left: EDINBURGH, Nov. 1841. Bottom: DUNDEE ... ABERDEEN ...

MA135 THE SCOTTISH PROVIDENT INSTITUTION FOR ASSURANCES AND ANNUITIES ON LIVES
a Bottom Left: [MESSRS. BOLSTER, PRINTERS, CORK.] Bottom Right: Office 96 South Mall. (Manuscript)(1d Envelope)

MA136 SCOTTISH UNION FIRE AND LIFE INSURANCE COMPANY
a Top Left: Chief London Office--No. 449, WEST STRAND. Bottom Right: F. G. SMITH, Secretary to the London Board.

MA137 UNITED KINGDOM LIFE ASSURANCE (Printed in Blue)
a Middle Left: On the 1st of July, THE BOARD...March 1834: Bottom Centre: Agents, EDINBURGH ... AMSTERDAM ...
b Middle Left: On the 1st of July, 1841, THE BOARD...March 1834: Bottom Centre: Agents, AMSTERDAM ... ROTTERDAM ...
c Middle Left: On the 1st of July, 1841, THE BOARD...March 1834: Bottom Centre: Agents, AMSTERDAM ... ST. JOHN'S, NEW BRUNSWICK ...
d Middle Left: On the 1st of July, 1841, THE BOARD...policy for L1000. Bottom Centre: Agents, AMSTERDAM ... ROTTERDAM ...

MA138 UNITED MERCANTILE AND TRAVELLERS' ASSOCIATION AND GENERAL MUTUAL LIFE ASSURANCE & ANNUITY SOCIETY
a Top Centre: TRUSTEES. Bottom Right: JAMES DRANSFIELD, ...

MA139 UNIVERSAL LIFE ASSURANCE SOCIETY (Printed in Blue)
a Details Unknown.

MA140 YORKSHIRE FIRE AND LIFE INSURANCE COMPANY
a Top Centre: CAPITAL L500,000. Bottom Right: Applications to be made to Mr. W. L. NEWMAN, ...

MA141 UNKNOWN COMPANY
a Bottom Left: JOHN PIM, Agent to Life and Fire Assurances, Annuities, Loans, &c., 12, Castle Court, Budge Row.

Stamp and Tax Offices

MA201 ABERDEEN

a Top Centre: Stamps and Taxes, Aberdeen,...5th April, 1841. Bottom Middle: Note.--Your receipt...Office of... (Manuscript Insertion)
b Top Centre: LAND AND ASSESSED TAXES--COUNTIES OF ABERDEEN AND KINCARDINE...12th May, 1841.
c Top Centre: LAND... Top Right: STAMPS AND TAXES, 2, ADELPHI COURT, ABERDEEN, 15th March, 1842.
d Top Centre: LAND... Top Right: STAMPS AND TAXES, No. 2, ADELPHI COURT, ABERDEEN, 1st May, 1842. Middle: the Sub-Collector at ...

MA202 AYR

a Top Centre: To the Collector of Taxes for Ayrshire...Ayr, 22d April, 1841.
b Top Right: STAMPS AND TAXES, Ayr, 22d May, 1841.
c Top Right: STAMPS AND TAXES, AYR, 15TH MARCH, 1842. Middle: ..., the Sub-Collector at...(Manuscript Insertion)
d Top Right: STAMPS AND TAXES, Ayr, 2d May, 1842.

MA203 BANCHORY

a Top Centre: Stamps and Taxes, Aberdeen,...5th April, 1841. Bottom Middle: Note.--Your receipt...Office of Banchory(Banchory in Manuscript)
b Top Centre: LAND... Top Right: STAMPS AND TAXES, No. 2, ADELPHI COURT, ABERDEEN, 1st May, 1842. Middle: the Sub-Collector at ...

MA204 BANFF

a Top Right: STAMPS AND TAXES, BANFF,...184
b Top Right: STAMPS AND TAXES, BANFF, 1st May, 1842. Middle: the Sub-Collector at...(Manuscript Insertion)

MA205 BATHGATE

a Top Right: Stamp and Tax Office, Bathgate, 7th March, 1842. Bottom Right: JOHN ... WALTER BLACK, Sub-Collector.

MA206 BIGGAR

a Main Heading: PAYABLE AT BIGGAR. Top Right: GLASGOW, 15th March, 1842.
b Details Unknown. Main Heading: PAYABLE AT BIGGAR. Top Right: 66, MILLER STREET, Glasgow, 2d May, 1842.

MA207 BRISTOL

a Top Right: Stamp Office, Bristol,
b Top Right: Stamp Office, Bristol, 184
c Top Right: Bristol Stamp Office,
d Top Right: Bristol Stamp Office, 184

MA208 CAMPBELTOWN

a Top Right: Campbeltown, 15th March, 1842.

MA209 COLDSTREAM

a Top Right: COLDSTREAM, 5th April 1841.

MA210 CUPAR

a Top Centre: COUNTY OF FIFE. Middle: ...the Sub-Collector for the District of ... Bottom Left: Cupar 2d April, 1841. (1d Envelope)
b Details Unknown. Top Centre: COUNTY OF FIFE. Middle: ...Sub-Collector ... District of ... Bottom Left: Cupar 10 May, 1841. (1d Envelope)
c Top Centre: Stamps and Taxes Cupar 15th March 1842.
d Top Centre: Stamps and Taxes Cupar, 2d May, 1842.

MA211 DUMBARTON

a Main Heading: PAYABLE AT DUMBARTON. Top Right: GLASGOW, 15th March, 1842.
b Main Heading: PAYABLE AT DUMBARTON. Top Right: 66, MILLER STREET, Glasgow, 2d May, 1842.

MA212 DUMFRIES

- a Top Right: STAMP AND TAX OFFICE, DUMFRIES, 25th March, 1841. ..., with the least possible delay. (Manuscript Insertion)
- b Top Right: STAMP AND TAX OFFICE, DUMFRIES, 25th March, 1841. Dumfries, with the least possible delay. (Dumfries in Manuscript)
- c Top Right: STAMP OFFICE, DUMFRIES, 15th March, 1842.

MA213 DUNBLANE

- a Top Right: COUNTY CESS OFFICE, PERTH, 15th March, 1841. Middle: Receipts are...Office in Dunblane.

MA214 DUNDEE

- a Top Centre: LAND AND ASSESSED TAXES, 1840-41. Bottom Left: Stamp and tax Office, Dundee, 11th May, 1841.
- b Top Right: Stamp and Tax Office, Castle Street, Dundee, 15th March, 1842.

MA215 DUNFERMLINE

- a Top Centre: COUNTY OF FIFE. Middle: ...the Sub-Collector ... Dunfermline(Manuscript) Bottom Left: Cupar 2d April, 1841. (1d Envelope)

MA216 DUNSE

- a Top Right: STAMP OFFICE, Dunse 12 August 1841. (Dunse and Date in Manuscript)
- b Top Right: STAMP OFFICE, DUNSE, 15th March, 1842.

MA217 EARLSTOWN

- a Top Right: STAMP OFFICE, Earlstown 10th August 1841. (Earlstown and Date in Manuscript)

MA218 EDINBURGH

- a Top Right: COUNTY AND CITY CESS OFFICE, 60, NORTH BRIDGE, EDINBURGH. Letter Text Begins: SIR, With reference...
- b Top Right: COUNTY AND CITY CESS OFFICE, 60. NORTH BRIDGE, NEW BUILDINGS, Edinburgh, ... 1841. (Day and Month Manuscript)
- c Top Right: COUNTY AND CITY CESS OFFICE, 60 NORTH BRIDGE, EDINBURGH, ... 1842. (Day and Month Manuscript)
- d Top Right: COUNTY AND CITY CESS OFFICE, 60 NORTH BRIDGE, EDINBURGH, .. April 1842. (Day Manuscript)
- e Top Right: COUNTY AND CITY CESS OFFICE, 60 NORTH BRIDGE, EDINBURGH, .. May 1842. (Day Manuscript)
- f Top Right: COUNTY AND CITY CESS OFFICE, [60 NORTH BRIDGE, EDINBURGH, Letter Text Begins: SIR, I regret...

MA219 ELGIN

- a Details Unknown. 15th March 1842
- b Details Unknown. 14th July 1843

MA220 EYEMOUTH

- a Top Right: STAMP OFFICE, ... August 1841. (Eyemouth and Date in Manuscript)

MA221 FALKIRK

- a Top Right: Stamp and Tax Office, Falkirk, 8th March, 1842.

MA222 FORFAR

- a STAMP & TAX OFFICE, FORFAR, 15th March, 1842.

MA223 FOULDEN

- a Top Left: Name & Foulden(Manuscript) Top Right: STAMP OFFICE, DUNSE, 15th March, 1842. At Bottom: Name & Foulden(Manuscript)

MA224 GREENOCK

- a Main Heading: LAND AND ASSESSED TAXES, Due ... 25th March, 1841. Middle: ...Greenock. Bottom Left: CESS OFFICE, GLASGOW, ...
- b Main Heading: ARREARS OF TAXES COUNTY OF RENFREW. Middle: of the ... in Greenock, Bottom Left: ..., GLASGOW, 12th MAY, 1841.

c Top Right: STAMP AND TAX OFFICE, GREENOCK, 15th March, 1842. Middle: the Sub-Collector at …(Manuscript Insertion of City name)
d Top Right: STAMP AND TAX OFFICE, GREENOCK, 15th March, 1842. Middle: the Sub-Collector at …(Deleted, indicating Greenock)
e Top Right: STAMP AND TAX OFFICE, GREENOCK, 15th March, 1842. Bottom Right: J. DRUMMOND, Collector.
f Details Unknown. LAND AND ASSESSED TAXES, 2nd May 1842

MA225 HADDINGTON
a Top Right: STAMP AND TAX OFFICE, HADDINGTON, 18th March, 1842.
b Top Right: STAMP AND TAX OFFICE, HADDINGTON, 19th March, 1842.

MA226 HAMILTON
a Main Heading: PAYABLE AT HAMILTON. Top Right: 66, MILLER STREET, Glasgow, 2d May, 1842.

MA227 HAWICK
a Top Right: Stamp and Tax=Office, JEDBURGH, 15th March, 1842. Middle: … appealed ...), …Hawick ... (Tax Collector & Town Manuscript)

MA228 INVERARAY
a Top Right: Stamps and Taxes INVERARAY, .. March 1842. (Manuscript Insertion of Date)
b Details Unknown. (2d Letter Sheet)

MA229 INVERNESS
a Main Heading: LAND TAX, DUE 25TH MARCH, 184.. (Year Manuscript) Centre: Land Tax,…L Stamp,…….. (Amounts Manuscript)
b Main Heading: ARREARS OF TAXES. COUNTY OF INVERNESS Bottom Left: Castle, Inverness, ..May, 1841. (Date Manuscript)
c Bottom Left: Inverness, 15th March, 1842. Bottom Right: A. I. ROBERTSON.
d Main Heading: LAND TAX, DUE 25TH MARCH, 184.. (Year Manuscript Insertion) Centre: Stamp,…….. (Amount Manuscript Insertion)
e Top Right: STAMPS AND TAXES, INVERNESS, 2ND MAY, 1842.
f Details Unknown. ASSESSED TAXES DUE 25TH MARCH 184

MA230 JEDBURGH
a Top Right: JEDBURGH, JUNE 30 1841. (Date Manuscript) Bottom Left: COUNTY RATES, ….L PRISON ASSESSMENT,(Amounts Manuscript)
b Top Right: JEDBURGH, Augt 6th 1841. (Month & Date Manuscript) Bottom Left: COUNTY RATES, ….L PRISON ...,(Amounts Manuscript)
c Top Right: JEDBURGH, 25 April 1842. (Date, Month, & Year Manuscript) Bottom Left: COUNTY RATES, ….L PRISON ASSESSMENT,

MA231 KELSO
a Top Right: Stamp and Tax=Office, JEDBURGH, 1ST APRIL, 1841. Middle Right: ... Kelso Lower Left: at the TAX-OFFICE, ….. (Manuscript)
b Top Right: Stamp & Tax=Office, JEDBURGH, 10TH MAY, 1841. Top Right: …Kelso Mail ... Lower Right: …Taxes … Kelso... (Manuscript)
c Top Right: Stamp and Tax=Office, JEDBURGH, 15th March, 1842. Middle: …appealed against it), Middle Left: Kelso(Manuscript) the said…

MA232 KILMARNOCK
a Top Right: STAMPS AND TAXES, AYR, 15TH MARCH, 1842. Middle: …, the Sub-Collector at Kilmarnock(Kilmarnock Manuscript Insertion)

MA233 KINROSS
a Top Centre: ARREARS OF TAXES. COUNTY OF KINROSS. Middle: or to ..., at Kinross,… Bottom Left: Cupar, 10th May 1841. (1d Envelope)

MA234 KIRKWALL
a Top Right: STAMPS AND TAXES. Kirkwall, 15th March, 1842. Middle: against it,) or to MR. ROSS … Stromness(Deletion beginning at MR.)
b Top Right: STAMPS & TAXES. Kirkwall, 6th May, 1842. Middle: Having neglected to attend…

MA235 LANARK

a Main Heading: PAYABLE AT LANARK. Top Right: 66, MILLER STREET, Glasgow, 2d May, 1842.

MA236 LARGS

a Top Right: STAMPS AND TAXES, Largs, 22d May, 1841. (Ayr Deleted & Largs Manuscript Insertion)

MA237 LEITH

a Top Right: TOWN CLERK'S OFFICE, LEITH. Middle Left: I also beg to remind you, … 25th of March last, …

b Top Right: TOWN CLERK'S OFFICE, LEITH, 15th March, 1842. Middle Left: the 25th instant, …

MA238 LESLIE

a Top Centre: ARREARS OF TAXES. … DUE 25th MARCH 1841. Middle: or to the Sub-Collector, at Leslie(Manuscript)(1d Envelope)

b Top Right: Stamps and Taxes Cupar, 2d May, 1842. Middle: …(Manuscript Name Insertion) the Sub-Collector at Leslie(Manuscript)

MA239 LINLITHGOW

a Top Right: Stamp and Tax Office, Stirling, 15th May, 1841. Middle: … hands of Mr. Andrew Nimmo, Linlithgow; …

b Top Right: Stamp and Tax Office, Linlithgow, 7th March, 1842. Middle: … Assessment is due and payable on the 25th instant,

MA240 LONDON, REGISTRAR OF BIRTHS AND DEATHS

a Printed Address: To The ….. Registrar of Births and Deaths, ….. District. Inside: Top Right: DOWNING STREET, September .., 1841.

MA241 MELROSE

a Top Right: Stamp and Tax=Office, JEDBURGH, 1ST APRIL, 1841. Middle: …at the TAX-OFFICE, … Bottom: … Melrose(Manuscript)

MA242 MONTROSE

a Details Unknown. Top Right: Stamp and Tax Office, 15 March, 1842.

MA243 NEWCASTLE

a Top Right: Stamp Office, Newcastle Bottom Left: Pringle & Co. lithog.

b Top Right: Stamp Office, Newcastle Bottom Left: Pringle & Co. lithog. (Salutation & Closing Changed by Manuscript)

c Top Right: Stamp Office, Newcastle, Bottom Right: Your obedient Servant,

d Top Right: Stamp Office, Newcastle, Bottom Right: Your obedient Servant,(Salutation & Closing Changed by Manuscript)

MA244 PERTH

a Top Right: COUNTY CESS OFFICE, PERTH, .. March, 1841. (Date Manuscript Insertion) Middle: … MR. GLOAG, Commercial Bank, Perth.

b Top Right: COUNTY CESS OFFICE, PERTH, .. August, 1841. (Date & Month Manuscript) Middle: … MR. GLOAG, Commercial Bank, Perth.

c Top Right: TAX OFFICE, PERTH, …..1842. (Date Manuscript) Middle: Commercial Bank, Perth, on or before the .. Instant. (Date Manuscript)

d Details Unknown. Tea Office, Perth 1842

e Top Right: COUNTY CESS OFFICE, PERTH. (Date, Month & Year Manuscript Insertion) Bottom Right: A. D. STEWART.

MA245 PORTSOY

a Top Right: STAMPS AND TAXES, BANFF, 1st May, 1842. Middle: …, the Sub-Collector of Portsoy(Portsoy Manuscript Insertion)

MA246 STIRLING

a Top Right: Stamp and Tax Office, Stirling, 15th May, 1841. Bottom Right: JOHN MURRAY, COLLECTOR. (1d Letter Sheet)

b Top Right: Stamp and Tax Office, Stirling, 29th May, 1841. (1d Letter Sheet)

c Top Right: Stamp and Tax Office, Stirling, 15th March, 1842. (1d Envelope)

MA247 STONEHAVEN
- a Main Heading: LAND AND ASSESSED ... Top Right: ... ABERDEEN, 1st May, 1842. Middle: the Sub-Collector at Stonehaven(Manuscript)

MA248 STRANRAER
- a Top Right: STRANRAER, 15th March, 1842. Middle: ..... the Sub-Collector at ..... (Tax Collector Name & Town Manuscript Insertion)

MA249 STRATHAN
- a Main Heading: LAND TAX, DUE 25TH MARCH, 184.. (Year Manuscript) Centre: Strathan Land Tax,...L Stamp,........ (Strathan Manuscript)

MA250 STROMNESS
- a Top Right: STAMPS AND TAXES. Kirkwall, 15th March, 1842. Middle: against it,) or to MR. ROSS the Sub-Collector at Stromness, ...

MA251 TAX TEMPLATE FOR SCOTTISH CITIES
- a Top Right: STAMP OFFICE, ...August 1841. (City and Day of Month to be Entered in Manuscript)

MA252 THURSO
- a Top Centre: COUNTY OF CAITHNESS. LAND AND ASSESSED TAXES, Due 25th March, 1841.
- b Top Right: STAMPS & TAXES, THURSO, 15th March, 1842.

MA253 YORK
- a Main Heading: Mr. ..... Stamp Office, York. ..... 1841(Name, Date, & Month Manuscript Insertions)
- b Main Heading: Mr. ..... Stamp Office, York. ..... 184. (Name, Date, Month, & Last Digit of Year Manuscript Insertions)
- c Printed Address: Mr. ..... Stamp Office Main Heading: Mr. ..... Stamp Office, York. ..... 184. (Name, Date, Month, & Year Manuscript)

Banks

MA301 BARNETT HOARES & COMPANY
- a Top Flap: Please to Pay Barnett Hoares and Co. on account of Ipswich Bank. (Ordinary Letters)(1d Envelope)
- b Top Middle: Please to Pay Barnett Hoares and Co. on account of Ipswich Bank. (Ordinary Letters)(1d Letter Sheet)
- c Top Middle: Please to Pay BARNETT HOARES AND CO. on account of IPSWICH BANK. (Capital Letters)(1d Letter Sheet)

MA302 BATE & ROBINS
- a Top Centre: Enclosed ... on account of BATE & ROBINS, Stourbridge Old Bank, ... 184(Amount, Day, Month, & Last Digit of Year Manuscript)

MA303 THE DEVON & CORNWALL BANKING COMPANY
- a Details Unknown.

MA304 DORSETSHIRE BANK
- a Main Heading: Dorsetshire Bank. STURMINSTER..... 18.. Bottom Right: For Williams, Cox, & Co.

MA305 EAST OF ENGLAND BANK
- a Top Flap: ________184., Please credit to the East of England Bank, Stowmarket, L _______(Spaces for Manuscript Insertions)(1d Envelope)
- b Middle: ________184., Please credit to the East of England Bank, Stowmarket, L _______(Spaces for Manuscript Insertions)(1d Letter Sheet)
- c Top Middle: East of England Bank Lynn(Hand-Stamped in Orange-red)(1d Letter Sheet)

MA306 MESSRS. EVERETT, RAVENHILL, AND COMPANY
- a Top Right: Warminster & Wiltshire Bank, ... 184. MESSRS. EVERETT, RAVENHILL, and Co., ...

MA307 MANCHESTER AND LIVERPOOL DISTRICT BANK
- a Main Heading: Manchester and Liverpool District Bank, Manchester, 17th August, 1840.

MA308 OAKES, BEVAN & COMPANY
- a Top Centre: _____1841. Please pay to Messrs. Barclay & Co. L _____ on account of Oakes, Bevan & Co. Stowmarket Bank. (1d Letter Sheet)
- b Top Centre: _____1842. Please pay to Messrs. Barclay & Co. L _____ on account of Oakes, ... Bank. (1 Changed to 2)(1d Letter Sheet)
- c Top Centre: _____184.. Please pay to Messrs. Barclay & Co. L _____ on account of Oakes, ... Bank. (Year Digit Manuscript)(1d Letter Sheet)

MA309 PRESCOTT, GROTE, & COMPANY (Printed in Black) Middle Right: ... to Messrs. Prescott, Grote & Co.,
- a Top Right: Lynn Regis, ... 184. (Day and Month Manuscript Insertions)

MA310 SHEFFIELD & ROTHERHAM BANK, SHEFFIELD
- a Top Flap Outside: R. I. Bingham(Agent for the Bank)(2d Envelope)

MA311 SOUTHERN BANK OF SCOTLAND
- a Main Heading: Southern Bank of Scotland, Dumfries, ... 184. (Day and Month Manuscript Insertions)

MA312 UNION BANK
- a Main Heading: UNION BANK, Top Right: Burlington, ... 184. (Day and Month Manuscript Insertions)

MA313 WILLIAMS, DEACON, AND COMPANY
- a Top Flap: Please to pay Messrs. Williams, Deacon, and Co., on account of the Guildford Bank. (1d Envelope)

Individual Firms, Organisations, etc., Advertising Their Own Goods or Services

MA401 ACKWORTH SCHOOL
- a Top Right: Ackworth School .. Month .. 1840(Number of Month and Day Manuscript Insertions)
- b Main Heading: MONITORIAL SCHOOL. Bottom Left: Ackworth School, .. month .. 184. (Day, Month, and Last Digit of Year Manuscript)
- c Main Heading: UPPER SCHOOL .. CLASS. (Class Manuscript) Bottom Left: Ackworth School, .. month .. 184. (Manuscript Insertions)
- d Main Heading: UPPER SCHOOL .. CLASS. (Class Manuscript) Bottom Left: The inclosed ... School, .. month .. 184. (Manuscript Insertion)

MA402 DR. ALLISON
- a Main Heading: DR ALLISONS' UNPARALLELED REMEDY AND CERTAIN CURE FOR THE TOOTHACHE,

MA403 THOMAS ALLSOP
- a Main Heading: RAILWAYS.

MA404 ANTI DRY-ROT COMPANY
- a Main Heading: ANTI DRY-ROT COMPANY. (KYAN'S PATENT.)

MA405 J. ARTER
- a Top Right: 1, Princes Buildings, Bottom Right: J Arter

MA406 ASSOCIATION FOR THE PROMOTION OF THE FINE ARTS IN SCOTLAND
- a Top Centre: ASSOCIATION FOR THE ... Bottom Left: Edinburgh, May 17, 1841.

MA407 THE BANNATYNE CLUB
- a Printed Address: THE SECRETARY OF THE BANNATYNE CLUB, ...
- b Printed Address: Club List from .... To THE SECRETARY...(Club Name Manuscript Insertion)

MA408 T. C. BATES

- a Main Heading: ORGAN AND PIANO-FORTE MANUFACTORY, Top Right: ... STOCK OF MUSICAL INSTRU-
- b Main Heading: ORGAN AND PIANO-FORTE MANUFACTORY, Top Right: ... STOCK OF MUSICAL INSTRUMENTS,
- c Main Heading: ORGAN AND PIANO-FORTE MANUFACTORY, Top Left: THE SEMI-COTTAGE, OR PICCOLO PIANO-FORTE,

MA409 WILLIAM AND E. H. BENTALL

- a Top Right: Boxtead, January 1st, 1842. Middle Right: WILLIAM BENTALL.

MA410 JOHN BESEMERES & SONS

- a Main Heading: LIST OF ARTICLES MANUFACTURED BY JOHN BESEMERES & SONS, Bottom: No Message
- b Main Heading: LIST OF ARTICLES MANUFACTURED BY JOHN BESEMERES & SONS, Bottom: Every garment is kept ready...
- c Main Heading: LIST OF ARTICLES MANUFACTURED BY JOHN BESEMERES & SONS, Bottom: Light Portable Waterproof Trunks, ...
- d Main Heading: LIST OF NECESSARIES FOR A CADET, FURNISHED BY JOHN BESEMERES & SONS,
- e Main Heading: LIST AND ESTIMATE ... AN INFANTRY CADET, PROCEEDING TO INDIA BY THE CAPE OR LONG SEA ROUTE ...
- f Main Heading: LIST AND ESTIMATE ... AN INFANTRY CADET, PROCEEDING TO INDIA. MANUFACTURED AND FURNISHED BY ...
- g Main Heading: LIST AND ESTIMATE OF NECESSARIES FOR AN ASSISTANT-SURGEON, PROCEEDING TO INDIA.

MA411 ADAM AND CHARLES BLACK

- a Centre: THE ROD AND THE GUN Bottom: ADAM AND CHARLES BLACK ...
- b Top Left: Republished from the Seventh Edition Bottom Left & Right: ADAM AND CHARLES BLACK ...
- c Top Left: SCIENTIFIC TREATISES Bottom Centre: ADAM AND CHARLES BLACK ...
- d Top Centre: ENCYCLOPAEDIA BRITANNICA. Bottom Centre: ADAM AND CHARLES BLACK ...

MA412 JOHN BRIGHT

- a Main Heading: BRIGHT'S NUTRITIOUS FARINA, ...(Printed in Blue)

MA413 BRITISH and FOREIGN SCHOOL SOCIETY

- a Main Heading: British and Foreign School Society.

MA414 BROADHEAD & ATKIN

- a Main Heading: BROADHEAD & ATKIN. Middle: BRITANNIA METAL. Bottom: SHEFFIELD

MA415 CHALONER, HOUGHTON & FLEMING

- a Main Heading: To Timber-merchants, ... Bottom Right: CHALONER, HOUGHTON, & FLEMING, BROKERS. (1d Envelope)

MA416 CHELMSFORD AND ESSEX AGRICULTURAL SOCIETY

- a Printed Address: To the Churchwardens or Overseers Parish of ...(Name Manuscript) Main Heading: To the Honorable the House of Commons ...

MA417 CHELTENHAM ANNIVERSARY OF THE CENTENARY FETE

- a Main Heading: CHELTENHAM ANIVERSARY OF THE CENTENARY FETE Bottom: Further ... Public. (Ordinary Type)
- b Main Heading: CHELTENHAM ANIVERSARY OF THE CENTENARY FETE Bottom: Further ... Public. (Ordinary & Bold Type)
- c Top Left: WILLIAM HAINES. Top Centre: Blank Area Top Right: LAMB COMMERCIAL & FAMILY HOTEL,
- d Top Left: WILLIAM HAINES. Top Centre: Blank Area Top Right: BELL HOTEL AND COMMERCIAL INN.
- e Top Left: WILLIAM HAINES. Top Centre: Entrance Gate Picture(Pasted Into Blank Area) Top Right: LAMB COMMERCIAL & FAMILY HOTEL,
- f Top Left: WILLIAM HAINES. Top Centre: Entrance Gate Picture(Pasted Into Blank Area) Top Right: BELL HOTEL AND COMMERCIAL INN.

MA418 CHUDLEIGH UNION LODGE
a Main Heading: UNION LODGE, NO. 650. Chudleigh .. ….. 1840. (Day and Month Manuscript Insertion)

MA419 CLERK OF THE UNION
a Printed Address: To the Clerk of the __________ Union,(Underlined Space, Name a Manuscript Insertion) Inside: Blank.
b Printed Address: To the Clerk of the __________ Union, … Inside Main Heading: LAW WORKS PUBLISHED BY SHAW & SONS, …
c Printed Address: To the Clerk of the __________ Union, … Inside Main Heading: SHAW'S SHEET HOLDER, …
d Printed Address: To the Clerk of the __________ Union, … Inside Top Right: LANDLORD … Bottom: LONDON: SHAW AND SONS, …
e Printed Address: To the Clerk of the __________ Union, … Inside Top Right: A LIST … Bottom: LONDON: SHAW AND SONS, …

MA420 PETER CUMMING
a Main Heading: BOT OF PETER CUMMING … Glasgow.

MA421 CURRALL & SON
a Main Heading: CROSBY-HALL WINE ESTABLISHMENT, … Top Left: CURRALL & SON, in gratefully …

MA422 JOHN DALLENGER
a Main Heading: JOHN DALLENGER, AUCTIONEER, APPRAISER, ESTATE AGENT, AND ACCOUNTANT, WICKHAM MARKET.
b Main Heading: JOHN DALLENGER, AUCTIONEER, APPRAISER, … ACCOUNTANT, late of WICKHAM MARKET. ("late of" is Manuscript)

MA423 DELIANSON CLARK AND COMPANY
a Main Heading: PATENT OFFICE, -- BRITISH AND FOREIGN, … Top Centre: DELIANSON CLARK AND CO., …

MA424 GEORGE AND WILLIAM EAGLESFIELD
a Details Unknown. Prices of Shares.

MA425 ROBERT BEST EDE
a Top Right: R. B. EDE'S PORTABLE CHEMICAL LABORATORIES & CABINETS. (Printed in Black)
b Top Right: R. B. EDE'S PORTABLE CHEMICAL ... Bottom: Sold by JOHN S. GOWING, Bookseller, SWAFFHAM. (Printed in Black)
c Top Right: R. B. EDE'S PORTABLE CHEMICAL ... Bottom: Sold by JOHN THEW, Bookseller, LYNN(Printed in Black)
d Top Right: R. B. EDE'S ... (Printed in Black) Two Boxes: THESE POSTAGE…(Printed in Red) Bottom: ...JOHN S. GOWING, Bookseller …
e Main Heading: NOW PUBLISHING, Middle: DORKING: ROBERT BEST EDE. Left Middle: EXTRACT ..., JANUARY, 1841. (Printed in Black)

MA426 EDINBURGH and GLASGOW RAILWAY COMPANY
a Centre: The Directors of the EDINBURGH and GLASGOW RAIL-... (2d Letter Sheet)

MA427 C. M. FIRTH
a Top Right: C. M. FIRTH, GENERAL PRINTER, 7 St. Michael's Alley…

MA428 JOHN FOSTER & SON
a Top Right: BIGGLESWADE, January 1st, 184 Bottom Right: JOHN FOSTER & SON.

MA429 J. GREEN
a Centre: 63. GRAND PARADE. J. GREEN'S …

MA430 CHARLES HALE
a Top Left: CHANTS. Left Side: Benedictus. Jones. Crotch.
b Top Left: CHANTS. Left Side: C. Hale. Battishill. Morrington.
c Top Left: CHANTS. Left Side: Henry Latre. C. Hale. Robinson.

d Top Left: DISMISSAL. Top Right: Haydn.
e Left Side: Labitsky.
f Left Side: Gabrielen Walzer. Top Right: J. Strauss.
g Left Side: Philomelen Walzer. Top Right: J. Strauss.
h Left Side: La Rosa Walzer. Top Right: J. Strauss.

MA431 SAMUEL HANSON & SON
a Main Heading: Bot. of Samuel Hanson & Son, ... Oranges, Lemons, ...(Last Line)
b Main Heading: Bot. of Samuel Hanson & Son, ... No Bags will be allowed ...(Last Line)

MA432 J. & H. HAYCROFT
a Main Heading: FARM AND GARDEN SEED WAREHOUSE, Top Left: J. & H. HAYCROFT beg to inform their Patrons ...

MA433 JAMES HEELEY & SONS
a Top Centre: JAMES HEELEY & SONS, PATENTEES & MANUFACTURERS, ...

MA434 R. HENDRIE
a Main Heading: HENDRIE'S OLD BROWN WINDSOR SOAP

MA435 G. K. HOLMES
a Main Heading: THE SQUARE, RETFORD. Bottom Right: MR. G. K. HOLMES, SOLICITOR,

MA436 R. HOOPER & SONS
a Top Right: QUEENHITHE, LONDON, ... 18.. (Day, Month, & Year Manuscript) Bottom Right: Your ... Servants, R. HOOPER & SONS.

MA437 HULL SUNDAY SCHOOL UNION
a Main Heading: Hull Sunday School Union, Bottom Left: December, 1840.

MA438 G. HYDE & COMPANIES
a Main Heading: UTILITY COMBINED with ECONOMY G. HYDE & Cos. (Printed in Dark Blue)

MA439 JOSEPH JONES
a Main Heading: JOSEPH JONES, Stationer, Broad Street, Hereford, Bottom Right: MISCELLANEOUS STOCK.

MA440 T. KERSLAKE
a Main Heading: CHEAP NEW BOOKS, ... T. KERSLAKE, Top Left: AINSWORTH'S Latin Dictionary, ...
b Main Heading: CHEAP NEW BOOKS, ... T. KERSLAKE, Top Left: BAXTER's Saint's Rest, ...

MA441 KING'S COLLEGE HOSPITAL
a Top Flap: KING'S COLLEGE HOSPITAL ... Inside: This Hospital ... Bottom Flap: Donations ... (NoCoat of Arms)(1d Envelope)
b Main Heading: KING'S COLLEGE HOSPITAL,(With Coat of Arms)(1d Letter Sheet)
c Main Heading: KING'S COLLEGE HOSPITAL,(With Coat of Arms & 2 Vertical Lines Separating 3 Columns)(1d Letter Sheet)

MA442 LAVARS & ACKLAND
a Main Heading: JUST PUBLISHED Top Left: LAVARS & ACKLAND Lithographers, Bristol.

MA443 JOSIAH LAWRENCE
a Top Left: Detachd. Lever Watches ... Middle Left: Josiah Lawrence Watch & Clock Manufacturer, ...

MA444 LAWRIE & KNIGHT
a Top Left: LAWRIE & KNIGHT'S POST-OFFICE LETTER PAPER, ... Bottom Left: 41, DUNDAS STREET, EDINBURGH.

MA445 LEEDS SUNDAY SCHOOL UNION
a Details Unknown.

MA446 LONDON AND CROYDON RAILWAY
- a Main Heading: LONDON AND CROYDON RAILWAY. Bottom: SUNDAYS. Every HALF HOUR ... in the Evening.
- b Main Heading: LONDON AND CROYDON RAILWAY. Bottom: DAY TICKETS.--In order ... from Croydon. (Printed in Blue)

MA447 LUXFORD & COMPANY
- a Top Flap: LUXFORD & CO., 65, RATCLIFF HIGHWAY, BOOKSELLERS, STATIONERS, BOOKBINDERS,(1d Envelope)

MA448 THE MANCHESTER AND LIVERPOOL PLATE GLASS COMPANY
- a Main Heading: GREAT REDUCTION IN THE Price of Plate Glass. THE MANCHESTER AND LIVERPOOL PLATE GLASS COMPANY,

MA449 MASSON & HOGGINS
- a Main Heading: FOR SYDNEY ... Bottom Right: MASSON & HOGGINS, ...

MA450 METROPOLITAN BENEFIT SOCIETIES' ASYLUM
- a Top: METROPOLITAN Picture Heading: BENEFIT SOCIETIES' ASYLUM,

MA451 THE MILTON PRESS
- a Main Heading: THE MILTON PRESS PRINTING ESTABLISHMENTS Bottom Right: COPPER-PLATE. (Printed in Black)
- b Main Heading: CHEAP AND ELEGANT PRINTING. Bottom Right: ENGRAVING. (Printed in Black and Green)

MA452 MIMPRISS & COMPANY
- a Main Heading: These Circulars may be had at 10d. A Dozen. Bottom: Willey, Printer 151 High Street, Cheltenham.
- b Main Heading: These Circulars may be had at 10d. A Dozen. Bottom: A LARGE SUPPLY OF WRIGHT AND ALLBRIGHT'S ...
- c Main Heading: MIMPRISS & Co., (LATE WIGHT,) Bottom: M. & Co. will feel greatly obliged for early intimation of any new Publication ...

MA453 R. W. MOORE
- a Top Middle: R. W. MOORE. Share and Stockbroker. 68 THREADNEEDLE STREET LONDON

MA454 EDWARD NEWMAN
- a Top Left: A HISTORY OF BRITISH FERNS. ... Bottom Right: EDWARD NEWMAN will feel much obliged for any specimens,

MA455 THE NEWRY TELEGRAPH (Printed in Red)
- a Top Flap: THE NEWRY TELEGRAPH ... Bottom Flap: PRINTING, ... Side Flaps: Circulation Particulars(1d Envelope)
- b Details Unknown(1d Letter Sheet)

MA456 NORTHERN REVERSION COMPANY
- a Main Heading: Northern Reversion Company, Bottom Left: In order, as far as possible, to facilitate ...

MA457 OBBARD AND COMPANY
- a Main Heading: OBBARD AND COMPANY, Bottom: GREEN GLASS.
- b Main Heading: OBBARD AND COMPANY, Bottom: BRITISH SHEET PLATE GLASS,

MA458 PAGET
- a Details Unknown(Printed in Blue)(1d Letter Sheet)
- b Main Heading: PAGET, WORKING CUTLER, ... Bottom: The following is copied verbatim ... (2d Letter Sheet)

MA459 J. H. PARKER
- a Top Right: Oxford, June, 1840. Bottom Right: Your obedient Servant, J. H. PARKER.

MA460 HENRY PENNY
- a Top Left: Henry Penny's much approved Metallic Paper ... Middle: OPINIONS OF THE PRESS(Underlined Twice)

b Top Left: Henry Penny's much approved Metallic Paper … Middle: OPINIONS OF THE PRESS(Underlined Once)

MA461 PENNY & SONS

a Main Heading: PENNY & SONS' CHEAP AND ELEGANT ASSORTMENT OF … Bottom: PUBLISHED THE 1st OF NOVEMBER.

MA462 JOHN AND NATH'L PHILIPS AND COMPANY

a Top Right: Manchester .. … 184. (Day, Month, & Year Manuscript Insertion) Bottom Right: for John & Nath'l Philips & Co.

MA463 JOSEPH PLOWMAN

a Top Left: PLOWMAN'S IMPROVED COPYIST, … Bottom Right: MR. W. BADDELEY'S …

MA464 THE RAILWAY MAGAZINE AND COMMERCIAL JOURNAL

a Top Centre: THE RAILWAY MAGAZINE, … Bottom Centre: KELLY & Co., Printers, …

MA465 JOHN RICHARDS AND COMPANY

a Top Left: Law Books, &c. MIRROR OF PARLIAMENT, Bottom Right: TAMLYN'S TREATISE on the …

b Top Left: MIRROR OF PARLIAMENT, Bottom Right: CHARNOCK'S STORY'S LAWS …

c Top Left: MIRROR OF PARLIAMENT, Bottom Right: TAMLYN'S TREATISE on the …

d Top Left: WESTERN'S CONVEYANCING, Bottom Right: CHARNOCK'S STORY'S LAWS …

e Top Left: Law Books, &c. REPORTS OF CASES Bottom Right: Rouse on Copyhold Enfranchisement.

MA466 RIDLEY'S (Printed in Blue)

a Main Heading: RIDLEY'S AUCTION AND ESTATE AGENCY OFFICES

MA467 FREEMAN ROE

a Main Heading: FREEMAN ROE, Plumber and Engineer. Bottom: Sent to any part or Town or Country.

MA468 THE CONSECRATION OF ST. STEPHEN'S CHAPEL

a Main Heading: THE CONSECRATION OF ST. STEPHEN'S CHAPEL, … Bottom: Copies of the Consecration Service, …

MA469 SALISBURY DIOCESAN CHURCH BUILDING ASSOCIATION

a Details Unknown.

MA470 THE SCOTSMAN

a Main Heading: THE SCOTSMAN. Bottom Left: SCOTSMAN OFFICE, 257, HIGH STREET, Edinburgh, July 1840.

MA471 WILLIAM SHAW

a Main Heading: TWO ESTABLISHMENTS Bottom Left: earliest attention, and every effort ... (1d Envelope)

b Main Heading: TWO ESTABLISHMENTS Bottom Left: earliest attention, and every effort ... (1d Letter Sheet)

c Main Heading: TWO ESTABLISHMENTS Bottom Left: earliest tatention, and every effort …(attention misspelled)(1d Letter Sheet)

MA472 SHAW BROTHERS

a Main Heading: REDUCED POSTAGE! PENNY STAMPED COVERS, Bottom: Shaw Brothers providing for their circulation, …

MA473 SHAW AND SONS

a Main Heading: WORKS PUBLISHED BY SHAW & SONS, 136, 137 AND … Top Left: TO THE CLERGY, VESTRY CLERKS …

b Main Heading: WORKS PUBLISHED BY SHAW & SONS, 136, 137 AND … Top Left: POOR LAWS.

c Address Panel: TO POSTMASTERS. … (Printed in Red) Main Heading: WORKS PUBLISHED … Top Left: POOR LAWS.

d Main Heading: WORKS PUBLISHED BY SHAW & SONS, 136, 137 AND … Top Left: SAVINGS' BANKS …
e Main Heading: EXTENSION OF VACCINATION, Bottom: BY SHAW & SONS, 136, 137 AND 138, FETTER LANE.
f Main Heading: LAW WORKS PUBLISHED BY SHAW AND SONS, 137 AND … Top Left: To Surveyors of the Highways
g Main Heading: LAW WORKS PUBLISHED BY SHAW AND SONS, 137 AND … Top Left: A PRACTICAL TREATISE …
h Main Heading: LAW WORKS PUBLISHED BY SHAW AND SONS, Top Left: POPULATION CENSUS.
i Main Heading: LAW WORKS RECENTLY PUBLISHED BY SHAW AND SONS, 137 AND … Top Left: TITHE COMMUTATION MAPS.
j Top Left: PUBLISHED BY SHAW & SONS, … PRISON REGULATIONS. Bottom Right: TITHE COMMUTATION PRACTICE.
k Top Left: PUBLISHED BY SHAW & SONS, … TO MAGISTRATES, … Bottom Right: REMARKS …
l Main Heading: SHAW'S SHEET HOLDER, Bottom: London: SHAW and SONS. 137 & 138, Fetter Lane.
m Top Left: THE OVERSEER'S GUIDE Top Right: A PRACTICAL GUIDE … CHURCHWARDENS
n Top Left: TO MAGISTRATES, … Top Right: LANDLORD AND TENANT. Bottom: LONDON: SHAW AND SONS, FETTER LANE
o Top Left: TO MAGISTRATES, … Top Right: SHERIFF FORMS AND BOOKS. Bottom: LONDON: SHAW AND SONS, FETTER LANE

MA474 CHAS. SMITH

a Main Heading: STATIONERY. CHAS. SMITH, 87 Princes St. EDINBURGH, Bottom Right: *not Political.

MA475 SOCIETY FOR THE EXTINCTION OF THE SLAVE TRADE, AND THE CIVILIZATION OF AFRICA

a Bottom Left: Shortly will be Published, An Abridgement … Bottom Right: Shortly … by Subscription... (1d Letter Sheet)
b Bottom Left: Shortly will be Published, An Abridgement … Bottom Left: POST-OFFICE COVERS, … One Shilling ... (1d Letter Sheet)
c Bottom Left: Just Published, price 1s. Bottom Left: POST-OFFICE COVERS, … One Shilling …. (1d Letter Sheet)
d Bottom Left: Just Published, price 1s. Bottom Left: POST-OFFICE COVERS, … 1s and 2s …(1d Letter Sheet)
e Bottom Left: Just Published, price 1s. Bottom Left: POST-OFFICE COVERS, … 1s and 2s …(2d Letter Sheet)
f Bottom Left: POST-OFFICE COVERS, … 1s and 2s … Bottom Right: Recently Published, by Subscription …(1d Letter Sheet)

MA476 THE SOUTHAMPTON DISTRICT COMMITTEE

a Main Heading: DR. TO THE SOUTHAMPTON DISTRICT COMMITTEE, FOR PROMOTING CHRISTIAN KNOWLEDGE, …

MA477 J. R. STEBBING

a Main Heading: BY APPOINTMENT, TO HER ROYAL … J. R. STEBBING, Bottom Left: A LICENSED HAWKER.

MA478 WILLIAM STRONG

a Main Heading: VALUABLE, IN(Unreadable), AND CHOICE BOOKS, BY WILLIAM STRONG, BOOKSELLER, 26, CLARE STREET, BRISTOL,

MA479 TAYLOR'S

a Main Heading: A SELECTION FROM TAYLOR'S … Bottom Right: Xenophonti's Opera …

MA480 THOMAS TODD

a Details Unknown. Notice of new publication.

MA481 THOMPSON, M'KAY & COMPANY

a Main Heading: THOMPSON, M'KAY & CO., 8 PIER-STREET, … Bottom: Goods for the above Places …

MA482 CHARLES TURNER

- a Top Right: No. 9, Broad Street, Bloomsbury, London. Bottom Right: Your obedt. Servt Charles Turner(Manuscript Signature)

MA483 TWEEDDALE PATENT DRAIN TILES

- a Main Heading: TWEEDDALE PATENT DRAIN TILES. Bottom: Tweeddale Patent Drain Tile and Brick Office, ..., September 1840. (1d Envelope)
- b Main Heading: TWEEDDALE PATENT DRAIN TILES. Bottom: Tweeddale … Office, ..., September 1840. (Printed in Blue)(1d Letter Sheet)

MA484 UNWIN'S MERCANTILE PRINTING OFFICE

- a Main Heading: UNWIN'S MERCANTILE PRINTING OFFICE AND COMMERCIAL STATIONERY WAREHOUSE, …

MA485 JOHN WAILES

- a Main Heading: BERZELIUS' INK, Bottom: Sold Wholesale by the Proprietor, …

MA486 GEORGE WATSON

- a Main Heading: GEORGE WATSON, OLD … Bottom Right: Postage Covers … 10 dozen.
- b Main Heading: GEORGE WATSON, OLD … Bottom Right: Postage Covers … 10 dozen. Bottom Right: A fine-tuned Organ, …
- c Main Heading: GEORGE WATSON, OLD … Bottom Right: Postage ... (Manuscript Deletion) Bottom Right: A fine-tuned Organ, …

MA487 WAREING WEBB

- a Top Flap Outside: WAREING WEBB LIVERPOOL(1d Envelope)
- b Bottom Flap Outside: Webb, L'pool. (1d Letter Sheet)
- c Bottom Flap Outside: Webb, L'pool. (2d Envelope)
- d Bottom Flap Outside: Webb, L'pool. (2d Letter Sheet)

MA488 WELSHMAN NEWSPAPER

- a Main Heading: Welshman Newspaper Bottom Right:'WELSHMAN" OFFICE. CARMARTHEN, SOUTH WALES. 184 .

MA489 THE WESTMINSTER REVIEW

- a Main Heading: ORDER FOR ADVERTISEMENTS, … WESTMINSTER ... Top Left: To Mr SAMUEL CLARKE, 13 Pallmall East, London.
- b Main Heading: ORDER FOR ADVERTISEMENTS, … WESTMINSTER ... Top Left: To Mr HENRY HOOPER, 13 Pallmall East, London.
- c Main Heading: Contents of the Westminster Review (No. LXVI), just published.
- d Main Heading: JUST PUBLISHED, THE WESTMINSTER REVIEW … NO. LXVII, FOR SEPTEMBER,
- e Top Left: Cheap and Superior … Bottom Left: Letterpress and Copperplate …

MA490 WHITMARSH'S ROYAL VICTORIA SUSSEX HOTEL

- a Main Heading: TUNBRIDGE WELLS. Bottom: WHITMARSH'S, Royal Victoria SUSSEX HOTEL, …

MA492 WILLIAM WHITWELL

- a Top Right: Kendal, .. Month, .. 184. Bottom Right: William Whitwell.

MA493 WILLEY

- a Details Unknown. Printer, 151, High Street, Cheltenham. Works published by…

MA494 C. WILSON

- a Main Heading: C. WILSON, STATIONER, … Bottom Left: EVENING MAIL Top Second Column: ENGLISH CHRONICLE
- b Main Heading: C. WILSON, STATIONER, … Bottom Left: EVENING CHRONICLE Top Second Column: ENGLISH CHRONICLE
- c Main Heading: C. WILSON, STATIONER, … Top Second Column: MARK LANE EXPRESS

APPENDIX 2

Protective Overprints or Underprints

These overprints (on the face of the stamps) or underprints (on the backs of the stamps) were made to defeat petty pilfering of stamps. At the time it was a common practice for the public to pay small accounts by means of stamps; the Post Office co-operated inasmuch as they were prepared to redeem such stamps for cash over the counter.

The Oxford Union Society had in 1858 adopted the practice of printing their initials on the face of the stamps that they provided free to their members. This was unofficially done but it was permitted until 1870 when the Society was informed that they must conform with the practice of having the protective initials officially printed on the backs of their stamps, this practice having commenced in 1867.

Including the Oxford Union Society only five firms or organizations availed themselves of the official co-operation in this matter of protective underprinting and the privilege was withdrawn in 1882. These official underprints were done by Perkins, Bacon & Co. or De La Rue & Co. and were printed *under the gum.*

Apart from the unofficial underprints made by the authorised bodies, some sixty firms and organizations overprinted or underprinted their stocks of stamps and these are listed. The unofficial and private underprints differ from the official underprints in being printed *over* the gum. Later the same purpose was served by firms puncturing the stamps with their initials and this practice still continues. Some firms embossed their stamps and examples for the 1d. stamps of 1840 and 1841 are known with this security protection. Examples of these are rarely found, however, and a listing is probably impractical.

Stamps privately overprinted by local councils for receipt purposes occasionlly passed through the post and these are outside the scope of this Catalogue. Examples most often found occur on the 1881 1d. lilac.

Prices

It is hoped to publish prices for unpriced listings in the future. All prices quoted are for used examples.

Where several plates are listed the cheapest is priced; scarcer plates will be worth more.

W. J. BARRON & SONS LONDON.	BEDDOE, HULBERT & CO.	BORROWMAN, PHILLIPPS & Co.
1	2	3

1868. W. J. Barron & Sons., London. Unofficial Underprint Type 1 in black. Vertical underprint, reading upwards.

PP1 1d. lake-red (G1), Plates 117, 129, 130, 134, 145, 154, 156 . . . *from* £300

(b) Vertical underprint, reading downwards

PP1A 1d. lake-red (G1), Plate 155 . . . .

1874. Beddoe, Hulbert & Co. Unofficial Underprint Type 2 in black. (a) Vertical underprint, reading upwards.

PP2 1d. lake-red (G1), Plates 174, 178, 181, 190, 193, 195, 196, 198, 201 to 204, 209, 210, 212 to 214, 218 to 220, 222 to 224 . . . . *from* £275

PP3 2d blue (G3), Plate 13 . . . .

PP4 1d Venetian red (K3) . . . .

(b) Vertical underprint, reading downwards

PP5 1d. lake-red (G1), Plates 202, 209, 210, 212 . . . .

1871. Borrowman, Phillips & Co. Unofficial Underprint Type 3 in black.

PP6 1d. lake-red (G1), Plates 150, 152, 155, 170, 171, 174, 177, 180, 185 to 187, 194, 198, 202, 214 . . . . *from* £275

J. & C. BOYD & CO. 7 FRIDAY ST.	J. & C. BOYD & CO. 7 FRIDAY ST.	BROWN, DAVIS & CO. LONDON.	BROWN, DAVIS & CO., LONDON.
4	5	6	7

1867. J. & C. Boyd & Co., 7 Friday St. Official Underprint Type 4 in red or blue (2d.).

PP7 1d. lake-red (G1), Plates 73, 74, 78, 79, 85, 87, 89, 90, 102, 103, 105, 107, 108, 111 to 113, 115, 118 to 121, 124, 125, 127, 129 to 134, 136, 139, 140, 143, 145, 146, 148 to 150, 152, 154, 155, 159, 160, 162 to 167, 169 to 172, 177, 179, 181, 183, 185, 187, 189, 192 to 195, 198, 199, 205 to 207, 209, 213, 224 . . . . *from* 30·00

PP8 2d. blue (G2), Plate 9 . . . . 75·00

PP9 2d. blue (G3), Plate 13 . . . . 75·00

The 1d. Plate 139 exists unused.

J. & C. Boyd & Co. Unofficial Underprint Type 5 in black.

PP10 1d. rose-red (C13), Plate R16 . . . . —

J. & C. Boyd & Co. Unofficial Underprint Type 5 in red.

PP11 1d. rose-red (C10), Plates 52, 55, 57, R17 . . . . *from* £120

PP12 1d. rose-red (C12), Plates 50, 51 . . . . —

PP12a 1d. rose-red (C13), Plate R15 . . . . —

PP13 1d. lake-red (G1), Plates 72 to 74, 78 to 81, 84, 85, 87 to 94, 97 . . . . *from* £100

PP14 2d. blue (G2), Plate 9 . . . . £175

The 1d. Plate 90 is known unused.

1868. Brown, Davis & Co., London. Unofficial Underprint Type 6 in black. (a) Vertical underprint, reading upwards.

PP15 1d. lake-red (G1), Plates 113, 118, 120, 121, 124, 125, 127, 129, 134, 137, 140, 141, 143 to 146, 148, 149, 151, 154, 155, 157, 159, 161, 162, 164, 195 . . . . *from* £275

(b) Vertical underprint, reading downwards

PP16 1d. lake-red (G1), Plate 143 . . . .

(c) Unofficial underprint Type 7, in black

PP17 1d. lake-red (G1), Plates 148, 154 . . . .

PP17A $\frac{1}{2}$d. rose-red (G4), Plates 1, 4, 8 . . . .

8 9 10 11

1868. M. Bs. Unofficial Underprint Type 8 in blue.

PP18 1d. lake-red (G1), Plate 119 . . . .

The origin of this underprint is unknown.

1868. The City Bank, London. Unofficial Underprint Type 9 in black.

PP19 1d. lake-red (G1), Plates 106 to 108, 121, 127, 165 . . . . *from* £275

PP20 4d. vermilion (J57), Plate 10 . . . .

1874. Cocker Brothers Limited, Sheffield, Unofficial Underprint Type 10 in black.

PP21 1d. lake-red (G1), Plates 174, 191, 195, 196, 198, 199, 208, 212, 215, 218 . . . . *from* £275

1872. L. Cohen, London. Unofficial Overprint Type 11 in black.

PP22 3d. rose (J345), Plates 9 and 10 . . . . *from* £275

No. PP22 may also show "LONDON" (part) below the name.

12 (Large "&") 13 14

15 (Small "&") 16 17 18

Types **12/14** are official underprints printed under the gum.

1867. Copestake, Moore, Crampton & Co., London. Underprint as Type 12. (a) Official Underprint in red.

PP23 1d. lake-red (G1), Plates 74, 76, 78 to 81, 90, 92, 96, 97, 100 to 120, 122, 123, 125, 127, 129 to 150, 152, 154 to 160, 162 to 164, 166 to 169, 171, 172, 174 to 181, 183 to 189, 191, 192, 194, 196 to 202, 204 to 207, 211, 213, 214, 215, 219, 224 .... *from* 24·00

a. Underprint double £300

PP24 1½d. lake-red (G6), Plates (1) and 3 .... *from* 75·00

a. Error of lettering: OP–PC for CP–PC (Plate 1) ....

(b) Underprint in blue

PP25 2d. blue (G2), Plates 9 and 12 .... *from* 65·00

PP26 2d. blue (G3), Plates 13, 14 and 15 .... *from* 42·00

1867. Copestake Moore, Crampton & Co., London. Official Underprint Type 13 in red.

PP27 ½d. rose-red (G4), Plates 1, 3 to 6, 8 to 15 and 20 .... *from* 55·00

Plates 5 and 13 exist unused.

1867. Copestake, Moore, Crampton & Co., London. Official Underprint Type 14 by De La Rue in the colour of the stamp.

PP28 3d. rose (J30, J33), Plates 5 and 8 .... *from* £130

PP29 3d. rose (J38, J42, J43, J44), Plates 14, 18, 19, 20 .... *from* £110

PP30 6d. violet (J76/7), Plates 8 and 9 .... *from* £180

PP31 6d. grey (J84), Plate 14 .... £175

PP32 1s. green (J104), Plate 4 .... —

PP33 1s. green (J112), Plate 12 .... —

a. Underprint inverted ....

PP34 1d. Venetian red (K3) .... 60·00

Copestake, Moore, Crampton & Co., London. Various Unofficial Underprints. (a) Underprint as Type 13 but smaller, in red.

PP35 ½d. rose-red (G4), Plates 10 and 11 .... —

(b) Underprint Type 15, in red

PP36 1d. lake-red (G1), Plates 71, 73, 74, 78, 79, 81, 89 to 92, 95, 96, 98, 99, 101, 103 to 125, 127, 129 to 132, 134 to 138, 140 to 150, 152 to 163, 165 to 168, 170 to 176, 178 to 184, 186, 191, 202, 204 .... *from* 30·00

a. Underprint inverted (Plates 111, 165)........
b. Additional underprint (inverted) on the face (Plate 106)........
c. Additional underprint on the face (Plate 103)........

PP37 1½d. lake-red (G6), Plate (1) .... 60·00

PP38 2d. blue (G2), Plates 9, 12 .... *from* 85·00

PP39 2d. blue (G2), Plate 12 (*in violet*) .... 85·00

PP40 2½d. rosy mauve (J1, J3), Plates 1 and 3 .... *from* £130

PP41 2½d. rosy mauve (J5), Plate 4 .... £130

PP42 3d. rose (J10), Plate 5 .... £130

PP43 4d. vermilion (J55, J56, J58), Plates 8, 9, 11 .... *from* £130

PP44 10d. red-brown (J97), Plate 1 .... —

(c) Underprint Type 16, in black

PP45 $\frac{1}{2}$d. rose-red (G4), Plate 5 . . . . —

(d) Underprint Type 16, in red

PP45A $\frac{1}{2}$d. rose-red (G4), Plate 9 . . . . —

(e) Underprint Type 17 vertically in black

PP46 1d. lake-red (G1), (upt. reads upwards), Plates 99, 101, 103, 104, 106, 113, 115 to 118, 121, 123 to 125 . . . . *from* 60·00

PP47 1d. lake-red (G1), (upt. reads downwards), Plates 92, 101, 103, 105 to 107, 114, 116 . . . . *from* 60·00

(f) Underprint Type 17, vertically in red

PP48 1d. lake-red (G1) (upt. reads upwards), Plate 118 . . . . 75·00

PP49 1d. lake-red (G1) (upt. reads downwards), Plates 106 and 111 *from* 75·00

Copestake, Hughes, Crampton & Co., London. Unofficial Underprint Type 18 in red; 2d. in blue. (a) Underprint vertical.

PP50 $\frac{1}{2}$d. rose-red (G4), Plate 12 . . . . —

(b) Underprint horizontal

PP51 $\frac{1}{2}$d. rose-red (G4), Plates 13, 14, 19 . . . . —

PP52 1d. lake-red (G1), Plates 134, 140, 146, 158 to 170, 172, 174, 177, 179, 182 to 188, 190, 192 to 194, 196 to 200, 204 to 206, 208 to 213, 216, 217, 218, 219, 220, 222, 223 . . . . *from* 75·00

b. Underprint inverted (Plate 183) . . . .

c. Underprint doubled (Plate 74) . . . .

PP53 2d. blue (G3), Plate 15 . . . .

PP54 2$\frac{1}{2}$d. rosy mauve (J6, J10, J12), Plates 5, 9, 11 . . . . —

PP55 6d. grey (J86), Plate 16 . . . . —

PP56 1d. Venetian red (K3) . . . . —

Wm. Dawbarn & Co LIVERPOOL	W.Dawbarn&Co. LIVERPOOL.	DEBENHAM. TEWSON, & FARMER. 80 CHEAPSIDE, E.C.	M.DE COSTA ANDRADE & CO.
19	20	21	22

1868. Wm. Dawbarn & Co., Liverpool. Unofficial Overprint Type 19 in black. (a) Vertical overprint, reading upwards.

PP57 1d. lake-red (G1), Plates 125, 137, 138, 148, 171, 172 . . . . . . *from* £130

(b) Vertical overprint, reading downwards

PP58 1d. lake-red (G1), Plates 110, 113, 118, 119, 121 to 125, 127, 129, 130, 135 to 150, 152 to 154, 156, 158 to 163, 165 to 168, 170 to 175, 177 to 179, 181, 186, 187 . . . . *from* £130

Used on cover
a. Overprint double . . . .

The 1d. Plate 154 is known unused.
The 1d. Plate 136 has been found with an overprint in yellow.

1873. W. Dawbarn & Co., Liverpool. Unofficial Underprint Type 20 in black. (a) Vertical underprint, reading upwards.

PP59 1d. lake-red (G1), Plates 170, 171, 174, 176, 181, 184, 186, 187, 190 to 198, 200, 202 to 205, 207, 209, 214, 217, 218, 221, 223. . . . .

Plate nos. 221 and 223 exit unused.

(b) Vertical underprint, reading downwards

PP60 1d. lake-red (G1), Plates 171, 183, 200, 206 . . . .

1868. Debenham, Tewson & Farmer, 80, Cheapside, E.C. Unofficial Underprint Type 21 in black. (a) Vertical underprint, reading upwards.

PP62 1d. lake-red (G1), Plates 110, 125, 130, 131, 136 . . . .

(b) Vertical underprint, reading downwards

PP63 1d. lake-red (G1), Plate 222 . . . .

1868. M. De Costa Andrade & Co. Unofficial Underprint Type 22 in black. Vertical underprint, reading upwards.

PP64 1d. lake-red (G1), Plates 112, 116 . . . .

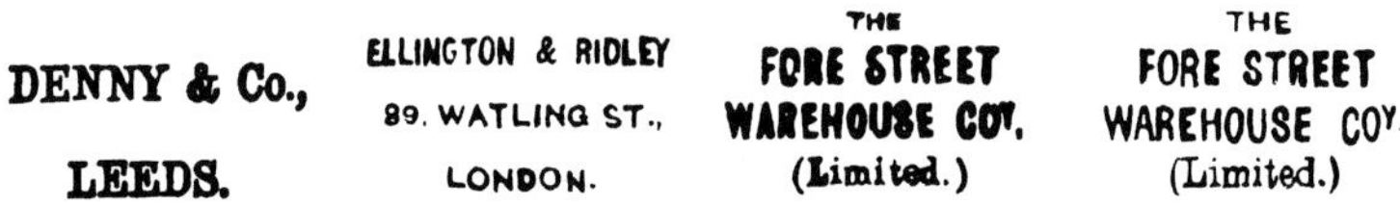

22A | 23 | 24 (Small "Limited") | 24A (Large "Limited")

1868. Denny & Co., Leeds. Unofficial Underprint Type 22A in black. Vertical underprint, reading downwards.

PP64A 1d. lake-red (G1), Plate 99 . . . .

186(?). Ellington & Ridley, 89, Watling Street, London, Unofficial Underprint Type 23 in black. Vertical underprint, reading downwards.

PP65 1d. lake-red (G1) Plate 119 . . . . £300

1868. The Fore Street Warehouse Coy. (Limited). Unofficial Underprint Type 24 in black. (a) Vertical underprint, reading upwards.

PP67 1d. lake-red (G1), Plates 111, 113, 117 to 125, 127, 129 to 132, 134, 136 to 168, 170 to 190, 192 to 202, 204, 207 to 212, 214 to 216, 218, 219, 221 . . . . *from* £120

PP68 1½d. lake red (G6), Plates (1) and 3. . . . .

PP69 2d. blue (G3), Plates 13, 14 and 15 . . . .

PP70 1s. deep green (J109), Plate 9 . . . .

PP71 1d. Venetian red (K3) . . . .

PP72 1d. lilac, 14 dots (K7) . . . .

(b) Vertical underprint, reading downwards

PP73 ½d. rose-red (G4), Plate 5 . . . .

PP74 1d. lake-red (G1) Plates 134, 143, 146, 153, 176, 177, 191 to 193, 195, 196, 208, 210, 220 . . . .

PP75 3d. rose (J41, J45A), Plates 17 and 21. . . . .

PP76 1d. lilac, 14 dots (K7). . . . .

PP77 1d. lilac, 16 dots (K8). . . . .

(c) Unofficial underprint Type 24A, in black

PP78 1d. Venetian red (K3) . . . .

PP79 1½d. Venetian red (K4) (upt. reads upwards) . . . .

PP79A 1½d. Venetian red (K4) (upt. reads downwards). . . . .

PP80 2½d. rosy mauve, (J4), Plate 3 (upt. reads upwards). . . . .

PP81 2½d. blue (J19), Plate 17 (upt. reads upwards) . . . .

PP81A 2½d. blue (J22), Plate 20 (upt. reads upwards). . . . .

PP81B 2½d. blue (J25), Plate 21 (upt. reads upwards). . . . .

G. E. R.	F. E. Gaddum, Manchester.	B. H. & H.	H. H.	James Harvey B. Stortford.
25	25A	26	27	28

1873. Great Eastern Railway. Official Underprint Type 25 in red.

PP82 1d. lake-red (G1), Plates 95, 111, 124, 134, 148, 149, 151, 155 to 158, 163, 168, 171, 174, 175, 176, 178, 181, 184, 185, 189 . *from* 90·00

1872. F. E. Gaddum, Manchester, Unofficial Underprint Type 25A in black. Vertical underprint, reading downwards.

PP83 1d. lake-red (G1), Plate 161 . . . .

1868. B.H. & H. Unofficial Underprint Type 26 in black. (a) Vertical underprint, reading upwards.

PP84 1d. lake-red (G1), Plate 120 . . . . £275

(b) Vertical underprint, reading downwards

PP84A 1d. lake-red (G1), Plate 122 . . . .

1869. H.H. Unofficial Underprint Type 27 in black.

PP85 1d. lake-red (G1), Plates 124, 154, 171, 186, 188, 198 . . . . . .

PP86 2d. blue (G3), Plates 13 and 14 . . . .

The 1d. Plates 171, 188, 198 and 2d. Plates 13 and 14 exist unused.

1868. James Harvey, B. Stortford. Unofficial Underprint Type 28 in black.

PP87 1d. lake-red (G1), Plates 113, 134, 155, 158, 164, 167, 170, 172 to 174, 176 to 179, 182, 184, 186, 188, 191 to 193, 195, 199, 201, 207, 210 . . . . *from* £275

Harvey and Portway, B. Stortford.	Property of A. & S. Henry & Co. Belfast.	Property of A. & S. Henry & Co. Glasgow.	A. & S. H. & CO.
29	**30**	**31**	**31A**

1868. Harvey and Portway, B. Stortford. Unofficial Underprint Type 29 in black.

PP88 1d. lake-red (G1), Plates 110, 113, 115, 123, 125, 127, 140, 151, 156, 160 . . . . *from* £275

1864. A. & S. Henry & Co. Belfast. Unofficial Underprint Type 30 in black. (a) Vertical underprint, reading upwards.

PP89 1d. lake-red (G1), Plates 81, 98, 99 . . . . *from* £275

(b) Unofficial underprint Type 31, vertically in black

PP90 1d. lake-red (G1) (upt. reads upwards), Plates 73, 93, 97, 102, 107, 123 to 127, 145, 148, 149, 179 . . . .

PP91 1d. lake-red (G1) (upt. reads downwards), Plates 102, 107, 154 . . . .

PP92 1½d. lake-red (G6) (upt. reads downwards), Plates (1), 3 . . . .

(c) Unofficial underprint Type 31A, vertically in black

PP93 1d. lake-red (G1) (upt. reads upwards), Plate 158 . . . .

Property of A. & S. Henry & Co. Portland-st., Manchester	Mr. Mitchell Henry's Committee 82, Market-st.	HOLLOWAY 244	C.T. HOOK & Co.
32	**33**	**34**	**35**

(d) Unofficial underprint Type 32. Vertical underprint in black, reading upwards

PP94 1d. lake-red (G1), Plates 73, 97, 98, 101, 102, 104, 106, 107, 110, 111, 113, 118, 119, 120, 125, 127, 130 . . . . *from* £275

PP95 2d. blue (G2), Plates 9 and 12 . . . .

PP96 2d. blue (G3), Plate 13 ....

PP97 3d. rose (J30), Plate 5 ....

PP97A 4d. vermilion (J58/9), Plates 11 and 12 ....

PP98 6d. violet (J75/7), Plates 6, 8 and 9 ....

PP99 1s. green (J104), Plate 4 ....

PP99A 2s. blue (J118), Plate 1 ....

(e) As last but underprint Type 32, reading downwards

PP100 1d. lake-red (G1), Plates 79, 92, 93, 97, 99 to 103, 105, 107, 109 to 111, 113, 115, 119, 122 to 125, 130, 133 to 135 ....

PP101 2d. blue (G2), Plates 9 and 12 ....

PP102 2d. blue (G3), Plate 13 ....

PP103 3d. rose (J30), Plates 5 and 6 ....

PP104 4d. vermilion (J58), Plate 11 ....

PP105 6d. violet (J75/7), Plates 6, 8 and 9 ....

PP106 1s. green (J104/5), Plates 4 and 5 ....

1864. Mitchell Henry's Committee, 82 Market Street, Unofficial Underprint Type 33 in black.

PP110 1d. lake-red (G1), Plates 79, 92, 102, 110, 111, 113, 118, 119, 153 .... *from* £300

It has been suggested that the origin of No. PP110 was Manchester.

186(?). Holloway 244 (Strand, London). Unofficial Overprint Type 34 in blue.

PP111 1d rose-red (C10), Plates 43, 47, 55, 57 .... *from* £325

PP112 1d rose-red (C12), Plates 50 and 51 ....

PP113 1d rose-red (C13), Plate R16 ....

This overprint was reported to have been a wooden handstamp applied to the stamp stock of Holloway's Pills and Ointment from about 1860–64.

1868. C. T. Hook & Co. Unofficial Overprint Type 35 in black.

PP114 1d lake-red (G1), Plate 117 ....

HUGH JONES & CO LONDON.	H. J. & Co WOOD STREET	Moses, Levy & Co., 2 & 3, Aldgate.	LINOLEUM COMPY. (Limited)
36	37	38	39

1866. Hugh Jones & Co., London. Unofficial Underprint Type 36 in black. (a) Vertical underprint, reading upwards.

PP115 1d. lake-red (G1), Plates 102, 105, 107, 109 to 112, 115 to 121, 123, 124, 213 .... *from* £275

PP116 2d. blue (G3), Plate 13 ....

(b) Vertical underprint, reading downwards

PP117 1d. lake-red (G1), Plates 107, 111, 123 . . . .

PP118 2d. blue (G2), Plate 12 . . . .

1866. H. J. & Co., Wood Street, Unofficial Underprint Type 37 in black, reading downwards.

PP119 1d lake-red (G1), Plates 102 and 120 . . . .

1864. Moses, Levy & Co., 2 and 3, Aldgate. Unofficial Underprint Type 38 in black. (a) Vertical underprint, reading upwards.

PP120 1d lake-red (G1), Plate 193 . . . . £300

(b) Vertical underprint, reading downwards

PP121 1d. lake-red (G1), Plate 91 . . . .

PP122 2d. blue (G3), Plate 13 . . . .

PP122A 6d. lilac (J72), Plates 4, 5 . . . .

PP123 6d. violet (J76), Plate 8 . . . .

PP124 1s. green (J103), Plate 4 . . . .

1868. Linoleum Compy. (Limited). Unofficial Underprint Type 39 in black, reading upwards.

PP125 1d. lake-red (G1), Plates 107, 111, 122, 130, 136 . . . .

40

41
(Letters $1\frac{1}{2}$ mm high)

42

1878. Messhirrefi. Unofficial Overprint Type 40 in black, reading upwards.

PP126 1d lake-red (G1), Plate 218 . . . . £275

1864. Samuel, Montagu & Co. Unofficial Underprint. (a) Type 41 (letters $1\frac{1}{2}$ mm high) in black.

PP127 1d. lake-red (G1), Plates 72, 76, 78, 80, 81, 85, 86, 87, 92, 95, 96, 100, 101, 103 . . . . *from* £275

PP128 2d. blue (G2), Plate 9 . . . .

PP129 3d. rose (J28), Plate 4 . . . .

PP130 4d. vermilion (J55/6), Plates 8 and 9 . . . .

a. Underprint inverted (Plate 8) . . . .

PP131 6d. lilac (J73/4), Plates 5 and 6 . . . .

PP132 6d. violet (J75), Plate 6 . . . .

PP133 1s. green (J103), Plate 4 . . . .

(b) Underprint as Type 41 (letters 2 mm high) in black

PP134 2d. blue (G2), Plate 9 . . . .

PP135 6d. lilac (J73), Plate 5 . . . .

PP136 1s. green (J103), Plate 4 . . . .

1868. W. M. & Co. Unofficial Underprint Type 42 in black. (a) Vertical underprint, reading upwards.

PP139 2d. blue (G2), Plate 9 . . . .

(b) Vertical underprint, reading downwards

PP140 1d. lake-red (G1). Plates 115, 185 . . . .

PP141 2d. blue (G2), Plate 12 . . . .

(c) Underprint horizontal

PP142 1d. lake-red (G1), Plate 115 . . . .

43 44 45 46

1868. Naylor, Benzon & Co., London. Unofficial Underprint Type 43 in black.

PP143 1d. lake-red (G1), Plates 111, 115, 118, 119, 122, 127, 131, 135, 137, 139, 141, 142, 144, 145, 148, 149, 152, 155, 157 . . . . . . *from* £300

PP143A 2d. blue (G3), Plate 13 . . . .

PP144 3d. rose (J31, J35), Plates 6, 10 . . . .

PP144A 4d. vermilion (J58), Plate 11 . . . .

PP145 6d. violet (J77), Plates 8, 9. . . . .

PP145A 1s. green (J105), Plate 5 . . . .

PP146 5s. rose (J121), Plate 1. . . . .

1881. Ogilvie & Moore, Cork. Unofficial Underprint Type 44 in purple.

PP147 1d. lilac, 16 dots (KB) . . . .

1858 (November). Oxford Union Society. Unofficial Overprint Type 45 in red on the face of the stamps. (a) Vertical overprint, reading upwards.

PP148 1d. rose-red (C10), Plates 27, 34, 36, 39, 41, 42, 43, 44, 46 to 49, 52, 55 to 62, 66, 68 . . . . *from* 24·00

Used on cover	60·00
a. Overprint double	£225
b. Stop after "S" inverted (at top)	
PP149 1d. rose-red (C12), Plate 50	75·00
Used on cover	£150
PP150 1d. rose-red (C13), Plates R15, R16	*from* 75·00
Used on cover	£120
PP151 1d. lake-red (G1), Plates 71 to 74, 76, 78 to 107, 109 to 119, 121, 123, 125, 129 to 135, 137, 139, 140, 142	*from* 24·00
Used on cover	90·00
a. Overprint double, Plates 93, 95, 112	*from* £225
b. Watermark inverted (Plate 101)	

(b) Vertical underprint, reading downwards

PP152 1d. rose-red (C10), Plates 46, 47, 52, 57	*from* 75·00
Used on cover	£150
PP153 1d. lake-red (G1), Plates 95, 97, 101	*from* 75·00
Used on cover	£150

1871 (January). Oxford Union Society. Official Underprint Type 46 in red on the back of stamps. (a) Vertical underprint, reading upwards.

PP154 1d. lake-red (G1), Plates 119, 124, 130, 134 to 136, 146, 150, 155, 156, 159, 160, 162 to 166, 169 to 171, 174, 177, 179, 182, 183, 185, 197, 199, 204, 205, 208, 212, 213, 215, 218	*from* 36·00
a. No stop after "O"	60·00

(b) Vertical underprint, reading downwards

PP155 1d. lake-red (G1), Plates 134, 143, 150, 156, 205, 212, 213	*from* 70·00
Used on cover	—
a. No stop after "O"	£110

1880. Oxford Union Society. Unofficial Underprint as Type 45 in carmine. (a) Vertical underprint, reading upwards.

PP156 1d. lake-red (G1), Plates 199, 200, 223	—
PP157 1d. Venetian red (K3)	70·00
PP158 1d. lilac, 14 dots (K7)	£170
PP159 1d. lilac, 16 dots (K8) (carmine underprint)	90·00
PP160 1d. lilac, as PP159 but underprint in various other shades, brown-red to violet	£170

(b) Vertical underprint, reading downwards

PP161 1d. lake-red (G1), Plates 199, 200, 202, 205, 208, 218, 221, 223, 225	*from* 65·00
PP162 1d. Venetian red (K3)	70·00
PP163 1d. lilac, 14 dots (K7)	£200
PP164 1d. lilac, 16 dots (K8) (carmine underprint)	90·00
PP165 1d. lilac, as PP164 but underprint in various other shades, brown-red to violet	—

P P S O	H ROSSELL & Co SHEFFIELD	R & S. M.	G.S.S. & Co.
47	48	49	50

1874. PPSO. Unofficial Overprint Type 47 in purple on face of stamp.

PP166 1d lake-red (G1), Plate 176 . . . .

1873. H. Rossell & Co., Sheffield. Unofficial Underprint Type 48 in black.

PP167 $\frac{1}{2}$d. rose-red (G4), Plate 1 . . . .

PP168 1d. lake-red (G1), Plates 140, 168, 170, 184, 191, 198 . . . . .

1870. R. & S. M. (Ryland & Sons, Manchester). Unofficial Underprint Type 49 in black.

PP169 1d. lake-red (G1), Plates 181 and 182 . . . .

PP170 $\frac{1}{2}$d. rose-red (G4), Plate 6 . . . .

1868. G. S. S. & Co. Unofficial Underprint Type 50 in black. (a) Vertical underprint, reading upwards.

PP171 1d. lake-red (G1), Plates 105 . . . .

(b) Vertical underprint, reading downwards

PP171A 1d. lake-red (G1), Plate 109 . . . .

(c) Underprint horizontal

PP172 $\frac{1}{2}$d. rose-red (G4), Plates 4 to 6, 10, 11, 13, 14, 20 . . . .

PP173 1d. lake-red (G1), Plates 111, 118, 123, 125, 140, 144, 148 to 150, 153, 154, 156, 158, 159, 166, 168 to 170, 175, 177, 184, 187, 189, 191, 192, 195, 197, 200, 201, 204, 205, 214 . . . . *from* £275

a. Overprint inverted, Plate 140 . . . .

PP173B $1\frac{1}{2}$d. lake-red (G6), Plate (1) . . . .

PP174 2d. blue (G3), Plates 13, 14, 15 . . . .

PP175 $2\frac{1}{2}$d. rosy mauve (J14), Plate 13 . . . .

PP176 3d. rose (J30), Plate 5 . . . .

PP176A 9d. straw (J96), Plate 4 (underprint inverted) . . . .

PP177 1d. Venetian red (K3) . . . .

J. S. & Co. 68, Up. Th. St.	The Property of Schwann. Modera & Co., London.	SMITH, ELDER & C.O. LONDON.	SMITH & LISTER.
51	52	53	54

1868. J. S. & Co. 68, Up. Th. St. (James Spicer & Co.). Unofficial Underprint Type 51 in black.

PP178 $\frac{1}{2}$d. rose-red (G3), Plate 11 . . . .

PP179 1d. lake-red (G1), Plates 114, 117, 122, 123, 125, 129 to 131, 134 to 136, 138 to 140, 144, 145, 147, 150 to 152, 156, 159, 164, 167, 168, 171, 173, 174, 177, 187, 191, 192, 195, 201, 205, 207, 220 . . *from* £300

1870. Schwann, Modera & Comp., London. Unofficial Underprint Type 52 in black.

PP180 1d lake-red (G1), Plate 138 . . . .

PP180A 3d. rose (J30), Plate 5 . . . .

1864. Smith, Elder & Co., London. Unofficial Underprint Type 53 in black

PP181 1d lake-red (G1), Plates 84, 87, 96, 97, 107 . . . . *from* £300

PP182 4d vermilion (J56), Plate 9 . . . .

1868. Smith & Lister. Unofficial Underprint Type 54 in black.

PP183 1d lake-red (G1), Plates 120, 129, 137, 138, 151 . . . . *from* £300

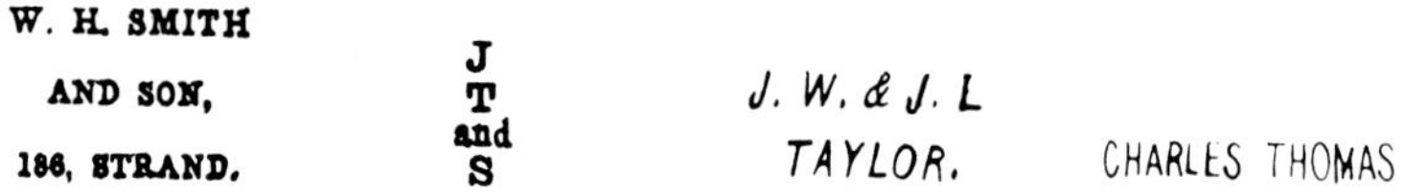

55 56 57 58

1867. W. H. Smith and Son, 186 Strand. Official Underprint Type 55 in red or blue (2d.). (a) Underprint reading upwards

PP187 1d. lake-red (G1), Plates 92, 97, 103, 109, 119, 121, 124, 131, 134, 147, 152, 164, 169, 173, 174, 183 . . . . *from* 38·00

PP188 2d. blue (G2), Plate 9 . . . . £130

PP189 2d. blue (G3), Plate 14 . . . . £130

(b) Underprint reading downwards

PP190 1d. lake-red (G1), Plates 73, 74, 78, 102, 111, 114, 124, 147 *from* 42·00

PP191 2d. blue (G2), Plate 9 . . . . £150

Essays of a sans-serif W. H. Smith underprint on the 1867 1s., Plate 4, are known. Other Essays in various colours are known on the 1d. Plate 95 (overprints as well as underprints). These last differ from the official underprints in that the address is omitted.

1864. J. T. and S. (Joseph Travers & Sons). Unofficial Overprint Type 56 in red.

PP192 1d lake-red (G1), Plate 90 . . . .

The 1d. Plate 90 exists unused only.

1872. J. W. & J. L. Taylor. Unofficial Underprint Type 57. (a) Underprint in black (letters 2$\frac{1}{2}$ mm high).

PP193 1d lake-red (G1), Plates 155, 172 . . . .

(b) As last but not italic (letters 3 mm high) in black

PP194 1d. lake-red (G1), Plate 163 . . . .

1868. Charles Thomas. Unofficial Overprint Type 58 diagonally in black.

PP195 1d lake-red (G1), Plate 111 . . . .

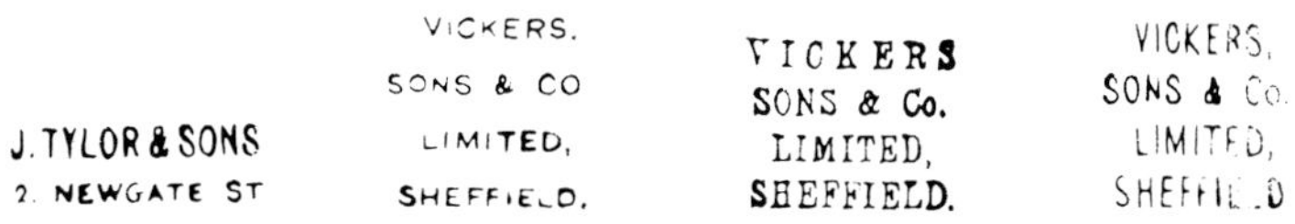

59 60 61 62

1868. J. Tylor & Sons, 2 Newgate St. Unofficial Underprint Type 59 in black. (a) Vertical underprint, reading upwards.

PP196 1d. lake-red (G1), Plates 119, 120, 122, 124, 134, 138, 140, 143, 144, 147, 149 to 152, 154, 156, 161, 167, 171, 173, 174, 177, 185, 192, 198, 201, 212 . . . . *from* £300

(b) Vertical underprint, reading downwards

PP197 1d. lake-red (G1), Plates 146, 170, 183, 201, 202, 207, 213 .

1868. Vickers Sons & Co. Limited, Sheffield. (a) Unofficial Underprint Type 60 in black.

PP198 1d. lake-red (G1), Plates 105, 120, 122 to 124, 129, 131, 133, 135, 138 to 140, 143 to 145, 147 to 152, 154, 155, 157 to 161, 163, 165, 166, 168, 170, 171, 173, 174, 175, 177, 178, 181, 182, 184, 185, 191 to 193, 196, 198, 199 . . . . *from* 90·00

PP199 1½d. lake-red (G6), Plate 3 . . . .

PP200 2d. blue (G3), Plates 14 and 15 . . . .

PP200A 2½d. blue (J24), Plate 22 . . . .

PP201 3d. rose (J34), Plate 9 . . . .

PP202 4d. vermilion (J60), Plate 13 . . . .

(b) Unofficial Underprint Type 61, in black

PP203 1d. lake-red (G1), Plates 134, 198, 202 . . . .

PP204 1½d. lake-red (G6), Plate 3 . . . .

PP205 2d. blue (G3), Plate 15 . . . .

PP206 6d. grey (J85), Plate 15 . . . .

(c) Unofficial Underprint Type 62, in black

PP207 1d. lake-red (G1), Plates 130, 150, 182, 192 . . . .

PP207A 1½d. lake-red (G6), Plate 3 . . . .

F. P. W. & CO.	F. P. W. & CO.	G.H.W.& CO ST. PAUL'S	W&Co
63	64	65	66

1868. F. P. W. & Co. Unofficial Underprint Type 63 in black. (a) Vertical underprint, reading upwards.

PP208 1d lake-red (G1), Plates 106 to 108, 114 . . . .

PP209 2d. blue (G3), Plate 13 . . . .

(c) Unofficial Underprint, reading downwards

PP210 1d. lake-red (G1), Plates 106, 114 . . . .

(c) Unofficial underprint Type 64, vertically in black reading upwards

PP211 1d. lake-red (G1), Plates 111, 113, 118, 121, 124, 127, 132, 134, 135, 137, 147, 150, 152, 160, 162, 174, 177, 184, 187, 193, 194, 197 to 199, 208, 211 . . . .

PP212 1½d. lake-red (G6), Plate 3 . . . .

PP213 2d. blue (G3), Plates 14 and 15 . . . .

PP213A 3d. rose (J30), Plate 5 . . . .

(c) Vertical underprint, reading downwards

PP214 1d. lake-red (G1), Plates 106, 107, 114, 117, 118, 122, 124, 130, 132, 133, 135, 137, 138, 140, 144, 149 to 151, 155, 156, 158, 165, 170, 171, 175, 182, 186, 188, 192 to 195, 198, 202, 203, 205, 206, 209 . . . .

PP215 1½d. lake-red (G6), Plate 3 . . . .

PP216 2d. blue (G3), Plates 13 to 15 . . . .

PP216A 2½d. rosy mauve (J3), Plate 3 . . . .

PP217 4d. vermilion (J58), Plate 11 . . . .

PP217A 4d. sage-green (J65), Plate 16 . . . .

1866. G. H. W. & Co. St. Paul's (G. Hitchcock Williams & Co.). Unofficial Underprint Type 65 in black, reading upwards.

PP218 ½d. rose-red (G4), Plate 3 . . . .

PP219 1d. lake-red (G1), Plates 100 to 103, 107 to 125, 127, 129 to 136, 138 to 156, 158 to 170, 172, 174, 177 . . . . *from* £300

PP220 2d. blue (G3), Plate 13 . . . .

1875. W. & Co., Unofficial Overprint Type 66 in black.

PP221 1d lake-red (G1), Plates 179, 184, 198 . . . .

W.W.&CO.	WILLIAM WHITELEY LONDON.
67	68

1872. W. W. & Co. Unofficial Underprint Type 67 in black. (a) Vertical underprint, reading upwards.

PP222 1d. lake-red (G1), Plates 159, 168, 174, 176, 189 . . . . *from* £275

(b) Vertical underprint, reading downwards

PP223 1d. lake-red (G1), Plates 159, 174 . . . .

1877. William Whiteley, London. Unofficial Underprint Type 68 in red.

PP224 1d lake-red (G1), Plate 205 . . . .

PP225 1d. Venetian red (K3) . . . .

a. Underprint inverted . . . .

No. PP224 is known only with the underprint inverted.

APPENDIX 3

"Specimen" and "Cancelled" Overprints

From 1840 to 1873 examples of stamps of new denominations and of those differing fundamentally in design from their predecessors were distributed with circulars to Postmasters in the United Kingdom and Ireland and also to a few British Postmasters overseas. Changes in plate numbers or in the style of the corner lettering were not considered to be fundamental changes for this purpose. From 1847 the stamps used for this purpose were cancelled with the word "SPECIMEN". Thus the first new issue to be so cancelled was the 1847 Embossed Shilling.

Also many issues, including 1849 printings of the imperforate Penny Red-brown and Twopence Blue, were cancelled "SPECIMEN" for use as official reference copies and for other official purposes. It later became the practice to preserve sheets or blocks of six of printings from different plates which varied in shade from their predecessors to serve as colour standards for matching future printings and these were cancelled "SPECIMEN", or later "CANCELLED". However, the "CANCELLED" Type **14A** was used mainly by the printers on samples of their work for the purpose of securing contracts from other countries. There is another form of large "Cancelled" applied in manuscript diagonally upwards which is found on archive material which is now on the market.

In 1879 examples of the then current British stamps were cancelled "SPECIMEN" and sent to the International Bureau of the Universal Postal Union for distribution to the member nations. This practice continued for new issues involving new values or colours and major changes in design throughout the Victorian period. However, from 1892 only stamps with face values above 1s. were overprinted "SPECIMEN", the lower values being sent unoverprinted. Consequently the 1892 4½d., and 1900 ½d. and 1s. overprinted "SPECIMEN" were only used for official purposes.

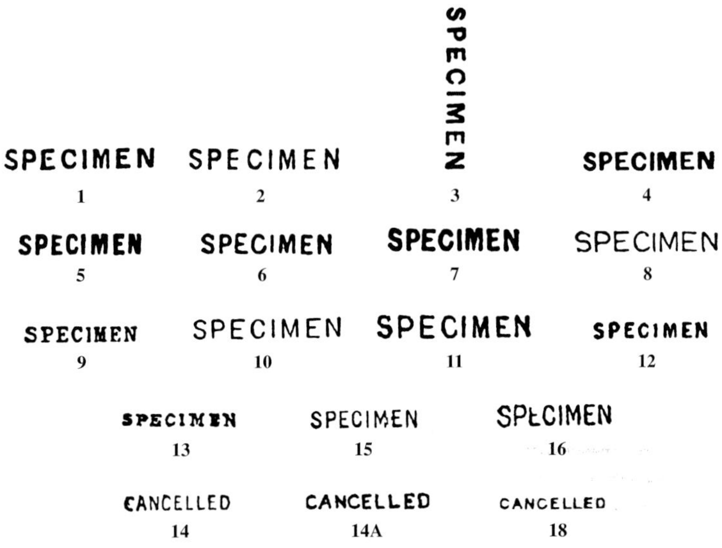

It is understood that at some time one of the departments of the Post Office had in its possession a whole-world collection of postage stamps and items of postal stationery which had been received as specimens from the U.P.U. by the postal authorities of one of the British-controlled territories and returned to the Post Office as surplus to requirements. To avoid having to take this material on charge, the Post Office auditors cancelled all the items, whether or not they had been previously overprinted "SPECIMEN". For this purpose they used a large serifed "SPECIMEN" handstamp measuring

22½ × 2¾ mm and a very large sans-serif "CANCELLED" measuring over 40 × 6 mm and capable of cancelling several stamps with one strike. Many of these stamps were stuck down and/or additionally pen-cancelled. Whilst it is clear that these overprints were British and official, the stamps bearing them cannot have the same status as the official reference specimens and they are therefore not listed.

A few overseas receiving authorities also cancelled British stamps received from the U.P.U. with "SPECIMEN" or its foreign equivalent, but these are not listed.

All the types of "SPECIMEN" and "CANCELLED" overprints referred to in the lists in this volume are illustrated in this Appendix.

The table below gives the dimensions and dates of use of the various overprints:

	Dimensions	*Dates of Use*
Type **1***	19¾ × 2½ mm	1847–70
Type **2**	20 mm × 2¾–3 mm	1854–73
Type **3**	21 × 2½ mm	1855
Type **4**	18 × 2½ mm	1856
Type **5**	16½ × 2¾ mm	1862–67
Type **6***	18¼ mm × 2¾–3 mm	1860–87
Type **7**	18¼ mm × 3 mm	*c.* 1861
Type **8**	19½ × 2½ mm	1862–77
Type **9***	14¾ × 1¾–2 mm	1871–1900
Type **10***	20 × 2½ mm	1874–87
Type **11***	20¼ × 3 mm	1876–1900
Type **12**	15½ × 1¾ mm	1881–87
Type **13**	15¼ × 1½ mm	1883–92
Type **14***	14½ × 1¾ mm	1883–1900
Type **14A**	17½ × 1¾ mm	*c.* 1873
Type **15***	14½ mm × 2–2¼ mm	1891–1902
Type **16**	15½ × 2½ mm	1891–1902
Type **18**	14¼ × 1½ mm	1900–1907

The Types marked above with asterisks represent groups of overprints which differ in style (and also in dimensions where indicated). Care should therefore be exercised, since overprints of these groups not identical to the illustrations above are not necessarily forgeries. Reference should also be made to the dates of use given for each Type.

Types **3**, **4**, **5**, **14**, **14A** and **18** were printed from type-set formes by De La Rue and all the rest are believed to have been handstamped at Somerset House by the Inland Revenue, so that sight variations in dimension can be found.

Forgeries. Beware of forged overprints and more particularly of fakes made by using perforated copies bearing genuine overprints and trimming them to pass as imperforates, especially wing-margined copies where it is possible to leave one wide margin.

Inverted Overprints. Genuine inverted overprints are known but as varieties they are outside the scope of the listings.

APPENDIX 4

Postage Rates

Postage rates from 1635 have been researched from official records and the following extract is reproduced with the kind permission of the Post Office. The rates given apply only to the period covered by this Catalogue.

Letter Post. The Treasury was empowered to regulate rates of postage, and subsequent changes have been made by Treasury Warrant.

Date	*Rates of Charge*	
5 December 1839	½oz.	4d.
	1oz.	8d.
	2oz.	1s. 4d.

Then 8d. for each additional oz. up to 16oz.

Date	*Rates of Charge*	
10 January 1840	½oz.	1d.
	1oz.	2d.
	2oz.	4d.

Then 2d for each additional oz. up to 16oz. The weight limit was abolished in 1847.

Date	*Rates of Charge*	
1 April 1865	½oz.	1d.
	1oz.	2d.
	1½oz..	3d.

The 1d. for each additional ½oz.

Date	*Rates of Charge*	
5 October 1871	1oz.	1d.
	2oz.	1½d.

Then ½d. for each 2oz. up to 12oz. Then 1d.for each additional oz.

Date	*Rates of Charge*	
1 July 1885	1oz.	1d.
	2oz.	1½d.

The ½d. for each additional 2oz.

Date	*Rates of Charge*	
22 June 1897	4oz.	1d.

The 1½d. for each additional 2oz.

Imperial Penny Postage. The rate for the then colonies of 1d. was introduced on 25 December 1898. The rate was extended to the United States in 1908.

Postcards. The Postcard was first introduced in Austria in 1869 and, because of their great popularity, were issued by the British Post Office in 1870. The charge for sending a postcard throughout the period covered by this Catalogue was ½d. and the maximum size allowed was 5½″× 3½″. In 1882 the reply Postcard came into use. It was not until 1894 that permission was granted for the use of private postcards to which an adhesive stamp could be affixed. These became very popular following the introduction of the picture postcard.

Printed Papers (Introduced as "Book Post"). A Book Post was set up on the recommendation of Rowland Hill. The charge was 6d. per 1lb. and was restricted to one book per package. This rule was relaxed soon after to cover second-hand books and the sending of more than one book in a package. This service was a great boon to the subscribing Lending Libraries.

Date	*Rates of Charge*	
21 February 1848	6d. per lb. up to 14lb.	

From 1855 regulations modified to permit practically any printed matter to be sent by the Book Post.

Date	*Rates of Charge*	
1855	4oz.	1d.
	8oz.	2d.
	16oz.	4d.

Then 2d. for each additional ½lb. up to 14lb.

Date	*Rates of Charge*	
1866	4oz.	1d.
	8oz.	2d.

Then 1d. for each additional 4oz. up to 14lb.

Date	*Rates of Charge*	
1 October 1870	2oz.	½d.

Then ½d. for each additional 2oz. up to 5lb. Newspapers ½d. per copy irrespective of weight.

Date	*Rates of Charge*	
22 June 1897	2oz. only	½d.

Because the Letter Rate became 1d. for 4oz. and ½d. for each additional 2oz. the Book Post applied only to packets up to 2oz. in weight.

Express Service. The Treasury authorized an expenditure of £1,100 by the Post Office in 1891 for a limited local service in London. This was the beginning of the Express Service as it is today.

SERVICE I. Express by Post Office messenger all the way. This was introduced in London and selected provincial towns on 25 March 1891 and extended to the whole country in August the same year.

Date	*Charges*
25 March 1891	2d. for first mile 3d. for each succeeding mile

There was an additional 1s. for distances over 2 miles where no public conveyance was available: plus ordinary postage.

1892. Postage no longer levied but a weight charge of 1½d. per 1lb. after the first lb. was imposed.

Date	*Charges*
July 1893	3d. per mile with a weight charge of 1½d. a lb. after the first lb.

1898. Weight charge reduced to 1d. per lb. after first lb.

1900. Weight charge abolished.

SERVICE II Special Delivery at the request of the sender. This was introduced as a new service in August 1891. In London the fee in no case exceeded 3d. unless delivery was affected from the GPO or Head District Post Office to an address outside the postal delivery of those offices when full fee was charged.

Date *Charges*

August 1891. Full ordinary postage plus 2d. for the first mile and 3d. for each succeeding mile, and in addition 1s. fee for distances over 2 miles where no public conveyance was available.

July 1893	3d. per mile with a weight charge of 1½d. per lb. after the first lb.

Date *Charges*

1898. Weight charge reduced to 1d. per lb. after the first lb.

1900. Weight charge abolished.

SERVICE III. Express delivery at the request of the addressee. Introduced in July 1893 together with the new charges for Services I and II. The charges were the same as for Service I.

SERVICE V. Express delivery of message received by telephone. This was a new service introduced in July 1893. The charge included the usual amount for the telephone call, a writing down fee (minimum charge 3d. for 30 words., 1d. for every additional 10 words) and Express charges as for Service I.

Official Parcel Post. A general official Parcel Post Service was introduced on 1 August 1883.

Date	*Rates of Postage*	
1 August 1883	1lb.	3d.
	2lb.	6d.
	5lb.	9d.
	up to 7lb.	1s. 0d.
1 May 1886	1lb.	3d.
	2lb.	4½d.
	3lb.	6d.
	4lb.	7½d.
	5lb.	9d.
	6lb.	10½d.
	7lb.	1s. 0d.
	8lb.	1s. 1½d.
	9lb.	1s. 3d..
	10lb.	1s. 4½d.
	up to 11lb	1s. 6d.

Date	*Rates of Postage*	
1 June 1897	1lb.	3d.
	2lb.	4d.
	3lb.	5d.
	4lb.	6d.
	5lb.	7d.
	6lb.	8d.
	7lb.	9d.
	8lb.	10d.
	9lb.	11d.
	up to 11lb.	1s. 0d.

APPENDIX 5

Circular Delivery Companies

Prior to 1870 there was no cheap "printed paper" service provided by the British Post Office for the delivery of addressed printed circulars, and similar material, which were becoming increasingly important to the many retail businesses which had been set up during the economic expansion of the 1860s.

In the autumn of 1865 an Edinburgh printer, Robert Brydone, advertised the services of the Edinburgh & Leith Circular Delivery Company and its associated parcels delivery company. The venture was an immediate success, although Robert Brydone was declared bankrupt in September 1866. His difficulties appear to have been very short-lived, however, as he then moved to London, leaving his father in charge of the Edinburgh companies.

Once in London Robert Brydone formed the London Circular Delivery Company which amalgamated with the Metropolitan Circular Delivery Company in April 1867 under the management of Manuel Eyre. There were, by now, other companies, either independent or connected to Brydone's network, in Aberdeen, Dundee, Edinburgh, Glasgow and Liverpool. Brydone and Eyre now expanded with the London & Districts Circular Delivery Company and the National Circular Delivery Company which was intended to transfer circulars between the companies in the various cities.

Robert Brydone is thought to have left the London companies in July 1867.

It is possible that he had a premonition of disaster as the Post Office moved against the London & Metropolitan Circular Delivery Company the following month for violating the official postal monopoly. They had previously obtained a legal opinion that:

"No letters or printed circulars, folded or enclosed in a sealed envelope, could legally be collected and delivered otherwise than by the official Post Office.

Letters conveyed by messenger specially employed by the senders or writers were exempted from exclusive privilege, but that no one could legally collect such letters for delivery".

London & Metropolitan lost the case and, in consequence, the circular delivery companies ceased trading around September 1867, or possibly reverted to the delivery of unaddressed and unfolded circulars which fell outside the Post Office monopoly.

USE. It seems likely that many of the circulars were delivered without stamps being attached, although a few issues have survived on cover or circular. It is possible that only individually addressed items were so treated. Notes on known cancellations are provided in the listings.

PRINTING PROCESS. All genuine circular delivery company issues were printed by lithography.

CRAYON MARKS. It is believed that these were applied, usually in blue, by the stamp dealer W. S. Lincoln after he had been informed that it was an offence to sell such issues in unused condition.

ILLUSTRATIONS. In this section the stamp illustrations are shown $\frac{3}{4}$ size. Company cancellations are shown full size.

PRICES. These are for unused examples without defects. Examples with crayon marks, as described above, are generally worth 50% of the unused price.

ABERDEEN CIRCULAR DELIVERY COMPANY

1

1867 (May). *P* 13

CD1	**1**	$\frac{1}{2}$d. yellow-brown	£110
CD2		$\frac{1}{2}$d. slate-blue	12·00

Printed in sheets of 130 (10 × 13).

CLARK & CO, EDINBURGH

2

1866 (Feb.). *Imperf.*

CD3	**2**	($\frac{1}{4}$d.) blue	24·00

Printed in sheets of 72 (8 × 9), made up of two alternating transfer types, over 25mm wide and the other 23$\frac{1}{2}$mm.

DUNDEE CIRCULAR DELIVERY COMPANY

3

1867 (May). *Imperf.*

CD4	**3**	$\frac{1}{4}$d. reddish purple	£110
CD5		$\frac{1}{2}$d. dull scarlet	£110

Printed in sheets of 130 (10 × 13).

EDINBURGH & LEITH CIRCULAR DELIVERY COMPANY

4

Monogram cancellation

1865 (Oct.)–**66.**

CD6	**4**	$\frac{1}{4}$d. green (*roul* 7)	22·00
		a. Imperf between (vert pair)	£350
		b. Perf 11$\frac{1}{2}$	55·00
CD7		$\frac{1}{4}$d. slate-blue (*roul* 7)	15·00
		a. Imperf between (horiz pair)	£210
CD8		$\frac{1}{4}$d. grey-lilac (*imperf*)	15·00
		a. Perf 11$\frac{1}{2}$	£150

CD9		$\frac{1}{4}$d. olive-grey (*imperf*)	15·00
		a. Perf 11$\frac{1}{2}$	15·00
		b. Roul 7	75·00
		c. Pin perf 10$\frac{1}{2}$	75·00
CD10		$\frac{1}{4}$d. dull mauve (*imperf*) (Jan. 1866)	7·50
		a. Perf 11$\frac{1}{2}$	60·00

No. CD7 has been reported imperforate

Stamps known used on cover or circular:
No. CD6
No. CD6b
No. CD7
No. CD9
No. CD9a
No. CD10a

Loose stamps known with monogram cancellation:

No. CD6b	£150
No. CD10a	£150

Printed in sheets of 64 (8 × 8) (Nos. CD6/7) or 60 (10 × 6) (others).

5

1866 (Dec.). *Imperf.*

CD11	**5**	$\frac{1}{4}$d. grey-lilac	8·50
		a. Pin perf 10$\frac{1}{2}$	22·00
CD12		$\frac{1}{2}$d. yellowish green	22·00
		a. Pin perf 10$\frac{1}{2}$	30·00
		ab. Imperf between (vert pair)	£375

Printed in sheets of 66 (11 × 6).

6

1867 (Feb.). Inscr. "12 ELDER STREET". *Imperf.*

CD13	**6**	$\frac{1}{4}$d. red-brown	7·50
		a. Roul 7	£150
CD14		$\frac{1}{4}$d. black/*lemon-yellow*	£225
		a. Roul 7	£150

Stamps known used on cover or circular:
No. CD14a

Printed in sheets of 144 (12 × 12).

FORGERIES: $\frac{1}{4}$d. in green (*imperf* or *roul* 13) or grey-blue (*imperf*). These either have inscriptions in sans-serif letters, instead of serif, or are printed in typography instead of lithography.

EDINBURGH & LEITH PARCEL DELIVERY COMPANY

7

1865 (Oct). *Inscr*. "12 St ANDREW SQUARE". *Roul* 7.

CD15	**7**	($\frac{1}{4}$d.) yellowish green	£175
CD16		(2d.) yellow-bistre	12·00
CD17		(3d.) red-brown	£175

Nos. CD15/17 have been reported imperforate.

Stamps known used on cover or circular:
No. CD15 . . . .
No. CD16 . . . .
No. CD17 . . . .

Loose stamps used with monogram cancellation:
No. CD15 . . . . £375

Printed in sheets of 240 (20 × 12).

8

1866 (Mar.). *Imperf.*

CD18	**8**	2d. yellow	12·00
		a. Roul 7	75·00
		ab. Imperf between (vert pair)	£375
		b. Pin perf $10\frac{1}{2}$	60·00
CD19		3d. brown-red	12·00
		a. Roul 7	55·00
		b. Pin perf $10\frac{1}{2}$	55·00
		ba. Imperf on three sides (perf at right only)	

Printed in sheets of 60 (10 × 6).

FORGERIES: 3d. (*imperf*) in lilac, bright violet, deep blue, red-orange, yellow or green.

GLASGOW CIRCULAR DELIVERY COMPANY

9

1866 (Dec.). *Horizontally laid paper. Imperf.*

CD20	**9**	$\frac{1}{4}$d. black	7·50
		a. Pin perf $10\frac{1}{2}$	24·00
		ab. Imperf between (horiz pair)	£375
CD21		$\frac{1}{2}$d. dull scarlet	7·50
		a. Pin perf $10\frac{1}{2}$	30·00

Printed in sheets of 66 (11 × 6).

FORGERIES: $\frac{1}{4}$d. (*imperf.*) in black or orange; $\frac{1}{2}$d. (*imperf*) in vermilion or black; 1d. (*imperf*) in carmine-lake. All on wove paper and showing a curved vertical line extending downwards from the upright of the second "R" in "CIRCULAR".

LIVERPOOL CIRCULAR DELIVERY COMPANY

10

1867 (Apr).

CD22	**10**	$\frac{1}{4}$d. sepia (*imperf*)	24·00
CD23		$\frac{1}{4}$d. brown (*perf* 13)	11·00
CD24		$\frac{1}{2}$d. state-lilac (*perf* 13)	9·50
		a. Blank impression (in pair with normal)	£725

No. CD24a occurs on R.1/18. Early sheets show a very weak impression on this position which was subsequently completely erased to form No. CD24a.

Printed in sheets of 198 (18 × 11) (Nos. CD22, CD24) or 99 (9 × 11) (No. CD23).

LONDON & METROPOLITAN CIRCULAR DELIVERY COMPANY

London Circular Delivery Company

11

1866 (Sept). *Thick soft paper without wmk. (a) Imperf.*

CD25	**11**	$\frac{1}{4}$d. deep blue	9·50
CD26		$\frac{1}{2}$d. greenish grey	7·50
CD27		$\frac{1}{2}$d. deep dull purple	9·50
CD28		$\frac{1}{2}$d. dull mauve	27·00

(b) Clean-cut perf $11\frac{3}{4}$ *(large holes)*

CD29	**11**	$\frac{1}{4}$d. deep blue	12·00
CD30		$\frac{1}{2}$d. greenish grey	9·50

(c) Pin perf $10\frac{1}{2}$–11

CD31	**11**	$\frac{1}{4}$d. deep blue	27·00
CD32		$\frac{1}{2}$d. greenish grey	£150
CD33		$\frac{1}{2}$d. deep dull purple	18·00

(b) Rough perf $11\frac{1}{2}$

CD34	**11**	$\frac{1}{4}$d. deep blue	£225
CD35		$\frac{1}{2}$d. deep blue (*error of colour*)	£200

Printed in sheets of 66 (11 × 6)

1867 (Mar). *Hard wove paper showing papermaker's watermark* "A COWAN & SONS" *or* "EXTRA SUPERFINE A C & S". *Rough perf* $11\frac{1}{2}$.

CD36	**11**	$\frac{1}{4}$d. deep blue	38·00
CD37		$\frac{1}{2}$d. dull purple	12·00

The sheet watermarks exist either upright or inverted. Stamps showing part of the watermark are worth a premium.

Stamps known used on cover or circular
No. CD36 . . . .

Printed in sheets of 66 (11 × 6).

PROOFS: $\frac{1}{4}$d. indigo (*imperf*) on thin hard wove paper (*Price* £375).

FORGERIES: $\frac{1}{4}$d. blue (*imperf*) with central shield mis-shapen and value too bold. $\frac{1}{2}$d. blue-grey (often found with horizontal ink line) with serif, instead of sans-serif, capitals.

Metropolitan Circular Delivery Company

12

1867 Mar). *Rough perf* 11$\frac{1}{2}$. *(a) Very thin soft wove paper without wmk.*

CD38	**12**	$\frac{1}{4}$d. rose-carmine	10·00
		a. Imperf between (horiz pair)	£350
		b. Imperf between (vert pair)	£360

(b) Hard wove paper showing papermaker's watermark "A COWAN & SONS" *or* "EXTRA SUPERFINE A C & S". *Rough perf* 11$\frac{1}{2}$.

CD39	**12**	$\frac{1}{4}$d. rose-carmine	10·00
CD40		$\frac{1}{2}$d. orange	24·00
		a. Imperf. between (horiz. pair)	£350
		b. Imperf. between (vert pair)	£300

Nos. CD39/40 with the sheet watermarks either upright or inverted. Stamps showing part of the watermark are worth a premium.

(shield)

(address)

Company cancellations

Stamps known used on cover or circular
No. CD38 . . . .

Loose stamps used with oval cancellations, as above, in red
No. CD38 . . . . 75·00

Covers, without stamps, are also known showing these cancellations or a similar type without "LIMITED" on the centre bar of the shield.

Printed in sheets of 66 (11 × 6).

PROOFS: $\frac{1}{4}$d. rose (*imperf*) (*Price* £375) and $\frac{1}{4}$d. yellow-orange (*rough perf* 11$\frac{1}{2}$) (*Price* £150) on thick soft wove paper.

FORGERIES: $\frac{1}{4}$d. rose (*imperf*) and $\frac{1}{2}$d. yellow (*imperf*) (both often found with horizontal ink line) with value in serif, instead of sans-serif, capitals.

London & Districts Circular Delivery Company

13

1867 (Apr). *(a) Imperf*

CD41	**13**	$\frac{1}{4}$d. yellow-green	18·00
		a. Error. Claret	£225
CD42		$\frac{1}{2}$d. claret	75·00

(b) P 13

CD43	**13**	$\frac{1}{4}$d. yellow-green	12·00
		a. Error. Claret	60·00
CD44		$\frac{1}{2}$d. claret (*shades*)	12·00

Nos. CD41a and CD43a occur on the ten impressions of the fifth horizontal row in the sheet of the $\frac{1}{2}$d. which show the face value as $\frac{1}{4}$d.

Stamps known used on cover or circular
No. CD44 . . . .
Printed in sheets of 130 (10 × 13).

NATIONAL CIRCULAR DELIVERY COMPANY

14

1867 (Apr). *P* 13.

CD45	**14**	$\frac{1}{4}$d. light green	£100
CD46		$\frac{1}{2}$d. blue	18·00
CD47		$\frac{3}{4}$d. brown-ochre	27·00
CD48		1d. brown-rose	18·00

Printed in sheets of 130 (10 × 13).

CIRCULAR DELIVERY COMPANY LIMITED

Following the verdict of August 1867 in favour of the Post Office, Manuel Eyre attempted to circumvent the decision by setting up a limited company which would only handle material belonging to its shareholders. Such efforts were unsuccessful, however, and the company ceased trading after a further court case went against it in June 1868. An appeal followed, but this was finally dismissed on 2 June 1869. This was the end for the circular delivery companies, but their activities had not been in vain as the Post Office reduced the printed paper rate to $\frac{1}{2}$d. for up to 2 ounces on 1 October 1870.

The following stamps were prepared, but not used for postal purposes.

15

1867 (Feb). *Inscr. with names of different cities, one on each horizontal row, and with the individual letters* "TNDC" *at the corners of each design. Thin to medium wove paper. P* 12.

CD49	**15**	$\frac{1}{4}$d. green	10·00
		a. Imperf	30·00
CD50		$\frac{1}{2}$d. blue	10·00
		a. Imperf	30·00
CD51		$\frac{3}{4}$d. brown-lilac	10·00
		a. Imperf	30·00
CD52		1d. scarlet	10·00
		a. Imperf	30·00

Printed in sheets of 81 (9 × 9) with each horizontal row showing a different inscription in the following sequence: Dundee, Manchester, Glasgow, Liverpool, Aberdeen, Birmingham, London, Metropolitan, Edinburgh & Leith.

PROOFS: Reprinted die proofs (8) produced in black on thick cartridge or medium to thick wove paper in 1929. (*Price* £125 *each*).

FORGERIES: Many forgeries exist of this issue, but most can be easily identified by the omission of the "TNDC" corner letters. The only forgeries to include the corner letters are probably contemporary with the stamps themselves and can be identified by differences in the lettering and the value. These only exist imperforate and are on medium wove paper, usually gummed. The $\frac{1}{4}$d. exists in green, the $\frac{1}{2}$d. in blue or green, the $\frac{3}{4}$d. in slate-grey and the 1d. in scarlet.

16

1868 (Feb). *National issue. Thin, hard wove paper. P* 11$\frac{1}{2}$.

CD53	**16**	($\frac{1}{4}$d.) green	18·00
CD54		($\frac{1}{2}$d.) deep blue	18·00
CD55		($\frac{3}{4}$d.) brown-lilac	30·00
CD56		(1d.) scarlet	18·00

Printed in sheets of 81 (9 × 9).

FORGERIES: Imperforate forgeries exist of all values in similar shades, but showing the comma after "15" in the address omitted. Other forgeries of the $\frac{1}{4}$d. and 1d. only occur on soft paper, either imperforate or pin-perforated, generally with the stamp margins far wider than on the originals.

APPENDIX 6

College Stamps

Introduction. The rights of the various Oxford and Cambridge colleges to provide their own delivery services appear to date from the medieval foundations of the two universities. Such rights were recognised by Act of Parliament in 1656 and confirmed by another in 1710.

These delivery services, organised by the domestic staff and sometimes employing special messengers, operated within a limited area of the university concerned and were only available to members of the organising college.

To simplify accounting some of the colleges, starting with Keble in 1871, introduced adhesive stamps and such use had spread to eight colleges in Oxford and three in Cambridge by 1886. On 28 January 1886 the Postmaster-General, Lord John Manners, raised official objections to the college posts and a meeting of Oxford college representatives on 11 February agreed to withdraw the stamps and the postal stationery which had accompanied them. The college delivery services continued to operate, however, and it is known that Keble College continued the use of its postal stationery for at least another ten years.

REPRINTED DIE PROOFS. Certain of the Oxford designs were reprinted from the original dies on up to three separate occasions. The reprints were made on behalf of Professor A. S. Napier, a prominent collector of College Stamps.

Except Nos. CS5 and CS12 the dies or plates were all defaced with a diagonal line cut from the NW to SE corner of the design and are now in a museum.

December 1893 reprints — On thick hard wove paper of CS1, CS3, CS4, CS9, CS10 and CS17. On thick hard laid paper of CS5 and CS12. The proofs were used to illustrate an article by Prof. Napier in the December 1893 issue of Gibbons Monthly Journal.
(*Prices from* £400)

March 1897 reprints — On very thick soft 'cartridge' paper of CS1, CS3, CS4, CS9, CS10, CS17. These proofs normally show wide margins and the full impression of the die (a small copper plate measuring 82 mm. × 49 mm.) is usually plainly outlined.
(*Prices from* £400)

October 1897 reprints after defacement of the dies — On thick wove cream paper of CS1, CS3, CS4, CS9, CS10, CS17. (*Prices from* £400)

PRICES. Those in the left-hand column are for mounted mint stamps and those in the right-hand column for examples used on cover. Loose stamps without gum are worth a percentage of the prices quoted for mint, depending upon their scarcity.

ALL SOULS' COLLEGE, OXFORD

CANCELLATIONS. Not normally cancelled

1

(Litho. Supplied by Spiers and Son)

1884 (26 Jan.). *P*11½.

			Mint	*On Cover*
CS1	**1**	(½d.) ultramarine	40·00	£1700
		Block of four	£200	
		a. Imperf between (vert pair)	£400	

Printed in sheets of 40 (5 × 8).

Original die proof. In black on white wove paper, struck 1884 (*Price* £1000).
Reprints exist see Introduction.

BALLIOL COLLEGE, OXFORD

2

(Embossed, probably by Emberlin and Son)

1885. *P* 11½ × *imperf.*

CS2	**2**	(½d.) scarlet	75·00	
		a. Tête-bêche (vert pair)	£700	

Printed in vertical strips of 17 with the lower part of each strip inverted to produce a *tête-bêche* pair.

These stamps were delivered on 19 January, 1885, but were never used for the college delivery service.

EXETER COLLEGE, OXFORD

CANCELLATIONS. Various manuscript marks including "E" with a line drawn through it, signatures or initials.

3

(Litho. Supplied by Emberlin and Son)

1882 (11 Nov.). *P* 12

CS3	**3**	(½d.) salmon-red	25·00	£600
		Block of four	£125	

Printed in sheets of 96 (12 × 8) using blocks of six transfers from a single die engraved on a copper plate.

Original die proof. In black on white wove paper, struck 1882. (*Price* £1500).
Reprints exist see Introduction.

HERTFORD COLLEGE, OXFORD

CANCELLATIONS. A cancellation showing a cross pătée fitchée was prepared, but examples are rare.

4

(Des S. Spiers. Litho. Supplied by Spiers and Son)

1879. *P* $11\frac{1}{2}$ *with some sheets having the outer edges imperforate.*

			Mint	*On Cover*
CS4	**4**	($\frac{1}{2}$d.) bright mauve	15·00	£2200
		Block of four	75·00	
		a. Imperf between (horiz. pair)	£325	

Printed in sheets of 35 (5 × 7).

Original die proof. In black on white wove paper, struck December, 1875. (*Price* £1500).
Reprints exist see Introduction.

Remainders exist in two shades, imperforate and without gum, from reserve stock kept by the supplier. An attempt was subsequently made by contemporary collectors to provide some of these sheets with gum (*Price, imperf.* £2, *block of four* £10). Some of these gummed remainders were unofficially perforated 12.

KEBLE COLLEGE, OXFORD

CANCELLATIONS. The official cancellation supplied for use with the embossed issue showed five dots arranged as on a dice face. This was sometimes imitated by a similar marking in pencil. The use of the dot cancellation continued to at least 1881. Examples so cancelled are scarce.

5

(Embossed on surface-coloured paper by Spiers and Son)

1871 (29 Nov.)–**73.** *Rough perf* $10\frac{1}{2}$ *with the outer edges of the sheet imperforate.*

CS5	**5**	($\frac{1}{2}$d.) vermilion	£250	£850
		a. *Tête-bêche* (vert pair)	£2250	
		b. Perf 12 (1.72)	£200	£1000
		ba. *Tête-bêche* (vert pair)	£1400	
CS6		($\frac{1}{2}$d.) magenta (1873)	£200	£1700

The sheet format is unknown, but the lower rows were inverted to produce vertical *téte-bêche* pairs. Reprints of No. CS5 exist see Introduction.

(Embossed on surface-coloured paper by Emberlin and Son)

1876. *P* 11 × *imperf.*

			Mint	*On Cover*
CS7	**5**	($\frac{1}{2}$d.) magenta	£400	£2800

Printed in vertical strips, possibly of 13 or 14 stamps.

Colour Trials. Embossed on bright crimson, emerald or bright ultramarine surface-coloured paper. Roul $7\frac{1}{2}$ between stamps. Struck in sheets, probably of 30, by Emberlin and Son in 1876 (*Price* £375).

6

(Des. S. Spiers, Litho. Supplied by Spiers and Son)

1876 (Oct.). "S" of "Spiers" well formed, round "o" in Son" and Oxford." *P* $11\frac{1}{2}$.

CS8	**6**	($\frac{1}{2}$d.) ultramarine	65·00	£600
		Block of four	£375	

Printed in sheets of 48 (6 × 8) divided into two panes of 24 by a horizontal gutter. Imprints applied individually to the impressions on the stone.

1879 (June). "S" of "Spiers" poorly drawn, oval "o" in Son" and "Oxford." *P* $11\frac{1}{2}$.

CS9	**6**	($\frac{1}{2}$d.) ultramarine	50·00	£450
		Block of four	£325	

Printed in sheets as No. CS8, but with the imprints engraved on the copper die from which the transfers were made.

Original die proof. In black on brown paper, struck June, 1879. (*Price* £1700).
In black on white wove paper, struck June, 1879. (*Price* £1700).

Reprints exist see Introduction.

7

(No. imprint. Chevron blunt)

(Litho. Supplied by Emberlin and Son)

1882 (May). *P* 11½.

CS10	**7**		(½d.) ultramarine	10·00	£300
			Block of four	50·00	
		a.	Imperf between (vert pair)	£200	
		b.	Imperf between stamp and left margin	70·00	
		c.	Imperf between stamp and central gutter	70·00	

Printed in sheets of 48 (6 × 8) divided into two panes of 24 by a horizontal gutter.

Original die proof. In black on card, struck 1882. (*Price* £1500).
In black on wove paper, struck 1882. (*Price* £1500).

Reprints exist see Introduction.

Gummed labels showing the college crest, taken from a die used for envelope flaps, are said to have been used as 2d. parcel stamps in 1876–77.

LINCOLN COLLEGE, OXFORD

CANCELLATIONS. By pencil mark or smudge.

8

(Des, eng and recess by Allan Wyon, London)

1877 (June)–**84.** *P* 14½.

				Mint	*On Cover*
CS11	**8**		1d. deep blue	95·00	£850
			Block of four	£450	
		a.	*Prussian blue* (1882)	75·00	£700
		b.	*Deep dull blue* (1884)	75·00	£700

Printed in sheets of 30 (6 × 5).

Plate proofs. In black on cartridge paper imperforate, struck June, 1877. (*Price* £300).
In indigo on toned wove paper imperforate, struck between 1877 and 1879. (*Price* £125).

MERTON COLLEGE, OXFORD

CANCELLATIONS. Nos. CS12/13 were normally left uncancelled but examples of Nos. CS14 can sometimes be found with pencil marks.

9

(Embossed as **Type 9** on surface-coloured paper by Emberlin and Son)

1876 (1 June)–**77.** *P* $12\frac{1}{2}$ × *imperf.*

			Mint	Complete Stamp on Cover	Partial Stamp on Cover
CS12	**9**	($\frac{1}{2}$d.) bright blue	£325	£2200	£1500
		a. *Perf* $11\frac{1}{2}$–12 × imperf. milky blue (1877)	£425	£2200	£1500
		ab. Double embossing, one inverted	£2000		

Printed in vertical strips of 13.

No. CS12 with deep embossing, cutting the paper, meant that some examples on cover have the centre pushed out and used instead of the complete stamp. This does not apply to other college stamps.

Only one example of No. CS12ab is known.

Reprints of No. CS12 exist see Introduction.

1882. *As* **Type 9,** *but redrawn. Imperf* × *P* $11\frac{1}{2}$.

			Mint	On Cover
CS13	**9**	($\frac{1}{2}$d.) dull blue	£750	£2750

As redrawn for No. CS13 the design shows the shield and letters larger. The circles in the design are also of different widths with the outer and inner thick. On No. CS12 the inner circle is thin. The right-hand corner of the shield points to the "E" on the 1882 printing instead of the space between the "E" and "R".

Printed in horizontal strips.

10

(Litho. Supplied by Emberlin and Son)

1883 (29 Jan.). *P* 11½.

CS14	**10** (½d.) mauve	35·00	£450
	Block of four	£175	

Printed in sheets of 48 (6 × 8) divided into panes of 24 by a horizontal gutter, using blocks of four transfers from a single die engraved on a copper plate.

QUEENS' COLLEGE, CAMBRIDGE

CANCELLATIONS. Not normally cancelled.

11

(Des E. Temperley. Litho. Supplied by W. P. Spalding)

1883 (Oct). *P* 11½ *with the outer edges of the sheet imperforate.*

CS15	**11** (½d.) bright green	30·00	£2750
	Block of four	£150	

Printed in sheets of 96 (12 × 8).

ST. JOHN'S COLLEGE, CAMBRIDGE

CANCELLATIONS. Usually a manuscript cross in ink or whorl in indelible pencil.

12

(Litho. Supplied by W. P. Spalding)

1884 (Jan.). *P* 11½ *with the outer edges of the sheet imperforate.*

		Mint	*On Cover*
CS16	**12** (½d.) scarlet	25·00	£3250
	Block of four	£125	

Printed in sheets of 96 (12 × 8).

ST. JOHN'S COLLEGE, OXFORD

CANCELLATIONS: Various manuscript markings, in ink or pencil.

13

(Litho. Supplied by Emberlin and Son

1884 (19 Jan.). *P* 12

CS17	**13**	(½d.) grey-blue	10·00	£400
		Block of four	50·00	
		a. Imperf between (pair)	£300	

No. CS17a should show no trace of perforation indentations between the stamps.

Printed in sheets of 96 (12 × 8), using blocks of six transfers from a single die engraved on a copper plate. The two halves of the sheet were printed *téte-bêche* to one another, but these were separated into blocks of 6 × 8 before delivery.

Original die proofs. In black on paper, struck January, 1884 (*Price* £1500).
In black on card, struck January, 1884 (*Price* £1500).
Reprints exist see Introduction.

SELWYN COLLEGE, CAMBRIDGE

CANCELLATIONS. Usually a cross or pen stroke.

14

(Litho on surface-coloured paper. Supplied by W. P. Spalding)

1882 *Imperf.*

			Mint	*On Cover*
CS18	**14**	(½d.) black on magenta	70·00	£2750

The stamps were supplied already separated, but it is believed that there may have been 480 in the printer's sheet. Examples sometimes show an offset of the design on the reverse.

Further Reading

The list below is representative of major works relating to British postal history, stamps and postmarks of the reign of Queen Victoria. Initially, culled from *A List of Books on the Postal History, and Adhesive Postage and Revenue Stamps of Great Britain,* compiled by Arnold M. Strange (2nd edition, Great Britain Philatelic Society, London, 1971). Later publications to date are also included.

POSTAL HISTORY

Archer, Michael Scott. *The Welsh Post Towns before 1840.* (1969. Phillimore & Co. Ltd., Chichester.)

Bennett, Edward. *The Post Office and its Story.* (1912. Seeley, Service & Co. Ltd., London.)

Bonython, Elizabeth and Burton, Anthony. *The Great Exhibitor: The Life and Work of Henry Cole.* (2003. V & A Publications, London.)

Cole, Henry. *Fifty Years of Public Work by Sir Henry Cole, K.C.B. (*1884. 2 vols. George Bell & Sons, London.)

Edwards, Eliezer. *Sir Rowland Hill, K.C.B. (*1879. Frederick Warne & Co., London.)

Ellis, K. *The Post Office in the Eighteenth Century.* (1958. The Oxford University Press.)

Farrugia, Jean. *Life and Work of Sir Rowland Hill, 1795–1879.* (1979. National Postal Museum, London.)

Farrugia, Jean and Gammons, Tony. *Carrying British Mails.* (1980. National Postal Museum, London.)

Feldman, Hugh. *Letter Receivers of London 1652 to 1857.* (1999. 2 vols. Stuart Rossiter Trust, and the Postal History Society.)

Fryer, Gavin and Ackerman, Clive (Eds). *The Reform of the Post Office in the Victorian Era and its Impact on Economic and Social Activity* (based on Sir Rowland Hill's journal and ancillary papers). (2000. 2 vols, Royal Philatelic Society, London.)

Gammons, Tony. *The Early Days of the Postal Service.* (1986. National Postal Museum, London.)

Goodwyn, Charles W. *Royal Reform.* (1999. Stuart Rossiter Trust, Bristol.)

Graveson, Samuel. *Penny Postage Centenary.* (1940. The Postal History Society, London.)

Grimwood-Taylor, James. *The British Postal Reforms of 1839 to 1840.* (1990.)

Grimwood-Taylor, James. *The Post in Scotland.* (1990. Stamp Publicity Board, London.)

Hemmeon, J. C. *The History of the British Post Office.* (1912. Harvard University Press.)

Henderson, J. R. *Post Offices in Scotland. (*1966. Correction slip (32 pp) in 1968. The Scottish Postmark Group.)

Hill, George Birkbeck. *The Life of Sir Rowland Hill and the History of Penny Postage.* (1880. 2 vols. Thos. De La Rue Ltd., London.)

Hill, Col. H. W., C.M.G., D.S.O. *Rowland Hill and the Fight for the Penny Post.* (1940. Frederick Warne & Co., London.)

Hill, Pearson. *The Post Office of Fifty Years Ago.* (1887. Cassell & Co., Ltd., London.)

Hill, Rowland. *Post Office Reform. Its Importance and Practicability.* (1838. 4th edn. Charles Knight & Co., London.)

Hill, Rowland. *The State and Prospect of Penny Postage, as Developed in the Evidence Taken before the Postage Committee of 1843 etc.* (1844. London.)

Hodgson, K. and Sedgewick, W. A. *The Scottish Additional Halfpenny Mail Tax 1813–1839.* (1974. Jonathan Partridge, Sheffield.)

Johnson, Peter. *Mail By Rail: The History of the TPO & Post Office Railway.* (1995. Ian Allan Ltd., Shepperton, Surrey.)

Johnson, Peter. *The Travelling Post Office 1838–2004.* (2004. Royal Mail, London; British Philatelic Bulletin Publication No. 10.)

Joyce, Herbert. *The History of the Post Office from Its Establishment Down to 1836.* (1893. Richard Bentley & Son, London.)

Kay, George F. *Royal Mail, The Story of the Posts in England from the Time of Edward IV to the Present Day.* (1951. Rockliffe Publishing Corporation Ltd.)

Lewins, William. *Her Majesty's Mails. An Historical and Descriptive Account of the British Post Office. (*1865. 2nd edn. Sampson Low & Son, Marston, London.)

Lovegrove, J. W. *Herewith My Frank . . .* (1991. 2nd Edn. The Author, Winchester, Hants.)

Mackay, James A. *Scotland's Posts.* (2000. The Author, Glasgow.)

Marshall, C. F. Dendy. *The British Post Office from its Beginnings to the End of 1925.* (1926. Oxford University Press.)

Melville, Fred J. *Origins of the Penny Post.* (1930. Philatelic Institute, London.)

Murray, Sir Evelyn, K.C.B., Secretary to the Post Office. *The Post Office.* (1927. Putnam & Co., Ltd., London.)

Oxley, G. F. *The English Provincial Local Posts 1765–1840.* (1973. The Postal History Society, London.)

Oxley, G. F. *British Postal Rates to Europe 1836–1876.* (1992. The Postal History Society, Beckenham, Kent.)

Pawlyn, Tony. *The Falmouth Packets 1689–1851.* (2003. Truran Books Ltd, Redruth.)

Robertson, Alan W. *Great Britain Post Roads, Post Towns and Postal Rates 1637–1839.* (1961. Reprinted 1974. Robson Lowe Ltd., London.)

Robinson, Howard. *The British Post Office. A History.* (1948. Princeton University Press.)

Robinson, Howard. *Carrying British Mails Overseas.* (1964. George Allen & Unwin Ltd., London.)

Rowse, David. *Joshua Bacon—1790–1863. The Printer of Banknotes and the First Postage Stamps.* (2000. Great Britain Philatelic Society, London.)

Sanford, O. R. and Salt, Dennis. *British Postal Rates 1635–1839.* (1991. The Postal History Society, London.)

Smith, A. D. *The Development of Rates of Postage.* (1917. George Allen & Unwin Ltd., London.)

Smyth, Eleanor C. *Sir Rowland Hill, The Story of a Great Reform Told by his Daughter.* (1907. T. Fisher Unwin, London.)

Staff, Frank. *The Penny Post 1680–1918.* (1964. Paperback edn. 1992. Lutterworth Press, Cambridge.)

Todd, T. *William Dockwra and the Rest of the Undertakers. The Story of the London Penny Post 1680–1682.* (1952. C. J. Cousland & Sons, Ltd., Edinburgh.)

Uniform Penny Postage Provisionals of Great Britain 1840–1853. (1948. Sovenir Catalogue of the David Miller Brown Collection. The Postal History Society, London.)

Vale, Edmund. *The Mail Coachmen of the Late Eighteenth Century.* (1960. Cassell & Co., Ltd., London.)

Wellsted, Hilary. *Express Service 1891–1971.* (1986. Postal History Society, Tonbridge.)

White, Brian. *A Look at the Night Mail: Travelling Post Offices – A History.* (2006, Moorside Publishing Ltd, Bridlington.)

Willcocks, R. M. *England's Postal History with Notes on Scotland, Wales and Ireland.* (1975. The Author, Blackheath, London, SE3.)

Willcocks, R. M. and Jay, B. *British County Catalogue, Vol. 1,* 1978. (Covers Cambridgeshire, Essex, Hampshire, Leicestershire, Norfolk, Northamptonshire, Nottinghamshire, Oxfordshire, Rutland, Suffolk and Warwickshire.)

Willcocks, R. M. and Jay, B. *British County Catalogue of Postal History, Vol. 2. (*1982. Covers four cities, Birmingham, Bristol, Liverpool, Manchester and nine counties, Buckinghamshire, Cornwall and Isles of Scilly, Devon, Hertfordshire, Isle of Wight, Middlesex, Shropshire, Surrey, Sussex and Channel Islands.)

Willcocks, R. M. and Jay, B. *British County Catalogue of Postal History, Vol. 3.* (1983. Covers London.)

Willcocks, R. M. and Jay, B. *British County Catalogue of Postal History, Vol. 4.* (1988. Covers Bedfordshire, Berkshire, Cheshire, Dorset, Hampshire, Isle of Man, Kent, Lancashire, Staffordshire and Yorkshire.)

Willcocks, R. M. and Jay, B. *British County Catalogue of Postal History, Vol. 5.* (1990. Covers Cumberland, Durham, Gloucestershire, Herefordshire, Lincolnshire, Northumberland, Somerset, Westmorland, Wiltshire and Worcestershire.)

GENERAL

Alcock, R. C. and Meredith, C. W. *British Postage Stamp Varieties Illustrated, Q.V. Surface-printed Issues to K.G.VI.* (1949. R. C. Alcock Ltd., Cheltenham.)

Alderfer, David & Rosenblum, Larry. *Introduction to the Stamps of Great Britain.* (2004. Amos Press, Sidney, Ohio, U.S.A.)

Arman, F. Marcus. *The Reginald M. Phillips Collection of 19th Century British Postage Stamps.* (1966. G.P.O., London.)

Brauers, Theo. *Scarce Victorian Postage Stamps of Great Britain on cover.* (2003. Forschungsgemeinschaft Grossbritannien e.V. (FgGB), Düsseldorf, Germany.)

Briggs, Asa. *Victorian Things. (*London 1988, 2nd Edn., 1996.)

Courtney, Nicholas. *The Queen's Stamps: The Authorised History of the Royal Philatelic Collection.* (2004. Methuen, London.)

Daunton, Martin J. *Royal Mail: The Post Office since 1840.* (1985. Athlone Press, London and New Hampshire, U.S.A.)

Davies, Peter and Maile, Ben. *First Post From Penny Black to the Present Day.* (1990. National Postal Museum, London and Quiller Press Ltd., Norfolk.)

Farrugia, Jean. *A Guide to Post Office Archives.* (1987. Post Office Archives, London.)

Hamilton, Patrick. *British Stamps. A Description of the Postage Stamps of the United Kingdom.* (1948. Peter Davies, London. Supplement published by Harris Publications Ltd., London, 1954.)

Hyde, Rikki C. *Great Britain: Numbers Issued 1840–1910.* (1990. 2nd Edn. Stanley Gibbons Publications Ltd.)

Jefferies, Hugh. *The Queen's Stamps.* (2002. Royal Philatelic Collection, London.)

Lowe, Robson. *The Encyclopaedia of British Empire Postage Stamps, 1661–1951.* (1952. 2nd Edn. Robson Lowe Ltd., London. Reprinted in Billig's Philatelic Handbook series (Vols. 34/35). HJMR Co., North Miami, Florida.)

Lowe, Robson. *The British Postage Stamp of the Nineteenth Century.* (1979. 2nd Edition. The National Postal Museum, London.)

Mackay, James A. *Great Britain. The Story of Great Britain and her Stamps.* (1967. Philatelic Publishers, London.)

Mackay, James. *British Victorian Stamps.* (1997. British Philatelic Bulletin Publication No. 4, Royal Mail, London.)

Mackay, James A. *British Stamps.* (1985. Longman Group Ltd., London.)

Mackay, James A. *Under the Gum—Background to British Stamps 1840–1940.* (1997. James Bendon Ltd., Limassol, Cyprus.)

Madden, Don & Louis, Karl. *The Dublin Find: The most important stamp find in GB philately.* (2006. Mike Jackson Publications, Melton Mowbray.)

Morgan, Glenn. *British Stamp Printers.* (2006. Royal Mail, London. British Philatelic Bulletin Publication No. 12.)

Morley, Walter. *Walter Morley's Catalogue and Price List of the Stamps of Great Britain* (includes fiscals, railway, deed stamps and stationery). (1897. 2nd edn. Walter Morley, London.)

Muir, Douglas. *Victorian Innovation 1837–1901.* (2005. British Postal Museum & Archive, London. Exhibition brochure.)

Oliver, Sidney A. R. and Vallancey, F. Hugh. *The Postage Stamps of Great Britain, 1840–1922, Stamp Collecting.* (1923. London.)

Philbrick, F. A. and Westoby, W. A. S. *The Postage and Telegraph Stamps of Great Britain.* (1881. Sampson, Low, Marston, Searle & Rivington, London for the Philatelic Society, London.)

Rose, Stuart. *Royal Mail Stamps—A Survey of British Stamp Design.* (1980. Phaidon Press, Oxford.)

Todd, T. *A History of British Postage Stamps.* (1949. Duckworth, London.)

West, Richard & Muir, Douglas N. *The Story of Definitive Stamps.* (1994. Royal Mail, London.)

Westoby, William A. S. *Descriptive Catalogue of all the Postage Stamps of the United Kingdom of Great Britain and Ireland, Issued during Fifty Years.* (1892. Sampson, Low, Marston, Searle & Rivington, London.)

Wijman, J. J. *The Postage Stamps of Great Britian and their History.* (1986. Jeeboer Press, The Netherlands.)

Wilson, Sir John, Bart, *The Royal Philatelic Collection.* (1952. The Dropmore Press, London.)

Wright, Hastings E. and Creeke Jr., A. B. *A History of the Adhesive Stamps of the British Isles Available for Postal and Telegraph Purposes.* (1899. The Philatelic Society, London. A supplement was published in 1903.)

PHILATELIC PERIODICALS DEVOTED TO GREAT BRITAIN

The British Philatelist. (1908–54. Chas. Nissen & Co., Ltd., London.)

Gibbons Stamp Monthly (*British Stamps* supplement from October 1981, January, April and July 1982, monthly since October 1982.)

British Philatelic Bulletin (From 1963. (title was *Philatelic Bulletin*, 1963–83.) The Post Office, London.)

The GB Journal. (From 1956. The Great Britain Philatelic Society, London.)

The G.B. Philatelic, (1961–65. The Regent Stamp Co., Ltd., London.)

The Philatelist and Philatelic Journal of Great Britain (From 1981. (The P.J.G.B., 1891–1980, was wholly devoted to Great Britain after March 1966.) Christie's Robson Lowe Ltd., London.)

Britannia News. Published by GB collectors club in Netherlands, Studiegroep Britannia.

Cross Post. Published by Friends of Postal Heritage (formerly Association of Friends of the National Postal Museum).

GBCC Chronicle. Published by Great Britain Collectors Club in USA.

Rundbrief. Published by GB collectors society in Germany, Forschungsgemeinschaft Grossbritannien e.V. (FgGB).

MULREADY LETTER SHEETS AND ENVELOPES

Bodily, Ritchie, Jarvis, Chris and Hahn, Charless. *British Pictorial Envelopes of the 19th Century.* (1984. The Collectors Club of Chicago, Illinois, U.S.A.)

Evans, E. B. *A Description of the Mulready Envelope and of Various Imitations and Caricatures of its Design, etc.* (1891. Stanley Gibbons Ltd., London. S. R. Publications and Stanley Gibbons Ltd., London, 1970 facsimile edition.)

Huggins, A. K. *British Postal Stationery.* (1970. The Great Britain Philatelic Society, London. Reprinted with amendments 1971.)

Lowe, Malcom G. *The Mulready Advertisements.* (1983. Mulready Research Foundation, California U.S.A.)

LINE-ENGRAVED STAMPS

Alcock, R. C. *The Alphabets of the British Line-Engraved Stamps.* (1937. 2nd Edn. R. C. Alcock Ltd., Cheltenham.)

Alcock, R. C. and Holland, F. C. *Hand-engraved Plates 50 and 51. Alphabet IV.* (1948. R. C. Alcock Ltd., Cheltenham.)

Alcock, R. C. *Reserve Plate 15. One Penny Rose-Red on White Paper. Alphabet II.* (1947. R. C. Alcock Ltd., Cheltenham.)

Alcock, R. C. *Reserve Plate 16. One Penny Rose-Red on White Paper. Alphabet II.* (1947. R. C. Alcock Ltd., Cheltenham.)

Bacon, Edward D. *The Line-Engraved Postage Stamps of Great Britain Printed by Perkins, Brown & Co.* (1920. Chas. Nissen & Co. Ltd., London.)

Bacon, Edward D. Supplement to the above. (1929. Chas. Nissen & Co., Ltd., London.)

Bacon, Edward D. *The Essays, Proofs, Colour Trials and Reprints of the Line-Engraved Postage Stamps of Great Britain Printed by Perkins, Bacon & Co., Ltd., London.* (1936. Chas. Nissen & Co., Ltd., London.)

Brown, Roland and Fisher, H. W. *The Plating of the Penny 1840–1864.* Vols. I and II devised and compiled by Roland Brown and edited by H. W. Fisher; vols. III, IV and V compiled and edited by H. W. Fisher: *Vol. I, Plates 1–45* (Revised ed. 1979); *Vol. II, Plates 46–91* (1973); *Vol. III, Plates 92–131* (1976); *Vol. IV, Plates 132–175* (1980); *Vol. V, Plates 176–204, Reserve Plates 1 to 6* (1984). The Great Britain Philatelic Society, London.

Current, Tom. *Handbook of British Philately.* (1980. Part 1, section 1-Identification of line engraved stamps 1840–79, Lord Byron Stamps, Portland, Oregon, U.S.A.)

Dagnall, H. *John Dickinson and his Silk-Thread Paper.* (1975. The Author, Leicester.)

Eddison, H. W. *Penny Red-Brown Die II—Alphabet III. On Blued Paper. Plates 22–26, 28–30, 32, 40.* (R. C. Alcock Ltd., Cheltenham.)

Gardiner-Hill, Clive. *The Stamps of Great Britain. The Line-Engraved Issues. Archer plates, 1841 Penny Red.* (1950. R. C. Alcock Ltd., Cheltenham.)

Gardiner-Hill, Clive. *The Stamps of Great Britain. Archer Plates, 1841 Penny Red Die I. Alphabet I. Plates 92–101.* (1950. 2nd edn. Banbury.)

Gardiner-Hill, Clive. *The Stamps of Great Britain.The Line-Engraved Issues. 1841 Penny Red. Die 1. Alphabet 1. Plates 102–131. Constant Varieties.* (1950. 2nd Edn. R. C. Alcock Ltd., Cheltenham.)

Gardiner-Hill, Clive. *The Stamps of Great Britain. The Line-Engraved Issues. 1841 Penny Red. Die I. Alphabet I. Plates 102–131.* (1951. R. C. Alcock, Ltd., Cheltenham.)

Goldsmith, David and Danzig, Robert. *The Cancellations of the 1841 Penny Red.* (1991. Philatelic Imprint, London.)

Holland, F. C. *Reserve Plate 17. Die II. Alphabet III.* (1949. R. C. Alcock Ltd., Cheltenham.)

Jackson, Mike. *May Dates.* (1999. The Author, Melton Mowbray, Leics.)

Litchfield, P. C. *Guide Lines to the Penny Black.* (1949. Reprinted 1979. Robson Lowe Ltd., London.)

Marshall, C. F. Dendy. *A Study of the Line-Engraved Twopence Postage Stamps of Great Britain.* (1929. Harris Publications Ltd., London.)

Melville, Fred J. *The Stamps of Great Britain: Line-Engraved Stamps, The British Philatelist.* (1926. Chas. Nissen & Co., Ltd., London.)

Messenger, W. de L. M. *The Line-Engraved Halfpenny – A critical Analysis of the Production of the first halfpenny stamps of Great Britain.* (2005. Great Britain Philatelic Society, London.)

Muir, Douglas N. *The Postal Reform and The Penny Black. A New Appreciation.* (1990. National Postal Museum, London.)

Nissen, Charles and McGowan, Bertram. *The Plating of the Penny Black Stamps of Great Britain, 1840.* (1922. Chas. Nissen & Co., London. Stanley Gibbons Ltd., London & Ringwood. Reprinted 1998.)

Osborne, H. *British Line-Engraved Stamps—Repaired Impressions.* (1950. H. F. Johnson, London.)

Osborne, H. *British Line-Engraved Stamps. Twopence Blue. Studies of Plates 1 to 15.* (1948. H. F. Johnson, London.)

Osborne, H. *Twopence—Plate Nine. A Study of the Plate and its Repairs.* (1939. Chas. Nissen & Co., Ltd., London.)

Osborne, H. *The Ray-Flaws of the Plates 1 and 2 of the Penny Black Postge Stamps of Great Britain.* (1932. Chas. Nissen & Co., London.)

Proud, Edward B. *Penny Black Plates.* (1985. Proud-Bailey Co., Ltd., Heathfield, E. Sussex.)

Rigo de Righi, A. G. *The Story of the Penny Black and its Contemporaries.* (1980. National Postal Museum, London.)

Rowse, David. *"Rainbow Trials" May–December 1840.* (2000. Great Britain Philatelic Society, London.)

Seymour, J. B. *The Postage Stamps of Great Britain. Part I. The Line-Engraved Issues, 1840–1853.* (1967. 3rd edn. Edited by John Easton, The Royal Philatelic Society, London.)

Seymour, J. B. *The Stamps of Great Britain. Part II. With Addenda and Corrigenda to Part 1. The Remainder of the Line-Engraved Issues, and Embossed Adhesives and Surface Printed Issues up to 1865.* (1937. 1st edn. The Royal Philatelic Society, London, For 2nd Edn., see under W. R. D. Wiggins.)

Stanton, J. B. M. *The Varieties and Characteristics of the 1d. Red Line-Engraved Stamps, 1841–1864.* (1958. Chas. Nissen & Co. Ltd., London.)

Statham, K. W. *The Essential Guide to the Great Britain Line Engraved 1d and 2d Stars 1840–1864.* (17 volumes, published by Eric Paul Ltd., Marple, Cheshire, last three volumes published 2003.)

Stone, J. W. W. *The Repairs of the 1841 One Penny Plates 1–40.* (1974. R. C. Alcock Ltd., Cheltenham.)

Tonna, G. C. *Penny Red Stars Die II, Alphabet III (Plates 22 to 68, R.17) 1855–1862. Part I–AA to JL.* (1980. The Author, Kirkcudbrightshire.)

Tonna, G. C. and Madden, Don. *Penny Red Stars Die II, Alphabet III (Plates 22 to 68, R.17) 1855–1862. Part 2–KA to TL.* (1996. Mike Jackson Publications, Melton Mowbray, Leicestershire.)

Wiggins, W. R. D. *The Postage Stamps of Great Britain. Part II. The Perforated Line-Engraved Issues.* (1962. 2nd edn. The Royal Philatelic Society, London.)

Wiggins, W. R. D. *The Plating of Alphabet II, Plates 1 to 21.* (1974. Robson Lowe Ltd., London.)

Wiggins, W. R. D. *Repaired Impressions 1855–79 One Penny Die II.* (1982. Robson Lowe Ltd., Bournemouth.)

Wiggins, W. R. D. and Tonna, G. C. *The Plating of Alphabet III Plates 22 to 68 and R17, together with Alphabet IV (Plates 50 and 51) and Alphabet II (R15 and R16).* (Comprises photographs of practically every stamp (5 vols), 1973–74.)

Worms, Percy de. *Perkins, Bacon Records,* 2 vols. (1953. The Royal Philatelic Society, London.)

EMBOSSED STAMPS

Beaumont, K. M. and Adams, H. C. V. *The Postage Stamps of Great Britain, Part III.* (1954. The Royal Philatelic Society, London.)

Melville, Fred J. *Great Britain: Embossed Adhesive Stamps.* (1910. The Melville Stamp Books, London.)

Seymour, J. B. *The Postage Stamps of Great Britain. Part II* (see under Line-Engraved Stamps.)

Todd, T. *The Embossed Octagonal Postage Stamps of Great Britain.* (No date. The Vallancey Press Ltd., London.)

SURFACE-PRINTED STAMPS

Akerman, G. C. *Queen Victoria. The Plating of the Half Penny 1887–1900.* (1970. The Great Britain Philatelic Society, London.)

Beaumont, K. M. and Adams, H. C. V. *The Postage Stamps of Great Britain. The Embossed Issues. The Surface-Printed Issues of Queen Victoria and King Edward VII.* (1954. The Royal Philatelic Society, London. Revised 1964 by K. M. Beaumont and John Easton.)

Easton, John. *The De La Rue History of British and Foreign Postage Stamps, 1855 to 1901.* (1958. Faber & Faber for the Royal Philatelic Society, London.)

Huggins, Alan. *The De La Rue Punch Book, A Philatelic Journal of Great Britain* monograph. (1979. Robson Lowe Ltd., London.)

Lee, R. A. G. *The Penny Lilac—Part I. Frame Damage, and Part II. Damage and Minor Varieties of Four Segments, Letters and Ovals.* (1963 and 1990 (Part II). The Great Britain Philatelic Society, London.)

Seymour, J. B. *The Postage Stamps of Great Britain. Part II. The Surface Printed Issues up to 1865.* (1937. The Royal Philatelic Society, London.)

Simpson, Ray C. and Sargent, Peter J. *Stamp Perforation: The Somerset House Years 1848 to 1880.* (2004. The Royal Philatelic Society, London.)

Wiseman, W. A. *Great Britain: The De La Rue Years 1878–1910.* (1984. Vol. 1. Bridger & Kay Ltd., London.)

Wiseman, W. A. *Great Britain: The De La Rue Years 1878–1910.* (1990. Vol. 2. Stanley Gibbons Publications Ltd., London and Ringwood.)

"SPECIMEN" STAMPS

Bendon, James. *UPU Specimen Stamps,* (1988. The Author, Limassol, Cyprus.)

Samuel, Marcus and Huggins, Alan. *Specimen Stamps and Stationery of Great Britain.* (1980. The Great Britain Philatelic Society, London.)

POSTAL FISCAL STAMPS AND REVENUES

Booth, R. G. *A Catalogue of the Adhesive Revenue Stamps of the U.K., Isle of Man and Channel Islands.* (1976. J. M. Booth, Newcastle upon Tyne.)

Fiscal Philatelic Society, *The Catalogue of the Adhesive Revenue and Fee Stamps of the United Kingdom.* (1906–09. The Fiscal Philatelic Society, London.)

Frank, Samuel B. and Schonfield, Josef. *The Stamp Duty of Great Britain and Ireland.* (1970–74. 3 vols. Mamaroneck, New York.)

Frank, Samuel B., Schonfield, Josef and Barber, William A. *The Impressed Duty Stamps of Great Britain 1694 to the Present.* (1981. W. A. Barber, Stamford, Connecticut U.S.A.)

Kay, A. B. *A List of the Impressed Duty Stamps of Great Britain and Ireland.* (1924. Bridger & Kay Ltd., London.)

TELEGRAPH STAMPS

Bacon, E. D. *The Stamps of the Electric Telegraph Company (Great Britain). Issues of 1851 to 1861.* Chas. Nissen & Co., Ltd., London, 1927

Hiscocks, S. E. R. *Telegraph and Telephone Stamps of the World,.* (1984. The Author, Woking, Surrey.)

Jackson, H. T. *The Preparation of the Post Office Adhesive Telegraph Stamps of Great Britain.* (1970, Rugby.)

Jackson, H. T. *The Post Office Telegraph Stamps of Great Britain, 1869–1881.* (1971. Rugby.)

Langmead, Peter and Huggins, Alan K. *The Telegraph Stamps and Stationery of Great Britain 1851–1952.* (2003. Great Britain Philatelic Society, London.)

Lister, Raymond. *Private Telegraph Companies of Great Britain and their Stamps.* (1961. The Golden Head Press Ltd., Cambridge.)

McDonald, A. *Telegraph Stamps of Great Britain.* (1959. The Author, London.)

COLLEGE AND CIRCULAR DELIVERY CO. STAMPS

Bellamy, F. A. *A Concise Register of the College Messenger Postage Stamps, Envelopes and Cards used in the Universities of Oxford and Cambridge,* 1871–1885. (1925. Oxford.)

Cummings, Hayman. *The College Stamps of Oxford and Cambridge.* (1904. The Author, Oxford.)

Harman, Christopher. *Great Britain: The Stamps of the Circular Delivery Companies and Their Forgeries.* (1990. Cinderella Stamp Club and Frank Godden Ltd.)

Lister, Raymond. *College Stamps of Oxford and Cambridge.* (1966. Cambridge.)

West, Vincent. *The Post Office and the Colleges.* (2004. Great Britain Philatelic Society, London.)

PERFINS (APPENDIX 2)

Gault, Roy (ed). *The "Tomkins" Catalogue of Identified G.B. Perfins* (2004. 10th edn, The Perfin Society.)

POSTMARKS

Alcock, R. C. *Scots Local Cancellations Illustrated, 1854–1860.* (1984. R. C. Alcock Ltd., Cheltenham.)

Alcock, R. C. and Holland, F. C. *British Postmarks. A Short History and Guide.* (1978. 2nd Edn. R. C. Alcock Ltd., Cheltenham. Combines three earlier works by the same authors.)

Alcock, R. C. and Holland, F. C. *The Maltese Cross Cancellations of the United Kingdom.* (1971. Revised Edn. R. C. Alcock Ltd., Cheltenham.)

Auckland, Bruce. *The Postal Markings of Scotland to 1808.* (1978, William Carson, Ayr.)

Batchelor, L. E. and Picton-Phillips, D. B. *Pre-Victorian Stamps & Franks.* (1971. Picton Publishing, Chippenham.)

Brummell, George. *Postmarks of the British Isles. A Short History with Notes on Collecting.* (1930. Bournemouth Guardian Ltd., Bournemouth.)

Brummell, George. *British Post Office Numbers, 1844–1906.* (1946. R. C. Alcock Ltd., Cheltenham.)

Brummell, George. *A Short Account of the Franking System in the Post Office, 1652–1840.* (1936. Bournemouth Guardian Ltd., Bournemouth.)

Brummell, George. *The Local Posts of London, 1680–1840.* (1938. R. C. Alcock Ltd., Cheltenham.)

Chapman, Ken. *British Post Office Numbers by County.* (1985. Harry Hayes, Batley, West Yorkshire.)

Cohen, Stanley F. *Squared Circle Postmarks of the London Suburban District Offices.* (1983. Harry Hayes, Batley, Yorks.)

Cohen, Stanley F. *London Fancy Geometric Postmarks (Early Combined Daters and Obliterators of 1880–1909.* 1984. Harry Hayes, Batley, Yorks.)

Cohen, Stanley F., Barette, Maurice, Hine, J. and Williams, A. M. *Collecting British Squared Circle Postmarks.* (2006, 2nd Edn. Stanley F. Cohen and distributed by Vera Trinder Ltd., London.)

Current, Tom. *The Numeral Cancels of Ireland, 1844–1906.* (1979. Lord Byron Stamps, Portland, Oregon U.S.A.)

Dubus, Léon. *London Cancellations, Repairs and Re-Cuttings from 1840.* (1969–70. 2 vols. Robson Lowe Ltd., London.)

Hawkins, R. *Date Stamps of the General Post Branch Offices in London, 1829–1858.* (1980. Vera Trinder Ltd., London.)

Hendy, John G. *The History of the Postmarks of the British Isles from 1840 to 1876.* (1909. Compiled from official records, Supplement to *Gibbons' Stamp Weekly,* London.)

Hewlett, M. A. *Picton's Philatelic Handbook No. 1.* (1979. B.P.H. Publications Ltd., Chippenham, Wilts.)

Holland, F. C. *Introduction to British Postmark Collecting.* (1971.)

Jay, Barrie. *The British County Catalogue of Postal History, Vol. 3, London* (2005. 2nd edition, London Postal History Group.)

Lowe, Robson. *The Encyclopaedia of British Empire Postage Stamps, 1661–1951.* (1952. 2nd Edn. Robson Lowe Ltd., London. Reprinted in Billig's Philatelic Handbook series (Vols. 34/35). HJMR Co., North Miami, Florida.)

Mackay, James A. *Scottish Postmarks.* (1978. The Author, Dumfries.)

Mackay, James A. *The Circular Name Stamps of Scotland.* (1978. The Author, Dumfries.)

Mackay, James A. *Postmarks of England and Wales.* (1988. 2nd Edn. The Author, Dumfries.)

Mackay, James A. *The Parcel Post of the British Isles.* (1982. The Author, Dumfries.)

Mackay, James A. *Irish Postmarks since 1840.* (1982. The Author, Dumfries.)

Mackay, James A. *Official Mail of the British Isles.* (1983. The Author, Dumfries.)

Mackay, James A. *Registered Mail of the British Isles.* (1983. The Author, Dumfries.)

Mackay, James A. *Scottish Twin-Arc Postmarks, with Stampers Numbers 1894 to 1963.* (1983. The Author, Dumfries.)

Mackay, James A. *Skeleton Postmarks of England & Wales* (2006. 3rd edn compiled by P. G. Awcock & J. R. Frost. British Postmark Society, Hemel Hempstead.)

Mackay, James A. *Surcharged Mail of the British Isles.* (1984. The Author, Dumfries.)

Mackay, James A. *Scottish Numeral Postmarks.* (1988. The Author, Dumfries.)

Meredith, C. W. *Scots Local Cancellations.* (1953. Revised 1964R. C. Alcock Ltd., Cheltenham.)

Meredith, C. W. *Old Irish Postage Stamps and Franks.* With Priced Catalogue by Walter Morley. (1923. Walter Morley, London.)

Midland (GB) Postal History Society, *Undated Circular Marks of the Midland Counties.* (1989. 3rd Edn. John Calladine, Gloucester.)

Midland (GB) Postal History Society, *The Undated Straight Line and Numbered Receiving House Marks of the Midland Counties 1840–1860.* (1988. John Calladine, Gloucester.)

Moy, John A. E. *The Use of the 1894 Coded Time System in British Post Offices.* (1999. The Author, East Horsley, Surrey.)

Parmenter, J. *A Priced Catalogue of Horizontal Oval Single Cancellations of the London District Post, Suburban Offices and the East Central District.* (1974. Peter A. Forrestier Smith, Bishops Stortford, for the London Postal History Society.)

Pearson, George R. *Special Event Postmarks of the United Kingdom,* Vol. 1: The Early Years 1851–1962. (1991. 4th Edn. British Postmark Society, Herts.)

Pipe, W. T. and Blackman, G. J. *Postmarks of British Railway Stations.* (1994. Railway Philatelic Group.)

Rockoff, S. David & Jackson, Mike. *Encyclopaedia of the Maltese Cross Cancellations of Great Britain and Ireland* (2006. Mike Jackson Publications, Melton Mowbray.)

Sandford Jr., Oliver R. *The Postal Markings of England, London and Wales, 1661–1900.* (1986. Lord Byron Stamps, Portland Oregon, U.S.A.)

Scottish Postmark Group, Edinburgh:

Dotted Circle Postmarks of Scotland. (1962.)

Experimental Duplex Cancellations of Scotland. (1963.)

Scots Local Name Stamps. (1964.)

The Mileage Marks of Scotland. (1966.)

Numbered Postmarks of Scotland, Vol. 1. (1968.)

Penny Posts of Edinburgh and District. 1773–1839. (1972.)

Smith, Brian. *London's Postal History Section E, Inland Office Cancellation 1844–1868—The Horizontal Diamonds*. (1992. London Postal History Group, Carshalton Beeches, Surrey.)

Stitt Dibden, W. G. *Late Fee and Too Late Stamps*. (1967. The Great Britain Philatelic Society, London.)

Todd, T. *William Dockwra and the Rest of the Undertakers. The Story of the London Penny Post, 1680–1682*. (1952. C. J. Cousland & Sons, Ltd., Edinburgh.)

Traill, R. G. and Holland, F. C. *The Sideways Duplex Cancellations of England and Wales*. (1975. R. C. Alcock Ltd., Cheltenham.)

Vallancey, Hugh. *British Postmarks. With Special Reference to the '1844' and subsequent Obliterations*. (1935. The Vallancy Press Ltd., London.)

Walker, Derek (ed). *The British County Catalogue of Sussex Postal History*. (2006. Sussex Postal History Society, Worthing.)

Westley, H. C. *The Postal Cancellations of London 1840–1890 with the Dates when they were Issued*. Compiled from G.P.O. records. (1950. H. F. Johnson, London.)

Whitney, J. T. *Collect British Postmarks*. (1997. 7th Edition. Colin G. Peachey and V. Brian Crookes, British Postmark Society, Hemel Hempstead, Herts.)

Willcocks, R. M. and R. W. and Bentley, Wilfred. *The Spoon Experiment, 1853–58*. (1960. Blackheath, London.)

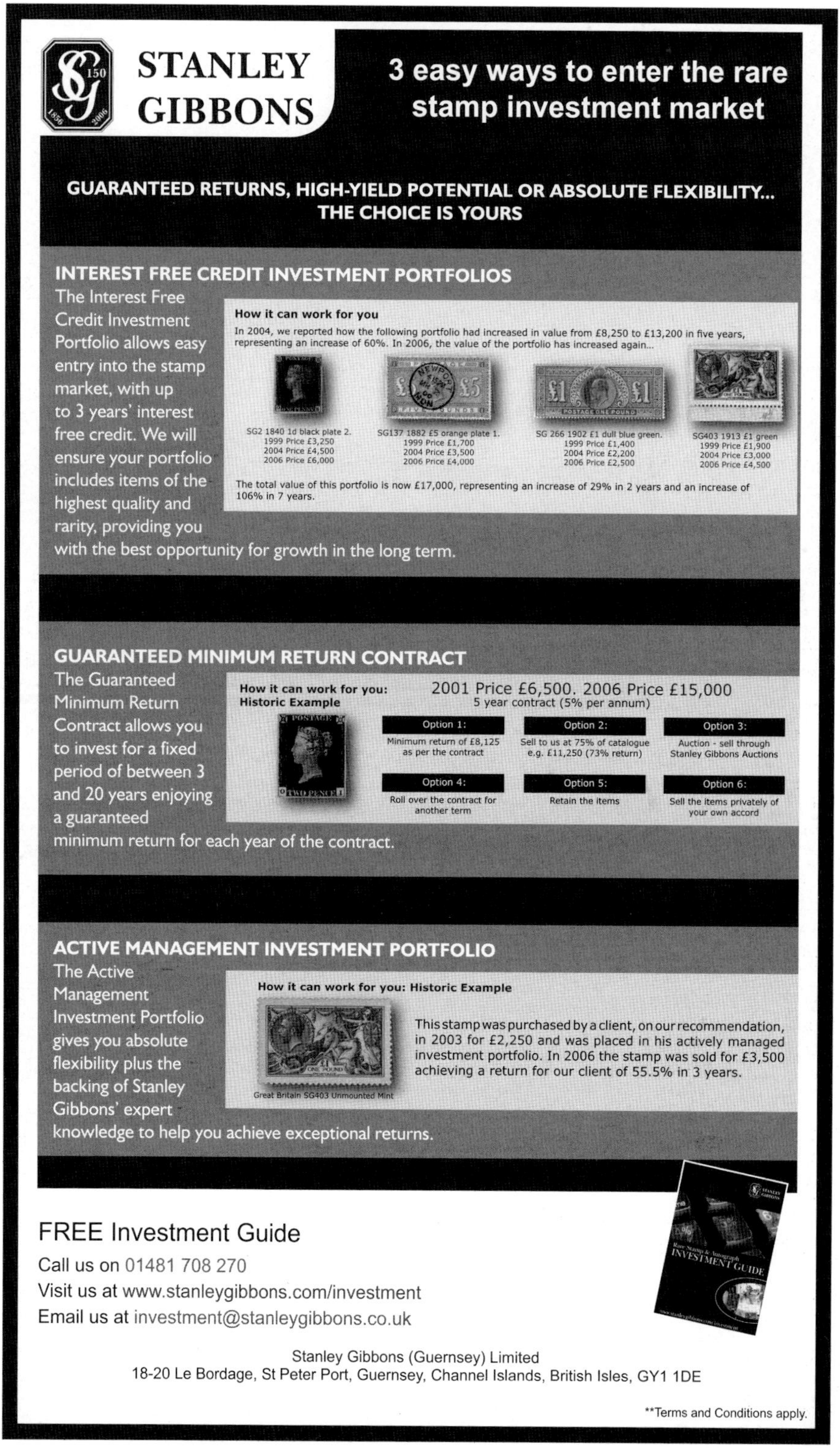
STANLEY GIBBONS
150
1856 2006
3 easy ways to enter the rare stamp investment market
GUARANTEED RETURNS, HIGH-YIELD POTENTIAL OR ABSOLUTE FLEXIBILITY... THE CHOICE IS YOURS
INTEREST FREE CREDIT INVESTMENT PORTFOLIOS
The Interest Free Credit Investment Portfolio allows easy entry into the stamp market, with up to 3 years' interest free credit. We will ensure your portfolio includes items of the highest quality and rarity, providing you with the best opportunity for growth in the long term.
How it can work for you
In 2004, we reported how the following portfolio had increased in value from £8,250 to £13,200 in five years, representing an increase of 60%. In 2006, the value of the portfolio has increased again...
SG2 1840 1d black plate 2. 1999 Price £3,250 2004 Price £4,500 2006 Price £6,000
SG137 1882 £5 orange plate 1. 1999 Price £1,700 2004 Price £3,500 2006 Price £4,000
SG 266 1902 £1 dull blue green. 1999 Price £1,400 2004 Price £2,200 2006 Price £2,500
SG403 1913 £1 green 1999 Price £1,900 2004 Price £3,000 2006 Price £4,500
The total value of this portfolio is now £17,000, representing an increase of 29% in 2 years and an increase of 106% in 7 years.
GUARANTEED MINIMUM RETURN CONTRACT
The Guaranteed Minimum Return Contract allows you to invest for a fixed period of between 3 and 20 years enjoying a guaranteed minimum return for each year of the contract.
How it can work for you: Historic Example
2001 Price £6,500. 2006 Price £15,000
5 year contract (5% per annum)
Option 1: Minimum return of £8,125 as per the contract
Option 2: Sell to us at 75% of catalogue e.g. £11,250 (73% return)
Option 3: Auction - sell through Stanley Gibbons Auctions
Option 4: Roll over the contract for another term
Option 5: Retain the items
Option 6: Sell the items privately of your own accord
ACTIVE MANAGEMENT INVESTMENT PORTFOLIO
The Active Management Investment Portfolio gives you absolute flexibility plus the backing of Stanley Gibbons' expert knowledge to help you achieve exceptional returns.
How it can work for you: Historic Example
This stamp was purchased by a client, on our recommendation, in 2003 for £2,250 and was placed in his actively managed investment portfolio. In 2006 the stamp was sold for £3,500 achieving a return for our client of 55.5% in 3 years.
Great Britain SG403 Unmounted Mint
FREE Investment Guide
Call us on 01481 708 270
Visit us at www.stanleygibbons.com/investment
Email us at investment@stanleygibbons.co.uk
Rare Stamp & Autograph INVESTMENT GUIDE
Stanley Gibbons (Guernsey) Limited
18-20 Le Bordage, St Peter Port, Guernsey, Channel Islands, British Isles, GY1 1DE
**Terms and Conditions apply.

COLLECT
GREAT BRITAIN STAMPS

From Stanley Gibbons, THE WORLD'S LARGEST STAMP STOCK

Priority order form
Four easy ways to order

Phone:
020 7836 8444
Overseas: +44 (0)20 7836 8444

Fax:
020 7557 4499
Overseas: +44 (0)20 7557 4499

Email:
lmourne@stanleygibbons.co.uk

Post:
Lesley Mourne, Stamp Mail Order Department Stanley Gibbons Ltd, 399 Strand London, WC2R 0LX

Customer Details

Account Number ______________________

Name ______________________

Address ______________________

______________________ Postcode ______________________

Country ______________________ Email ______________________

Tel No ______________________ Fax No ______________________

Registered Postage & Packing £3.60

I enclose my cheque/postal order for £............ in full payment. Please make cheques/postal orders payable to Stanley Gibbons Ltd. Cheques must be in £ sterling and drawn on a UK bank

Please debit my credit card for £.......... in full payment. I have completed the credit card section below.

Card Number

☐☐☐☐☐☐☐☐☐☐☐☐☐☐☐☐

Start Date (Switch & Amex) ☐☐☐☐

Expiry Date ☐☐☐☐

Issue No (Switch) ☐☐

Signature ______________________ Date ______________

COLLECT
GREAT BRITAIN STAMPS

From Stanley Gibbons, THE WORLD'S LARGEST STAMP STOCK

Priority order form
Four easy ways to order

Condition (mint/ UM/used)	Country	SG No.	Description	Price	Office use only

Postage & Packing	£3.60
Grand Total	£

Minimum price. The minimum catalogue price quoted is 10p. For individual stamps, prices between 10p and 95p are provided as a guide for catalogue users. The lowest price charged for individual stamps or sets purchased from Stanley Gibbons Ltd is £1

Please complete payment, name and address, details overleaf